T0207087

Lecture Notes in Computer Science   10896

Commenced Publication in 1973
Founding and Former Series Editors:
Gerhard Goos, Juris Hartmanis, and Jan van Leeuwen

More information about this series at http://www.springer.com/series/7409

Klaus Miesenberger
Georgios Kouroupetroglou (Eds.)

Computers Helping People with Special Needs

16th International Conference, ICCHP 2018
Linz, Austria, July 11–13, 2018
Proceedings, Part I

 Springer

Editors
Klaus Miesenberger
Johannes Kepler University Linz
Linz
Austria

Georgios Kouroupetroglou
National and Kapodistrian University
   of Athens
Athens
Greece

ISSN 0302-9743   ISSN 1611-3349   (electronic)
Lecture Notes in Computer Science
ISBN 978-3-319-94276-6   ISBN 978-3-319-94277-3   (eBook)
https://doi.org/10.1007/978-3-319-94277-3

Library of Congress Control Number: 2018947426

LNCS Sublibrary: SL3 – Information Systems and Applications, incl. Internet/Web, and HCI

Printed on acid-free paper

This Springer imprint is published by the registered company Springer Nature Switzerland AG
The registered company address is: Gewerbestrasse 11, 6330 Cham, Switzerland

Preface

Welcome to the ICCHP 2018 Proceedings!

ICCHP's mission for inclusion and participation in the information society strives for better Assistive Technology (AT) and eAccessibility for support, enhancement and restoration of resources for people with disabilities and compensating limita-  tions of standardized Human–Computer Interaction (HCI). This mission continues to gain even more importance owing to the ongoing ICT revolution (Internet/Web of Things/Ubiquitous computing/Cloud-based services).

ICCHP had the honor to accompany and support the revolutionary developments of AT and eAccessibility over the past three decades. With its roots going back almost 30 years, it provides an outstanding and most comprehensive overview of these revolutionary developments supporting the full inclusion and participation of people with disabilities in all domains of society. The ICT revolution brings along an increased potential for inclusion and participation, but also risks for exclusion and thus the responsibility for implementing eAccessibility.

This provokes a growing number of challenging research questions. Old boundaries of concepts dissolve, new approaches and fresh thinking are needed: not only in technical terms, but also in legal, social, economic, pedagogic, and other terms. The UN Convention on the Rights of People with Disabilities (UNCRPD) is the globally accepted reference and expression of the societal transformation toward effective inclusion and participation of all people with disabilities in society. The UNCRPD refers to AT, eAccessibility, eInclusion, and Design for All as preconditions and means of support.

These are exactly the core topics of ICCHP. Since the first conference in Vienna (Austria) back in 1989, ICCHP has evolved as a unique and one of the few long-term references of R&D with evidence on how Information and Communication Technologies (ICT), AT, and eAccessibility have been implemented and have significantly contributed to the improvement of the life of people with disabilities. By addressing all these aspects, ICCHP invites and provides a platform for a holistic discussion on improving the lives of people with disabilities in every corner of our world.

ICCHP is proud to contribute with its scientific excellence to these outstanding social developments. All 21 volumes of past proceedings, covering more than 2,400 reviewed articles,[1] are a unique source for learning and understanding the theoretical, methodological, and pragmatic specializations of our field and for reflecting on the inclusion movement. This collection of work, with its unique user focus, offers a

---

[1] Owing to the increasing interest in ICCHP, the last two conferences published their proceedings in two volumes.

significant body of evidence for the enormous but often neglected impact on usability for all users regardless of their abilities.

In 2018, the proceedings of the 16th conference are delivered to you as a compendium of the new and exciting scholarly and practical work going on in our field. Again, in a highly competitive process, 136 experts formed the scientific committee compiling at least three reviews for each of the 356 submitted contributions. A panel of 12 conference chairs selected and accepted 101 submissions as full papers and 78 as short papers based on the expert reviews, which you find now in the two volumes of the proceedings. This two-phase selection procedure guarantees the high scientific quality making ICCHP unique in our field. The concept of organizing "Special Thematic Sessions" again helped to structure the proceedings and the program in order to support a deep focus on highly desirable selected topics in the field as well as to bring new and interesting topics to the attention of the research community.

ICCHP hosts a high-quality and fully accessible meeting for scientists, users, practitioners, educators, and policy makers. In addition to the traditional paper sessions, the forum also includes industry representatives showing their new products and looking for new ideas. In particular, ICCHP welcomes young researchers, the next generation of experts in our field, and encourages them to contribute to the Young Researchers Consortium as well as to the Coding for a Cause competition. Additionally, the conference affords spaces and times for less formal discussions – an important factor supporting the transfer of knowledge so needed in our endeavors.

We welcomed the attendees' valuable contribution to ICCHP 2018 and encourage them and their colleagues to become regular participants in its most important mission, which is also recognized through patronage of the United Nations Educational, Scientific and Cultural Organization (UNESCO). It is here that research, innovation, and practical endeavors in important topics of AT and eAccesibility can come together to be shared, explored, and discussed.

July 2018

Klaus Miesenberger
Georgios Kouroupetroglou

Organization

ICCHP Committees

General Chair

Kouroupetroglou, G.   University of Athens, Greece

Steering Board

Bühler, C.   TU Dortmund University, FTB, Germany
Burger, D.   INSERM, France
Murphy, H. J.   California State University Northridge, USA
Suzuki, M.   Kyushu University, Japan
Tjoa, A. M.   Technical University of Vienna, Austria
Wagner, R.   University of Linz, Austria

Publishing Chair

Miesenberger, K.   University of Linz, Austria

Program Chairs

Archambault, D.   Université Paris 8, France
Debevc, M.   University of Maribor, Slovenia
Fels, D   Ryerson University, Canada
Kobayashi, M.   Tsukuba University of Technology, Japan
Manduchi, R.   University of California at Santa Cruz, USA
Penaz, P.   University of Brno, Czech Republic
Weber, G.   Technische Universität Dresden, Germany
Zagler, W.   Vienna University of Technology, Austria

Young Researcher Consortium Chairs

Archambault, D.   Université Paris 8, France
Chen, W.   Oslo and Akershus University College of Applied
                    Sciences, Norway
Fels, D.   Ryerson University, Canada
Fitzpatrick, D.   Dublin City University, Ireland
Kobayashi, M.   Tsukuba University of Technology, Japan
Morandell, M.   University of Linz, Austria
Pontelli, E.   New Mexico State University, USA
Prazak-Aram, B.   AIT Austrian Institute of Technology GmbH, Austria
Weber, G.   Technische Universität Dresden, Germany

Workshop Chairs

Petz, A.   University of Linz, Austria
Pühretmair, F.   KI-I, Austria

International Program Committee

Abascal, J	Euskal Herriko Unibertsitatea, Spain
Abbott, C.	King's College London, UK
Abou-Zahra, S.	W3C Web Accessibility Initiative (WAI), Austria
Abu Doush, I.	American university of Kuwait, Kuwait
Andrich, R.	Polo Tecnologico Fondazione Don Carlo Gnocchi Onlus, Italy
Augstein, M.	University of Applied Sciences Upper Austria, Austria
Azevedo, L.	Instituto Superior Tecnico, Portugal
Batusic, M.	Fabasoft, Austria
Bernareggi, C.	Università degli Studi di Milano, Italy
Bernier, A.	BrailleNet, France
Bosse, I.	Technische Universität Dortmund, Germany
Bu, J.	Zhejiang University, China
Christensen, L. B.	Sensus, Denmark
Chutimaskul, W.	King Mongkut's University of Technology Thonburi, Thailand
Conway, V.	WebKeyIT, Australia
Coughlan. J.	Smith-Kettlewell Eye Research Institute, USA
Craddock, G.	Centre for Excellence in Universal Design, Ireland
Crombie, D.	Utrecht School of the Arts, The Netherlands
Cudd, P.	University of Sheffield, UK
Darvishy, A.	ZHAW, Switzerland
Darzentas, J.	University of Aegean, Greece
Debeljak, M.	University of Ljubljana, Slovenia
DeRuyter, F.	Duke University Medical Centre, USA
Diaz del Campo, R.	Antarq Tecnosoluciones, Mexico
Draffan, E. A.	University of Southampton, UK
Dupire, J.	CNAM, France
Emiliani, P. L.	Institute of Applied Physics "Nello Carrara", Italy
Engelen, J.	Katholieke Universiteit Leuven, Belgium
Galinski, Ch.	InfoTerm, Austria
Gardner, J.	Oregon State University, USA
Hakkinen, M. T.	Educational Testing Service (ETS), USA
Hanson, V.	University of Dundee, UK
Harper, S.	University of Manchester, UK
Heimgärtner, R.	Intercultural User Interface Consulting (IUIC), Germany
Höckner, K.	Hilfgemeinschaft der Blinden und Sehschwachen, Austria

Hoogerwerf, E.-J.	AIAS Bologna, Italy
Huenerfauth, M.	Rochester Institute of Technology, USA
Inoue, T.	National Rehabilitation Center for Persons with Disabilities, Japan
Iversen, C. M.	U.S. Department of State (retired), USA
Kalinnikova, L.	University of Gävle, Sweden
Koumpis, A.	University of Passau, Germany
Kouropetroglou, Ch.	ALTEC, Greece
Kozuh, I.	University of Maribor, Slovenia
Kremser, W.	OCG, HSM, Austria
Küng, J.	Johannes Kepler University Linz, Austria
Lewis, C.	University of Colorado at Boulder, USA
Lhotska, L.	Czech Technical University in Prague, Czech Republic
Magnusson, M.	Moscow State University, Russia
Matausch, K.	KI-I, Austria
Mavrou, K.	European University Cyprus, Cyprus
Mayer, Ch.	AIT Austrian Institute of Technology GmbH, Austria
McSorley, J.	Pearson, USA
Mihailidis, A.	University of Toronto, Canada
Mohamad, Y.	Fraunhofer Institute for Applied Information Technology, Germany
Mrochen, I.	University of Silesia in Katowice, Poland
Müller-Putz, G.	TU Graz, Austria
Muratet, M.	INS HEA, France
Normie, L.	GeronTech-Israeli Center for Assistive Technology and Aging, Israel
Nussbaum, G.	KI-I, Austria
Ono, T.	Tsukuba University of Technology, Japan
Panek, P.	Vienna University of Technology, Austria
Paredes, H.	University of Trás-os-Montes e Alto Douro, Portugal
Parson, S.	University of Southampton, UK
Petrie, H.	University of York, UK
Pissaloux, E.	Université Rouen, France
Pontelli, E.	New Mexico State University, USA
Rassmus-Groehn, K.	Lund University, Sweden
Raynal, M	University of Toulouse, France
Rice, D.	National Disability Authority, Ireland
Seeman, L.	Athena ICT, Israel
Sik Lányi, C.	University of Pannonia, Hungary
Simsik, D.	University of Kosice, Slovakia
Slavik, P.	Czech Technical University in Prague, Czech Republic
Sloan, D.	The Paciello Group, UK
Snaprud, M.	University of Agder, Norway
Sporka, A.	Czech Technical University in Prague, Czech Republic
Stepankova, O.	Czech Technical University in Prague, Czech Republic
Stephanidis, C.	University of Crete, FORTH-ICS, Greece

Stiefelhagen, R.	Karlsruhe Institute of Technology, Germany
Stoeger, B.	University of Linz, Austria
Takahashi, Y.	Toyo University Japan
Tauber, M.	University of Paderborn Germany
Teixeira, A.	Universidade de Aveiro, Portugal
Teshima, Y.	Chiba Institute of Technology, Japan
Truck, I	Université Paris 8, France
Uzan, G.	Université Paris 9, France
Vigo, M.	University of Manchester, UK
Vigouroux, N.	IRIT Toulouse, France
Wada, C.	Kyushu Institute of Technology, Japan
Wagner, G.	Upper Austria University of Applied Sciences, Austria
Watanabe, T.	University of Niigata, Japan
Weber, H.	ITA, University of Kaiserslautern, Germany
White, J	Educational Testing Service (ETS), USA
Yamaguchi, K.	Nihon University, Japan
Yeliz, Y.	Middle East Technical University, Cyprus

Organizing Committee

Bieber, R.	Austrian Computer Society, Austria
Feichtenschlager, P.	Integriert Studieren, JKU Linz, Austria
Haider, S.	Integriert Studieren, JKU Linz, Austria
Heumader, P.	Integriert Studieren, JKU Linz, Austria
Höckner, K.	Austrian Computer Society, Austria
Koutny, R.	Integriert Studieren, JKU Linz, Austria
Miesenberger, K.	Integriert Studieren, JKU Linz, Austria
Murillo Morales, T.	Integriert Studieren, JKU Linz, Austria
Pavlicek, R.	Masaryk University Brno, Czech Republic
Penaz, P.	Masaryk University Brno, Czech Republic
Petz, A.	Integriert Studieren, JKU Linz, Austria
Pölzer, St.	Integriert Studieren, JKU Linz, Austria
Seyruck, W.	Austrian Computer Society, Austria
Schult. Ch.	Integriert Studieren, JKU Linz, Austria
Verma, A.	Integriert Studieren, JKU Linz, Austria

ICCHP Roland Wagner Award Nomination Committee

Bühler, Ch.	TU Dortmund, FTB Vollmarstein, Germany
Burger, D.	BrailleNet, France
Draffan, E.A.	University of Southampton, UK
Fels, D.	Ryerson University, Canada
Miesenberger, K.	University of Linz, Austria
Zagler, W.	TETRAGON, Austria

ICCHP Roland Wagner Award Winners

Award 8, ICCHP 2016 in Linz, Austria

Dominique Burger, BrailleNet, France

Award 7, ICCHP 2014 in Paris, France

- Art Karshmer (✝ 2015), University of San Francisco, USA and
- Masakazu Suzuki, Kyushu University, Japan

Award 6, ICCHP 2012 in Linz, Austria

TRACE Centre of University Wisconsin-Madison, USA

Award 5, ICCHP 2010 in Vienna, Austria

- Harry Murphy, Founder of CSUN's Center on Disabilities, USA and
- Joachim Klaus, Founder of the SZS at KIT, Germany

Award 4, ICCHP 2008 in Linz, Austria

George Kersher and the Daisy Consortium

Award 3, ICCHP 2006 in Linz, Austria

Larry Scadden, National Science Foundation

Award 2, ICCHP 2004 in Paris, France

Paul Blenkhorn, University of Manchester

Award 1, ICCHP 2002 in Linz, Austria

WAI-W3C

Once again we thank all those helping in putting ICCHP 2018 together and thereby supporting the AT field and a better quality of life for people with disabilities. Special thanks go to all our supporter and sponsors, displayed at http://www.icchp.org/sponsors-18.

Contents – Part I

Accessible eLearning - eLearning for Accessibility/AT

Personalized Access to TV, Film, Theatre, and Music

Digital Games Accessibility

Accessibility and Usability of Self-Service Terminals, Technologies and Systems

Universal Learning Design

Empowerment of People with Cognitive Disabilities Using Digital Technologies

**Augmented and Alternative Communication (AAC),
Supported Speech**

Contents – Part II

3D Printing in the Domain of Assistive Technologies (AT) and Do It Yourselves (DIY) AT

**Tactile Graphics and Models for Blind People and Recognition
of Shapes by Touch**

Access to Artworks and Its Mediation by and for Visually Impaired People

Digital Navigation for People with Visual Impairments

Mobile Healthcare and mHealth Apps for People with Disabilities

Web Accessibility in the Connected World

A Holistic Decision Support Environment for Web Accessibility

Yehya Mohamad[1]([✉]), Carlos A. Velasco[1], Nikolaos Kaklanis[2],
Dimitrios Tzovaras[2], and Fabio Paternò[3]

[1] Fraunhofer Institute for Applied Information Technology (FIT),
Schloss Birlinghoven, 53757 Sankt Augustin, Germany
{Yehya.mohamad,Carlos.velasco}@fit.fraunhofer.de
[2] Information Technologies Institute, Centre for Research and Technology Hellas,
6th Klm. Charilaou-Thermi Road, P.O. BOX 60361, 570 01 Thessaloniki, Greece
{nkak,Dimitrios.Tzovaras}@iti.gr
[3] CNR-ISTI, HIIS Laboratory, Via Moruzzi 1, 56124 Pisa, Italy

Abstract. This paper presents the architecture of a decision support environment for large-scale assessment of compliance against web accessibility recommendations and legislations. The proposed decision support environment aims at integrating, extending and further enhancing existing web accessibility solutions making them customizable to the needs of different stakeholders, transferable to different sectors in web and mobile environments, in order to minimize costs and development time by also increasing scalability and improving their accessibility and usability.

Keywords: Web accessibility · Decision support system
Accessibility guidelines

1 Introduction

It is important to realise that people with disabilities are not just a tiny minority of the population of the European Union. The lowest estimate, based on currently defined impairment categories, indicates their total number at around 44 Million persons (nearly 13% of the population of the EU). Designing for people with disabilities is becoming an increasingly important topic for a variety of reasons, especially due to the recent legislation (European Web Accessibility Directive, WAD[1]) published on 2 December 2016 and entered into force on 22 December 2016 in Europe promoting the rights of disabled people. In this direction, accessibility has become necessary due to the rapid growth of online information and interactive services provided by web and mobile applications. Some examples are online banking and shopping, public services, social networks. The lack or absence of accessibility contributes to the exclusion or partial exclusion of many people from society.

---

[1] http://data.europa.eu/eli/dir/2016/2102/oj .

© The Author(s) 2018
K. Miesenberger and G. Kouroupetroglou (Eds.): ICCHP 2018, LNCS 10896, pp. 3–7, 2018.
https://doi.org/10.1007/978-3-319-94277-3_1

Making web and mobile apps more accessible results in a better user experience for all, not just for users with disabilities. Simple changes that make applications more user-friendly can bring huge improvements for everyone. Accessibility also benefits businesses with economic gains, as they can reach a larger customer base when it is supported. Web accessibility is not just about technical standards, web architecture and design. It is an issue in terms of political will and moral obligation, now enshrined in the United Nations Convention on the Rights of Persons with Disabilities (UNCRPD). Article 9 of the Convention, to which the EU is a party, requires that appropriate measures are taken to ensure access for persons with disabilities, on equal basis with others, to inter alia information and communication technologies, including the Internet. By that, people with disabilities will have better access to the websites and mobile applications of public services. Web Accessibility Evaluation is an assessment procedure to analyse how well the Web can be used by people with different levels of disabilities. However, there are two main categories of web testing tools: - Tools for accessibility testing and repair, like Siteimprove, AccVerify, imergo® [7], WaaT [6], egovMon, AChecker, SortSite, TAW, Deque, MAUVE etc. The metrics implemented by these tools correspond (more or less accurately) to official (W3C WAI or Section 508) accessibility criteria. - Tools for usability testing (e.g. WebXM, LIFT, WebCriteria) that are based on usability guidelines. A comprehensive list of such tools can be found on W3C/WAI website[2]. Having an automated way of evaluating the accessibility of Web pages opens the way to perform large-scale analysis of Web accessibility. Large-scale accessibility evaluations of the Web are not yet well established. This may be due to the dependency of computational resources for large-scale analysis [1]. Current assessment tools had a number of limitations: First, most of these tools allow validating and or evaluating only single webpages, or in rare cases, single websites [5]. However, in the real world it is more useful to evaluate the accessibility of collections of websites grouped by topic or territory and to monitor the evolution of their accessibility over time, providing a high-level view of whether progress is being made. To mitigate this problem, work is typically conducted on evaluating smaller scale collections of Web documents [2]. These processes are based on sampling methods, such as those defined in UWEM [3]. However, there is always a significant sampling bias induced by these methods [4]. In this paper, the general design and architecture of a decision support environment for large scale web accessibility assessment are presented.

2   Architecture of the Proposed Infrastructure

In the current situation introduced before, a holistic and hybrid approach to Web accessibility assessment is still missing. This approach will provide developers, designers, experts and policy makers with an integrated web accessibility support environment. This will be obtained with a dynamic and personalised environment that will enable them, on one hand, to design accessible software applications and, on the other hand, to understand their problems, and analyse and test their accessibility. Within this approach, the challenge is to find the way in which technology can be best used to increase

---

[2] https://www.w3.org/WAI/ER/tools/ .

accessibility, usability and quality of software applications and services. The presented architecture integrates both new ICT driven concepts and user-oriented approaches with methodologies and tools regarding web accessibility assessment. Within this context, and by using lessons learnt from relevant research and best practices (WCAG, ARIA, EARL, etc.), this architecture aims at developing a new scalable, interoperable and integrated web accessibility assessment and Decision Support Environment (DSE) system as an accessible-driven solution with a user-centred approach. Instead of a simple developer and designer-aid framework, the designer/developer communities will have a user-centred environment to get access to the different parts of the methodological approaches they need. The resulting instances of this architecture will be installable in several ways e.g. as standalone environment, software as a service (SaaS), platform as a service (PaaS) or just as an API for integration with CMSs or IDEs (See Fig. 1.).

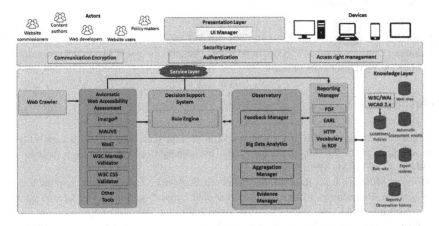

Fig. 1. Architecture of the proposed infrastructure

The core components of the software platform can be split into 4 logical layers: (1) The **knowledge layer** that includes all the knowledge/data needed for the proper functioning of the large scale components (e.g. list of web sites to be evaluated, guidelines and policies to be considered in web accessibility assessment, rule sets, etc.) as well as the knowledge/results that will be extracted (e.g. ontologies[3] that describe the guidelines of WCAG 2.x and ARIA standards in a semantic manner, etc.). (2) The **service layer** that includes all the core software modules of the large scale cloud-based architecture. In this layer we include our accessibility validation tools (Imergo, MAUVE, Waat), tools for validating the Web sites content, and other relevant tools. (3) The **security layer** that is responsible for the security, authentication and access rights management. (4) The **presentation layer**, which includes all the user interfaces that enable user interaction with the large-scale services. We aim to provide adaptive ways to report the detected accessibility issues, also depending on the target communities (developers, end users, web site commissioners, etc.).

---

[3] http://www.accessible-eu.org/index.php/ontology.html .

3 Conclusions and Future Work

This paper presents the high-level design of a large scale infrastructure that offers the following functionalities: (1) Automatic web accessibility assessment. (2) Decision support to accessibility experts for detecting further barriers that need further manual investigation. (3) guidance to developers in repairing accessibility errors, (4) presentation of aggregated results through an Observatory using advanced visual analytics methods enabling different stakeholders such as web commissioners, policy makers and the general public to examine changes in the accessibility of various websites. The proposed infrastructure provides also APIs to external tools like CMSs for checking webpages during design and content authoring to make them "born accessible".

We also plan to empirically validate the results of such accessibility infrastructures with the relevant communities.

Acknowledgments. This work was partially funded by the European Commission H2020 programme; Contract number 780206; WADcher. The authors would like to acknowledge the support of the WADcher consortium.

References

1. Lopes, R., Gomes, D., Carriço, L.: Web not for all: a large scale study of web accessibility. In: Proceedings of the 2010 International Cross Disciplinary Conference on Web Accessibility (W4A), p. 10. ACM, April 2010
2. Mirri, S., Muratori, L.A., Roccetti, M., Salomoni, P.: Metrics for accessibility on the Vamolà project. In: Proceedings of the 2009 International Cross-Disciplinary Conference on Web Accessibility (W4A), pp. 142–145. ACM, April 2009
3. Bühler, C., Heck, H., Perlick, O., Nietzio, A., Ulltveit-Moe, N.: Interpreting results from large scale automatic evaluation of web accessibility. In: Miesenberger, K., Klaus, J., Zagler, Wolfgang L., Karshmer, Arthur I. (eds.) ICCHP 2006. LNCS, vol. 4061, pp. 184–191. Springer, Heidelberg (2006). https://doi.org/10.1007/11788713_28
4. Brajnik, G., Mulas, A., Pitton, C.: Effects of sampling methods on web accessibility evaluations. In: Proceedings of the 9th International ACM SIGACCESS Conference on Computers and Accessibility, pp. 59–66. ACM, October 2007
5. Paternò, F., Schiavone, A.G.: The role of tool support in public policies and accessibility. ACM Interact. **22**(3), 60–63 (2015)
6. Oikonomou, T., Kaklanis, N., Votis, K., Kastori, G.E., Partarakis, N., Tzovaras, D.: Waat: personalised web accessibility evaluation tool. In: Proceedings of the International Cross-Disciplinary Conference on Web Accessibility, p. 19. ACM (2011)
7. Carlos, V., Denev, D., Stegemann, D., Mohamad, Y.: A web compliance engineering framework to support the development of accessible rich internet applications. ACM. https://doi.org/10.1145/1368044.1368054, 978-1-60558-153-8

Certification in the Field of eAccessibility and eInclusion

Focusing on Certification Aspects Regarding Web Accessibility

Christian Galinski[1(✉)], Klaus Höckner[2(✉)], and Reinhard Koutny[3(✉)]

[1] Infoterm, International Information Centre for Terminology, Vienna, Austria
christian.galinski@chello.at
[2] Hilfsgemeinschaft der Blinden und Sehschwachen Österreichs, Vienna, Austria
hoeckner@hilfsgemeinschaft.at
[3] Johannes Kepler Universität, Linz, Austria
Reinhard.Koutny@jku.at

Abstract. There are different kinds of certification. In the field of eAccessibility and eInclusion (eAcc&eIncl) web accessibility (WA) is aiming at the highest degree of semantic interoperability. This can largely be achieved by compliance to pertinent standards, such as the W3C's Web Accessibility Initiative (WAI) guidelines – in particular WCAG 2.0. Technical and legal regulations concerning WA are getting more demanding by the day. Standards-based certification schemes can prove the technical compliance to WA standards or show that a WA expert is abreast with technical developments and regulations.

Keywords: eAccessibility and eInclusion · Web accessibility
Certification of websites · Certification of experts' competences and skills

1 Introduction

eAccessibility and eInclusion (eAcc&eIncl) demands the highest dimensions of semantic interoperability: including that the 'content' of (increasingly ICT-supported) interhuman communication *must not* be corrupted whatever the language or modality (spoken, written and other) used and user interface required (re. responsive design). The Recommendation on software and content development principles 2010 formulated at ICCHP 2010, addressed these requirements and was adopted by several committees in the field of standardization. [1] Today, W3C's Web Accessibility Initiative (WAI) guidelines – in particular WCAG 2.0 [2] – are a prerequisite to achieve WA. They also serve as ideal basis for standards-based certification schemes.

© Springer International Publishing AG, part of Springer Nature 2018
K. Miesenberger and G. Kouroupetroglou (Eds.): ICCHP 2018, LNCS 10896, pp. 8–12, 2018.
https://doi.org/10.1007/978-3-319-94277-3_2

2   The Role of Standards-Based Certification

'Certification' here refers to the confirmation of certain characteristics of an object, person, or organization. It can be carried out in the form of first-party certification (whereby an individual or organization providing the good or service offers assurance that it meets certain claims), second-party certification (whereby an association to which the individual or organization belongs provides the assurance) and third-party certification (which involves an independent assessment declaring that specified requirements pertaining to a product, person, process, or management system have been met). Any of these, especially the latter, may be based on regulations – whether legal or technical regulations. Technical regulations primarily refer to standards.

Certification can be applied to: products (incl. electric-electronical devices and ICT hardware), software/tools (e.g. with respect to interoperability), data/content resources, processes, services, human resources (with respect to personnel certification or experts' competences and skills), training (including training organization, trainers' competences and skills, training material and tools).

This contribution focuses on certification schemes for WA experts and on the increasingly legally obligatory technical requirements for WA – for instance in public procurement not least due to EU Directive 2014/24/EU [3].

3   Technical Aspects of Web Accessibility (WA)

Recommendation 2010 states that "...*multilinguality, multimodality, eInclusion and eAccessibility need to be considered from the outset in software and content development, in order to avoid the need for additional or remedial engineering or redesign at the time of adaptation, which tend to be very costly and often prove to be impossible.*"

To comply with this recommendation, a fundamental requirement was close user involvement from the very beginning of the software engineering process in project Web Accessibility Certificate Austria (WACA). Therefore, we have chosen an agile software engineering process, that focuses on stakeholder engagement and short iterations aiming to implement sets of user requirements defined for every sprint.

The prototype of the portal allows the management and support of the certification process. Following use cases are already covered by this tool (additional uses case will likely follow in the future, to better automatize, digitize and support the process).

- Create a new instance representing a website which will be evaluated
- Assign website owner to website
- Assign one or multiple evaluators to a website
- Assign one or multiple auditors to a website
- Undertake a (self) evaluation done by an evaluator
- Undertake an audit of an evaluation done by an auditor
- Certification of website after successful audit by certification authority

Multiple roles were defined to perform these use cases. Due to different user rights, users, who can have one or more roles, can only perform a subset of these use cases. Following rules were defined:

- Website owner: Can read website and evaluations to get an overview of the progress of the evaluation
- Evaluator: Can define the initial scope of the website which will be evaluated and can create evaluations
- Auditor: Can create audits and can extend scope of a website and add evaluations the extended scope
- Certification authority: Can create website instances and assign evaluators and auditor in the system
- Anonymous user: Can check the certification status of a website and can read the evaluation report

The prototype of the certification portal is based on Drupal 8 CMS (Content Management System). Reasons to choose Drupal over other CMSs are the modular architecture and the flexible structure due to the concept of content types, which is comparable to non-primitive data types. This allows the rapid recreation of processes and objects involved. Besides, because of the modular approach every page and view can be individualized easily.

By means of the approach applied in this project, the process to achieve technical WA is largely facilitated. This also makes it easier to pass certification requirements for the resulting web user interfaces. But, of course, it needs the right software experts' competences and skills to fulfill tasks like the above.

4 WA Professional Competences and Skills

In order to avoid efficiency loss and costs in the process of software development, i.e. the companies and persons producing or programming websites, it is necessary to find or train the required WA professional competences and skills. Therefore, the CWAE (Certified Web Accessibility Expert) [4] certification scheme according to EN ISO/IEC 17024 was established in Austria in cooperation with the Austrian Chamber of Commerce – in practice with its subsidiary company Incite, which is responsible for Certification for Companies and Persons in the field of ICT and Consulting. CWAE is a personal certification scheme for persons, that requires to have at least experience (namely in the form of 2 real projects, that have to be presented in front of a certification commission) and education in the field of Web Accessibility. It is possible to acquire the certificate directly by the candidate him/herself. However, if support to upgrade existing competences and skills is needed, a 3-day-course for refreshing the knowledge is offered.

5 Lessons Learned

1. A sufficient knowledge of standards – especially in the field of eAccessibility & eInclusion – is important for avoiding risks (e.g. in the form of liability cases) and improving sustainability of the organization, its systems and services – not to mention the protection of formal and informal caregivers and the end-users. EU project IN LIFE (INdependent LIving support Functions for the Elderly) revealed the need for both, the development of new standards (or new aspects to be standardized) and existing standards to be harmonized. [5]
2. 'Content' in connection with interhuman communication is underrepresented in standardization efforts, which needs extension towards higher dimensions of semantic interoperability. This also requires the stronger inclusion of 'users' in software design.
3. Standardisation and certification are 'twins' in the sense that good certification schemes are often based on pertinent standard(s), and certification can be a powerful means to enforce standards. Besides, standards and certification schemes in the fields of eAccessibility & eInclusion are – more than anywhere else – aiming at comprehensive 'interoperability' (IOp) comprising also cross-border, cross-culture and cross-language interoperability which increasingly includes data and content (as well as pertinent methods) used by assistive technology (AT).

6 Outlook

Given the fact that high-level experts' competences and skills are necessary to achieve higher efficiency in the development of accessible websites, certification of both the experts' competences and skills and the technical achievement in the form of accessible websites are complementary. Given the huge dimension of WA – to fulfil requirements of multilinguality and multimodality in the Internet – efforts towards WA certification should be geared towards coordination at international level. Same applies to pertinent standardisation efforts which can form the basis for certification schemes.

Acknowledgment. This paper draws on results of "INdependent LIving support Functions for the Elderly" (IN LIFE), project no. 643442 co-funded by the EC under HORIZON 2020, the EU Framework Programme for Research and Innovation.

References

1. Management Group of the ITU-ISO-IEC-UN/ECE Memorandum of Understanding on eBusiness standards (MoU/MG). Recommendation on software and content development principles (2010). http://isotc.iso.org/livelink/livelink/fetch/2000/2489/Ittf_Home/MoU-MG/Moumg476Rev.1.pdf. (MoU/MG/12 N 476 Rev.1) (2012)
2. World Wide Web Consortium (W3C). Web Content Accessibility Guidelines 2.0 (identical with ISO/IEC 40500:2012 Information technology — W3C Web Content Accessibility Guidelines (WCAG) 2.0)

3. European Union (EU). Directive 2014/24/EU of the European Parliament and of the Council of 26 February 2014 on public procurement and repealing Directive 2004/18/EC. http://eur-lex.europa.eu/legal-content/EN/TXT/?uri=CELEX%3A32014L0024
4. https://www.incite.at/ausbildung/de/zertifizierungen/certified-webaccessibility-expert/
5. IN LIFE (INdependent LIving support Functions for the Elderly) Consortium, DELIVERABLE 9.8: Dissemination & Standardisation Plan 2018

Correlating Navigation Barriers on Web 2.0 with Accessibility Guidelines

Letícia Seixas Pereira[✉] and Dominique Archambault

Université Paris 8 Vincennes-Saint-Denis,
2 Rue de la Liberté, 93526 Saint-Denis, France
leticia.seixas-pereira02@univ-paris8.fr

Abstract. The constant emergence of new resources and interaction possibilities brought by web 2.0 brings a constant urge of keeping in track how those new elements can affect the interaction of people with disabilities and how far current re-search has managed to address existing problems. This paper presents the results of an empirical study designed to gather navigation barriers affecting blind people when interacting with some widely used web widgets – such as Popup windows, Auto Suggest Lists, etc. The aim is to correlate those barriers with WCAG 2.0 and ARIA guidelines. From this point of view, it is possible to determine which barriers are being covered by current guide-lines and which ones are still on the wild. As conducting users' evaluations are really costly, the more barriers can be eliminated beforehand, the more useful those sessions can be.

Keywords: Web accessibility · User evaluation · Accessibility guidelines
Navigation barriers · Web 2.0

1 Introduction

Once characterized by static pages and a passive environment, the web is currently a dynamic structure, that, through the use of several components (widgets), it combines a desktop interface and functionalities with the wide range of a web application [6, 10]. However, concerning the accessibility of these pages, all this interactivity represents a problem for users with disabilities, since assistive technologies are still trying to cope with this interaction model and dynamic updates [5, 6]. Furthermore, in order to make an accessible web 2.0 it is essential to comprehend how users interact with these dynamic contents and highly interactive components [6]. With that in mind, we correlated WCAG guidelines and WAI-ARIA recommendations that can be applied on the development of accessible web widgets. Following that, an empirical study was conducted with eleven blind users to gather a collection of barriers faced by them when interacting with dynamic components. The goal of this research was to link both specifications and analyze how far they can assure an accessible dynamic environment and which problems are still not covered by them.

© The Author(s) 2018
K. Miesenberger and G. Kouroupetroglou (Eds.): ICCHP 2018, LNCS 10896, pp. 13–21, 2018.
https://doi.org/10.1007/978-3-319-94277-3_3

2 Background

Power et al. [13] and Vigo and Harper [15], concentrate the efforts on the perspective of understanding user behavior and navigation strategies, however, with different goals. While the first one aims towards personalized web applications for people with disabilities, the second one aims towards navigation problems in real-time. Moreover, about code standardization, one significant attempt to create accessible dynamic content is WAI-ARIA. Published in 2014 by the W3C, it adds roles, states and properties to HTML tags to identify user features and their connection and states. It also offers the resource of communicating some updates to the screen reader [16]. Regarding methods for evaluating the accessibility on dynamic updates, Abu Doush et al. [1] and Fernandes et al. [9], proposed the evaluation of these pages by triggering all JavaScript events, i.e. generating all possible code changes, in order to check code compliance with WAI-ARIA and WCAG 2.0 specifications respectively. However, one considerable problem still remains: although it is essential to enable users to access the information, it is also extremely important being sure that they are able to make efficient use of it [4], i.e. that they understand interact with the content. Yet, this subject is not yet being sufficiently addressed by current researches. Given that, we aim to connect all those points, by finding out existing gaps between currently guidelines and navigation barriers, through gathering interaction problems from an empirical study and correlating them with WCAG 2.0 guidelines and WAI-ARIA Authoring Practices 1.1.

3 Method

We conducted an exploratory study case with eleven blind users who undertook several tasks on a variety of pre-defined websites, in order to observe their interaction and gather a collection of problems encountered by them while performing online activities.

3.1 Website Selection

Websites to be used was first based on a list provided by Alexa[1] web analytics tool, with the most accessed ones in France and, to ensure a dynamic sample, the sites at the top of the list were analyzed from the tell-signs described by [7]. Those who had the highest number of web widget were selected. Next, we elaborated tasks for each website based on its main activities as well its own purpose and also considering an activity that required an interaction with the widgets available on their pages.

---

[1] http://www.alexa.com.

3.2 Participants

This study was conducted with eleven blind users, between 36 and 66 years old. Most of them self-declared as experienced users and working with computer related activities, while the other two participants declared having an average familiarity with computers and internet. One participant used Voice Over and the rest of them used JAWS as their main screen reader software. Some of them used NVDA as a second screen reader during the evaluations, changing between tasks. Five of them counted with a braille display to assist their navigation. To exclude some external factors, all evaluations were conducted in their familiar environment (home/work places) and their usual assistive technologies, computers and software configurations were used.

3.3 Design

Evaluations began with us informing the participants about the study goal and how it would be conducted. Next, we ask them to sign a consent form and applied a profile form. The participants were encouraged to report any problems, using the "think aloud" verbal protocol [8], and after finishing the tasks from a website, they were asked to summarize their difficulties and how they affected task execution. Each evaluation was registered by an external digital camcorder and additional notes.

4 Data Analysis

In the first place, all data collected (notes, videos, forms and user reports) from participants was reviewed to identify barriers during their interaction with selected websites and their respectively widgets. Each barrier was labeled and categorized by the following items: (1) widget: corresponding element; (2) severity (minor/significant/critical): level of disruption caused by the barrier (from a minor shift in the interaction to an interruption of current task); (3) signalized/identified: whether the barrier has been signalized by the user or identified by the researcher; (4) impact: description of the consequences of the barrier in the interaction and task execution; (5) description: description of the barrier itself. Further, a second round of categorization was realized to highlight the instances of same barriers. For this, each instance was classified by its frequency, assistive technology used, user experience (from 1: none to 5: advanced), severity and general description. The final step consisted in correlate each final barrier with WCAG 2.0 guidelines and WAI-ARIA authoring practices to determine which of these barriers could be avoided by using recommendations and to identify the gap between development specifications and interaction barriers.

5 Results

For the first round of data analysis, a total of 43 instances of single barriers from an interaction with some web widget were identified and categorized (Table 1).

Table 1. Example of a single barrier identified and categorized

Inappropriate identification of the element "Tabs"	
Widget:	Tabs
Severity:	Critical
Signalized/Identified:	Identified

Impact: Even with the content being "available", the participant did not know how to manipulate it, as he understood it as a non-clickable element, providing a wrong result consciously.

Description: The participant was able to locate the desired content corresponding area. However, he could not identify that the information was arranged in tabs, not realizing that there were other contents hidden by that element.

From that, it was possible to detect the recurrence of 10 types of barriers, described as Final Barriers, with the following five widgets: Tabs, AutoSuggestList, Popup content, Carrousel and Collapsible panels. As the goal of this work was, by identifying existing barriers on the interaction of people with disabilities with web widgets, investigate how current efforts handles the accessibility of those elements, we correlated these barriers with WCAG 2.0 guidelines and WAI-ARIA Authoring Practices 1.1. It is important to stress that, as an accessibility evaluation, several barriers were also identified, however, only those linked, directly or indirectly, to the selected web widgets were categorized and further analyzed. Next, from all barriers categorized, we highlight those with the highest level of severity or frequency in Tables 2, 3 and 4.

From that we propose more guidance to support the development of accessible widgets. For the elements presented in described barriers, besides the items from W3C [16], to guarantee the accessible development of these elements, we add that:

- PopUp Content: (1) Users must be able to identify the opening of this element, being notified that new content is available as a result of a previous action; (2) As a modal dialog, keyboard should be moved to this descendent window, since users cannot interact with content outside an active dialog window; (3) Functionalities available through this element must be part of a set of consistently identified features;

Table 2. Final Barrier 1: lack of feedback from a PopUp Content.

Lack of feedback from a PopUp Content	
Frequency:	14 occurrences
Assistive technology:	6 Jaws, 2 NVDA, 4 braille display
Average user experience:	5 (Advanced)
Severity:	9 critical, 4 minor, 1 significant

Description: When accessing features that trigger a PopUp Content, by not receiving the expected feedback – since they assume that after accessing a functionality, a new page is loaded – it occurs a disruption in their interaction. Depending on its implementation, this code is or added or made visible, but, in both cases, this content is not highlighted in an equivalent way.

WCAG 2.0 related guidelines:

- Guideline 1.3: Success Criteria 1.3.1, 1.3.3: Content created should be presented in different ways without losing information or structure. Also, this structure must be reflected in the code, i.e. *programmatically determined*, and should not rely on sensory characteristics. But, when a PopUp is triggered and opened, visually, it is possible to recognize the highlight of the information, that, without the proper screen reader notification, it is not perceived.
- Guideline 2.4: Success Criterion 2.4.3: In a navigation sequence, components should receive focus in an order that preserves meaning, helping users locate themselves. Keyboard focus was not located inside the modal box, i.e. inside the functionality, and the primary window that should be blocked was navigable by the keyboard.
- Guideline 3.2: Success Criterion 3.2.4: Pages should appear and operate in predictable ways and, components that have the same functionality within a set of web pages should be identified consistently. But, while some menu options linked to another page, other triggered a PopUp Content, making their behavior completely unpredictable by the user.
- Guideline 4.1: Success Criterion 4.1.2: It assists a maximum compatibility with assistive technologies *programmatically determined* by the use of states, properties and their corresponding values. By using HTML tags name, role and value, assistive technologies could provide notifications on changes in those pages, avoiding the lack of feedback.

WAI-ARIA 1.1 related Authoring Practices 1.1:

- 3.8 Dialog (Modal): <dialog>: Indicates that the element is a descendent window.

Table 3. Final Barrier 2: difficulty in the perception of contents and sections in a Carousel.

Difficulty in the perception of contents and sections in a Carousel	
Frequency:	7 occurrences
Assistive technology:	7 Jaws, 3 NVDA, 1 Voice Over, 5 braille display
Average user experience:	5 (Advanced)
Severity:	7 minor

Description: Since the structure of the code does not reflect the visual structure of the element, users have a different perception of contents and sections of a page. They were not able to understand that both content – the list of information and the one highlighted at the moment by the element are at the same hierarchy level. Without the visual identity that groups all related information, they cannot distinguish those sections and contents from each other.

WCAG 2.0 related guidelines:

- Guideline 1.3: Success Criteria 1.3.1, 1.3.2, 1.3.3: Content should be presented in different ways without losing information or structure and it should maintain its structure and relationships presented in the same way, containing the same meaningful sequence and also it should not rely on sensory characteristics for being understood and operated. But, a content available by a Carousel when presented by a screen reader, did not reflected the same hierarchy and grouping that the visual one, changing its meaning and its relevance.
- Guideline 2.2: Success Criteria 2.2.3: As the Carousel is a based time widget, it should provide users enough time to read and use its content. Also, timing should not be an essential part of the activity, however, as the highlighted information changed, it also changed the hierarchy of main headings, altering the general page structure.
- Guideline 2.4: Success Criteria 2.4.10: Section headings should be used to organize the content and to help users navigate, find content and determine where they are. But, by changing the highlighted information, Carousel also changed headings structure, leaving the user extremely disoriented.

WAI-ARIA 1.1 related Authoring Practices 1.1: No recommendation was found.

- Carousel: (1) Elements at the same hierarchy level should be equally identified in the code, respecting their corresponding section grouping; (2) Page main structure and information should not be altered without a user action or a notification; (3) If what is changed is only visual, i.e., one content at a time being visually highlighted from a list, it should be kept along with control layout and presentation code (CSS);
- Tabs: (1) Titles of tabs and their corresponding contents must have the same logical structure as that displayed visually when read by the screen reader; (2) Users must be able to recognize the titles of the element and also manipulate them only with the use of the keyboard; (3) Visual hierarchical structure of the tabs must be reflected in the code so that the software is able to accurately reproduce the available content.

Table 4. Final Barrier 4: inappropriate identification of the element "Tabs".

Inappropriate identification of the element "Tabs"	
Frequency:	9 occurrences
Assistive technology:	5 Jaws, 1 NVDA, 2 braille display
Average user experience:	5 (Advanced)
Severity:	5 critical, 2 significant, 2 minor

Description: Since the code structure does not reflect the visual, if the identification is not adequate, the user does not identify the logic – title, link, list of information – in the content. In such cases, or he does not know how to interact with the element, not having access to the information at all, or he accesses information that does not correspond to the expected one.

WCAG 2.0 related guidelines:

- Guideline 1.3: Success Criteria 1.3.1, 1.3.2, 1.3.3: Content should maintain its structure and relationships presented in the same way, containing the same meaningful sequence, also it should not rely on sensory characteristics for being understood and operated. But, the content provided, when presented by the screen reader, is not equivalent to the structure visually displayed, representing different relationships and navigation sequences.
- Guideline 2.4: Success Criteria 2.4.3, 2.4.6, 2.4.10: Users must be able to locate themselves and section headings and focus order should reflect the same structure as the visual one.

WAI-ARIA 1.1 related Authoring Practices 1.1:

- 3.2.1 Tabs: <tablist>: container for a set of tabs; <tab>: tab control; <tabpanel>: tab container.

6 Conclusions

As already shown in several researches [2, 3, 11, 12, 14, 17], relying only in accessibility guidelines is not enough to ensure an accessible website, especially if taking into account the growth on web 2.0 related technologies. Automatic evaluation tools are capable to identify a great number of possible barriers, however, some of them can only be perceived through real user interaction. From the conducted study case we analyzed how currently guidelines such as WCAG 2.0 and WAI-ARIA combined can and should be used to promote web accessibility for dynamic pages. We also perceived that there is still a gap in accessibility guidelines, since it depends on the interpretation of the relationships between the elements present in the page. For that, it becomes necessary more studies on how users interact with these widgets to check which barriers are still not covered by current guidelines in order to direct our efforts.

As this is an ongoing research, future studies include users with different kinds of disabilities and also the development of a tool for assisting dynamic pages evaluations based on navigation barriers, evolving these conclusions into code checking items.

Acknowledgments. This work was supported by Coordenação de Aperfeiçoamento de Pessoal de Nível Superior (CAPES), Brazil, grant Doutorado Pleno no Exterior.

References

1. Abu Doush, I., Alkhateeb, F., Al Maghayreh, E., Al-Betar, M.A.: The design of RIA accessibility evaluation tool. Adv. Eng. Softw. **57**, 1–7 (2013)
2. Brajnik, G.: Validity and reliability of web accessibility guidelines. In: Proceedings of the 11th International ACM SIGACCESS Conference on Computers and Accessibility ISSU, pp. 131–138 (2009)
3. Brajnik, G., Yesilada, Y., Harper, S.: Testability and validity of WCAG 2.0. In: Proceedings of the 12th International ACM SIGACCESS Conference on Computers and Accessibility - ASSETS 2010, p. 43. ACM Press (2010)
4. Brown, A., Jay, C., Harper, S.: Audio presentation of auto-suggest lists. In: Proceedings of the 2009 International Cross-Disciplinary Conference on Web Accessibililty (W4A), pp. 58–61 (2009)
5. Brown, A., Jay, C., Harper, S.: Tailored presentation of dynamic web content for audio browsers. Int. J. Hum. Comput. Stud. **70**(3), 179–196 (2012)
6. Chen, A.Q.: Widget identification and modification for web 2.0 access technologies (WIMWAT). ACM SIGACCESS Access. Comput. **96**, 11–18 (2010)
7. Chen, A.Q., Harper, S., Lunn, D., Brown, A.: Widget identification: a high-level approach to accessibility. World Wide Web **16**(1), 73–89 (2013)
8. Ericsson, K.A., Simon, H.A.: Protocol Analysis: Verbal Reports as Data. Revised edition (1993)
9. Fernandes, N., Costa, D., Neves, S., Duarte, C., Carriço, L.: Evaluating the accessibility of rich internet applications. In: Proceedings of the International Cross-Disciplinary Conference on Web Accessibility - W4A 2012, p. 13. ACM Press (2012)
10. Fortes, R.P.M., Antonelli, H.L.: Avaliação de Acessibilidade e Usabilidade em RIA. In: Anais do XXII Simpósio Brasileiro de Sistemas Multimídia e Web, vol. 3, Minicursos, Teresina, Piauí, 8 a 11 de novembro 2016 (2016)
11. Leuthold, S., Bargas-Avila, J.A., Opwis, K.: Beyond web content accessibility guidelines: design of enhanced text user interfaces for blind internet users. Int. J. Hum. Comput. Stud. **66**(4), 257–270 (2008)
12. Power, C., Freire, A., Petrie, H., Swallow, D.: Guidelines are only half of the story: accessibility problems encountered by blind users on the web. In: Proceedings of the 2012 ACM Annual Conference on Human Factors in Computing Systems - CHI 2012, p. 433. ACM Press (2012)
13. Power, C., Petrie, H., Swallow, D., Murphy, E., Gallagher, B., Velasco, C.A.: Navigating, discovering and exploring the web: strategies used by people with print disabilities on interactive websites. In: Kotzé, P., Marsden, G., Lindgaard, G., Wesson, J., Winckler, M. (eds.) INTERACT 2013. LNCS, vol. 8117, pp. 667–684. Springer, Heidelberg (2013). https://doi.org/10.1007/978-3-642-40483-2_47
14. Rømen, D., Svanæs, D.: Validating WCAG versions 1.0 and 2.0 through usability testing with disabled users. Univers. Access Inf. Soc. **11**(4), 375–385 (2012)

15. Vigo, M., Harper, S.: Real-time detection of navigation problems on the World 'Wild' Web. Int. J. Hum. Comput. Stud. **101**, 1–9 (2016)
16. W3C: WAI-ARIA Overview (2018). http://www.w3.org/WAI/intro/aria.php
17. WAI: Involving Users in Evaluating Web Accessibility (2010). http://www.w3.org/WAI/eval/users.html

A Public Barrier Tracker to Support
the Web Accessibility Directive

Diane Alarcon[1], Kim Andreasson[1], Justyna Mucha[2], Annika Nietzio[3],
Agata Sawicka[4], and Mikael Snaprud[5(✉)]

[1] DAKA advisory AB, Varberg, Sweden
[2] University of Agder (UiA), Kristiansand, Norway
[3] Forschungsinstitut Technologie und Behinderung (FTB),
der Evangelischen Stiftung Volmarstein, Wetter, Germany
[4] Kristiansand, Norway
agasawi@gmail.com
[5] Tingtun AS, Lillesand, Norway
mikael.snaprud@tingtun.no
http://www.DAKAadvisory.com
http://www.uia.no
http://www.ftb-esv.de
http://www.tingtun.no

Abstract. In this paper we propose the *Public Barrier Tracker (PBT) –*
a comprehensive solution that supports both filing and handling of user
feedback on web accessibility. We give an overview of some existing
approaches for gathering user feedback on accessibility barriers and outline the PBT functionality. The PBT can also offer further support for
the implementation of the WAD: The collected data could be useful for
monitoring and reporting as well as the enforcement mechanism.

1 Introduction

In 2016 the European Parliament adopted the *Directive (EU) 2016/2102 on
the accessibility of the websites and mobile applications of public sector bodies*
(Web Accessibility Directive, WAD). The Directive is a result of a long lasting effort aiming at increasing accessibility of public online services across the
European Union. The Directive not only provides a set of minimum accessibility
requirements, but also defines a methodology for regular monitoring of accessibility. The website's owner has a central responsibility for ensuring accessibility. Compliance with the accessibility requirements shall be declared through a
mandatory accessibility statement. The statement must also provide information
regarding the enforcement procedure and describe a feedback mechanism. This
mechanism shall enable "any person to notify the public sector body concerned
of any failure of its website or mobile application to comply with the accessibility
requirements" (WAD, Article 7, paragraph 1(a)).

A. Sawicka—Accessibility expert.

© The Author(s) 2018
K. Miesenberger and G. Kouroupetroglou (Eds.): ICCHP 2018, LNCS 10896, pp. 22–26, 2018.
https://doi.org/10.1007/978-3-319-94277-3_4

The feedback mechanism gives users the opportunity to report on noncompliance with WAD. This is an important element in achieving web accessibility. Direct feedback from end users can help capture crucial issues. User-reported barriers are likely to be those that are currently difficult to detect with automatic or expert web accessibility tests. For the feedback mechanism to be effective, it needs to be easy to use, and it needs buy-in from website owner so that the users can see that their comments are acted upon and lead to real improvements.

2 Gathering User Feedback About Accessibility Issues: Overview of Existing Approaches

The most common way of gathering user feedback is through an open comment form where users can send their remarks to the website's owners. In recent years, several initiatives have been established, aiming at collecting feedback on web accessibility, but also on issues such as physical barriers or other problems in streets and buildings. This section gives a brief overview of such initiatives.

Meldestelle für Digitale Barrieren (Digital barrier helpdesk) [1] is a German project run by the disability organisation BAG Selbsthilfe. The initiative collects reports about accessibility problems in websites, electronic documents and public service terminals. Barriers can be reported through a form on the project website, a browser addon or an Android application. Moreover, users can report barriers by email, phone, fax and via a specialised sign-language service. All reports are stored in a database and analysed by the project team who then contacts the website owner with information about the barrier and a recommendation how to remove it. The strengths of this initiative are: multiple ways of reporting, many areas of accessibility covered, and individual handling of each report.

FixTheWeb [2] is a campaign to raise awareness for web accessibility issues. Persons with disabilities can report accessibility problems by using a web form, email, Twitter or a browser plugin. Reports can be submitted anonymously but users are encouraged to provide an email address for questions. FixTheWeb is a community effort relying on volunteers to handle the reports, i.e. confirm that the issue exists and contact the website owner. More than 54% of all reports turned out to be incorrect (spam or issues not caused by the website). 39% of the contacted website owners acknowledged the report and 25% fixed the issue. The strengths of this initiative are: awareness raising, empowerment of persons with disabilities (only they can submit reports), individual handling of each report.

Web Forms Provided on Public Sector Bodies' Websites. Some websites provide a feedback mechanism to report web accessibility issues. They use a web form to collect detailed information about the location and type of problem and the circumstances. Sometimes the link to the feedback page is available in the footer of the website, i.e. on every page. In other cases the link is provided only on the contact page or on another specific page, which are hard to find. In these approaches the feedback is handled directly by the public body.

FixMyStreet [3] collects reports about potholes, broken street lights etc. The reports are sent to the municipality via the official email address provided for such complaints and are published on the FixMyStreet website. Municipalities can subscribe to the FixMyStreet service which allows them to integrate the reporting with their back-office system. FixMyStreet is handling a large number of reports – about 8000 per week. The strengths of this initiative are the simple process, integration with back-office systems and large number of reports.

W3C Contacting Organizations about Inaccessible Websites [4]. The W3C Web Accessibility Initiative (WAI) has compiled a list of tips for contacting organizations about inaccessible websites. The step-by-step guide describes how to clearly identify and describe the problem so that it can be solved. There are many tips for communication, e.g. regarding the follow-up discussion with the goal of getting a response and achieving the removal of the barrier.

The experiences of these initiatives can inform the implementation of the feedback mechanism for the WAD. Howemver, none of them covers all the required features. In the next section, we outline the main functions of the proposed PBT solution and discuss how it addresses the WAD requirements.

3 The Public Barrier Tracker (PBT)

PBT provides a mechanism for gathering user feedback regarding web accessibility directly on a website. It uses an approach where JavaScript is included on a webpage to add the service. In addition there is a fall-back solution for those who do not use JavaScript. The reports are processed by the website owner who can accept a report and assign it to a web developer or reject it. The status of each report is tracked in a public interface so anyone knowing the report number can look it up. This allows users who want to remain anonymous to monitor the progress. Users who provide their contact information and give consent will receive updates on the issues directly.

The PBT database allows the users to have insight into how the barriers are handled. Further interaction is also possible, e.g. a user confirming that a barrier has been removed or a web developer searching for similar issues and how those were addressed. In addition, PBT also provides a powerful tool for implementing other aspects of the WAD.

3.1 Potential Synergies of PBT with Other WAD Requirements

The feedback mechanism of the WAD has the double function of providing an effective way for users to obtain information and services that are provided online in an inaccessible way and a channel for users to inform public sector bodies of accessibility barriers.

Reports from WADEX (The WAD Expert group) emphasize that the accessibility statement should encourage users to send feedback and that the process should be made as easy as possible [5]. However, so far no particular advice is given on how the use of feedback could be promoted in practice. The PBT solution offers a cohesive framework for a user feedback tool with focus on automatic facilitation of feedback gathering and handling. This provides advantages for both users and developers. The tracking functionality will increase the user engagement.

The data collected by PBT can also support other aspects of the WAD. PBT will support barrier classification consistent with the WAD accessibility requirements defined in Articles 4, 5 and 6. Furthermore, the PBT solution will support filing of the complaints through the implemented enforcement procedures (Article 9). Accessibility reports that are not addressed in an adequate manner may be sent directly to the enforcement agency. Alternatively, enforcement agencies may use the PBT database to discover public sector bodies that do not handle user requests adequately.

Finally, the PBT database will provide a rich repository of data on the accessibility problems that are encountered by users, where the problems are most prominent, how they are addressed, etc. Such information will be valuable both for reporting, as well as for fine tuning of the evaluation guidelines and monitoring methodologies (Article 8).

3.2   Potential Challenges in Implementation and Use

The PBT implementation is not yet completed. A first prototype is available. User testing and improvements of the implementation are planned. To successfully establish a PBT service it has to give good support to the users filing barrier reports and it has to be easy to implement for the site owners.

Challenges include how to strike a balance between barrier details to request from the users and the ease of use. The PBT user interface must be accessible and easy to use but it should also allow users to provide all the details needed to inform the repair process.

PBT needs to take into account the upcoming General Data Protection Regulation and will for allow anonymous and personalized feedback. In both cases, issues of data protection will have to be addressed. One of the challenges is to avoid that users provide personal data inadvertently.

PBT may be implemented as a feedback solution by an individual website owner. However, the approach would be most powerful when adopted by a greater number of organisations – for example as a sectoral or national solution, or ideally as an approach recommended at the European level. This would allow PBT not only to function as an effective mechanism for submitting user feedback on a particular issue, but also as a tool for gathering important data to support effective implementation of the WAD at large.

Acknowledgements. The PBT project is financially supported by the Swedish Post and Telecom Authority (PTS) innovation competition.

References

1. BAG Selbsthilfe: Abschlussbericht des Modellprojekts Barrieren Melde- und Monitoringstelle (2017). http://barrieren-melden.de/images/stories/docs/2017-Barrieren-MeMo-Abschlussbericht.pdf. Accessed 08 Jan 2018
2. FixTheWeb: www.fixtheweb.net. Accessed 08 Jan 2018
3. FixMyStreet: www.fixmystreet.com. Accessed 23 Jan 2018
4. W3C/WAI: Contacting Organizations about Inaccessible Websites. www.w3.org/WAI/users/inaccessible. Accessed 08 Jan 2018
5. Web Accessibility Directive Expert Group: Reports and and meeting notes (2017). http://ec.europa.eu/transparency/regexpert/index.cfm?do=groupDetail.groupDetail&groupID=3475. Accessed 01 Feb 2018

CrowdAE: A Crowdsourcing System with Human Inspection Quality Enhancement for Web Accessibility Evaluation

Liangcheng Li[1], Jiajun Bu[1(✉)], Can Wang[1], Zhi Yu[1], Wei Wang[1], Yue Wu[1], Chunbin Gu[1], and Qin Zhou[2]

[1] Alibaba-Zhejiang University Joint Institute of Frontier Technologies, Zhejiang Provincial Key Laboratory of Service Robot, College of Computer Science, Zhejiang University, Hangzhou 310027, China
{liangcheng_li,bjj,wcan,yuzhirenzhe,wangwei_eagle, wy1988,guchunbin}@zju.edu.cn

[2] Information Center, China Disabled Persons' Federation, Beijing 100034, China
zhouqin@cdpf.org.cn

Abstract. Crowdsourcing technology can help manual testing by soliciting the contributions from volunteer evaluators. But crowd evaluators may give inaccurate or invalid evaluation results. This paper proposes an advanced crowdsourcing-based web accessibility evaluation system called *CrowdAE* by enhancing the crowdsourcing-based manual testing module of the previous version. Through three main process namely learning system, task assignment and task review, we can improve the quality of evaluation results from the crowd. From the comparison on the two years' evaluation process of Chinese government websites, our *CrowdAE* outperforms the previous version and improve the accuracy of the evaluation results.

Keywords: Web accessibility evaluation · Crowdsourcing

1 Introduction

In the era of the ongoing World Wide Web, the disabled populations are experiencing various difficulties in accessing information on the Web. Although many efforts have been made on web accessibility, a lot of accessibility problems still remain in websites [1]. Web Accessibility Evaluation (WAE) is a work to find the potential accessibility problems and provide suggestions for amelioration [2]. Among many evaluation methods quantifying the accessibility feature, conformance testing is the most widely adopted as analytic judging method based on some formal guidelines [3], with the hybrid process of automatic testing and manual testing.

Since most of the checkpoints in web accessibility evaluation still need manual testing, the main challenge is the burdensome and expensive work for an evaluator to evaluate a medium-size website. Crowdsourcing technology can help by soliciting the contributions from volunteer evaluators. However, the web accessibility evaluation is a

© Springer International Publishing AG, part of Springer Nature 2018
K. Miesenberger and G. Kouroupetroglou (Eds.): ICCHP 2018, LNCS 10896, pp. 27–30, 2018.
https://doi.org/10.1007/978-3-319-94277-3_5

professional work [4], so the evaluators who lack certain expertise may give inaccurate or invalid evaluation result, causing negative effects on web accessibility evaluation.

In consideration of the previous weaknesses on crowdsourcing system, we provide an advanced WAE system which is called *CrowdAE* by enhancing the quality of human inspection in manual testing process. The core three mechanisms around the manual testing, namely learning system, task assignment and task review. We integrate them into previous crowdsourcing-based evaluation system and make the comparison between two- year evaluation results. The results show that our *CrowdAE* outperforms the previous web accessibility evaluation system.

2   Related Work

WAE has been widely studied and many countries contribute on it with some accessibility evaluation methods and metrics supported. South America countries rely on automatic evaluation tools to evaluate e-government websites [5]; Turkey also performs automatic testing on evaluating its government websites based on WCAG guideline [6]. Although most evaluation checkpoints can be achieved via automatic process, there still require manual testing to evaluate the semantic or operative checkpoints [7].

As insufficient evaluators evaluating the large-scale websites is burdensome and expensive in manual testing, crowdsourcing technology is applied which can integrate the power of crowds to finish evaluation tasks. Previously, Li et al. propose a crowdsourcing-based system with proper task assignment to let volunteer crowds participate in evaluation in China, which has been used for accessibility evaluation on Chinese government websites since 2016. However, this crowdsourcing system still lack complete mechanism for dealing with the crowd, such as novice training, quality control.

3   System Architecture and Work Flow

The *CrowdAE* is a synthetic online web accessibility evaluation system. Based on the Chinese authoritative standard YD/T 1761-2012, the *CrowdAE* provides four sub-modules to accomplish the whole evaluation process as following: (1) Sampling, crawling and rendering. A sampling algorithm is plugged in to select typical pages according to some criteria, these pages are downloaded and rendered for the further evaluation. (2) Automatic testing. Accessibility evaluation that can be done automatically by tools are examined at this module and an automatic evaluation result will be generated. (3) Crowdsourcing-based manual testing. For accessibility evaluation requiring human judgement, we will leverage contributions from a wide range of volunteer evaluators, including people with disabilities. The crowdsourcing system has built-in mechanisms including training evaluators, assigning tasks, evaluating results submitted and task review. Generally, a result for an accessibility check is based on decisions from multiple evaluators. If results are divergent, the system will rely on task review to settle the disagreements. (4) Result presentation. The results from automatic testing and manual testing will be combined for analyzation via several assessment metrics, then they will be generated into the final evaluation report. Figure 1 shows the details.

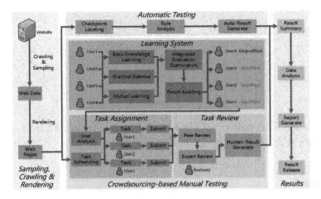

Fig. 1. The architecture of *CrowdAE*. The arrows and blocks with different color show the work flow of the web accessibility evaluation process. (Color figure online)

The core module of *CrowdAE* is the Crowdsourcing-based Manual Testing, which is consist of learning system, task assignment and task review. The novice evaluators first need participate in the learning system for training accessibility evaluation skills, they can learn basic theory of web accessibility as well as make practical evaluation for self-checking, with a sample recommendation method assisting by providing the similar examples for the current learning page. Meanwhile, the evaluators can make online discussion on difficulties in mutual learning mode. Then each evaluator is suggested to take an integrated test for qualification of evaluation. Once some evaluators are qualified for formal accessibility evaluation, they are received some formal evaluation tasks scheduled by task assignment algorithm with personalized analysis and submit their evaluation results. For each task, multiple evaluators are required to judge for the checkpoints on the web page. If one feels confused about a task, he/she can choose to give up and work for another task which the system assigns dynamically. After that, task review including peer review and expert review is proposed for checking the validity of the previous evaluation results based on some evaluation metrics. Finally, the human results in manual testing are generated for the final result generation.

4 Observation in Real World

We perform the web accessibility evaluation on 30 Chinese government websites in 2017, which have been also evaluated in 2016. We recruit 30 new different volunteer evaluators with different ages and vocations to participate in evaluation in 2017 under our new *CrowdAE*. These volunteers are training for grasping accessibility knowledge for two weeks in learning system, after passing the qualification test they will participate in formal accessibility evaluation. With the comparison of the evaluation results under the China Web Accessibility Evaluation System (CWAES) in 2016, we check the results according to the review and count the consistent ones for accuracy rate. From the Fig. 2 we can find that the accuracy of tasks increases under *CrowdAE*.

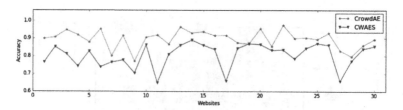

Fig. 2. The accuracy of evaluation tasks in 30 websites under *CrowdAE* (red line) in 2017 and *CWAES* (blue line) in 2016. (Color figure online)

5   Conclusion

The *CrowdAE* mainly enhances the human inspection in web accessibility evaluation. With the mechanism in manual testing which are learning system for novice evaluators, task assignment for analyzing the preference and ability of evaluators, and task review for task quality control, the web accessibility evaluation is improved with high task accuracy and more volunteer evaluators. The experiment also proves that the *CrowdAE* outperforms in real world accessibility evaluation, and the crowdsourcing idea will bring more focuses, participations and contributions on web accessibility.

Acknowledgement. This work is supported by the National Natural Science Foundation of China (Nos. 61173185 and 61173186), the National Key Technology R&D Program of China (No. 2012BAI34B01 and 2014BAK15B02), and the Hangzhou S&T Development Plan (No. 20150834M22).

References

1. Sullivan, T., Matson, R.: Barriers to use: usability and content accessibility on the Web's most popular websites. In: ACM Conference on Universal Usability, pp. 139–144 (2000)
2. Abou-Zahra, S.: Web accessibility evaluation. In: Harper, S., Yesilada, Y. (eds.) Web Accessibility. Human-Computer Interaction Series, 1st edn, pp. 79–106. Springer, London (2008). https://doi.org/10.1007/978-1-84800-050-6_7
3. Brajnik, G., Yesilada, Y., Harper, S.: Is accessibility conformance an elusive property? A study of validity and reliability of WCAG 2.0. ACM Trans. Access. Comput. **4**(2), 8 (2012)
4. Brajnik, G., Yesilada, Y., Harper, S.: The expertise effect on web accessibility evaluation methods. Hum.-Comput. Interact. **26**(3), 246–283 (2011)
5. Lujan-Mora, S., Navarrete, R., Penafiel, M.: E-government and web accessibility in South America. In: First International Conference on E-democracy & E-government, pp. 77–82 (2014)
6. Akgül, Y., Vatansever, K.: Web accessibility evaluation of government websites for people with disabilities in Turkey. J. Adv. Manag. Sci. **4**, 201–210 (2016)
7. Brajnik, G.: A comparative test of Web accessibility evaluation methods. In: Proceedings of the 10th International ACM SIGACCESS Conference on Computers and Accessibility, pp. 113–120 (2008)

Is Web-Based Computer-Aided Translation (CAT) Software Usable for Blind Translators?

Silvia Rodríguez Vázquez[1(✉)], Dónal Fitzpatrick[2], and Sharon O'Brien[2]

[1] University of Geneva, 40, Bd. du Pont d'Arve, 1211 Geneva, Switzerland
silvia.rodriguez@unige.ch
[2] Dublin City University, Glasnevin, Dublin 9, Ireland
{donal.fitzpatrick,sharon.obrien}@dcu.ie

Abstract. In spite of the progress made to date in the area of Human-Computer Interaction (HCI), recent experience reports by end users as well as research work have suggested that leading desktop-based Computer-Aided Translation (CAT) tool providers fail to consider the particular needs of screen reader users when developing their software. The study presented in this paper was conducted to assess the usability of two popular online CAT tools (Matecat and Memsource) that could serve as an alternative solution to inaccessible desktop applications. Findings indicate that Matecat is significantly more usable than Memsource, although changes would be needed in the former for blind translators to be able to perform a translation job completely autonomously and efficiently. Overall, our study suggests that accessibility awareness is still low in the translation technology industry, and that further research and development is needed in to guarantee equal opportunities for all in the translation market.

Keywords: Computer-Aided Translation · Web accessibility · Blind translators
Usability

1 Introduction and Motivation

Computer-aided translation (CAT) tools are the most popular example of translation technology and, over the last years, knowing how to use them has become an indispensable skill for translators to access the job market. Beyond the traditional goals of increasing quality and productivity levels, translation technologies are now designed, more than ever, to be as enjoyable and easy to use and learn as possible. In order to achieve the latter, translation software providers try to account for different end user profiles by designing cross-device, cross-platform solutions and multimodal interfaces.

Nevertheless, and in spite of the progress made to date in the area of Human-Computer Interaction (HCI), recent experience reports by end users as well as research work have suggested that leading desktop-based CAT tool providers fail to consider the particular needs of screen reader users when developing their software [6, 7]. Although some efforts have been devoted in the past to developing translation tool prototypes that particularly target blind translators [1], we contend that, for them to be treated equally

© Springer International Publishing AG, part of Springer Nature 2018
K. Miesenberger and G. Kouroupetroglou (Eds.): ICCHP 2018, LNCS 10896, pp. 31–34, 2018.
https://doi.org/10.1007/978-3-319-94277-3_6

as their sighted peers at a professional level, accessibility should be built into the development and design practices of the commercial tools available on the market.

Taking into account the conclusions drawn in prior research work about the low level of accessibility featured by the most popular desktop-based CAT tools [7], we conducted a follow-up study to explore the potential of web-based CAT tools as a more suitable solution for blind translators. Our study, which took place over a period of two months (May–June 2016), was grounded on the belief that web development techniques are more standardised than most of the computer programming styles available and, therefore, a higher level of accessibility can be achieved. To the best of our knowledge, this is the first experimental study on the use of translation technology conducted with screen reader users. This novel focus on accessibility is not only motivated by the potential social impact that the availability of fully accessible commercial CAT tools could have, it also aligns with the recent research interest shown on user centred factors in translation technology design and evaluation, with an increasing number of studies revolving around the translators' needs in terms of UX [5] and multimodal software [8, 9].

2   Method

The goal of the study was two-fold: on one hand, it sought to assess the usability of two Machine Translation-integrated (MT) online CAT tools (Matecat[1] and Memsource[2]) and, on the other hand, it aimed at identifying the most recurrent accessibility issues in this type of software, with a view to developing a quick "accessibility checklist" for current and future online CAT tool developers. Due to space restrictions, this paper will only present the overall results of the former. In the study, we followed a classic usability evaluation approach, where a cohort of blind translators, mainly recruited through the RoundTable mailing list,[3] were requested (i) to conduct a simple post-editing exercise (i.e. translation and revision of machine-translated text in their mother tongue) and (ii) to provide information about their interaction with the software.

More specifically, translators were asked to report any issues encountered while trying to perform the post-editing exercise via a validated frustration experience form, used in prior work for HCI studies of similar nature [2, 3]. Once the interaction finished, participants completed a survey, inspired by the Computer System Usability Questionnaire (CSUQ) [4]. The survey also included several questions intended to measure the participants' confidence in having successfully completed the task requested.

The two tools chosen were the only ones among a selection of six popular web-based post-editing environments which, during a pre-test, met the basic accessibility requirements needed for the study to be feasible. Participants were allowed to use their own assistive technology (screen reader only or screen reader in combination with their refreshable Braille display), as well as to test the tools with different browsers, should

---

[1]   https://www.matecat.com/ Last access: 29th January 2018.

[2]   https://www.memsource.com/ Last access: 29th January 2018.

[3]   http://lists.screenreview.org/listinfo.cgi/theroundtable-screenreview.org   Last   access: 29th January 2018.

they find it appropriate. They all performed the experiment using Windows as the main operating system.

The 11 participants (8 female, 3 male) included representatives from seven different nationalities: Austria (N = 3), Germany (N = 2), Italy (N = 2), Canada (N = 1), Egypt (N = 1), Poland (N = 1) and UK (N = 1); who had a translation background with a university degree (BA or MA), and whose self-rated computer skills on a 5-point scale were excellent (N = 5), good (N = 5) and adequate (N = 1). From the 11 participants, six had a translation job at the time of the study, while the other five were working in related fields, such as transcription, revision or public administration.

3 Usability Evaluation: Key Findings

In total, each tool was tested by 10 translators (nine translators tested both tools, one translator tested only Matecat and one translator tested only Memsource). As illustrated in Fig. 1, findings indicate that, overall, blind translators participating in the study found that Matecat (average score $\bar{x} = 4.20$, sd = 0.51) was significantly more usable (p < 0.001) than Memsource (average score $\bar{x} = 2.37$, sd = 1.13). A significant difference was also found between both tools when particularly looking at the system usefulness subscale (Matecat, average score $\bar{x} = 4$, sd = 0.11; Memsource, average score $\bar{x} = 1.64$, sd = 0.63; p < 0.001). It is also worth noting that blind translators reported a higher level of confidence in having successfully completed the translation task in the case of Matecat, which is in line with the CSUQ results.

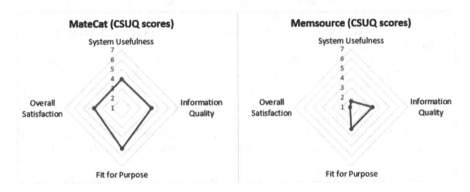

Fig. 1. Overall CSUQ scores (on a 7-point scale) for Matecat (radar chart, left) and Memsource (radar chart, right)

Paradoxically, the qualitative data collected through the frustration experience forms reveals that, in the case of Matecat, 48.15% of the issues reported were found in the translation editor, usually considered as the main working environment (as opposed to the general settings and project management sections of this type of tool). Some examples included difficulties while editing the MT suggestion or copying parts of the source segment into the target language segment. This can be explained by the fact that, while only 27.59% of the frustration experiences logged by participants when interacting with

Memsource referred to the translation editor, these seemed impossible to overcome for all screen reader users. In contrast, most translators using Matecat figured out a coping strategy to bypass the issues found in the translation environment, either by fixing the problem themselves or by finding alternative solutions to carry out the task requested.

4 Concluding Remarks

From a general perspective, the usability evaluation carried out suggests that changes would be needed in the tools tested for screen reader users to be able to perform a translation job autonomously and efficiently, although those would be minor in the case of Matecat. Additionally, the quantitative and qualitative data gathered have contributed not only to identifying current challenges faced by blind translators when using the two tools evaluated, but also to provide important insights into which general recommendations could be followed by translation technology providers to adopt an accessible design approach when developing their software.

References

1. Al-Bassam, D., Alotaibi, H., Alotaibi, S., Al-Khalifa, Hend S.: EasyTrans: accessible translation system for blind translators. In: Miesenberger, K., Bühler, C., Penaz, P. (eds.) ICCHP 2016. LNCS, vol. 9759, pp. 583–586. Springer, Cham (2016). https://doi.org/10.1007/978-3-319-41267-2_83
2. Ceaparu, I., et al.: Determining causes and severity of end-user frustration. Int. J. Hum.-Comput. Interact. **17**(3), 333–356 (2004)
3. Lazar, J., et al.: What frustrates screen reader users on the web: a study of 100 blind users. Int. J. Hum.-Comput. Interact. **22**(3), 247–269 (2007)
4. Lewis, J.R.: IBM computer usability satisfaction questionnaires: psychometric evaluation and instructions for use. Int. J. Hum.-Comput. Interact. **7**(1), 57–78 (1995)
5. Moorkens, J., O'Brien, S.: Assessing user interface needs of post-editors of machine translation. In: Kenny, D. (ed.) Human Issues in Translation Technology: The IATIS Yearbook. Routledge, Oxford (2017)
6. Owton, T., Mileto, F.: Translation tools and software - help or hindrance? (2011). http://www.euroblind.org/newsletter/2011/november-december/en/translation-tools-and-software-help-or-hindrance
7. Rodríguez Vázquez, S., Mileto, F.: On the lookout for accessible translation aids: current scenario and new horizons for blind translation students and professionals. J. Transl. Educ. Transl. Stud. **1**(2), 115–135 (2016)
8. Teixeira, C.S.C., Moorkens, J.: Creating a tool for multimodal translation and post-editing on touch-screen devices. In: Translating and the Computer (TC39) Conference, London, UK (2017)
9. Torres-Hostench, O., et al.: Testing interaction with a mobile MT postediting app. Int. J. Transl. Interpret. Res. **9**(2), 138–150 (2017)

An Image-Based Visual Strategy for Working with Color Contrasts During Design

Frode Eika Sandnes[1,2(✉)] iD

[1] Department of Computer Science, Oslo Metropolitan University, Oslo, Norway
frodes@oslomet.no
[2] Faculty of Technology, Kristiania University College, Oslo, Norway

Abstract. Many websites do not satisfy minimum contrast requirements. One reason could be that designers must select colors through trial and error using contrast calculators. This paper presents a visual framework for working with color contrasts. The foreground and background colors are detected automatically, and views are presented to simulate how a design is viewed with different levels of reduced vision. Moreover, saturation-brightness plots are introduced to help make valid color choices. Color corrections are proposed and visualized.

Keywords: Color contrast · Low-vision · WCAG2.0 · Visual design

1 Introduction

WCAG2.0 [1] gives concrete advice on how to ensure sufficient color contrast on web pages. The minimum requirement is a contrast ratio of 4.5:1 between the foreground body text and the background and a contrast ratio of 3:1 for headings (criterion 1.4.3), while the enhanced criterion (1.4.6) specifies a contrast of 7:1 for body text and 4.5:1 for headings. The recommendation is mathematical, and many web developers therefore use contrast calculators for validation. Such contrast calculators are often used when a design is finished. Moreover, the user needs to experiment through trial and error to find alternative color combinations that meet the contrast requirements. The calculators require color vectors as input, and these may be cumbersome to retrieve.

This paper therefore explores an interactive visualization tool that allows a designer to visualize the effects of a design when perceived by individuals with low vision. Moreover, if the design does not meet the contrast requirements the tool suggests corrected colors and visualizes how the design appears with these colors. The tool is intended to be quick and convenient to use with the aim that it is used during the design phase instead of afterwards. It is not limited to html pages as it works with design mockups drawn in paint programs, ordinary user interface designs, mobile interfaces as well as html-pages. The framework is intended to work alongside the designers' preferred tools.

K. Miesenberger and G. Kouroupetroglou (Eds.): ICCHP 2018, LNCS 10896, pp. 35–42, 2018.
https://doi.org/10.1007/978-3-319-94277-3_7

2   Background

The successful reading of text is affected by factors such as correct input [2–4] and readability [5–7] which especially affect individuals with dyslexia [8]. Sufficient contrast is an absolute prerequisite to perceive text visually both by human and machine [9], and visual reading is the preferred modality for individuals with working vision [10, 11]. Individuals who are diagnosed as being technically blind employ other modalities such as audio [12, 13] and haptic feedback [14]. Early work on contrast of printed text was dominated by Tinker and colleagues [15]. Later works has studied contrast on various output devices such as CRT-displays [16], LCD-displays [17] and electronic paper [18]. Issues addressed include display quality [19], color combinations [20–22], polarity effects [23, 24] and text size [14].

WCAG2.0 gives concrete advice on what constitute sufficient contrast. Yet, a lack of contrast is a common problem. Since WCAG2.0 became part of the legislature on universal design in Norway, the Norwegian agency that oversees these regulations has found contrast problems in many cases since official audits were introduced. One may speculate to the reasons why a lack of contrast is still a problem despite the concrete requirements and color contrast tools. One reason may be that some designers are unaware of these requirements and tools. Another explanation may be that designers forget to check for contrast compliance. More likely is that designers use their impressionistic judgement of what constitute sufficient contrast.

There have been relatively few studies on the process of selecting colors and color picking interfaces. Exceptions include the exploration of bimanual color selection [25], color-selection for image retrieval [26], the effects of various visual color representations in color pickers [27], the design of palettes for color blindness [28] and software tools for color scheme design [29, 30]. Reinecke et al. [31] described a tool to compare colors under different lighting conditions. Webster [32] pointed out that there is no support for contrast calculations in traditional color selection tools.

In our previous work [33] we explored specialized color selection palettes with built-in contrast visualizations, both for RGB-based palettes [34] and HSB-based palettes [35]. We also visualized contrast requirements in the color spaces including RGB, HSB and CIElab [36]. Recently, Tigwell et al. [37] developed a specific tool to help designers select colors that satisfies the WCAG2.0 color contrast constraints.

3   Method

Three visualizations tools are proposed herein, namely contrast filters, contrast enhancers and saturation-brightness plots. The contrast filter is used to visually assess how well information in a design is perceived by users with different levels of reduced vision. The contrast enhancer is a tool that analyses the design and proposes corrected foreground colors that satisfy the WCAG2.0 contrast requirements. Finally, the saturation-brightness plot (SB-plot), is an analysis tool for understanding color choices. Foreground and background colors are plotted in the saturation-brightness plane where "safe" areas with sufficient contrast are indicated.

3.1 Contrast Filter

An image contrast filter was built using the luminosity contrast definitions in the WCAG2.0 documentation. For each pixel in the input image the contrast with the background color is computed. If the contrast meets the requirement the original pixel color is used, otherwise the background color is used.

To determine the background color of an image it is necessary to find the color that occur the most frequently. The following algorithm was devised. The image is dived into a 3 × 3 grid and the middle section is used for analysis. This approach means that borders and other peripheral elements do not affect the result. It assumes that the central part of the image is the most important. A 3D histogram is constructed from these pixel values according to the RGB components. Since pixel colors often vary the two least significant bits are ignored. The histogram had 64 × 64 × 64 bins. Next, the histogram entry with the highest count is the background color, and the entry with the second highest count is the foreground. Finally, the average color of the pixels with this histogram entry were calculated.

Figure 1 shows the original image of a text with low contrast, and the image committed to the contrast filter a threshold of 3:1. We can just about see the contours of the letter, but we are unable to perceive the text. Figure 2 shows the filter applied to Google Maps. With a contrast threshold of 3:1 some of the text is still readable, but the subtle indication of roads are gone. With a contrast threshold of 4.5:1 the text becomes much harder to perceive, and with a contrast threshold of 7:1 all the text disappeared. Only the notification (bell icon in the top right corner) survived.

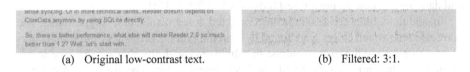

(a) Original low-contrast text.   (b) Filtered: 3:1.

Fig. 1. Contrast filtering of an image with low contrast text.

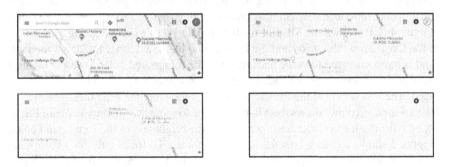

Fig. 2. Inspecting the contrast of Google Maps (original, 3:1, 4.5:1 and 7:1).

Figure 3 shows the contrast filter applied to an image of a Microsoft Office color picker when choosing a white background. It is apparent which colors are contrast safe. Any type of color picker, or background color, can be used.

Fig. 3. Color picker: Valid colors with white background: original, 3:1, 4.5:1 and 7:1. (Color figure online)

3.2 SB-Plots

The selected colors were plotted in the saturation-brightness plane to help designers understand their color choices, their freedom and the formal constraints. All varieties of hues are projected onto the same SB-plot. The rationale is that color choices are primarily focused around hues, and contrast adjustments are thus best performed by either adjusting the brightness or saturation. A SB-plot has two components, namely color choices and threshold regions. The horizontal axis represents brightness going from dark (left) to bright (right), and the vertical axis represents the saturation going from unsaturated (top) to saturated (bottom).

The background and foreground colors are represented using a green and red cross, respectively. Shades of grey are used to signal contrast levels where white signals invalid brightness and saturation choices in relation to the background color. Light, medium and dark grey denote contrast thresholds of 3:1, 4.5:1 and 7:1.

In addition, blue crosses indicate corrected foreground color suggestions. The corrected foreground colors were found by searching for the brightness-saturation coordinates that satisfy the given contrast thresholds yet with the shortest distance to the brightness-saturation coordinate of the background color. The foreground color is adjusted since it occupies fewer pixels. If the background color was altered the overall impression of change would be stronger. Also, fixing contrast problems in one area of the design may introduce new contrast problems elsewhere.

Figure 4 (left) shows the SB-plot for the Google Maps example in Fig. 2. Clearly, both the foreground (blue text) and the background has a high brightness, but the foreground is more saturated than the background. The foreground color is nearly meeting the contrast requirement of 3:1, but the shaded area shows that its intensity must be reduced. The less saturated the foreground color is the more the brightness needs to be reduced. Figure 4 (right) shows the SB-plot for the low-contrast text example in Fig. 1. Also, here the contrast is increased by reducing the brightness of the foreground color.

Figure 2 shows a design containing several colors. To focus only on a color-pair, each area of interest is cropped and inserted into the tool (see Fig. 5). Figure 5 also illustrates the SB-plots for text samples based on hue contrasts. The only way to improve the contrast in the red-blue example is to increase the brightness so it matches the brightness of the foreground, which may seem counterintuitive, and to reduce the saturation. To meet the strictest contrast requirements the foreground color needs to be highly unsaturated. This example illustrates that brightness adjustments may not always

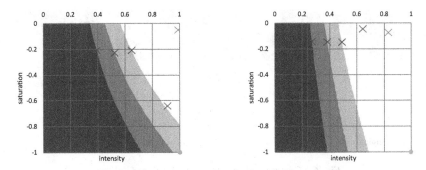

Fig. 4. SB-plot for Fig. 2 (left) and Fig. 1 (right). (Color figure online)

be the right solution. The green-red example (right) shows that sufficient contrast is achieved by either increasing or lowering the brightness of the foreground.

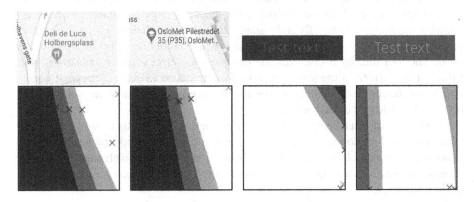

Fig. 5. SB-plots. (Color figure online)

3.3 Contrast Enhancer

The suggested corrected foreground color is visualized by replacing the colors of the foreground pixels with the adjusted color. To increase the realism of the visualization we do not want to adjust the colors of other foreground colors. We therefore only altered the colors of pixels that were within a certain radius of the foreground pixel. A radius was chosen by taking half the distance between the foreground color and the background color. Figure 6 illustrates the contrast enhancement in practice for three examples used here-in given the three contrast thresholds. Note that no foreground color can be found that meets the 7:1 contrast requirement for the red-green text.

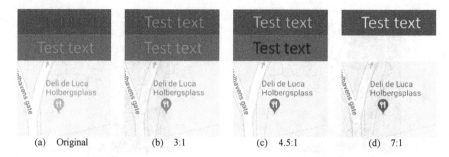

(a) Original   (b) 3:1   (c) 4.5:1   (d) 7:1

Fig. 6. Contrast enhancement. (Color figure online)

4 Conclusions

An approach to working with color contrasts was presented. The approach is intended to be simple and quick to use by hiding the technical details of color contrasts yet allowing the designer to rapidly and visually validate color choices. Using their native graphical tools designers can easily determine which colors on their color palette are valid. The tool thereby encourages the designers to select color combinations with sufficient contrast from the start. SB-plots are introduced to get a conceptual understanding of the contrast problems and possible solutions which at the same time maintain the visual profile of the color scheme.

Next, contrast enhancements allow the designers to view designs with foreground colors corrected for contrast. The method is image-based and works on designs drawn in non-web design tools, screenshots of existing applications and web pages. Universal accessibility requires training [38], and the strategy presented may be used for pedagogical purposes.

References

1. W3C, WCAG2.0. https://www.w3.org/TR/WCAG20/
2. Sandnes, F.E., Huang, Y.P.: Chording with spatial mnemonics: automatic error correction for eyes-free text entry. J. Inf. Sci. Eng. **22**, 1015–1031 (2006)
3. Sandnes, F.E.: Evaluating mobile text entry strategies with finite state automata. In: Proceedings of the 7th International Conference on Human Computer Interaction with Mobile Devices & Services, pp. 115–121. ACM (2005)
4. Sandnes, F.E., Jian, H.-L.: Pair-wise Variability Index: Evaluating the Cognitive Difficulty of Using Mobile Text Entry Systems. In: Brewster, S., Dunlop, M. (eds.) Mobile HCI 2004. LNCS, vol. 3160, pp. 347–350. Springer, Heidelberg (2004). https://doi.org/10.1007/978-3-540-28637-0_35
5. Eika, E.: Universally designed text on the web: towards readability criteria based on antipatterns. Stud. Health Technol. Inform. **229**, 461–470 (2016)

6. Eika, E., Sandnes, F.E.: Assessing the reading level of web texts for WCAG2.0 compliance —can it be done automatically? In: Di Bucchianico, G., Kercher, P. (eds.) Advances in Design for Inclusion. AISC, vol. 500, pp. 361–371. Springer, Cham (2016). https://doi.org/10.1007/978-3-319-41962-6_32

7. Eika, E., Sandnes, F.E.: Authoring WCAG2.0-compliant texts for the web through text readability visualization. In: Antona, M., Stephanidis, C. (eds.) UAHCI 2016. LNCS, vol. 9737, pp. 49–58. Springer, Cham (2016). https://doi.org/10.1007/978-3-319-40250-5_5

8. Berget, G., Sandnes, F.E.: Do autocomplete functions reduce the impact of dyslexia on information searching behaviour? a case of Google. J. Am. Soc. Inf. Sci. Technol. **67**, 2320–2328 (2016)

9. Huang, Y.P., Chang, Y.T., Sandnes, F.E.: Ubiquitous information transfer across different platforms by QR codes. J. Mob. Multimed. **6**, 3–13 (2010)

10. Sandnes, F.E.: What do low-vision users really want from smart glasses? faces, text and perhaps no glasses at all. In: Miesenberger, K., Bühler, C., Penaz, P. (eds.) ICCHP 2016. LNCS, vol. 9758, pp. 187–194. Springer, Cham (2016)

11. Sandnes, F.E., Eika, E.: Head-mounted augmented reality displays on the cheap: a DIY approach to sketching and prototyping low-vision assistive technologies. In: Antona, M., Stephanidis, C. (eds.) UAHCI 2017. LNCS, vol. 10278, pp. 167–186. Springer, Cham (2017). https://doi.org/10.1007/978-3-319-58703-5_13

12. Sandnes, F.E., Tan, T.B., Johansen, A., Sulic, E., Vesterhus, E., Iversen, E.R.: Making touch-based kiosks accessible to blind users through simple gestures. Univ. Access Inf. Soc. **11**, 421–431 (2012)

13. Gomez, J.V., Sandnes, F.E.: RoboGuideDog: guiding blind users through physical environments with laser range scanners. Procedia Comput. Sci. **14**, 218–225 (2012)

14. Lin, M.W., Cheng, Y.M., Yu, W., Sandnes, F.E.: Investigation into the feasibility of using tactons to provide navigation cues in pedestrian situations. In: Proceedings of the 20th Australasian Conference on Computer-Human Interaction: Designing for Habitus and Habitat, pp. 299–302. ACM (2008)

15. Tinker, M.: A, Paterson: D. G.: Studies of typographical factors influencing speed of reading. J. Appl. Psychol. **15**, 241 (1931)

16. Mathews, M.L.: Visual performance with coloured CRT displays: research update. Appl. Ergon. **20**, 58 (1989)

17. Stone, D.S., Fisher, K., et al.: Adults' prior exposure to print as a predictor of the legibility of text on paper and laptop computer. J. Read. Writ. **11**, 1–28 (1999)

18. Lin, P.H., Lin, Y.T., et al.: Effects of anti-glare surface treatment, ambient illumination and bending curvature on legibility and visual fatigue of electronic papers. Displays **29**, 25–32 (2008)

19. Nasanen, R., Karlsson, J., et al.: Display quality and the speed of visual letter search. Displays **22**, 107–113 (2001)

20. Greco. M, Stucchi. N., et al.: On the portability of computer-generated presentations: the effect of text-background color combinations on text legibility. Hum. Factors **50**, 821–833 (2008)

21. Hall, R.H., Hanna, P.: The impact of web page text-background colour combinations on readability, retention, aesthetics and behavioural intention. Behav. Inform. Technol. **23**, 183–195 (2004)

22. Ling, J., van Schaik, P.: The effect of text and background colour on visual search of Web pages. Displays **23**, 223–230 (2002)

23. Buchner, A., Baumgartner, N.: Text – background polarity affects performance irrespective of ambient illumination and colour contrast. Ergon. **50**, 1036–1063 (2007)

24. Lee, D.S., Shieh, K.K., et al.: Effect of character size and lighting on legibility of electronic papers. Displays **29**, 10–17 (2008)
25. Gonzalez, B., Latulipe, C.: BiCEP: bimanual color exploration plugin. In: CHI 2011 Extended Abstracts on Human Factors in Computing Systems, pp. 1483–1488. ACM (2001)
26. van den Broek, E.L., Kisters, P.M.F., Vuurpijl, L.G.: Design guidelines for a content-based image retrieval color-selection interface. In: Dutch HCI 2004, pp. 14–18. ACM (2004)
27. Douglas, S.A., Kirkpatrick, A.E.: Model and representation: the effect of visual feedback on human performance in a color picker interface. ACM T. Graph. **18**, 96–127 (1999)
28. Troiano, L., Birtolo, C., Miranda, M.: Adapting palettes to color vision deficiencies by genetic algorithm. In: Keijzer, M. (ed.) Proceedings of the 10th Annual Conference on Genetic and Evolutionary Computation, pp. 1065–1072. ACM (2008)
29. Meier, B.J., Spalter, A.M., Karelitz, D.B.: Interactive color palette tools. IEEE Comput. Graphics Appl. **24**, 64–72 (2004)
30. Moretti, G., Lyons, P.: Tools for the selection of colour palettes. In: Proceedings of the SIGCHI-NZ Symposium on Computer-Human Interaction, pp. 13–18. ACM (2002)
31. Reinecke, K., Flatla, D. R., Brooks, C.: Enabling designers to foresee which colors users cannot see. In: Proceedings of the 2016 CHI Conference on Human Factors in Computing Systems, pp. 2693–2704. ACM (2016)
32. Webster, M.: Integrating color usability components into design tools. Interactions **21**, 56–61 (2014)
33. Sandnes, F.E.: On-screen colour contrast for visually impaired readers: selecting and exploring the limits of WCAG2.0 colours. In: Black, A., Lund, O., Walker, S. (eds.) Information Design: Research and Practice, pp. 405–416. Routledge (2016)
34. Sandnes, F.E., Zhao, A.: An interactive color picker that ensures WCAG2.0 com-pliant color contrast levels. Procedia-Comput. Sci. **67**, 87–94 (2015)
35. Sandnes, F.E., Zhao, A.: A contrast colour selection scheme for WCAG2. 0-compliant web designs based on HSV-half-planes. In: Proceedings of SMC2015, pp. 1233–1237. IEEE (2015)
36. Sandnes, F.E.: Understanding WCAG2.0 color contrast requirements through 3D color space visualization. Stud. Health Technol. Inform. **229**, 366–375 (2016)
37. Tigwell, G.W., Flatla, D.R., Archibald, N.D.: ACE: a colour palette design tool for balancing aesthetics and accessibility. ACM Trans. Access. Comput. **9** (2017). Article no. 5
38. Whitney, G., Keith, S., Bühler, C., Hewer, S., Lhotska, L., Miesenberger, K., Sandnes, F.E., Stephanidis, C., Velasco, C.A.: Twenty five years of training and education in ICT Design for All and Assistive Technology. Technol. Disabil. **3**, 163–170 (2011)

Multilevel Accessibility Evaluation
of Institutional Websites in Tunisia

Imen Gharbi[1,3], Amina Bouraoui[1,2(✉)], and Narjess Bellamine Ben Saoud[3]

[1] Riadi GLORY, University of Manouba, Manouba, Tunisia
Imen.gharbi@issit.utm.tn, hannibal.a@topnet.tn
[2] Institut Supérieur des Technologies Médicales-ISTMT,
University of Tunis El Manar, Tunis, Tunisia
[3] Ecole Nationale des Sciences de l'Informatique, University of Manouba, Manouba, Tunisia
narjes_bellamine@yahoo.fr

Abstract. Actually several public and private services are more and more popular on the Web, even though they are intended to be usable for everyone regardless of age, disability and environment or technology limitations, their accessibility remains a real issue. This might be a factor of discrimination and exclusion of a large proportion of users. To raise awareness about web accessibility, this paper focuses on evaluating the accessibility of a sample of institutional websites in Tunisia. The evaluation was not limited to automatic and manual check but it was extended to accessibility tests involving end-users. The results show that the accessibility guidelines are often violated and in some cases are not adopted at all.

Keywords: Web accessibility · Website evaluation · WCAG 2.0

1 Introduction

Nowadays, no one can deny that the Web is becoming an extremely powerful source of information browsed by a huge number of users having various skills and abilities. Unfortunately, a large population of users, mainly in developing countries, is usually facing a wide range of obstacles that prevent it from gaining access to online content. Despite the existence of well-defined guidelines and recommendations, most websites do not provide equal access to all since they still suffer from problems that enhance accessibility barriers. According to the National Institution of Statistics [1], there were approximately 242 thousand people living with various disabilities in Tunisia in 2014 (2.5% of the population). Given that this number is expected to rise in the future, it is crucial to raise the awareness of designers and developers toward access barriers. Therefore, we conducted a survey to study the current accessibility status of Tunisian Web. This paper is structured as follows. In the first section, we present an overview of the accessibility evaluation process. In the second section, we describe our methodology. In the third section, we summarize the findings of the evaluation process. Finally, the last section is dedicated to the conclusion and future works.

K. Miesenberger and G. Kouroupetroglou (Eds.): ICCHP 2018, LNCS 10896, pp. 43–46, 2018.
https://doi.org/10.1007/978-3-319-94277-3_8

2   Related Work

There are several studies focusing on Web accessibility issues that have been conducted by researchers either in developing or developed countries. Based on a sample of websites, each of these studies narrowly targeted online accessibility on a specific domain such as higher education [2–6], government [7–9] and banking [10]. Most of these evaluations were carried out only via automated tools, while a limited number was performed by a combination of automated and manual testing or/and involved end-users' investigation. Regarding the accessibility standard guidelines, the authors of these evaluations, referred to WCAG 1.0 [11], WCAG 2.0 [12] or the Section 508 [13].

All these studies confirm the existence of a variety of accessibility problems in the majority of examined sites. Even the websites whose stakeholders claimed adherence to accessibility recommendations, are not providing adequate levels of accessibility.

To the best of our knowledge, no study on accessibility of Tunisian websites was led. Thus, this paper presents the first publically available results of Web accessibility analysis of institutional websites in Tunisia.

3   Evaluation Methodology

To carry out our evaluation, we chose to examine the accessibility of the most frequently viewed institutional websites. This list includes 15 higher education institutions' websites, the ministry of secondary education's website, the ministry of higher education's website, the student orientation portal, the scholarship and university services' portal, the catalog of university resources, the employment portal and the public contests' portal. Assuming that if the home page is not accessible, users may certainly have trouble to access other pages of the site, in the present case, the assessment mainly concerned each site's home page. To check more heterogeneous amount of information such as multimedia content, forms and tables, other pages can also be consulted.

To evaluate the compliance of the selected websites to the WCAG 2.0, we conducted a multilevel evaluation procedure based on a combination of automatic evaluation tools (automated tests), deep manual analysis (conformance reviews) and tests involving end-users (user testing).

3.1   Automated Tests

During this stage we resorted to multiple tools. First, we used two open source web-based evaluation tools namely A-Tester [14] and AChecker [15]. Second, we used AInspector Sidebar [16], a Firefox browser add-on. These tools provide assessment based on a variety of international accessibility guidelines but each one has its own capabilities and limitations to cover errors.

After carefully analyzing the reports generated by these automated tools and comparing results, we were convinced that there were potential checkpoints that could not be identified, so we should not rely on automated tests alone. Accordingly, manually inspection and end-users' judgment are still required.

3.2 Conformance Reviews

A deep manual evaluation was carried out by each of the authors, to assess specific guidelines for each selected webpage since not all accessibility checkpoints can be fully automated. These assessments include checking for the validity of alternative texts, of data tables' structure, of links content and destinations, of forms and also for the navigation via keyboard. Thus, this manual inspection is time-consuming but relatively cost-effective to check conformance with accessibility guidelines.

3.3 User Testing

Users involved in this testing phase were neatly selected to best represent the target audience in term of disability and Web experience. Thus, aiming to cover most cases where users may face difficulties to access online content, we appealed to people with limited abilities due to aging (declines in vision), disadvantaged individuals using obsolete devices and slow Internet connection, persons suffering from different types of disabilities (visual, auditory, physical and cognitive) equipped or not with assistive technologies. User testing was carried out with 18 participants over a period of three months. To ensure effectiveness of this assessment, we were carefully observing participants' behavior during testing sessions, to identify accurate barriers actually faced by each type of impairment in real situations. After that, we classified these barriers by level of priority according to WCAG 2.0.

4   Evaluation Findings

The tests using the aforementioned tools showed that all the examined Web pages do not satisfy the lowest conformance level defined in WCAG 2.0 at Level-A. In addition to HTML and CSS errors, the most frequent errors involved are: lack of text equivalent, problems of color contrast, absence of skip links, inadequate navigation markup (headings), etc. Thus, minimum requirements to allow access for all are not reached. In fact, accessibility guidelines are often violated and in most cases are not adopted at all. This result was also confirmed by manual evaluation and also via tests involving end-users. More than 60% of the problems experienced by target users during tests were not detected by automated tools such as the difficulty of using assistive technologies. Added to that, the impossibility for people with motor impairments to browse websites without assistance since they do not support keyboard navigation. We also noticed that users with cognitive disabilities meet challenges to interact with 73% of selected Web pages due to their layout complexity and information overload. These issues were not detected neither by automated tools nor by conformance reviews.

5   Conclusion and Future Work

The accessibility of institutions' websites plays an important role to the integration of disabled persons. In this paper, a multilevel evaluation process has been conducted to explore the accessibility status of a representative list of institutional websites. In light of this evaluation, we highlight the critical accessibility status of Tunisian websites, which denotes a potential risk of exclusion for disabled. This is due to the fact that Web developers still ignore the importance of online accessibility and lack knowledge on recommendations. The real problem lies in underestimation of the disabled's rights in Tunisia since no strict regulations are introduced to give higher priority for Web accessibility. We hope via this work to make Web developer community and Tunisian authorities aware of the importance of the Web accessibility and that concrete actions to support access for all are still needed. Following this study, Web developers have been provided with a collection of rules and best practices most adapted for Tunisian context in order to promote the compliance with accessibility standards and to raise the overall quality of websites.

References

1. NIS Statistics page. http://www.ins.tn/fr/statistiques. Accessed 08 Nov 2017
2. Comeaux, D., Schmetzke, A.: Accessibility of academic library web sites in North America: current status and trends (2002-2012). Libr. Hi tech **31**(1), 8–33 (2013)
3. Kurt, S.: The accessibility of university web sites: the case of Turkish universities. Univ. Access Inf. Soc. **10**(1), 101–110 (2011)
4. Aziz, A., et al.: Assessing the accessibility and usability of Malaysia higher education website. In: Proceedings of International Conference on User Science and Engineering, i-USEr 2010, Shah Alam, pp. 203–208 (2010)
5. Comeaux, D., Schmetzke, A.: Web accessibility trends in university libraries and library schools. Libr. Hi Tech **25**(4), 457–477 (2007)
6. Hackett, S., Parmanto, B.: A longitudinal evaluation of accessibility: higher education web sites. Internet Res. **15**(3), 281–294 (2005)
7. Lazar, J., Beavan, P., Brown, J., et al.: Investigating the accessibility of state government web sites in Maryland. In: Langdon, P.M., Clarkson, J., Robinson, P. (eds.) Designing Inclusive Interactions, pp. 69–78. Springer, London (2010). https://doi.org/10.1007/978-1-84996-166-0_7
8. Kuzma, J.: Global E-government web accessibility: a case study (2010)
9. Narashiman, N.: Accessibility of government websites in India: a report (2013)
10. Kaur, A., Diksha, D.: Banking websites in India: an accessibility evaluation. CSI Trans. ICT **2**(1), 23–34 (2014)
11. WCAG 1.0 Documents. https://www.w3.org/WAI/intro/wcag10docs. Accessed 05 Feb 2018
12. WCAG 2.0 Errata. https://www.w3.org/WAI/WCAG20/errata/. Accessed 05 Feb 2018
13. Section 508. https://www.section508.gov/. Accessed 05 Feb 2018
14. A-Tester. http://www.evaluera.co.uk/. Accessed 17 Apr 2017
15. AChecker. https://achecker.ca/checker/index.php. Accessed 20 Apr 2017
16. AInspector Sidebar. https://addons.mozilla.org/fr/firefox/addon/ainspector-sidebar/. Accessed 12 Mar 2017

The Inaccessibility of Video Players

Gian Wild[✉]

AccessibilityOz, Melbourne, VIC, Australia
gian@accessibilityoz.com

Abstract. We conducted a series of tests of 37 major video players, both free and paid, on the market. Initially we tested on a PC on Google Chrome and excluded video players that contained what we called "show-stoppers": serious accessibility failures. The remaining video players were then tested with people with vision impairments reliant on various screen readers. Any video players that contained show-stoppers were excluded from any additional testing. Thirdly, we tested on two different mobile devices, again excluding video players that contained show-stoppers. Finally, we tested with an iPad and a Bluetooth keyboard. At the end of the testing only two players remained: AblePlayer and OzPlayer.

Keywords: Accessibility · Video players · WCAG2 · W3C · Media player

1 Why Is Video Important?

Video is now ubiquitous. One third of all online activity is watching video [1], over two-thirds of all internet traffic is video [2] and over half of all video content is accessed via a mobile device [3]. Over 500 million people watch video on Facebook every day [4] – that's over 100 million hours of video [5]! On YouTube, the numbers are even higher – over 1 billion hours of video are watched every day [6].

2 Video and Accessibility

Web accessibility is about making sure web sites, web applications and mobile apps (including video) are accessible to people with disabilities. The estimate of people with disabilities in the US is approximately 19% of the population – that's 56.7 million people [7].

Web accessibility of web sites is best achieved by following the Web Content Accessibility Guidelines, Version 2.0 created by the World Wide Web Consortium (W3C). The W3C states that "following these guidelines will make content accessible to a wider range of people with disabilities, including blindness and low vision, deafness and hearing loss, learning disabilities, cognitive limitations, limited movement, speech disabilities, photosensitivity and combinations of these" [8]. The W3C Web Content

---

The original version of this chapter was revised: The affiliation of the author was corrected. The correction to this chapter is available at https://doi.org/10.1007/978-3-319-94277-3_100

© The Author(s) 2018
K. Miesenberger and G. Kouroupetroglou (Eds.): ICCHP 2018, LNCS 10896, pp. 47–51, 2018.
https://doi.org/10.1007/978-3-319-94277-3_9

Accessibility Guidelines, Version 2.0, contain specific techniques for providing accessibility features within video.

Almost everyone understands the need for accessibility features like transcripts, captions and audio descriptions for people with disabilities: these features also are important to people without a disability when viewing video. Over 85% of all Facebook video is viewed without sound [9] – and, if a video has captions, a user is almost twice as likely to finish the video than if it did not have captions [10]. We all know Google is blind and deaf and we see that in revenue as well – videos with transcripts earn 16% more revenue than videos without transcripts [11]. And what has been dubbed the "Broadchurch effect" (due to the strong accents in the BBC drama "Broadchurch"), the BBC found that 80% of people who use captions are not using it for accessibility reasons [12].

To provide accessible video solutions, web site owners must provide a variety of accessibility features. One of the requirements is that the video player itself must be accessible. Lack of accessibility in video players can be the consequence of a number of things, but usually includes inadequate keyboard access, inoperable captions and non-existence of audio descriptions and transcripts.

3   Testing Video Player Accessibility

We tested the following video players: AblePlayer; Acorn; Adobe; AFB; Amazon; AMI Player; Brightcove; Facebook; JW Player; Kaltura; MediaElement; MediaSite; Ooyala; OzPlayer; Panopto; PayPal; Plyr; RAMP; Video.js; Vidyard; Vimeo; Viostream; Wistia; Yahoo; YouTube; and YouTube embed.

We conducted four rounds of testing:

- Round 1: Desktop testing on Google Chrome, Windows 10;
- Round 2: User testing with a vision-impaired user using a screen reader;
- Round 3: Mobile testing on iPhone and Android devices; and
- Round 4: Mobile testing on an iPad with a Bluetooth keyboard.

We identified certain "show-stoppers" that were failures of the four non-interference clauses in WCAG2: If technologies are used in a way that is not accessibility supported, or if they are used in a non-conforming way, then they do not block the ability of users to access the rest of the page [13].

3.1   Round 1 Testing

Initially we conducted testing on Google Chrome version 61.0.3163 under Windows 10. A series of tests were undertaken including whether the video player supported audio descriptions, whether the transcript was accessible to the keyboard and whether the volume of the player could be modified. Video players were deemed to include show-stoppers if any of the following occurred:

- Audio plays automatically; unless the user is made aware this is happening or a pause or stop button is provided – failure of WCAG2 Level A Success Criterion 1.4.2: Audio Control);

- Video contains a keyboard trap (i.e. users cannot escape from the video using the keyboard) – failure of WCAG2 Level A Success Criterion 2.1.2 No Keyboard Trap; and/or
- Full-screen video contains a reverse keyboard trap (i.e. users cannot escape from full-screen mode using the keyboard) – failure of WCAG2 Level A Success Criterion 2.1.2 No Keyboard Trap.

At the conclusion of Round 1 testing only the following eight video players remained: AblePlayer; JW Player; Kaltura; OzPlayer; Panapto; Plyr; and YouTube embed.

3.2 Round 2 Testing

Experienced vision-impaired users tested the remaining eight video players on the following combinations of screen reader/operating system and browser:

- JAWS with Windows 10 with: Internet Explorer; FireFox; and Chrome
- NVDA with Windows 10 with: Internet Explorer; FireFox; Chrome; and Edge
- VoiceOver with iOS Safari
- TalkBack with Android Chrome

A series of tests were undertaken including whether the player's controls were labelled, button status was announced appropriately and fast-forwarding and rewinding was available to the screen reader user. A video player was deemed to include a show-stopper if the video could not be played– not a failure of WCAG2, but deemed a significant failure. Only one video was excluded at the end of this round of testing: Panopto.

3.3 Round 3 Testing

We tested the remaining seven video players Google Pixel 1, Android 8.0, Chrome and iPhone 7+, iOS 10.3.2, Safari. A series of tests were undertaken including whether the mobile video player supported captions and/or audio descriptions, whether the volume of the video player could be modified and whether color contrast was sufficient. A video player was deemed to include a showstopper if any of the following occurred:

- Video could not be played – not a failure of WCAG2, but deemed a significant failure;
- Video could not be paused) – failure of WCAG2 Level A Success Criterion 2.2.2 Pause, Stop, Hide; and/or
- Video crashed the browser – not a failure of WCAG2, but deemed a significant failure.

Three video players: Kaltura, MediaSite and YouTube contained embedded show-stoppers. The remaining four video players were: AblePlayer; JW Player; OzPlayer; and Plyr.

3.4   Round 4 Testing

We tested the remaining four video players on an iPad, iOS 10, Safari, Zagg keyboard. We tested only one task via the keyboard on the iPad: whether the controls could be operated by the keyboard. A video player was deemed to include a showstopper if any of the following occurred:

- Video could not be played – not a failure of WCAG2, but deemed a significant failure;
- Video could not be paused – failure of WCAG2 Level A Success Criterion 2.2.2 Pause, Stop, Hide; and/or
- Video crashed the browser – not a failure of WCAG2, but deemed a significant failure.

Two video players: JW Player and Plyr, contained show-stoppers. The remaining two video players were: AblePlayer; and OzPlayer.

4   Conclusion

This is the third year that this testing has been conducted. As in previous years, Able-Player and OzPlayer were the only two video players that do not contain show-stoppers. Although we have seen improvements – such as more video players supporting audio descriptions – we have also seen the advent of new show-stoppers such as reverse keyboard traps. For every show-stopper encountered there will be thousands – perhaps hundreds of thousands – of people who cannot watch the video. As one of our screen reader testers said:

> "Video is a very important source of information and is a remarkable aspect of our culture now. Blind individuals must not be excluded from access to data provided in video content. You can't see, but you can understand."

References

1. Video Marketing: The future of content marketing. https://www.forbes.com/sites/forbesage ncycouncil/2017/02/03/video-marketing-the-future-of-content-marketing/#5417a4be6b53
2. Cisco Visual Networking Index: Forecast and methodology, 2016–2021. https://www.cisco.com/c/en/us/solutions/collateral/service-provider/visual-networking-index-vni/complete-white-paper-c11-481360.html
3. Global Video Index, Q2 (2016). http://go.ooyala.com/rs/447-EQK-225/images/Ooyala-Global-Video-Index-Q2-2016.pdf
4. Million people are watching Facebook videos everyday. http://tubularinsights.com/500-million-watch-facebook-video/
5. Facebook hits 100M hours of video watched a day, 1B users on groups, 80M on Fb lite. https://techcrunch.com/2016/01/27/facebook-grows/
6. People now watch 1 billion hours of YouTube per day. https://techcrunch.com/2017/02/28/people-now-watch-1-billion-hours-of-youtube-per-day/
7. Nearly 1 in 5 people have a disability. https://www.census.gov/newsroom/releases/archives/miscellaneous/cb12-134.html

8. Understanding compliance. https://www.w3.org/TR/UNDERSTANDING-WCAG20/conformance.html
9. 85 percent of Facebook video is watched without sound. https://digiday.com/media/silent-world-facebook-video/
10. PLYmedia: Subtitles increase online video viewing by 40%. http://www.subply.com/en/news/NewsItem_SubPLY_Trial_Results.htm
11. 8 Best practices to optimize e-commerce video landing pages for search. http://tubularinsights.com/8-practices-optimize-video-landing-pages-search/
12. Ofcom: Television access services. https://www.ofcom.org.uk/__data/assets/pdf_file/0016/42442/access.pdf

Using Semi-supervised Group Sparse Regression to Improve Web Accessibility Evaluation

Yue Wu[1], Zhi Yu[1], Liangcheng Li[1], Wei Wang[1], Jiajun Bu[1(✉)],
Yueqing Zhang[2], and Lianjun Dai[3]

[1] Alibaba-Zhejiang University Joint Institute of Frontier Technologies, Zhejiang
Provincial Key Laboratory of Service Robot, College of Computer Science,
Zhejiang University, Hangzhou 310027, China
{wyl1988,yuzhirenzhe,liangcheng_li,
wangwei_eagle,bjj}@zju.edu.cn
[2] University of Liverpool, Liverpool, England, UK
704787221@qq.com
[3] China Disabled Persons' Federation Information Center,
Beijing 100034, China
dailianjun@cdpf.org.cn

Abstract. Web accessibility evaluation checks the accessibility of the website
to help improve the user experiences for disabled people. Due to the massive
number of web pages in a website, manually reviewing all the pages becomes
totally impractical. But the complexities of evaluating some checkpoints require
certain human involvements. To address this issue, we develop the semi-
supervised group sparse regression algorithm which takes advantages of the
high precision of a small amount of manual evaluation results along with the
global distribution of all the web pages and efficiently gives out the overall
evaluation result of the website. Moreover, the proposed method can tell the
importance of each feature in evaluating each checkpoint. The experiments on
various websites demonstrate the superiority of our proposed algorithm.

Keywords: Accessibility evaluation · Semi-supervised
Group Sparse Regression

1 Introduction

With the development of the Internet, the number of the web pages in a website has a
rapid growth in the past decade. As a result, manually reviewing all the pages to
perform the web accessibility evaluation requires an unacceptable time cost and
becomes totally impractical. To overcome this issue, we propose a novel semi-
automatic web accessibility evaluation approach which inherits the advantages of both
automatic accessibility evaluation and sampling based accessibility evaluation and
overcomes their shortcomings. It first samples a small amount of web pages for human
experts to evaluate, then uses these evaluation results together with all the other
unevaluated pages to train a semi-supervised group sparse regression model, and finally

© Springer International Publishing AG, part of Springer Nature 2018
K. Miesenberger and G. Kouroupetroglou (Eds.): ICCHP 2018, LNCS 10896, pp. 52–56, 2018.
https://doi.org/10.1007/978-3-319-94277-3_10

gives out the accessibility score for all the pages according to the predict model. The experts' accessibility evaluation results guide the training process and the large amounts of unevaluated data are used as a constraint to guarantee the generalization of the model.

2 Related Work

The automatic accessibility evaluation approaches can only detect violations of some simple accessibility regulations and often appears as a small tools or plug-ins for the web browsers, such as works proposed in [1, 2]. Nowadays, the most common way to perform web accessibility evaluation is manual evaluation after sampling. In the beginning, the accessibility scores of homepages are used to represent the results of websites [3, 4]. Later researches show that homepages are not enough to reflect the accessibility level of websites [5], so the sampling range expands to the entire website. Instead of uniform random sampling which may lose important pages, many clustering based accessibility evaluation approach have been developed. Harper et al. proposes a DOM block clustering based sampling and accessibility evaluation method which achieves an 80% coverage by evaluating between 0.1–4% of pages [6]. Mucha et al. proposes another clustering based approach that clusters the web pages according to the barriers detected and selects representative pages for the accessibility score calculation [7]. The method proposed in [8] uses only URLs to select candidate pages, so the following accessibility evaluation process only need to crawl the sample pages. This greatly reduces the waiting time before doing the evaluation. All these methods mentioned above only evaluate the sampled pages. This indicates that the final accessibility scores heavily depend on the quality of sampling. Zhang et al. proposes the active-prediction method which uses the active learning to selected samples, then trains a predict model with the sample result and finally uses the model to predict the accessibility score for all the other pages [9]. Note that the predict model are trained only by the sampled pages, the generalization may be limited. So, we propose the semi-supervised group sparse regression which uses the results of sampled pages along with the unevaluated pages to train a more generalized predict model and achieves better results.

3 The Proposed Approach

As we know that web pages consist of thousands of HTML tags and the structures of these pages are highly related to the HTML tags, so we can use the number of tags' occurrences to represent a web page. Let $X = [x_1, x_2, \ldots, x_N]^T$ be the pages crawled from a website where N is the total number of pages, $x_i \in \mathbb{R}^M$ denotes a web page and M is the number of tags. Let X_S denote the sampled pages and Y_S denote pass rate of each checkpoint. Active learning is used to select the samples like the method proposed in [9]. S denotes the similarity matrix calculated with k nearest neighbors and heat kernel. Our goal is to find a regression model to predict the pass rate of each checkpoint for all pages, that is:

$$Y = XW + \mathbf{1}b \tag{1}$$

With the evaluated sample pages, the coefficient W can be easily calculated by minimizing $\|Y_S - X_S W - b\|_F^2$. As we know that web pages using the same template usually share similar evaluation result. So, we add a constraint to the model to make use of the unevaluated pages that is $\min \sum_{i,j} \|y_i - y_j\|_2^2 S_{ij} = \min 2\mathrm{tr}\left(W^T X^T L X W\right)$ where L is the Laplacian matrix. To prevent overfitting and make coefficients concentrate on important tags, an $L_{2,1}$-norm regularization term $\|W\|_{2,1}$ is added and the final objective function becomes:

$$\mathrm{argmin}_W \|Y - XW - \mathbf{1}b\|_F^2 + \alpha \mathrm{tr}\left(W^T X^T L X W\right) + \beta \|W\|_{2,1}. \tag{2}$$

By using $\mathrm{tr}\left(\mathbf{W}^T U W\right), U_{ii} = 1/(2\|w_i\|_2)$ to approximate $\|W\|_{2,1}$, we develop an iterative algorithm to efficiently solve this optimization problem and obtain the coefficient matrix W with the bias term b. Then the pass rate of all the unevaluated pages can be predicted by the regression model and the importance of the tags to each checkpoint can be measured by the corresponding coefficients in W.

4　Experimental Result

We conduct experiments on a real-world web accessibility evaluation dataset which is the official websites of ministries, commissions and provincial governments in China evaluated during June 1th to December 10th, 2016. And our proposed methods are compared with the supervised one which only uses the evaluated pages to train the regression model without the help of the unevaluated pages.

The experimental result in Fig. 1 shows that our semi-supervised model outperforms the supervised one and the average accuracy of SGSR is 91.53% which demonstrates the effectiveness of our proposed method.

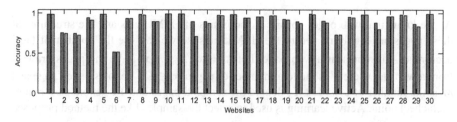

Fig. 1. The predict accuracies on 30 websites. The blue bar shows the results of our proposed semi-supervised group sparse regression (SGSR) while the red bar are the results of group sparse regression (GSR) without the constraint of unevaluated pages. Clearly SGSR performs better than GSR. (Color figure online)

5 Conclusion, Future Work and Acknowledgments

In conclusion, a novel semi-supervised predict model is introduced into the web accessibility evaluation which makes it possible to automatically evaluate almost every page in a website and avoid missing critical pages. Moreover, with the help of the regression coefficients, experts are able to tell which tags or HTML structures are more related to certain checkpoints and pay more attention to them when doing accessibility evaluations.

In the future, we plan to implement the proposed methods as a module in our CrowdAE system which is a crowdsourcing system with human inspection quality enhancement for web accessibility evaluation and whose evaluation results are now listed in the China Government Website Evaluation Index. We believe that this will reduce the evaluation time costs and bring us a more accurate result.

This work is supported by Alibaba-Zhejiang University Joint Institute of Frontier Technologies, Zhejiang Provincial Natural Science Foundation of China (No. LZ13F02 0001), the National Natural Science Foundation of China (Nos. 61173185 and 61173 186), the National Key Technology R&D Program of China (No. 2012BAI34B01 and 2014BAK15B02), and the Hangzhou S&T Development Plan (No. 20150834M22).

References

1. Nietzio, A., Eibegger, M., Goodwin, M., Snaprud, M.: Following the WCAG 2.0 techniques: experiences from designing a WCAG 2.0 checking tool. In: Miesenberger, K., Karshmer, A., Penaz, P., Zagler, W. (eds.) ICCHP 2012. LNCS, vol. 7382, pp. 417–424. Springer, Heidelberg (2012). https://doi.org/10.1007/978-3-642-31522-0_63
2. Klein, E., Bolfing, A., Riesch, M.: Checking web accessibility with the content accessibility checker (CAC). In: Miesenberger, K., Fels, D., Archambault, D., Peňáz, P., Zagler, W. (eds.) ICCHP 2014. LNCS, vol. 8547, pp. 109–112. Springer, Cham (2014). https://doi.org/10.1007/978-3-319-08596-8_16
3. Lazar, J., Beere, P., Greenidge, K.D., Nagappa, Y.: Web accessibility in the Mid-Atlantic United States: a study of 50 homepages. Univers. Access Inf. Soc. 2(4), 331–341 (2003)
4. Lazar, J., Greenidge, K.D.: One year older, but not necessarily wiser: an evaluation of homepage accessibility problems over time. Univers. Access Inf. Soc. 4(4), 285–291 (2006)
5. Hackett, S., Parmanto, B.: Homepage not enough when evaluating web site accessibility. Internet Res. 19(1), 78–87 (2009)
6. Harper, S., Moon, A.A., Vigo, M., Brajnik, G., Yesilada, Y.: DOM block clustering for enhanced sampling and evaluation. In: Proceedings of the 12th Web for All Conference, p. 15. ACM (2015)
7. Mucha, J., Snaprud, M., Nietzio, A.: Web page clustering for more efficient website accessibility evaluations. In: Miesenberger, K., Bühler, C., Penaz, P. (eds.) ICCHP 2016. LNCS, vol. 9758, pp. 259–266. Springer, Cham (2016). https://doi.org/10.1007/978-3-319-41264-1_35

8. Zhang, M., Wang, C., Bu, J., Yu, Z., Zhou, Y., Chen, C.: A sampling method based on URL clustering for fast web accessibility evaluation. Front. Inf. Technol. Electron. Eng. **16**(6), 449–456 (2015)
9. Zhang, M., Wang, C., Yu, Z., Shen, C., Bu, J.: Active learning for web accessibility evaluation. In: Proceedings of the 14th Web for All Conference on the Future of Accessible Work, p. 16. ACM (2017)

Accessibility and Usability of Mobile Platforms for People with Disabilities and Elderly Persons: Design, Development and Engineering

On the Development of a Harmonized, User-Centered Terminology for Current and Upcoming ICT Devices, Services and Applications

Bruno von Niman[1,4(✉)], Martin Böcker[2,4], and Angel Boveda[3,4]

[1] Vonniman Consulting, Dalen 13, 13245 Saltsjö-Boo, Sweden
bruno@vonniman.com
[2] Dr. Böcker & Dr. Schneider GbR, Constance, Germany
boecker@humanfactors.de
[3] Wireless Partners SLL, Sangenjo 5, 28034 Madrid, Spain
angel.boveda@wirelesspartners.es
[4] ETSI TC Human Factors Specialist Task Force 540, Sophia Antipolis, France

Abstract. Unfamiliar terms used in the user interface (UI) of an Information and Communication Technology (ICT) device, service or application may present an obstacle to users, if unfamiliar with them or uncertain about their technical meaning and intended functionality. The availability of a harmonised, user-centred terminology benefits users with functional variations, such as those with literacy difficulties, or people with varying visual needs or cognitive capabilities. This paper presents on-going standardization work, focusing on improving the overall usability and accessibility through the development of recommendations addressing terminology harmonization among devices, services and applications to a well-defined degree, in areas not intended to convey a certain brand-specific feature or image.

Keywords: Harmonization · Terminology · User-centered

1 Background

Unfamiliar terms used in the UI of an ICT device, service or application may present an obstacle to users, if uncertain about their technical meaning or intended functionality. Furthermore, terms may be introduced by manufacturers to denote new features, or to distinguish own features from those offered by competitors. Most technical terms are not intended for brand-related positioning or differentiation. In the absence of a common terminology for the most frequently used and common elements, the use of terms differs considerably among manufacturers and service providers.

This paper presents an alternative, with focus on improving the overall user experience and accessibility through the development of recommendations addressing terminology harmonization (to a well-defined degree) among devices, services and applications.

K. Miesenberger and G. Kouroupetroglou (Eds.): ICCHP 2018, LNCS 10896, pp. 59–63, 2018.
https://doi.org/10.1007/978-3-319-94277-3_11

A common terminology can be employed to help prevent negative effects such as increased user difficulties in understanding and accessing complex, ambiguous and inconstantly-used terms leading to unnecessary confusion, increased efforts in user education and costs for user support, limited feature discovery, unclear user expectations and a limited uptake in use (as users may be reluctant to use fuzzy features) [2], or even increased cognitive complexity and subsequent learning efforts.

The need for harmonization increases as new features and services are being introduced at an increased pace in the world of agile ICT development and as new device and service providers continue to enter today's dynamic market.

In addition, as network operators' business models develops, end-user loyalty may decrease. The introduction of new features without the timely and instant availability of accessible user documentation impacts on the usability and accessibility of ICT.

2 Approach and Addressed Users

While terms may be introduced by manufacturers to denote new features, or to distinguish own features from those offered by competitors, most technical terms are not intended for brand-related differentiation. In the absence of a common terminology for the most frequently used and common elements, the use of terms differs considerably among manufacturers and service providers.

This paper describes an alternative, focusing on improving the overall user experience through the development of recommendations addressing terminology harmonization (to a well-defined degree) among devices, services and applications (in areas not intended to convey a certain brand-specific feature or image).

A common terminology can be employed to help prevent negative effects such as increased user difficulties in understanding complex, ambiguous and inconstantly-used terms leading to unnecessary confusion, increased efforts in user education and costs for user support, limited feature discovery, unclear user expectations and a limited uptake in use (as users may be reluctant to use fuzzy features), or even increased cognitive complexity and subsequent learning efforts.

The need for harmonization increases as new features and services are being introduced continuously, at an increased speed in the world of agile ICT development and as new device and service providers continue to enter today's dynamic market.

In addition, as network operators' business models change, end-user loyalty to network operators and device manufacturers may decrease. The introduction of new features without the timely and easy availability of user documentation is another factor with a considerable impact on the usability and accessibility of ICT.

Intended *readers* of the ETSI Guide under development will include device manufacturers, application developers, service providers, network operators, technical writers and developers of marketing materials, national and international standards bodies and regulatory institutions.

Its intended *users* are those designing, developing, implementing and deploying user interfaces for and interaction with ICT devices, services, and applications.

All users are expected to benefit from this work, including young and older people and specifically, people with functional limitations (e.g. within the cognition area [3]).

3   Method and Collaborative Processes

The development work reported will be conducted in a close collaboration with experts representing the ICT industry and interested and relevant stakeholders and will be based upon a combination of desk research, expert knowledge and an industry-wide collaboration, consultation, review and consensus process, in three main phases:

1. Identification of objects and activities to be addressed;
2. Collection of terms used by major providers; and
3. Analysis, selection and presentation of the recommended terms.

The most common functional areas (see clause 3 below) will be identified, grouped and selected to be covered by the work.

For each functional area, relevant and representative providers will be selected and the terms used by them for the most frequently used, specific objects and activities of the respective functional areas will be collected in the five languages (English, French, German, Italian and Spanish) covered by the reported work.

In the final phase of the work, the collected terms will be reviewed and the recommended terms will be selected, based on a variety of checks (e.g. for consistency between manufacturers (i.e. prevalence of certain terms)) and described and presented with focus on practical use, as reported in detail in [1].

During this process, a Reference group consisting of domain experts will be established and used to discuss, review and validate the selections and assist in the harmonization effort. Experts interested to contribute are invited to visit our homepage for additional details and the latest draft and contact us to identify the optimal forms of collaboration.

4   Results

The result will consist of a detailed list of terms listed in the Guide, providing principles of use and deployment and the terms themselves, grouped and presented by the five language-specific versions of the basic commands. At the moment of the writing of this paper, the following functional groups are intended to be covered:

1. Basic and interaction-related terms;
2. Non-functional, interaction-related terms (that also covers the most common accessibility and assistive device connectivity-related terms);
3. Telephony services;
4. Media handling;
5. Messaging;
6. Navigation and maps;
7. Banking and payments;

8. eHealth services;
9. Travel services;
10. Searching and browsing;
11. Social media;
12. Photography and imaging;
13. Games and tools; and
14. Miscellaneous (as, and if necessary).

Due to space limitations, further details are not provided here but interested readers are invited to visit our homepage and download the latest draft, or contact the authors directly during the development phase.

The final result will have to be approved by the ETSI Human Factors Committee (TC HF), as well as the representatives of the ETSI Membership community, consisting of some 800 member organizations, non-exhaustively including user representatives, standards bodies, startups, research entities, SMEs developing, deploying or using ICT, accessibility, user and disability associations, network operators, policy makers and most of the largest ICT corporations.

5   Conclusions, Recommendations and Future Steps

The aim of our work is a quick uptake and the widest possible support in product implementations in the widest possible range – eased by the easy and free, on-line availability of the publication and its unrestricted use.

We intend to openly report about our experiences, in order to ease and optimize possible future updates and expansions.

Future expansion possibilities envisaged include updated vocabularies and expanded language coverage (e.g. to the official EU/EFTA ones, or minority languages used in Europe).

Acknowledgements. This work, performed during 2017–2019, is co-funded by the European Telecommunications Standards Institute (ETSI), the European Commission (EC) of the European Union (EU) and the European Free Trade Association (EFTA).

References

1. ETSI DEG 203 499: Human Factors (HF); User-centered terminology for existing and upcoming ICT devices, services and applications. Draft under development, for publication in July 2019. This is the topic of this paper!
2. ETSI EG 202 132 v1.1.1 (2004–08): Human Factors (HF); User Interfaces; Guidelines for generic user interface elements for mobile terminals and services. www.etsi.org
3. ETSI EG 203 350 v1.1.1 (2016–11): Human Factors (HF); Guidelines for the design of mobile ICT devices and their related applications for people with cognitive disabilities

Can We Improve App Accessibility
with Advanced Development Methods?

Elmar Krainz[1,2]([✉]), Klaus Miesenberger[2], and Johannes Feiner[1]

[1] FH JOANNEUM, Kapfenberg, Austria
{elmar.krainz,johannes.feiner}@fh-joanneum.at
[2] Johannes Kepler University, Linz, Austria
klaus.miesenberger@jku.at
http://www.fh-joanneum.at
https://www.jku.at/iis

Abstract. The number of mobile apps is rising. This can be seen in the Android Play Store were more than 3.5 million different apps are available. However, most apps have some problems with accessibility. This paper addresses the following research question: Can we improve the accessibility of apps with the help of advanced software development methods? Taking the model-driven development approach into consideration, the design and the development of an accessible app prototype is possible.

In the present study 42 developers compared the new model-driven method with the standard app development approach. The evaluation of the development process shows that model-driven development can improve the accessibility of mobile apps significantly.

Keywords: Mobile apps · Model-driven development · Accessibility

1 Introduction

The number of mobile apps is rising. Actually, there are more than 3.5 million[1] different apps available in the Android Play Store. Unfortunately, most apps have some problems with accessibility (A11Y). A quick inspection of the top apps in Google's Play Store shows issues in the proper implementation of A11Y. The Accessibility Scanner[2] reports for apps like WhatsApp, Messenger and Instagram problems with contrast of texts and images, missing object descriptions or too small touch target sizes. Table 1 presents the accessibility errors of nine top apps analysed with Accessibility Scanner.

Who needs accessible apps? According to the World Report on Disability [1] 15,3% of the world population have prevalence for a moderate disability and 2.9% have a severe impairment. Within the European Union about 80 million

---

[1] https://www.statista.com/statistics/266210.
[2] https://support.google.com/accessibility/android/answer/6376570.

© Springer International Publishing AG, part of Springer Nature 2018
K. Miesenberger and G. Kouroupetroglou (Eds.): ICCHP 2018, LNCS 10896, pp. 64–70, 2018.
https://doi.org/10.1007/978-3-319-94277-3_12

Table 1. Accessibility issues of 9 app automatically checked with Accessibility Acanner

App	Nr Problems	Description
Messenger	15	Missing object label, text contrast, touch target size
Whatsapp	12	Image contrast, text contrast,
Instagram	4	Touch targets size, text contrast
Amazon	13	Missing object label, text contrast, touch target size
Spock	7	Touch target size, object description, text contrast
Pinterest	5	Text contrast., missing object label,
Snapchat	11	Text contrast, wrong object description, touch targets size, missing object label
Wish	18	Image contrast, text contrast, missing label, touch target size
Twitter	9	Missing label, touch target size, image contrast

people are affected by disabilities[3]. Recently, the European Commission enacted the Directive (EU) 2016/2102 which should ensure that mobile applications of public sector bodies are accessible [2].

To solve this problem, it is important to give software developers tools to include accessibility from the beginning. The research at hand presents a model-driven development approach to create accessible apps and presents the evaluation in an empiric study with developers. This paper addresses the following research question: Can we improve the accessibility of apps with the help of advanced software development methods?

2 Background

Accessibility in software is defined in standards, such as ISO [3] or WCAG 2.0 [4]. Adopted versions (see [5]) adjust the standards for the mobile domain. Volter and Brambilla [6,7] used Model-driven Development (MDD) when designing and implementing mobile applications. Furthermore, Kraemer presents Android apps based on UML activities [8] and Parada [9] used UML modelling and code generation for Android apps. For cross-platform apps Heitkotter [10] added role-based app variability for model-driven development.

Approaches to combine accessibility and MDD can be found in Andrews and Hussain, who introduces the framework *Johar* for accessible applications [11]. Gonzales et al. created an accessible media player based on a model [12]. Zouhaier et al. are heading in the same direction with their research on the adaption of accessible UIs based on models [13]. The generation of accessible user interfaces in ubiquitous environments is presented in [14].

---

[3] http://ec.europa.eu/ipg/standards/accessibility/index_en.htm.

3   Model-Driven Development for Accessible Apps

As aforementioned, the integration of accessibility in the software development process could increase the accessibility of the resulting products. With the model-driven development approach following Krainz et al. [15, 16], one can design and develop an accessible app prototype. The first step is the description of the model in Domain Specific Language (DSL) in form of an XML file. The model describes the screen, the user interface elements and the interaction within the app. A generator transforms the model into an Android app prototype with proper implementation for the platform specific assistive technologies and the additional supportive add-ons like speech-to-text input integration. Finally, developers add native functionality for the mobile application. Figure 1 presents the process from the model in XML via the generation tool to the smart phone app.

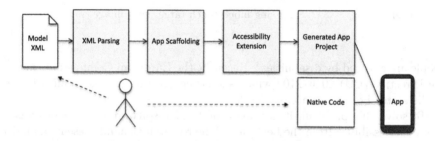

Fig. 1. Model-driven Development Process.

This paper presents the evaluation of the model driven development approach. To evaluate the utility of the app generation tool *Accapto* [15] and the accessibility of the resulting app we conducted an empiric study with developers.

3.1   Evaluation of Accessibility

The evaluation of accessibility is based on guidelines like the WCAG [4] or platform specific rules like the Material Design Guideline for Accessibility[4]. This work shows a method to rate and compare the accessibility of an app. The evaluation was performed in three consecutive steps:

1. Rating the support of the assistive technologies like the screen reader *Talkback* from very good (1) to very bad (5).
2. Automatic check with Accessibility Scanner to find, for example, insufficient contrast. The number of errors is taken into account.
3. Manual checks of the user Interface e.g. the position of widgets from very good (1) to very bad (5).

---

[4] https://material.io/guidelines/usability/accessibility.html.

Table 2. Accessibility evaluation

Assistive Technologies

1	Screenreader	1
2	Tabbing	1
3	External keyboard	2

average {1,33}

Accessibility Scanner

4	Touch size	0
5	Image contrast	0
6	Text contrast	0
7	Missing label	0
8	Double label	0
9	Wrong implantation of accessibility	0

sum {0}

Manuelle Checks

10	Clear and simple texts	2
11	Clear navigation	2
12	Readable font size	3
13	Possibility of magnification	4
14	Position of the ui elements	3

average {2,8}

Overall Accessibility Rating {4,13}

Table 2 shows a single items of the accessibility check. Each rule are based on the WCAG definitions. For example rule 5 *Image contrast* is related to WCAG success criterion *1.4.3 Contrast (Minimum)*. The result of the complete check is a single numeric value, which allows to compare the accessibility of two similar apps. A lower value means better accessibility.

3.2 Empiric Study with Developers

In this study 42 participants were involved, each one had moderate to good experience with programming within Android app development. The developers had to perform two tasks. The first task was the implementation of a simple Android application. The participants were divided into two groups, one started with conventional app development, while the other used the model-driven approach with *Accapto*. Afterwards, in the second task all participants had to rate the accessibility of the resulting app with the help of the evaluation method mentioned above.

Results: First, in a post-questionary all participants were asked about their own impression of the resulting accessibility. They had to rate in a scale form 1 (very good) to 10 (very bad). Developers using the model-driven method reported an average of 3,3 compared to 5,2 of the other group. Figure 2, left shows the differences in a box plot diagram. The first impressions is that model-driven development leads to better accessibility. To strengthen this result we compared the evaluation results of both groups.

The analysis of the accessibility evaluation (where a lower value indicated better accessibility) the group using model-driven development had better values for accessibility (mean = 6.19, SD = 5.97) than the group with the classical development approach (mean = 12.29, SD= 9,7). The box plot diagram of the evaluation is presented in Fig. 2 (right). Table 3 shows the complete accessibility rating ob both developer groups.

With the *Wilcoxon-Mann-Whitney-test* we draw a conclusion of the generality of this result. The following statistical hypothesis is defined to answer this question.

- **Null Hypothesis H0**
  $\mu_0 = \mu_1$: App accessibility of model driven development is the same as standard development.
- **Alternative Hypothesis H1**
  $\mu_0 \neg \mu_1$: App accessibility of model driven development is not the same as standard development.

The Wilcoxon-Mann-Whitney test demonstrated that in the group using model-driven development where better values of accessibility (mean = 6.19, SD = 5.96) than in the group using the standard development approach (mean = 12.29, SD = 9.69). With a p-value of p = 0.0007789 lower than 0.05, we reject the hypothesis H0 of statistical equality of means of two groups. The data analysis of the model-driven development and the standard procedure shows a significant difference in the accessibility of the resulting app. The model-driven approach with Accapto creates apps with better accessibility from the beginning.

Table 3. Statistics of Accessibly Evaluation

Model-driven Development (n=21)

	Overall	AssistiveTechologies	Errors A11y Scanner	Manual Checks
mean	6,19	1,80	2,10	2,38
var	35,53	0,40	31,99	0,20
SD	5,96	0,63	5,66	0,45
median	4,40	1,58	0,00	2,40

Android Development (n=21)

	Overall	AssistiveTechologies	Errors A11y Scanner	Manual Checks
mean	12,29	2,97	6,76	2,56
var	93,93	1,02	79,89	0,32
SD	9,69	1,01	8,94	0,57
median	13,07	2,67	6,00	2,40

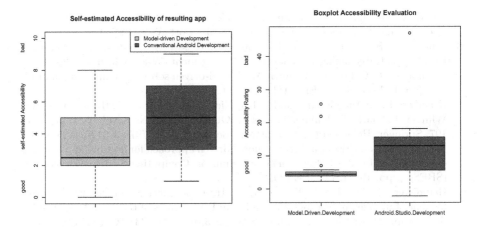

Fig. 2. Accessibility rating: Self-estimated accessibility (left) and evaluation results of created app (right).

4   Conclusion

This work tries to answer the question: Can we improve app accessibility with advanced development methods? With the model-driven development approach developers start the implementation process by modelling the app interaction followed by the automatic code generation. In this step many accessibility features can be included form the beginning.

The automatic model-to-code transformations cover missing attributes for assistive technologies. The proper implementation of the app prototype and the enrichment with other supportive features helps to create accessible apps. The evaluation of the development process shows that model-driven development can improve the accessibility of mobile apps. The design is still limited to simple workflows and user interface elements, but can be extended in further version of *Accapto*.

References

1. WHO: World report on disability. Technical report, World Health Organization (2011)
2. European Union: Directive (eu) 2016/2102 of the european parliament and of the council of 26 october 2016 on the accessibility of the websites and mobile applications of public sector bodies, October 2016
3. ISO. ISO, DIS 9241–171: ergonomics of human-system interaction - part 171: Guidance on software accessibility, p. 2008. Standard, International Organization for Standardization (2008)
4. Caldwell, B., Reid, L.G., Cooper, M., Vanderheiden, G.: Web content accessibility guidelines (WCAG) 2.0. W3C recommendation, W3C, December 2008. http://www.w3.org/TR/2008/REC-WCAG20-20081211/

5. Patch, K., Spellman, J., Wahlbin, K.: Mobile accessibility: How wcag 2.0 and other w3c/wai guidelines apply to mobile. Technical report, W3C (2015)
6. Völter, M., Stahl, T., Bettin, J., Haase, A., Helsen, S.: Model-Driven Software Development: Technology, Engineering. Management. Wiley, Chicheste (2013)
7. Brambilla, M., Cabot, J., Wimmer, M.: Model-driven software engineering in practice. Synth. Lect. Softw. Eng. 1(1), 1–182 (2012)
8. Kraemer, F.A.: Engineering android applications based on UML activities. In: Whittle, J., Clark, T., Kühne, T. (eds.) MODELS 2011. LNCS, vol. 6981, pp. 183–197. Springer, Heidelberg (2011). https://doi.org/10.1007/978-3-642-24485-8_14
9. Parada, A.G., de Brisolara, L.B.: A model driven approach for android applications development. In: 2012 Brazilian Symposium on Computing System Engineering (SBESC), pp. 192–197. IEEE (2012)
10. Heitkötter, H., Majchrzak, T.A., Kuchen, H.: Cross-platform model-driven development of mobile applications with md². In: Proceedings of the 28th Annual ACM Symposium on Applied Computing, SAC 2013, pp. 526–533. ACM (2013)
11. Andrews, J.H., Hussain, F.: Johar: a framework for developing accessible applications. In: Proceedings of the 11th International ACM SIGACCESS Conference on Computers and Accessibility, pp. 243–244. ACM (2009)
12. González-García, M., Moreno, L., Martínez, P.: A model-based tool to develop an accessible media player. In: Proceedings of the 17th International ACM SIGACCESS Conference on Computers & Accessibility, ASSETS 2015, pp. 415–416. ACM, New York (2015)
13. Zouhaier, L., Hlaoui, Y.B., Ayed, L.J.B.: A MDA-based approach for enabling accessibility adaptation of user interface for disabled people. In: ICEIS, vol. 3, pp. 120–127 (2014)
14. Miñón, R., Abascal, J., Aizpurua, A., Cearreta, I., Gamecho, B., Garay, N.: Model-based accessible user interface generation in ubiquitous environments. In: Campos, P., Graham, N., Jorge, J., Nunes, N., Palanque, P., Winckler, M. (eds.) INTERACT 2011. LNCS, vol. 6949, pp. 572–575. Springer, Heidelberg (2011). https://doi.org/10.1007/978-3-642-23768-3_85
15. Krainz, E., Miesenberger, K.: Accapto, a generic design and development toolkit for accessible mobile apps. Stud. Health Technol. Inform. 242, 660–664 (2017)
16. Krainz, E., Feiner, J., Fruhmann, M.: Accelerated development for accessible apps – model driven development of transportation apps for visually impaired people. In: Bogdan, C., et al. (eds.) HCSE/HESSD -2016. LNCS, vol. 9856, pp. 374–381. Springer, Cham (2016). https://doi.org/10.1007/978-3-319-44902-9_25

Group-Based Expert Walkthroughs to Compensate for Limited Access to Target User Groups as in Case of Chronically Ill Patients

Henrike Gappa[✉], Gaby Nordbrock, Yehya Mohamad, and Carlos A. Velasco

Fraunhofer Institute for Applied Information Technology (FIT), Schloss Birlinghoven,
53757 Sankt Augustin, Germany
{henrike.gappa,gaby.nordbrock,yehya.mohamad,
carlos.velasco}@fit.fraunhofer.de

Abstract. Involvement of real end users right from the beginning of an IT project is understood nowadays as good practice particularly in research projects where new and innovative concepts are to be investigated. In some situations, this is not feasible though, because this would cause unreasonable burden on target users, e.g., in case of chronically ill older patients or it is simply not possible, because administrative hurdles like permission by ethical committees need to be overcome, therefore it is necessary to install substituting methods. In the PICASO project (Personalised Integrated Care Approach for Service Organisations and Care Models for Patients with Multi-Morbidity and Chronic Conditions) this was achieved by implementing group-based expert walkthroughs where experts with different work-domain expert knowledge, in this case from usability, accessibility, clinical practice and software development, walked through an application by following typical usage scenarios target users are supposed to achieve. In contrast to the original method outcomes of walkthroughs were documented in form of software requirements, i.e. essential functionalities and features of the envisioned application instead of usability and accessibility issues. This way a reference document for developers evolved that closed the gap in bringing user requirements to application development.

Keywords: Group-based expert walkthrough · Usability inspection
User requirement engineering · Software requirements

1 Introduction

Involvement of real end users right from the beginning of an IT project is under-stood as good practice nowadays particularly in research projects where new and innovative concepts are to be investigated. The goal is to ensure that developments are useful and easy to use by the intended target user group. For this purpose user requirements are collected at the beginning of a research project which can be achieved by various methods among those are focus groups, interviews with users representing the target user groups and ethnographic methods such as participatory observation of the domain context. Such field studies help to understand the context-of-use and typical usage

© The Author(s) 2018
K. Miesenberger and G. Kouroupetroglou (Eds.): ICCHP 2018, LNCS 10896, pp. 71–74, 2018.
https://doi.org/10.1007/978-3-319-94277-3_13

scenarios of the envisioned application can be deduced which altogether build the base for elicitation of user requirements.

User requirements are descriptions of how a system is expected to perform from the user's perspective. They are intended to serve as primary source of in-formation for developers when determining system architecture and specifications as well as required software functionalities and features. To communicate user requirements in a suitable format they provide at its core a short but precise description of the user's need, a rationale for that and most important a fit criterion which states in a quantified manner when a user need is met, e.g. by providing a specified feature [1].

However, complexity of development projects has been rapidly increasing, so user requirements of the end application are not fully understood even after the phase of user requirements gathering has been completed resulting in high volatility of defined requirements. Beyond this, user needs and fit criteria cannot all be defined as precise as needed to serve as encompassing source for derivation of software requirements which is a precondition for creating an application that suits the domain context and is characterised by good usability and accessibility. It is rather to expect that user requirements will need substantial refinement and enhancement by new ones actually requiring further user involvement to ensure suitability to users' needs. In some situations this is not feasible though, because this would cause unreasonable burden on target users, e.g., in case of chronically ill older patients or it is simply not possible, because administrative hurdles like permission by ethical committees need to be overcome. Therefore it is necessary to install substituting methods. In the PICASO project (Personalised Integrated Care Approach for Service Organisations and Care Models for Patients with Multi-Morbidity and Chronic Conditions)[1] this was achieved by implementing group-based expert walkthroughs where experts with different work-domain knowledge, in this case from usability, accessibility, clinical practice and software development, walk through an application by following typical usage scenarios target users are supposed to achieve.

The PICASO project focuses on the needs of patients with multi-morbidity conditions such as Parkinson disease and rheumatism often combined with cardiovascular diseases and aims to build an ICT based integrated care platform to improve their treatment situation. It supports collaborative sharing of care plans across sectors in a cloud-based health platform ensuring data privacy. Furthermore, PICASO aims to stimulate the independence and empowerment of patients by offering home care applications to support self-management and self-monitoring of their diseases. For this purpose a mobile application was to develop which presents to patients a daily schedule with tasks to do like on-time medication intake, measuring blood pressure, taking weight, do self-recordings such as well-being ratings in accordance to the care plan defined by their physicians. To support patients in managing their tasks as required, reminders are provided. Moreover, patients are presented results of their measurements and self-recordings in form of combined graphs or tables also in retrospective to receive better understanding of their health situation and mutually reinforcing factors.

---

[1] http://www.picaso-project.eu/.

2   Group-Based Expert Walkthroughs for Achievement of Software Requirements

As already mentioned the PICASO platform consists of applications for medical professionals like physicians as well as for chronically ill patients who could be involved in the initial phase of user requirements gathering in PICASO but not later on, so group-based expert walkthroughs were initiated to support the process of feeding collected user requirements into technical realisation of the envisioned applications. During these walkthroughs clinicians experienced with e-health applications, software developers and usability experts with a background in accessibility walked through early and evolving prototypes to discuss user requirements and how to satisfy these in terms of software requirements. Since partners in PICASO are situated in different European countries group sessions were organized as desktop-sharing sessions where developers presented the current status of their application. The presentation was aligned to typical usage scenarios users of this application need to accomplish. During the walkthroughs it was evaluated whether users would know what is the next step, which control or element should be selected to achieve the task goal as well as appropriateness of layout and work flow. Thereby arising lacks or weaknesses in functionality and accessibility were raised by experts from their individual point of view. The needs of chronically ill older people suffering from Parkinson disease or rheumatism which often causes inhibited fine motor skills were taken into account in particular. By bringing together expert knowledge from different domains usability issues could be identified, where relevance for the target user group can be assumed and feasible design solutions determined [2]. This is understood as one of the advantages of group-based expert walkthroughs.

Group-based expert walkthroughs are based on the methodology of the Cognitive Walkthrough developed by Catherine Wharton [3] which can be considered a well-established usability evaluation technique that has proven to provide excellent results in regard to identifying usability issues related to successful task achievement [4]. In PICASO this method was developed further in that usability professionals documented results of group-based expert walkthroughs not as a list of usability and accessibility issues as in the original method, but rather in form of software requirements, i.e. a description of required functionalities and features of the discussed application. This description was circulated among all group members and feedback collected until finally a reference document evolved that described agreed essential software requirements of viable PICASO applications. This reference document was understood as a very valuable source of information by PICASO developer to better transfer user requirements to software requirements on which base development takes place. In the upcoming user study it will be evaluated if and how usability and accessibility issues raised here will match with usability and accessibility issues discussed in the PICASO walkthroughs.

3 Conclusions

Installing group-based expert walkthrough sessions to compensate for limited access to target user groups like chronically ill older patients appeared to be a feasible solution in PICASO. This approach might work as well in similar situations such as when recruiting a critical number of test participants turns out to be impossible. In development projects recruitment of test participants with required characteristics, e.g. certain disabilities, often poses a problem. Beyond this, group-based expert walkthroughs offer the opportunity to meet more frequently during the development phase as it would be reasonable with real test users. Thereby, an iterative design approach is supported that is suitable to reduce the gap between understanding users' needs and actually implementing them. The approach followed in PICASO to document outcomes of PICASO walkthroughs in form of software requirements, i.e. required functionalities and features of the application aimed for rather than usability and accessibility issues turned out to be a powerful driving force to put user requirements into technical realization.

Acknowledgments. This work was partially funded by the European Commission H2020 programme; Contract number 689209; PICASO. The authors would like to acknowledge the support of the PICASO consortium.

References

1. Robertson, S., Robertson, J.R.: Mastering the Requirement Process. Addison Wesley, London (1999)
2. Følstad, A.: Group-based expert walkthrough. In: Scapin, D., Law, E. (eds) R3UEMS: Review, Report and Refine Usability Evaluation Methods, The 3rd COST294-MAUSE International Workshop, Athens, 5 March 2007, pp. 58–60. ESF, COST (2007)
3. Wharton, C., Rieman, J., Lewis, C., Polson, P.: The cognitive walkthrough method: a practitioner's guide. In: Nielsen, J., Mack, R. (eds.) Usability Inspection Methods, pp. 105–140. John Wiley & sons Inc., New York (1994)
4. Power, C., Fox, J.: Comparing the comprehensiveness of three expert inspection methodologies for detecting errors in interactive systems. Saf. Sci. **62**(2014), 286–294 (2014)

Modular Human-Computer Interaction Platform on Mobile Devices for Distributed Development

Sebastian Ritterbusch[1,2(✉)], Patrick Frank[1], and Vanessa Petrausch[3]

[1] iXpoint Informationssysteme GmbH, Ettlingen, Germany
{sebastian.ritterbusch,patrick.frank}@ixpoint.de
[2] VWA-Hochschule, Stuttgart, Germany
[3] Karlsruhe Institute of Technology, Studycentre for the Visually Impaired,
Karlsruhe, Germany
vanessa.petrausch@kit.edu

Abstract. For people with visual disabilities, mobile devices have become an indispensable part for independent and self-determined living. Increasing performance of mobile devices and availability of mobile sensors and actors can improve the usability and applicability of mobile solutions. The wide range of modalities available for communication and interaction with mobile devices increase the gap between Human-Computer Interaction (HCI) research and actual implementation on mobile devices. We propose the use of a Domain Specific Language to enable the distributed development of modular and individually adaptable HCI implementations on an improving and exchangeable mobile platform.

Keywords: Human-Computer Interaction · Mobile computing
Development cycle · Multi-modal interaction

1 Introduction

The availability of versatile mobile computing platforms with wireless connectivity opened new Human-Computer Interaction (HCI) models for blind users making mobile devices like smartphones an indispensable helping device. Following [1], usable information starts with localization, object detection, beacons, body orientation, and many more, and does not end with recent advances in image recognition, that is now available on mobile platforms. Already in [2], demand for the design of user interfaces for all, raises the need of new development and evaluation cycles to keep track with technological and scientific advances, and to maintain solutions. There are still many open question of research into multi-modal non-visual interaction [4], and how experiments can be designed and suitable developed given the rich sensory information of mobile platforms. This concludes to a user-centered design process [3] to recognize and understand individual capabilities, and accommodate to them during development. This paper presents a solution, where a user-centered design is feasible by abstraction of data sources,

© Springer International Publishing AG, part of Springer Nature 2018
K. Miesenberger and G. Kouroupetroglou (Eds.): ICCHP 2018, LNCS 10896, pp. 75–78, 2018.
https://doi.org/10.1007/978-3-319-94277-3_14

sensors and actors using a Domain Specific Language (DSL). The shortened development and distribution cycle enables distributed HCI experts implement, and experiment with modalities, while users and testers validate the approaches for immediate feedback. At the same time, hardware and mobile developers improve its implementation for several operating systems.

2   Problem Statement and Related Work

The survey papers [3,4] mention various mobile solutions to assist people with visual disabilities. In contrast to them, the developed platform does not aim at a specific application, and offers general programmatic access to data networks, provided sensors and actors to communicate with the user.

The main aim is to enable distributed development, testing and evaluation of multi-modal HCI models on mobile devices for several platforms, support both sensors and actors on mobile devices, and external devices such as orientation sensors, vibration bands and mobile Braille displays with low-latency responses.

3   Methodology

Integral part of the platform is the use of a DSL to enable full versatility how data is processed, how the user is informed, and how the system reacts to user interaction. The DSL should enable full access to sensors, actors and data, while each module is encapsulated from other HCI models and modules. A main aspect is the abstraction of access to data, sensors, actors and external hardware from the actual HCI modules. Furthermore, special care was needed to manage access to serialized actors, such as the narration unit for mobile devices. Using priority queues, the modules can inform about severity of information, to help the system which information to deliver first.

This structure also promotes the distribution of the development, which is enabled by a client-server approach, where developers can easily upload their modules to a server, which is queried by all installed clients that are permitted access to development version. This reduces the time for development updates from the HCI side to clients a matter of less than a minute. All modules have four states: paused and unregistered, registered and inactive, active and muted, active. Every module needs to be registered, activated and unmuted before using the module within the system. This behaviour promotes easy testing of different modules, since they can be loaded individually.

Another advantage of modular development and the usage of the DSL is the abstraction from app programming itself. This allows people with different implementation skills to contribute their experience in the design of barrier-free HCI interfaces without having pronounced programming skills. As an example, modules can offer nearly unlimited individualization for users, and simplify testing and evaluation of various HCI modes just by switching in options. Listing 1.1 shows an example of two menu options for a haptic anklet by defining the vibration intensity as a number and the delay between two vibrations. Default values can be set with the `value` parameter. These simple manipulations of the options and the short update cycles allow a quick adjustment and testing of the modules in direct and immediate feedback with actual users, which promotes efficient and a new level of user-centered programming.

```
function registerModule()
 local moduleOptions = {
  vibInt = {
   label = {de = "Intensitaet [%]",
            en = "Intensity [%]" },
   description = {de = "Staerke der Vibration", en = "Strength of vibration"},
   kind = "entry:number",
   value = "30"
  },
  vibrationDelay = {
   ...
   kind = "entry:number",
   value = "1500"
  }
 }
```

Listing 1.1. Register function in theModule Options

Also, modules may read available sensors on demand, or are informed about changed readings via call-back functions, enabling fast responses to changed conditions or requests.

4   Results

The development platform has already been tested by implementation of several HCI modules for aiding blind persons in their urban mobility, or help researching HCI modalities: A module for a simple acoustic compass informs the user about the heading of the smartphone, in degrees, cardinal directions or in clock directions. A so-called radar module informs about objects or points of interest that are registered in OpenStreetMap or a city administration database in a circular pattern. For free space traversal, a module supporting GPS and compass orientation helps to reach a point in a given distance and heading, using narrative output or haptic feedback. Using a routing module, the user can be guided on a computed path between two points supporting safe pedestrian routing.

Additionally, various hardware was successfully accessed over Bluetooth by modules, such as vibration bands for arms or feet, or orientation sensors such as the TI SensorTag to easily query head or body orientation. For efficient sonification, an analogue synthesizer simulation and head-related transfer function support offer a wide range of acoustic feedback. A communication protocol to a computer with state-of-the-art neural-network optical object detection was successfully established. Finally, yet importantly, a mobile Braille display is supported, to give haptic feedback to the user.

The app programmers provided the framework for all these modules, so that experts in supporting barrier-free interactions with the external devices could easily implement the individual modules. For example, the focus could be placed on the design of vibration patterns, which optimally support a user in a navigation task by implementing the control of the individual vibration motors at various events in a vibration module without having to have detailed knowledge of application programming. Since no extensive programming environment needs to be used to develop the modules, people with visual impairment or people without programming skills can efficiently participate in the development of the app without having to familiarize themselves with IDEs. This approach is currently successfully used in a diversity team of seeing and blind developers, skilled app developers and HCI experts.

Finally, a simulation module offered an efficient platform for Wizard-of-Oz tests for successfully evaluating the usage of the app with its various modalities to inform the user about routing hints and obstacles. The test was carried out with ten visually impaired users and shows that not only can the development be made efficient and barrier-free, but also that the app is promising as an application in the area of support for the visually impaired.

5   Conclusion

The modular HCI platform for mobile devices has proven its applicability, supporting multi-modal, user-centered and customized feedback to the user. Its extensibility offers more hardware sensors, actors, as well as mobile platforms to be integrated. In addition, other groups may provide HCI modules to the platform, enabling fast development, evaluation and testing cycles for new solutions to aid people with visual disabilities in their independent and self-determined life.

Depending on its distribution platform, some large manufacturers do not allow uploading new code on installed systems at the end-users. This seems a drawback to the original approach to fast development and distribution cycles. Actually, this does not influence the development phase, where real-time update are not forbidden. For end-users, the well-tested modules will be distributed as App updates as included code.

The platform is an integral part of the TERRAIN Project[1], helping visually impaired humans for a self-determined and individual mobility in an urban environment.

References

1. Bradley, N.A., Dunlop, M.D.: An experimental investigation into wayfinding directions for visually impaired people. Pers. Ubiquitous Comput. 9(6), 395–403 (2005)
2. Stephanidis, C.: User interfaces for all: new perspectives into human-computer interaction. In: User Interfaces for All-Concepts, Methods, and Tools, vol. 1, pp. 3–17 (2001)
3. Hakobyan, L., Lumsden, J., O'Sullivan, D., Bartlett, H.: Mobile assistive technologies for the visually impaired. Surv. Ophthalmol. 58(6), 513–528 (2013)
4. Csapó, Á., Wersényi, G., Nagy, H., Stockman, T.: A survey of assistive technologies and applications for blind users on mobile platforms: a review and foundation for research. J. Multimodal User Interfaces 9(4), 275–286 (2015)

---

[1] http://www.terrain-projekt.de/, federally funded by BMBF, 07/2016–06/2019.

Accessible
System/Information/Document Design

Review on Smart Solutions for People with Visual Impairment

Mostafa Elgendy[✉] and Cecilia Sik Lanyi

University of Pannonia, Egyetem Street 10, Veszprem 8200, Hungary
mostafa.elgendy@virt.uni-pannon.hu, lanyi@almos.uni-pannon.hu

Abstract. Nowadays, over a billion people are estimated to be living with disabilities. The lack of support services make them overly dependent on their families and prevent them from being socially included. A good solution is to use Mobile Assistive Technologies (MAT) to perform tasks in everyday lives, but one of the most important and challenging tasks is to create a solution which offers the assistance and support they need to achieve a good quality of life and allows them to participate in social life. This paper reviews researches within the field of MATs to help people with visual impairment in their daily activities like navigation and shopping.

Keywords: Smartphones · Assistive technology · People with visual impairment
Navigation · Shopping

1 Introduction

Mobile technologies like smartphones and smart glasses are becoming more and more popular in recent years. Studies show that more than 56% of users in the world use mobile technologies which have a lot of capabilities like Wi-Fi, cameras, and GPS. Mobile technologies can be used to develop new solutions for people with visual disabilities and this is called MAT [1]. MATs have the potential to enhance the quality of life via improved autonomy and safety. Furthermore, it encourages them to travel outside their normal environment and to interact socially. A lot of researches have been made to help people with visual impairment in navigation and independent shopping. In this review these solutions are discussed and how to overcome their drawbacks.

2 Mobile Assistive Technology Solutions

People with visual impairment are moving from one place to another to finish their daily activities using traditional assistive devices like white cane or guide dog which provide only limited assistances [2]. Therefore it is important to complement these traditional assistive devices and not to replace them. A lot of researches have been done to allow people with visual problems to navigate indoor and outdoor and also to avoid obstacles [3–6]. Moreover, they face a lot of challenges and obstacles while they are shopping

K. Miesenberger and G. Kouroupetroglou (Eds.): ICCHP 2018, LNCS 10896, pp. 81–84, 2018.
https://doi.org/10.1007/978-3-319-94277-3_15

alone in a public place e.g. preparing shopping list, navigating in-side shops and identifying items [7–9].

2.1 Navigation

A system was developed to navigate inside buildings and avoid obstacles [3]. It uses a wearable module which contains; a Radio-Frequency Identification (RFID) reader and Wi-Fi component to get user position efficiently, an ultra-sonic to detect obstacles and a voice controller for giving directions to the user. On the server side it tries to calculate the shortest path using the Dijkstra algorithm, makes the localization process and runs an obstacles avoidance algorithm. This system allows user acting smoothly by minimizing response time and detects obstacles in a range from 3 cm to 6 m. However further work is needed to validate the effectiveness of proposed method. Also components like Wi-Fi, or RFID tags must be in place and needs a lot of maintenance.

Flores and co-workers [4] have used algorithms based on Hidden Markov Model (HMM) to detect and record the sequence of turns and number of steps between turns along the doctor's office route. After a visit, the user consults smartphone which reads the list of turns taken in reverse order using voice commands to safely trace back to the waiting room. This system helps the user to navigate indoor, but it assumes that the person only takes turns at discrete angles and this is not always true. Also it needs a lot of experiments with participants using a white cane in order to understand what is necessary for correct tracking of the gait of blind walkers.

Kammoun et al. provide a system which uses vision module to extract relevant visual information from the environment for object localization and user positioning [5]. To get user position, the system looks for nearby automatically loaded landmarks according to the estimated location of the user. These visual landmarks are used to refine the current GPS position. However, as the system is intended to be used in noisy environment the sounds should be as short as possible while still allowing good localization performance. Also the creation of landmarks needs to be automatically generated but now it is performed manually from recorded videos of the evaluation test site.

Walking straight provides a solution to help visually impaired people walking in a straight path using a smartphone's gyroscope and compass [6]. It uses the updated gyroscope values to remove the effects of body sway, and then use it to compute an average heading for each walking period, which is compared to the desired heading. If there is any deviation, it sends alarm signal to the user. However manual selection of the correct heading needs to be automatic. Furthermore, sensor reliability should also be improved. The smart phone orientation has to be fixed to a specific direction which prevents the user from using phone for some other tasks while walking.

2.2 Independent Shopping

Third eye is an automatic shopping assistant system that helps the user in the selection of the desired item from a grocery store shelf [7]. It consists of smart glasses with which the distance of objects can be properly located and identified. It is connected to a back-end server system that supports real-time video analytics. User wears a glove with a camera on the hand to grasp a product. Third Eye provides audio commands or tactile vibration patterns to guide the user's steps and hands toward the desired item. However, this system uses the navigation skills that visually impaired people already have so it needs to be completely automated. The feedback latency needs to be reduced so it can be used more effectively. Finally, the system uses a video streaming via Wi-Fi to the server which drained the battery power.

Shopping by Blind People developed a system that uses RFID to help people with visual impairment searching for products from the shelf during shopping [8]. User can easily scan any product to get details about it, e.g. the name of the product, and receive messages helping to navigate and reach it. Moreover, it allows making a shop-ping list and editing it, this way you can get total bill through voice message after the shopping. Store keeper uses a server to store product details and how to reach them. However, the products database is not enough to cover all the items, and the update frequency is slow. Also, in a noisy environment using voice commands requires wearing headphones and in many instances this would not be recommended. Finally, technology such as servers, Wi-Fi, or RFID tags must be in place.

López-de-Ipiña and co-workers proposed a system which allows people with visual impairment to navigate using voice messages by combining RFID reader and a smart-phone [9]. Also, it allows them to identify products with phone's camera using QR codes placed on product shelves. Moreover, it provides a web-based management component to easily configure the system, generating and binding barcode tags for product shelves and RFID tag markers attached to the supermarket floor. This system is simple to deploy, so conventional shopping could be altered and blind user could use their usual devices. However in a noisy environment, the use of the audio channel could require wearing headphones, and in many instances this would not be recommended. Also technology such as servers, Wi-Fi, or RFID tags must be in place.

3   Conclusion

Multiple technologies have been developed to help people with visual problems to navi-gate outdoor, indoor and to avoid obstacles. Also a lot of applications were de-signed to allow them to navigate and identify items while shopping.

Solutions related to navigation tried at first to figure out know where the visually impaired are standing which can be achieved in different ways. It can be done using dead reckoning which estimates your location based on the last known one. Also some installed tags like RFID, IMU, Infrared IR, Ultrasound identification (USID), Beacons, Barcodes, QR codes and markers can be used. These tags store information about loca-tion and surrounding environment, then visually impaired people use tag reader to iden-tify current location. Moreover they can use GPS for outdoor places or using some systems which depend on computer vision. After identifying user place and orientation, these systems tried to calculate the path to destination using some algorithms like Dijk-stra to start navigation. During navigation user can identify obstacles and distance to them using sensors like Ultrasonic sensor, IMU and Laser scanner or using computer vision techniques. Solutions related to shopping save time for visually impaired people by allowing preparing shopping list using techniques like converting speech to text; converting handwriting to text which can be stored in a data-base as a shopping list; and finally converting this text to speech during shopping to allow the user to identify the shopping list. Also they tried to allow visually impaired people to shopping without any help from others by using some technologies like Google Glasses, Smartphones and Cameras to identify products based on QR code and barcode or using computer vision techniques.

All proposed solutions tried to give feedback to the user using sound commands or haptic vibrations. All of these solutions tried to use high storage capacity for storing the required data and also need significant computing power, this way all of these solutions tried to use notebook carried in the pack, using server for processing and storing all data or using cloud computing. But the most important thing is to consider the experience of the visually impaired people in the early design process to allow more usability solutions [10].

Acknowledgement. The authors acknowledge the financial support of Széchenyi 2020 under the EFOP-3.6.1-16-2016-00015.

References

1. Domingo, Mari Carmen: An overview of the Internet of Things for people with disabilities. J. Netw. Comput. Appl. **35**(2), 584–596 (2012)
2. Wachaja, A., et al.: Navigating blind people with walking impairments using a smart walker. Auton. Robots **41**(3), 555–573 (2017)
3. Tsirmpas, C., et al.: An indoor navigation system for visually impaired and elderly people based on Radio Frequency Identification (RFID). Inf. Sci. **320**, 288–305 (2015)
4. Flores, G.H., Manduchi, R., Zenteno, E.D.: Ariadne's thread: robust turn detection for path back-tracing using the iPhone. In: Ubiquitous Positioning Indoor Navigation and Location Based Service (UPINLBS), 2014. IEEE (2014)
5. Kammoun, S., et al.: Navigation and space perception assistance for the visually impaired: the NAVIG project. IRBM **33**(2), 182–189 (2012)
6. Panëels, S.A., et al.: The walking straight mobile application: helping the visually impaired avoid veering. Georgia Institute of Technology (2013)
7. Zientara, P.A., et al.: Third Eye: a shopping assistant for the visually impaired. Computer **50**(2), 16–24 (2017)
8. Kesh, S.: Shopping by blind people: detection of interactions in ambient assisted living environments using RFID. Int. J. **6**(2) (2017).
9. López-de-Ipiña, D., Lorido, T., López, U.: Indoor navigation and product recognition for blind people assisted shopping. In: Bravo, J., Hervás, R., Villarreal, V. (eds.) IWAAL 2011. LNCS, vol. 6693, pp. 33–40. Springer, Heidelberg (2011). https://doi.org/10.1007/978-3-642-21303-8_5
10. Yuan, C.W., et al.: Constructing a holistic view of shopping with people with visual impairment: a participatory design approach. Univ. Access Inf. Soc. 1–14 (2017)

Accessible EPUB: Making EPUB 3 Documents Universal Accessible

Thorsten Schwarz$^{(\boxtimes)}$, Sachin Rajgopal, and Rainer Stiefelhagen

Karlsruhe Institute of Technology, Studycentre for the Visually Impaired,
Engesserstr. 4, 76131 Karlsruhe, Germany
thorsten.schwarz@kit.edu
http://szs.kit.edu

Abstract. Current document standards have the characteristic that they can only serve one group of users under the aspect of vision (sighted, visually impaired or blind reader). Wouldn't it be nice if one documentformat could combine all properties in one document? This paper presents a new approach of an universal accessible version of EPUB 3 documents, which will allow sighted, visually impaired and blind readers to use and share the same EPUB 3 document by an "integrated switching mechanism" to change the output format. Furthermore, we will introduce a simple word processing tool that allows to easily create such accessible EPUBs without knowing how an EPUB file is constructed or created.

Keywords: EPUB · EPUB 3 · Accessible documents

1 Introduction

In recent years, accessibility has become increasingly important, especially for accessible documents. Several nations have passed regulatory laws that ensure equal treatment of all people and ensure that documents are accessible to all [1].

The currently dominant formats for accessible electronic documents are Microsoft Word and PDF (Portable Document Format) documents, or more precisely PDF/UA (PDF/Universal Accessibility) documents. First of all, both formats have a predefined page size. While this is useful for printed documents, a computer screen can rarely display all contents of the document to the detriment of visually impaired people [2]. Therefore, an electronic document format - like HTML - without a fixed document size containing semantic and structural information and a fixed reading order would be better suited to meet the requirements of accessibility.

Furthermore, different "selectable" forms of presentation would be advantageous, especially for graphics or mathematical formulas. For example, formulas in the LATEXsource code for blind users or high-contrast images for users with limited residual vision. This could be combined with EPUB 3 [2].

© Springer International Publishing AG, part of Springer Nature 2018
K. Miesenberger and G. Kouroupetroglou (Eds.): ICCHP 2018, LNCS 10896, pp. 85–92, 2018.
https://doi.org/10.1007/978-3-319-94277-3_16

This is exactly where we come in with our new EPUB approach, which combines all three versions in one document. But why is EPUB the format of our choice?

EPUB stands for **E**lectronic **PUB**lication and is a format primarily used for books in an electronic format (E-Book). The EPUB format was created by the International Digital Publishing Forum (IDPF) and the current version is 3.1 which is a minor update to EPUB 3 [3]. EPUB uses XML based formats like XHTML, and thus also uses the accessibility standards and guidelines already established in many nations like the Web Content Accessibility Guidelines (WCAG) [4]. This was done as reading systems can have different screen sizes and the EPUB content can therefore be reflowable. Font type and size can also be adapted to the individual needs of the users. Visually impaired people could therefore adjust the document to their preferences in font style, size and color. The EPUB 3 specification also contains guidelines for accessibility so these features are built in and not an afterthought [5].

The EPUB working group has also made important changes from EPUB 2 to EPUB 3 which improve the accessibility of documents. For example, mathematical equations can now be displayed in MathML and there is better navigation and more support for Cascading Style Sheets (CSS). However, not all of these changes are yet supported by EPUB readers and devices [6].

Creating EPUBs, however, is not as simple as word documents. There are several editors available, but the issues of them will be presented in Sect. 2.1. Accessible EPUB is an attempt to remedy these issues and simplify the process so that accessible documents for STEM subjects can be created without intricate knowledge of EPUBs.

2   Related Work

Of course, there are already works that have tried to generate different accessible formats. Takaira et al. [7] created a tool which analyzes a PDF document and outputs different kinds of textbooks by detecting the structure of the document properly assigning the tags. Leporini et al. [8] have created the tool "Book4All" to convert PDF-E-Books into a more accessible format. This was done by analyzing the PDF and converting it into the XML based Intermediate Book Format. This can then be converted into XHTML or Daisy [9]. Coming back to EPUB, Book4All was also developed to create EPUBs and Lenzi and Leporini [10] found out that while there are difficulties using voiceover with EPUBs, this can be improved by using the tags and attributes properly. Bartalesi and Leporini [11] carried out an online survey in their work and asked 25 users to rate "enriched" EPUB in comparison to the original PDF format regarding accessibility and usability. 50% of respondents preferred EPUB over other E-Book formats, while 13% said EPUB was equivalent. The sample group also felt that it was easier to access content in EPUBs and use the table of contents than in PDFs. Furthermore, 80% of blind users were unable to read images in PDFs correctly with their screen reader, while the corresponding value for EPUBs was less than 50%. 64% of users found the EPUB's document structure easy to understand.

2.1 Existing EPUB Editors

There are a number of different ways to create EPUB documents [12]. Adobe InDesign[1] is one way and is suitable for publishers, but it has no built-in MathML support and it is a commercial program that is unaffordable to most user groups. LibreOffice in its latest version 6.0 is able to export Writer documents to EPUB, too. This and perhaps Microsoft Word (with installed EPUB macros) are maybe the easiest options to create an EPUB document. Nevertheless, these versions have to be edited in special EPUB editors to meet proper accessibility levels. For example, alternative texts for images or LaTeXsource code alternatives for mathematical formulas.

Some EPUB editors are pure WYSIWYG editors (What You See Is What You Get), but important functions such as mathematical equations and semantic information are usually missing. EPUB editors where the program code has to be edited are limited to persons with programming experience. Sigil [13], for example, is such a popular open source WYSIWYG EPUB editor with many features, but important features such as text alternatives for images can only be added manually with coding.

After all, most editors are not able to produce the kind of universal accessible document we want out of the box, nor accessible to visually impaired or blind people.

3 Specifications of Our "Accessible EPUB"

3.1 EPUB Creation Process

First of all, what is needed to create an EPUB file and then get it accessible? An EPUB file is nothing more than a ZIP file[2] [14], but renamed from "*.zip" to "*.epub". If you change the file extension and extract the file contents, the individual files, such as XHTML and image files, can be opened and edited. The creation of an EPUB document can therefore be briefly described in three steps:

1. create content documents (texts, images, etc.) in formats such as XHTML and SVG,
2. create the package document "package.opf" and
3. compression of the data including metadata in a ZIP file.

The package document consists of five sections describing how the EPUB document is structured [5].

3.2 EPUB Switching Mechanism

The introduction shows that although EPUB 3 is a promising format, the lack of easy-to-use editors means that not everyone can create accessible EPUB documents. Therefore, the main objective of this work is to lay the foundations

---

[1] https://www.adobe.com/products/indesign.html.

[2] ZIP is an archive file format that supports lossless data compression.

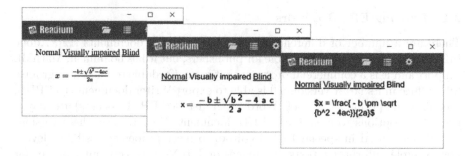

Fig. 1. EPUB in 'Normal', 'Visual impaired' and 'Blind' mode (from left to right).

for such EPUB documents. On the one hand, there is a suitable basic structure that unifies all format versions, and on the other hand, a suitable editor that gets the mentioned problems/restrictions under control for the end user or document creator.

This means that, at the end of the day, it should be easy for teachers and other educators to create an EPUB document that can be used by blind, visually impaired and sighted people. By a simple switch in the document, the CSS can be adapted to the needs of the target group with one click (see Fig. 1).

For example, the text alternatives for mathematical equations (e.g. the LATEXsource code) and images are displayed automatically when the blind version is selected [5]. The switching mechanism can be done either with JavaScript or via CSS. Although JavaScript is easier to use, not all EPUB readers or devices support JavaScript and the EPUB specification does not require JavaScript to be supported [5]. The CSS version is much more limited because all content has to be inserted into a single XHTML file and CSS selectors are not fully supported yet, but CSS support is included in the EPUB specification. Ultimately, we need an EPUB framework that can be used by most end devices, as well as a suitable easy-to-use editor.

Unfortunately a unified accessible standard for the EPUB documents could not be found, as EPUB readers do not support all features mentioned in the EPUB 3 specifications. As a result, Accessible EPUB allows users to create documents either with CSS or JavaScript as basis for the switching mechanism. It is possible that when EPUB readers either have widespread support for CSS 3 or the specification makes JavaScript support mandatory, one of the standards will establish itself. Until then it is better to design both to allow users to have a choice.

3.3   Editor "Accessible EPUB"

"Accessible EPUB" is a WYSIWYG program written in C# (. NET) that serves to create accessible EPUB documents using the switching mechanism (see Fig. 2). The process of creating documents should be as simple as possible so that even people with little experience in using special software can use the program.

Primary target groups are, for example, teachers or implementation centers that have a need for accessible documents for different user groups.

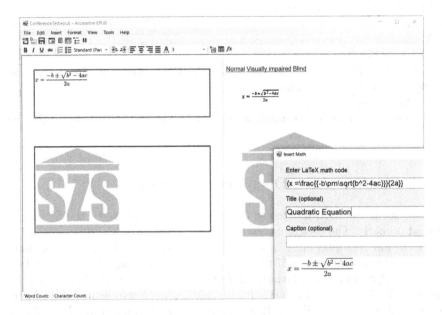

Fig. 2. Accessible EPUB editor

A feature is to allow the user to have immediate feedback to their actions. Any text or other content written in the editor on the left side is immediately shown on the right side (Fig. 2). The user can switch between normal, visually impaired and blind versions of the content within the preview browser.

One of the goals of this project is to create documents for STEM subjects. In other EPUB editors, like Sigil or Adobe InDesign, there is no possibility of adding MathML without coding it in. Equations have to be inserted as normal text or as images. As discussed earlier in this paper, MathML is preferable due to is superior presentation and the ability to interact with equations, such as highlighting a part of an equation. Therefore adding a easy way to insert equations was of particular importance in this program. The equation insertion tool can be seen in Fig. 2. It accepts LaTeXcode and the result is shown in a panel in the bottom half of the screen. In case of an error, the panel is highlighted with a red border. This immediate feedback should improve the usability of the program.

Tables and images are inserted similarly. When inserting images, the user has to enter some alternative text to ensure the accessibility of the document. Entering a caption and title is optional. All of these will be put in a figure element, and if the user moves it, the caption and alternative text will move it. Editing commands commonly found in word processors are also present in a toolbar at the top of the program.

Some of the main features of our "Accessible EPUB" editor are:

1. It creates an EPUB document with the switching mechanism without having to customize the source code.
2. It includes an equation editor which accepts LaTeXas input and inserts the MathML equivalent, SVG image and the alternative text of the equation, as shown in Fig. 2.
3. It provides the ability to insert images with title, caption and alternative text, the last one being mandatory.
4. Is able to insert tables.
5. It gives the possibility to mark up sections using the HTML styles (h1, h2, p, etc.).

4   Evaluation of the Document Standard

The document standard was tested on various programs to see if the EPUB can be read properly. The programs tested include Adobe Digital Editions, Calibre, AZARDI and Readium on Windows 10, iBooks under iOS and Reasily under Android. The test examined if they supporte the following: the CSS standard, the JavaScript standard, MathML and screen reader support. The results are shown in Table 1. Several other software readers were tested, like the Bluefire Reader and the Icecream Ebook Reader, but they don't support MathML. Adobe Digital Editions is an exception, but is among the better known readers so it was included in the comparison. A first problem was the often missing MathML support. EPUB 3 was approved by the IDPF in 2011, but MathML support is still not common. Even major companies like Adobe do not have MathML support in their Adobe Digital Editions. Another point is the support of JavaScript. Only the open source program Calibre supports JavaScript in connection with the storage of sessions, so that the EPUB document retains its appearance until the program is closed. Session and local storages are typically used in web browsers to store personal website settings. A negative aspect of Calibre is that it does

Table 1. Features supported by several EPUB readers

	CSS	JavaScript	MathML	Screen reader
Adobe Digital Editions	✗	✗	✗	✓
Calibre	✗	✓	✓	✗
AZARDI	✗	✗	✓	✓
Readium	✓	✗	✓	✓
iBooks	✗	✗	✓	✓
Bluefire Reader	✗	✗	✗	✗
Icecream Ebook Reader	✗	✗	✗	✗
Reasily	✓	✗	✓	✓

not support any screen reader. Another example is Apple's iBooks, which supports JavaScript but does not allow access to the local or session storage. While the initial page changes its style, other pages remain in their default state. Only by leaving iBooks and reopening it, the view is currently adjusted. Reasily for Android supports the same features as Readium and the Android screen reader (Talk Back) works fine.

CSS 3 support in the form of CSS selectors is also very rare. Only the Windows program Readium supports this and is therefore the only reader that can handle the CSS standard. However, Readium sometimes has problems with selectors that the Gecko-based Mozilla Firefox does not have, for example, so the support can be improved. Readium also supports MathML and screen readers. This makes it the only Windows tool currently available to screen reader users that supports these standards. AZARDI is mentioned by the DAISY consortium as an EPUB reader with screen reader support. It shows MathML formulas in the sighted version, but it does not support both CSS and JavaScript switching. Furthermore, a link for switching can be clicked, but it is shown as normal text and not as a hyperlink, so users can't differentiate between them.

The document standard we created makes extensive use of the new features of EPUB 3, and this is where the problem lies. Even seven years after its approval, support for EPUB 3 is not yet widespread. There is still a lack of suitable readers (on the hardware and software side). The website "EPUB 3 Support Grid[3]" gives a comprehensive overview of which function is supported by which reading system.

5   Future Work

There is still some room for improvement in the compatibility of the EPUB standard, so that it will also be possible to use the documents better with "older" EPUB readers. The JavaScript document standard supports multiple HTML files as content documents. If the reader system supports local or session storage, it remembers which version is to be displayed across several HTML files. Accessible EPUB does not yet support this. Adding this feature would allow users to create longer documents and manage individual sections.

Future development will focus on usability and simplified import of other document standards. Currently, users can already import text and HTML documents with certain restrictions so that they can keep their work in these formats. The tool PANDOC can serve as a basis for many formats. Furthermore, images and formulas will not yet be in the format specified by the document standard during an import, so a wizard will be added that works through each image and formula and allows the user to enter alternative texts.

Another feature advanced users may want is a source code editor. A code viewer is already available, but currently displays the entire file with the inner workings. The user should not be able to see it, since the processing increases the error possibilities in the document.

---

[3] http://epubtest.org/testsuite/epub3/.

We are also considering whether we will start developing suitable readers for various end devices.

6   Conclusion

An EPUB document standard has been developed to allow visually impaired, blind and normal-sighted users to use the same document while meeting their respective accessibility requirements. An editor called "Accessible EPUB" was created so that users without programming knowledge can create accessible documents. The document standard uses EPUB 3, which is not yet fully supported by most EPUB reading systems. It is planned to add features to improve the usability of Accessible EPUB.

References

1. WebAIM: Webaim (web accessibility in mind): World laws: Introduction to laws throughout the world, 30 Jan 2018. https://webaim.org/articles/laws/world/
2. IDPF: Understanding epub 3, 29 Jan 2018. http://epubzone.org/epub-3-overview/understanding-epub-3
3. IDPF: Epub 3 specification, 29 Jan 2018. http://www.idpf.org/epub/301/spec/epub-overview.html
4. W3C: Web content accessibility guidelines (wcag) 2.0, 29 Jan 2018. https://www.w3.org/TR/WCAG20/
5. Garrish, M., Gylling, M.: EPUB 3 Best Practices. Oreilly and Associate Series. O'Reilly, Newton (2013)
6. IDPF: Epub 3 changes from epub 2.0.1, 29 Jan 2018. http://www.idpf.org/epub/30/spec/epub30-changes.html
7. Takaira, T., Tani, Y., Fujiyoshi, A.: Development of a unified production system for various types of accessible textbooks. In: Miesenberger, K., Bühler, C., Penaz, P. (eds.) ICCHP 2016. LNCS, vol. 9758, pp. 381–388. Springer, Cham (2016). https://doi.org/10.1007/978-3-319-41264-1_52
8. Calabrò, A., Contini, E., Leporini, B.: Book4All: a tool to make an e-book more accessible to students with vision/visual-impairments. In: Holzinger, A., Miesenberger, K. (eds.) USAB 2009. LNCS, vol. 5889, pp. 236–248. Springer, Heidelberg (2009). https://doi.org/10.1007/978-3-642-10308-7_16
9. DAISY-Consortium: Baseline for accessible epub3, 29 Jan 2018. http://www.daisy.org/baseline
10. Bartalesi Lenzi, V., Leporini, B.: Investigating an accessible and usable epub book via VoiceOver: a case study. In: Holzinger, A., Ziefle, M., Hitz, M., Debevc, M. (eds.) SouthCHI 2013. LNCS, vol. 7946, pp. 272–283. Springer, Heidelberg (2013). https://doi.org/10.1007/978-3-642-39062-3_17
11. Bartalesi, V., Leporini, B.: An enriched ePub eBook for screen reader users. In: Antona, M., Stephanidis, C. (eds.) UAHCI 2015. LNCS, vol. 9175, pp. 375–386. Springer, Cham (2015). https://doi.org/10.1007/978-3-319-20678-3_36
12. DAISY-Consortium: Tools for creating epub 3 files, 29 Jan 2018. http://www.daisy.org/daisypedia/tools-creating-epub-3-files
13. Marković, S., Schember, J., Hendricks, K., Massay, D.: Sigil is a multi-platform epub ebook editor, 29 Jan 2018. https://sigil-ebook.com/
14. Garrish, M.: What is EPUB 3?. O'Reilly Media, Newton (2011)

Design for Me?

Charlotte Magnusson[⊠], Per-Olof Hedvall, and Björn Breidegard

Lund University, PO Box 118, 221 00 Lund, Sweden
{charlotte.magnusson,per-olof.hedvall,
bjorn.breidegard}@certec.lth.se

Abstract. In this paper, as a generative contrast to the notion of design "for all", we present and discuss the potential benefits of a design "for me" approach, where the design process from the starts from, and initially is targeted at, just one person. Given many things developed for a user group or a constructed average user, in this text we describe starting from design for a single user as an alternative approach for achieving useful and useworthy designs. We provide an example from the development of an assistive device as the starting point and discuss how and why this alternative approach should be of interest for everyone interested in usability.

Keywords: Design · User-centered · Method

1 Introduction

This paper deals with the ever-increasing interest for Design for All and ways of gaining better understanding of different users and their lives. As a generative contrast to the notion of "for all" we present and discuss the potential benefits of a "for me" approach, where the design process from the start and on is targeted at just one person. The research is based on a ten-year development of an assistive communication system for a girl suffering from a severe traumatic brain injury. The tension between "Design for Me" and "Design for All" was initially brought forward by Anderberg [1].

Today there is a range of tools and methods available for anyone who wants to develop usable systems. User centered design [14] has been around for a long time, and participatory design [2, 4, 7, 11] or versions of it are widely used. Usability testing is common practice (as in usability engineering [20]) and there are also more abstract tools such as Personas [8] to help bring developers close to the users. The importance of context has been pointed out [24], and is receiving an increasing amount of attention as more and more applications are developed for mobile devices.

Another dominating design approach is represented by the Design for All (European), Universal Design (American) and Inclusive Design (British) family of related approaches. They are strongly rooted in Ergonomics and Human Factors [10] and are based on mainstream solutions in standard products and environments. The goal of Universal Design is to design "products and environments to be usable by all people, to the greatest extent possible, without the need for adaptation or specialized design" [23]. This focus has strong political overtones and attempts to include the individual while striving for solutions on a broad level [19]. Universal Design rests on the notion that a

© Springer International Publishing AG, part of Springer Nature 2018
K. Miesenberger and G. Kouroupetroglou (Eds.): ICCHP 2018, LNCS 10896, pp. 93–99, 2018.
https://doi.org/10.1007/978-3-319-94277-3_17

diversity of people demands a diversity of ways to achieve equal results and strives towards creating an inclusive flexibility, supporting all people in fulfilling their needs, wishes and dreams. Hence, Universal Design highlights the connection between flexibility and equality. How to best achieve this flexibility is still up for debate.

Although user centered approaches involve users and situations, and often explore individual cases [13], we argue in this paper that there is often an underlying assumption that to be able to design useful systems one needs to get an understanding of the "average user" – we see no point in listing all studies where it is reported that a certain (preferably large) number of users participated in studies performed to evaluate the usability of existing or future technology.

So, although there is an increasing use of ethnologically inspired methods for observing and involving users, we suggest that there also is a common underlying assumption which states that if you understand average users and average situations you will get designs suitable for a wide range of users and situations. Newell et al. [19] highlight the need for user-sensitive inclusive design and stress the need for developers and designers to establish methods and methodology to achieve a real empathy with their user groups.

In this paper we take our inspiration from work with developing assistive solutions, and suggest that it may be fruitful to question this underlying assumption and consider what we, inspired by Anderberg [1], call "design for me".

To make our case, we start with a concrete example.

2 Example

Our example comes from the development of an assistive device for a teenage girl who sustained a severe head injury when she was kicked by a horse. She was unable to speak, and her mobility was extremely limited. With difficulty, she was able to move the little finger on her right hand. The parents of this girl contacted our research team asking for "a tool that will enable our daughter to say yes or no". The first device, called the Minimeter [5], was a computer-based communication tool that recorded extremely small movements of the little finger. The girl in question only needed to wear a rubber thimble with a small magnet. The second step in this development was to change from using a small magnet to making use of a video camera to decode facial expressions and head movements (Fig. 1).

The product was developed in close collaboration with the girl and her family. After a working system had been designed, it became obvious that there were more users who needed this type of technology, and smaller adjustments were made in order to adapt the system to different users.

The technological and educational advances have been user guided: the individual has been the driving force. Improvements have progressed hand in hand with ongoing user trials. All aspects have been individually adapted to each person's very special abilities and limitations. But the reason for using this example in the present article is that which was designated for one user has proven to be useful for another (with only minor modifications). In this way, instead of starting with designing for many users at

Fig. 1. The Minimeter system.

once, we started with designing for a single user and then expanded our concept to include a larger target group.

The project went on for more than ten years, and we observed how the assistive system came to wider and wider use. What started as a highly specialized system targeted at one particular girl has, as the system has matured and gotten more and more robust and flexible, come to be used by about twenty other persons with similar disabilities. We learnt a lot during the development, such as the importance of continuous feedback, that have influenced other projects on assistive technology and what we focus on also when teaching and doing research on Universal Design.

3   Why Is This Relevant?

Before discussing more in detail, the methodological implications of the suggested shift of perspective, we start by discussing why this rather extreme example from the assistive technology sector is relevant to a wider audience.

When designing for persons with disabilities there are a couple of facts that become very obvious:

(1) The developer is typically not the user. As a designer or developer you cannot use yourself as a reference - you have to work very close to real users.
(2) The situation the developer is in while doing the development is usually very different from the situation the user is in when using the system. Thus you explicitly have to consider how to bring the real context of the user into the development process.

Both these observations are really valid for most development work. Although on a theoretical level most developers are aware that they are not typical users (point 1), it is still common to test novel designs "in house" and/or with colleagues. Point 2 becomes particularly relevant for the development of mobile systems. The developer is usually seated in front of a desk, while the user of the mobile system may be walking, cycling, driving etc. Thus, we argue that there is a strong link between HCI in general and the assistive sector, not only in that developers of assistive systems use methods used also by non-assistive sector, but also that it should be fruitful for designers everywhere to take a closer look at methods and techniques used when developing assistive systems.

4 Design for Me

With the above in mind we are suggesting designers and developers should consider methods where the design process starts with one person. In the process a design which really suits this person should be developed – and once a working design is reached this may then be extended to encompass more users. With this suggestion we are not thinking of just an interface element – we are talking about a full application designed to suit a single person, "me" [1]. If we compare this to the usual design methods, we could say that using this perspective ensures that the product at least fits one person really well. The usual design methods on the other hand, can be expected to lead to a design which is hopefully reasonably ok on an average level, but which may not fit anyone perfectly.

In addition, persons with disabilities may serve as extreme [3] and inspiring cases helping developers consider alternative solutions and to think "out of the box".

"If we understand what the extremes are, the middle will take care of itself"
(Dan Formosa, PhD, Smart Design, from the documentary "Objectified")

By now, there are several established concepts pointing towards the benefits and values of bringing in the informative far ends of user spectrums into design processes, such as extreme users [6] and lead users [17, 18]. Design for me offers a starting point that engages deeply in people's lived perspectives [16] and is initially targeted at just one person. Designing for one person has its virtues in itself. At the same time, it relates not only to the tension between the extreme and the average, but also to the tension between what's special and mainstream. Over time, knowledge gained from designing for several "one persons" can be utilized in broader approaches in creating an understanding of what flexibility is needed in creating useworthy solutions for all. The user's perspective is still just as extreme, "me", but it then also becomes part of mainstream flexibility.

5 Discussion

It is well known that it is important to bring real people and contexts into the design process. At the same time it is usually costly to get to know a large number of users and situations – and in industrial practice time saving methods such as Personas [8] are often used. While a well-constructed Persona can contain much useful information about the users it is also on some level an average construct. The kind of surprises (and design inspiration) generated by a real person and his or her lived perspective is usually lost in the process – typical personas are after all constructs synthesized from several persons. An additional problem with personas is the personal focus. In real life the abilities and preferences of a person depends on the situation (as is noted in situated design [15]) as well as on the personality. An obvious example is how a person on the move may be considered to be situationally impaired [22]. It could be argued that a combination of personas and scenarios may be the solution, but again: both are fictional – or at least filtered – versions of the reality.

If we turn to the more user centered and participatory design tradition it is clear that the above problems are avoided – although, as was observed initially, it can be very costly and time consuming to involve many users in real life situations. Living labs [9] may be one way around this hurdle, but living labs take time and effort to establish and maintain. We also question the assumption implicit in many works in this field, which is that it is better the more users you involve. As we argued above, there is a risk that by combining several persons and situations you may end up filtering away features rated high by some and low by some in favor of features rated average by everyone.

Although it is not uncommon in user centered design approaches to do small scale design activities with one or a few users, we are arguing that these are often left too early in favor of studies and activities involving more users (and where averaging/filtering takes place). We have found it useful to keep the "for me" perspective longer in order to be able to get a deeper and richer understanding of the design space, the user and the context/situation.

To start the design process with designing for a single person, understanding this person in detail, solves some of the above problems. The design team gets access to the full complexity resulting from a real person in real situations – and since only one user is involved the cost/effort involved is easier to manage. With one person involved it becomes easier to observe this kind of behaviors noted in [12] as well as to learn from them and iterate the design. In some cases, for instance when working with persons with profound disabilities, "design for me" might be the only starting point feasible.

The obvious counter argument is the risk of choosing the wrong starting point. Just like in all other iterative design processes, if you start at the wrong point you may never converge to a good solution. In addition, there is also the risk of getting stuck in a local minimum.

Thus, we are not suggesting this as the only method that can be used when discussing design and development processes. What we argue is that a "design for me" approach can provide a design team with a valuable additional tool in their methodological toolbox, and that such a tool may provide important input which otherwise might be hard to obtain.

6 Conclusion

In this paper we have outlined how starting from design for a single user can be an alternative approach for achieving useful and useworthy designs. Compared to "design for one" [21] where one designs for many but strive to adapt to the individual, our approach is conceptually opposite: we suggest starting with one person and then extending to more.

After more than twenty years of research together with people with multiple and profound disabilities, "design for me" is by now a well-established approach within our research department. It is often used in combination with other activities as part of larger research designs or as part of studies built on several cases. We argue that changing the perspective from "average design" to "design for me" may provide insights helpful for developers and designers, insights that otherwise would be lost. We are not proposing our method as a silver bullet recipe solving all usability problems – but we feel the "design for me" perspective may provide substantial benefits, particularly within the assistive field where it will contribute to enhancing state-of-the-art.

More work remains to be done in order to develop this method when it comes to the design of mainstream products for a mass market – the intention of this paper is simply to start this process by highlighting the values of designing for me as an end in itself and as part of striving towards inclusive, useworthy solutions for all.

Acknowledgements. We want to thank everyone involved in the Minimeter project. In addition we want to thank NordForsk for funding the ActivAbles project and the EU for funding the STARR project.

References

1. Anderberg, P.: FACE-disabled people, technology and Internet. Lund University (2006)
2. Bødker, S., Kyng, M., Ehn, P., Kammersgaard, J., Sundblad, Y.: A UTOPIAN experience: on design of powerful computer-based tools for skilled graphic workers. In: Bjerknes, G., Ehn, P., Kyng, M. (eds.) Computers and Democracy - A Scandinavian Challenge, pp. 251–278. Gower Publishing (1987). http://pure.au.dk/portal/en/publications/a-utopian-experience (405d1260-c86f-11de-a30a-000ea68e967b)/export.html
3. Bødker, S., et al.: Creativity, cooperation and interactive design. In: Proceedings of 3rd Conference on Designing Interactive Systems: Processes, Practices, Methods, and Techniques, pp. 252–261 (2000)
4. Bødker, S., Iversen, O.S.: Staging a professional participatory design practice - moving PD beyond the initial fascination of user involvement. In: Proceedings of Second Nordic Conference on Human-Computer Interaction, pp. 11–18, January 2002
5. Breidegard, B.: Doing for understanding – on rehabilitation engineering design. Lund University (2006)
6. Brown, T., Katz, B.: Change by design. J. Prod. Innov. Manag. **28**(3), 381–383 (2011)
7. Bφdker, S., et al.: Cooperative design: techniques and experiences from the Scandinavian scene. In: Readings in Human–Computer Interaction, pp. 215–224 (1995)
8. Chang, Y., et al.: Personas: from theory to practices. In: Proceedings of Nordic Conference on Human-Computer Interaction: Building Bridges, Nord 2008, pp. 439–442 (2008)
9. Dell'Era, C., Landoni, P.: Living lab: a methodology between user-centred design and participatory design. Creat. Innov. Manag. **23**(2), 137–154 (2014)
10. Dong, H.: Shifting paradigms in universal design. In: Universal Access in Human Computer Interaction, pp. 66–74 (2007)
11. Ehn, P.: Work-oriented design of computer artifacts. Umeå University (1988)
12. Gaver, W., et al.: Anatomy of a failure: how we knew when our design went wrong, and what we learned from it. In: SIGCHI Conference on Human Factors in Computing Systems, pp. 2213–2222 (2009)

13. Gaver, W.W., et al.: Cultural probes and the value of uncertainty. Interactions **11**(5), 53 (2004)

14. Gould, J.D., Lewis, C.: Designing for usability: key principles and what designers think. Commun. ACM **28**(3), 300–311 (1985)

15. Greenbaum, J., Kyng, M.: Introduction: situated design. In: Design at Work, pp. 1–24. L. Erlbaum Associates Inc., Hillsdale (1992)

16. Hedvall, P.-O.: The Activity Diamond – Modeling An Enhanced Accessibility. Lund University (2009)

17. von Hippel, E.: Lead users: a source of novel product concepts. Manag. Sci. **32**(7), 791–805 (1986)

18. Luthje, C., Herstatt, C.: The Lead User method: an outline of empirical findings and issues for future research. R D Manag. **34**(5), 553–568 (2004)

19. Newell, A.F., et al.: User-sensitive inclusive design. Univers. Access Inf. Soc. **10**(3), 235–243 (2011)

20. Nielsen, J.: Usability Engineering. Morgan Kaufmann Publishers Inc., San Francisco (1993). https://dl.acm.org/citation.cfm?id=529793

21. Ringbauer, B., Peissner, M., Gemou, M.: From "Design for All" towards "Design for One" – a modular user interface approach. In: Stephanidis, C. (ed.) UAHCI 2007. LNCS, vol. 4554, pp. 517–526. Springer, Heidelberg (2007). https://doi.org/10.1007/978-3-540-73279-2_58

22. Sears, A., et al.: When computers fade: pervasive computing and situationally induced impairments and disabilities. In: Proceedings of HCI International, vol. 2, pp. 1298–1302 (2003)

23. Story, M., et al.: The universal design file: designing for people of all ages and abilities. Des. Res. Methods J. **1**(5), 165 (1998)

24. Wixon, D., et al.: Contextual design: an emergent view of system design. In: Proceedings of the SIGCHI Conference on Human Factors in Computing Systems Empowering People - CHI 1990, pp. 329–336 (1990)

Calculation of the User Ability Profile in Disability Situations

Karim Sehaba[✉]

University of Lyon 2, LIRIS UMR CNRS 5205, 69676 Lyon, France
karim.sehaba@liris.cnrs.fr

Abstract. The abilities profile represents the physical, cognitive and perceptual properties of the individual. This type of profile is used in the adaptive system dedicated to persons with disabilities to adapt the content, presentation and the interaction modalities to the user. In most existing works, the abilities profile is static, whereas the abilities can be altered by the situation of the individual and his environment. This article focuses on the calculation of the abilities profile in disturbance situation, such as the fatigue, cognitive overload or noise. In this framework, our objective is to determine the operational capacities of an individual by considering his theoretical capacities and the disturbances, related to his state and/or his environment, which can alter his capacities. By theoretical capacity, we mean the capacity of the individual in optimal conditions, without any disturbance. To achieve this goal, we propose models of representation of profile capacities and disturbances as well as a method that calculates the impact of the disturbances on the capacities by considering their weakening and the forgetfulness of disturbances.

Keywords: Capacity profile · Disturbance situation · Adaptive system

1 Introduction

The user profile is one of the most important components in adaptive systems. Indeed, it is according to the profile that this type of system adapts its behavior to the properties and characteristics of each user [5, 6]. Among the profile information, we have: [1]: the user's knowledge, interests, goals, past experiences, individual traits and abilities. In this article, we are interested in the ability profile that represents the physical, cognitive and perceptual properties of the user [2].

Formally, the ability profile is usually represented by a set of properties $P = \{p1 = v1, p2 = v2...\}$, where pi is the name of the property related to a given capacity, and vi is its value, with $vi \in [0, 1]$. In existing adaptive systems, the capability profile is usually static. Thus, whatever the state of the individual and his environment, vi remains unchanged. For example, the visual ability of an individual without visual impairment is pvisual = 1 regardless of his situation and this throughout the execution of the system.

This model of representation is not adapted to temporal disability situations. It's a disturbance situation that can alter the abilities of the individual [3, 4]. For instance, the visual ability can be altered by several factors, as: fatigue, cognitive overload or sleepiness. In general, the capacities are not necessarily stable and static and can thus evolve according to several factors intrinsic to the individual and/or his environment.

The objective of our work is to develop models that allow to calculate the abilities profile taking into account the disturbance situation. By disturbance situation, we mean all the factors, related to the individual or his environment, which can diminish the capacity of the individual. This situation can appear, persist in time, then disappear. In this context, the research questions of this study are as follows:

- How to calculate the impact of a disturbance on a given capacity?
- How to merge the impact of several disturbances on a given capacity?
- How to take into account the forgetting of the disturbances (once disappeared) and the weakening of the capacity (if the disturbances persist at the time) in the calculation of the operational capacities?

For this, we propose representation models of ability profile and disturbances situation, and methods that calculate the operational abilities based on theoretical abilities and disturbances situation.

2 Related Work

From a computational point of view, the updating of the user profile according to his activities has been the subject of several research works, in particular in the field of Technology-Enhanced Learning. In this context, the profile of the learner evolves according to his learning. For example, for a knowledge about a given concept, i.e. c, the learner, and through the interaction with educational resources related to c, will improve this knowledge. Thus, his knowledge will go from $c = vi$ to $c = vi + 1$ with $vi + 1 > vi$.

Among the update models, we focused on Ontologies, Bayesian Networks and Rule-Based Systems [7, 8]. These different models were designed and used to update the profile, especially the knowledge and skills of the learner. Nevertheless, the updating of the capacity profile in disability situations is thus not adapted to the learning situation. In fact, the profile properties in this situation do not cover all the specificities intrinsic to the disability situation:

- Temporality of the disturbances: generally, the more the disturbance situation is present, the more its impact is weighing on the capacities of the user.
- Considering the forget of disturbances: the disappearance of certain disturbances, such as fatigue, requires a certain time for the individual to regain his theoretical capacity;
- Fusion of several disturbances: it is a question of calculating the impact of several disturbances on a given capacity at a given moment. This merger must respect these properties:
  - The higher the cardinality of the disturbances, the greater their impact on the ability of the individual,
  - The capacity is impacted by the disturbance whose effect is greater, to which is added the effects of other disturbances;

To answer these specificities, we have developed an approach to calculate the operational profile in disability situations. The principle of our method is presented in the following section.

3   Our Method

Definitions of the concepts of our approach:

- Disturbance: a temporal situation related to the state of the individual or his environment that may diminish one or more of his abilities.
- Theoretical capacity: the capacity of the individual in optimal conditions (without any disturbance). It is considered to be fixed.
- Operational capacity: the real capacity considering the situation of disturbance. It is measured according to the theoretical capacity of the individual and the alteration rate caused by the disturbances.
- Alteration rate: measures the impact of disturbances on the capacity.

The principle of our approach is to calculate the effect E_{ij} of each of the disturbances on a given capacity. Then, it is a question of merging these different effects in order to measure the rate of alteration caused by all the significant disturbances. The operational capacity is thus calculated according to the theoretical capacities and the rate of alteration. This treatment is done after each lapse of time.

Formally, the set of physical and cognitive capacities is represented by the vector C with $C = [c_1, ..., c_n]$, where $c_i \in [0, 1]$. The value 0 indicates the absence of the capacity and 1 is the maximum intensity of the capacity. The operational capacity Cop is calculated as a function of the theoretical capacity Cth and the rate of alteration T caused by the situation of disturbances: $Cop = T * Cth$. The set of disturbances is also represented by a vector, i.e. $G = [g_1, ..., g_m]$ such that $g_j \in d_j$, where d_j is the definition domain of g_i. Recall that the disturbances are temporal. Thus, the disturbance g_j at time t_k is represented by $g_j(t_k)$. We assume that the disturbances are independent of each other. From this representation, we have proposed methods to calculate:

- The impact of a disturbance on a given capacity by considering the effect of this one on the capacity, the decay of the capacity over time and the forgetfulness of the disturbance. The first one measure the value of the capacity confronted with a situation of disturbances at a given moment. The capacity decay models the evolution of this one during the situation of disturbances. Indeed, the more the disturbance persists in time the more its impact can be more and more important. The forgetting the disturbance models the evolution of the capacity between the moment when the disturbance becomes insignificant and the moment when it reaches its theoretical value. Indeed, the disappearance of certain disturbance, such as fatigue caused by physical effort, requires a certain time for the individual to regain his theoretical physical capacity.
- Operational capacity in a situation of disturbance. For this, we propose formalisms allowing to calculate the rate of alteration caused by several disturbances.

4   Conclusion and Planned Activities

Our approach is being applied to calculate the operational capacity of hearing in a situation of disturbances related to cognitive overload and environmental noise. First, we measure the impact of each of these two disturbances on hearing ability, then we calculate the impact of these two disturbances on the audition, the rate of alteration and the operational hearing ability that ensuing. The first results demonstrate that the proposed approach produces the expected behavior. Our future work would focus on the application of our approach in the field of home automation. It is a question of adapting the parameters of the various devices to the needs of comfort and security of persons with situation disabilities. The impact of this contribution will be detailed.

References

1. Brusilovsky, P., Millán, E.: User models for adaptive hypermedia and adaptive educational systems. In: Brusilovsky, P., Kobsa, A., Nejdl, W. (eds.) The Adaptive Web. LNCS, vol. 4321, pp. 3–53. Springer, Heidelberg (2007). https://doi.org/10.1007/978-3-540-72079-9_1
2. Vidhya, B., Nalini, V.: Server transcoding of multimedia data for cross-disability access. In: Proceedings SPIE the International Society for Optical Engineering, pp. 45–56. International Society for Optical Engineering (1999)
3. Gonzalez, C., Best, B., Healy, F.A., Kole, J.A., Bourne, L.E.: A cognitive modeling account of simultaneous learning and fatigue effects. Cogn. Syst. Res. **12**, 19–32 (2011)
4. Saeki, T., Fujii, T., Yamaguchi, S., Harima, S.: Effects of acoustical noise on annoyance, performance and fatigue during mental memory task. Appl. Acoust. **65**(9), 913–921 (2004)
5. Hussaan, A.M, Sehaba, K.: Adaptive serious game for rehabilitation of persons with cognitive disabilities. In: The 13th IEEE International Conference on Advanced Learning Technologies, Beijing, China, pp. 65–69 (2013)
6. Sehaba, K., Courboulay, V., Estraillier, E.: Interactive system by observation and analysis of behavior for children with autism. In: 8th European conference for the advancement of assistive technology in Europe (AAATE 2005), pp 358–362. IOS Press, Lille, September 2005
7. Xing, J., Ah-Hwee, T.: Learning and inferencing in user ontology for personalized Semantic Web search. Inf. Sci. **179**(16), 2794–2808 (2009)
8. Vrieze, P.: Fundaments of Adaptive Personnalisation. Ph.D. Dutch Research School for Information and Knowledge Systems (2006)

Template Based Approach for Augmenting Image Descriptions

Akshansh Chahal[✉], Manshul Belani, Akashdeep Bansal,
Neha Jadhav, and Meenakshi Balakrishnan

Indian Institute of Technology - Delhi, Hauz Khas, New Delhi, India
akshanshchahal@gmail.com

Abstract. With the increasing focus on digital learning, it has become extremely important that digital content is available with ease. However, a lot of this digital content is not generated keeping Universal Access in mind. Most of such content available is either completely inaccessible or only partially accessible to the print disabled people. One of the major gaps in accessibility of digital content, especially electronic books is the lack of alternative texts for diagrams and ineffective descriptions in cases they are present. The paper discusses the design of a template, which can help in augmenting descriptions for textbook diagrams. The template consists of various components, which are populated using the information present in the diagram or from the text surrounding the diagram in the textbook. This template provides means for generation of comprehensible diagram descriptions, which not only help the user to visualize the diagram but also create a mental model of the layout of the diagram. Observations made during the user study validate the effectiveness of these augmented descriptions.

Keywords: Accessibility · Blind · Visually impaired · eBooks
Template · Augmentation · Image · Description

1 Introduction

E-books are increasingly becoming an effective tool for enhancing the practical learning aspects in a classroom setting. Such books are also exciting for print-disabled and blind readers because their properties make them ideal for finding alternative forms of access [1]. Developments in technology have also improved access to these e-books using assistive technologies. However, most assistive technologies fail when it comes to accessibility of diagrams. This can be due to lack of alternative text description or at times insufficient descriptive text [2]. Because of this, visually impaired students often fail to keep pace with diagram understanding with their sighted peer group.

The paper presents the design of a template, to augment descriptions of diagrams present in digital textbooks and assist the students in better visualization of the diagrams. The template aims to include information required for the contextual understanding of diagram as well as build a mental model of the layout of diagram elements.

Our template is composed of attributes including the objects, number of objects, relative position of objects, interaction between the objects and the overview of the

© Springer International Publishing AG, part of Springer Nature 2018
K. Miesenberger and G. Kouroupetroglou (Eds.): ICCHP 2018, LNCS 10896, pp. 104–112, 2018.
https://doi.org/10.1007/978-3-319-94277-3_19

image. The template has been generated keeping in view the experimental setup diagrams in High School Chemistry books. Evaluation with high school students shows that the descriptions containing information covering all the aspects of the template are easily understandable and help the students in perceiving a mental model of the apparatus.

2 State of the Art

Most of the previous work done in image caption or description generation has been focused on four underlying techniques. The most recent technique is the use of Convolutional Neural Networks to identify tags or captions related to images and then using techniques like Recurrent Neural Networks, word2vec, GloVe for sentence generation. In [3], an attention-based model is trained using standard backpropagation techniques and maximizing stochastically a variational lower bound. [4] generates image descriptions by extracting image features using a CNN model, which are fed into a RNN or Long Short term memory network (LSTM) to generate brief descriptions in valid English. Such techniques require large datasets for improved accuracy of generated descriptions.

The second technique is based on finding an image most similar to the test image from the training set and returning the caption related to that particular training image. [5] associates images with sentences drawn from a pool of human written image descriptions. [2] also generates descriptions for query image by selectively combining existing human composed phrases describing visually similar images. [6] performs Flickr queries to collect a large body of images on the internet with associated visually descriptive text, using this photo collection to generate an image description. Both these techniques have the shortcoming that they result in single line descriptions of images which are in most cases not enough to understand the concept. In addition, they depend on large datasets of captioned images for training and validation, which may not be easily generated for particular categories of images.

The third technique involves first retrieving similar captioned images from a large database then modifying these retrieved captions to fit the query. [2] uses visual recognition to predict individual image elements followed by retrieval of pre-existing visually relevant phrases from human composed descriptions for these image elements. The human composed phases are selectively combined to generate descriptions for the query image. This again requires a large dataset of human annotated images to generate rich in content descriptions.

The fourth technique requires generating templates, which are to be filled based on results of object detection and attribute discovery. [7, 8] touch upon the approach by collecting three types of data about the input image, objects, attributes and prepositions and generates sentence descriptions using this information. [9] similarly uses an object, adjectives and prepositions based template to generate image descriptions. [1] also uses a Nouns-Verbs-Scenes-Prepositions based template. [10] describes a series of template based image description models using the images as bags of regions or visual dependency representation approaches.

3 Methodology Used

3.1 First Approach

With computer vision techniques being extensively used in wide range of applications, many technological giants provide an intelligent suite of Application Programming Interfaces (APIs) for tasks such as image tagging, object detection, object recognition, face recognition, video tagging. Some APIs also generate a description for images. Our first approach was to use one such computer vision based API to augment description for images. These APIs were tested for two sets of images - general life images (e.g. Fig. 1) and science textbook images (e.g. Fig. 2) - using 6 APIs namely Cloudsight [11], Amazon (Rekognition) [12], Google [13], Microsoft [14], Clarifai [15], and IBM [16] (using an open source tool, Cloudy Vision [17]). Some of these APIs give only captions or tags whereas some give both.

rekognition_tags	People (.99) , Person (.99) , Human (.99) , Musical Instrument (.97) , Musician (.97) , Performer (.97) , Electric Guitar (.70) , Guitar (.70) , Face (.51) , Selfie (.51)
cloudsight_captions	Ed Sheeran

Fig. 1. Results for a general life image using computer vision APIs.

For 40 general life images, we obtained an average confidence of 95% (the APIs also return their confidence for the result). However, for 40 science textbook images we obtained an average confidence of about 70% (Ranging from 40% to 97%, with higher confidence tags being "diagram" or "drawing" in most of the cases). Such tags are not very useful when trying to visualize the diagram. We concluded that such APIs in the current state are not helpful for us in augmenting image descriptions for science textbook images. These APIs are not able to identify the content in these images with confidence because they have not been trained on enough number images from such specific domain. Therefore, we worked towards designing, developing, testing and validating a General Template, comprising of sections, which provide layout as well as contextual details of the diagram. The description generated using this template would hence be more effective in visualizing as well as understanding the diagram.

3.2 Second Approach

A set of diverse images were chosen from the standard Science Textbook of 9th and 10th Grades by National Council for Educational Research & Training (NCERT), India. Descriptions for these images were first written manually, to understand different aspects of the images to be taken care of. This helped us to identify the different components necessary for effective augmentation of images. For designing the template we chose the domain of experimental setup diagrams. The initial draft of the template,

Fig. 2. Results for a science textbook diagram using computer vision APIs.

designed based on these descriptions, comprised of sections as broad as the total number of objects to the details about the interaction between these objects. To validate the initial template we conducted a small informal study with the teachers and students of the National Association for the Blind, Delhi. We came to know about the sources from which the students try to understand the images, like tactile books, handmade artefacts (using thread, matchsticks etc. pasted on a sheet to depict some diagram), or by giving reference to something they use in daily life. The teachers told us how they would describe a particular image (out of the sample images) to students. We interacted with students to understand the difficulty they face in accessing and perceiving digital book diagrams/images. The feedback from this exercise helped us in refining and updating the template to its final version as described in Table 1.

Table 1. Template sections and sources

	Template section	Source of content
1	Overview	Image caption
2	Number of objects	From image processing
3	What are the objects?	From the labels (e.g. Beaker, Burner, Test tube)
4	Any specific placement?	From label positioning (Left to right, top to bottom, or none)
5	How are the Objects placed?	Relative positioning of the objects (e.g. x is at the top, y is on the left of x)
6	How are the objects interacting?	This has to be extracted from the text surrounding the image. (e.g. beaker heated using the burner)

We analyzed the template with the set of images to find out that most of the information to fill the template can be extracted from the information already present in the book. Information required to fill the template (and to finally augment descriptions) can be extracted from the image, image caption, image labels and text surrounding the image in the textbook as depicted in Figs. 3 and 4 (The green underlined parts of the descriptions are obtained from the image caption and the surrounding text, the blue parts from the relative positioning of the labels in the image).

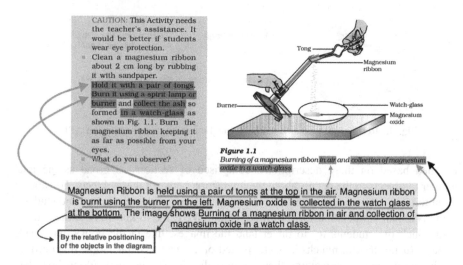

Fig. 3. Illustration of mapping the sources for generating description. (Color figure online)

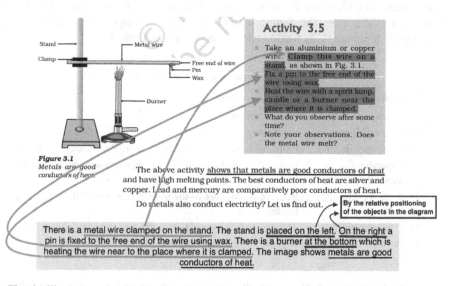

Fig. 4. Illustration of mapping the sources for generating description (Color figure online)

The relative positioning of the objects in the image can be obtained using the relative positioning of the labels in the image. This is because in all the images under consideration, the relative positions of the labels is same as that of the objects, and all the objects are labeled in every case. The information about the interaction between the objects is present in the image caption and the text surrounding the image.

4 User Study

4.1 Dataset

For testing and validating the template, a set of 30 images were selected for which the descriptions were generated using the template. It was done manually with an assumption that all the information required to fill different sections of this template is available to us. This assumption was made in order to have the descriptions ready to be verified by the students for efficacy, verbosity and understandability. The diagrams covered all the experimental setup diagrams from 9th and 10th NCERT textbooks. These diagrams were randomly divided into 6 mutually exclusive sets of diagrams containing 5 diagrams per set.

4.2 Focus Group

The study was conducted with 22 students from special as well as inclusive schools. The students were within the age group of 13–18 years, who have had some exposure to science concepts and experimental setups in their course of study. 19 out of 22 users were digital book readers, 13 of which being comfortable or very comfortable with the digital content. 6 had an average comfort level with eBooks, while 3 users were not comfortable at all.

4.3 Methodology

The users were narrated with the manually generated descriptions and were asked some simple questions focusing on the visual and conceptual aspect of the image. They were also enquired about the qualitative aspect of the descriptions. The users were allowed to hear the description more than once. The number of times the user heard the description, the time taken to hear each iteration of description and the answers to the questions were noted to collate quantitative as well as qualitative results.

4.4 Evaluation Metric

Quantitative results were analyzed with the questions sets relating to the image sets. Each diagram in the set included three questions based on the placement of apparatus and interaction between objects, which helped to evaluate the description in quantitative terms. For qualitative analysis, users were asked to rate the ease of use, verbosity and effectiveness of descriptions in helping to visualize the image.

Quantitative Results. The average accuracy of image understanding or visualization based on questions asked per image was found to be 82.42% with the standard deviation of 11.43. Average time required to understand one image was 2.77 min with a standard deviation of the 1.08. Each image was heard on an average 2.17 times with a standard deviation of 0.61. Manually written description helped students with prior knowledge of apparatus helped slightly better with the accuracy of 86.10% with compared to people who had no knowledge of apparatus managing accuracy of 77.99%.

Qualitative Results. Qualitative measures were measured to analyze ease of understanding of diagrams, the verbosity of the description and visualization level from the description. Out of 22 users, 14 ($\sim63\%$) found image descriptions either very easy or easy to understand. None of the students found the descriptions to be very difficult to understand and only one student found it to be difficult. Seven of the remaining users found description average. 95% of the users found the description to be non-verbose. 18 out of 22 ($\sim82\%$) students rated the visualization of images based on the descriptions to be good or very good. Only one student found the visualization to be not good while three students found it to be fair. The following charts illustrate these results (Figs. 5 and 6).

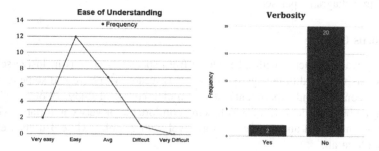

Fig. 5. (a) Ease of understanding against number of users (b) Verbosity of Description

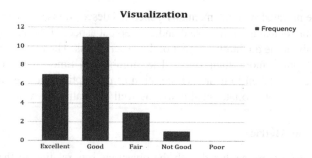

Fig. 6. Visualization level against number of users

Students helped us to find gaps present in the description by suggesting some modifications to the manually filled descriptions. Suggestions were related to apparatus and their positioning. In cases where apparatus functioning was not known, a little description regarding apparatus or their correlation with everyday life objects would help in better understanding of the description. For instance, the spatula can be related with a spoon. Positioning can be improved by referring objects which are described earlier, this will make sure that description lines are connected and in flow helping to visualize the set-up. If diagram setup was with more number of objects, students were interested in more explanation regarding positions. If students are listening to description more, they get a clear understanding of apparatus setup and interaction between them. More user-friendly language and first-time tactile feel of the diagram was desired by some students.

5 Scientific and Practical Impact or Contributions to the Field

Most of the work done in image description generation, even if it is for assisting the visually impaired people, is targeted for the general life images comprising of images from the domains like vehicles, animals, humans, natural landscapes etc. Our work focuses on making textbook diagrams more accessible to the visually impaired by augmenting descriptions for these diagrams. The image captions and the text surrounding the images in the textbooks are not sufficient to visualize or understand the image. We therefore amalgamate these (caption and surrounding text) along with information from the diagrams (labels, positioning of objects) to augment the information for better understanding of diagrams. With our augmented description of the images, users are able to comprehend the images in the text-books more effectively than before.

6 Conclusion and Planned Activities

The description generated for images in the textbook, using the presented template enhances the visualization of diagrams, making them more comprehensible, and therefore accessible to the visually impaired users. This in turn, increases the efficiency of the user while accessing such materials and will help user to study independently. We are currently developing algorithms based on object detection and image- processing techniques in order to automate the process of populating the subsections of the template like what objects are present in the diagram, positions of the objects, interaction between objects. Template content should be stitched using Natural Language Processing techniques which con-sider text surrounding the diagram and text present in the diagram to augment the description for the image. Therefore, we aim to develop an automated system for augmenting image description for text-book diagrams.

References

1. Yang, Y., Teo, C.L., Daumé III, H., Aloimonos, Y.: Corpus-guided sentence generation of natural images. In: Proceedings of Conference on Empirical Methods in Natural Language Processing, Edinburgh, Scotland, UK, pp. 444–454, July 2011
2. Kuznetsova, P., Ordonez, V., Berg, A.C., Berg, T.L., Choi, Y.: Collective generation of natural image descriptions. In: Proceedings of the 50th Annual Meeting of the Association for Computational Linguistics, Jeju, Republic of Korea, pp. 359–368, July 2012
3. Xu, K., Ba, J., Kiros, R., Cho, K., Courville, A., Salakhudinov, R., Zemel, R., Bengio, Y.: Show, Attend and Tell: Neural Image Caption Generation with Visual Attention. arXiv: 1502.03044v3 [cs.LG], April 2016

4. Elamri, C., de Planque, T.: Automated Neural Image Caption Generator for Visually Impaired People (2016)
5. Hodosh, M., Young, P., Hockenmaier, J.: Framing image description as a ranking task: data, models and evaluation metrics. J. Artif. Intell. Res. **47**, 853–899 (2013)
6. Ordonez, V., Kulkarni, G., Berg, T.L.: Im2Text: Describing images using 1 million captioned photographs. In: Advances in Neural Information Processing Systems 24 (NIPS 2011) (2011)
7. Kulkarni, G., Premraj, V., Ordonez, V., Dhar, S., Li, S., Choi, Y., Berg, A.C., Berg, T.L.: BabyTalk: understanding and generating simple image descriptions. IEEE Trans. Pattern Anal. Mach. Intell. **35**(12), 2891–2903 (2013)
8. Mitchell, M., Dodge, J., Goyal, A., Yamaguchi, K., Stratos, K., Han, X., Mensch, A., Berg, A., Berg, T., Daume, H.: Midge: generating image descriptions from computer vision detections. In: 13th Conference of the European Chapter of the Association for Computational Linguistics, pp. 747–756 (2012)
9. Li, S., Kulkarni, G., Berg, T.L., Berg, A.C., Choi, Y.: Composing simple image descriptions using web-scale N-grams. In: Fifteenth Conference on Computational Natural Language Learning, pp. 220–228 (2011)
10. Elliott, D., Keller, F.: Image description using visual dependency representations. In: 2013 Conference on Empirical Methods in Natural Language Processing, pp. 1292–1302 (2013)
11. https://cloudsight.ai/
12. https://aws.amazon.com/rekognition/
13. https://cloud.google.com/vision/
14. https://azure.microsoft.com/en-in/services/cognitive-services/computer-vision/
15. https://www.clarifai.com/
16. https://www.ibm.com/watson/services/visual-recognition/
17. https://github.com/goberoi/cloudy_vision

PDF Accessibility: Tools and Challenges

Alireza Darvishy[(✉)]

Institute for Applied Information Technologies, Zurich University of Applied Sciences,
Steinberggasse 13, 8400 Winterthur, Switzerland
alireza.darvishy@zhaw.ch

Abstract. This paper presents a comparison of different post-processing software tools to make PDF documents accessible. The comparison is based on different qualitative and verifiable criteria. In addition, this paper gives an overview of different standards of PDF accessibility for people with visual impairments using screen-reader software. PDF formats, potential barriers for visually impaired users, PDF accessibility standards, and available software solutions are described in more detail. A discussion including challenges for further work is presented at the end of the paper.

Keywords: PDF accessibility · Visually impaired users · Screen readers
Tagged PDF

1 Introduction

While a plain piece of text might be perfectly accessible as such, the situation becomes much more complex as soon as a document gets larger. Navigation soon becomes an important aspect, as visually-impaired users cannot simply scan through lots of pages to get a sense of orientation. Good structure is essential, with proper headings serving as identifiers for different parts of the document.

Additionally, purely visual elements such as illustrations, drawings and pictures need an alternative textual description such that assistive technologies, like screen readers, can read out a description of the graphical content. Furthermore, complex layouts might need additional meta-information about the flow of text to ensure that assistive technologies can process content in its logical order. The various document formats have their own, although often similar, ways to add such metadata to documents.

PDF has become the de-facto standard for fixed-format document exchange and publishing. It is partially based on PostScript used for printing. PDF files are therefore more like a set of instructions on how to visually produce a given page, rather than a structured representation of content, such as HTML. Its contents are inherently less accessible due to the missing structure.

To alleviate this issue, version 1.4 of the standard ISO 32000-1 introduced "tagged PDF," adding structural metadata. Sequences of rendering commands can be assigned a tag describing its logical significance. For example, a command drawing a line of text can have a tag marking it as a heading. Embedded images and line drawings can be

© Springer International Publishing AG, part of Springer Nature 2018
K. Miesenberger and G. Kouroupetroglou (Eds.): ICCHP 2018, LNCS 10896, pp. 113–116, 2018.
https://doi.org/10.1007/978-3-319-94277-3_20

tagged as figures. Tags also can contain additional attributes, such as an alternative textual description.

All tags themselves can be structured hierarchically, forming the tag tree of a document. Aside from the hierarchical structure of elements, this tree also specifies the order in which elements should be read. This order enables assistive technologies to process content in its logical, semantically correct order instead of the order in which the rendering commands appear in the file.

2   PDF Accessibility Guidelines and Standards

The World Wide Web Consortium (W3C) publishes the Web Content Accessibility Guidelines (WCAG) currently in its second version. These guidelines are based on four basic principles for accessibility: perceivable, operable, understandable and robust. While the guidelines themselves are focused on web content (possibly represented as HTML), a subset of them also applies to documents in general.

ISO standard 14289 [1], also known as PDF/UA, defines further requirements for accessible PDF files and complements WCAG 2.1. The standard does not define new extensions to the PDF standard, but merely defines how existing facilities should be used to provide accessible documents. It puts forward requirements for processors, assistive technologies, and PDF files. The standard also outlines detailed requirements for different types of elements (headings, tables, lists, formulas, embedded content, etc.).

The Matterhorn Protocol outlines a testing model to ensure a document's accessibility in regards to PDF/UA. It consists of 136 failure conditions, of which 89 are testable by software. The conditions are organized in 31 checkpoints, categorizing the different aspects of a document covered by PDF/UA requirements. It's important to keep in mind that while the majority of conditions in the Matterhorn Protocol are machine-testable, the most critical aspects of accessibility – such as the correct structuring and proper reading order – still have to be verified manually. This process usually also requires the human verifier to be able to see the document in order to make these judgments and thus is an inherently inaccessible task.

3   Producing Accessible PDF Documents

Since accessible PDF documents are mainly based on correct tagging, tag structures should be included where possible when authoring a document. Some popular authoring software incorporates PDF/UA support. Major examples include: Adobe Acrobat [2], Microsoft Office, LibreOffice [3], and CommonLook [4].

Alternatively, an existing PDF file can be enhanced for accessibility with a suitable post-processing tool after its initial creation. Examples of such tools include Adobe Acrobat, PDFix [5], axesPDF QuickFix [6], CommonLook, and PAVE [7, 8]. The following section describes a comparison of these PDF accessibility post-processing tools, based on verifiable ad-hoc criteria (Table 1). This list may not be complete.

Table 1. Comparison of post-processing tools for PDF accessibility

Tool name	Free of charge	Open-source	Multilingual	Web-based	Creates accessibility report	Manual tag manipulation available
Adobe Acrobat	No	No	Yes (many languages)	No (installation needed)	Yes	Yes
PDFix	Yes	No	No (English only)	Yes	No	No
axesPDF QuickFix	No	No	Yes (English, German)	No (installation needed)	Yes	Partially
CommonLook	No	No	No	No	Yes	Yes
PAVE	Yes	Yes	Yes (English, German)	Yes	Yes	Yes

The first four criteria above describe how widely available a tool is to users world-wide: a free or low-cost tool can obviously be accessed by more users, as can a tool available in multiple languages. Being open-source allows users to adapt and expand a tool according to different needs, while web-based tools eliminate the need for users to install specialized software onto a given device. The next criterion refers to accessibility reports, which enable communication of accessibility issues with different stakeholders involved in the creation of the PDF document. Finally, many aspects of PDF accessibility are not possible without human interaction, such as adding alternative text for an image. As such, the option of manual manipulation is important, as it provides added flexibility for users when amending documents.

This comparison does not describe all important aspects of PDF post-processing tools. A highly important aspect, for example, is ease-of-use for non-experts, as well as handling large PDF files in an efficient way. However, these features are beyond the scope of this research. For web-based tools, it is also important that they provide mechanisms to protect the privacy and security of the content uploaded to their platforms. It is not known to which degree privacy and security are addressed by all tools. Additionally, none of the presented tools provides mechanisms to interpret and describe mathematical formulas and scientific graphs such that they can later be presented to a screen reader user.

4   Discussion and Future Challenges

This paper presented an overview of different aspects of PDF accessibility, as well as a comparison of different PDF accessibility post-processing tools, based on verifiable criteria.

There are several different tools available nowadays to produce accessible PDFs that comply with the corresponding standards. There are still some issues, however, regarding scientific PDF documents containing mathematical formulas or scientific graphs. Although considerable research work has been done in recognizing mathematical formulas from PDFs or images [9–11], and there are some research proto-types available that are able to recognize mathematical formulas in PDFs or image files [12, 13], there is still no easy way to make scientific PDF documents accessible. One possibility to make scientific graphics (such as charts, graphs, and maps) accessible in PDFs is to manually write an alternative text that explains the content of the graphic. However, this is time-consuming and not pragmatic. Hence, future research and development must be done in order to make scientific PDF documents accessible. To that end, the recognition of mathematical formulas in PDF documents has to be further improved and integrated into a tool such as PAVE, and an intuitive way to generate automated alt-text explaining the contents of graphs and formulas must be found. This would allow millions of technical and scientific authors to easily create PDF documents that are accessible to readers with visual impairments, which in our opinion is well worth the effort.

References

1. ISO 14289-1:2014. https://www.iso.org/standard/64599.html
2. Adobe Acrobat Pro. https://acrobat.adobe.com/us/en/acrobat/acrobat-pro.html
3. LibreOffice. https://www.libreoffice.org
4. Common Look. https://commonlook.com
5. PDFix. https://pdfix.net/
6. AxesPDF. https://www.axes4.com/axespdf-quickfix-overview.html
7. PAVE. http://pave-pdf.org/index.en.html
8. Darvishy, A., Nevill, M., Hutter, H.-P.: Automatic paragraph detection for accessible PDF documents. In: Miesenberger, K., Bühler, C., Penaz, P. (eds.) ICCHP 2016. LNCS, vol. 9758, pp. 367–372. Springer, Cham (2016). https://doi.org/10.1007/978-3-319-41264-1_50
9. Álvaro, F., Sánchez, J.-A., Benedí J.-M.: Recognition of printed mathematical expressions using two-dimensional stochastic context-free grammars. In: International Conference on Document Analysis and Recognition, pp. 1225–1229 (2011)
10. Álvaro, F., Sánchez, J.-A., Benedí, J.-M.: An integrated grammar-based approach for mathematical expression recognition. Pattern Recognit. 51(Suppl. C), 135–147 (2016)
11. Baker, J.B., Sexton, A.P., Sorge, V.: MaxTract: Converting PDF to LaTeX, MathML and Text. In: Jeuring, J., Campbell, J., Carette, J., Dos Reis G., Sojka, P., Wenzel, M., Sorge, V. (eds.) Intelligent Computer Mathematics, pp. 422–426 (2012)
12. Maxtract. School of Computer Science, University of Birmingham. http://www.cs.bham.ac.uk/research/groupings/reasoning/sdag/maxtract.php
13. Mathematical Expression Recognition. http://cat.prhlt.upv.es/mer/

An Evaluation of the Displaying Method on the Braille Learning System for the Sighted: For Understanding of the Mirror Image Relation

Yuko Hoshino[1] and Akihiro Motoki[2,3(✉)] (iD)

[1] Graduate School of Literature, Tsurumi University, 2-1-3 Tsurumi, Tsurumi-ku,
Yokohama-shi, Kanagawa 230-8501, Japan
[2] School of Literature, Tsurumi University, 2-1-3 Tsurumi, Tsurumi-ku,
Yokohama-shi, Kanagawa 230-8501, Japan
motoki-a@tsurumi-u.ac.jp
[3] Graduate School of Educational Informatics Education Division, Tohoku University,
27-1 Kawauchi, Aoba-ku, Sendai, Miyagi 980-8576, Japan

Abstract. The present work evaluates the effectiveness of adding blank cells to the 3DCG display of braille characters in the braille learning system for sighted learners to understand the mirror image relation between the written and read characters. The results of tests indicate the effect of the addition of blank cells to the 3DCG display in advancing the understanding of the mirror image relation.

Keywords: Braille · Displaying method · Blank cells · Mirror image relation
Sighted

1 Introduction

Braille, a set of characters consisting of raised dots arranged in cells, enables visually impaired to communicate with others. The system was invented by Louis Braille, a French educator who was blind himself.

The braille system for the Japanese language was developed by Kuraji Ishikawa, a teacher at Tokyo Blind and Dumb School. A character of Japanese braille consists of six dots in a cell, of which three represent a consonant, and the three others a vowel, of a syllable of the language. A character of Japanese braille thus corresponds to a syllabic character of Japanese.

A braille text is read from left to right by touching the raised dots in left-aligned lines. Braille characters must therefore be written from right to left as right-aligned lines of recessed dots. The configuration of the recessed dots formed on the backside of the paper is thus a mirror image of raised dots on the front side. This circumstance is referred to as the "mirror image relation" hereinafter.

Several systems have been developed to support sighted learners of braille. Putnam and Tiger [1] wrote a program for learning English braille. Evaluation by four sighted students proved that the program enabled all the learners to understand the relationship of braille characters and corresponding printed letters.

© The Author(s) 2018
K. Miesenberger and G. Kouroupetroglou (Eds.): ICCHP 2018, LNCS 10896, pp. 117–121, 2018.
https://doi.org/10.1007/978-3-319-94277-3_21

Motoki [2] developed and evaluated a Web-based system to support sighted braille learners. The system intended to familiarize learners with the basic rules of Japanese braille as well as the mirror image relation by providing three-dimensional computer graphic (3DCG) images of braille characters. Tests in which the learner filled circles corresponding to points to be indented when writing braille characters revealed two types of errors indicating lack of understanding of the mirror image relation: Error 1 in which each character is singly inverted in the order in the original string, and Error 2 in which the entire string is correctly inverted but left-aligned. He suggested that such errors were caused by inadequate specifications of the 3DCG. It provided the same number of cells to fill with braille characters as needed for an actual text, which meant that no hint was given as to right- and left-alignment of characters. Since this may have impeded clear understanding of the mirror image relation on the learner's part, he pointed out the necessity of an improved 3DCG system.

Hoshino and Motoki [3] proposed an improved 3DCG display design including additional blank (entirely flat) cells after the braille cells proper, and determined experimentally the number of the blank cells to be added for braille strings consisting of 1–10 characters. However, effects of this measure on learning have not been evaluated.

The purpose of the present work is to evaluate the effectiveness of the 3DCG braille display with added blank cells proposed by Hoshino and Motoki [3] for supporting sighted learner's understanding of the mirror image relation. Two 3DCG systems were made available for the test participants.

2   Participants and Setting

Tests were performed with 39 undergraduate students studying library service for the handicapped. All the participants were sighted native speakers of Japanese.

Tests utilized two types of braille learning systems including different 3DCG systems: System N without a blank cell and System A with added blank cells. Figure 1 shows examples of braille characters displayed in each system.

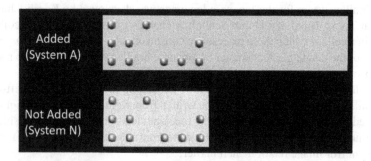

Fig. 1. Examples of braille characters displayed in the two 3DCG systems

The participants were divided into a control group and an experimental group. The control group, consisting of 17 students, used System N, while the experimental group of 22 students used System A.

A test concerning braille was performed on the control group on May 27, 2016 without prior notice to know the knowledge level of the group. The group was then permitted to use System N and asked to practice braille writing in arbitrary schedules. A similar test was performed on July 22, or eight weeks after the release of the system, without prior notice.

Likewise, a test was performed on the experimental group on June 2, 2017 without prior notice. The group was permitted to use System A on June 16, or two weeks after the test, and asked to practice braille writing. A similar test was performed On July 21, or five weeks after the release of the system, without prior notice.

All the test consisted of questions of an equivalent level. The full score was set to 15 points. The average and standard deviation of the scores in each test were calculated. In addition, the proportion of students who gave Errors 1 and 2 was calculated to evaluate the effectiveness of studies on the mirror image relation.

3   Results

The tests before the system release yielded average scores of 2.12 (S.D. = 4.21) for the control group and 0.82 (S.D. = 2.92) for the experimental group. The scores in the tests after the system release rose to 5.65 (S.D. = 4.3) and 7.45 (S.D. = 5.26), respectively.

The participants in each group were divided into subgroups according to the difference between the scores in the two tests, and the population percentages of individual subgroups within each group were calculated. The two groups were compared in terms of the population percentages in individual subgroups (Fig. 2).

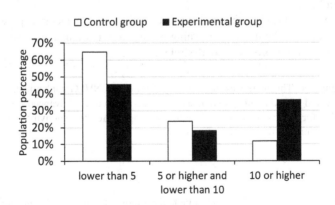

Fig. 2. Relative population in subgroups within the two groups

Figure 2 indicates that, for the experimental group, the population percentage of the subgroup with score difference of 10 or higher is greater than that with score difference of 5 or higher and lower than 10, while the population percentage decreases monotonously with increasing score difference in the control group. This tendency can be attributed to the introduction of blank cells in the 3DCG display used by the experimental group in the tests.

The control group yielded Error 1 answers by 24% of the members and Error 2 by 6%. The experimental group gave no Error 1 but Error 2 answers by 5%. A significant difference between the control and experimental group was observed for Error 1 only, which suggests effectiveness of the 3DCG with additional blank cells in improving learner's understanding of the need of reversing the entire string when producing a braille text.

4   Conclusion

The present work evaluates the effectiveness of adding blank cells to the 3DCG display of braille characters in supporting learners to understand the mirror image relation between the written and read characters.

Two groups of subjects were asked to practice braille, each using a braille learning system including a different 3DCG systems. Tests on braille were performed before and after the practice to assess the learning effect. The group that used the 3DCG system with added blank cells showed a higher proportion of participants who improved the scores by 10 points or more in the second test. A characteristic error found in a previous study in which braille characters were singly inverted in the order in the original string instead of inverting the entire string did not appear in the group using the 3DCG system with added blank cells.

These results indicate the effect of the addition of blank cells to the 3DCG display in advancing the understanding of braille. Particularly the addition of blank cells provided learners with a clear indication that the entire string must be inverted when writing a braille text.

While the present study concerns Japanese braille only, character display with additional blank cells will be useful in learning braille for other languages. Similar studies on non-Japanese braille systems are desirable.

Acknowledgments. This work was supported by JSPS KAKENHI Grant Number JP17K00444. The authors would like to thank the students who take the lecture "Advanced Library Services (library service for the handicapped)". Finally, we appreciated the anonymous reviewers for comments that improved this paper.

References

1. Putnam, B.C., Tiger, J.H.: Teaching braille letters, numerals, punctuation, and contractions to sighted individuals. J. Appl. Behav. Anal. **48**(2), 466–471 (2015)
2. Motoki, A.: Improvement and evaluation of braille learning support system for an understanding of mirror image relation. Educ. Inf. Res. **31**(3), 31–40 (2015)
3. Hoshino, Y., Motoki, A.: A study on the displaying method to assist the intuitive understanding about braille mirror image. Educ. Inf. Res. **33**(2), 31–36 (2017)

Optical Braille Recognition

Thorsten Schwarz[✉], Reiner Dolp, and Rainer Stiefelhagen

Studycentre for the Visually Impaired, Karlsruhe Institute of Technology,
Engesserstr. 4, 76131 Karlsruhe, Germany
thorsten.schwarz@kit.edu
http://szs.kit.edu

Abstract. Analog production methods for braille material, like braille typewriter or thermoforming processes, are still in use. Thereupon exists the wish to archive and preserve those materials, e.g. by digitalizing it. Research in the field of braille writing system detection and braille transcription has been sparse. Therefore we present a system to digitize printed Braille-documents.

Keywords: Optical braille recognition · Twin shadow
Ink suppression

1 Introduction

Braille is still one of the most important aids in the inclusion of blind people. On the one hand there are several Braille media or tactile graphics, which are only analogue and not digital. On the other hand, e.g., sighted teachers must proofread exams for blind pupils in Braille. But how, if they are not trained in Braille? Digitization makes it possible to convert, archive and reproduce data. Similarly, the method can be used to make Braille media readable for a blind student and a sighted teacher alike. In addition, there are different Braille notations or standards that can be easily transferred from one system to another by digitization. Therefore, we need a system that enables us to scan and digitize different Braille media and automatically convert them into archivable text.

For such a system there are a few points to consider. Depending on the type system, a Braille character consists of six or eight Braille dots. The translation of a vector from Braille to another font is not unique, but depends on the type system used. Braille varies according to state and language. A further problem is, e.g., that a Braille character can be transliterated to a letter, to a markup, to words or to word fragments (shortening) depending on the context of the Braille character.

In Braille printing, the font becomes visible or palpable by deformation of the paper. Here, we have the next challenge to recognize Braille correctly. Different printing techniques for Braille lead to different paper deformations. Too thin paper or too much force during embossing can lead to cracks in the deformed paper. Furthermore, other techniques like swell paper, thermoforming or even 3D printing can lead to different dot shapes. The next step is the Braille dimension.

K. Miesenberger and G. Kouroupetroglou (Eds.): ICCHP 2018, LNCS 10896, pp. 122–130, 2018.
https://doi.org/10.1007/978-3-319-94277-3_22

It can be observed that the standards hardly differ in terms of the proportions (point sizes and distances as well as Braille character sizes). In some Braille writing systems there are even signs to indicate "underlining, block, bold or oblique printing" or other highlightings. Those make recognition more difficult.

2   Related Work

A chronological overview of Optical Braille Recognition (OBR) work is presented in *An Insight into Optical Braille Character Recognition since its Conceptualisation* [1]. An overview of other existing papers is given in the review paper by Isayed and Tahboub [2] as well as Shreekanth and Udayashankara [3]. Flatbed scanners are often used. The same applies to the use of column and row profiles for the detection of rotation, raster and set points. Some works require a book page as a Braille medium. This means that the Braille text in a block must be placed on a rectangular medium.

   In 1986, Calders et al. [4] described the construction of an apparatus for the digitization of Braille, which illuminates a Braille medium at a flat angle with parallel light and takes photographs using mirrors and trying to achieve uniform lighting. Mennens et al. [5] use a A3 scanner for data acquisition. They evaluated their system on a small data set of seven documents. Hentzschel and Blenkhorn [6] use the difference between two binarized images using different light sources to detect the Braille points. There are several approaches [7,8], which detect points by mating gloss spots and shadows and classify them as Braille points of the current (recto) or declining (verso) side. Antonacopoulos et al. [8] present a complete recognition system that recognizes interdot Braille and different Braille systems. A procedure for error correction using a dictionary is presented. Wong et al. [9] suggest a system that first detects the position of a half Braille sign - only one column of the Braille dot matrix - and then uses a neural network for Braille detection. Namba et al. [10] perform a classification with a cellular neural network. For this purpose, a multi-layered perceptron is constructed for evaluation. Babadi et al. [11] model a Braille page with a Gaussian Mixture Model. Zhang and Yoshino [12] constructed a system that uses the camera of a mobile phone. First, horizontal lines corresponding to the line orientation are detected. To group characters together, the distances between points are compared. The description of the paper is short, incomplete and does not contain an evaluation. In addition, some of the approaches have at least one of the following shortcomings: (a) They do not deal with different Braille writing systems. (b) Many of them use a Lookup Table for transliteration, which do not solve the problem of ambiguity. (c) Recognition of Braille in interdot Braille is not considered. Which in particular, it is claimed that a procedure can be extended easily to interdot Braille without evaluation. This is generally not the case. (d) The existence of computer Braille. According to intention, most procedures can be easily adapted from Braille characters with six dots to Braille characters with eight dots. For other procedures, such as [11], this must be shown first. Moreover, there is no golden standard for the evaluation of the different systems and small data sets are sometimes used for evaluation. Thus, comparison of the systems is not easy.

3   The Optical Braille Scanner

In our setup a controlled lighting environment was designed for data acquisition (Fig. 1). The lighting environment allows the software configuration of illuminance and direction and therefore reproducible images. For this work, the lighting environment is used to produce parallel lighting with light beams orthogonal to the left and right sides of the paper. The light sources are mounted at the most flat, pointed angle possible. The goal is a long shadow cast and a strong highlight through the Braille dots. The image is taken parallel to the plane of the print medium for the channels red, green, blue with a bit depth of q of 8bit (rgb888) each with an 8 megapixel camera. In processing, however, only the grayscale image is used, since the color channels hardly differ. The image is cut to 2048×2048 pixels. This simplifies processing on a graphics card (GPU). A Braille point is projected in the image plane onto a partial image with an edge length of about 13 to 15 pixels. This corresponds to a significantly lower resolution than using a flatbed scanner. In this paper, Braille detection can be divided into the steps shown in Fig. 2, which are discussed below.

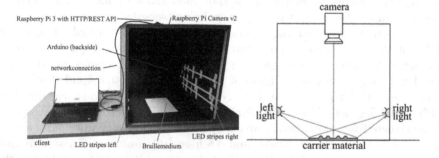

Fig. 1. Experimental setup (left); Position of main elements (right) (Color figure online)

We chose a camera solution because we were trying to find a cost-effective approach that would eventually run on a mobile device.

3.1   Background and Black Ink Suppression

Two shots I^L and I^R of the identical scene are created, but with different lighting. After taking the two pictures with different illumination, the following simple routine is used to separate the paper/object from the background (see the black background in Fig. 3): (1) removing the gradient generated by the illumination, by using a local threshold value method; (2) removing all related components, other than the largest, or removing all related components below a certain size; and (3) convex filling of the remaining context components.

For processing, the subtraction of the images $I^{L-R} = I^L - I^R$ is used, as it allows a distinction between the glossy side and the shady side of a Braille dot according to the sign of the pixel value (Fig. 3). Hentzschel's twin shadow approach [6] used a similar design with one lamp on each side and one lamp on the right to the print medium. In the second step the black print of the object is removed by the mentioned twin shadow approach.

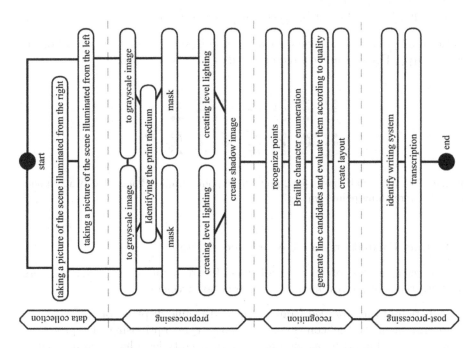

Fig. 2. Steps of the Optical Braille Scanner

Fig. 3. Input images with left I^L/right I^R and $I^{|L-R|} = |I^L - I^R|$ (left to right).

3.2   Braille Dot and Character Recognition

Template matching, as in [5], is used to separate Braille dots from the object/media layer. A pattern consisting of n pixels in the size of a Braille dot and all subimages of the difference image are checked for conformity.

Afterwards all possible Braille characters are searched out of the point cloud P_{recto}. To identify a character candidate from two set points (p_1, p_2), the following is needed (see Fig. 4).

1. the position of the Braille points p_1 and p_2 within the Braille dot matrix of the Braille character,
2. the rotation of the vector $\boldsymbol{p_1 p_2}$ relative to the vector $\boldsymbol{d_h}$ between Braille point 1 and Braille point 4,
3. as well as the scaling of the vector $\boldsymbol{p_1 p_2}$ to vector $\boldsymbol{d_h}$.

To form all possible characters, each possible Braille dot mask is placed on the vector $\boldsymbol{p_1 p_2}$. Each Braille character found is now clearly defined.

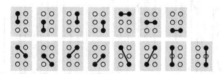

Fig. 4. Overview of all masks for 2 points in 6-point Braille. Black filled Braille points mark the stretching points (p_1, p_2).

3.3   Line Formation and Layout Recognition

The search space for solving the problem of line recognition is very large. Therefore two types of improvements can be used for acceleration:

- reduction of the observed Braille signs and Braille displays, or
- Improvement of the convergence behaviour by optimising the processing sequence and aborting as soon as a certain quality level has been reached.

The following *greedy* algorithm is used to create a complete solution for the medium from the set of potential lines:

1. The list of lines is sorted in ascending order according to their quality rating. The line with the best rating is now the first item in the list.
2. The list of rows is sorted by a stable sorting algorithm according to the number of row instances. Those have their maximum for lines that are the best choice for the characters of the considered line in the local environment of the characters.
3. The list of rows is sorted in descending order by a sorting algorithm according to the length categories, and secondary by the number of row instances, and tertiary by the quality score.

4. Now the first element of the list is removed iteratively. If the element consists only of Braille dots that have not yet been added to the solution, the element is added to the solution. This step is repeated until the list empty.

The reading order of similarly oriented lines can be defined by simple sorting by the y-coordinate and x-coordinate of the first Braille character of the line. If you sort in ascending order, the first line read is at the beginning of the list and the last line read is at the end of the list.

3.4   Braille Transliteration

Among the common methods of language detection, a character-based n-gram model is suitable, since the order of the lines and words does not have to be fixed yet. This makes it possible to determine the language of a line, but also to use the language model as a metric. This applies to the ranking of the individual candidates in the recursion step of the line formation algorithm as well as to the ranking of complete lines.

The open source Liblouis library [13] is used to translate the Braille writing system into a normal print system. This is used by screen readers such as NVDA, Orca and JAWS. Liblouis can be used for both rule-based and dictionary-based translation. A transcription to a writing system is defined by a translation table. The language tables are designed for the translation of the normal alphabet to the Braille alphabet. A table consists of a list of mapping rules (opcodes). The translation direction that is relevant for this work is possible by reverse execution of the derivation rules (back-translation), if this is possible.

4   Evaluation

Depending on the type system, an error in a character can affect the characters that follow the transcription. If a single Braille dot is not recognized, the word changes completely. Obviously, the minimum error propagation is zero. This is the case if the transcription of one character does not affect its successor. The maximum corresponds to the text length. We evaluate our system by measuring: (a) the minimum error rate $ER(M)$:

$$ER(M) = \frac{\#Substitutions + \#Cancellations + \#Insignments}{|M|} \, ,$$

(with an accuracy $ACC(M) = 1 - ER(M)$), (b) the point error rate $ER(P_{recto})$, (c) the character error rate $ER(Chr_Z)$, and (d) the transcription error rate $ER(T)$. Whereby Chr_Z describes the set of Braille characters of the lines selected for the layout and T the set of characters in the transcription. The above described error propagation shall now be considered empirically. For this purpose, starting from a set of M consisting of pairs with correct Braille/normal print transcriptions, the Braille text is falsified and the error rate in the transcription of the falsified Braille text is considered. To create the set M, a random character position i is selected from a longer text in normal print and the character sequence with character positions $i - 100$ to $i + 100$ is extracted. This character sequence T is transcribed by the library Liblouis to de-de-g2 Braille to get the text line L. In L, n random Braille points are falsified to get $\hat{L}$. Then $\hat{L}$ is transcribed to $\hat{T}$ and the transcription error rate $ER(T)$ is calculated by comparing T and $\hat{T}$. This process was repeated for every n one hundred times and averaged with the median. With an error propagation of 1.7 in the median per distorted Braille point, this appears to be low. However, the transcription error rate of the Liblouis library for a transcription cycle without falsification of a Braille dot (round trip) is high at 47 in the median on a text fragment with 201 black characters. The library's high transcription error rate seems to be caused by too frequent expansion of syllables to words. This suggests that the actual error propagation has a lower value. The validity of the result is called into question by the high rate of transcription errors for a transcription cycle without falsification. Obviously, the transcription is not correct in most cases if the Braille writing system is not correctly recognized. The presented algorithm depends on the length of the input. Each supported language selected a random position in the document for each word count k, extracted the next k words and the script for the extracted word sequence was detected by the algorithm. If the detected writing system corresponds to the actual writing system, the test was positive. The procedure only works satisfactorily from 200 to 300 Braille characters in length. The Braille page used in our tests consists of about 500 Braille characters. The procedure is therefore suitable for recognizing the language of a document, but not for classifying individual lines consisting of fewer than 30 characters. Braille point detection works reliably. Errors are mostly false positive detection, which are omitted in the characters and line selection and thus do not cause an error in the transcription. Observable reasons for false positive detection are defects in the cell structure of the paper or dog ears. The only detectable erroneously negative detection that could be observed was caused by Braille dots placed too close to the edge of the paper, as the implementation used only adapts templates to regions that are completely part of the print medium. If an error occurs in the character assignment. Some or all Braille characters are also wrongly selected until the end of the line. Lines consisting of only one or two characters are problematic for the procedure. The number of pages at the end of the document is mostly wrongly recognized and provides a significant portion of the total error in character assignment. Another reason for errors in recognition is incorrectly offset printed Braille dots. Overall, the error of 0.08 percent for point recognition and 0.90 percent for character recognition seems to be very small. It should be noted, however, that on average there are more than six erroneous characters per document page, with an average of 4.5 erroneous characters in the median (Table 1).

Table 1. Results of the evaluation

Total number of points	14786	Total number of characters	5829
Median point error rate	0.08%	Median character error rate	0.90%
Median accuracy	99.92%	Median drawing errors	99.10%

5 Conclusion

A new system was designed to digitize nearly flat media printed on one side with Braille in different Braille writing systems. New contributions to the current state of research include, in particular, an improved twin-shadow approach to the removal of normal print, which facilitates the recognition of Braille points. An algorithm was also developed to identify Braille displays on a point cloud without making assumptions about the macrotypography of the print medium. Initial investigations have also been made into the recognition of a Braille system. The entire system was tested on the basis of various Braille documents.

In the future, further questions have to be clarified and possible improvements of the system have to be considered, as: twin shadowing approach on mobile devices, stochastic line search, segment correction, scaling variance and lighting independence, preservation of document semantics, interdot Braille, tactile graphics and computer Braille.

References

1. Srinath, S., et al.: An insight into optical braille character recognition since its conceptualisation. Int. J. Comput. Appl. **33**, 1 (2011)
2. Isayed, S., Tahboub, R.: A review of optical braille recognition. In: 2015 2nd World Symposium on IEEE Web Applications and Networking, p. 1 (2015)
3. Shreekanth, T., et al.: A review on software algorithms for optical recognition of embossed braille characters. Int. J. Comput. Appl. **81**(3), 25 (2013)
4. Calders, P., Mennens, J.E., Frangois, G.E.: Optical pattern recognition of braille originals. In: 1986 International Symposium/Innsbruck International Society for Optics and Photonics, p. 229 (1986)
5. Mennens, J., et al.: Optical recognition of braille writing using standard equipment. IEEE Trans. Rehabil. Eng. **2**(4), 207 (1994)
6. Hentzschel, T., Blenkhorn, P.: An optical reading system for embossed braille characters using a twin shadows approach. J. Microcomput. Appl. **18**(4), 341 (1995)
7. Kitchings, R.T., Antonacopoulos, A., Drakopoulos, D.: Analysis of scand braille documents. In: Document Analysis Systems, Bd. 14, p. 413. World Scientific (1995)
8. Antonacopoulos, A., Bridson, D.: A robust braille recognition system. In: Marinai, S., Dengel, A.R. (eds.) DAS 2004. LNCS, vol. 3163, pp. 533–545. Springer, Heidelberg (2004). https://doi.org/10.1007/978-3-540-28640-0_50
9. Wong, L., Abdulla, W., Hussmann, S.: A software algorithm prototype for optical recognition of embossed braille. In: Proceedings of the 17th International Conference on Pattern Recognition, ICPR 2004, Bd. 2, p. 586. IEEE (2004)

10. Namba, M., Zhang, Z.: Cellular neural network for associative memory and its application to braille image recognition. In: The 2006 IEEE International Joint Conference on Neural Network Proceedings IEEE, p. 2409 (2006)
11. Babadi, M.Y., Nasihatkon, B., Azimifar, Z., Fieguth, P.: Probabilistic estimation of braille document parameters. In: 16th IEEE International Conference on Image Processing (ICIP), p. 2001. IEEE (2009)
12. Zhang, S., Yoshino, K.: A braille recognition system by the mobile phone with embedded camera. In: Second International Conference on IEEE Innovative Computing, Information and Control, ICICIC 2007, p. 223 (2007)
13. Group, L.: Liblouis manual. http://liblouis.org/documentation/liblouis.html

Accessible eLearning - eLearning for Accessibility/AT

Accessible eLearning - eLearning for Accessibility/AT

Introduction to the Special Thematic Session

E. A. Draffan[1]([⊠]) and Peter Heumader[2]

[1] WAIS, ECS, University of Southampton, Southampton, UK
ead@ecs.soton.ac.uk
[2] University of Linz, Linz, Austria

Abstract. The special thematic session on eLearning for accessibility and assistive technologies is made up of a wide range of papers that illustrate a variety of approaches to teaching and learning that comes under the title 'eLearning' such as gamification, use of apps, online presentation tools and MOOCS. Successful inclusion of those with disabilities as well as those who wish to enhance their knowledge can be achieved by ensuring ease of access to the platform of choice, the type of content available, whilst enhancing user motivation and appreciation.

Keywords: eLearning · Gamification · MOOCs · Online learning
Accessibility

1 Introduction

ELearning has been described as "the use of new multimedia technologies and the Internet to improve the quality of learning by facilitating access to resources and services as well as remote exchanges and collaboration" [1]. Accessible eLearning is about inclusion, enabling those with disabilities equal access not only to the platform used to present the learning materials, but also to the materials themselves. Some users may wish to make use of assistive technologies (AT) such as screen readers, text to speech and magnification. Others may require alternative formats in order to engage with the content, such as captions for videos, audio descriptions or transcripts or even multiple representations of content. Whereas, most eLearners are seen in the context of what they can do with technology, often discussions around disability are more negative in nature where it is about what cannot be done [2]. Illustrating the positive outcomes that can come from the development of accessible eLearning platforms and materials is essential for the inclusion agenda to gain traction within the online learning community.

A recent study in the UK with 105 Higher Educational institutions and 13 case studies gathered from 59 individuals, found that "sixty per cent of providers rated themselves as at least halfway towards being fully inclusive and all providers reported that they are moving forward with an inclusive support agenda" [3]. From the report it was clear that, even in one country, "despite having institution wide policies and procedures there can

K. Miesenberger and G. Kouroupetroglou (Eds.): ICCHP 2018, LNCS 10896, pp. 133–137, 2018.
https://doi.org/10.1007/978-3-319-94277-3_23

be a lack of consistency in terms of how university-wide inclusive policies are implemented." However, throughout the report staff and student skills training with the need for improved digital accessibility and use of assistive technologies, were seen as essential elements for removing barriers to inclusion.

Nevertheless, one of the challenges related to inclusion and eLearning is gauging the skills of the user as well as the degree to which digital accessibility has been achieved. The following sections of the paper examine the challenges discussed by authors working in five different settings.

2 Gamification

Patzer et al. (2018) [5] present the challenge of needing to teach skills to learners who have only reached a basic level of education. The form of gamification used involved the use of videos with encouraging feedback at all stages with hints when answers were incorrect and a move to the next stage with badges when successful. The adaptation of difficulty levels in response to users' skills could be seen as motivating and was effective, in that no one felt excluded from the learning process. Varying levels of knowledge about gamification and being in a competition did not appear to have an impact on results. However, the challenge mentioned by the authors was to know the degree of gamification knowledge prior to engaging with the learning and the extent of learners' computer skills. In the study, a lack of computer skills meant that extra support was needed.

3 Apps

The field of digital music in terms of inclusion for those with disabilities is not well researched according to Niediek et al. [6] even though there are numerous music apps on portable technologies and digital music creation is possible. There are specialists working with those who have disabilities and supporting music creation using assistive technologies, but very rarely in the general classroom alongside other musicians. Niediek et al. set out to involve these specialists in an enquiry based research project that provided an insight into the challenges faced in these situations. Initial findings show that, despite the reservations of teachers regarding the use of digital devices, in many cases not related to the creation of music, it was possible to mix the use of music created digitally with traditional musical instrument playing. Where this mix was successful with adaptations being made to digital devices and apps for those with disabilities and a range of skills being taken into account, inclusive teaching practices were not considered an issue. However, the jury is out as to how one measures talent in an 'elaborated music' setting and whether this can be considered part of the norm in most music teaching situations.

4   Sign-Bilingual Teaching

Individuals who are pre-lingual deaf often fail to gain high levels of literacy skills because they have limited access to spoken language that means they have "fewer experiences with words and do not over learn their meanings" [7]. Volpato et al. (2018) [8] noted that this can result in a lack of ability to engage with written information, as those who are deaf mainly use a national sign language based on gestures rather than spoken language. The challenge that many teachers face is a lack of skills to cope with bilingual situations in the classroom (spoken and signing) and this can cause barriers to inclusion for those who are deaf. By providing an online Moodle set of interactive resources with signing in the language of choice, alongside the classroom teaching, deaf students were given the chance to experience a teacher discussing the topics with a written language version as well as the signed option being available. Bite-sized modules provided in a customized order and self-correcting exercises with visual feedback provide motivation. However, the challenge of assessing student skills remained, although options for multiple representations of content and the introduction of additional language support prior to the start of the course helped.

5   An Open Authoring Tool for Accessible Slide Presentations

Jane Hart in her eleventh annual survey of 'The Top 200 Tools for Learning 2017' received responses from "2,174 learning professionals from 52 countries worldwide" [9] who said that PowerPoint was their second most often used tool in the workplace and third most used in educational settings after YouTube and Google Search. The popularity of using slides to present knowledge is undeniable, but Elias et al. (2018) [10] have highlighted the possible challenges faced by those with disabilities when accessing content in this format. The authors found six elements that content providers needed to make sure were accessible when developing online slide presentations in the open authoring SlideWiki platform. However, there was no way of knowing how skillful slide authors would be at coping with the six accessibility requirements. A survey took place to discover author preferences. Should they be encouraged to complete the tasks with guidance or should the process happen automatically, or were there degrees of accessibility support in between these two? The results highlighted a dilemma as most authors wished to be encouraged to make accessibility changes with guidance but complete the process in a few minutes. This may not be possible if accessibility knowledge is negligible. However, the challenge to make automatic accessibility correction acceptable to both authors and learners with disabilities remains an issue.

6   Accessible MOOCs

The authors of two papers about developing accessible MOOCs with content on the subject of digital accessibility have highlighted very different issues in their papers, but have in common the topic of increased support to aid access to content. One paper discusses the development of an Accessible MOOC Platform (AMP) to provide ease of use, with the ability to personalize the way content is presented for those with cognitive impairments (Cinquin et al. 2018) [11]. The other paper presents the issue of ease of access to additional information in multiple formats when a topic is complex (Draffan et al. 2018) [12]. As has been shown in the papers presented so far, eLearning does not always offer content providers with the chance to evaluate the skills of their learners prior to offering a course. The accessible MOOC papers illustrate that the idea of providing multiple ways of presenting knowledge can be an effective way of encouraging inclusion in an educational setting for a wide range of skills and abilities.

7   Discussion and Conclusion

The thread that appears to be running through all the papers presented on the subject of Accessible eLearning - eLearning for Accessibility/AT is one of skills. This applies to both the teacher and the learner whatever their situation. The need to enhance digital literacy, confidence and accessibility knowledge by offering extra support, whether this is by encouraging the development of platforms that are easy to use or the enhancement of knowledge through the provision of multiple formats. Inclusive education is a multi-faceted concept [13] made up of many elements including the policies and procedures put in place by institutions and governments and the way inclusion is considered alongside mainstreaming. It is clear from the studies undertaken by the various authors, that there remains the need to make adaptations to standard forms of presentation as well as teaching and learning practices. Ease of access and strategies that offer extra support with multimodal alternative formats provided at all levels are vital in order to keep learners motivated and willing to remain engaged with eLearning in all its forms.

References

1. eEurope: Bringing knowledge within reach (2005). http://ec.europa.eu/information_society/doc/factsheets/005-e-Learning.pdf. Accessed 22 Mar 2018
2. Seale, J.: When digital capital is not enough: reconsidering the lives of disabled university students. Learn. Media Technol. **38**(3), 256–269 (2013)
3. Williams, M., Pollard, E., Langley, J., Houghton, A-M., Zozimo, J.: Models of support for students with disabilities: report to HEFCE (2017). http://dera.ioe.ac.uk/30436/1/modelsofsupport.pdf. Accessed 22 Mar 2018
4. W3C Web Content Accessibility Guidelines 2.0 (WCAG 2.0). https://www.w3.org/WAI/intro/wcag. Accessed 22 Mar 2018
5. Patzer, Y., Russler, N., Pinkwart, N.: Gamification in inclusive eLearning. In: Unpublished Paper for the 16th International Conference on Computers Helping People with Special Needs (2018)
6. Niediek, I., Gerland, J., Sieger, M., Zielbauer, S.: Music Apps in inclusive classroom – a spotlight into practice. In: Unpublished Paper for the 16th International Conference on Computers Helping People with Special Needs (2018)
7. Easterbrooks, S.R., Maiorana-Basas, M.: Literacy and deaf and hard-of-hearing students. In: Educating deaf learners: creating a global evidence base, pp. 149–172 (2015)

8. Volpato, L., Hilzensauer, M., Krammer, K., Chan, M.: Teaching the national written language to deaf students: a new approach. In: Unpublished Paper for the 16th International Conference on Computers Helping People with Special Needs (2018)

9. Hart, J.: Top 200 tools for learning 2017. http://c4lpt.co.uk/top100tools/analysis/. Accessed 22 Mar 2018

10. Elias, M., James, A., Lohmann, S., Wald, M.: Towards an open authoring tool for accessible slide presentations. In: Unpublished Paper for the 16th International Conference on Computers Helping People with Special Needs (2018)

11. Cinquin, P.A, Guitton, P., Sauzéon, H.: Towards truly accessible MOOCs for persons with cognitive disabilities: design and field assessment. In: Unpublished Paper for the 16th International Conference on Computers Helping People with Special Needs (2018)

12. Draffan, E.A., Leon. M., James, A., Aljaloud, S., Wald, M.: Completion, comments and repurposing a digital accessibility MOOC. In: Unpublished Paper for the 16th International Conference on Computers Helping People with Special Needs (2018)

13. Mitchell, D.: Inclusive education is a multi-faceted concept. CEPS J. Center Educ. Pol. Stud. J. 5(1), 9 (2015)

Completion, Comments and Repurposing a Digital Accessibility MOOC

E. A. Draffan[✉], Manuel Leon, Abi James, Saud Aljaloud, and Mike Wald

WAIS, ECS, University of Southampton, Southampton, UK
ead@ecs.soton.ac.uk

Abstract. The 'massive' and 'open' nature of Massive Open Online Courses (MOOCs) can provide powerful dissemination tools to raise awareness of topics in need of public attention, such as digital accessibility and its impact on assistive technology users. The subject is a wide-ranging one when taught from the point of view of those who may have sensory, physical and/or cognitive impairments coping with a myriad of digital activities on a daily basis. These may range from creating and viewing documents, surfing the web to using a mobile or a washing machine. An analysis of the interactions and learning experiences of those who completed the FutureLearn Digital Accessibility MOOC was conducted, using a combination of statistical and qualitative methods. Preliminary results indicate a progressive loss of participants over time, which is to be expected with MOOCs. However, certain measures such as the number of comments per participant, completed steps, and the "likes" count suggest a relatively high degree of engagement from this particular learning community. After examining the topics that triggered most participation, a suggestion has been formulated to repurpose parts of the course in order to exploit its most engaging sections and offer alternative forms of support for those activities that required more explanation.

Keywords: MOOCs · Digital accessibility · Elearning · Professionals
Dissemination · Repurposing

1 Introduction

The Erasmus + European project "MOOCs for Accessibility Partnership" (MOOCAP) [1] set out to provide education on accessible design in Information, Communication and Technology (ICT) covering a wide range of topics that would be of interest to all those involved in the delivery and consumption of digital products, publications and services. Over the course of three years, the project team delivered a series of Massive Open Online Courses (MOOCs) and online courses, all available as Open Educational Resources (OERs) with a Creative Commons Attribution 4.0 International Licence. The introductory course aimed to help learners understand how "those with sensory, physical and cognitive impairments may be disabled by barriers encountered when using digital technologies." [2] The MOOC did not require any previous knowledge about the topics covered, but set out a series of accessibility skills that could be acquired if a learner completed the course over five weeks. 9642 learners registered on the three runs that

© The Author(s) 2018
K. Miesenberger and G. Kouroupetroglou (Eds.): ICCHP 2018, LNCS 10896, pp. 138–145, 2018.
https://doi.org/10.1007/978-3-319-94277-3_24

were held in 2016–2017 and of those who signed up 5,604 (58%) stayed to at least view one step at any time in any course week. According to FutureLearn [3] "the average number of learners on a course is 50% of joiners".

Research has shown there is a wide variation in the reasons for dropping out of courses [4] due to internal and external factors [5, 6]. Examples include:

- "No real intention to complete,
- Lack of time,
- Course difficulty and lack of support,
- Lack of digital skills or learning skills,
- Bad experiences,
- Expectations,
- Starting late and
- Peer Review" [7].

When developing the Digital Accessibility MOOC, the project team was aware of the high dropout rates and wanted to ensure the course platform was accessible, easy to use and encouraged interaction with tutors and mentors. Ease of use checks with assistive technologies showed that FutureLearn fulfilled the accessibility criterion and offered captions and transcriptions for all the videos or audio files uploaded to the system. There was the added bonus of an embedded discussion forum so that learners could easily comment on the content. Researchers have suggested that FutureLearn is a social learning platform because comments appear alongside each step or activity, rather than requiring the learner to work in an unrelated discussion area on the website. The former tends to encourage increased interaction between learners and this was seen as being important, where those participating on each course run outnumbered the teachers and mentors [8].

Those creating the MOOC (eight university departments in seven different countries) were aware that their contributions varied in content style and topic from discussing different types of disability with personas to complex accessibility standards related to web page design and development. The authors of this paper, coming from a partner university, were interested to see how many learners completed the various activities presented on the Digital Accessibility MOOC, as well as how many actively engaged with content and their peers. By analyzing the comments from the various steps and activities alongside completion levels it was felt there might be the possibility of seeing which topics encouraged engagement and which should be the focus of future courses and in particular suitable for repurposing into an alternative format and offered as additional Open Educational Resources.

2 Method

The initial task was to discover how many learners completed each step. Questioning whether there were any anomalies or was there a general level of dropout over the course of the five weeks? A step (as seen in a FutureLearn MOOC) is made up of a single topic page that may contain a short video or audio clip with text, possibly images and usually a question to engender discussion. Steps are grouped as activities, which are rather like a section in a chapter of a book. The chapter becomes the week of activities in the online course. There followed an analysis of the number of comments in each step compared to the number of learners. The learner's unique ID was used due to data protection and where steps required no commenting these were omitted. It was felt this comparison might illustrate different levels of engagement to the types of content or topic. Any replies to comments were omitted from the analysis as these tended to show appreciation or question the previous comment rather than the content within the course. The results were aligned with the number of 'likes' on each original comment about the content to illustrate more active engagement with the topic being discussed.

Finally, an analysis of the comments found in the reflection steps, offered at the end of each week, was undertaken to find any discussion that might be related to particular topics. It was felt that this task would not only offer an insight into the learning outcomes, but also whether adaptations should be made to the way a topic was presented.

3   Results

Of the 5,604 joiners on the three runs of the Digital Accessibility MOOC only 4185 were active learners. According to FutureLearn these learners are "those (of any role) who have completed at least one step at any time in any course week, including those who go on to leave the course." Recording the completion of a step is dependent on the learner manually selecting the 'mark as complete' button. When analysing the 98 steps over the five weeks it was found that the rate of completion dropped from 2465 learners per step to 839 learners. This was not unexpected as stated at the beginning of the paper and it was found that the rate of attrition was relatively uniform after the first week (see Fig. 1).

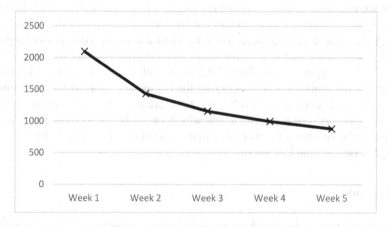

Fig. 1. The average number of participants who completed a step per week

Moreover, despite encouragement from mentors on the Digital Accessibility MOOC to engage with the questions posed at the end of many steps or to be reflective at the end of each week and to discuss topics independently of the teaching staff, it was found that the majority of learners still failed to regularly comment. Swinneton et al. [8] discovered in their research, on average 47% of those using the discussion area only make one or two comments. On the Digital Accessibility MOOC the average number of comments per learner was 6–7 throughout the three runs.

Further inspection of the data showed that the average percentage of learners who completed an activity and commented on the topics in the reflection step provided each week, varied very little: 21–27% over the five weeks. However, when linking this to the percentage of 'likes' for particular comments it became clear that there was a distinct difference marking out week 4. It had the second lowest number of comments relating to the reflection step (214) with the second highest number of likes for the comments about the content (415) (Table 1).

Table 1. Number of comments and likes compared to the number of learners per week

Reflective Step	Number of learners who completed the step	Number of comments made	Number of comment "likes"
Week 1	1699	467	489
Week 2	1308	332	352
Week 3	1085	223	325
Week 4	937	214	415
Week 5	829	199	276

On inspection of week four's content, spread over 20 steps, there were fewer questions compared to the other weeks. Only nine steps had questions, and there were three quizzes to break up the amount of content and allow learners time to self-assess their knowledge building. Questions in the activity steps asked for answers that related directly to a web accessibility activity such as the one asked after Step 4.7 "What barriers can a web form have for people with limited dexterity?" The reflection steps at the end of each week always had the same three questions namely:

1. What have you found to be good, useful or interesting this week?
2. What actions will you now take to learn more about these topics and take the lessons forward in your life and work?
3. What questions, if any, have arisen for you?

So the question asked, was why this particular reflection step caused an increased amount of engagement? There were nearly twice the number of likes per comment, compared to other reflection steps (34% to 66%). It was decided that a thematic analysis of the comments might show what had made this particular reflection step different from the others. An initial familiarisation with the content of the 214 comments showed that learners had sometimes answered all three of the questions in one comment. Data within the comments was coded and a thematic analysis undertaken [9]. Four themes appeared, an appreciation of the week's content in terms of helpfulness and raising awareness, mentions of complexity, the need for further materials and the wish to revisit materials with other comments relating to particular web accessibility questions. Table 2 shows the worked-out themes from the comments (with percentages) found in the week four reflection step.

Table 2. Themes for classifying comments provided in the week four reflection step.

Theme	Comments	Percentage
Appreciate materials	118	45%
Complexity	23	9%
Further materials required	12	5%
Materials need revisiting	32	12%
Other themes related to activities	75	29%
Total	260	100%

4   Discussion

By examining the content of activities for week four, it became clear that this was not only a very full week, but also the activities might be considered quite complex, because it was about web content accessibility standards and the barriers to ease of access for those with disabilities. It included Web Content Accessibility Guidelines (WCAG), conformance and user testing often undertaken by developers or those involved with online content development. However, when posing questions for reflection, with guidance to help learners think about general aspects of the week's activities, the most popular answers showed appreciation to those who provided the content. This gratitude was welcoming, but made the authors of this paper wonder whether the actual reflection questions needed to change in order to provide a better understanding of the learner outcomes.

However, research has shown that when learners participate actively with comments such as replying or liking, it shows more active engagement with the course [10] which could be said to be true of week four as there were comments that revealed a deep interest in the subject. Those who managed the activities often said how much they appreciated the amount of information and external links. The minority who mentioned the complexity of it all (9%) or were new to the subject often praised the way it had been broken down into steps, but still wanted an equivalent of a 'Dummies guide' with key points and less technical language.

There were other comments about the amount of links and resources provided and how they would need to be revisited or shared with colleagues at a later date. These comments highlighted the fact that time may have been an issue, with a sense of overload in terms of the amount of reading material provided. The idea of offering slides with key points and even smaller mini chunks of content with diagrams for the crucial elements might have helped learners cope better in this type of situation. Videos and audio recordings were purposely kept below three minutes and in the reflections, no one said they were too long. Transcripts and captions were offered and the former could be downloaded and kept for reference.

There was an awareness that the materials would only be available for 14 days after the course unless further access was purchased. On the other hand, it was pointed out that, for this particular course, all the materials had been made available and could be repurposed in different formats, once gathered from the MOOCAP project website.

When examining the comments regarding particular activities (29%) it was clear that practical advice, such as the use of web accessibility testing tools, was also highly valued. Several learners on the course shared their expertise in their comments. One of the limitations of a MOOC is the difficulty of providing hands on experience from a distance. The repurposing of this aspect of the course with more interactive online activities, illustrating how the tools worked, where they were useful and where they failed to pick up accessibility errors, would have provided improved support. This could have helped those learners who were educationalists rather than developers.

Finally, the problem of having to leave the MOOC platform to read or interact with other websites could be considered a weakness of all online learning where there are hyperlinks out to similar areas of interest. Not knowing the skills and interests of the learners who join a MOOC can make it difficult for content providers. A judgement has to be made as to the level and complexity of knowledge provided and in the case of the Digital Accessibility MOOC there was a tacit understanding that the content would be offered at several levels with the external links providing basic and/or advanced support materials. All the resources had clear explanations, but these could have been presented with indications as to the level of knowledge required, perhaps on a sliding scale from basic to advanced or college level to post graduate.

5   Conclusion

Many researchers have commented on the way learners fail to complete MOOCs based on course completion figures, the gaining of a certificate or the passing of tests. It could be said that this way of measuring the success of a MOOC fails to address the diversity of those participating and what they may wish to achieve. The Digital Accessibility MOOC had two main groups of participants namely educators and those in Information Technology professions and when reviewing the comments in the week four reflection step, it was clear that members of both groups had engaged with the content. However, the reasons for engagement included the wish to pass information on to others and use of the knowledge gained in daily work, as well as showing a genuine desire to participate with particular topics despite their complexity. Some learners were willing to share their knowledge when others included questions in amongst their comments and topic specific threads developed. This process of discussion, commenting and liking comments has resulted in researchers highlighting the potential for social learning via MOOC platforms. However, as Tubman et al. [11] point out "MOOC environments have unique challenges for pedagogy which are not present in other socioconstructivist learning environments: the scale and diversity of participation". Nevertheless, these peer on peer interactions can be very valuable as a way of raising awareness about learners' positive and negative feelings and when problems are arising.

Even with a very small number of comments from one reflective step taken from one week in the Digital Accessibility MOOC it was possible to prioritise the type of activity that should be repurposed into alternative formats in order to better support some learners. For example, the highlighting of crucial elements of the content into a series of online interactive slides, such as offered by SlideWiki [12], that can be made available as open education resources (using the Creative Commons licence CC-BY 4.0), would offer support to those wishing to share the information as well as collaborate on the topic. The addition of metadata to provide information to learners about the level of each activity may also be useful to prevent concerns about complexity, but a true appreciation on the part of authors as to the time it takes to absorb materials is hard, due to the diversity of those participating as mentioned before.

Most MOOCs offer content in a variety of layouts, with use of text and multimedia, as a whole course and rarely offer their content in ways that can be easily repurposed. As part of the development of the content for the Digital Accessibility MOOC as well as to facilitate the collaboration of experts within different countries, institutions and fields, a "stepwise" process for authoring was organized. Each learning object was carefully documented, with accessibility metadata and grouped in small chunks of information making up the various activities [13]. These individual artefacts such as single images, audio files to videos with their transcripts and caption files plus text based content in separate word processed documents can be adapted to suit all levels of education. The concept of offering multiple ways of learning has been recognised as an effective way of encouraging inclusive teaching and learning practices with "multi-modal opportunities in terms of representation, engagement and expression" [14].

References

1. MOOCAP Erasmus + Project Home page http://gpii.eu/moocap/. Accessed 31 Jan 2018
2. FutureLearn 'Why Join the Course'. https://www.futurelearn.com/courses/digital-accessibility. Accessed 31 Jan 2018
3. FutureLearn Course Run Measures. https://partners.futurelearn.com/data/stats-dashboard/. Accessed 31 Jan 2018
4. Breslow, L.B., Pritchard, D.E., DeBoer, J., Stump, G.S., Ho, A.D., Seaton, D.T.: Studying learning in the worldwide classroom: research into edX's first MOOC. Res. Pract. Assess. **8**, 13–25 (2013)
5. Halawa, S., Greene, D., Mitchell, J.: Dropout prediction in MOOCs using learner activity features. Experiences Best Pract. Around MOOCs **7**, 3–12 (2014)
6. Lu, X., Wang, S., Huang, J., Chen, W., Yan, Z.: What decides the dropout in MOOCs? In: Bao, Z., Trajcevski, G., Chang, L., Hua, W. (eds.) DASFAA 2017. LNCS, vol. 10179, pp. 316–327. Springer, Cham (2017). https://doi.org/10.1007/978-3-319-55705-2_25
7. Onah, D.F., Sinclair, J., Boyatt, R.: Dropout rates of massive open online courses: behavioural patterns. In: Proceedings of the EDULEARN14, pp. 5825–5834 (2014)
8. Swinnerton, B., Hotchkiss, S., Morris, N.P.: Comments in MOOCs: who is doing the talking and does it help? J. Comput. Assist. Learn. **33**(1), 51–64 (2017)
9. Braun, V., Clarke, V.: Using thematic analysis in psychology. Qual. Res. Psychol. **3**(2), 77–101 (2006)
10. Ferguson, R., Clow, D.: Examining engagement: analysing learner subpopulations in massive open online courses (MOOCs). In: Proceedings of the Fifth International Conference on Learning Analytics and Knowledge, pp. 51–58. ACM, March 2015

11. Tubman, P., Oztok, M., Benachour, P.: Being social or social learning: a sociocultural analysis of the FutureLearn MOOC platform. In: 2016 IEEE 16th International Conference on Advanced Learning Technologies (ICALT), pp. 1–2. IEEE (2016)
12. SlideWiki EU Open Courseware Project. https://slidewiki.org/. Accessed 31 Jan 2018
13. Draffan, E.A., Wald, M., Dickens, K., Zimmermann, G., Kelle, S., Miesenberger, K., Petz, A.: Stepwise approach to accessible MOOC development. Studies in health technology and informatics **217**, 227 (2015)
14. Department of Education, Inclusive Teaching and Learning in Higher Education as a route to Excellence (2017). https://www.gov.uk/government/publications/inclusive-teaching-and-learning-in-higher-education. Accessed 31 Jan 2018

Towards Truly Accessible MOOCs for Persons with Cognitive Disabilities: Design and Field Assessment

Pierre-Antoine Cinquin[✉], Pascal Guitton, and Hélène Sauzéon

Bordeaux University & INRIA, Talence, France
{pierre-antoine.cinquin,pascal.guitton,
helene.sauzeon}@u-bordeaux.fr

Abstract. MOOCs are playing an increasingly important role in education systems. Unfortunately, MOOCs are not fully accessible. In this paper, we propose design principles to enhance the accessibility of MOOC players, especially for persons with cognitive disabilities. These principles result from a participatory design process gathering 7 persons with disabilities and 13 expert professionals. They are also inspired by various design approaches (Universal Design for Learning, Instructional Design, Environmental Support). We also detail the creation of a MOOC player offering a set of accessibility features that users can alter according to their needs and capabilities. We used it to teach a MOOC on digital accessibility. Finally, we conducted a field study to assess learning and usability outcomes for persons with cognitive and non-cognitive impairments. Results support the effectiveness of our player for increasing accessibility.

Keywords: Accessibility · Cognitive disabilities · MOOC · Participatory design Ability based design · Usability

1 Introduction

Even if the situation of Persons with Disabilities (PWDs) is improving due to inclusion policies aimed at combating discrimination, there are still many areas where disability is somewhat overlooked. This is particularly the case for education: the representation of PWDs decreases drastically between primary school and higher education. Lower qualification leads to adverse consequences in the professional world, where unemployment rates for PWDs are much higher than average.

As online e-learning platforms such as MOOCs (Massive Online Open Courses) are playing an increasingly key part in our education and training systems [1], they could allow PWDs to develop new skills, thus facilitating access to employment. Unfortunately, MOOCs are lacking in terms of accessibility, which contributes to PWD's social exclusion. Even if sensory and motor disabilities are beginning to be considered when designing accessible interfaces, this is rarely the case for cognitive impairments (attention, memory…). Although they are very common, they are often referred to as invisible

© Springer International Publishing AG, part of Springer Nature 2018
K. Miesenberger and G. Kouroupetroglou (Eds.): ICCHP 2018, LNCS 10896, pp. 146–153, 2018.
https://doi.org/10.1007/978-3-319-94277-3_25

disabilities because they are not very well-known outside of the family, medical or specialized environment [2].

Our overall goal is to enable the development of MOOCs that are accessible for many different learners, by including as much as possible those with cognitive impairments. The main contributions of this paper are:

1. The design and the implementation of a truly accessible MOOC player based on the pre-existing design principles as well as those from a participatory design, which included both PWDs and (scientific or professional) experts.
2. A field study on the use and efficiency (follow-up measures) of this MOOC player in a "real life" context, i.e. a real MOOC that we built and broadcast (5800 registered users coming from 60 countries).

2   Related Work

2.1   Accessibility Design Approaches

Several design frameworks have specifically addressed cognition-related issues. The most known are: Cognitive Load - Instructional Design [3] which aims to reduce distractive and non-instructional information and promoting opportunities to process target information; Universal Design for Learning [4] that proposes using specialized instructional strategies and compensatory devices like speech-to-text transcribers, and Environmental support for cognition [5] that suggest to reduce the demands and attentional cost of tasks, and spare cognitive functions. Those frameworks are fully compatible with recent advances in accessible computing concepts, such as Ability-based Design [6]. It refocuses the accessibility issue on capability rather than disability to adapt a system to what a person can do. For instance, it recommends the possibility for users to adapt the interface instead of specifically designing an interface for PWDs. As a virtuous circle, these adaptations potentially provide benefits for all users. Edwards [7] has shown that it is not a matter of placing a patch on existing systems, but of offering user-driven change. In a MOOC context, where many different people are involved, we think that it is important to take this approach to give all users the best chance to succeed, regardless of their conditions.

2.2   Accessibility and MOOCs

There has been little research activities on MOOC accessibility [8]. Most of the studies on MOOC accessibility were published after 2013 and focus on physically impaired learners. They are essentially based on the assessment of accessibility in relation to "mainstream" accessibility guidelines (*e.g.*, WCAG 2.0 [9]) and unfortunately they include few or no PWDs in the evaluation [10].

Most of existing MOOCs are not fully accessible. In 2014, Bohnsack and Puhl [11] showed that most MOOC platforms had a lack of correct language markers or accessible design. This study concluded that accessibility was not considered when developing these platforms, effectively excluding PWDs and not fulfilling the claim that MOOCs are open to everyone. Nevertheless, some projects try to overcome this lack of accessibility. The EU4ALL project [12] provides a framework to satisfy eLearning accessibility needs of higher students by using already existing standards and guidelines to customize presentations of several Learning Management Systems. In a different way, Sánchez-Gordón and Luján-Mora [13] propose a plugin for the OpenEdx platform, which adapts the content of the course according to the learner's preferences, needs and competences following a set of predefined adaptation rules.

Although these two studies illustrate real progress in the design of MOOC systems, shifting from a technology to a human-centered approach. Unfortunately, the authors did not assess their systems with real learner and their progress should perhaps be considered as claims rather than ground truth of effective accessibility. Moreover, it is noteworthy that today, no study actually addressed the MOOC accessibility for cognitive impairments (attention, memory…).

3   Design of Aïana, An Accessible MOOC Player

A Participatory Design (PD) process was conducted to define the users' needs in terms of basic and specific accessibility features for Aïana. It consisted in meetings and interviews with 7 students with disabilities (age > 18 years) and 13 expert professionals. PWDs exhibited varied neurodevelopmental diseases or neuropsychological syndromes to be representative of cognitive needs that they encountered. To specifically address the needs of persons relative to their cognitive capabilities, we listed and consigned the successes and requests of PWDs in situations closely related to MOOC experience during interviews. This preparatory phase led to a first set of ideas for accessibility features conceptualized in paper mockups (Iteration Loop 1) then software mockup (Iteration Loop 2) in an iterative process. Finally, ideas selected during these two PD session loops were integrated into a first version of Aïana, our MOOC player. This version was then evaluated during a field study.

3.1   Key Design Features

In this section, the features from the participatory design sessions are presented. They are organized into two main purposes: self-configuration vs. access.

Self-configuration
Allows users to select the desired streams, and then configure the position and location of their display window and of the buttons of the interface.

- **Separation of streams:** Classically, a MOOC consists of several types of information (video, slides, subtitles) merged together in a single stream (video most often). We built our MOOC using a different principle by explicitly separating all information streams into different windows.
  Goal: Allow the user-selection of the more useful stream for using screen-readers or for optimizing the learning task.

- **Selection of useful streams:** Users can configure their work space in Aïana by selecting which streams they want to watch, read and listen. This choice can be made at any time and can be modified whenever users wish to do so.
  Goal: Enhance task-relevant information, for instance for people for whom few information can be processed such as in cases of cognitive slowing-down or with a decrease of divided-attention or working memory.
- **Spatial organization:** Users can either keep the initial layout as it is when Aïana is first launched, or modify it as they please. They can resize and move each of the control buttons and display windows. These modifications can be made at any time and can be renewed whenever users wish to do so.
  Goal: Enhance task-relevant information, for instance to avoid distractors for persons with selective attention deficits or spatial disorders such as in schizophrenia or in attention disorder syndromes.
- **User profile:** By combining these features, users can dynamically configure their own MOOC player to suit their wishes and abilities. These settings form the users' profile. If a user needs evolve due to personal or contextual changes (*e.g.*, MOOC topic, MOOC contents, etc.), then they can reconfigure the player's interface.
  Goal: Promote self-determination perception in users, particularly those related to autonomy as motivational leverage for online e-learning.
- **Social Learning:** Users can save this profile on their computer and therefore to share it, with people who have disabilities close to their own for instance. On a voluntary basis, these exchanges can help create communities of Aïana users, who can exchange and potentially help each other.
  Goal: Promote social interactions and community building, particularly between proficient and less proficient Aïana users.

Access
Allows users to access the stream of information they have selected and navigate through the courseware sequence (start, stop, forwards, backwards, bookmark, *etc.*).

- **Additional Window:** Unfamiliar terms or abbreviations are often explained only once, the first time they occur. We added an information window providing short texts and simple icons. This additional information is intended to assist users in their understanding, for instance by providing the meaning of an abbreviation or by indicating with an alert icon where their attention is required.
  Goal: Externalize non-relevant sub-tasks, for instance for persons with working memory and long-term memory impairments.
- **Time Markers:** To take notes, learners must pause the video, resulting in a stuttered playback of the video which can make course hard to follow. With Aïana, users can put tags on the timeline to mark specific moments of the course so they can quickly and easily access a specific piece of information that they were unable to fully process the first time they play the video.
  Goal: Optimize processing opportunities; for instance, for persons needing specific repetitions or for persons with difficulties for achieving simultaneous tasks (*i.e.*, listen and write) as in the cases of a cognitive slowing-down or attention disorders.

- **Semantic Navigation:** The standard functions for navigating video streams should be enhanced with new features, notably regarding concept-driven navigation in MOOC sessions. In Aïana, the course contents are divided into main instructional units (each containing information which must be considered as a whole to fully understand a given concept) that are presented using one or more slides. It is possible to navigate across the instructional units: users can either return to the previous one in the event of a misunderstanding if they wish to deepen their understanding, or they can move forward if they are already familiar with the current concept.

  Goal: Encourage knowledge use in MOOC navigation, for instance for persons with understanding disorders due to impairments in processing speed, attention working memory, or memory.

- **Different teacher displays:** Classically, teachers are filmed looking into the camera lens forcing users to process simultaneously, but separately, the communication stream uttered by teacher and the slide's contents. We proposed a classic frontal face view and a profile view such as the teacher's gaze is oriented to the slide.

  Goal: Enhance task-relevant information by supporting joint attention and by avoiding direct face-to-face interaction, for instance for persons with social particularities (such as schizoaffective disorder or autism).

4 Field Assessment

Aïana was used during two sessions of a MOOC dedicated to digital accessibility (5 weeks per session). 651 persons signed the consent form and completed the profile survey (end of week 1) including 94 PWDs (14%). Of these, 146 completed the course and answered all our surveys, including 24 PWDs (19.67%). Among these 24 participants, 8 declared at least one cognitive disability (designated COG group) and 16 declared at least one sensory or motor disability and no cognitive disability (designated NON-COG group). Disability was assessed by a questionnaire derived from the function disabilities taxonomy (sensory, motor/mobility, etc.) according to the International Classification of Functioning, Disability and Health [14]. It included 20 items, of which 8 were about sensorial capabilities, 3 about motor capabilities and 9 about cognitive capabilities (for instance: *I have difficulty reading text, I have difficulty staying focus, I have problems with memorization...*).

4.1 Assessment Procedure

To study the impact of Aïana's features, three outcomes were analyzed:

- **Usability score** using the standardized questionnaire System Usability Scale (SUS) [15]. This questionnaire fits perfectly within an online environment [16].
- **Learning score** by a learning scale using multiple-choice questions. For each course video (each lasting between 2'31 and 10'23, average duration = 6'12) participants were asked to complete an assessment composed of 3 items on average. Each of the 30 assessments was then marked to give a percentage of success. We calculated two

scores: once at mid-point (average over the first 14 assessments) and once at the end of the MOOC (average of all assessments).

- **Self-Determination** (SD) scores using a 9 items-rating scale inspired from [17] that assesses the three SD dimensions (Autonomy, Competence and Relatedness). SD is a key factor of technology accessibility and acceptance [18] and of e-learning progress [19], notably for older adults and PWDs [*e.g.*, 20].

4.2 Results

Overall, all learners achieved high learning performance regardless of their disability condition (Table 1). Thus, the functionalities allowed them to access all the instructional material provided through the entire MOOC. Similarly, the Aïana usability results at the end of the MOOC reached a "good" usability level (average of 75) according to Bangor [21]. Before starting the MOOC sessions, we proposed a video-based demonstration and an illustrated user manual as recommended in the field of adoption of assistive technology [22], allowing a good understanding of the offered functionalities amongst learners. Consequently, this video and this manual could have occasion a boost on the subsequent SUS scoring. Furthermore, although group difference failed the significance (p = .607), the mean examination of SUS score reveals that COG (74.75) was slightly more proficient than NON-COG (66.34) until mid-point.

Table 1. Means (and standard deviation) for learning, usability scores (across times: Mid- vs. End-point) and for SD achieved scores according to group condition

		NON-COG	COG
Learning score *(max. score = .100)*	*Mid-point*	.87 (.08)	.78 (.15)
	End-point	.89 (.08)	.89 (.09)
Usability score *(max. score = 100)*	*Mid-point*	66.34 (21.53)	74.75 (21.65)
	End-point	75.46 (23.53)	75.81 (13.57)
SD score *(max. score = 5)*	**Autonomy**	3.46 (.23)	3.94 (.33)
	Competence	3.31 (.24)	3.71 (.34)
	Relatedness	3.20 (.25)	3.04 (.25)

Additionally, Aïana provided a good SD support to PWD needs in terms of autonomy and competence, known as important components for learners' intrinsic motivation. In distance learning, improving the intrinsic motivation of learners (*i.e.*, self-determination) decreases the attrition rate of online learning platforms [23]. This is even truer in the case of PWD, where the lack of accessibility can lead to a bigger effort to self-regulate their learning. Finally, regarding the participation rate, we compare our results to other MOOCs thanks to a recent paper studying eight MOOCs [24]. For the first week, we observed a slightly higher rate of PWD with Aïana (14%) than in other MOOCs (10.75%). At the end of the last week, the difference is much significant: 19.67% with Aïana versus 11.3%. Aïana seemed to make it possible to better keep PWDs throughout the MOOC. This is a promising result that truly accessible MOOC players improve opportunities for the educational inclusion of PWDs.

5   Limitations and Future Work

The user interface of this first version of Aïana has yet to be improved. As already noted, the current version promoted self-configuration according to users' abilities and preferences, but no adaptive features are included, Future works will address this issue to fully cover the principles of the ability-based design. The continuation of the iterative process will also allow us to increase the number of participants and therefore reinforce the statistical results and the diversity of disabilities of potential MOOC users. A tracking log of user's interactions with Aïana is currently under implementation. Its analysis should enable us to highlight the relevance of designed features.

Regarding the SD scores elicited by Aïana, it would be interesting to think about functionalities that strengthen the relatedness component. In MOOC, the social part is usually handle outside of the courses' material (in a forum or a chat) and it may be interesting to include it directly into the player, mimicking the social presence induced by a classroom. Such new functionalities should be modulated according to user capabilities for cognitively managing additional distractors.

We have successfully designed a MOOC player to support inclusive e-education. Results presented here provide evidence of its good usability value and its positive impact (learning and SD) for PWDs, notably for those with cognitive impairments.

References

1. Clark, R.C., Mayer, R.E. (eds.): e-Learning and the Science of Instruction (2016). https://doi.org/10.1002/9781119239086
2. Matthews, C.K., Harrington, N.G.: Invisible disability. In: Braithwaite, D.O., Thompson, T.L. (eds.) LEA's Communication Series. Handbook of Communication and People with Disabilities: Research and Application, pp. 405–421 (2000)
3. Sweller, J.: Cognitive load theory, learning difficulty, and instructional design. Learn. Instr. **4**(4), 295–312 (1994). https://doi.org/10.1016/0959-4752(94)90003-5
4. Rose, D.H., Meyer, A.: A Practical Reader in Universal Design for Learning. Harvard Education Press, Cambridge (2006)
5. Morrow, D.G., Rogers, W.A.: Environmental support: an integrative framework. Hum. Factors J. Hum. Factors Ergon. Soc. **50**(4), 589–613 (2008). https://doi.org/10.1518/001872008x312251
6. Wobbrock, J.O., Kane, S.K., Gajos, K.Z., Harada, S., Froehlich, J.: Ability-based design. ACM Trans. Accessible Comput. **3**(3), 1–27 (2011). https://doi.org/10.1145/1952383.1952384
7. Edwards, A.D.: Computers and people with disabilities. In: Extra-Ordinary Human-Computer Interaction, pp. 19–43. Cambridge University Press, December 1995
8. Iniesto, F., Rodrigo, C.: Strategies for improving the level of accessibility in the design of MOOC-based learning services. In: 2016 International Symposium on Computers in Education (SIIE) (2016). https://doi.org/10.1109/siie.2016.7751841
9. Web Content Accessibility Guidelines (WCAG) https://www.w3.org/WAI/intro/wcag
10. Sanchez-Gordon, S., Luján-Mora, S.: Research challenges in accessible MOOCs: a systematic literature review 2008–2016. Universal Access in the Information Society (2017). https://doi.org/10.1007/s10209-017-0531-2

11. Bohnsack, M., Puhl, S.: Accessibility of MOOCs. In: Miesenberger, K., Fels, D., Archambault, D., Peňáz, P., Zagler, W. (eds.) ICCHP 2014. LNCS, vol. 8547, pp. 141–144. Springer, Cham (2014). https://doi.org/10.1007/978-3-319-08596-8_21

12. Rodriguez-Ascaso, A., Roldán Martínez, D., Raffenne, E., Buendía García, F., Boticario, J.G., Montandon, L., Santos, O.C.: Accessible lifelong learning at higher education: outcomes and lessons learned at two different pilot sites in the EU4ALL project. JUCS J. Univ. Comput. Sci. 18(1) (2012). https://doi.org/10.3217/jucs-018-01-0062

13. Sánchez Gordón, S., Luján Mora, S.:. Adaptive content presentation extension for open edX. Enhancing MOOCs accessibility for users with disabilities. In: ACHI 2015, pp. 181–183 (2015)

14. World Health Organization: International Classification of Functioning, Disability and Health (ICF). World Health Organization, Geneva (2001)

15. Brooke, J.: SUS-A quick and dirty usability scale. Usability Eval. Indus. 189(194), 4–7 (1996)

16. Van Selm, M., Jankowski, N.W.: Conducting online surveys. Qual. Quant. 40(3), 435–456 (2006). https://doi.org/10.1007/s11135-005-8081-8

17. Vallerand, R.J.: Toward a hierarchical model of intrinsic and extrinsic motivation. Adv. Exp. Soc. Psychol. 29, 271–360 (1997). https://doi.org/10.1016/s0065-2601(08)60019-2

18. Lee, Y., Lee, J., Hwang, Y.: Relating motivation to information and communication technology acceptance: self-determination theory perspective. Comput. Hum. Behav. 51, 418–428 (2015). https://doi.org/10.1016/j.chb.2015.05.021

19. Roca, J.C., Gagné, M.: Understanding e-learning continuance intention in the workplace: a self-determination theory perspective. Comput. Hum. Behav. 24(4), 1585–1604 (2008). https://doi.org/10.1016/j.chb.2007.06.001

20. Dupuy, L., Consel, C., Sauzéon, H.: Self-determination-based design to achieve acceptance of assisted living technologies for older adults. Comput. Hum. Behav. 65, 508–521 (2016). https://doi.org/10.1016/j.chb.2016.07.042

21. Bangor, A., Kortum, P.T., Miller, J.T.: An empirical evaluation of the system usability scale. Int. J. Hum. Comput. Interact. 24(6), 574–594 (2008). https://doi.org/10.1080/10447310802205776

22. Kizilcec, R.F., Saltarelli, A.J., Reich, J., Cohen, G.L.: Closing global achievement gaps in MOOCs. Science 355(6322), 251–252 (2017). https://doi.org/10.1126/science.aag2063

23. Zahed-Babelan, A., Moenikia, M.: The role of emotional intelligence in predicting students' academic achievement in distance education system. Procedia Soc. Behav. Sci. 2(2), 1158–1163 (2010). https://doi.org/10.1016/j.sbspro.2010.03.164

24. Iniesto, F., McAndrew, P., Minocha, S., Coughlan, T.: What are the expectations of disabled learners when participating in a MOOC? In: Proceedings of the Fourth 2017 ACM Conference on Learning @ Scale - L@S 2017 (2017). https://doi.org/10.1145/3051457.3053991

Gamification in Inclusive eLearning

Yasmin Patzer[(⊠)], Nick Russler, and Niels Pinkwart

Humboldt-University Berlin, Unter den Linden 6, 10099 Berlin, Germany
patzer@informatik.hu-berlin.de
https://cses.informatik.hu-berlin.de/en/

Abstract. The usage of gamification elements in learning contexts is getting more and more attention, as it can help increase learners' motivation. Nevertheless accessibility and inclusion are seldom considered yet. In this paper an inclusive gamification concept for an eLearning course is presented. The main target group are people with poor basic education in hospitality industry. The developed gamification concept has been tested in a first small pilot study.

Keywords: Gamification · eLearning · Inclusion

The awareness of the importance of inclusion all over society has been increasing over the last years. One big milestone on the way to inclusion is the UN convention on the rights of persons with disabilities. It includes the access to education, no matter what the limitations of a person are. As the importance of eLearning in educational contexts is increasing as well, accessibility and inclusion are requirements that need to be fulfilled here as well. Gamification elements are used increasingly in learning environments to support learner motivation. There are also already some ideas and research on designing for accessible gamification, but not yet in combination with inclusive eLearning. This paper addresses this research gap.

There is a lot of research on inclusion, eLearning and gamification, but not on the combination of all three of them. Inclusive eLearning is a yet rarely researched field with just a few authors' publications [1,2]. Publications on gamification and accessibility are also rare [3]. There are some, which combine those two but rather with a focus on how to use gamification to spread accessibility [4] than on how to make gamification accessible. There are also some publications on how gamification can be used in socio-technical systems that realize different levels of accessibility, such as [5–7]. Yet, as argued, these approaches do not consider the specific requirements of eLearning scenarios.

In cooperation with KOPF, HAND + FUSS and Arbeit und Leben Berlin-Brandenburg (DGB/VHS), we designed and developed an eLearning course for people with poor basic education. The course is technically based on the inclusive eLearning platform LAYA [2]. As part of this research, we technically integrated accessible gamification elements in this platform.

© The Author(s) 2018
K. Miesenberger and G. Kouroupetroglou (Eds.): ICCHP 2018, LNCS 10896, pp. 154–158, 2018.
https://doi.org/10.1007/978-3-319-94277-3_26

In the course a sequence of videos guides the learner and builds up a realistic story setting in a hotel. Aim of the course is to improve the learners' basic literacy focused on requirements of the hospitality industry. This is addressed by ten different exercises on IT-topics. These exercises are offered on three different levels of difficulty targeting different levels of reading, writing and media literacy skills. To increase the motivation during this learning process gamification elements are included. The gamification concept for this course [8] embeds the learning into a story with characters and tasks and makes the learner the protagonist. Good performance and challenging exercises are rewarded with trophies and badges, which the learner collects throughout the whole course.

Fig. 1. In-between-page

Following the collection pattern learners collect badges for each solved exercise. The colour of the badges depends on the level of difficulty: bronze for easy, silver for medium and gold for difficult. Related to the exercise content each exercise has an own pictogram shown on its' badges. In Fig. 1 for instance the learner receives a bronze badge for the phishing mail exercise. It is accompanied by the sentence "You have solved the exercise phishing mail correctly". Like the badge colour itself, the text depends on the level of difficulty.

Besides badges learners can collect trophies. The upper part of Fig. 1 shows a trophy with the above text "Wow, you have already solved three exercises without mistakes!". Trophies are not dependent of single exercises but of solving exercises on the first try. There are three different trophies for one ("PC-Knowledgeable"), two ("Power-User") or three ("PC-Professional") solved exercises without mistakes, with additional complimenting text. The laptop pictogram in the trophy, as well as the names of the trophies, is connected to the content of the course as a whole. The trophies themselves are a motivational prize for good performance. Suitable pictograms have been chosen for badges and trophies. To prevent an interruption of the learning process, the text is in easy language and also available as audio. A major requirement was to not create barriers by the in-between-page. Therefore trophies and badges follow the WAI-ARIA recommendations for informative graphics.

Another gamification element, that has been used in this course are recommendations to change the difficulty level of the exercises. These recommendations appear at the bottom of the in-between -page, if the learner solved two exercises without mistakes or was not able to solve two exercises in a row. He is then asked if he wants to increase or decrease the difficulty of the exercises. As illustrated in Fig. 1 the learner has the choice to follow the recommendation or not (and continue on the level that was set before).

After finishing the whole course the learner is presented the completion-page, where all the collected badges and the best received trophy are shown. Beneath each badge the name of the exercise is written, to simplify the relation between badge and exercise for the user. Furthermore, the learner gets congratulations for finishing the course and is additionally complimented for the number of exercises he performed without mistakes. If he did so for more than half the exercises, this is emphasized as well. This design follows the gamification principle "Designing for the Novice, Considering the Elder" [9]. At the bottom of this page is a button for restarting the course, in case learners want to repeat the course to collect badges on a higher difficulty level.

A small pilot study was conducted with nine participants, of whom five had poor basic education and four had no impairments. The focus on participants with poor basic education was chosen, as this is the main target group of the eVideo course. The other four participants were experts on technical development and design and therefore included in this first pilot. All participants were observed as they were using the course for at least 50 min. At the end of this practical sequence the completion-page was opened, although it was not possible to go through the whole course in 50 min. But as the gamification concept should be evaluated, users needed to see this page as well. Afterwards, problem centred guided interviews were conducted to enquire the participant's opinions on the course. They were asked about their usage of digital media and if they already had any experiences with eLearning or gamification. Most of the participants already knew gamification elements from games or learning games. Furthermore, the participants were asked about the different gamification elements in this course and what they liked or disliked about these. Except for one participant with no computer experience, who did not take notice of the trophies and badges during the course, all study participants liked these gamification elements and also the differentiation on difficulty. The recommendations on changing the difficulty were also perceived quite positively. Some users said that the question if they wanted to increase the difficulty made them feel confident. We also asked the participants if they would have liked a form of a social competition in the course - e.g. with high scores. Here the opinions varied. Some participants loved this idea and said they would have been even more motivated, while others stated that they were learning for their own progress and thus would not want to be part of a competition.

The results of the lessons learned during system development and of the small-scale pilot evaluation can be summarized as follows:

1. The adaptation of the included gamification elements and mechanisms has not been perceived as a barrier. It has either been perceived as motivating or was ignored.
2. The offer to adapt the difficulty level, based on an automatic assessment of the learner's performance, can be meaningful, motivating and effective in an inclusive eLearning system.
3. As impairments often come along with poor media skills, precognition of gamification principles cannot be assumed.
4. Independent of impairments or previous knowledge, gamification in form of social competition might be motivational, but should be optional.

Further studies with a more heterogeneous user bases are necessary to make sure that the course is as accessible and inclusive as possible. A question for further research could be if the positive perception of the tested gamification patterns differs for people with other impairments and needs. And if it does, what adaptations are necessary to make the gamification elements more inclusive?

References

1. Draffan, E.A., Wald, M., Dickens, K., Zimmermann, G., Kelle, S., Miesenberger, K., Petz, A.: Stepwise approach to accessible MOOC development. Stud. Health Technol. Informat. **217**, 227 (2015)
2. Patzer, Y., Pinkwart, N.: Inclusive e-learning - towards an integrated system design. In: Cudd, P., De Witte, L. (eds.) Studies in Health Technology and Informatics, vol. 24. IOS Press, Amsterdam (2017)
3. Johnson, D., Deterding, S., Kuhn, K.A., Staneva, A., Stoyanov, S., Hides, L.: Gamification for health and wellbeing: a systematic review of the literature. Internet Interv. **6**, 89–106 (2016)
4. Spyridonis, F., Daylamani-Zad, D., Paraskevopoulos, I.T.: The gamification of accessibility design: A proposed framework. In: 2017 9th International Conference on Virtual Worlds and Games for Serious Applications (vs-games), pp. 233–236. IEEE (2017)
5. Korn, O., Muschick, P., Schmidt, A.: Gamification of production? A study on the acceptance of gamified work processes in the automotive industry. In: Chung, W., Shin, C.S. (eds.) Advances in Affective and Pleasurable Design: Proceedings of the ahfe 2016 International Conference on Affective and Pleasurable Design, pp. 433–445. Springer International Publishing, Cham (2017). https://doi.org/10.1007/978-3-319-41661-8_42
6. Seaborn, K., Edey, J., Dolinar, G., Whitfield, M., Gardner, P., Branje, C., Fels, D.I.: Accessible play in everyday spaces: mixed reality gaming for adult powered chair users. ACM Trans. Comput. Hum. Interact. (TOCHI) **23**(2), 12 (2016)

7. Jent, S., Janneck, M.: Gamification für blinde und sehbehinderte Menschen. In: Burghardt, M., Wimmer, R., Wolff, C.,Womser-Hacker, C. (eds.) Mensch und Computer 2017 – Tagungsband, pp. 341–344. Regensburg: Gesellschaft für Informatik e.V (2017)
8. Russler, N.: Gamification in inklusivem E-Learning. Master Thesis. Humboldt-University Berlin, Department of Informatics (2018)
9. Zichermann, G., Cunningham, C.: Gamification by Design: Implementing Game Mechanics in Web and Mobile Apps. O'Reilly Media Inc., Sebastopol (2011)

Music Apps as Inclusive Engines? – A Spotlight into Practice

Imke Niediek[1,2(✉)], Marvin Sieger[1], and Juliane Gerland[2]

[1] University Siegen, Adolf-Reichwein Straße 2, 57068 Siegen, Germany
imke.niediek@uni-siegen.de
[2] FH Bielefeld, University of Applied Sciences, Interaktion 1, 33619 Bielefeld, Germany

Abstract. In this paper we present first findings from interviews with twelve experts from four different sub-fields of music education regarding their views upon challenges and chances of Apps and digital music-instruments in (inclusive) music education settings with students with and without disabilities.

Keywords: Music education · Inclusion · Music apps · Expert interviews

1 Introduction

In the field of inclusive music education digitalization is still not very popular. Although there are some projects exploring the potential for making music together, really few research is done in that area. In this paper, we present first findings of our initial research in the field of musical education with digital devices and music Apps in educational settings with young people with and without disabilities. Our research is situated within the project "be_smart" (engl. "Importance of specific music Apps for participation of young people with complex disabilities in cultural education") funded by Federal Ministry of Education and Research (Germany) (Funding line: Digitization in Cultural Education) and runs from Oct 2017 to Sept 2021.

2 Approach

Many teenagers with severe disabilities use electronic devices to cope with everyday life, like e-wheelchairs, environmental control or even smart home systems. In the field of arts and cultural education, however the use of digital devices is (still) not very common. Digital devices have to struggle against reservations of teachers and parents. They seem to be persist in the area of education at a broad level [1, 2].

Although there are numerous projects were young people with and without disabilities make music together, inclusive music education is usually based on conventional instruments [3]. This is a bit of a surprise because sensor-based digital music devices may offer potentials in new forms of creative expression and identity development [4, 5] and provide an interface design fittingly for people with special needs. Creative artists

© Springer International Publishing AG, part of Springer Nature 2018
K. Miesenberger and G. Kouroupetroglou (Eds.): ICCHP 2018, LNCS 10896, pp. 159–162, 2018.
https://doi.org/10.1007/978-3-319-94277-3_27

and performers have already recognized the potential of digitalization for their work and have utilized all kinds of electronic and digital devices for their branch.

Therefore it's a crucial part of the project to address and classify beliefs of music teachers in different music education settings. In the context of this paper we present findings from interviews with experts from four different sub-fields regarding their view upon digital music-instruments in (inclusive) music education settings. Inclusive settings are considered in this project as any kind of group or individual activities in which common ground differences projected by actors become to some extent suspended or (temporarily) irrelevant.

3   Methods and Methodology

With respect to previous observations we outlined four tentative subfields for the interviews: (A) inclusive cultural/music education projects where digital devices might be included, (B) experts on the adaption of digital devices for children and young adults with (severe) disabilities, (C) experts for music education for students with severe physical disabilities (without focus on digital devices), (D) experts regarding the use of digital devices with music Apps. The experts were selected through individual acquisition in the relevant networks, web research and personal recommendations. All experts have a certain urge to present their know-how and to voice their stance regarding their professional experiences, if approached adequately. The interview outlines are based on a consistent epistemic structure to un-cover possible conjoint dimensions, but are provided with customized questions to match the individual expertise of the particular interview partner. The question outlines are underpinned by the following dimensions: (1) culture/ cultural education (2) media (usage) (3) disability. Finally twelve semi-structured telephone interviews (three for each sub-field A to D) have been conducted, transcribed and analyzed. The sample and the interview outline were compiled acquire narration based information from gatekeepers and experts in the respective sub-fields [6]. Task at hand was to obtain exclusive and extensive statements, narrations and insights, based in the respective field and to get a grasp of the predominant cultural patterns of interpretation within. In the long run the goal is to ground a (saturated) middle range theory [7] which addresses the challenges and chances which go along with the use of digital music instruments in inclusive music settings.

4   First Findings

The tentative assumption, that there are certain reservations projected by parents, teachers and professionals in the field of music and cultural education towards digital devices in educational settings, can be confirmed by the findings from the interview material to a certain degree: Some of the references by the experts insinuate that some of the staff in music/cultural education tend to classify digital devices as "not appropriated for teaching matters". This finding seems to be especially true for interviewees of group (C). In cases of "severe disability" as a fundamental part of a professional context the "human" as mediator resp. as assistant seem to have a significantly different relevance, than in regular educational settings. Furthermore experts within the field of "App music" (D) indicate the common belief, that "mediation" and dissemination of knowledge, should be exclusively tied to the (analogue) hands of the educational staff. However, both findings have to be carefully examined via deep case analysis in the further course. It seems that these claims are underpinned by a more or less latent fear of losing the attention of the pupils, respectively the "exclusive" power of supervision in an educational setting.

On one hand there are clear-cut references that digital devices in educational settings are responsible for transporting potentially harmful content (primarily explicit content such as pornography or violence drenched stuff) into child´s room or classroom. This is a rather shallow, but nonetheless common and wide-spread claim. In the same category resides the belief, that digital devices are "un-social" because especially children and teenagers would tend to spend a lot of time on interacting with the device instead of paying attention to curricular demands or interacting with classmates. On the other hand there can be found a more subtle notion, which implies, that digital technologies could be utilized to steer/regulate educational settings entirely. This implication culminates ultimately in the ascription, that such technology has the potential to dissolve or annul educational settings as a whole. This solicitude is by far more latent, but seems to have a big impact on interpretations, ascriptions, narrations and beliefs: A coherent conclusion to this proposition is the concern that educational staff could become dispensable (digital devices as existential threat).

Beside the reservations interviewees also made observations that point to the great potential of digital devices for inclusive music classes: Especially in private music schools an open minded-ness towards digital devices can be found. Governmental regulations regarding curricular guidelines here apply just on a very basic level in comparison to public schools. Thus, some private music schools have already institutionalized to customize digital devices for musical purposes and to embed them into musical practice. There is currently a more and more widespread approach in music education noticeable to equip tablets with music Apps and supplemental extend the tablets with interfaces to match the requirements of (varying) individual needs. To a certain degree some of the experts concede, that this development is related to the competition of private music schools among themselves.

Furthermore, experts indicate that "inclusion" is not a goal that needs to be achieved in future, but already a reality in their field of work. Primary objective is to find a suitable instrument for the student. It would not be a fundamental issue, which instrument that is, nor if it's a "conventional" or "digital" instrument. Thus, following the narration of the experts it's first and foremost relevant, that one finds the right tool for musical self-expression. The criteria for "in group" membership (or inclusion) regarding the schools is thus for the main part dedication and musical talent/achievement. However, our findings indicate, that this "freedom" is foiled by a normative stance regarding what is considered to be "well formed" (or well played) music and by ascriptions regarding who is considered to be talented and who is not. Further research has to show if this normative stance works as a barrier against digital devices and music Apps as well as against full inclusive music classes.

5   Conclusion

Music as medium provides a potential for communication and interaction beyond the constraints of lexical organized language. The references made by the experts indicate, that if one wants to establish an adequate workflow it would be pivotal to customize a setting within two continua: The first continuum (or dimension) ranges from "basal" to "complex". This means on one hand to estimate what kind of inter-face/instrument is suitable for a person and on the other hand to estimate how "elaborated" the comprehension regarding the medium music is (skill level/ability). It seems obvious in this context that one has to pay attention to the implicit and explicit indications made by the particular individual. The second continuum comprises the spectrum of "individual" and "group" practice. Several of the experts refer to the necessity that for matters of "learning" respectively getting a "grasp" for an instrument the addressee needs to be granted phases of individual practice, action and the possibility of "group withdrawal". This would be as crucial, as phases of playing music in group settings.

The transitions within these continua as well as intersections are thus fluent and dynamic and this is in fact the crucial point which can be drawn from for (inclusive) educational settings in general. An educator would have to consider this dynamic relations, develop a grasp for "applying" them in an appropriated way and implement them in the first place by simply increasing the degrees of freedom in an educational setting. For this matter digital devices especially tablets and music Apps should hold the flexibility to utilize them for these kinds of settings.

References

1. Kranefeld, U., Heberle, K., Lütje-Klose, B., Busch, Th: Herausforderung Inklusion? Ein mehrperspektivischer Blick auf die JeKi-Praxis an Schulen mit gemeinsamem Unterricht (GU). In: Clausen, B. (ed.) Teilhabe und Gerechtigkeit, pp. 95–114. Waxmann, Münster, New York (2014)
2. Langner, A.: Kompetent für einen inklusiven Unterricht. Eine empirische Studie zu Beliefs, Unterrichtsbereitschaft und Unterricht von LehrerInnen. VS Springer, Wiesbaden (2015)
3. Gerland, J.: Inklusive Regel statt exklusiver Ausnahme? Inklusive Entwicklung von Musikschulen und Professionalisierung der Lehrkräfte. Üben & Musizieren, vol. 01, pp. 12–15 (2016)
4. Partti, H., Karlsen, S.: Reconceptualising musical learning: new media, identity and community in music education. Music Educ. Res. 12(4), 369–382 (2010)
5. Brown, A.R., Stewart, D., Hansen, A., Stewart, A.: Making meaningful musical experiences accessible using the iPad. In: Keller, D., Lazzarini, V., Pimenta, M. (eds.) Ubiquitous Music. Computational Music Science. Springer, Cham (2014). https://doi.org/10.1007/978-3-319-11152-0_4
6. Gläser, J., Laudel, G.: Experteninterviews und qualitative Inhaltsanalyse als Instrumente rekonstruierender Untersuchungen, 3rd edn., VS, Wiesbaden (2009)
7. Merton, R.K.: Social Theory and Social Structure, Enl edn. The Free Press, New York (1968)

Teaching the National Written Language
to Deaf Students: A New Approach

Laura Volpato[1]([⊠]) [iD], Marlene Hilzensauer[2] [iD], Klaudia Krammer[2], and Melanie Chan[2]

[1] Università Ca' Foscari, Dorsoduro 3246, 30123 Venice, Italy
laura.volpato@unive.at
[2] Alpen-Adria-Universitaet, Universitaetsstrasse 65-67, 9020 Klagenfurt, Austria
{marlene.hilzensauer,klaudia.krammer,melanie.chan}@aau.at

Abstract. Deaf people across Europe struggle to have equal access to written information as the main language of instruction in school is the spoken language. The "Deaf Learning" project (2015-1-PL01-KA204-016) aims at improving the above-mentioned situation by developing a face-to-face course supported by a Moodle course according to the needs of young deaf adults. Within the project, the partners developed a framework for lessons ranging from A1 to B2 (on the basis of the Common European Framework for Languages, CEFR) to improve reading and writing skills in the respective national languages. The teaching materials for level A1 consist of 30 lessons in pdf printable version, and 6 Moodle lessons. To make the course suitable for the very heterogeneous group of deaf learners, the structure of the lessons was designed so that teachers can adapt it to the needs of the deaf students. The Moodle lessons are kept simple and visual; they include sign language videos, images, and H5P interactive contents. The teaching materials have been tested in Italy for the main target group (17 participants aged 16–25 years) and in Austria for all other interested parties (3 participants aged over 30 years) through face-to-face lessons. The participants' feedback was incorporated into the materials.

Keywords: Sign language · Deaf education · E-learning · Inclusive learning
Bilingual approach

1 Educational Problems: The State-of-the-Art

As they cannot hear, deaf people are visually oriented and prefer to use the visual channel for communication. Each country has its own sign language(s)[1] and dialectal variants. The national sign language is the first language or the preferred one for many deaf people. However, they live surrounded by a hearing majority that mainly communicates through the national spoken/written language(s). In most European countries, spoken language is the language of instruction in schools – a language that does not meet the communication needs of deaf people. Lip-reading is very hard to do over extended periods of time and only 30–40% [7] of the information are visible on the mouth, i.e. deaf people

---

[1] A country can have more than one national sign language, as it can have more than one national written/spoken language.

© The Author(s) 2018
K. Miesenberger and G. Kouroupetroglou (Eds.): ICCHP 2018, LNCS 10896, pp. 163–171, 2018.
https://doi.org/10.1007/978-3-319-94277-3_28

have to guess most of the contents. Although international research shows the efficiency of the bilingual teaching method (sign language and written language) for deaf students, it is still rare in Europe [9–11]. When leaving compulsory school, deaf students often have large gaps in their national written language knowledge. This leads to the fact that deaf people do not have equal access to written information. That, among other things, reduces their chances on the labor market and leads to a low self-esteem.

In Italy as well as in Austria and in other European countries, even teachers and tutors for special needs are not specifically trained to teach deaf students (e.g., most have a very low sign language competence) [1, 10]. As a result, the educational plans, which should be tailored to the deaf individuals, are often limited and lack adequate methodological settings.

Depending on the type of school, the sign language support differs. In mainstream schools there is normally no sign language support; in inclusive classes, deaf students are provided with interpreting services only for a few hours a week and not for every subject; besides, they have to concentrate on the signing of the interpreter and they find it very difficult to take notes or participate actively in the lesson. There are too few interpreters and they would need a special training for most of the school subjects, especially in secondary and higher education. Even in most schools for the deaf, sign language support is limited, as mostly spoken language is the language of instruction.

These problems with teaching the national written language result in poor reading and writing competencies [2, 3, 5, 10, 13].

2   A Proposed Solution

To improve the above-mentioned situation, the "Deaf Learning" project (2015-1-PL01-KA204-0165; homepage: www.pzg.lodz.pl/deaflearning)[2] developed a face-to-face course supported by a Moodle course according to the needs of the deaf target group, namely young deaf adults aged between 16 and 25 years. All of the partners[3] have experience within the educational field of the deaf.

2.1   Structure of the Course

Within the project, the partners developed a framework for lessons ranging from A1 to B2 (on the basis of the Common European Framework for Languages, CEFR). The teaching materials for the A1 level were fully prepared (in a pdf printable version), including a Moodle course for the six A1 lessons of the first theme.

The course is divided into five themes/topics: Relationships, Sport and Free-Time, Money, Travel, School and Career. Each topic consists of six lessons, which have been

---

[2] "The European Commission support for the production of this publication does not constitute an endorsement of the contents which reflects the views only of the authors, and the Commission cannot be held responsible for any use which may be made of the information contained therein".

[3] The project consortium consists of five partners: Poland as coordinator; Austria, Italy, Lithuania and the United Kingdom.

planned by taking into account both the target group, with all its specific features, and the language teaching strategies currently in use for regular second language learners.

A lesson cycle was developed: it starts with the presentation of the new topic and ends with the assessment of that same topic and the introduction of the following one. One of the specific features of the course is that this proposed lesson cycle can be easily adapted to the needs of the deaf students, as they are a heterogeneous group of learners [6], whose initial language competence is very difficult to assess. Within this cycle, either the course modules can be placed in different order, or the teacher can spend more time on one module and skip another one. Sign language plays a crucial role in the education of most deaf students, even if they are at different competence levels: it is the only element capable of bringing deaf learners together, raising their interest and motivation. Therefore, the lessons follow sign-bilingual methods such as Purposeful Concurrent Use, Preview-View-Review and Translation [4].

2.2   The Supporting Moodle Courses

Nowadays Moodle has spread in all areas of e-learning, from language education to vocational trainings. This is one of the main reasons behind the choice of Moodle as the tool for the e-learning course. For the students who have already worked with Moodle it will be easy to use the "Deaf Learning" courses. The others will be able to transfer the experience they will gain here also to other contexts. In addition to this, Moodle has the advantage that it is relatively easy to handle, and it offers the possibility to include videos and interactive exercises in a much easier way than e.g. WordPress, which had been used in a previous project.

The Moodle courses are based on the materials developed for the face-to-face course. For deaf students, it is vital to keep the structure as uncluttered, simple and visual as possible. Sign language videos and images are provided wherever they are needed (with a focus on grammar topics and explanations). Moodle offers various possibilities of how to structure the course. For the Austrian version (Moodle version 3.4), a thematic structure was chosen.

The texts developed for the course had to be adapted and simplified to allow independent learning without the help of a teacher. Where possible, the visual attractiveness of the contents was improved by using H5P interactive contents like "Accordion" (e.g. for the different types of questions) and "Course presentation" (e.g. for different forms of greetings).

Students can try out what they have learned in the face-to-face course with interactive exercises (for the Austrian course, also done with H5P), e.g. identifying nouns or verbs in a text with "Mark the words". Most of these exercises are self-correcting and they give the students a visual feedback as well, e.g. they show which nouns/verbs were missed by highlighting them.

H5P also allows the use of videos within exercises. For example, the students can practice their vocabulary by first watching videos of signs in their native sign language and then writing down the respective word in the written language of their country.

3 Practical Impact

At the beginning, the course aims at introducing any new topic in sign language and at activating the written vocabulary related to the lesson. Slowly, the familiar code makes way for the unfamiliar one: the written national language. The second step is achieved through comparisons between the respective signed and written languages (contrastive method), pointing out the similarities and the differences between both systems. In order to test this approach, trial lessons were held in Italy and in Austria. While Italy focused on the main target group, i.e. young deaf people aged 16–25, Austria delivered the lessons to older deaf people (aged over 30). Since the final products of the project will be open access resources, we expect older deaf people to also benefit from them. Similarities and differences were observed during the trials in AT and IT.

3.1 Trial Lessons in Italy

In Italy, 11 lessons of 80–100 min were delivered to a group of 17 students. The lessons were divided into two main sessions according to the division in themes. Session 1 consisted of 6 lessons A1 level, theme 1 (Relationships). Session 2 consisted of 5 lessons A1 level, theme 2 (Sport and Free-time). 10 students aged 16–25 were involved in session 1; the lessons took place during school hours, hosted by the secondary Specialized School for the Deaf I.S.I.S.S. Magarotto in Padua. 5 out of the 10 students were not Italian but moved to Italy during their childhood or later. 9 students were involved in session 2; the lessons took place in the afternoon, after school hours, at the residential house of the above-mentioned school. 2 out of the 9 students were not Italian. All students were deaf or hard of hearing and they were all sign language users. The teacher was a hearing native speaker of Italian with very good sign language competence.

All partners agreed to use online assessment tools already available for (hearing) second language learners and proposed a list of such websites. The assessment of the Italian deaf students' competence in the national written language was attempted repeatedly because of two main reasons: the students' resistance against the idea of being assessed; and the failure of the feedback delivery system of the first website employed. One side effect of this situation was that results from two websites could be compared, showing whether the results were different or equal. Two different online language tests were administered[4]. From the first website only 3 out of 6 participants received the results (P1 = B1; P2 = A2; P3 = A2). From the second website, all 6 received their results: most of the respondents' competence in Italian showed to be higher than A2. In particular, the three participants who completed both tests and received proper feedback scored as follows: P1 = B1; P2 = A2/B1; P3 = A2/B1. Even if three participants are not enough to draw significant conclusions, the comparison between the first and the second assessment shows that the latter gave slightly higher results than the first one. It is

---

[4] Assessment session 1: http://www.torredibabele.com/it/Corsi_di_lingua_italiana/Test_on_line.html; assessment session 2: https://www.esl.ch/it/soggiorno-linguistico/tests-online/test-d-italiano/index.htm.

unlikely that the higher scores are the result of an actual improvement, given that one session is probably too short a time to trigger an increase in the language competence.

The lessons were delivered in written form through Keynote presentation and supported through Italian Sign Language (LIS) according to the sign-bilingual strategies of Purposeful Concurrent Use and Preview-View-Review [4]. Other materials which were employed are: an interactive smart board, portable white boards, a regular blackboard, pens, paper, and computers. After each lesson, the teacher noted down the duration of the lesson, the rate of attendance, which activities had been successful or unsuccessful, and some personal comments.

At the end of the second session, due to the gradual decrease in the rate of attendance, the students were asked for an interview, in order to find out the reasons of the attendance phenomenon. Only 6 students agreed to be interviewed. The questions investigated their likes and dislikes for the lessons, their preferences among the proposed activities, and their suggestions to improve the course. The interviews were carried out in LIS with the support of written text, and they were video-recorded.

All the important remarks collected through the trials and the interviews can be related to three main issues: lack of motivation, need for flexibility, and heterogeneity. Starting from heterogeneity, the group of learners has proved to vary extremely concerning the competence in both sign and written language. Some grammar elements typically included in the A1 level were not grasped by the learners assessed as B1, and vice-versa, higher-level topics were well mastered by students assessed as A2. Despite knowing from the existing literature [12, 14] which peculiarities are found amongst written Italian productions by deaf people, the grammar difficulties arose unexpectedly from different students at different times during the lessons. With the students being such a heterogeneous group, it was necessary to adapt the lesson to individual needs; for instance, the teacher had to spend some time individually with each student to revise previous topics. This required the teacher to show a great deal of flexibility. Finally, motivation proved to be the biggest obstacle to the learning process. As previously mentioned, most deaf learners struggle with the national language during their school years and they refuse to face it again, especially if they are in their last years of secondary school, when they already imagine a learning-free future. In order to foster their inner motivation, the partners agreed to interview deaf role-models who achieved high job positions and possess a good competence in the national written language. During the lessons, some strategies to raise motivation were used, such as: give the students more responsibility (e.g. assign specific roles in tasks); use their competitiveness in a positive way (e.g. language games in teams); and praise the students' efforts.

3.2   Trial Lessons in Austria

The trial lessons in Austria lasted from September 2017 to February 2018; all lessons of the first three themes of A1 were taught. The setting of the trial lessons, as well as the participants (number and age) were quite different from the ones in Italy. In Austria, the trial lessons took place at the Alpen-Adria-Universitaet Klagenfurt with three deaf participants. These participants were all co-workers at the university and competent sign language users. As mentioned before, most deaf people have problems with learning their written national language, regardless of their age. Although the main target group of "Deaf Learning" are young adults (16–25 years), those who are older and want to improve their national written language competence should not be excluded. Therefore, deaf co-workers who were older than 30 years offered to test whether the course content and the methods are appropriate for this extended target group. All three participants showed great interest in improving their written language competence.

As it was done in Italy, an online assessment task of written German competence was administered[5] before starting with the trial lessons. According to CEFR, all three participants showed a B1 language competence. The teacher was a hearing native speaker of German with very good sign language competence.

At B1 level, students are expected to be familiar with – at least – the basic grammar concepts and terminology (e.g. word classes, declination, and inflection) of a language. It can also be assumed that at this language level, students are able to read and understand the content of a text. As it turned out during the trial lessons, this was not the case[6]. Especially during the grammar module of the lessons, their self-confidence and threshold of frustration were rather low. They often struggled with the grammar terminology and the (grammar) content. After being taught German for at least 9 years in compulsory education (with spoken German as language of instruction), their grammar knowledge was shockingly low, which must be seen as the logical consequence of the respective teaching method. For example, they could mostly add the correct article to a common noun, but they were unable to use the correct declined forms of the articles. It must be noted that the problems of the deaf participants (declination, flection, word-order as well as a limited vocabulary) coincide with the problems described in the literature [2, 8, 13].

The limited vocabulary constitutes a major obstacle to gaining information from a text. As it turned out during the trial lessons, the participants had problems with reading a text and answering questions about it. At this language level (A1), the texts are very short and easy to understand, nevertheless the deaf participants were often unable to extract the relevant information from the text. Creating short texts on their own proved also a very difficult task for them. They clearly preferred exercises where they were asked to combine phrases or to put given words/sentences into the correct order. It was easier for them, when, before writing an actual text, they had the opportunity to experiment with role-playing. According to their feedback, understanding and writing a text was much easier for them this way.

What pushed their motivation was a positive competitiveness when they exchanged their work. While correcting each other's work, they also asked more questions than during the normal class.

The feedback of the deaf participants from the trial lessons was included in the development of the final version of the teaching materials. Overall, they liked the visual layout. In some cases, small alterations to exercises and/or texts were done by the course designers, based on the deaf participants' suggestions.

---

[5] The test did not include any listening or talking exercises (https://www.alpha.at/de/deutschlernen/einstufungstest-deutsch/).

[6] This shows that the language competence test that was used did neither capture the full range of their knowledge nor the respective lack of it.

3.3 Common Grounds and Differences Between Italy and Austria

It was interesting to compare the experience from the trial lessons in Italy with the one from Austria, as the age of the participants as well as the setting of the lessons were quite different.

First, the common grounds: both groups (in AT and IT) had a far poorer competence with regard to their written language than their hearing peers and exhibited a rather low level of tolerance towards frustration. Due to their education experience, they give up much easier than most of their hearing peers would. Both in IT and in AT the knowledge concerning the national written language differed between the participants. This is consistent with the international literature, which describes deaf students as a hetero-geneous learning group [6]. Some grammar themes from A1 were unknown to the participants, whereas they were quite familiar with themes from higher levels like B1. The teachers in both countries had to react flexibly to meet the needs of the different students - far more than when teaching hearing students.

Looking at the differences, it turned out that the motivation of the participants to attend the lessons was higher in AT than in IT. The explanation is quite simple: the Austrian participants had the advantage of being familiar with the teacher, they were able to attend the lessons during their normal working hours and at their working place, while the Italian students were busy with other school matters as well. The participants in Austria also had experienced the importance of a good written language competence in their lives – being aware of the consequences of the lack of it.

The trial lessons in IT and AT showed that there are some key facts for successful lessons with this learning group: it is very important to create a positive, welcoming and comfortable learning environment, more than with hearing students. They need the feeling of being "safe" and that making mistakes is an important part of the learning process instead of a failure on their side (as they remember from their previous school experience). The teachers should be able to flexibly adjust their teaching to the different knowledge levels of the students. This might imply to deviate from the prepared lesson plan as well as from the lesson cycle. It turned out that offering deaf students an active role and individual responsibility during the lessons as well as helping them discover what knowledge they already possess served well to awaken the interest of the partici-pants and to motivate them further.

4 Conclusion and Planned Activities

The challenge in this project was to create written national language courses, which took into consideration two peculiarities: first, they had to meet the learning needs of deaf students and second, they had to be suitable for "false" foreign language learners. In fact, deaf people have a certain command of their written national language – as it is the language of the majority and they learned it at school – whereas foreigners normally do not have this knowledge when beginning to learn another language. However, the language competence of the deaf students is mostly poor, which leads to the conclusion that the teaching methods in the schools are not at all suitable for those deaf students who use sign language as their first language. Based on this fact, the "Deaf Learning" project designed a structured course for teaching the national written languages of the five partner countries (i.e. English, German, Italian, Lithuanian, and Polish). The course takes into account the needs of deaf students and their preference for visually based learning. This course provides the target group, and all those who are interested in improving their competence in the respective national written languages, with an opportunity to work on their reading and writing skills, tailor-made to their needs and preferences. It is a crucial first step towards an equal access to education.

The further course of action will consist of different dissemination activities to promote the course in the project partners' countries. As mentioned above, many teachers of the deaf are not trained enough for this special learning group. It is therefore crucial to spread the information about this course and especially the course method amongst schools for the deaf, inclusive schools, and teachers of the deaf as well as the deaf themselves via national/regional deaf associations.

During the trial lessons, it turned out that the students would need a preparatory course to understand linguistic concepts like noun and verb as well as the different building blocks of written and signed languages. Therefore, the Polish coordinator of "Deaf Learning" will submit a follow-up project consisting of 18 e-learning lessons with signed videos and short assessment activities. The lessons will focus on both general language knowledge (e.g., what is language, what are language families, bilingualism, etc.) and on the aforementioned general concepts (e.g. how do languages express movement/activities).

References

1. Bertone, C., Volpato, F.: Le conseguenze della sordità nell'accessibilità alla lingua e ai suoi codici. EL. LE, vol. 1, no. 3, pp. 549–580 (2012)
2. Eisenwort, B., Vollmann, R., Willinger, U., Holzinger, D.: Zur Schriftsprachkompetenz erwachsener Gehörloser. Folia Phoniatrica et Logopaedica **54**(5), 258–268 (2002). https://doi.org/10.1159/000065198
3. Eisenwort, B., Willnauer, R., Mally, B., Holzinger, D.: Selbsteinschätzung und Wünsche gehörloser Erwachsener in Österreich bezüglich ihrer Schriftsprachkompetenz. Folia Phoniatrica et Logopaedica **55**(5), 260–266 (2003). https://doi.org/10.1159/000072156
4. Gárate, M.: ASL/English bilingual education (Research Brief No. 8). In: Visual Language and Visual Learning Science of Learning Center. Washington, DC (2012). http://vl2.gallaudet.edu/files/3813/9216/6289/research-brief-8-asl-english-bilingual-education.pdf. Accessed 18 Apr 2018
5. Holzinger, D., Fellinger, J., Strauß, U., Hunger, B.: Chancen Hörgeschädigter auf Eine Erfolgreiche Schulische Entwicklung (CHEERS). Eine Studie gefördert von der Gesundheitsabteilung des Landes Oberösterreich und dem Fond Gesundes Österreich (2006). https://www.barmherzige-brueder.at/unit/issn/sprachundtherapiezentrum/wissenschaft. Accessed 21 Mar 2018
6. Knoors, H.: Language use in the classroom: accommodating the needs of diverse deaf and hard-of-hearing learners. In: Diversity in Deaf Education, pp. 222–223 (2016)
7. Krammer, K.: Einblicke in das Leben einer 'Laut'-losen Minderheit. Gehörlose Frauen in Kärnten. Veröffentlichungen des Zentrums für Gebärdensprache und Hörbehindertenkommunikation, Band 14. Klagenfurt (2008). https://www.aau.at/wp-content/uploads/2017/11/zgh-veroeffentlichung-bd-14.pdf. Accessed 21 Mar 2018

8. Krammer, K.: Schriftsprachkompetenz gehörloser Erwachsener. Veröffentlichungen des Forschungszentrums für Gebärdensprache und Hörgeschädigtenkommunikation, Band 3. Forschungszentrum für Gebärdensprache und Hörgeschädigtenkommunikation, Klagenfurt (2001)
9. Krausneker, V.: Viele Blumen schreibt man "Blümer". Soziolinguistische Aspekte des blingualen Wiener Grundschul-Modells mit Österreichischer Gebärdensprache und Deutsch. Sozialisation, Entwicklung und Bildung Gehörloser, Band 3. Signum, Hamburg (2004)
10. Krausneker, V., Schalber, K.: Sprache Macht Wissen. Zur Situation gehörloser und hörbehinderter SchülerInnen, Studierender & ihrer LehrerInnen, sowie zur Österreichischen Gebärdensprache in Schule und Universität Wien. Abschlussbericht des Forschungsprojekts 2006/2007. Auftraggeber: Innovationszentrum der Universität Wien, Verein Österreichisches Sprachen-Kompetenz-Zentrum (mit Unterstützung der Abt I/8 des bm:ukk). Fassung 2 (2007). http://www.univie.ac.at/oegsprojekt. Accessed 21 Mar 2018
11. Swanwick, R., Gregory, S.: Sign Bilingual Education: Policy and Practice. Douglas McLean Publishing, Coleford (2010). https://doi.org/10.1080/13670050903474069
12. Trovato, S.: Insegno in segni. Linguaggio, cognizione, successo scolastico per gli studenti sordi. Raffaello Cortina Editore, Milano (2014)
13. Vollmann, R., Eisenwort, B., Holzinger, D.: Zweitsprache Muttersprache: Die schriftsprachliche Deutsch-Kompetenz österreichischer Gehörloser. Zeitschrift für Interkulturellen Fremdsprachenunterricht 5(2) (2000). http://tujournals.ulb.tu-darmstadt.de/index.php/zif/article/view/622/598. Accessed 21 Mar 2018
14. Volterra, V., Bates, E.: Selective impairment of Italian grammatical morphology in the congenially deaf: a case study. Cognit. Neuropsychol. 6(3), 273–308 (1989)

Towards an Open Authoring Tool
for Accessible Slide Presentations

Mirette Elias[1], Abi James[2(✉)], Steffen Lohmann[3], Sören Auer[4],
and Mike Wald[2]

[1] University of Bonn, Bonn, Germany
melias@uni-bonn.de
[2] University of Southampton, Southampton, UK
a.james@soton.ac.uk, mw@ecs.soton.ac.uk
[3] Fraunhofer IAIS, Sankt Augustin, Germany
steffen.lohmann@iais.fraunhofer.de
[4] Technische Informationsbibliothek, Hannover, Germany
soeren.auer@tib.eu

Abstract. Creating and sourcing accessible Open Educational Resources is a challenge. Although slides are one of the primary forms of educational resources, there has been little focus on what is required to make slides containing different media accessible and how to encourage authors to improve accessibility. This paper examines the components within slide presentations that impact accessibility and will evaluates six different approaches for encouraging authors to add accessibility issues. Authors indicated a preference for being encouraged and guided to resolve issues rather than allowing for automatic corrections.

Keywords: Open Educational Resources · OpenCourseWare
Slide presentations · Accessibility · Inclusive design · Slide authoring
SlideWiki

1   Introduction

Open Educational Resources (OERs) are openly licensed and freely available learning materials that can be used in e-learning contexts and beyond. One of the key advantages of OERs is that the license allows for the content to be reused, remixed, and repurposed [8]. Often, OERs are published on the Web in the form of OpenCourseWare (OCW), with resources organized into courses and complemented by tools for collaboration and evaluation. Learners may include those with disabilities who encounter barriers to their accessibility needs and preferences. These needs and preferences should be addressed by OCW systems that aim to be inclusive and accessible to all.

To ensure OERs are accessible, it is important to provide teachers and learners with disabilities with appropriate user interfaces (UIs) for reading, browsing, and authoring the materials. An OER can be represented in various formats,

© Springer International Publishing AG, part of Springer Nature 2018
K. Miesenberger and G. Kouroupetroglou (Eds.): ICCHP 2018, LNCS 10896, pp. 172–180, 2018.
https://doi.org/10.1007/978-3-319-94277-3_29

including text documents, slides, videos, and audio files. While considerable research has been conducted on the accessibility of individual media and text documents [11], one of the most common e-learning formats is slides for use in lectures and other teaching contexts.

Slides are created to represent information concisely with a structured layout in order to help learners easily recall knowledge. A slide *deck* comprises of a collection of slides which can make up a course, lecture, or any other form of presentation on a specific topic. One slide can be considered to be the equivalent to a paragraph of text in that it should convey a single topic or concept. However, whereas a paragraph usually only contains text, a slide can include different types of media, such as images, tables, audio, and videos. Slides are also widely used independently of a presenter, as they provide a readable and printable version of the content. Furthermore, they can be exported to other types of formats, such as static PDF documents or video slideshows.

Slides can pose particular accessibility challenges due to the frequent use of images, bulleted lists, and tables. In addition, the spatial layout of content on a slide is often used to convey information. The experience for a disabled user accessing these different types of content can be highly dependent on the quality of the accessibility information (such as the captions, audio descriptions, and 'alternative' text) used to annotate the slide. While some annotations can be automated, the authors of the slides are usually most suited to undertake this task, as they are the subject experts.

This work addresses the following research question: What accessibility annotations should be included in a presentation slide and how can authors be encouraged to undertake actions to improve the accessibility of their slide content?

This research is conducted in the context of the SlideWiki EU project[1], which involves the development of a large-scale accessible OCW platform for OERs. The platform provides a means for creating and presenting slides online, in HTML, where authors can collaboratively edit and share their content. This offers the opportunity for the OERs to be accessible to assistive technologies, which can be used by authors and learners with disabilities. It is therefore necessary that both the content and the platform conform with digital accessibility standards. In addition, as the platform provides a collaborative slide creation tool, the accessibility of the content must be maintained even when authors edit and create different versions of the slides. Throughout the project, feedback on the platform design and use has been provided by a range of organizations involved in trials. Our methodology is organized into four steps:

1. Define the main components of the slides, and the accessibility needs for each component, to enable the content to meet the relevant accessibility guidelines [4,5,7,9] and IMS Access For All (AfA) specification [2].
2. Identify which of these accessibility needs can be met through functionality within the slide creation tool and which will require action by content authors.
3. Identify approaches that can be used within a slide creation tool for ensuring authors undertake the necessary actions to ensure their content is accessible.

---

[1] https://slidewiki.eu.

4. Gather feedback from authors on prototypes of the approaches that could be developed to improve the accessibility of their slides.

2   Accessibility Requirements of Slides

As a first step to identify the accessibility requirements of slides, an analysis was undertaken of the relevant components and properties of slides and decks. A deck has three components: (1) meta-data, (2) outline, and (3) slides.

The *deck meta-data* defines the properties of a deck (e.g., language, date, topic). It also contains the *theme* defining the visual presentation of the content within the deck. Each theme uses Cascading Style Sheets (CSS) to set the font size, font type, font color, and background color. As the theme is used to set the visual elements of a deck, this can be used to manage accessibility by offering color and font combinations that meet accessibility guidelines. The default theme of the platform includes high contrast and common color combinations for those visual difficulties. The inclusion of additional meta-data concerning the accessibility of a deck and its content may also be useful for educators when searching for OERs. Such meta-data could be used to report decks that contain slides that have been checked for accessibility or to report the complexity of the text within the slides. This could be linked to the needs for learners to filter search results [6].

The *outline* refers to the structure and organization of the slides within the deck, which is important for users to be able to navigate through the slides and recognize the structure of the presentation using different assistive tools. Each slide in the index contains an ID and a name, which is human-readable when viewing the structure of the deck. The slide name is equivalent to a page or document title and is independent of the title used within the slide content. To meet accessibility guidelines, authors should be encouraged to give each slide within a deck a unique name.

A *slide* is the fundamental part of a deck; it can be composed of:

- The slide layout, which defines the location of the different content components within the slide and may also convey meaning.
- The slide content, which is made up of elements that may contain a heading, normal text (a short paragraph), a list, symbols and equations, tables, charts and images, hyperlinks, or embedded media such as a video.

A slide can only be considered to be fully accessible when each of the content elements within it meets the accessibility requirements for that type of media. In addition, the information indicated by the layout must be conveyed appropriately through the reading order and accessibility annotations. Predefined layouts, for example, with inputs boxes using predefined styles for the slide heading and a box for text and list content, can assist authors with managing the reading order if they are encouraged to use them. However, there is always a risk that authors will convey information through the layout (for example, if they use a number of components to create a diagram) and this will need to be described to readers who rely on non-visual access through accessibility annotations.

In order for the content created within the slide editor to be accessible, the following must be met: (i) comply with accessibility guidelines, and (ii) allow authors to annotate the content with additional accessibility information [1]. The first step taken to meet these requirements was to select an authoring toolbar that conforms to the W3C Authoring Tool Accessibility Guidelines 2.0 (ATAG 2.0) [3]. While such an authoring tool can generate accessible content, a review of the potential slide content elements identified six areas that would require input from the slide author, as outlined in Table 1.

Table 1. Accessibility requirements for the slide content elements

Slide content element	Accessibility added by the system	Author actions required to improve accessibility
Slide title	Set as heading using the respective HTML tag	Ensure that each slide has a unique title
Text box	Authoring toolbar creates appropriate HTML tags text styling, lists and hyperlinks	Ensure that lists and styles are added using the authoring toolbar
Image	Interface provided for adding *alt* text and captions to images	Ensure that the *alt* text is meaningful. Where multiple images are combined to form a diagram, the *alt* text should describe the diagram appropriately
Embedded content	An *iframe* can be accessed using the keyboard, alternative input devices and assistive technologies. An interface is provided for adding a title or caption for embedded element	Ensure that each *iframe* has a title and that the site provides accessible controls. If the content contains video or audio media, and it does not have closed captions and/or an audio description, then a transcript and description should be provided in the speaker notes or attached to the slide
Equations	Equations are embedded within slides as MathML	Ensure authors avoid adding equations as images
Tables	Tables are created as HTML, and an interface is provided for setting headers and adding a caption or text summary	Define which rows and/or columns are headers and provide a caption or text summary of the table

3   Approaches for Ensuring Authors Address the Accessibility Requirements of Slides

As part of an iterative, user-centered design process, six approaches were identified for encouraging authors to improve the accessibility of their slides:

1. **Require:** Require authors to address accessibility issues on each slide before they save their deck. Authors would be notified of accessibility issues and the actions they need to undertake to make their slides accessible before they can publish their slides as OER.
2. **Guidance:** Assist authors to make their content accessible as they create it. Authors would be presented with guides and hints on how to make their slides more accessible as they add content.
3. **Encourage:** Encourage authors to check and correct accessibility issues once they have created a slide. Authors would be informed of potential accessibility issues when they attempt to save a slide and be encouraged to address the issues.
4. **Rate:** Encourage authors to make their slides accessible by including accessibility as a factor in rating and search results. The number of accessibility issues would be considered as a factor in rating decks and ordering search results. Decks with the least number of issues would be rated higher.
5. **Crowd-source:** Encourage other users to improve the accessibility of slides in an attempt to crowd-source accessibility enhancements. Users could add accessibility information to other authors' decks. This would increase their prestige on the platform as they will have contributed content. However, their changes to the deck may not be as accurate as the annotations that would have been created by the original author.
5. **Automatic:** Attempt to automatically fix accessibility issues. Some techniques can be used to automatically improve the accessibility of slide content, but this may result in incorrect accessibility annotations being added to slides.

Each approach presents different advantages and disadvantages to authors and users who rely on accessibility conformance. This must be balanced against the goal of encouraging authors to create OERs, with the potential to be accessible through an efficient and satisfying user experience.

In order to establish which approach would be most effective to encourage authors to create accessible slides, a survey was distributed to lecturers and teachers creating content within the SlideWiki project. Each approach was explained in the survey with an illustrate mock-up. Authors were requested to rank each approach using a five point Likert scale. In addition, the survey included a question about how much time the authors were willing to spend on accessibility issues per slide, and a free-text question were provided for additional comments. Thirteen authors responded to the survey; their results are presented in Fig. 1.

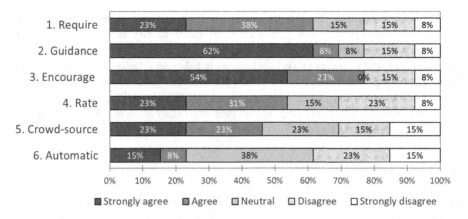

Fig. 1. Chart of the responses by slide authors to questions of whether they agreed with each proposed approach to improving the accessibility of slides.

The approaches "encourage" and "guidance" received the most positive responses from authors with 77% and 69% in agreement, respectively. This shows that many authors would like to be made aware of potential accessibility issues and would like information on how to address these issues. Responses for the "require" approach, which would ensure that authors addressed accessibility issues before publishing their deck, were also positive overall with 62% of respondents agreeing with this approach. Automatically correcting accessibility issues was the least popular approach with only 23% responding positively. Comments from authors indicated that they were concerned about the quality of automatic annotations and their content being altered without their approval. Similarly, there were mixed views on whether other users should be allowed to improve the accessibility of authors slides using the "crowd-source" approach, as concerns were raised about changes being made to authors' slides without their knowledge. Authors did not show a clear preference on whether decks should be rated on their accessibility.

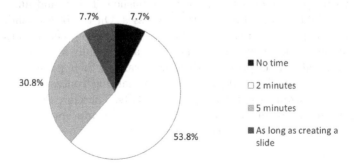

Fig. 2. Chart of responses by slide authors to the question "How long are you willing to spend on improving the accessibility of a slide?"

Figure 2 illustrates the amount of effort that authors would be willing to spend on accessibility issues. Authors were asked to say how long they were prepared to spend on fixing accessibility issues on a slide: (i) no time, (ii) two minutes, (iii) five minutes or (iv) as long as it takes to create a slide. More than half of the respondents indicated that they felt two minutes was a reasonable time to fix accessibility issues on a slide, and 38.5% were willing to spend longer than two minutes. Only one respondent indicated they were not willing to spend any time on addressing accessibility issues.

4   Discussion

Despite slide presentations being one of the most common forms of learning material, there has been little work on investigating how these can be made accessible to all users. Accessibility guidance has tended to focus on materials that form a linear document or web page. By considering common elements in slides, six areas were identified as requiring authors input (cf. Table 1). This is a more straightforward list of requirements for authors to review than WCAG2.0 [4], which contains at least 60 success criteria.

Responses from authors indicate that there is a preference to be encouraged to improve the accessibility of slides, as long as the process is efficient and not too time consuming. However, the two approaches that are preferred by the authors ("encourage" and "guidance") would rely on their judgment and goodwill to resolve issues.

The survey was small; it was clear that quality and content ownership as well as the usability of the accessibility approach would affect how likely authors were to engage with improving the accessibility of slides. Improving accessibility cannot be separated from usability. It is important to ensure that the tools for creating accessible content are efficient and effective, as poor usability could result in a lower usage and mitigate the objective of creating more accessible content.

Of particular interest were the concerns about the quality of the automatic accessibility annotations. Authors want to be able to check and confirm any amendments to their slides before they are published. This would limit the efficiency and usability gains of automated processes. On the other hand, the use of automatically generated image descriptions is increasing, and studies of their use in social media tools have shown that blind and visually impaired users tend to accept automatic descriptions if they are aware of their possible ambiguity [10]. However, the quality and provenance of learning content is particularly important when encouraging the adoption of OERs. Therefore, having a level of ambiguity within accessibility annotations may not be appropriate in a learning context and requires further investigation.

5   Conclusion

Encouraging authors of OERs and OCW to consider the needs of disabled learners and to meet accessibility requirements is vital for inclusion. Despite the wide use of slide presentations in education, few studies have considered the related accessibility requirements. This paper has reviewed the elements that make up slide presentations, and has determined which of these can impact the experience of users with accessibility needs. By providing a slide editing tool for creating accessible content, there are mainly six elements commonly used within slides that require the author to undertake actions to ensure the slides are accessible. Willingness to spend time fixing accessibility issues is increased if support is offered, as long as it is an efficient process. As a result of this work, it is intended that the SlideWiki platform will warn authors of potential accessibility issues and provide them with guidance as they create content. The authors' concerns about automatic correction of accessibility issues should be noted and future studies are needed to consider whether the impact of providing potentially inaccurate accessibility information benefits or hinders learners.

Acknowledgments. This research has been supported by the EU project SlideWiki (grant no. 688095).

References

1. How to Make Presentations Accessible to All. Web Accessibility Initiative (WAI) (2012). https://www.w3.org/WAI/training/accessible
2. IMS Access For All. IMS Global Learning Consortium (2012). https://www.imsglobal.org/activity/accessibility
3. Authoring Tool Accessibility Guidelines (ATAG2.0). WWW Consortium (W3C) (2015). https://www.w3.org/TR/IMPLEMENTING-ATAG20/
4. Caldwell, B., Cooper, M., Reid, L.G., Vanderheiden, G.: Web content accessibility guidelines (WCAG2.1) (2008). https://www.w3.org/TR/WCAG20/
5. Dattolo, A., Luccio, F.L.: A review of websites and mobile applications for people with autism spectrum disorders: towards shared guidelines. In: Gaggi, O., Manzoni, P., Palazzi, C., Bujari, A., Marquez-Barja, J.M. (eds.) GOODTECHS 2016. LNICST, vol. 195, pp. 264–273. Springer, Cham (2017). https://doi.org/10.1007/978-3-319-61949-1_28
6. Elias, M., Lohmann, S., Auer, S.: Ontology-based representation of learner profiles for accessible opencourseware systems. In: Różewski, P., Lange, C. (eds.) KESW 2017. CCIS, vol. 786, pp. 279–294. Springer, Cham (2017). https://doi.org/10.1007/978-3-319-69548-8_19
7. Accessibility requirements suitable for public procurement of ICT products and services in Europe. Standard 1.1.1 (2014–02), European Telecommunications Standards Institute, France (2014)
8. Hilton III, J., Wiley, D., Stein, J., Johnson, A.: The four 'R's of openness and ALMS analysis: frameworks for open educational resources. Open Learn. **25**(1), 37–44 (2010)

9. James, A., Draffan, E., Wald, M.: Designing web-apps for all: how do we include those with cognitive disabilities? Stud. Health Technol. Inform. **242**, 665–668 (2017)
10. MacLeod, H., Bennett, C.L., Morris, M.R., Cutrell, E.: Understanding blind people's experiences with computer-generated captions of social media images. In: Proceedings of the 2017 CHI Conference on Human Factors in Computing Systems, pp. 5988–5999. ACM (2017)
11. Teixeira, A., Correia, C.J., Afonso, F., Cabot, A.G., López, E.G., Tortosa, S.O., Piedra, N., Canuti, L., Guzmán, J., Sol, M.Á.C.: Inclusive open educational practices: how the use and reuse of OER can support virtual higher education for all. Eur. J. Open Dist. E-learn. **16**(2), 56–65 (2013)

Personalized Access to TV, Film, Theatre, and Music

A Preliminary Observation on the Effect of Visual Information in Learning Environmental Sounds for Deaf and Hard of Hearing People

Yuu Kato, Rumi Hiraga$^{(\boxtimes)}$, Daisuke Wakatsuki, and Keiichi Yasu

Tsukuba University of Technology, Amakubo 4-3-15, Tsukuba 305-8520, Japan
rhiraga@a.tsukuba-tech.ac.jp
http://rhiraga.info

Abstract. Environmental sounds (ES) give us fundamental information about the world around us and are essential to our safety as well as our perception of everyday life. With improvements in noise reduction techniques, hearing aids and cochlear implants show better performance in the understanding of speech by deaf and hard of hearing (DHH) people. On the other hand, DHH children have little chance to learn ES. We are developing an ES learning system with visual information so that those with severely handicapped children could enjoy learning ES. In this paper, we describe a preliminary observation of including visual information as well as sound in learning ES.

Keywords: Environmental sound · Visual information
Hearing-impaired people

1 Introduction

Deaf and hard of hearing (DHH) people learn to understand speech if they have opportunities to learn "sound". Though speech has been the focus of sound for DHH, we are surrounded by non-speech sounds such as music and environmental sound (ES) in everyday life. There are many DHH who like music and even professional musicians with hearing impairment. On the other hand, few DHH have studied ES in their childhood, although ES can convey much information. We predict an approaching earthquake by sensing rumbling, we stop walking or change direction to avoid an approaching car, and we feel the high summer through the sounds of cicadas. These so-called ES are the keys to deciding our actions and give us a taste of everyday life. In other words, if DHH do not recognize ES well, they cannot react appropriately to warning sounds or might feel less affected by or isolated from their environment.

Many researchers work on speech, both in analysis and synthesis fields, and practical use has been made of many results. Thus, the performance of cochlear implants (CI) and hearing aids (HA) is getting better in terms of understanding

© Springer International Publishing AG, part of Springer Nature 2018
K. Miesenberger and G. Kouroupetroglou (Eds.): ICCHP 2018, LNCS 10896, pp. 183–186, 2018.
https://doi.org/10.1007/978-3-319-94277-3_30

speech. This implies that CI and HA are well adapted to listening to speech by eliminating sounds other than speech as noise. Different from music, which can be approached by DHH themselves, ES have received less interest from DHH. Among the few research results about ES and DHH, most of them are on ES recognition by CIers [1,2].

We, including a deaf person as an author, understand the importance of ES and developed an ES learning system for hard of hearing children [3]. Though the system was well appreciated by hard of hearing children and their teachers and parents, it was not good enough for the profoundly deaf because the learning was only with sounds. We are going to extend the system by involving visual information of ES so that deaf children as well as other hard of hearing children who wear CI or HA that have high performance in terms of avoiding sounds other than speech can use it to learn ES.

As a preliminary study to see the effect of visual information in learning ES, we conducted an experiment. Although we could not conclude the effectiveness of visual information in learning ES, participants appreciated the visual information. We could see the effectiveness of learning ES in identifying ES. We were also able to understand the importance of contents and the way to visualize them for ES learning.

2   Method

Material: We chose 59 ES on the basis of previous research [4] for an identification test. We used sounds from commercial CDs and from free sources. As visual information, we used waveforms of the sounds.

Participants: We asked two sensorineural and congenital deaf college students (both aged 21, M: 2, using hearing aids in both ears) to participate in the experiment. We call them S1 and S2.

Procedure: (1) A participant takes an ES identification test. (2) We measure the minimum sound pressure (MSP) of the ES by the participant. (3) The participant learns the ES. (4) MSP measurement. (5) Identification test. (6) Subjective evaluation.

Among the un-identifiable sounds, 20 sounds were chosen randomly for learning. Half of them were presented with visual information during the learning. We call the learning only with sound the A-method (A) and that with both sound and visual information the AV-method (AV). A participant could learn an ES for up to 15 min or quit learning it if he was confident in recognizing the ES.

MSP was recorded when a participant understands a proposed ES. We define MSP as the minimum sound pressure level to understand a sound, not only recognize the sound. In order to measure MSP of a sound, a participant is told the name of the sound, listens to the sound whose sound pressure level increases from smaller to larger, and then notifies us that he understands the sound. The sound pressure level of the participant's notification is the MSP. A lower MSP implies that a participant could recognize the ES with less listening effort.

3 Results

Table 1 shows the results of the identification tests, MSP, and the elapsed time for learning an ES. The MSP difference and elapsed learning time are the averages of ten ES in each of the learning methods. If the MSP difference before and after learning (subtracting the MSP value of after learning from that of before learning) is less than zero, it implies that a participant could recognize the sound after learning it with less effort. There were no significant differences in the MSP difference in both methods by both participants by t-test. There were no significant differences in the elapsed learning time in both methods by both participants by t-test either.

Table 2 shows ES that were identified after learning. An asterisk shows that the MSP after learning was the smallest among the learned ES. Double asterisks show that the elapsed learning time was the shortest among the learned ES.

The free comments described by the participants are as follows.

- S1: Waveforms help me understand the features of a sound.
- S2: I had less of a burden in learning with the AV-method than with the A-method.

Table 1. Results of ES learning experiment. Numbers after '/' are those of ES used in identification tests.

		S1	S2
Num. of identified ES before learning		5/59	7/59
MSP difference before and after learning (dB)	A	2.15	−2.23
	AV	−1.98	−0.36
Elapsed learning time (seconds)	A	93.3	43.6
	AV	71.4	48.7
Num. of identified ES after learning	A	3/10	4/10
	AV	2/10	4/10

Table 2. Identified ES after learning. *: the MSP after learning was the smallest. **: the elapsed learning time was the shortest.

	S1	S2
A	Glass breaking, Toilet flushing, Ice cubes into glass	Jackhammer, Horse neighing, Bowling strike, Sneezing
AV	Car horn*, Pool balls colliding	Toilet flushing*, Clearing throat**, Clapping, Blowing nose

4 Discussion

There were no differences in learning effects in terms of MSP and elapsed learning time between the two methods. One possible reason for the lack of differences between the two learning methods is the choice of contents to show and their visualization. Solely showing a waveform was not good enough for learning unidentified ES. On the other hand, the participants subjectively appreciated the AV-method, as shown in their free comments.

As shown in Table 2, some of the identified ES after learning were learned with the shortest time and with the smallest MSP. These ES are learned by the AV-method. Besides the participants' subjective opinions of preference to the AV-method, it indicates the possibility of the AV-method giving the smaller burden to learn ES for DHH, especially deaf people.

A simple calculation shows the effectiveness of ES learning. Since S1 could identify 25% of un-identified ES after learning (5 of all 20 learned sounds), if he learned all 54 un-identified sounds, then he could expect to identify 13 more sounds after learning. Similarly, S2 could identify 40% of un-identified ES after learning, and he could expect to identify 21 more sounds after learning.

These results suggest that DHH could improve their understanding of ES by learning them. Thus, we are going to continue exploring better visualization on the basis of sound analysis and develop an ES learning system. As ES visualization for learning is currently possible through recent sound analysis and visualization research, the ES learning system proposed by a DHH herself will be an embodiment of an assistive technology from the view of a deaf person.

Acknowledgments. This work was supported by JSPS KAKENHI Nrs. JP2628001, JP15K01056, JP15K1614, and the Sasakawa Scientific Research Grant from the Japan Science Society.

References

1. Shafiro, V., Gygi, G., Cheng, M.Y., Vachhani, J., Mulvey, M.: Perception of environmental sounds by experienced cochlear implant patients. Ear Hear. **32**(4), 511–523 (2011)
2. Looi, V., Arnephy, J.: Environmental sound perception of cochlear implant users. Cochlear Implants Int. **11**(4), 203–227 (2010)
3. Hiraga, R., Kato, Y., Matsubara, M., Terasawa, H., Tabaru, K.: A learning system for environmental sounds on tablets: toward a teaching resource for deaf and hard of hearing children. In: Proceedings of the Conference on Universal Language Design, pp. 310–314 (2016)
4. Shafiro, V.: Development of a large item environmental sound test and the effects of short-term training with spectrally degraded stimuli. Ear Hear. **29**(5), 775–790 (2008)

Implementation of Automatic Captioning System to Enhance the Accessibility of Meetings

Kosei Fume[(⊠)], Taira Ashikawa, Nayuko Watanabe, and Hiroshi Fujimura

Corporate Research and Development Center, Toshiba Corporation,
1, Komukai-Toshiba-cho, Saiwai-ku, Kawasaki 212-8582, Japan
kosei.fume@toshiba.co.jp

Abstract. In terms of information accessibility tools for hearing-impaired people, in order to understand meetings, expectations for real-time captioning utilizing speech recognition technology are increasing, from manual handwritten abstracts. However, it is still difficult to provide automatic closed captioning with a practical level of accuracy stably, without regard to various speakers and content. Therefore, we develop a web-based real-time closed captioning system that is easy to use in contact conferences, lectures, forums, etc., through trial and feedback from hearing-impaired people in the company. In this report, we outline this system as well as the results of a simple evaluation conducted inside and outside the company.

Keywords: Automatic speech recognition · Captioning
Information accessibility · Meeting support systems

1 Introduction

With the progress of speech recognition technology in recent years, the accuracy of speech recognition has improved. In addition, the applications and uses of speech recognition technology have been expanding [4,11]. One such application is the expectation for automatic captioning as an information accessibility tool [1]. The application consists of recognizing the speaker's voice in real time in classes and lectures at a school, meetings in the company, business contacts, etc. and displaying the closed caption on a handheld tablet or the equipment installed in the room [2,10,12]. Until now, note-taking and abstract writing have been provided as a general guarantee of information accessibility for hearing-impaired persons. However, due to the fact that conventionally, information accessibility has been guaranteed and provided as a service by volunteers, NPO organizations, or specialized skills providers, there are constraints on the time and place, as well as for the service receiving side. It was not possible to ignore these constraints and it was difficult to provide sufficient services to people in need in the required scenarios.

K. Miesenberger and G. Kouroupetroglou (Eds.): ICCHP 2018, LNCS 10896, pp. 187–194, 2018.
https://doi.org/10.1007/978-3-319-94277-3_31

2 Background

In actual usage scenarios, there are many variations in the contents of an utterance, speaker, and speech style, even in the scenario of information transmission in classes or enterprises. In these various situations, it is very difficult to stably achieve practical-level recognition accuracy. While there are such technological difficulties, as a social request, the so-called "Act for Eliminating Discrimination against Persons with Disabilities" has been enforced since April 2016 in Japan, and rational consideration of these guidelines is required as a foundation.

In view of these circumstances, we conducted a questionnaire survey of 52 of our hearing impaired employees for the purpose of identifying problems as well as their requirements in places of business, such as meetings, that are indispensable to the completion of their daily tasks. As a result, I would like to try using it by all means (5 out of 5 stages), preferably would like to use (4 out of 5 stages), slightly want to use (3 out of 5 stages) was found to be over 80%. However, in disability grade 6, we wanted to act positively and scores of (5 and 4) remained at about 40%. In fact, the degree of expectation varied depending on the difference in grades. In terms of the difficulties often encountered at meetings, there are many items such as not understanding details and terms (77%), not understanding slight remarks or comments (83%), which are listed regardless of the degree of disability. However, there were also issues with not knowing the topic of an answer in addition to not knowing only the detail of the answer. This was found to be present at a ratio of about 20% from the 1st to 3rd grade, respectively.

3 Basic Concept of Automatic Captioning System

Based on the results of the questionnaire, the expectations for speech recognition are high, and real time subtitles are required. In particular, in information sharing places where time is limited mainly by hearing people, guaranteeing information accessibility tends to be forgotten. As a method embodying the concepts corresponding to this, we decided to verify the concrete functional specifications and validity through a lean start-up development method through use by the parties and stakeholders in regular business.

3.1 Target Scenes

The usage scenario assumes opportunities for providing information such as lectures and reporting meetings, etc., for information transmission within organizations such as companies and schools. As can be seen from the results of the questionnaire in the former stage, such usage scenarios are often indispensable in daily activities, but guaranteeing information accessibility for the disabled is often lost. Even in such a situation, the system itself can be easily set up directly by the disabled person or the speaker. In fact, the speaker realizes the provision of the subtitle service only with the burden of using an on-the-spot microphone.

3.2   Use Cases

In order to make it easy to use daily, it was implemented as an extension of a business-use PC and basic information was provided via a web application in Fig. 3. End users can view subtitles by loading a Web browser. In addition, by connecting a microphone to the PC, it is possible to capture the voice of the speaker. Furthermore, by using a general server/client configuration, the updating of the acoustic models and language models necessary for speech recognition, as well as in-house specialized terms and abbreviations, proper nouns, etc., can be collectively managed on the server-side.

Therefore, even as an end user, regardless of the equipment or location, the caption function in the same environment can be used if it is an in-house accessible PC. In addition, resources, such as acoustic models and user dictionaries, once created are shared in-house and can also be reused.

3.3   Automatic Speech Recognition Engine

This research attempts to improve accuracy by using the LSTM - CTC acoustic model [9] which simultaneously identifies phonemes, fillers, and phrases at the same time. In addition, the proposed Web application itself serves as the foundation, and it plays the role of collecting actual voice data directly connected to in-house tasks. In so doing, it is possible to disperse and prepare manually-required correct data creation work quickly.

3.4   Examination of User Interface

As for the subtitle presentation, given that it is a system to be used on a daily basis, it is important for the end user to make it intuitive, free from confusion, and to present captions that are easy to see.

Based on hearings at University etc., in addition to following the basic screens of white letters with a black background (Fig. 1) provided with general high contrast in subtitle presentation, other intentional displays from the hearing-impaired or non-speaker side take into consideration the requirement for an annotated display for the viewer. Therefore, an interactive screen was prepared (Fig. 2). These display styles can be changed at any time by the end user viewing subtitles by switching tabs as necessary.

In the interaction view in this proposal, the speech balloon is displayed so that the contents being corrected can be seen in real time. In manual typing, means for using cooperative work [6,7] and crowdsourcing [8] are proposed recently, and this system provides an interface with affinity that can be linked with such approach.

Also, regarding character error correction, unlike English phonetic characters, there is difficulty unique to Japanese which is ideogram. For example, pronunciation of "KA-ki" has an ambiguity as it may indicate the meaning of oysters, summer, floral or firearms.

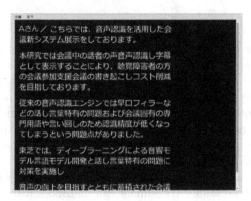

Fig. 1. Presentation type caption display

Therefore, in speech recognition, it is necessary not only to display the recognized phoneme but also to display the formatted Kana-Kanji sentence to the end user by considering the context before and after the word using natural language processing.

Furthermore, it takes time and effort to correct misrecognition by a corrector [3]. It is necessary to specify the correction range and input it by typing in consideration of the Kana-Kanji conversion result. In this method, this problem is addressed by enabling the use of UI with a small number of correction steps such as tablet and pen operation.

It is also available to allow users to easily create correspondence tables of unknown words and readings as user dictionaries. Therefore, even if the correct word can not be recognized during the conference or in the lecture, if the corrector registers the correct word and the reading set at that time, the correct recognition result can be output using the dictionary after that.

4   Lean Startup Development Based on In-House Trials

We constructed the above approach and asked hearing impaired people in the company to attempt to use the proposed system at conferences with the main purpose of communicating information within the business.

4.1   Improvement Based on User Feedback

In view of user feedback, the following functions which are highly effective and judged relatively easy to implement are subjected to function expansion and improvement at any time during the publication period. The functions are display recording status, display of sound level indicator, display the name of the audio device used for input, guidelines for using microphone, and user word registration function.

4.2 Analysis/Consideration of Accumulated Statistical Information

In order to focus on the hypothesis verification of the original concept and the fundamental problem derived therefrom, an overview of the actual usage scenario and level of utilization was conducted in the company actually using this system from August 18, 2015 to September 28, 2016.

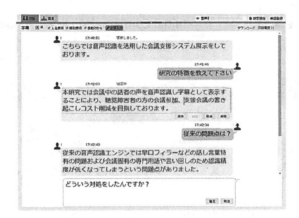

Fig. 2. Interactive type caption display

We execute an initial trial in more than 10 departments of our company where the hearing impaired staff and developers work. As a usage scenario, it was extremely useful at top-down conferences such as regular meetings and technical meetings once a week, especially when there are many participants. In addition, accumulated speech also had departments that exceeded 60 h, and it became clear that it was regularly used. On the other hand, if the presenter speaks without concern for microphone, there are many cases where the recognition precision is not good, or when other people talking by question and answer.

4.3 Prototype of Automatic Caption System for Lecture

In addition, we also focused on the fundamental issues in the scenes that end users actually use, following the trial results described thus far. In a busy business, the trouble of equipment preparation at startup and the height of the use hurdle due to a decrease in the speech recognition accuracy because of an incomplete sound setting or inadequate equipment setting could not be ignored. Practical correction means covering speech recognition errors and conveying accurate information as a tool guaranteeing information accessibility for the disabled.

In order to deal with these problems, we developed a system based on the configuration shown in Fig. 3 as a derived type of web system under internal verification.

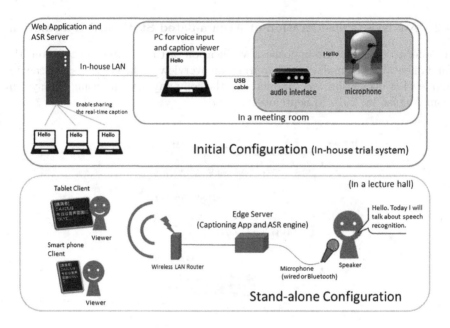

Fig. 3. Two types of system configuration

As a concept, it is a tool guaranteeing information accessibility for the disabled that allows end users to easily install, start up, use and close the system, while eliminating complicated operations as much as possible, avoiding setting fluctuations, all while being as simple and user-friendly as possible. Especially in lectures held at academic meetings and events, the environment is diverse and connections to external networks may become unstable in some cases. Even in the case where it was blocked from such an external network, it still was a system that could be easily used and separated.

4.4   Trial at External Conference

Furthermore, under the cooperation of the Information Processing Society in Japan, we tried the system for 2 days at the actual conference presentation venue.

Although it is common to use the Word Error Rate (WER) metric for speech recognition accuracy, usability evaluation has not been established yet and is being studied [5]. We conducted a sensory evaluation for paticipants by questionnaire. The paticipants who saw the caption and the results of 110 people who responded to the questionnaire are shown in Fig. 4.

In 5 grades, 5 is the best and 1 is worst. There are three perspectives, the mean on understandability is 3.15, the satisfaction level is 2.98, the necessity becomes 3.3. Although the necessity as guaranteeing information accessibility was recognized, many people found that it was a little short of the accuracy of subtitles, while on the other hand, there was an impression that it would be helpful to understand the content, although there was an error.

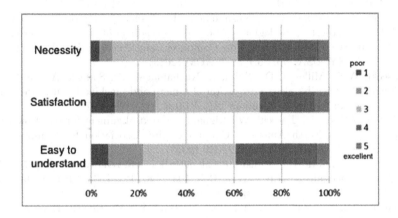

Fig. 4. Evaluation by conference participants

5   Conclusions

As a result of several trials, we believe that the proposed concept has been accepted as a means of realizing information accessibility for the disabled. However, sufficient consideration including the initial setting around the user is still necessary, and it is also obvious that it is difficult to implement unless departments divide understanding and actual work into tasks such as the registration of user word dictionaries, including operational maintenance.

Moving forward we will repeatedly test scenarios inside and outside the company, demonstrated our concepts against the above-mentioned issues, and improving system functions and GUIs based on feedback from actual use early on. Thus, we plan to refine it in order to transform it into a practical system.

References

1. Berke, L., Caulfield, C., Huenerfauth, M.: Deaf and hard-of-hearing perspectives on imperfect automatic speech recognition for captioning one-on-one meetings. In: Proceedings of the 19th International ACM SIGACCESS Conference on Computers and Accessibility. ASSETS 2017, New York, NY, USA, pp. 155–164. ACM (2017)
2. Fujitsu Social Science Laboratory Limited: LiveTalk. http://www.fujitsu.com/jp/group/ssl/products/software/applications/ud/livetalk/index.html
3. Gaur, Y., Metze, F., Miao, Y., Bigham, J.P.: Using keyword spotting to help humans correct captioning faster. In: 16th Annual Conference of the International Speech Communication Association, INTERSPEECH 2015, pp. 2829–2833 (2015)
4. Huang, X., Baker, J., Reddy, R.: A historical perspective of speech recognition. Commun. ACM **57**(1), 94–103 (2014)

5. Kafle, S., Huenerfauth, M.: Evaluating the usability of automatically generated captions for people who are deaf or hard of hearing. In: Proceedings of the 19th International ACM SIGACCESS Conference on Computers and Accessibility, ASSETS 2017, New York, NY, USA, pp. 165–174. ACM (2017)
6. Lasecki, W.S., Miller, C.D., Kushalnagar, R., Bigham, J.P.: Real-time captioning by non-experts with legion scribe. In: Proceedings of the 15th International ACM SIGACCESS Conference on Computers and Accessibility, ASSETS 2013, New York, NY, USA, pp. 56:1–56:2. ACM (2013)
7. Lasecki, W.S., Miller, C.D., Naim, I., Kushalnagar, R., Sadilek, A., Gildea, D., Bigham, J.P.: Scribe: deep integration of human and machine intelligence to caption speech in real time. Commun. ACM 60(9), 93–100 (2017)
8. Naim, I., Gildea, D., Lasecki, W., Bigham, J.: Text alignment for real-time crowd captioning. In: North American Chapter of the Association for Computational Linguistics, NAACL 2013, pp. 201–210 (2013)
9. Nasu, Y., Fujimura, H.: Acoustic event detection and removal using LSTM-CTC for speech recognition. IEICE Tech. Rep. 116(208), 121–126 (2016). (in Japanese)
10. NICT: SpeechCanvas. http://speechcanvas.nict.go.jp/
11. Ranchal, R., Taber-Doughty, T., Guo, Y., Bain, K., Martin, H., Robinson, J.P., Duerstock, B.S.: Using speech recognition for real-time captioning and lecture transcription in the classroom. IEEE Trans. Learn. Technol. 6(4), 299–311 (2013)
12. Shamrock Records Inc: UD Talk. http://udtalk.jp/

Detection of Input-Difficult Words by Automatic Speech Recognition for PC Captioning

Yoshinori Takeuchi$^{(\boxtimes)}$, Daiki Kojima, Shoya Sano, and Shinji Kanamori

Department of Information Systems, School of Informatics, Daido University,
10-3 Takiharu-cho, Minami-ku, Nagoya 457-8530, Japan
ytake@daido-it.ac.jp

Abstract. Hearing-impaired students often need complementary technologies to assist them in understanding college lectures. Several universities already use PC captioning. Captionists sometime input unfamiliar technical terms and proper nouns in a lecture inaccurately. We call these words "input-difficult words (IDWs)." In this research, we evaluate performance-detecting IDWs by using real lectures from our university. We propose a method to automatically extract IDWs from lecture materials. We conducted an experiment to measure performance-detecting IDWs from lectures by changing the interpolation weight of the language model. In this experiment, we used four real lectures. A high F-measure of 0.889 was achieved.

Keywords: PC captioning · Automatic speech recognition · Lecture
Hearing impaired

1 Introduction

To assist them in understanding college lectures, hearing-impaired students often need complementary technologies such as sign-language interpretation and PC captioning. Several universities already use PC captioning, and a system was developed that remotely transcribes the speech of a lecturer. Various groups have done work in this area. For instance, Kato *et al.* investigated the information required by remote captionists and ways to display that information on the monitors of the captionists [1]. In the approach they developed, content keywords are displayed on the monitor to aid the transcriber. Takeuchi *et al.* proposed a captioning system that inserts a mathematical formula image into the text. When a lecturer says a mathematical formula, the system extracts the corresponding mathematical formula image from the screen by using automatic speech recognition (ASR) and image processing technology and displays it on the monitors of the captionists. The captionists can input the mathematical formula by pressing a corresponding function key. Akita *et al.* proposed an automatic classification of ASR results and a presentation method based on the classification for efficient editing and quick presentation of caption texts [2]. They define

© Springer International Publishing AG, part of Springer Nature 2018
K. Miesenberger and G. Kouroupetroglou (Eds.): ICCHP 2018, LNCS 10896, pp. 195–202, 2018.
https://doi.org/10.1007/978-3-319-94277-3_32

the usability by syntactic correctness, errors, and redundant spoken expressions in ASR results and classify each unit of ASR results using hand-crafted rules and a machine learning framework. Gaur *et al.* introduced an approach that allows an audience or crowd workers to quickly correct errors that they spot in ASR output [3]. Their system allows the workers to simply type corrections for misrecognized words as soon as they spot them. The system then uses a keyword search to find the most likely position for the correction in the ASR output and stitches the word into the ASR output.

Because college lectures often deal with technical content, ideally, the captionists should understand the lecture content. However, it is sometimes difficult to secure such captionists, so volunteers who are nonprofessionals often perform PC captioning. If technical terms or proper nouns in a lecture are unfamiliar to them, they will sometimes input words inaccurately. We call these unfamiliar words "input-difficult words (IDWs)." With this in mind, Ikeda *et al.* proposed a system that detects IDWs by ASR and presents them to the captionists [4]. In our research, we evaluated the performance-detecting IDWs by using real lectures from our university.

There are some related works about detecting unfamiliar or unknown words by ASR. Qin proposed a method of automatically learning out-of-vocabulary (OOV) words in an ASR system [5]. It can recover the OOV word from speech. Illina and Fohr proposed an OOV word probability estimation using a recurrent neural network language model [6]. Mirzaei *et al.* proposed a method that detects difficult words listened to by using ASR errors [7]. In our work, while the IDWs were unfamiliar to the captionists, the lecturers knew those words very well. Therefore, we trained the language model of ASR to detect IDWs and display the detected words to the captionists.

When we performed PC captioning, the lecturer provided lecture materials (e.g., presentation slides, etc.) in advance. The captionists prepared PC captioning by using these materials. For example, a predictive conversion of kana and kanji was trained by typing IDWs in the materials. The preparation often takes a lot of time and is not easy. We propose a method of automatically extracting IDWs from lecture materials.

2   Detection of Input-Difficult Words

2.1   Extraction of Input-Difficult Words from Lecture Materials

We asked captionists to manually extract IDWs from the lecture materials. We used about 200 slides from four lectures, and captionists extracted about 600 IDWs. We divided the extracted words into two groups:

- technical terms and proper nouns,
- numbers and words including alphabetic characters.

The captionists were not familiar with the technical terms and proper nouns they encountered. Historically significant years were not easy to remember and input. In the case of Japanese captioning, the captionists had to change the input mode of the keyboard when they type words that include alphabetic characters. Therefore, we extracted those words as IDWs.

We used term frequency-inverse document frequency (tf-idf) to extract technical terms and proper nouns. Term frequency (tf) represents the frequency of the term that occurs in a document and is defined as follows,

$$\text{tf}(t, d) = \frac{n_{t,d}}{\sum_{s \in d} n_{s,d}}, \tag{1}$$

where the numerator $n_{t,d}$ is the number of the occurrence of the term t in document d, and the denominator $\sum_{s \in d} n_{s,d}$ is the total number of the word in document d. Inverse term frequency represents a measure whether the term is common or rare across all documents and is defined as follows,

$$\text{idf}(t) = \log \frac{N}{\text{df}(t)}, \tag{2}$$

where the numerator N is the total number of documents and the denominator $\text{df}(t)$ is the number of documents where the term t appears. Tf-idf is defined as a product of tf and idf,

$$\text{tf-idf}(t, d) = \text{tf}(t, d) \cdot \text{idf}(t). \tag{3}$$

Tf-idf represents how important the term t is in the document d.

Numbers and words including alphabetic characters are extracted by checking the range of the character code.

We extracted the IDWs from the presentation slide of the lecture titled "Information Security." The following IDWs were extracted as examples: "stateless protocol," "proxy connection," "vulnerability," "same-origin policy," and "cross-site scripting."

2.2 Adaptation of the Language Model in ASR

Generating a topic-dependent language model and combining it with a general-purpose, a large-vocabulary language model [8,9] is effective in improving an ASR rate. In order to obtain a topic-dependent language model, we collected web documents related to the lectures. We used the IDWs as web search queries. Then, we trained a topic-dependent language model with the collected web documents. Finally, the model was interpolated with the existing general-purpose conversational model to generate a model appropriate for the style of the lectures. We interpolated the language model with the following equation,

$$p_A(w|h) = \lambda p_G(w|h) + (1 - \lambda)p_W(w|h), \tag{4}$$

where p_A, p_G and p_w are the probability of an adaptive language model, a general-purpose conversational language model, and a web-based language model, respectively, and λ is the interpolation weight. When λ is higher, the probability of the adaptive language model is more affected by a general-purpose conversational language model. When λ is lower, it is more affected by a web-based language model.

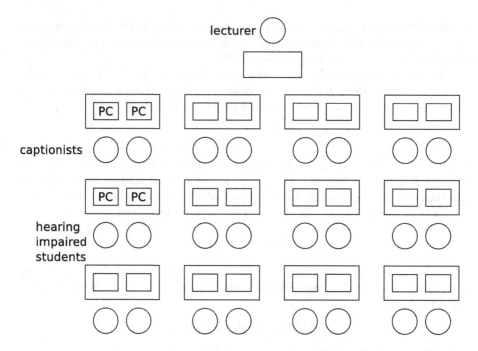

Fig. 1. Top view of the classroom: the captionists type what the lecturer says. The input text is sent to the hearing impaired students' PCs for them on read on their own displays.

3 PC Captioning with Input-Difficult Word Detection

Ikeda *et al.* developed a support system for lecture captioning using IDW detection [4]. We used their system to detect the IDWs in the lectures.

PC captioning is a method in which captionists transcribe a lecturer's speech. Hearing impaired students read the typed text. PC captioning is usually conducted by two captionists for lectures that are in Japanese. Figure 1 shows the captioning setup in the classroom.

We need to prepare for the PC captioning before a lecture. Figure 2 shows the preparation process. First, we obtain the lecture material (e.g., presentation slides, etc.) from the lecturer. Then, we extract the IDWs as described in 2.1. We collect web documents by conducting web searches of IDWs. We train a web-based language model from the web documents. Finally, we interpolate the web language model and the general-purpose conversational language model to obtain an adaptive language model. The interpolation weight λ affects the performance of the IDW detection rate. We then examine it by experimenting.

During the lecture, the system operates as follows. The speech of the lecturer is put into the system. ASR detects IDWs in their speech with the adaptive language model. The detected IDW is shown on the captionists' displays. Figure 3 shows this process. The captionists insert the IDWs into the text with the

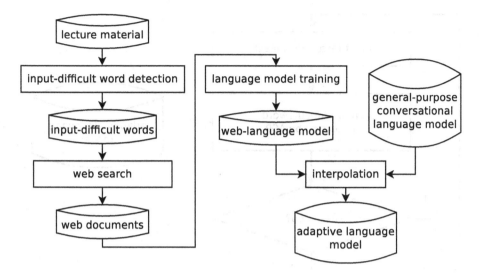

Fig. 2. Preparation process

function key. Then, the input text is shown on the displays of the hearing impaired students.

We implemented the automatic detection method of the IDWs. Therefore, the captionists didoes not need to prepare the PC captioning in advance. The spoken IDWs iswere displayed ion the captionists' monitors and can could be inserted into the text. The system can help captionists both in prepareation before the lecture and can help during the lecture.

4   Experimental Results and Discussion

We conducted an experiment to detect IDWs in lectures. We filmed 18 lectures in all. The course of two of the lectures were "digital signal processing" and "speech and image processing." Each lecture was about 90 min long. In this experiment, we used four lectures. Lectures 1 and 2 used the same lecture material. The IDWs were extracted from presentation slides of the lecture. Then, we generated a web-based language model from the collected web documents. We used a Palmkit [10] for training. Table 1 summarizes the number of IDWs and web documents. We changed the interpolation weight λ to adapt the language model in ASR. We used the SRI language modeling toolkit [11] for interpolation. To generate a general-purpose conversational language model, we used the corpus of spontaneous Japanese [12] database, which contains presentation speeches from academic conferences.

We detect the IDWs from the lectures speech by ASR with the adaptive language model. We calculated the following recall, precision, and F-measure as the performance index of the detection rate.

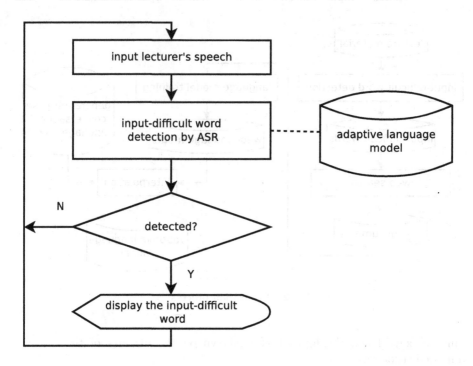

Fig. 3. Process during lecture

$$\text{Recall} = \frac{\text{Number of correct detection}}{\text{Number of uttered IDWs}}, \qquad (5)$$

$$\text{Precision} = \frac{\text{Number of correct detection}}{\text{Number of detected IDWs}}, \qquad (6)$$

$$\text{F-measure} = \frac{2 \cdot \text{Recall} \cdot \text{Precision}}{\text{Recall} + \text{Precision}}. \qquad (7)$$

Table 2 shows the results of the IDW detection.

High performance of F-measure (0.889) is achieved when λ is 0.1. Both recall (0.878) and precision (0.901) are higher than other λs. However, in lecture 4, F-measure (0.907) is highest when λ is 0.9. The value in lecture 4 does not change

Table 1. The number of input-difficult words and the size of collected web documents

Lecture	1	2	3	4
No. of acutual IDWs	12	12	9	14
No. of extracted IDWs	25	25	24	48
No. of total spoken IDWs	58	51	49	38
Size of web documents [kB]	6,586	6,586	5,683	15,164

Table 2. Input-difficult word detection results: the largest F-measure is printed in bold font

Lecture \ λ		0.1	0.2	0.3	0.4	0.5	0.6	0.7	0.8	0.9
1	Recall	0.810	0.776	0.672	0.724	0.741	0.707	0.707	0.672	0.621
	Precision	0.979	0.918	0.907	0.977	0.956	0.953	0.976	1.000	0.973
	F-measure	**0.887**	0.841	0.772	0.832	0.835	0.812	0.820	0.804	0.758
2	Recall	0.922	0.902	0.902	0.902	0.902	0.882	0.902	0.902	0.902
	Precision	0.979	0.958	0.958	0.958	0.979	0.978	0.979	0.979	0.958
	F-measure	**0.949**	0.929	0.929	0.929	0.939	0.928	0.939	0.939	0.929
3	Recall	0.918	0.878	0.878	0.878	0.816	0.816	0.776	0.755	0.735
	Precision	0.804	0.811	0.754	0.754	0.769	0.784	0.776	0.771	0.766
	F-measure	**0.857**	0.843	0.811	0.811	0.792	0.800	0.776	0.763	0.750
4	Recall	0.868	0.868	0.868	0.868	0.842	0.895	0.895	0.921	0.895
	Precision	0.846	0.917	0.917	0.917	0.842	0.872	0.872	0.854	0.919
	F-measure	0.857	0.892	0.892	0.892	0.842	0.883	0.883	0.886	**0.907**
Total	Recall	0.878	0.852	0.821	0.837	0.821	0.816	0.811	0.801	0.776
	Precision	0.901	0.898	0.875	0.891	0.885	0.894	0.898	0.897	0.899
	F-measure	**0.889**	0.874	0.847	0.863	0.852	0.853	0.853	0.846	0.833

very much compared to lectures 1 and 3. Increasing λ decreases recall and F-measure in lectures 1 and 3. Some IDWs such as "sine" and "cosine" are not detected when λ is high in lectures 1 and 3. These words are short and replaced with other words.

The same web-based language model is used in lectures 1 and 2. In lecture 2, there is no significant change of the values when λ is changed, while increasing λ decreases recall in lecture 1. As mentioned before, some IDWs are not detected when λ is high in lecture 1. However, these words are not uttered in lecture 2. When λ is low, the detection result is more affected by the web language model. The university lectures are professional and technical, so we applied more weight to the web-based language model than the general-purpose conversational language model.

5 Conclusion

We explained how some words are difficult for captionists to input and we defined IDWs. We proposed a method of automatically extracting IDWs from lecture materials and conducted experiments using recorded sounds from real lectures. A high performance of F-measure (0.889) is achieved when the weight parameter λ is 0.1.

We developed a method of automatically detecting IDWs so that captionists do not need to prepare PC captioning in advance. The spoken IDWs are displayed on monitors and can be inserted into text. The system can help captionists prepare before lectures and can help them during lectures.

In future work, we will evaluate the system's performance by using more lectures in order to check the appropriate value of λ. We plan to evaluate the performance of the lecture captioning system with real lectures.

This work was supported by JSPS KAKENHI Grant Number JP16K01574.

References

1. Kato, N., Kawano, S., Miyoshi, S., Nishioka, T., Murakami, H., Minagawa, H., Wakatsuki, D., Shirasawa, M., Ishihara, Y., Naito, I.: Subjective evaluation of displaying keywords for speech to text service operators. Trans. Hum. Interface Soci. 9(2), 195–203 (2007). (in Japanese)
2. Akita, Y., Kuwahara, N., Kawahara, T.: Automatic classification of usability of ASR result for real-time captioning of lectures. In: 2015 Asia-Pacific Signal and Information Processing Association Annual Summit and Conference (APSIPA), pp. 19–22 (2015)
3. Gaur, Y., Metze, F., Miao, Y., Bigham, J. P.: Using keyword spotting to help humans correct captioning faster. In: 16th Annual Conference of the International Speech Communication Association, pp. 2829–2833 (2015)
4. Ikeda, N., Takeuchi, Y., Matsumoto, T., Kudo, H., Ohnishi, N.: Support system for lecture captioning using keyword detection by automatic speech recognition. In: Miesenberger, K., Bühler, C., Penaz, P. (eds.) ICCHP 2016. LNCS, vol. 9759, pp. 377–383. Springer, Cham (2016). https://doi.org/10.1007/978-3-319-41267-2_53
5. Qin, L.: Learning out-of-vocabulary words in automatic speech recognition. Ph. D. thesis, CMU University (2013)
6. Illina, I., Fohr, D.: Out-of-vocabulary word probability estimation using RNN language model. In: Proceedings of the 8th Language & Technology Conference (2017)
7. Mirzaei, M.S., Meshgi, K., Kawahara, T.: Listening difficulty detection to foster second language listening with a partial and synchronized caption system. In: Borthwick, K., Bradley, L., Thouësny, S. (eds) CALL in a Climate of Change: Adapting to Turbulent Global Conditions Short Papers From EUROCALL 2017, pp. 211–216 (2017)
8. Munteanu, C., Penn, G., Beacker, R.: Web-based language modelling for automatic lecture transcription. In: Proceedings of the 8th Annual Conference of the International Speech Communication Association, No.ThD.P3a-2, pp. 2353–2356 (2007)
9. Kawahara, T., Nemoto, Y., Akita, Y.: Automatic lecture transcription by exploiting presentation slide information for language model adaptation, In: Proceedings of the ICASSP, pp. 4929–4932 (2008). (in Japanese)
10. Ito, A.: Palmkit (2009). http://palmkit.sourceforge.net/
11. Stolcke, A.: SRILM–an extensible language modeling toolkit. In: Proceedings of the ICSLP (2002)
12. Furui, S.: Recent advances in spontaneous speech recognition and understanding. In: Proceedings of the ISCA & IEEE Workshop on Spontaneous Speech Processing and Recognition, pp. 1–6 (2003)

A Cloud Robotics Platform to Enable Remote Communication for Deafblind People

Ludovico Orlando Russo[1,2], Giuseppe Airò Farulla[2(✉)], and Carlo Geraci[3]

[1] HotBlack Robotics, 10123 Torino, Italy
[2] Università Ca' Foscari Venezia, 30123 Torino, Italy
{ludovico.russo,giuseppe.airofarulla}@unive.it
[3] Institut Jean-Nicod, Département d'études cognitives,
ENS, EHESS, CNRS, PSL, 29, Rue d'Ulm, 75005 Paris, France
carlo.geraci76@gmail.com

Abstract. Cloud Robotics is the application of Cloud Computing and Internet of Things (IoT) technologies to the realm of robotics. This paradigm is gaining momentum in worldwide research as it allows to build robotic infrastructures leveraging on both IoT and the Cloud. These technologies are every day more pervasive in our lives and enhance service robotics (i.e., robotics applications meant to serve humans). We are developing a novel Cloud Robotics architecture empowered by hand tracking technology and 3D-printed bio-inspired robotic arms to enable remote on-line communication for deafblind people in tactile sign language, the communication system most natural to them.

Keywords: Cloud robotics · Service robotics · Tactile sign languages
Remote communication

1 Introduction

Communication is a fundamental condition required for social cohesion, which is typically achieved via language either in the speech or signed modality. The communication flow may happen in a variety of settings, one-to-one, many-to-one, one-to-many, many-to-many, and situations, in presence or remote face-to-face, live, or delayed broadcasting, etc. With the appropriate technologies and tools developed after the Network Society, there is virtually no difference in principle between spoken and sign languages [1].

The situation is radically different for Deafblind people that rely on tactile Sign Language (tSL). tSL is an adaptation of sign language from the visual modality to the tactile modality made by deaf signers [2]. In the prototypical

---

This research has been partially supported by the "Smart Cities and Social Innovation Under 30" program of the Italian Ministry of Research and University through the PARLOMA Project (SIN_00132).

K. Miesenberger and G. Kouroupetroglou (Eds.): ICCHP 2018, LNCS 10896, pp. 203–206, 2018.
https://doi.org/10.1007/978-3-319-94277-3_33

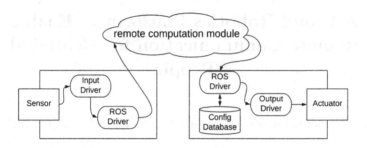

Fig. 1. General design of the communication pipeline.

setting, two tactile signers have to be in front of each other and the message is produced by the dominant hand, acting like the talking hand and received on the non-dominant hand, acting like the listening hand.[1] If one interlocutor is not Deafblind, then the message from the Deafblind person to the interlocutor is normally produced in the visual sign language. Variants of this setting are possible [2], still the one-to-one setting with the physical proximity constraint remains. This fact strongly constraints the interaction of Deafblind people with active society. In their everyday lives, they do not have many chances to talk with other people, unless they is a signer in the neighborhood.

The *PARLOMA*[2] project aims at developing a pipeline to allow Deafblind people to communicate on-line and remotely (i.e., like a *telephone*), hence over-coming the issue of spatial proximity. In previous contributions [3], we already introduced the background of the project, the actors, the main technology, and how signs from tSLs are sampled from the *input side* (gestures from the signer are captured by means of Computer Vision and low-cost hand tracking devices) and off-line reconstructed at the *output side* (gestures are conveyed to the inter-locutor by means of fully-fledged 3D-printed bio-inspired robot arms that can replicate the movements of real human arms). Going on-line is the key step developed in this research. We achieved this result with a Cloud Robotics archi-tecture that opens a communication pipeline and implements remote on-line communication to Deafblind signers.

The rest of the paper is organized as follows: Sect. 2 introduces the paradigm of Cloud Robotics and the architecture, Sect. 3 illustrates how we connect Deafblind users within PARLOMA. Section 4 concludes the paper.

2   Cloud Robotics and the General Architecture

Cloud robotics is an emerging field of robotics strictly linked to the realm of Internet of Things [4, 5]. It centers around the benefits of infrastructure and

---

[1] An example of tSL-based communication is given in https://www.youtube.com/watch?v=l11lahuiHLA.

[2] https://parloma.github.io.

services that are shared over the network to allow robots to benefit from powerful off-loaded communications resources. One of the building blocks of this paradigm is the Robot Operating System (ROS) [6]. ROS is an open-source, meta-operating system for robot software development, providing a collection of packages, software building tools and an architecture for distributed inter-process and inter-machine communication.

The paradigm of Cloud robotics is applied to the design of a communication pipeline in such a way that a sensor (or many sensors in parallel) on the input remotely controls one actuator (or many actuators in parallel) of the output (Fig. 1). This abstract architecture can be readily applied to many different implementations and can be customized on the needs of the users. The architecture is based on state-of-art approaches on the topic [7].

The implementation within PARLOMA requires that User A remotely controls an on-line hand tracking device which serves as the input device; a pair of anthropomorphic arms allows a (Deafblind) user B to receive the messages as if s/he were touching the hands of A. The message in visual SL is converted into tSL and conveyed to B, allowing remote communication between users A and B. An experience that would have required physical proximity is now possible with the two actors being in two distant locations. On the various possible implementations of this pipeline see Sect. 4.

3   Connecting Deafblind Signers

The main component of our architecture is the Cloud platform that connects the various devices in an on-line network [7]. The end-user experience is similar to that of typical video-communication tools.

A web-exposed GUI makes a contact list of locally registered accounts accessible to user A, who can select, and start a conversation with, user B. The platform then checks that the input device of user A is ready to transmit and that the output device of user B is ready to receive. A notification about a pending call is then send to user B, who can accept or decline through the same GUI [3]. If the request is accepted, a private virtual channel is established between users A and B via VPN server [8] and the ROS. This procedure guarantees privacy and functionality during the communication. The call can be terminated via the same GUI: this will cause the resources allocated for the private channel and for managing the I/O devices to be released and to become available to start a new conversation.

4   Conclusions and Future Remarks

Communication directed to Deafblind signers is a one-to-one experience that requires physical presence of both interlocutors. We developed a robotic based

---

[3] The details of the GUI and the notification to the Deafblind person, as well as the procedure to enable broadcasting communication, are under refinement so to be fully accessible to Deafblind users.

communication system to enlarge communication chances for Deafblind people. For this purpose, we used technologies and methodologies from the paradigms of IoT and Cloud Robotics. A web-based GUI allows a network of users to establish a peer-to-peer remote communication, hence by-passing the requirement of physical proximity. The hand-tracking module and the ROS allow the same message to be distributed (potentially simultaneously) to more than one receiver, hence by-passing the one-to-one experience. Indeed, PARLOMA enables a variety of settings allowing communication towards Deafblind signers to go beyond the one-to-one experience and physical proximity of the interlocutors. The hand-tracking module and the ROS allow the typical broadcasting one-to-many communication. Once paired to a GUI accessible memory device, it would allow delayed one-to-many broadcasting communication (e.g., on-demand daily news, tactile-books, etc.); a network open to multiple participants might in principle allow for a many-to-many non-overlapping communication (more work is envisaged to implement this component).

Future works will deal with an extensive validation of the proposed system with signers and tactile signers. Moreover, we plan to apply the same communication pipeline to allow users, even deafblind, to easily interact with robotic platforms different from bio-inspired arms. Industrial platforms could be easily controlled by means of gestures, thus paving the way to a future world where working consoles are really accessible and inclusive, and people coping with sensory disabilities can access to job positions and become more integrated in the active society.

References

1. McCaul, T.: Video-based telecommunications technology and the deaf community. Australian Communication Exchange Report (1997)
2. Edwards, T.: From compensation to integration: effects of the pro-tactile movement on the sublexical structure of tactile american sign language. J. Pragmatics **69**, 22–41 (2014)
3. Russo, L.O., Farulla, G.A., Pianu, D., Salgarella, A.R., Controzzi, M., Cipriani, C., Oddo, C.M., Geraci, C., Rosa, S., Indaco, M.: PARLOMA - a novel human-robot interaction system for deafblind remote communication. Int. J. Adv. Robot. Syst. **12**(57), 1–13 (2015)
4. Hu, G., Tay, W.P., Wen, Y.: Cloud robotics: architecture, challenges and applications. IEEE Netw. **26**(3), 21–28 (2012)
5. Kehoe, B., Patil, S., Abbeel, P., Goldberg, K.: A survey of research on cloud robotics and automation. IEEE Trans. Autom. Sci. Eng. **12**(2), 398–409 (2015)
6. Quigley, M., Conley, K., Gerkey, B., Faust, J., Foote, T., Leibs, J., Wheeler, R., Ng, A.Y.: ROS: an open-source robot operating system. In: ICRA Workshop on Open Source Software, Kobe, Japan, vol. 3, p. 5 (2009)
7. Russo, L.O.: Leveraging the Cloud to develop Service Robotics Applications. Ph.D. thesis, Politecnico di Torino (2017)
8. Wood, T., Shenoy, P.J., Gerber, A., van der Merwe, J.E., Ramakrishnan, K.K.: The case for enterprise-ready virtual private clouds. In: HotCloud (2009)

A Subjective Evaluation of Music Beat Recognition with Different Timbres by Hearing-Impaired People

Yuka Nakahara, Rumi Hiraga$^{(\boxtimes)}$, and Nobuko Kato

Tsukuba University of Technology,
Amakubo 4-3-15, Tsukuba 305-8520, Japan
rhiraga@a.tsukuba-tech.ac.jp
http://rhiraga.info

Abstract. For hearing-impaired people (HIs) to enjoy music more, one of the authors, who is profoundly deaf but enthusiastic about music, feels the choice of instrumental sounds is important. We conducted an experiment of beat tapping with 20 musical instruments involving one group of HIs using hearing aids and another group of HIs using cochlear implants. From the analysis of a subjective evaluation about each instrumental sound, we found the two groups differed in their perceptions of sounds. One reason for this difference seems to be the envelope of the sounds. Thus, we are going to analyze sounds to pursue suitable instrumental sounds for HIs.

Keywords: Beat perception · Musical instrument
Hearing-impairment

1 Introduction

This paper describes how hearing-impaired people (HIs) listen to timbre as basic research into enabling many more HIs to enjoy music. The music component of rhythm enables people to feel a sense of unity when listening to music at the same time and in the same place, such as at concerts. Even if HIs do not have fine pitch resolution, they can experience music through the vibrations it generates. On the other hand, we notice that many HIs who go to karaoke have difficulties knowing when to start singing even with the lyrics for guidance.

One of the authors, who is profoundly deaf with a hearing aid in her right ear but enthusiastic about music, learned to enjoy music at school thanks to teachers playing the piano or some other instruments. Since she could perceive music better with some instruments than others, she argued that the choice of instruments to present to HIs children is important in enabling them to appreciate music.

There are three possible methods to empower HIs to better appreciate music: (1) using special devices [1], (2) adjusting music for HIs, and (3) improving hearing ability [2]. We describe here an investigation into adjusting music rhythm,

© Springer International Publishing AG, part of Springer Nature 2018
K. Miesenberger and G. Kouroupetroglou (Eds.): ICCHP 2018, LNCS 10896, pp. 207–210, 2018.
https://doi.org/10.1007/978-3-319-94277-3_34

especially beat, for HIs. We use "beat" to mean the basic pattern of rhythm that represents the tempo of music. Several studies have tested how hearing people perceive beat [3,4]. Since these tests use real music with complicated timbres and rhythms, we found them difficult to apply to HIs. Though music recommendation systems with music information retrieval techniques have been widely developed [5], none of these systems takes music for HIs into account. By clarifying timbres that HIs can recognize, these tests and systems might be able to be adapted to HIs users.

In this paper, we describe an experiment of beat recognition with different instruments. A subjective evaluation found that the ease of listening to sounds and beat recognition depend on the envelope of a sound.

2   Method

Material: We prepared 16 different beats, all of which were 90 beats per minute, with the timbre of 20 instruments. First, we made a music score with Sibelius, score notation software, and then converted it into a sound file with Sibelius sound library. The score consists of four quarter notes of C4 for four measures in four-four time. The instruments used are listed in Table 1. The categories of the instruments are based on not Hornbostel-Sachs Classification but the classification of western music instruments used in orchestras. Some traditional instruments were also included. We excluded percussion instruments in order to see whether participants could perceive beats from instruments that only play melodies (and accompaniments). Sounds were presented to participants in a system using Presentation by Neurobehavioral Systems on a tablet (Windows Surface Pro3) with a pair of speakers (Genelec ONE). While listening, participants tapped the display along with the beat sound.

Participants: Nineteen HIs students participated in the experiment (aged: 21–23). Eleven used only hearing aid(s) (HA) (M:3), and the rest used at least one cochlear implant (CI) (M:4). Those who also used hearing aid in one ear and wore a CI in another ear were grouped in CI.

Procedure: (1) A participant practiced tapping and controlled the sound level. (2) The participant tapped the display in time with the beats. The tapping activity was repeated twice. (3) The participant answered a subjective evaluation. (4) To avoid the participant getting used to the beat, the participant executed simple calculations for half a minute. (5) The participant repeated steps (2) to (4) for 20 instrumental sounds.

Subjective evaluation: We presented four questions that participants marked from 1 (Strong no) to 5 (Strong yes): 1) Was the sound easy to hear? (EASY) (2) Did you hear sounds at higher pitches? (HIGH) (3) Was it easy to tap with the beats? (BEAT) (4) Did you like the instrumental sound? (LIKE).

Table 1. Instruments used in the experiment. The classification is based on the standard way of playing, and we did not insist on rigidness.

Family	Instruments
String	
Plucking	Mandolin (MDN), Class. guitar (CGT), Elec. guitar (EGT), Harp (HRP)
Rubbed	Violin (VIN), Cello (VCL)
Hammer	Piano (APF), Clavinet (CVN)
Brass	Trumpet (TRP), Trombone (TRB), Tuba (TUB), Horn (HRN)
Woodwind	Bassoon (BSN), Clarinet (CLN), Flute (FLT), Recorder (REC)
Others	Accordion (ACC), Harmonica (HMC), Shamisen (SHM), Sou (SOU)

3 Results

We analyzed the results for the four subjective evaluation questions with ANOVA to see the differences between 20 instrumental sounds and between the HA and CI groups.

3.1 Differences Between Instrumental Sounds for both Participant Groups

- EASY: [HA] Differences were found between REC and SHM ($p < 0.05$).
- HIGH: [HA] Differences were found between CGT and REC ($p < 0.01$) and CVN/SHM and REC ($p < 0.05$). [CI] Differences were found between CGT and TRP/TUB/SOU ($p < 0.05$).
- BEAT: [CI] Differences were found between REC and EGT/HRP/SHM ($p < 0.05$).

3.2 Differences Between Participant Groups for Each Instrument

- EASY: Differences were found for VCL ($p < 0.01$) and EGT ($p < 0.05$).
- LIKE: Differences were found for VCL ($p < 0.01$).

The results are shown in Table 2. Values in parentheses are mean values. Mean values of participant groups are presented in the order of HA and CI.

4 Discussion

We describe possible reasons for the results and suggest ways to utilize them.

- *Differences in listening to timbres between HA and CI groups.* The two groups produced different results for the subjective evaluation. HI children in special education classes use HAs, CIs, or both. When they have music classes, different children may hear or feel different things in the music, and some can recognize music with certain timbres while others cannot. For both HA and CI children to enjoy music at the same time, suitable musical instruments are suggested; for example, APF could be good, but not REC.

Table 2. Subjective evaluation. **: p<0.01, *: p<0.05

		Differences between instrumental sounds		Differences between participant groups
		HA	CI	
EASY	**	-	-	VCL (2.91/4.63)
	*	REC (2.36) and SHM (4.18)	-	EGT (3.64/4.75)
HIGH	**	CGT (2.27) and REC (4.45)	-	-
	*	CVN (2.8)/SHM (2.45) and REC (4.45)	CGT (2.13) and TRP/TUB/SOU (all 4.25)	-
BEAT	**	-	-	-
	*	-	REC (2.38) and HRP (4.50)/ EGT (4.63)/SHM (4.63)	-
LIKE	**	-	-	VCL (2.64/4.00)
	*	-	-	-

- *The effect of envelope.* The timbre of a recorder (REC) differed from other timbres more than once (Table 2). A possible explanation is the envelope of the sound. We are going to confirm the effect of the envelope in subjective evaluation by making sound files with eighth or sixteenth notes.
- *The effect of other sound features.* Envelopes of harp (HRP) and sou (SOU, a traditional Japanese instrument) resemble that of SHM because these instruments are played by plucking. Thus, we should analyze sounds with different features to explain the difference between these instruments.
- *The relationship between the subjective evaluation and an objective evaluation.* We need to analyze how HI participants follow the beat by analyzing results of the tapping experiment.
- *Future music assistive technology for HIs.* By gaining a basic understanding of beat perception by HIs, music systems such as beat assessment tests and music retrieval systems will be able to be adapted to HIs.

Acknowledgments. This work was supported by JSPS KAKENHI Nr. JP2628001.

References

1. hapbeat. http://hapbeat.com
2. Hansen, K. F., Hiraga, R.: The effects of musical experience and hearing loss on solving an audio-based gaming task. Appl. Sci. **7**(12), 1278 (2017)
3. Iversen, J.R., Patel, A.D.: The beat alignment test (BAT): surveying beat processing abilities in the general population. Proc. ICMPC **10**, 465–468 (2008)
4. Fujii, S., Schlaug, G.: The harvard beat assessment test (H-BAT): a battery for assessing beat perception and production and their dissociation. Front. Hum. Neurosci. **26**, 1196–1207 (2013)
5. Song, Y., Dixon, S., Pearce, M.: A survey of music recommendation systems and future perspectives. In: Proceedings of 9th International Symposium on Computer Music Modelling and Retrieval, pp. 395–410 (2012)

Subtitleformatter: Making Subtitles Easier to Read for Deaf and Hard of Hearing Viewers on Personal Devices

Raja Kushalnagar[1]([✉]) [iD] and Kesavan Kushalnagar[2]

[1] Gallaudet University, Washington DC 20002, USA
raja.kushalnagar@gallaudet.edu
[2] Rochester Institute of Technology, Rochester, NY, USA
krk4565@rit.edu

Abstract. For deaf or hard of hearing (DHH) viewers who cannot understand speech, many countries require video producers/distributors to provide speech-to-text over the video, also called subtitles that can be turned on or off by the viewer. These subtitles must comply with national subtitle quality standards. The growth in video capable personal devices has shifted viewers away from watching broadcast video on a standardized television display and towards watching video on interactive personal devices. However, personal devices range widely from tiny watch displays to enormous television displays, with different proportions which impact subtitle readability. SubtitleFormatter automatically formats subtitles according to a display's screen size and minimum font size for reading. A user study of subtitle formatting evaluates subtitle readability, and finds that viewers preferred SubtitleFormatted-segmented subtitles over wrap around (arbitrarily-formatted) subtitles.

Keywords: Subtitles · Speech-to-text · Deaf or hard of hearing

1 Introduction

Hearing loss is an invisible but significant barrier in daily life, including education and streaming television. In addition to approximately 2% of people born deaf or hard of hearing, approximately 31% of people over 65 have significant hearing loss [1]. Many rely on subtitles to access and enjoy videos.

Videos are a vital part of our shared cultural experience and shapes our identity as citizens. Subtitles provides accessibility to these individuals such that they are not shut out of society and culture. Subtitling laws and policies in many countries, including the United States, United Kingdom, Brazil and India, guarantee some access to video programming [2, 3].

These acts mandate aural-to-visual accommodations such as subtitles as shown in Fig. 1 which aids both people with disabilities, and people with situational accessibility

© The Author(s) 2018
K. Miesenberger and G. Kouroupetroglou (Eds.): ICCHP 2018, LNCS 10896, pp. 211–219, 2018.
https://doi.org/10.1007/978-3-319-94277-3_35

needs. For instance, subtitles have been shown to be useful across a wide range of situations, such as bars, restaurants, airports and to improve literacy skills in children and people learning English as a Second Language.

Fig. 1. Video with subtitles. The subtitles are the white letters at the bottom.

2 Background

In the United States, pre-prepared subtitles were included in national TV shows from 1973 [4], and real-time subtitles were included in television shows from 1982 [5]. The timeline for introducing subtitles in television was similar in most developed countries. For over 30 years, standards for subtitling [6] were developed and standardized for an average DHH viewer who watched analog broadcasts on non-interactive, fixed format television displays. The television screen resolution and proportions were set for standard resolution (e.g., NTSC: 720 by 480 pixels or PAL: 720 by 576 pixels with an aspect ratio of 4:3). This resolution and aspect ratio remained unchanged till the advent of digital broadcasts in the 2000s.

2.1 Subtitled Videos on Personal Devices

The advent of digital television on personal displays led to far more diversity in resolution, size and proportions. Viewers consume video programming personal devices with varying resolutions and aspect ratios. This diversity of personal display characteristics can influence a viewer's preferred size and number of caption lines. Although viewers can view videos anywhere, any time, and no longer be tethered to their couches, it becomes harder to fit subtitles on the widely varying sizes and proportions of personal devices. Viewing devices range from tiny smart watch displays to enormous television displays. While there has been a substantial body of research focused on a standardized speech-to-text presentation for all users watching television programs built over 30 years, there is scant research focused on adapting subtitles according to the display characteristics.

Currently, most video providers follow television captioning standards. When they do add features in their speech-text caption interfaces, these features create additional problems. For example, if the interface offers resizable fonts, and the font is made bigger, the caption lines will become too big for the video display and wrap around, which disrupts the reading process. To the best of our knowledge, no video platform provides a feature to reformat subtitles depending on screen size or user preferences.

3   Related Work

We focus on improving two parts of the closed caption reading process – the cognitive process of reading subtitles, and the process of segmenting and formatting subtitles to fit the video display.

3.1   Cognitive Process of Subtitle Reading

Prior research has shown that the cognitive process of reading subtitles that are a form of real-time speech-to-text is different from reading static text or print. Speech-to-text is short and regularly changes, while print is long, formatted and does not change [7]. Reading subtitles often takes relatively more time and energy than it does to listen to spoken or signed languages, and those watching subtitles must often split their attention between the subtitles and other visual information, such as whatever is happening on the TV screen [8].

This study focuses on how to divide up lines on subtitles to maximize readability and comprehension. Professionals format the subtitles manually to ensure that the number of words per line to a standard television display. When these subtitles are viewed on a smaller screen than the standard television screen, the subtitles should be made larger to maintain readability and the line width and count should be adjusted downwards. Then there is not enough screen real-estate to accommodate the subtitles, and the caption lines will become too big for the video display and wrap around, which disrupts the viewer's reading process as shown in Fig. 2. Conversely, on large displays,

Fig. 2. Picture on left – captions on small personal device display. The viewer increases subtitle size to comfortably read them. The size increase makes the line too long for the screen, and it wraps around, which impacts caption readability. Picture on right – captions on television display. The subtitles are formatted for this resolution and screen by default. The subtitles normally follow caption guidelines to maximize readability for most viewers of the video.

the font size does not have to grow as much as the video, and it may work to increase the number of simultaneously displayed lines.

Research on automatic caption segmentation seems to suggest it can have a positive impact, but is not conclusive. Perego et al. [9] found that segmenting subtitles in inappropriate places had no impact on sentence recall or eye movement. However, Rajendran et al. [10] found a significant difference in eye movement for different kinds of subtitle segmentation. Waller and Kushalnagar [11] suggest that segmentation may have an impact on our memory of the text.

4   SubtitleFormatter Design and Evaluation

We created a linguistically aware automatic formatting system, called SubtitleFormatter. The system automatically formats subtitles by parsing the text to break the text at linguistically appropriate places.

We conducted a user study to verify the utility of the system's parsing and breaking of subtitles. We compared the readability of unparsed subtitles versus human parsed subtitles that were generated by professional closed caption stenographers on both regular television screens and for small phone screens. We also compared the readability of unparsed subtitles versus automatic subtitles on both regular and small phone screens, to investigate whether the readability can reach the level and quality of human-parsed subtitles generated by professional closed caption stenographers.

4.1   Design

The SubtitleFormatter system analyzes the subtitles and the display so that it can format the subtitles according to the display. It has two parts – a linguistic analyzer and a display analyzer.

4.2   Linguistic Analyzer

The system incorporates the Stanford Parser which is an open-source statistical-based natural language processing processor [12]. The parser can produce a syntax tree for any given sentence or sentences in a text. For example, for the sentence "When it rains, the children like to play outside", the parser can display a syntax tree for the sentence as shown in Fig. 3.

It breaks down the sentence into phrases, which in turn are broken down into smaller and smaller phrases down to the level of words. The SubtitleFormatter system uses this information to identify optimal point breaks.

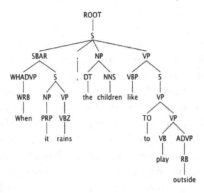

Fig. 3. The parse tree generated by the Stanford Parser for the sentence: "When it rains, the children like to play outside."

5 Evaluation

To evaluate caption segmentation and formatting, we evaluated the difference in readability between unparsed subtitles (A), human-parsed (H), and SubtitleFormatter-parsed (P) subtitles on a regular television display and on a personal phone.

For A, we counted the characters per line limit and split subtitles only after the line width was over the maximum in subtitling guidelines, as shown in Fig. 4 on right. For P, the program broke up the lines using as shown in Fig. 4 on left.

Fig. 4. Left: snapshot of SubtitleFormatter, where a break is inserted when it encounters a logical break according to the parse tree, and still less than the maximum length. Right: A snapshot of unparsed subtitles that was segmented and formatted automatically by inserting a break when the line has exceeded the maximum length.

5.1 Participants

We recruited 34 deaf and hard of hearing participants. All participants regularly use captions when watching online videos, TV, and other audio-video content. The participants ranged in age from 20 to 48 years old: 20 men, and 14 women. By ethnicity, 18 participants identified as white, 5 identified as black, 5 identified as Asian or Asian-American, 4 identified as Hispanic and 2 as multiracial.

5.2 Study

Each participant watched six 4-minute videos with A, H or P subtitles, with breaks in between. The survey and videos were shown either on a 40-inch television set or on iPhone 5 s. The entire experiment took 30–45 min. Half viewed the first three videos on a 40-inch high-definition (1920×1080) television display, and the next three videos on a 4-inch iPhone 5 (1136×640) display, and the other half watched in the reverse order. Each viewer watched all six videos in a balanced, randomized order. We gathered data from all participants through three parts – a Likert rating questionnaire, a comprehension questionnaire, a sentence completion task, and an eye-tracking data gathering part. After each video, the participants were given a sentence completion task in which they were presented with the beginning part of a sentence from the text. Afterwards the researcher explained the purpose of the study, and the participant was invited to add a comment on either the study or subtitles.

6 Results

The results from the following evaluations were grouped by Likert ratings, comprehension scores including sentence completion scores. The Shapiro-Wilk test indicated the observed values were not normally distributed, so non-parametric testing was done. The Wilcoxon Signed Rank tests was used to perform post-hoc comparisons between pairs of samples, with Bonferroni corrections to address the multiple comparisons.

6.1 Likert Ratings

Television Display
For the subjective responses, no significant differences were found: A vs. H: Wilcox = 54, $p > 0.05$; A vs. P: Wilcox = 45.5, $p > 0.10$; H vs. P: Wilcox = 48.5, $p > 0.05$.

For satisfaction, none of the three conditions had a significant impact on the ratings relative to each other: A vs. H: Wilcox = 48.5, $p > 0.05$; A Vs. P: Wilcox = 51, $p > 0.05$; H vs. P: Wilcox = 75.5, $p > 0.05$.

Phone Display
For the subjective and satisfaction responses, there was a significant difference between A vs. H, and A vs. P, but not H vs. P.

For satisfaction, there was no significant difference between A vs. H and A vs. P, but there was a significant difference between P and H: H vs. P: Wilcox = 14.8, $p < 0.05$.

6.2 Comprehension Scores

Television Display
For general comprehension questions, there was no significant difference: A vs. H: $t = 0.583$, $p > 0.05$; A vs. P: $t = 0.432$, $p > 0.05$; H vs. P: $t = -0.24$, $p > 0.05$.

For sentence completion, A was significantly different than either H or P: A vs. H: $t = -1.048$, $p < 0.05$; A vs. P: $t = 1.052$, $p < 0.05$, but not H vs. P: $t = 0.414$, $p > 0.05$.

However, participants got significantly more sentence completion questions correct for P than A: $t = 2.169$, $p < 0.05$, but not for the other pairwise comparisons.

Phone Display

For general comprehension, none of these means differed significantly: A vs. H: $t = 0.541$, $p > 0.05$; A vs. P: $t = 0.471$, $p > 0.05$; P vs. H: $t = 0.349$, $p > 0.05$.

For sentence completion, H was not significantly different than either of the other conditions: A vs. H: $t = -1.276$, $p > 0.05$; H vs. P: $t = 1.874$, $p > 0.05$.

However, participants got significantly more sentence completion questions for P vs. A: $t = 2.3224$, $p < 0.05$, but not for the other pairwise comparisons.

6.3 Comments

The participant comments were generally negative about unsegmented subtitles. They were generally positive about grammatically segmented subtitles, generated either by professionals, or SubtitleFormatter program, on both on small and large displays. When the participants had different comments between large and small displays, they said that the lines or words were too hard to see on small displays. On large displays, they said the lines were not complete, or that they did not like it and could not explain why. For human-segmented subtitles, 28 participants wrote comments, and 15 wrote down identical comments for both small and large displays. When they wrote the same comment for both, they said that it was easy to read, or that they could understand each line. When the participants had different comments between large and small displays, they generally said that the lines or words were too fast on small displays, and that on large displays, they said the lines were not complete.

7 Results

Participants significantly preferred H or P segmented subtitles for smaller screens, but not for bigger screens. They performed significantly better on sentence completion tasks for either P or H over A. However, they did not perform significantly better on either H or P over A for either large or small screens. The general lack of significant differences between H and A for bigger screens agrees with the assertion by Perego et al. that segmentation in captioning has little or no impact on readability. It is possible that human or SubtitleFormatter subtitles were easier to remember, but the difference from unsegmented subtitles did not rise to the level of significance.

The preference for human or SubtitleFormatter subtitles on smaller screens could be that when lines are shorter, the sentence concepts are more likely to be distributed on multiple lines and that breaking outside of phrases is likely to be confusing. The fact that segmentation has an impact on user preferences and sentence recall for smaller screens has important implications for captioning, as currently caption guidelines all encourage proper segmentation

The SubtitleFormatter supports viewer preferences for proportionately larger text on small screens by automatically adjusting caption line width according to screen size. It can be viewed as an automatic enhancement of accessibility for viewers who use captions, like how people with diverse magnification needs can benefit from automatic magnification. We present a novel approach to automatic subtitle segmentation which generates and selects optimal segmentation points according to SubtitleFormatter. SubtitleFormatter segmentation can be an inclusive approach for viewers who wish to follow best practice in segmentation guidelines and rules, or one that fits their own needs.

8   Future Work

Automatically formatting subtitles by display can also benefit people with limited English proficiency, or viewers with situational auditory barriers, e.g., quiet public spaces.

References

1. Pearson, J.D., Morrell, C.H., Gordon-Salant, S., Brant, L.J., Metter, E.J., Klein, L.L., Fozard, J.L.: Gender differences in a longitudinal study of age-associated hearing loss. J. Acoust. Soc. Am. **97**(2), 1196–1205 (1995)
2. United States Congress, Americans with Disabilities Act, Pub. L. No. 101-336, 104 Stat. 328. United States of America (1990)
3. National Congress of Brazil, Ley de Igualdad de Oportunidades para las Personas con Discapacidad (Law of Equal Opportunities for Persons with Disabilities) (1992)
4. NIDCD: Captions For Deaf and Hard-of-Hearing Viewers, NIH Publ., no. 4834 (2017). https://www.nidcd.nih.gov/health/captions-deaf-and-hard-hearing-viewers
5. Block, M.H., Okrand, M.: Real-time closed captioned television as an educational tool. Am. Ann. Deaf **128**(5), 636–641 (1983)
6. United States General Publications Office, 47 CFR 79.A.1. (2015)
7. Thorn, F., Thorn, S.: Television captions for hearing-impaired people: a study of key factors that affect reading performance. Hum. Factors **38**(3), 452–463 (1996)
8. Kushalnagar, R.S., Behm, G.W., Stanislow, J.S., Gupta, V.: Enhancing caption accessibility through simultaneous multimodal information: visual-tactile captions. In: ASSETS14 - Proceedings of the 16th International ACM SIGACCESS Conference on Computers and Accessibility (2014)
9. Perego, E., Del Missier, F., Porta, M., Mosconi, M.: The cognitive effectiveness of subtitle processing. Media Psychol. **13**(3), 243–272 (2010)
10. Rajendran, D.J., Duchowski, A.T., Orero, P., Martínez, J., Romero-Fresco, P.: Effects of text chunking on subtitling: a quantitative and qualitative examination. Perspectives (Montclair) **21**(1), 5–21 (2013)
11. Waller, J.M., Kushalnagar, R.S.: Evaluation of automatic caption segmentation. In: Proceedings of the 18th International ACM SIGACCESS Conference on Computers and Accessibility - ASSETS 2016, pp. 331–332 (2016)
12. Klein, D., Manning, C.D.: Accurate unlexicalized parsing. In: Proceedings of the 41st Annual Meeting on Association for Computational Linguistics - ACL 2003, vol. 1, pp. 423–430 (2003)

Study on Automated Audio Descriptions Overlapping Live Television Commentary

Manon Ichiki[1(✉)], Toshihiro Shimizu[1], Atsushi Imai[1], Tohru Takagi[2],
Mamoru Iwabuchi[3], Kiyoshi Kurihara[1], Taro Miyazaki[1], Tadashi Kumano[1],
Hiroyuki Kaneko[1,2,3], Shoei Sato[1], Nobumasa Seiyama[1], Yuko Yamanouchi[1],
and Hideki Sumiyoshi[1]

[1] NHK (Nippon Hoso Kyokai; Japan Broadcasting Corp.) Science and Technical Research
Laboratories, 1-10-11 Kinuta, Setagaya-ku, Tokyo 157-8510, Japan
{ichiki.m-fq,shimizu.t-hy,imai.a-dy,kurihara.k-fu,
miyazaki.t-jw,kumano.t-eq,kaneko.h-dk,satou.s-gu,
seiyama.n-ek,yamanouchi.y-fg,sumiyoshi.h-di}@nhk.or.jp
[2] NHK Engineering Systems, 1-10-11 Kinuta, Setagaya-ku, Tokyo 157-8510, Japan
takagi@nes.or.jp
[3] University of Tokyo, 4-6-1 Komaba, Meguro-ku, Tokyo 153-8904, Japan
mamoru@bfp.rcast.u-tokyo.ac.jp

Abstract. We are conducting research on "automated audio description (AAD)" which automatically generates audio descriptions from real-time competition data for visually impaired people to enjoy live sports programs. However, there is a problem that AAD overlaps with the live television commentary voice, making it difficult to hear each other's comment. In this paper, first, we show that the game situation is conveyed effectively when visually impaired persons listen to the AAD alone. Then we state the results of experiments on the following items to solve the overlap issue: (1) There is a difference in optimum volume level between live commentary and AAD, (2) The ease of listening differs depending on the difference in the characteristics of text-to-speech synthesizer for AAD, (3) Playing back AAD through a speaker placed differently from the TV speaker makes both voice sounds easier to listen to. We had clues to solve that depending on the presentation method of AAD, we can make AAD easy to listen to even when AAD overlaps the live television commentary.

Keywords: Audio description · Text-to-speech synthesizer · Visually impaired

1 Introduction

NHK is advancing research and development of audio description that can be automatically assigned to live TV sports programs. Current audio description in Japan is provided for recorded TV programs such as dramas, and the script for audio description is prepared in advance and is narrated without overlapping the broadcast audio. Therefore, applying such a method to live broadcasting is very difficult. In fact, audio description by announcers has been tried with live sports programs but is extremely difficult to produce.

© Springer International Publishing AG, part of Springer Nature 2018
K. Miesenberger and G. Kouroupetroglou (Eds.): ICCHP 2018, LNCS 10896, pp. 220–224, 2018.
https://doi.org/10.1007/978-3-319-94277-3_36

We are developing an automated audio description (AAD) system to add speech explaining a game situation to the sound of a live sports program so that visually impaired people can enjoy such programs. As shown in Fig. 1, the system consists of an explanation composer and text-to-speech synthesizer. When the system receives real-time competition data [1, 2], the explanation composer composes a new explanation appropriate to the situation. The text-to-speech synthesizer then conveys the explanation in natural speech [3, 4]. Generally, these metadata are intended to be used for television and the internet as text information, and have not been directly used for the visually impaired. This is the first trial in the world to attempt audio description with the visually impaired.

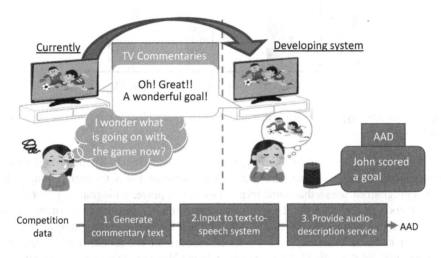

Fig. 1. ADD system we are developing consists of explanation composer and text-to-speech synthesizer.

2   Evaluation Experiments on Independent Effectiveness of AAD

We evaluated to what extent the content of a competition can be understood from automatic explanation sound alone. The evaluation sound was an AAD superimposed on the sound of the sports venue without commentary voice. We used the text-to-speech synthesizer using a corpus base (female). We compared different types of media to determine to what extent the visually impaired can understand a game situation. We conducted this subjective assessment with the following three types of media.

1. AAD superimposed on the sound of a venue without commentary
2. Simultaneous radio broadcasting audio
3. Simultaneous TV broadcasting audio

The experimental conditions are listed in Table 1, and the experimental results are shown in Fig. 2. The live TV commentary was evaluated to be "fair" because the announcer sometimes did not speak daringly if you look at the image, and the visually impaired participants had difficulty in understanding the game situation. On the other hand, the AAD and commentary on the radio were rated almost equal.

Table 1. Experimental conditions of subjective evaluation experiments in understanding content.

Participants	8 visually impaired individuals
Evaluation sound	Wheelchair basketball
	18 times for 30-s scene
Subjective assessment item	5-point evaluation

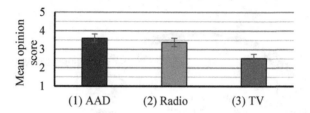

Fig. 2. Compared types of media to determine to what extent visually impaired can understand game situation.

As a result of an interview survey, some of the participants listened to television broadcasting and radio broadcasting at the same time as a way for them to enjoy the sports program. It seems that some information about player's biography, past records and others was provided for the live commentary on TV but main information was commentary of game situation on the radio. In fact, the rate of commenting on a game situation on the radio and television as objective information was compared and that this rate was high on the radio [5, 6]. However, in Japan, there are fewer sports programs on the radio than on television, and the number of TVs and radios that can be used together is limited. Therefore, providing AAD for television sports programs is effective for visually impaired people to enjoy such programs.

3   Issues with ADD Service

3.1   Issue with Overlapping of Broadcast Audio and Commentary Voice

Currently, an audio description service is produced with the limitation of overlapping with the live commentary voice. Regarding content with a large amount of information, such as a sports program, there are times when providing a service without audio overlap is physically difficult. Thus, we previously conducted a survey on the overlap ratio of the play-by-play commentary and audio description using actual programs of tennis and basketball programs [7]. For the tennis program, about 20% of the audio description temporarily overlapped with the play-by-play commentary. For the basketball program, about 70% of the audio description overlapped the play-by-play commentary.

3.2   The Method for Avoiding Overlap

We research the method for avoiding overlap between the commentary voices of the program and AAD as much as possible. We conducted basic study:

Experiment the Ease of Listening by the Difference in the Sound Voice Level between Television Commentary Voices and AAD. Participants are 240 sighted persons. As the evaluation stimulus, the commentary voices and AAD were mixed, and audio alone were presented. In this experiment, about 80% of the participant responded that the AAD was easy to understand when the sound volume level of AAD is raised to +4 dB or +8 dB.

Use Viewers' Attention to the Voice Sounds. In sports programs, viewers want to follow the progress of the game in some cases, and want to enjoy the atmosphere of the venue in other cases. They can get to know the progress of the game mainly through AAD. And they can enjoy the atmosphere of the game mainly through live television commentary. So we experimented if the characteristics of the text-to-speech synthesizer affects the ease of listening of the sounds viewers want to listen to. Experiment conditions are shown in Table 2.

Table 2. Conditions of the experiment on the ease of listening by using viewers' attention

Participants	20 sighted persons
Evaluation stimulus	Women's basketball
Live commentary	Male
Presentation method	Present the main voice sounds and the AAD overlapping each other
Text-to-speech synthe-sizers	4 types: A(woman), B(man), C(woman), D(man)
Subjective assessment item	Did you hear the content of the utterance well? Five-grade evaluation

In the experiment, participants listened to live commentary with attention. The experiment result significantly shows that live commentary was hard to listen to when it was obstructed by the AAD of text-to-speech synthesizer D. The reason seems to be that the characteristic of text-to-speech synthesizer D is similar to the voice of the live commentary and it was hard to distinguish them. This suggests that the synthesized voice that is similar in voice characteristic and speech style is unsuitable for the AAD.

Output AAD through a Speaker Different from the TV Speaker. Live commentary was output through the TV speaker, while AAD was output through the speaker near the participants. And the ease of listening of both voice sounds were evaluated. Participants were 10 visually impaired persons. Live commentary was presented through the TV speaker and the AAD was also presented through the TV speaker in one case, and through a speaker at hand in the other case. And participants chose which was easier to listen to. Evaluation was made at a number of points during a 20-min game. The result is that 74% of participants responded that both live commentary and AAD were easier to listen to when the latter was output through a speaker at hand. This presentation method is also advantageous when the whole family watches a sports program, because a visually impaired person who needs the AAD alone can listen through a speaker at hand.

3.3 Further Consideration

In order to put into practical use, we must consider of controlling the phase of AAD, using bone conduction for a way of listening to the AAD, putting in AAD at the appropriate timing and others.

4 Conclusion

The broadcast we aim at is to provide service everyone can enjoy regardless of disability. In this paper, we report that we developed an automated audio descriptions (AAD) system that automatically conveys the game situation in a sports program for visually impaired persons, and the method of presenting both the live television commentary and AAD simultaneously. It was confirmed that depending on the presentation method of AAD, we can make AAD easy to listen to even when AAD overlaps the live television commentary. We will continue to research a desirable method of presenting the commentary voices and AAD simultaneously.

References

1. International Olympic Committee. Olympic Data Feed. http://odf.olympictech.org/. Accessed 23 Mar 2018
2. Data creative & technology initiative for sports communities. http://www.datastadium.co.jp/. Accessed 23 Mar 2018. (in Japanese)
3. Taro, M.: Automatic generation of audio description for olympics/paralympics programs. In: NAB (National association of broadcasters) Show Conference, Broadcast Engineering and Information Technology Conference N256 (2017)
4. Kiyoshi, K.: Automatic Generation of Audio Description for Sports Programs, IBC (International Broadcasting Convention) (2017)
5. Shoei, S.: Speech Guides Helpful for Understanding Sports Broadcast, Spring Meeting of the Acoustical Society of Japan, 1-4-3, pp. 1547–1548 (2016). (in Japanese)
6. Shoei, S.: Utterance Classification for Automatic Audio Description of Sports Broadcasts, ITE Technical report, 11C-4 (2017). (in Japanese)
7. Atsushi, I.: A study on new service for overlapped audio information on TV programs. In: Proceedings of IEICE General Conference, H-4-11 (2016). (in Japanese)

Communication Support System of Smart Glasses for the Hearing Impaired

Daiki Watanabe[1], Yoshinori Takeuchi[2(✉)], Tetsuya Matsumoto[3], Hiroaki Kudo[3], and Noboru Ohnishi[3]

[1] Graduate School of Information Science, Nagoya University,
Furo-cho, Chikusa-ku, Nagoya 464-8603, Japan
watanabe.d@ohnishi.m.is.nagoya-u.ac.jp
[2] Department of Information Systems, School of Informatics, Daido University,
10-3 Takiharu-cho, Minami-ku, Nagoya 457-8530, Japan
ytake@daido-it.ac.jp
[3] Graduate School of Informatics, Nagoya University,
Furo-cho, Chikusa-ku, Nagoya 464-8603, Japan
{matumoto,kudo}@i.nagoya-u.ac.jp, ohnishi@nagoya-u.jp

Abstract. In this research, we propose a novel system for displaying captions of conversation content on smart glasses. We propose natural communication using smart glasses that is more like a conversation between hearing people than conventional communication methods such as sign language or handwriting. The system translates spoken words into text and displays them on the screen of the smart glasses. It equips four microphones, localizes the direction of the sound source, and distinguishes the angular direction of the sound source. Using signals from four microphones, the system can enhance voices. The voice enhancement technique is required to improve the automatic speech recognition rate in noisy environments. Experimental results showed that the system can estimate the angular direction of a voice and recognize more than 90% of words that are spoken. The subject experiment showed that the proposed system had a similarity score close to an existing smartphone application.

Keywords: Smart glasses · Automatic speech recognition
Sound localization · Voice enhancement · Hearing impaired

1 Introduction

When a hearing impaired person communicates with a hearing person, the hearing impaired person needs complementary methods such as sign language, writing, and lip reading. Both the hearing impaired person and the hearing person must understand sign language in order to communicate using it. They need writing instruments such as pens and paper in order to communicate by writing, and it is difficult to quickly write a lot of information. A hearing impaired

© Springer International Publishing AG, part of Springer Nature 2018
K. Miesenberger and G. Kouroupetroglou (Eds.): ICCHP 2018, LNCS 10896, pp. 225–232, 2018.
https://doi.org/10.1007/978-3-319-94277-3_37

person needs training in order to read lips, and it can be difficult to accurately lip read everything a person says. Even if a hearing impaired person needs or wants to converse, it may be difficult to actively participate in a conversation, or it may be assumed that they understand everything being said even when they do not. In this research, we propose a novel system that displays captions of conversation content on smart glasses.

Some systems using smart glasses have been developed. Suemitsu *et al.* proposed a system that provides conversation information on a see-through head-mounted display [1]. They designed a microphone array with irregular interval arrangement on a head-mounted display and focused on the target sounds over background noises. "Alarm Glasses for Deaf" are smart glasses that can alert hearing impaired people of danger [2]. It can translate loud sounds such as a car horns and screams into a visual alert or vibration.

Some smartphone applications that can assist communication between a hearing impaired person and a hearing person have been developed. KoeTra uses automatic speech recognition (ASR) to translate the voice of a hearing person into text [3]. This communication method requires both sides to use smartphones with each other, and it involves some difficulty for the hearing person. Therefore, when a hearing impaired person needs to ask for help, some of them hesitate to do so because they want to avoid inconveniencing others.

In this study, we propose smart glasses that make it easy for hearing impaired people to regularly communicate with anyone. The smart glasses we propose will enable more natural, conversational communication than conventional communication methods such as sign language and handwriting. The system translates voices into text and displays them on the screen of the smart glasses. It is equipped with four microphones and localizes the direction of the sound source. Using the sound localization technique, it can tell the angular direction of the speaker. This technique is used to detect the utterances of the person who is equipped. Using four microphones, it can enhance the speaker's voice. The voice enhancement technique is required to improve the ASR rate in noisy environments.

2   Communication Support System with Smart Glasses

2.1   Overview

We propose a system that can display the direction of a speaker and their conversation content on the screen of smart glasses. The reasons for using smart glasses are as follows:

- Only the hearing impaired wear the system; therefore, the hearing person does not need any equipment,
- Since conversation content is displayed on the scene being viewed, it is possible to communicate while looking at the speaker's face like in conversations between hearing people.

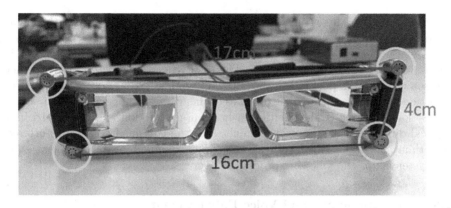

Fig. 1. Smart glasses with microphones

We attached four small microphones (ECM-CZ10, SONY) to the smart glasses (MOVERIO BT-200, EPSON). Figure 1 shows the smart glasses. The microphones are attached to the each corner of the smart glasses. When the microphones detect a voice, the system calculates the angular direction of the speaker by using the sound localization technique. Next, it emphasizes the voice signal by using the sound enhancement technique and reduces environmental noise with spectral subtraction methods. Then, the voice is translated into text by ASR. Finally, the direction of the speaker and the text of the voice are displayed on the screen of the smart glasses.

2.2 Estimation of Angular Direction of Arrival Sound

The angular direction of the arrival sound is estimated by simple sound localization technique. It can be calculated by the difference of the arrival time τ between two of the microphones,

$$\theta = \cos^{-1}\left(\frac{c\tau}{d}\right), \qquad (1)$$

where θ is the angular direction, c is the velocity of the sound and d is the distance between the two microphones. The time difference is estimated as the value when the cross-correlation function (2) reaches its maximum value.

$$\phi_{1,2}(\tau) = \frac{1}{T}\int_{-T}^{T} x_1(t)x_2(t+\tau)dt, \qquad (2)$$

where $\phi_{1,2}(\tau)$ is the cross-correlation function, $x_1(t)$ is a sound signal obtained by microphone 1, and $x_2(t)$ is a sound signal obtained by microphone 2.

The system estimates both the horizontal and vertical directions of the sound sources by using the pair of left and right microphones and the pair of upper and lower microphones. When the sampling frequency is 16 kHz, one sample time (1/16,000 s) difference between two microphones corresponds to about

10° in a horizontal direction. Therefore, the system cannot determine the angular direction with an accuracy of less than 10°. The system has less accuracy in a vertical direction because the vertical distance between two microphones is shorter than the horizontal distance. Therefore, the system determines whether the sound source is positioned above or below. The estimation of the vertical direction is used to detect the utterances of the equipped person. If the direction of the sound source is almost 0° in a horizontal direction and downward in a vertical direction, the system determines that the equipped person has uttered something. Since recognizing the speech of the equipped person is unnecessary, the system skips the following process.

2.3   Noise Reduction and Voice Enhancement

In order to improve the ASR rate in a noisy environment, we enhanced the voice signal and reduced the noise. First, a high-pass filter with a cutoff frequency of 200 Hz was applied in order to remove low frequency noise. Next, the phase of the signal recorded by each microphone was adjusted and the system added signals of the same phase in order to emphasize the voice signal. Then, the system reduced additive noise by a spectral subtraction method. Finally, a band-stop filter was applied in order to remove a large amount of background noise. The stop frequency was determined by the peak frequency component of the noise signal.

2.4   Automatic Speech Recognition

We used the Julius Dictation Kit v4.4 as a speech decoder. Julius is open-source, high-performance speech recognition software. In a Julius benchmark using 200 sentences of a JNAS test set, the recognition rate was 90.8% with a GMM-HMM acoustic model.

2.5   Displaying Information on the Smart Glasses

After the speech was recognized, the angular direction of the sound source and the results of the ASR were displayed on the smart glasses. Figure 2 shows an image of the scene visible on the smart glasses. The angle in degrees and the text are displayed near the center of the field of view.

3   Experimental Results and Discussion

3.1   Estimation of an Angular Direction of the Speaker

We placed the smart glasses with microphones 1 m above the floor. We played a voice using a loud speaker positioned 1 m away. Table 1 shows the angular direction of the input and the estimated angle.

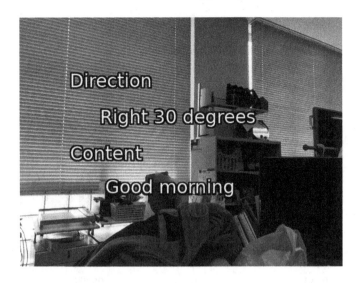

Fig. 2. Example of the screen displayed on the smart glasses

The system theoretically had an error of 10° in the horizontal direction, and the experimental results showed almost the same errors. Since it can be assumed that there are almost no cases in which multiple people exist within a range of several degrees, it is possible to visually recognize the person speaking. The system had more errors in the vertical direction. Experimental results show that the system successfully distinguished whether the sound source was above or below. The estimation of the vertical direction was only used for detecting the utterances of the equipped person.

3.2   Evaluation of the ASR

We placed the smart glasses with microphones 1 m above the floor. A hearing person spoke to the smart glasses from the front (0°), 30° to the right, and 30° to the left. We used the upper left and upper right microphones for the input of the ASR. 182 words from 20 sentences of daily conversation were spoken. We counted the words correctly recognized by the ASR. Table 2 summarizes the results of the recognition rate.

More than 90% of the words were correctly recognized by the ASR. The best results were obtained in the front direction. When the speaker spoke from the right side, the recognition rate was better when using the right-side microphone than when using the left-side one. The same was true for the recognition rate with the left-side speaker and microphone. This is because the distance to the microphone was closer and was less affected by the reflection of the sound from the smart glasses.

Table 1. Result of the estimation of an angular direction

Input angular direction	Estimated angle
Left 45°	Left 49°
Left 60°	Left 61°
Right 30°	Right 39°
Lower left	Left 39° and lower 32°
Upper left	Left 49° and upper 32°
Upper right	Right 39° and upper 32°

Table 2. Results of the recognition rate

Angle of incident of voice	Rate (right mic.)	Rate (left mic.)
Front	94.0%	95.1%
Right 30°	92.3%	91.8%
Left 30°	91.2%	92.3%

3.3 Evaluation by Subjects

We conducted experiments in which subjects communicated using the system. Figure 3 shows the arrangement of the experiment. Three subjects communicated. One subject put in earplugs and listened to music with headphones. Two loudspeakers were placed symmetrically about 3 m in front of the subjects and background noises were played during the experiment. We randomly repeated two sounds of inside a train station, two sounds from on the roadway, two sounds of inside a supermarket, and had silence every 30 s as background noises. The signal-to-noise ratio was about 10 dB.

After 3 min of conversation, they answered a questionnaire. For comparison, they communicated by writing and "KoeTra." There were 35 questions about the usefulness of the system in the questionnaire. Table 3 summarizes the questionnaire. We changed subjects seven times in the proposed system and four times in handwriting and KoeTra.

Table 3. Average score of the questionnaire

Method	Score of hearing impaired person	Score of hearing person
Proposed system	3.7	3.8
Handwriting	2.1	2.0
KoeTra	4.0	4.0

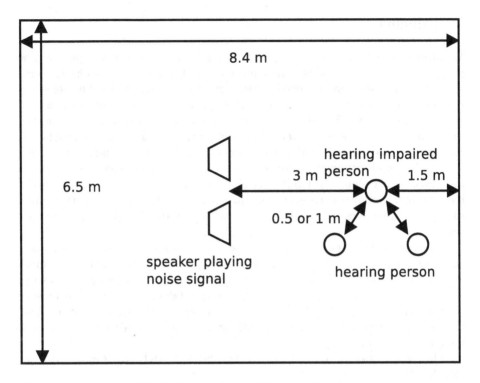

Fig. 3. Arrangement of the experiment

The proposed system had a similarity score close to KoeTra. KoeTra achieved a high recognition rate of ASR. However, it takes a little time to hand over the smartphone. The score of handwriting is low because of the time it takes to write on paper.

All the subjects stated that the display of sound direction was very appropriate and useful. The hearing impaired subjects could not pick up utterances outside their field of view. Only the proposed system has the great advantage of displaying the sound direction.

A total of 76 sentences of 499 words were spoken. The speech recognition rate was 61.9%, which got worse due to the noise played from the speakers. The average score in the questionnaire about the speech recognition was 3.0 (fair). We need to improve the recognition rate for better communication.

We measured the average time spent in the conversations. It was 39 s in the proposed system, 26 s in handwriting, and 36 s in KoeTra. Our system took the longest time. Due to the constraints of the hardware, the system could not start processing unless the recording of the sounds was finished. We need to improve the processing time. The handwriting took the shortest time. Some subjects did not write many sentences, instead writing singular words only. KoeTra sometimes failed in speech recognition, and it took a long time to redo the recognition in order to return the perfect recognition results.

4   Conclusion

We proposed a communication support system for hearing impaired people. The proposed system estimated the angular direction of voices and recognized speech. Small microphones were attached to the corners of smart glasses. The voice signals were processed to enhance the voices and reduce noise. The voice signals were recognized by ASR. The angular direction of the sound source and the results of speech recognition were displayed on the screen of the smart glasses. Hearing impaired people can use our system to look at the faces of hearing persons and understand their conversation content well by paying attention to their facial expressions and mouth movements. Our system is designed to always record sounds and process everything automatically before displaying the results so that the user does not have to bother with operating something every conversation.

Experimental results show that the system can estimate the angular direction of voices and recognize more than 90% of the words spoken. The experiment with subjects showed that the proposed system had a similarity score close to an existing smartphone application. The system takes a little time to present the recognition results. In future work, we will improve the accuracy of the ASR and the processing speed. Then, we will conduct more experiments to evaluate the effectiveness of the system.

This work was partly supported by JSPS KAKENHI Grant Number JP16K01574.

References

1. Suemitsu, K., Zenpo, K., Mizutani, K., Wakatsuki, N.: Captioning of conversational information on single channel microphone array. In: IEICE HCG Symposium, A-4-5, pp. 322–326 (2016). (in Japanese)
2. Alarm Glasses for Deaf. http://www.sparkawards.com/galleries/index.cfm?entry=7572B7F4-5056-A832-A2B0A52EDD972027. Accessed 31 Jan 2018
3. KoeTra App Support Page. http://www.koetra.jp/en/index.html. Accessed 31 Jan 2018

Development and Evaluation of System for Automatically Generating Sign-Language CG Animation Using Meteorological Information

Makiko Azuma[1]([✉]) [iD], Nobuyuki Hiruma[2], Hideki Sumiyoshi[1], Tsubasa Uchida[1], Taro Miyazaki[1], Shuichi Umeda[1], Naoto Kato[1], and Yuko Yamanouchi[1]

[1] NHK (Japan Broadcasting Corporation), 1-10-11 Kinuta, Setagaya-ku, Tokyo, Japan
azuma.m-ia@nhk.or.jp
[2] NHK Engineering System, Inc., 1-10-11 Kinuta, Setagaya-ku, Tokyo, Japan

Abstract. People who are born with hearing difficulties often use sign language as their mother tongue. The vocabulary and grammar of sign language differ from those of aural languages, so it is important to convey information in sign language. To expand sign-language services, we developed a system that accurately generates Japanese-Sign-Language computer-graphics (CG) animation from weather data. The system reads weather-forecast data coded in XML format distributed by the Japan Meteorological Agency and automatically generates CG animation clips to present them in sign language. We conducted two experiments to evaluate the system's performance in conveying weather information in sign-language CG animation to deaf participants, one was a comprehension evaluation to answer multiple-choice questions on the content and the other was a subjective evaluation on how easy the sign language was to understand and how natural it was on a 5-point scale (1: not understandable and unnatural and 5: understandable and natural). The overall percentage of correct answers was 96.5%. In the subjective evaluation, the average understandability was 4.43, and average naturalness was 4.13, suggesting that the participants highly appreciated the quality of sign-language CG animation. We also published a website in 2017 on which anyone can evaluate such animation regarding the latest weather forecast.

Keywords: Sign language · CG · Animation · Weather information
Evaluation experiment

1 Introduction

A closed-caption service for TV programs is not sufficient for deaf people who use sign language as their mother tongue; therefore, it is important to convey information in sign language. However, only a few TV programs are produced in Japanese Sign Language (JSL) in Japan. There are not many JSL interpreters in Japan, so it is not easy for a broadcaster to have them on site at any time, especially late in the night or early in the morning. NHK has been conducting research on sign-language CG animation for improving information accessibility for deaf people and designated weather information as the initial target. Our final target is the realization of sign-language broadcasting of weather information even when it is difficult to assign human sign-language casters.

There are several institutions working on translating from text data of aural languages to sign language, such as the Automatic Translation into Sign Languages (ATLAS) Project [1] and Research Lab. UTIC [2], but there is no system that can completely, automatically, and accurately generate sign language based on regularly updated data. NHK has been developing a Japanese-JSL machine-translation system, however, the system cannot be used in practical services because there is a problem with the accuracy. In especially about JSL, grammar has not been elucidated, so a Japanese-JSL machine-translation is more difficult than machine-translations between other natural-language combinations. Therefore, we have developed a system that completely, automatically, and accurately generates fixed pattern JSL CG animations using previously recorded fixed phrases from weather data.

2 Automatic Generation System of Sign-Language CG Animation Using Meteorological Information

2.1 Method

We developed a system that reads weather-forecast data coded in XML format distributed by the Japan Meteorological Agency (JMA) and automatically generates CG animation clips to present them in JSL. It automatically updates the sign-language animation based on the weather-forecast data via the Internet. Figure 1 shows the outline of the system. To ensure the accuracy of the JSL CG for weather information, templates are prepared in advance with variables such as weather-forecast terms and numerical values. The variables are determined by analyzing incoming weather-forecast data to complete the JSL sentence. The pre-fixed templates of natural JSL sentences were created by consulting native signers and sign-language interpreters. After this system has determined the complete JSL sentence, it selects JSL word-motion data to use in the database, enables smooth transition movements between two words using linear interpolation, and generates the motion data to represent the entire sentence. The motion data of each sign-language word were recorded using an optical motion capture system and stored in the Biovision Hierarchy (BVH) format. For the rendering engine, we adopted the TV program Making Language (TVML) system, which is a scripting language developed by NHK [3].

In addition to simple template completion, we introduced an advanced language-processing program, which analyzes incoming weather-forecast data and automatically revises the words and phrases to produce more natural sentences. For example, if a forecast predicts two consecutive days of sunny weather, the simple template completion is "It will be sunny today, and it will be sunny tomorrow," but this is awkward. With this system, the information can be expressed more naturally by saying, "Today's weather will be sunny, and it will continue through tomorrow."

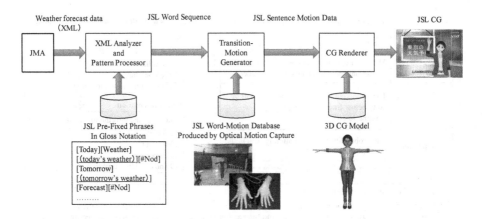

Fig. 1. Automatic-generation system of sign-language CG animation using weather-forecast data

2.2   Evaluation Experiments

We conducted experiments to evaluate the system's performance in conveying weather information in JSL CG animation to deaf participants. The participants were 5 deaf people aged from 20 s to 60 s (native signers) with Japanese ability required for understanding the questions and answering. We conducted two experiments, a comprehension evaluation to answer multiple-choice questions on the content and a subjective evaluation based on a 5-point scale on how easy the sign language was to understand and how natural it was (1: not understandable and unnatural and 5: understandable and natural). Regarding the comprehension evaluation, we presented JSL CG sentences on three topics, i.e., weather conditions, temperatures, and the probability of precipitation. The sentences were arranged in random order, although they were presented to all participants in the same order. A total of 136 sentences were presented, 114 on "weather," 6 on "temperature," and 16 on "precipitation." Figure 2 shows examples of presented sentences and multiple-choice questions. We described questions and answers in simple Japanese, and answers were in multiple-choice format. There were two reasons we adopted this method. One reason was to eliminate the linguistic load and differences in interpretations among the participants in understanding complicated Japanese sentences. The other reason was to evaluate the level of understanding of all participants directly and fairly. If we try to present questions in JSL and ask participants to answer in JSL, we need to ask JSL interpreters to translate from Japanese to JSL for the question, and from JSL to Japanese for the answer. This translation may include unique interpretations of each interpreter.

The participants were asked to answer questions about the topic, time information, and content in turn. When the participants answered the questions about the topic displayed on a screen, the screen changed and displayed the next question (about time information). After the participants finished all of the JSL CG animation clips, we asked questions to determine whether the JSL CG was easy to understand and natural. The participants gave their evaluation on a 5-point scale.

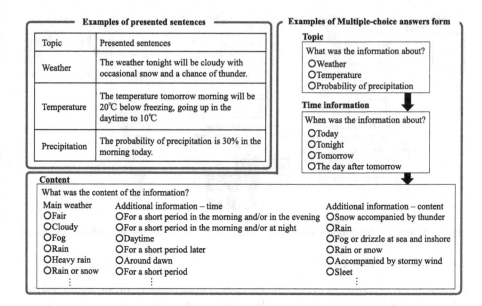

Fig. 2. Examples of presented sentences and multiple-choice questions

In the comprehension evaluation, the participants were asked several questions on each JSL sentence as the screen changed. We regarded their answers as correct only when they chose all the correct options. The overall percentage of correct answers was 96.5%. In the subjective evaluation, the average understandability was 4.43, and average naturalness was 4.13, suggesting that the participants highly appreciated the quality of JSL CG animation (Fig. 3). The results indicate that this system is useful for providing weather information in sign language.

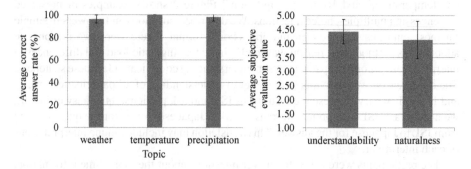

Fig. 3. Results of comprehension and subjective evaluations

3   Weather-Forecast Sign-Language CG-Animation Website

The system automatically generates JSL CG animation clips based on the latest weather forecasts and updates them as soon as it receives newer information through the Internet. After confirming the effectiveness of this system through the evaluation experiments, we published a website for evaluation in February 2017 on which anyone can evaluate the JSL CG animation of the latest weather forecast in order for us to receive a broad evaluation from the general public. People who visit this site can answer a questionnaire regarding JSL CG with the options of "understand well", "understand fairly well", "do not understand much", and "do not understand." They can also answer based on their age and JSL experience in multiple-choice format and post comments. Regarding the layout, we made it possible to select the place name from the map. This is because we thought that the placement of place names on the map rather than listing the place names written in Kanji would make it easier for the hearing-impaired to find the place name of interest, reducing their burden (Fig. 4).

Fig. 4. Weather-forecast sign-language CG-animation website (https://www.nhk.or.jp/strl/sl-weather/)

4   Conclusions and Planned Activities

We developed an automatic system for generating sign-language CG animation using weather-forecast data. We published a website for evaluation with which anyone can check and evaluate the sign language CG animation of the latest weather forecast. We will describe the questionnaire results sent to the published evaluation site and plan to improve this system based on evaluations from deaf people.

References

1. Lombardo, V., Battaglino, C., Damiano, R., Nunnari, F.: An avatar-based interface for the Italian Sign Language. In: International Conference on Complex, Intelligent, and Software Intensive Systems, pp. 589–594. IEEE Computer Society (2011)
2. Othman, A., Jemni, M.: Statistical Sign Language Machine Translation: from English written text to American Sign Language Gloss. IJCSI Int. J. Comput. Sci. Issues 8(5(3)), 65–73 (2011)
3. Kaneko, H., Hamaguchi, N., Douke, M., Inoue, S.: Sign Language Animation using TVML. In: ACM VRCAI 2010, pp. 289–292 (2011)

Digital Games Accessibility

Digital Games Accessibility
Introduction to the Special Thematic Session

Dominique Archambault[1]([⊠]) and Jérôme Dupire[2]

[1] Université Paris 8-Vincennes-Saint-Denis, THIM (E.A. 4004 CHArt),
Saint-Denis, France
dominique.archambault@univ-paris8.fr
[2] CNAM, Paris, France
jerome.dupire@cnam.fr

Abstract. Since a couple of decades, the video games area have spectacularly grown, and video games are now a genuine cultural and social object. Alongside with the pure entertainment finality, various application areas arose: "games with a purpose" are also aiming to teach, to monitor, to train, to treat, etc. By the way, people who play games became more diverse: from the younger to the elderly, nowadays everyone is potentially a gamer.

This wide diversity of users and products has led to pay a specific attention to their accessibility: how to ensure that nobody is not excluded from this strong cultural movement? The US legislation, through the CVAA, increased the focus on video/computer game accessibility, but still lots of efforts need to be done, especially regarding mainstream video games.

This session aims to bring together researchers, practitioners, to present and discuss new ideas and solutions dealing with video games accessibility issues.

Keywords: Computer games accessibility · Serious games

1 Introduction

A session about accessibility of games software have been organised at every ICCHP since 2002, so it is now the 9th. The Table 1 shows the different names of the session and the number of papers. Including this year's, we will have had 58 papers. The first year, the session themes were a bit wider ("software for the development of children") but only focused on young children. Then we decided to focus better theme of the session on entertainment software, while enlarging the group of users to any age. Since last ICCHP, in 2016, we have decided to rename it as "Digital Games Accessibility", which also includes Serious Games for the older ones.

The question of game accessibility arose at the turn of the new millennium. Indeed before 2000, the number of games that people with visual disabilities or

© Springer International Publishing AG, part of Springer Nature 2018
K. Miesenberger and G. Kouroupetroglou (Eds.): ICCHP 2018, LNCS 10896, pp. 241–244, 2018.
https://doi.org/10.1007/978-3-319-94277-3_39

Table 1. STS about accessibility of digital games software at ICCHP since 2002

Conference		Title of the session	Papers
2002	Linz	*Computers for the development of young disabled children*	5
2004	Paris	*Accessible Games and Entertainment*	4
2006	Linz	*Entertainment software accessibility*	5
2008	Linz	*Entertainment software accessibility: Towards generalised accessibility of computer games*	8
2010	Vienna	*Entertainment software accessibility*	5
2012	Linz	*Entertainment software accessibility*	8
2014	Paris	*Games and Entertainment Software: Accessibility and Therapy*	8
2016	Linz	*Digital Games Accessibility*	7
2018	Linz	*Digital Games Accessibility*	6
9 sessions			**58**

motor disabilities could play with was extremely low, close to zero. The questions at this point, and this can be assessed by the content or our 2002 session [1], were clearly focusing on specialised games for a group of users. Indeed the interaction in gameplay is usually very much linked to the device, which make it difficult to find a standard way of providing alternative for people who cannot access this device. In the 2002 session, several papers highlighted the need of focusing on abilities, instead of disabilities. [2] already points the question *"Can all young disabled children play at the computer ?"*, and answers it by replacing the question as analysing the possibilities, the abilities, to find the right software.

The 2007 state of the art paper [3] organise the field into 3 main categories: (1) specific games, (2) games for all and (3) accessible mainstream games. Today the first category, specific games, is still the winner with 4 papers (see Subsect. 2.1). The second category, which was here about specific games designed for being used by any users whatever way she/he accesses the computer (which is slightly different from fully accessible mainstream games), has been a important step [4,5]. It seems that researchers focus more now on how to improve accessibility of mainstream games (see Sect. 2.2), an long time objective from our community [6].

2   Content

2.1   Specific Games

As mentioned, we have four papers about specific games in this session, three of them about games to train a specific skill.

Computer games are often used to train a particular skill, these belong to a kind of games called *Serious Games*. This use of serious games is of great interest for people with disabilities, as for the rest of the population.

- Didier Schwab, Amela Fedja and Loïc Vial – *"The GazePlay project: open and free eye-trackers games and a community for people with multiple disabilities"* – propose a set of 13 mini-games intended to train people with multiple disabilities to use they eye gaze. This skill will be extremely important for them to to interact with their environment and to use AAC.
- Krzysztof Dobosz, Magdalena Dobosz and Marcin Wojaczek – *"Gamification of Cognitive Rehabilitation"* – designed rehabilitation exercises for different kinds of neurological patients, in the form of games.
- Szilvia Paxian, Veronika Szücs, Shervin Shirmohhamadi, Boris Abersek, Petya Grudeva, Karel Van Isacker, Tibor Guzsvinecz, and Cecilia Sik-Lanyi – *"Designing Trainer's Manual for the ISG for Competence project"* – present a manual intended for trainers introducing a set of games dedicated to training cognitive competence and describes how to use theses games.

The next paper can be added within this category of games, indeed to design specific computer games for people with disabilities, it is necessary to investigate how people with some limitations of activities can access some specific gameplay. This is a research field in itself. Papers in previous editions of this sessions have been focusing on how to propose an alternative gameplay with devices adapted to the player's situation [7,8].

- Barbara Leporini and Eleonora Palmucci – *"Accessible Question Types on a Touch-Screen Device: the Case of a Mobile Game App for Blind People"* – investigate methods to enable Visually Impaired Persons to use touch devices. They experimented various methods with a group of blind people in order to identify specific barriers encountered by Visually Impaired Persons and present a prototype to overcome these difficulties.

2.2 Mainstream Games

The two other papers are about the accessibility of mainstream games. This field have been explored since several years: [9] asked the question what's in a game and how to make a 3D shooter game accessible, while it is still a game; [10] proposed guidelines for games developers; [11] propose some modifications to make more accessible mainstream games.

- Jen Beeston, Christopher Power, Paul Cairns and Mark Barlet – *"Digital gaming with disabilities"* – Authors want to understand how persons with disability play mainstream computer games, and why do they play. They will present the results of a questionnaire survey involving 155 players.
- Thomas Westin, JaEun Jemma Ku, Jérôme Dupire, Ian Hamilton – *"Game Accessibility and W3C WCAG 2.0"* – considers online games in HTML5 and WebGL, and make some comparisons between WCAG 2.0 and some Games Accessibility Guidelines, in order to improve the WCAG with regards to this kind of games.

References

1. Archambault, D.: Computers for the development of young disabled children. In: Miesenberger, K., Klaus, J., Zagler, W. (eds.) ICCHP 2002. LNCS, vol. 2398, pp. 170–172. Springer, Heidelberg (2002). https://doi.org/10.1007/3-540-45491-8_37
2. Hildén, A., Hammarlund, J.: Can all young disabled children play at the computer? In: Miesenberger, K., Klaus, J., Zagler, W. (eds.) ICCHP 2002. LNCS, vol. 2398, pp. 191–192. Springer, Heidelberg (2002). https://doi.org/10.1007/3-540-45491-8_41
3. Archambault, D., Ossmann, R., Gaudy, T., Miesenberger, K.: Computer games and visually impaired people. Upgrade **VIII**(2), 43–53 (2007)
4. Ossmann, R., Archambault, D., Miesenberger, K.: Accessibility issues in game-like interfaces. In: Miesenberger, K., Klaus, J., Zagler, W., Karshmer, A. (eds.) ICCHP 2008. LNCS, vol. 5105, pp. 601–604. Springer, Heidelberg (2008). https://doi.org/10.1007/978-3-540-70540-6_85
5. Grammenos, D., Savidis, A., Georgalis, Y., Stephanidis, C.: Access invaders: developing a universally accessible action game. In: Miesenberger, K., Klaus, J., Zagler, W.L., Karshmer, A.I. (eds.) ICCHP 2006. LNCS, vol. 4061, pp. 388–395. Springer, Heidelberg (2006). https://doi.org/10.1007/11788713_58
6. Archambault, D., Gaudy, T., Miesenberger, K., Natkin, S., Ossmann, R.: Towards generalised accessibility of computer games. In: Pan, Z., Zhang, X., El Rhalibi, A., Woo, W., Li, Y. (eds.) Edutainment 2008. LNCS, vol. 5093, pp. 518–527. Springer, Heidelberg (2008). https://doi.org/10.1007/978-3-540-69736-7_55
7. Evreinova, T.V., Evreinov, G., Raisamo, R.: Non-visual gameplay: making board games easy and fun. In: Miesenberger, K., Klaus, J., Zagler, W., Karshmer, A. (eds.) ICCHP 2008. LNCS, vol. 5105, pp. 561–568. Springer, Heidelberg (2008). https://doi.org/10.1007/978-3-540-70540-6_80
8. García-Soler, A., Diaz-Orueta, U., Ossmann, R., Nussbaum, G., Veigl, C., Weiss, C., Pecyna, K.: Addressing accessibility challenges of people with motor disabilities by means of AsTeRICS: a step by step definition of technical requirements. In: Miesenberger, K., Karshmer, A., Penaz, P., Zagler, W. (eds.) ICCHP 2012. LNCS, vol. 7383, pp. 164–171. Springer, Heidelberg (2012). https://doi.org/10.1007/978-3-642-31534-3_25
9. Atkinson, M.T., Gucukoglu, S., Machin, C.H.C., Lawrence, A.E.: Making the mainstream accessible: what's in a game? In: Miesenberger, K., Klaus, J., Zagler, W.L., Karshmer, A.I. (eds.) ICCHP 2006. LNCS, vol. 4061, pp. 380–387. Springer, Heidelberg (2006). https://doi.org/10.1007/11788713_57
10. Tollefsen, M., Flyen, A.: Internet and accessible entertainment. In: Miesenberger, K., Klaus, J., Zagler, W.L., Karshmer, A.I. (eds.) ICCHP 2006. LNCS, vol. 4061, pp. 396–402. Springer, Heidelberg (2006). https://doi.org/10.1007/11788713_59
11. Laudanna, E., Bulgheroni, M., Caprino, F., Besio, S.: Making mainstreaming videogames more accessible: a pilot study applied to Buzz!^{TM} junior monster rumble for playstation. In: Miesenberger, K., Klaus, J., Zagler, W., Karshmer, A. (eds.) ICCHP 2010. LNCS, vol. 6179, pp. 235–242. Springer, Heidelberg (2010). https://doi.org/10.1007/978-3-642-14097-6_38

Accessible Player Experiences (APX): The Players

Jen Beeston[1]($\boxtimes$) (iD), Christopher Power[1,2] (iD), Paul Cairns[1,2] (iD), and Mark Barlet[2] (iD)

[1] Department of Computer Science, University of York, Deramore Lane, Heslington, York YO10 5GH, UK
jen.beeston@york.ac.uk
[2] The AbleGamers Foundation, PO Box 508, Charles Town, WV 25414, USA

Abstract. In research and practice into the accessibility of digital games, much of the work has focused on how to make games accessible to people with disabilities. With an increasing number of people with disabilities playing mainstream commercial games, it is important that we understand who they are and how they play in order to take a more user-centered approach as this field grows. We conducted a demographic survey of 154 players with disabilities and found that they play mainstream digital games using a variety of assistive technologies, use accessibility options such as key remapping and subtitles, and they identify themselves as gamers who play digital games as their primary hobby. This gives us a richer picture of players with disabilities and indicates that there are opportunities to begin to look at the accessible player experiences (APX) players have in games.

Keywords: Digital games · Accessibility · Disability

1 Introduction and Background

Currently, video games represent a significant part of our everyday modern lives, with UKIE[1] estimating that between 2.2 and 2.6 billion people play digital games worldwide. From online activity in social media, Twitch and player communities, we know that players with disabilities are increasingly part of what is a dynamic and growing community of digital game players, however there is very sparse research into who they are as players, the types of games they play and the prevalence of use of assistive technologies and accessibility settings in games. We surveyed 154 players with disabilities collected as part of the AbleGamers Player Panels programme, to direct future research as to the diversity of this distinctive population of players, and to inform design in terms of the diversity of breadth of technologies that are currently being used in digital games.

Researchers and designers alike acknowledge that there are not only barriers to playing digital games, but also accessibility concerns within the games themselves for those with individual and complex needs. Previously, researchers have considered the

---

[1] http://ukie.org.uk/research.

K. Miesenberger and G. Kouroupetroglou (Eds.): ICCHP 2018, LNCS 10896, pp. 245–253, 2018.
https://doi.org/10.1007/978-3-319-94277-3_40

barriers that players with disabilities encounter in games, with their efforts focused mainly on how technology can be adapted to enable them to play [1] and on creating bespoke games to investigate how games can be made playable for players with varying disabilities [9, 14]. Alongside this research, several charity organizations (e.g. AbleGamers, Gamers Outreach, Special Effect) and advocates of disabled gaming have established community and support for players with disabilities and created information to guide game developers to make adaptations and improvements [3]. Following on from this work, the successful integration of accessibility into many commercial titles means there are many people with disabilities playing online amidst non-disabled players. However, little is known about this audience and their player experiences. It is currently unclear what, if any, technology and accessibility options are being used by players with disabilities. Some academics have found that various methods that can be used to enable play, such as controllers [5], skill assistance [7] and difficulty adjustments [2] may impact upon the experience of play for those using them. For players with disabilities who may use these to play it is important to consider what effect this has on their experiences in games and in the social elements of the gaming hobby.

Digital games are widely recognised as a popular, enjoyable and even beneficial activity from which players can derive a sense of wellbeing [10]. Therefore, it is important that access to games should be universal and should not exclude people with disabilities. Most players view games as an end in themselves that provide experiences that are intrinsically valued [12]. However, rather than thinking about how players with disabilities play mainstream games that everyone plays, games are often positioned as a means to an end, particularly for rehabilitation and research is often focussed on creating bespoke games [9] or adapting and creating novel controllers [14]. This approach neglects the evidence that there are growing numbers of disabled players playing mainstream games alongside everyone else. Digital games are supporting real inclusion but little is known about how disabled players are gaining access to games and the experiences they have when they are playing, whether valued or not.

If we are to move research and practice beyond questions of basic access and enablement [16] it is important that we know more about players in the game space so we can begin to understand their accessible player experiences (APX) in games. Porter and Kientz [15] provide a useful starting point with a survey of 55 players with disabilities collected age, gender, impairment class, platforms played on, and types of games played and was also supplemented by interviews. They found that their participants had some incompatibilities with technologies that were barriers to their gaming, and that their sample tended towards single player games and less towards multiplayer games. Additionally, they spoke to games industry professionals about their current practises in making games accessible for players with disabilities. Their findings suggest that the games industry focus on the things that they are immediately aware of, such as a colleague having a specific need, such as colour remapping or subtitles. The motivation of the work reported in this paper is to provide a more comprehensive understanding of players with disabilities to inform and extend the focus of subsequent research and practice into accessible games.

2 Method

The AbleGamers Player Panels programme was created in a collaboration between the University of York and the AbleGamers Charity to provide a systematic means by which players with disabilities can have a voice in digital games research and development. The aim of the programme is to facilitate organisations looking to do user research or games testing with players with disabilities by putting them in touch with suitable players who have already declared an interest in taking part in such research. To enable such matchmaking and also to provide a better understanding of players with disabilities, the aim of this study is the collection of the necessary demographic information about the players.

The demographic survey was iteratively developed with collaboration between the AbleGamers team and players with disabilities. Players originally registered interest in the Player Panels through the AbleGamers Charity website, where they provided a small amount of demographic information including: contact information, age, current gaming platforms used, game genres played, and their motivation to register. The AbleGamers Player Panels registration requested that players only register if they want to be involved and be contacted by researchers and developers, have access to the internet and could fill out the online survey. The demographic questionnaire was available for all ages and for those with any form of disability that did not prevent them from completing the online questionnaire. This work and further research only included participants over the age of 18 and excluded those who have indicated that they have a cognitive disability. This was to safeguard those for whom consent could not be guaranteed at this stage.

A sample of 7 respondents from the California area took part in a telephone interview to trial further demographic questions and to inform questions about their gaming habits. From this, an initial draft demographic questionnaire was created and feedback elicited from 5 further registered respondents and from AbleGamers staff.

The final demographic survey contained demographic information, such as their contact information, preferences, gaming needs, current habits and technology usage, which can be used to identify participants for opportunities with organisations. Further, participants gave consent for the information to be used by AbleGamers and their partners for purposes of research.

3 Results

3.1 About the Players

Out of 154 respondents, 92 people identified as male, 38 female, 15 non-binary and 9 preferred not to say. The average age of respondents was 32. When asked about the length of a typical play session for them, 74 respondents said they played between 2 to 4 h at a time; 39 played 1 to 2 h, 32 played 5 h or more, and only 9 people reported a typical session as being 1 h or less. Respondents were asked to select as many of the items in Table 1 to describe their disabilities as required. It is worth noting that 'Other needs and preferences' was an open text item. This mainly seems to have been used to provide a more detailed description or the medical terms for their disability. To retain confidentiality, this information is not provided here.

Table 1. Disability information

Disability	Respondents
Autism	18
Hard of hearing	20
Deaf	7
Upper limb physical disabilities	91
Lower limb physical disabilities	81
Mental Health Difficulties	41
Learning Disabilities (e.g. dyslexia, SLP, ADHD, language etc.)	26
Blind	8
Colour vision deficient (e.g. red-green colour blind)	6
Low vision	25
Other needs and preferences	42

Many of the respondents identified themselves as gamers (96) and consider it to be their primary hobby (87). There were an almost equal number of people who considered themselves to be hardcore gamers (46) as those who identified as casual gamers (47). Very few people did not consider themselves a gamer (16) or only played games when they have nothing else to do (10).

3.2   What Are They Playing?

The gaming platforms rated as being used 'very often' by respondents were PC (104), followed by phone (53), PlayStation (52), Nintendo Switch (26), Xbox (24), then tablet (20). Out of those platforms, Nintendo Switch scored highest in the 'do not play' category, followed by Xbox, tablet, PlayStation, Phone, and then PC. It is quite possible that Nintendo Switch was least played since it was the newest gaming console listed in the options. The game types selected as played most often were Single Player (124), followed by Online Multiplayer (72), Cooperative Multiplayer (52), Competitive Multiplayer (40), One vs. One Multiplayer (26), and then Local multiplayer (17). Respondents were asked to provide their top 3 current favourite games. There were 255 different titles provided. Where games received more than one entry, a top favourite games list was created to show which were the most popular games (Table 2).

Table 2. Top favourite games

Rank	Top favourite games	Respondents	Best-selling games of 2017 by NPD Group
1	Destiny 2	13	Call of Duty: WWII
2	Overwatch	9	Star Wars: Battlefront II
3	Super Mario Odyssey	9	Super Mario Odyssey
4	PlayerUnknown's Battlegrounds	8	NBA 2K18
5	The Legend of Zelda: Breath of the Wild	8	Mario Kart 8
6	World of Warcraft	8	Madden NFL 18
7	The Elder Scrolls V: Skyrim	7	PlayerUnknown's Battlegrounds
8	Call of Duty World War II	6	Assassin's Creed: Origins
9	Hearthstone	6	The Legend of Zelda: Breath of the Wild
10	Rocket League	6	Grand Theft Auto V
11	Stardew Valley	6	FIFA 18

Source of ranked list: https://venturebeat.com/2018/01/18/december-npd-2017-nintendo-switch-leads-the-hardware-pack-in-a-3-29-billion-month/.

Note: Please see footnotes 2 in Sect. 4 for further top games lists by platform.

3.3   How Are the Players Accessing Games?

Participants were asked to indicate whether they used any items from a selection of assistive technologies (hardware) and accessibility options (software) or could specify in separate textbox if they used something not listed. Of the assistive technologies, 24 respondents provided information in the 'other' box. Items such as on-screen keyboard and using a converter to use keyboard and mouse on console were mentioned. One respondent mentioned that they used a handheld magnifying glass, but they did not specify exactly what they used this for. Customized controllers or alternative PC mouse were also selected as often used assistive technologies. Popular accessibility options items used were subtitles and key remapping/bindings used by 83 respondents (Table 3).

Table 3. Assistive gaming technology and in-game accessibility options

Assistive technology	Respondents	Accessibility options	Respondents
Eye gaze tracking	2	Text to speech	11
Customized controller	18	Speech to text	17
One handed controller	3	Subtitles	83
Screen reader	9	Colour blind options	7
Alternative PC mouse	17	Contrast or colour changes	29
VR headset	3	Mouse cursor enlargement	24
Alternative controller	7	Text enlargement	44
Other technology	24	Auditory or screen alerts	24
		Key remapping	83
		Other option	23

4 Discussion

The results show that this sample of players with disabilities are choosing to play mainstream, commercial games. Many of their favourite current games are aligned with current, top/most played games across the common gaming platforms[2] which strongly suggests that the gaming preferences of these players is no different from non-disabled digital game players. While this aligns with Porter and Kientz [15], Flynn and Lange [8] regarding the desire of players to play mainstream AAA titles, we differ in that our sample shows that more than half of our players favourite games are multiplayer games. Whether this is due to sampling bias, or due to a shift in demographics since that previous work, we have compelling evidence that players are engaging in both single player games, and online, community-based play.

Our findings show that there are some adaptations that are commonly used among this sample, such as customised controllers/PC mouse, subtitles and key remapping. This suggests that even such minimal accommodations provided in games can help to enable play for many players. PC was the most used gaming platform by participants. This is consistent with common wisdom that until recently PC gaming was more accessible than consoles as accessibility is more mature on that platform [15]. It will be important to revisit this in the near future now that a number of consoles are integrating middleware solutions for accessibility. Phone was the second most used platform by respondents which may be due to the ubiquity of the smartphone in modern life which is something that people are likely to own anyway rather than a separate platform for gaming.

Many of these players consider themselves to be *gamers*, and a substantial portion say that they are *hardcore gamers* which suggests that they identify deeply with the gaming hobby and invest substantial time and effort on the hobby [6]. If this is the case, there are social aspects to consider for these players within gaming, too. Previous studies suggest that features such as aim assist, difficulty settings, or different controllers can impact how players view not only their own ability and play experiences, but other players as well.

It is important to note that this sample of disabled players is likely subject to selection bias: these are players who currently play digital games and could complete our survey. As this survey was conducted to gain an overview of the AbleGamers Player Panels community, there are items which were not covered initially that could form the basis of further work. This may include covering: what assistive technologies or accessibility options/software players feel that they do not have but would help them, a broader look at what gaming platforms may be used (e.g. older consoles such as Nintendo Wii), a deeper look at who they are playing with and what their online multiplayer experiences are like.

More importantly, even though there will likely always be a need to address the implementation lag of new technologies to provide accessible options [16], we see that

---

[2] https://www.polygon.com/2018/1/5/16853706/ps4-games-top-psn-downloads-destiny-gta,   http://store.steampowered.com/stats/,   http://comicbook.com/gaming/2018/01/06/most-played-nintendo-switch-games/, https://www.microsoft.com/en-gb/store/most-played/games/xbox.

commercial mainstream games are reaching a point in the research domain where there is the opportunity to move beyond simply providing access to games. There is the opportunity to explore what it means for players to have accessible player experiences within games, leveraging the existing wealth of knowledge from the player experience research community.

5 Conclusions

The demographic survey we conducted shows that our participants are much like samples of the wider population of players. They are playing mainstream games, they identify as 'gamers' and give substantial amounts of their free time to the hobby. Since previous research has focussed on using games for therapeutic uses and rehabilitation, this work shows that, this may not be the only reason disabled people play games. Additionally, there may still be issues with control mechanisms for disabled players and mainstream games may not be entirely accessible, however despite this, there are still disabled players who do have access and do play mainstream games. Therefore, game designers and researchers can assume that people with disabilities want to play mainstream games with everyone else and will attempt to find a way to play. In terms of game design, since many of these players have reported using adaptations such as auditory alerts, key remapping, subtitles, alternative controllers, screen readers, this suggests that these minimal additions and modifications to games can accommodate for a substantial audience of disabled players. As such, it is becoming increasingly important for researchers and designers to consider not only the effectiveness of these adaptations but how these impact their overall APX of play and, consequently, their social experiences in playing games with others.

Acknowledgments. Thanks to the AbleGamers Charity for the collaboration on the Player Panels programme, and all the players who volunteered their time. This work is funded by EPSRC grant [EP/L015846/1] (IGGI) and the University of York Research Priming Fund.

References

1. Archambault, D., Gaudy, T., Miesenberger, K., Natkin, S., Ossmann, R.: Towards generalised accessibility of computer games. In: Pan, Z., Zhang, X., El Rhalibi, A., Woo, W., Li, Y. (eds.) Edutainment 2008. LNCS, vol. 5093, pp. 518–527. Springer, Heidelberg (2008). https://doi.org/10.1007/978-3-540-69736-7_55
2. Baldwin, A., Johnson, D., Wyeth, P.: Crowd-pleaser: player perspectives of multiplayer dynamic difficulty adjustment in video games. In: Proceedings of the 2016 Annual Symposium on Computer-Human Interaction in Play, pp. 326–337. ACM (2016)
3. Barlet, M.C., Spohn, S.D.: Includification: A Practical Guide to Game Accessibility. The Ablegamers Foundation, Charles Town (2012)
4. Bierre, K., Chetwynd, J., Ellis, B., Hinn, D. M., Ludi, S., Westin, T.: Game not over: accessibility issues in video games. In: Proceedings of the 3rd International Conference on Universal Access in Human-Computer Interaction, pp. 22–27 (2005)

5. Birk, M., Mandryk, R.L.: Control your game-self: effects of controller type on enjoyment, motivation, and personality in game. In: Proceedings of the SIGCHI Conference on Human Factors in Computing Systems, pp. 685–694. ACM, April 2013

6. Bosser, A.G., Nakatsu, R.: Hardcore gamers and casual gamers playing online together. In: Harper, R., Rauterberg, M., Combetto, M. (eds.) ICEC 2006. LNCS, vol. 4161, pp. 374–377. Springer, Heidelberg (2006). https://doi.org/10.1007/11872320_53

7. Depping, A.E., Mandryk, R.L., Li, C., Gutwin, C., Vicencio-Moreira, R.: How disclosing skill assistance affects play experience in a multiplayer first-person shooter game. In: Proceedings of the 2016 CHI Conference on Human Factors in Computing Systems, pp. 3462–3472. ACM, May 2016

8. Flynn, S., Lange, B.: Games for rehabilitation: the voice of the players. In; International Conference on Disability, Virtual Reality & Associated Technologies (ICDVRAT 2010), pp. 185–194 (2010)

9. Grammenos, D., Savidis, A., Georgalis, Y., Stephanidis, C.: Access invaders: developing a universally accessible action game. In: Miesenberger, K., Klaus, J., Zagler, Wolfgang L., Karshmer, Arthur I. (eds.) ICCHP 2006. LNCS, vol. 4061, pp. 388–395. Springer, Heidelberg (2006). https://doi.org/10.1007/11788713_58

10. Jones, C.M., Scholes, L., Johnson, D., Katsikitis, M., Carras, M.C.: Gaming well: links between videogames and nourishing mental health. Front. Psychol. 5, 260 (2014)

11. Juul, J.: A Casual Revolution: Reinventing Video Games and Their Players, pp. 8–12. MIT press (2010)

12. Juul, J.: Half-Real: Video Games Between Real Rules and Fictional Worlds. MIT press, Cambridge (2011)

13. Kulshreshth, A., LaViola, Jr., J.J.: Evaluating performance benefits of head tracking in modern video games. In: Proceedings of the 1st Symposium on Spatial User Interaction, pp. 53–60. ACM (2013)

14. López, S.A., Corno, F., Russis, L.D.: Design and development of one-switch video games for children with severe motor disabilities. ACM Trans. Accessible Comput. (TACCESS) 10(4), 12 (2017)

15. Porter, J.R., Kientz, J.A.: An empirical study of issues and barriers to mainstream video game accessibility. In: Proceedings of the 15th International ACM SIGACCESS Conference on Computers and Accessibility, p. 3. ACM, October 2013

16. Power, C., Cairns, P., Barlet, M.: Inclusion in the third wave: from access to experience. In: New Directions in the Third Wave of HCI. Springer (to appear)

17. Sherry, J.L., Lucas, K., Greenberg, B.S., Lachlan, K.: Video game uses and gratifications as predictors of use and game preference. Playing video games: motives, responses, and consequences 24(1), 213–224 (2006)

The Gazeplay Project: Open and Free Eye-Trackers Games and a Community for People with Multiple Disabilities

Didier Schwab[1(✉)], Amela Fejza[1], Loïc Vial[1], and Yann Robert[2]

[1] Univ. Grenoble Alpes, CNRS, Inria, Grenoble INP (Institute of Engineering Univ. Grenoble Alpes), LIG, 38000 Grenoble, France
{didier.schwab,loic.vial}@univ-grenoble-alpes.fr,
amela.fejza@grenoble-inp.org
[2] Anantaplex, Nanterre, France
yann.robert@anantaplex.fr

Abstract. In order to develop and enhance an augmentative and alternative communication (AAC), gaze is often considered as one of the most natural way and one of the easiest to set up in order to support individuals with multiple disabilities to interact with their environment. For children who start naturally from scratch, who have in addition such difficulties, it is a strong challenge even to acquire or to support the required basic knowledge. Games are often considered a good way to learn. Games designed for eye-trackers, i.e. electronic devices able to compute the position of the gaze, allow children to discover the power of their eyes and the consequences of the actions triggered by their gazes. Video games can be a good way to improve basic requirements as gaze fixation and gaze pursuit as well as conventions like rewards or dwell interactions often used in AAC tools. In this article, we present the GazePlay project which main contribution is a free and open-source software which gathers several mini-games playable with all eye-trackers including low cost ones.

Keywords: Eye-trackers · Games · Serious games
Children with multiple disabilities
Augmentative and alternative communication
Human-computer interaction · Eye-based interaction

1 Introduction

In order to develop and enhance an augmentative and alternative communication (AAC), gaze is often considered as being one of the most natural way and one of the easiest to set up in order to support individuals with multiple disabilities to interact with their environment. Of course, for children who start naturally from scratch, who have in addition such difficulties, it is a strong challenge even to acquire or to support the required basic knowledge. They have to learn the power of their eyes, the consequences of the actions triggered by their gazes but

© Springer International Publishing AG, part of Springer Nature 2018
K. Miesenberger and G. Kouroupetroglou (Eds.): ICCHP 2018, LNCS 10896, pp. 254–261, 2018.
https://doi.org/10.1007/978-3-319-94277-3_41

even to improve their extraocular muscles,... Games are often considered as a good way to learn. In the case of eye-tracking, video games could be a good way to improve basic requirements as gaze fixation and gaze pursuit as well as conventions like rewards or dwell interactions often used in AAC tools.

In this article, we present the GazePlay project which main contributions are

- *GazePlay*[1] a free and open-source software which gathers several mini-games playable with all eye-trackers including low cost ones. It permits people to access such games at a price which decrease from 2 000–3 000€ to 100–160€ excluding computer price.
- *TobiiStreamEngineForJava library*[2], a Java open library which links C++ library from Tobii to Java. With it help, is possible to develop software able to interact with Tobii's low-cost eye-trackers (Tobii EyeX, Tobii 4C).
- *GazePlay github*[3] a public repository hosted by GitHub which help us to manage GazePlay development. At the end of March 2018, eight people directly contribute to the code and dozens on ideas (including therapists and parents).

2   Eye, Gaze and Eye-Trackers

Eye is a sense organ that allows vision. It allows humans to see images in 3 dimensions and with colors. Eyes make specific motions [10,11]:

- *Saccade* happens when the eyes move from one point of interest to another.
- *Pursuit* happens when the eyes follow a moving target.
- *Fixation* happens when the eyes stop scanning the scene, and the vision is kept in one place so it can take detailed information about the object or the scene it is focused on.
- *Blinking* is a rapid closing then opening of the eyelids. When it occurs spontaneously, it protects the eye by moistening it. When it occurs voluntary, blinking can be used to reestablish a basic communication.

Naked-eye observations go back to the French ophthalmologist Louis Émile Javal (1839–1907), who noticed for the first time that reader's eyes do not skim fluently through the text while reading, but make quick movements mixed with short pauses where the eye gets fixated [6]. The very first eye tracker was created in 1908, again for an experiment about reading. At that time, eye-tracking was really intrusive and uncomfortable for the readers because they had to wear a type of contact lens with a small opening for the pupil. This lens was attached to a pointer which changed its position with the movement of the eye.

---

[1] https://gazeplay.net.
[2] https://github.com/coylz/TobiiStreamEngineForJava.
[3] https://github.com/schwabdidier/GazePlay.

Nowadays, eye-trackers are mainly infrared cameras which provide raw coordinates from which it is possible to estimate fixation, saccades, poursuites and/or blinking [4,8]. Several companies build eye-trackers, for marketing, virtual and augmented reality or to evaluate driver vigilance [5]. Eye-based interaction has been used for disabled people since the early 1980's [1] but main work about interaction is [3] where several solutions including dwell interaction which is often used to select in AAC softwares are discussed (see Sect. 3.1).

Until recently, eye-tracker were really expensive devices and were not affordable by the majority of families of disabled people. For instance, in France, the cost of a basic eye-tracker for disabled people is over 1200€ in the beginning of 2018 (it was the double one year before).

In 2013, the Eye-Tribe company is the first to have lowered the cost really much by creating cheap and more affordable eye-trackers with an elegant Java API and compatible with both Windows and OS X. Tobii, the most important firm to sell eye-trackers released their EyeX (2014, ≃100€) followed by the Tobii 4C (2016, ≃160€) and their C++ library. While the Eye-tribe was sold to Facebook for its Oculus division and is no longer developped, Tobii works a lot on their low-cost eye-trackers and their associated tools (multiple users, gaze trace, etc.).

Fig. 1. Two of the eye-trackers which permit to play with GazePlay: the Eye Tribe upper side, the Tobii 4C bottom side

These three eye-trackers can be used with GazePlay. We integrate directly eye-tribe library while our team has developed a Java Native Interface to build a java library, *TobiiStreamEngineForJava* which permits to use easily the Tobii EyeX and the Tobii 4C with Java (Fig. 1).

3 GazePlay

We present in the following GazePlay 1.3, the current development version of GazePlay we plan to release before the end of March, 2018. GazePlay is a free and open-source software which gathers 22 mini-games playable with an eye-tracker. It is compatible with all eye-trackers which are able to control the mouse cursor, with Tobii EyeX and Tobii 4C on Windows and the Eye Tribe Tracker on Windows or MacOs X. To help motivating the players, it is very easy to modify default images of the game. One player would prefer to play with Mickey Mouse while another would like to play with Princess Sofia, with his family or therapist. Another way to help motivating the players is to give them a reward (a big friendly smiley and applauses). Interface and games are fully translated in French, English and German (Fig. 2).

Fig. 2. Screenshot of the main menu of GazePlay development version on the 25th of March, 2018. They are currently 22 games (17 fully playable).

3.1   Games in GazePlay

GazePlay 1.3, gathers 17 playable games[4]. For each one, we aim to develop one or several skills for the children. We can consider that three kinds of skills are developed in GazePlay: action-reaction, selection, memorization skills.

Fig. 3. A child who plays the *creampie* game with an Eye Tribe tracker.

Action-Reaction Skill. The purpose of these games is to learn to the children that a gaze can have direct consequences. For instance, in the *creampie* game, the user throws a cream pie on the target when gaze looks at it (see Fig. 3); in *Block*, a big image is hidden by colored blocs. The player looks at a block to destroy it. When all blocs have disappeared, a reward is shown. In the *Ninja* game, the target explodes when the player looks at it.

Selection Skill. Selection with eye-tracker is not as easy as it is with a mouse. Blink is both not easy to capture with an eye-tracker and often very difficult to perform for a child with multiple disabilities. In AAC programs, an usual way to select an element (photo, image, pictogram, etc.) is to keep the gaze on this element. It is called, a dwell interaction [3]. A feedback is given as a circular progress bar. When it is full after a configurable time, the element is selected [7]. In *Magic Cards* several cards are displayed. One of the card hides an image. When the player stares at one card, it is turned. If (s)he finds the image, a reward is given to the player. Other games like *Memory* and *Where is it?* aim to train the selection skill.

---

[4] For a complete description of games see https://gazeplayeng.wordpress.com/games/.

Memorization Skill. The purpose of these games is to work on the short-term memory like in *memory* which has the same rules of the classic game. Several pairs of cards from 2 to 6 (following child/helper choice), face down. Then the player use a dwell interaction (see previous section) to turn over 2 cards. If both cards are the same, they disappear, otherwise they turn back over after few seconds to permit to the player to remember them. When all cards have been matched, the reward is given.

In other games, we aim to work on long-term memory. In the game *Where is the animal*, a sentence is pronounced and written to indicate to the player which animal to find (horse, dog, crocodile,...) and then several photos of animals are shown (from 4 to 9 following child/helper choice). Player selects photos until he finds the correct one. The same game is proposed with colors. An additional one is completely configurable i.e. parents/therapists can build their own games with their own photos. The sentence can be completed with pictograms for instance to learn them to the children (see Fig. 4). This game and the usage of pictograms was inspired by the community (see Sect. 4).

Fig. 4. Screenshot of the game *where is it?*, the question is asked associated with a pictogram from Makaton vocabulary [2].

3.2 Analysis

When a game is stopped by the helper, statistics are displayed and saved automatically. They includes charts which presents depending on the game, total active playtime, actual playtime, durations, reaction length, standard deviation,... A heatmap also shows gaze position on the screen. With these statistics, helpers get objective information to evaluate motivation and/or evolution of children (Fig. 5).

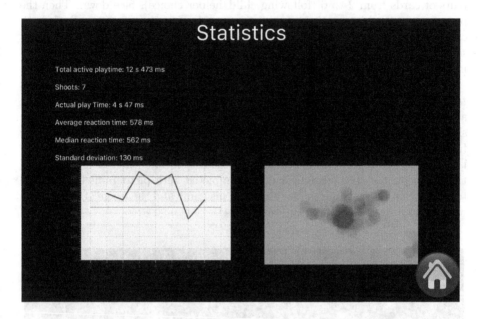

Fig. 5. Screenshot of statistics for an action-reaction focused game.

4   The Community as the Future of GazePlay

The project is open source under a GNU General Public License v3.0[5]. Anyone can modify it as long as (s)he distributes his/her code. It remains possible to sell customized version of GazePlay or services using GazePlay including therapies or tutorials.

The GazePlay project started with the first author who is both an associate professor in informatics and the father of a girl with multiple disabilities. Sharing experience with other parents especially the ones who already own eye-trackers and games for their children and with therapists [9], he worked with postgraduate students (second and third authors) to release first versions of GazePlay.

The code is hosted on GitHub. The repository permits to share code, information for developers, issues (enhancements, bugs, milestones, . . .) but also to find interesting projects. Due to his goal, some people (fourth author for instance) from the open source community helped us especially on the software engineering side and permitted to increase our efficiency. Similarly, we get regular feedback from many therapists who used GazePlay with children.

GazePlay was downloaded almost 800 times since its first release. We really hope that such a project can inspire others to build new projects related to people with special needs.

---

[5] https://www.gnu.org/licenses/gpl-3.0.en.html.

References

1. Friedman, M.B., Kiliany, G., Dzmura, M.: The eyetracker communication system. Johns Hopkins APL Tech. Dig. **3**(3), 250–252 (1982)
2. Grove, N., Walker, M.: The makaton vocabulary: Using manual signs and graphic symbols to develop interpersonal communication. Augmentative Altern. Commun. **6**(1), 15–28 (1990). https://doi.org/10.1080/07434619012331275284
3. Jacob, R.J.K.: What you look at is what you get: eye movement-based interaction techniques. In: Proceedings of the SIGCHI Conference on Human Factors in Computing Systems, CHI 1990, pp. 11–18. ACM, New York (1990). https://doi.org/10.1145/97243.97246
4. Jambon, F., Luengo, V.: Analyse oculométrique "on-line" avec zones d'intérêt dynamiques : application aux environnements d'apprentissage sur simulateur. In: Mollard, R., Franck Poirier, F.V. (eds.) Ergo'IHM 2012 - Conférence sur les nouvelles interactions, créativité et usages. p. publication en cours. Biarritz, France, October 2012. https://hal.archives-ouvertes.fr/hal-00873898, session plénière Ergo/IHM/IS
5. Kar, A., Corcoran, P.: A review and analysis of eye-gaze estimation systems, algorithms and performance evaluation methods in consumer platforms. IEEE Access **5**, 16495–16519 (2017). https://doi.org/10.1109/ACCESS.2017.2735633
6. Lupu, R.G., Ungureanu, F.: A survey of eye tracking methods and applications (2014)
7. Nguyen, V.B., Jambon, F., Calvary, G.: Gaze-Based Interaction: Evaluation of Progressive Feedback, pp. 153–158. ACM, October 2014. https://hal.archives-ouvertes.fr/hal-01090436. poster
8. Salvucci, D.D., Goldberg, J.H.: Identifying fixations and saccades in eye-tracking protocols. In: Proceedings of the 2000 Symposium on Eye Tracking Research & Applications, ETRA 2000, pp. 71–78. ACM, New York (2000). http://doi.acm.org/10.1145/355017.355028, https://doi.org/10.1145/355017.355028
9. Schwab, D.: Gazeplay : Creation of a community to help the development of a free and open-source plateform to make eye-tracker video games accessible to everyone. In: 5ème EUROPEAN RETT-SYNDROME CONGRESS, Berlin, November 2017
10. Tatler, B.W., Wade, N.J., Kwan, H., Findlay, J.M., Velichkovsky, B.M.: Yarbus, eye movements, and vision. i-Perception **1**(1), 7–27 (2010). https://doi.org/10.1068/i0382, http://www.ncbi.nlm.nih.gov/pmc/articles/PMC3563050/
11. Yarbus, A.L.: Eye Movements and Vision. Plenum, New York (1967)

Accessible Question Types on a Touch-Screen Device: The Case of a Mobile Game App for Blind People

Barbara Leporini[✉] and Eleonora Palmucci

ISTI - CNR, Via G. Moruzzi, 1-56124 Pisa, Italy
barbara.leporini@isti.cnr.it,
palmuccieleonora@gmail.com

Abstract. This study investigates accessibility and usability via screen reader and gestures on touch-screen mobile devices. We specifically focus on interactive tasks performed to complete exercises, answer questionnaires or quizzes. These tools are frequently exploited for evaluation tests or in serious games. Single-choice, multiple-choice and matching questions may create difficulties when using gestures and screen readers to interact on a mobile device.

The aim of our study is (1) to gather information on interaction difficulties faced by blind people when answering questions on a mobile touch-screen device, and (2) to investigate possible solutions to overcome the detected accessibility and usability issues. For this purpose, a mobile app delivering an educational game has been developed in order to apply the proposed approach. The game includes the typical question types and exercises used in evaluation tests. Herein we first describe the main accessibility and usability issues reported by a group of visually-impaired people. Next, the game and its different exercises are introduced in order to illustrate the proposed solutions.

Keywords: Accessibility · Mobile interaction · Visually-impaired users
Mobile games

1 Introduction

Several mobile and web applications exploit exercises and questions for practice and evaluation purposes. Activities like pairing words or ordering items are also widely used exercises in digital games. Thus, potential application fields may be learning systems (e.g., for foreign languages) and educational entertainment (e.g. serious games). Although several guidelines have been proposed in the literature [7, 8, 12], digital games and learning systems need to be further investigated in terms of accessibility and usability for visually-impaired people [1, 10]. This should especially be done for interaction with touch-screen devices via a gesture-based screen reader.

In our study we investigated the accessibility and usability of mobile user interfaces for screen reading users. We specifically focused on the interaction with questions and exercises widely used for quizzes, games or evaluation tests. Exercises such as pairing words or ordering elements may create a number of issues when interacting via screen reader and gestures on a touch-screen. Our purpose is to investigate how to overcome

© Springer International Publishing AG, part of Springer Nature 2018
K. Miesenberger and G. Kouroupetroglou (Eds.): ICCHP 2018, LNCS 10896, pp. 262–269, 2018.
https://doi.org/10.1007/978-3-319-94277-3_42

those issues. First, a group of visually-impaired users were asked to report their main accessibility and usability problems. Next, a mobile educational game was developed to test potential solutions proposed in order to enhance the interaction via screen reader and gestures with a case study.

This work focuses on the following goals:

(1) Gathering evidence of accessibility and usability issues encountered by the visually-impaired when interacting with exercises and questions on a touch-screen device;

(2) Designing various types of test typology that are commonly used for exercises and questions in the education context to practice specific topics, especially for an accessible gesture-based interaction on touch-screen devices.

To this aim, we developed a mobile app for touch-screen devices (tablet or smartphone) of an educational game composed of various exercises, which allowed us to test some technical solutions applied to different case studies on a touch-screen, especially for screen reading interaction.

In the previous work [5] the app was introduced to describe the design of the themes and layout in the user interface. This was done with the aim of providing equal auditory and visual content perception for sighted and non-sighted players. This paper describes the main mobile device interaction problems encountered with existing games and learning exercises. In addition, it illustrates how puzzles and exercises can be developed by describing the proposed solutions.

This paper is organized as follows: the next section introduces the methodology used; Sect. 3 reports the issues encountered by the visually-impaired when interacting with questions and specific tasks; Sect. 4 describes the proposed solutions applied to the various exercises on the mobile game. Conclusions ends the paper.

2 Method

Firstly the main accessibility and usability issues related to interaction with quizzes and exercises via a gesture-based screen reader were collected. This was done by interviewing a small group of visually-impaired people recruited by the local Italian Association for the Blind. The users were asked to report problems encountered when interacting with puzzles and exercises, in particular when carrying out specific actions. The common use cases in which the issues are encountered were also identified.

For our purposes, the main common types [6] used when preparing quizzes, tests for practicing and evaluating specific educational topics were considered in the users participatory study. The typologies of exercises and questions considered in the study are summarized as: Single-choice (just one answer is right); Multiple-choice (more than one answer may be right), Matching items (one item of a first list is paired with another one of the second list); True/False, Ordering items, Gap-filling (completing the sentence with an item).

On the basis of the reported accessibility issues, possible solutions have been proposed and applied to the exercises developed for a mobile game in order to make them more accessible for the visually impaired. In designing the different types of exercises, we considered the gestures available on a touch-screen which are compatible with the main screen readers for a smartphone/tablet. Examples of these are Voice-Over[1] for IOS systems and TalkBack[2] for Android platforms. This is important to ensure the App gestures are compatible with those available in the screen reader for touch-screen devices. We relied on simple gestures and VoiceOver-like interaction techniques with menus (single tap to hear an option and double tap to select it) in line with earlier accessibility work [4].

The mobile game prototype was developed using the Cordova Framework to design a cross-platform app. Since the user interface can be developed via X/HTML, CSS and JSs, the WAI-Aria suite [11] was used to enhance accessibility features. Studies like [2, 9] already applied WAI-Aria to ensure accessibility for the Web, in our work we test its efficacy for a mobile interface.

3 Exercise Types: Accessibility and Usability Issues

3.1 Participants

Five visually-impaired users were involved in our study. Their ages ranged from 25 to 70 years old. All of them had experience in using ICT and mobile devices with screen reading software: 2 people out of the 5 had experience of the Android-based devices and 3 people of the IOS operating system. All the users showed interest in a mobile digital game based on puzzles for a number of reasons. One important aspect is related to the lack of digital games for people with vision impairments. In addition, performing exercises or answering questions can be difficult, even impossible to accomplish due to the actions required, such as drag-and-drop. The issues described in this paper are essentially referred to mobile phone interaction. However, the users reported that they widely encountered these problems also with Web pages and applications. This implies a significant limitation in access to a number of online educational games or learning apps (e.g. for learning a foreign language).

3.2 Interaction Issues

Most interaction problems are related to the exploration mode used to detect text and items on the touch-screen. The exploration may be either (1) touch (i.e. slowly dragging one finger around the screen), or (2) swipe linearly to hear the items in order [3]. The main issues (from I1 to I6) reported by users can be summarized as:

I1 - Reading Question Content. The text is not always automatically read by the screen reader when a question is selected and displayed on the screen. Therefore, the user has to explore the screen with his/her finger in order to be able to read the text. For complex interfaces, especially in games, being able to explore and locate the right text can require a considerable effort for a non-sighted person.

---

[1] https://www.apple.com/accessibility/iphone/vision/.

[2] https://www.androidcentral.com/what-google-talk-back.

I2 - Finding Items. All the users stated that they often encounter problems in properly identifying the items related to possible answers. This occurs especially when the items are randomly or horizontally arranged. Even when they are listed in two columns, it may be very difficult to clearly identify the correct column (left or right) for an item. In this case, it is necessary to explore the screen by touch (exploration mode (1)) rather than with a swipe gesture (preferred by 4 out of 5 users interviewed). As a result, performing tasks such as matching items, ordering items or selecting answers might be unfeasible. This can occur also for True/False questions, i.e. even when there are only two answers. This may be because the position of the answers is not consistent for all the similar questions or the items are located very far from each other. Another reason could be that some elements might not be 'touched' when exploring by touch. For the users 'Left' and 'right swipe' exploration is considered a more reliable way to reach all the elements on the screen (4 out of 5 users expressed this preference).

I3 - Moving Items (Drag-and-Drop). Many exercises/questions require users to move or drag the items around the screen. This happens, for example, for ordering or pairing the items (e.g. matching exercises). When performing drag-and-drop, even if the user is able to identify and select the first item, it is practically impossible to, find and select the second one (the target element or position) while dragging the element. In practice, both exploration modes (touch or swipe) do not work with drag-and-drop exercises.

I4 - Awareness of Selected Status. In some exercises or questions the user is asked to select more than one answer (e.g. multi-choice questions). Once an item has been picked up, it is selected and the user cannot pick it up again. Other tasks can lead to a similar issue: difficulty for the user to understand if an item has already selected or not. In these cases, the screen reader is typically unable to perceive the elements already picked up (i.e. the questions already completed or the answers already selected). Accordingly, the user is constrained to proceed by trial and error (e.g. by clicking on the element again) or by remembering the elements previously chosen. This interaction is consequently inaccessible, and more importantly unusable.

I5 - Detecting Gaps to Fill In. All participants reported difficulties in detecting which blanks are to be filled in and how to edit them. Such an issue is related to the Gap-filling task (complete the sentence by filling in the blanks). This happens especially on mobile interfaces since the screen reader often interprets the entire phrase/paragraph as a single chunk. Consequently, the selection of gap fields becomes impossible.

I6 - Receiving Feedback and Confirmation. Task success/failure is often provided to the user in a visual manner. Therefore, a blind user can encounter several problems in detecting it. For instance, sometimes items are marked or just graphically rendered in a different way (e.g. changes to image, dimension, color, or position). So, even if the element is textual, getting information on status changes can be very difficult or impossible.

4   The Proposed Solutions

The game has been designed with eight different exercises. These exercises represent the various types of questions, which are usually used in a test environment. While the work [5] describes the exercises in terms of layout and themes to achieve an auditory perception equal to the visual rendering, this section explains the solutions proposed to enhance the interaction with specific tasks on a touch-screen. Specifically, through the development of the exercises we proposed potential technical solutions to solve the accessibility and usability issues summarized in the Sect. 3.

Features Common to All Exercises
All the exercises address issue I1 with regard to properly reading the question content. The question text has been arranged according to the graphical (and visual) layout in order to make it as attractive as possible. This is an example of a graphical interface which is difficult for a blind person to use. Since the layout may require a scattered arrangement of the elements for graphics purposes, detecting some items by touch (such as the question text) can become a very difficult task for a visually-impaired user.

We resolve this reading issue (I1) by using HTML tags and WAI-Aria attributes (e.g. "role", "aria-live", "aria-atomic", etc.). Interaction accessibility has been further improved in terms of touch accuracy. We noticed that the block size (i.e. the <div> width) affects the dimension of the tap-sensitive region: a larger <div> block requires a smaller touch accuracy to select the items. Consequently, some interface components have been enclosed in <div> blocks with a greater width. While this has a positive impact on screen reader interaction via gestures, it does not interfere with the visual rendering. As a result, the screen reader can detect an item regardless of its size and position within the block. As a result, detecting items is simpler for a visually-impaired user. See the green block in the Fig. 1 for an example: the 'True' is in a larger block (the color green has been used only to show the example).

Another issue common to the all exercises is related to feedback messages. As stated in issue I6, many difficulties are often connected to the graphical ways used for giving a feedback. To overcome this inconvenience, hidden <div> blocks have been added to the interface to provide information detectable only by the screen reader. Exercise 1 and exercise 3 are two examples.

Single-Choice (Exercise 1). This case has been implemented with a list of possible choices to be selected (only one right answer). The items are displayed in a column in the middle of the screen, thus facilitating exploration by touch (I2), as described above. Just one of them can be selected with a double tap. When tapping on an item, the answer is given and the game moves on to the next question. A graphical feedback is provided to the sighted user. Instead a feedback message is available to the screen reader to indicate the success/failure of the answer.

To make the feedback truly accessible (issue I6), a specific <div> block displaying the message has been added to the interface. The block is hidden so that only the screen reader is able to detect it. Moreover, to allow the screen reader to read it automatically, the added bloc needs to receive the focus.

Multiple-Choice (Exercise 2). The question implemented through this exercise displays all possible answers in a vertical column (Fig. 1) as in the 'single-choice puzzle'. The difference lies with the need to select more than one item and so how to proceed the next question. In the 'single-choice question' after tapping on a choice, the game moves directly to the next question. This approach cannot be applied to the multiple-choice question since more than one choice needs to be selected before proceeding. In addition, for this question type issue I4 had to be considered.

To implement a multiple-choice question, we made it possible to pick up the items one by one via a double tap. Once the item is chosen, it is displayed in bold (for visual rendering) and the screen reader announces "selected" to inform the user of their choice This result was obtained via WAI-Aria and a hidden-label detected only by the screen reader. The user can select the other items in the same way. On completion, a 'Confirm' button allows the player to proceed to the next question, this need to confirm the action makes this exercise different from the 'single-choice question'.

True or False (Exercise 3). For this question type (Fig. 1), selection is very simple since only two choices are available (true/false | yes/no | etc.). When selecting True or False, the screen reader announces 'right/wrong' (to overcome issue I6) and the next question is immediately displayed (as for the single-choice).

Some previously reported issues were related to how easy it is to locate the two choices by touch (I2). To avoid this potential problem we firstly introduced consistency in the location of the two answers (i.e. always in the same position). In this way the user can learn the given position for the two answers. Then, we worked on the tap-sensitive areas for the two choices, i.e. the <div> blocks enclosing the answers have been developed with a larger dimension.

In this exercise we also considered issue I4 related to more than one question being available. A predetermined number of questions is available: the user can select them one by one. Once a question has been answered, it can no longer be selected. When 'touch' locates an element related to a question already completed, the screen reader makes an announcement, for example, "Question already answered".

Fig. 1. Multiple-choice (on the left) and true or false (on the right) (Color figure online)

Matching Items (Exercise 4). This exercise consists in matching the items in two different sets. The items are displayed in two lists in two columns: one on the left and one on the right. It is common to complete the exercise using drag-and-drop to pair two items, however, this cannot be performed via screen reader and gestures.

To compensate for this, we designed a step by step selection process so as to match an item from one set with the corresponding one in the other set. The procedure is as follows: the first item in the left column is selected by a tap; the corresponding item on the opposite side can be picked up by another tap. At this point, the second item moves from the right to the left, pairing to the first one. Consequently, the two matching items are both shown on the left, marked as paired (Fig. 2). When finished to match all elements, on the right side there are no more items. The user confirms completion of the exercise via a specific button "End and Score". Through this approach the I3 issues related to drag-and-drop tasks are resolved. In addition, I2 (locating items) and I4 (awareness of selected status) issues are also considered in this exercise. In order to facilitate column detection (left and right), two hidden labels have been added before the two lists in order to inform the screen reader that the following elements are related to the left or right column.

Gap-Filling (Exercise 5). This exercise consists of a question to be completed by filling in the gaps. The sentence contains the ellipsis to indicate the missing term. To handle issue I5 (detecting gaps), the hidden label '[blank]' has been put in the position of the ellipsis to indicate the gap to the player. In order to avoid making editing too multifaceted, a list of potential answers is provided rather than asking the user to insert the word using the virtual keyboard. In this way, the puzzle is very similar to the 'single-choice puzzle', but the 'gap issue' has been solved. The items are visually arranged in a scattered order (see Fig. 2), but a blind user can perceive them in a regular list when exploring the interface via finger touch (i.e. I2). The solution was implemented with WAI-Aria techniques and hidden labels.

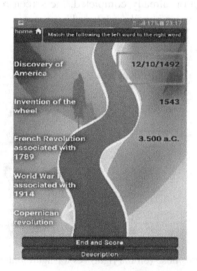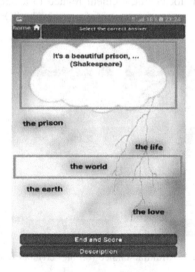

Fig. 2. Matching items (on the left) and gap-filling (on the right)

5 Conclusions

This work investigates the main accessibility difficulties encountered by screen reading users when interacting with touch-screen devices through gestures. Five blind users have been consulted to collect information on the problems arising when answering questions on a mobile device. Six accessibility and usability issues have been identified and summarized. A proposed solution aimed at avoiding those issues has been implemented via a mobile serious-game app for multiplatform systems. A few exercises have been designed. The app shows how exercises can easily be performed also via simple gestures (swipes and double taps) on a touch-screen by a blind user. The Cordova environment used to develop the app allows us to confirm that HTML tags and WAI-Aria techniques can support accessibility also for mobile multiplatform device with screen reader. In future, we plan to investigate interaction modalities for other typologies of exercises e structured user testing will be conducted.

References

1. Calvo, R., Iglesias, A., Moreno, L.: Accessibility barriers for users of screen readers in the Moodle learning content management system. Univ. Access Inf. Soc. **13**(3), 315–327 (2014)
2. Carvalho, L.P., Ferreira, L.P., Freire, A.P.: Accessibility evaluation of rich internet applications interface components for mobile screen readers. In: Proceedings of the 31st Annual ACM Symposium on Applied Computing, pp. 181–186. ACM (2016)
3. Google accessibility. Exploration by touch with Talkback. https://support.google.com/accessibility/android/answer/6006598?hl=en
4. Kane, S. Wobbrock, J.O., Ladner, R.E.: Usable gestures for blind people: understanding preference and performance. In: Proceedings of CHI 2011. ACM, New York (2011)
5. Leporini, B., Palmucci, E.: A mobile educational game accessible to all, including screen reading users on a touch-screen device. In: Proceedings of the 16th World Conference on Mobile and Contextual Learning, p. 5. ACM, October 2017
6. Madsen, H.S.: Techniques in Testing. Oxford University Press, New York and Oxford, viii + 212 pp. (1983). ISBN 0-19-434132-1
7. Mi, N., Cavuoto, L.A., Benson, K., Smith-Jackson, T., Nussbaum, M.A.: A heuristic checklist for an accessible smartphone interface design. Univ. Access Inf. Soc. **13**(4), 351–365 (2014)
8. Park, K., Goh, T., So, H.J.: Toward accessible mobile application design: developing mobile application accessibility guidelines for people with visual impairment. In: Proceedings of HCI Korea, pp. 31–38. Hanbit Media, Inc., December 2014
9. Spiliotopoulos, D., Dalianis, A., Kouroupetroglou, G.: Accessibility driven design for policy argumentation modelling. In: Stephanidis, C., Antona, M. (eds.) UAHCI 2014. LNCS, vol. 8516, pp. 101–108. Springer, Cham (2014). https://doi.org/10.1007/978-3-319-07509-9_10
10. Yuan, B., Folmer, E., Harris, F.C.: Game accessibility: a survey. Univ. Access Inf. Soc. **10**(1), 81–100 (2011)
11. W3C, WAI, Accessible Rich Internet Applications (WAI-ARIA) 1.1. Recommendation, 14 December 2017. https://www.w3.org/TR/wai-aria-1.1/
12. W3C, WAI, Web Content Accessibility Guidelines 2.0, WCAG 2.0. http://www.w3.org/TR/WCAG20/

Game Accessibility Guidelines
and WCAG 2.0 – A Gap Analysis

Thomas Westin[1(✉)], JaEun Jemma Ku[2], Jérôme Dupire[3], and Ian Hamilton[4]

[1] Department of Computer and Systems Science, Stockholm University,
Stockholm, Sweden
thomasw@dsv.su.se
[2] University of Illinois, Urbana, USA
jku@illinois.edu
[3] CNAM, Paris, France
jerome.dupire@cnam.fr
[4] Bristol, UK
i_h@hotmail.com

Abstract. Game accessibility is to remove unnecessary barriers for people with disabilities (PwD), within the limitation of game rules. Canvas in HTML5 and WebGL means that virtually every web browser is a game runtime environment. The problem is that web-based games can only be optimised to follow WCAG within limits of game rules and WCAG may not include what is needed for accessible games. The W3C Silver Taskforce is at the time of this writing preparing the next version of WCAG. This paper compares WCAG 2.0 and a set of current game accessibility guidelines (GAG), to answer: (1) Which similarities and differences can be found between WCAG 2.0 and GAG?; (2) How may these differences inform the W3C Silver Taskforce in the ongoing work to prepare the next version of WCAG?; and (3) How could the optimisation for accessibility in web-based games be performed? 107 GAGs were compared with WCAG 2.0, resulting in 61 survey questions plus comments and demographics, sent to experts and other users of WCAG. Semi-structured interviews were also conducted. Conclusions are that there is a clear gap but WCAG 2.1 bridges a few parts. Furthermore, the study seems relevant for the Silver Taskforce in understanding the demarcation line between apps in general and games and possibly for how extended reality applications could be made more accessible.

Keywords: Games · Accessibility · Web · Canvas · WebGL · Guidelines

1 Introduction

Games are defined by strict rules, differentiating from other types of computer applications by adding such deliberate obstacles: "playing a game is the voluntary attempt to overcome unnecessary obstacles." [1] Accessibility is to make a product or service (e.g.

I. Hamilton—Independent Accessibility Specialist.

© Springer International Publishing AG, part of Springer Nature 2018
K. Miesenberger and G. Kouroupetroglou (Eds.): ICCHP 2018, LNCS 10896, pp. 270–279, 2018.
https://doi.org/10.1007/978-3-319-94277-3_43

a game) usable to as many as possible, which means improved design for all. Thus, game accessibility can be defined as to remove unnecessary barriers for people with disabilities (PwD), within the limitation of game rules. Game accessibility has been researched since the early days of the digital game industry [2]. However, it was not until 2010 that it was legislated, under the 21st Century Communications and Video Accessibility Act 2010 (CVAA) in the USA. CVAA compliance requires Advanced Communications Systems (ACS) e.g. voice and text chat in games to be accessible. A detailed discussion of the CVAA and its impact on games is presented by Brooks [3].

Since the introduction of the Canvas tag in HTML5 and WebGL (support for hardware rendered real-time graphics without plugins), virtually every web browser is a game runtime environment. This means that web accessibility has to consider game accessibility within limits of game rules. The World Wide Web Consortium (W3C) has defined a set of Web Content Accessibility Guidelines 2.0 (here referred to as WCAG). A W3C working group called the Silver Taskforce[1] (TF) is currently preparing the next version of WCAG, i.e. after the interim version 2.1[2] (to be released). Following the WCAG requires that content is accessible, to different levels (A/AA/AAA) with Success Criteria, which poses several challenges in practice.

1.1   Problem and Research Questions

The problem is that web based games can only be optimised to follow WCAG within limits of game rules and WCAG may not include what is needed for accessible games. This paper presents and compares WCAG 2.0 and a set of current game accessibility guidelines (GAG), to try and answer these research questions (RQ): (1) Which similarities and differences can be found between WCAG and GAG?; (2) How may these differences inform the Silver TF in the ongoing work to prepare the next version of WCAG?; and (3) How could the optimisation for accessibility in web-based games be performed? Answering these questions is a prerequisite for further work in improving the WCAG with regards to Canvas and WebGL-based games.

2   W3C WCAG and the Silver Taskforce

As part of Accessibility Guidelines Working Group, Silver TF aims to include as many perspectives as possible by engaging with diverse stakeholders. Furthermore, Silver TF broadly communicates its efforts to keep the community informed and improve WCAG so that it can be inclusive of more disability and technologies[3]. The objective of the Silver TF is "to perform preliminary research and development for a successor to the Web Content Accessibility Guidelines (WCAG)"[4]. To achieve these goals, Silver TF has collaborated with researchers to compile the academic researches on WCAG. Also, Silver TF hosted a two-full day Design Sprint in March 2018 prior to CSUN Assistive

---

[1] https://www.w3.org/WAI/GL/task-forces/silver/wiki/Main_Page.
[2] https://www.w3.org/TR/WCAG21/#new-features-in-wcag-2-1.
[3] https://www.w3.org/WAI/GL/wiki/Goals_for_Designing_the_Silver_Process.
[4] https://www.w3.org/WAI/GL/task-forces/silver/wiki/Main_Page.

Technology conference. This was a brainstorming session with invited accessibility experts for the next version of WCAG. To prepare this, Silver TF looked at existing WCAG with three lenses: (1) Conformance; (2) Usability; and (3) Maintenance, which may also be useful to understand the gap in this study.

3   Game Accessibility Guidelines

Game Accessibility Guidelines[5] came about as a response to developer demand for game-specific accessibility resources, evolving from BBC's internal game accessibility standards and guidelines [4], which in turn were adapted from WCAG 2.0. Key goals for the project were to communicate information relevant to game developers in language that game developers understood and striking an effective balance between being detailed enough to be useful, while not too verbose that they become intimidating.

On the surface they appear similar in structure to WCAG, particularly the split between basic/intermediate/advanced, but these are in fact fundamentally different to A/AA/AAA in WCAG. In particular that they cannot be used as benchmarks to audit/ comply against, as what is appropriate to consider varies between games and genres. The categorization is based on a balance of how many people benefit, the level of impact on them, and developer cost/effort. They are further split by type of impairment[6]; vision, hearing etc., as these are easy for developers to relate to the kind of challenges present in their games. This pragmatism required for games is reflected in how the guidelines are implemented. The first action is to disregard guidelines that are not applicable to you; guidelines that would break your game if implemented. This varies significantly from game to game, e.g. avoiding all timing is an entirely reasonable accommodation in a turn-based strategy game such as Civilization, but it is not in a real-time game such as Call of Duty. This then leaves you with a tailored set of guidelines, based on what constitutes reasonable accommodations for your specific game design. The guidelines have formed the basis for academic marking criteria, government funding criteria, and a number of corporate internal guideline projects.

4   Related Research About Guidelines for Accessible Games

In the past many people have put a lot of effort into the topic of game accessibility guidelines and a selection are outlined below. While some guidelines focus on disabilities among seniors [5], others focus on a specific type of disability such as visual with audio games [6] and mobility and orientation [7] as well as hearing [8]. In addition to these guidelines found in research papers, BBC and the GAG, there are also well-defined guidelines developed by organisations such as AbleGamers [9], CEAPAT [10], and the IGDA Game Accessibility SIG [11]. A more generic set of guidelines of how to write about people with disabilities is also important to mention [12]. One reason to focus on GAG in this paper was that GAG has been continuously updated since 2012 (here Sep.

---

[5] http://gameaccessibilityguidelines.com/.

[6] https://www.w3.org/WAI/intro/people-use-web/diversity.

2017 update), while the other game accessibility related guidelines were published once (related to the quickly evolving game industry) and some focus on only one impairment. Another reason was that three of the authors were very familiar with or creators of GAG, which made it easier to identify the gap.

5   Methods

An exploratory survey approach was chosen combined with a comparative gap analysis to identify and confirm the gap between WCAG and GAG (RQ1, RQ2). RQ3 was answered by discussing the analysis and survey results with related research. The authors are more or less experienced users of WCAG; one is a WCAG expert with accessibility testing certificate from US government.

5.1   Gap Analysis

The gap analysis was made in three steps: (1) Both sets of guidelines were inserted side-by-side in a spreadsheet, with hyperlinks to each guideline to make it easy to look up a detailed description of each. A column to identify whether each guideline in GAG (Sep. 2017 update, available as a spreadsheet online[7]) could be related to guidelines in WCAG 2.0 was added, as well as a column to write a brief reason. There were 121 GAGs in total, of which 13 occur one or more times (total 27 instances). By removing the 14 extra instances there were 107 unique GAGs. (2) The second step in the gap analysis was to fill in the table, by evaluating whether each GAG was represented in WCAG. For this, the names of guidelines were used. If there was any uncertainty, a question mark (?) was added. (3) One author who was familiar with both GAG and WCAG followed up those with a question mark, by using the hyperlinks to read and compare the guidelines in detail. The evaluation and motivation were updated accordingly. If there was still uncertainty ('Y?') then it was included in the survey questions, along with those coded with 'N'. Of the 107 unique GAGs, 61 was found not (or were still uncertain) to be in WCAG. For these, feedback from other WCAG users was needed to validate the gap analysis through the online, exploratory survey.

5.2   Exploratory Survey Design and Selection

The population of WCAG experts is unknown to the best of the author's knowledge. Thus, an explorative survey approach was chosen to validate the gap analysis. Four different approaches to survey design were tried; (1) all GAGs coded with 'Y?' or 'N' were included as they were, with only minor edits such as adding "WCAG considers…". From the authors' internal discussion and one pilot test with a colleague, it was necessary to ease the work for respondents, while keeping as close to the origin as possible; (2) thematically grouped GAGs to 19 questions; (3) a mix of 1 and 2; and (4) as 1 but with rephrasing of GAG names, to lower the cognitive load for WCAG experts who could

---

[7] http://gameaccessibilityguidelines.com/excel-checklist-download/.

not be expected to also be game experts. The fourth approach was selected as it was judged by the authors as the best compromise of being close to the original GAG names and understandable by the survey respondents of WCAG users.

Demographic questions were (1) self-identification of disability; (2) years of WCAG use; (3) self-reported WCAG expertise; (4) role(s) when using WCAG; (5) industry; and (6) work title. Questions 1–4 were control questions to better interpret the results. 61 questions (one per GAG from gap analysis) were divided into Visual, Hearing, Motor, Speech, Cognitive, and General questions. The questions were designed as hypotheses with a 5-point Likert scale: "WCAG considers <GAG name>: 1 (Disagree) to 5 (Agree)". At the end of each section there was a comment field, and a final feedback field. There were 74 questions in total (including six demographics, six comments and one final question). The survey questions are available online[8]. The survey was submitted with permissions to W3C lists public-silver, wai-gl, wai-ig and aria. A one-time email was sent to 70 email opt-ins members of Silver researchers group. The survey was also spread via various social media channels, and introduced at the CSUN 2018 Silver TF Design Sprint with invited WCAG experts and others. The survey closed after 18 days.

5.3 Interviews

Before conducting the semi-structured interview, an online pilot interview was done with one of the survey respondents. Then we narrowed down and identified interview questions to ask. Three semi-structured interviews were conducted during the biggest Assistive Technology conference. The goal of the interview was to follow up survey answers which were hard to interpret; i.e. why some thought that WCAG considers certain GAG, while authors did not (in our gap analysis). Interviewees were two WCAG experts with more than 10–15 years of W3C WCAG involvement and a product manager overseeing accessibility testing for the company. The interview template was defined with four questions based upon preliminary survey results and a conceptual explanation of each GAG rule (see Results section). The interviews were conducted by: (1) asking four questions first; then (2) explain GAG concepts and ask to add comments for each question. Interviews were between 6–12 min long, recorded with audio, transcribed and coded with the MaxQDA™ software tool.

5.4 Ethical Considerations

The participation for the survey and interview was voluntary and could be withdrawn at any time. The informed consent forms for the interviews were collected and those for the online survey were waived because online survey poses no more than minimal risk nor has any personal identifiers. Before sending out online survey, permissions by relevant W3C working group chairs were obtained in writing. This research is also approved by University of Illinois Institutional Review board.

---

[8] https://tinyurl.com/y8bkdurm.

6   Results and Analysis

6.1   Preliminary Survey Results and Survey Redesign

In the 14 first survey responses to questions, a majority (>50%) respondents agreed (to a level of 4 or 5) in 5/61 questions. However, it was hard to understand why based on Likert scale data alone. Hence, we found a need to add one comment text field at the end of each section (Vision, Hearing…): "If you agreed (level 4 or 5) to any of the above, please explain". In addition, following text was added to increase the clarity based on preliminary survey feedback: "Do you think any of these are already covered by existing WCAG guidelines?".

6.2   Final Survey Results

34 responses were collected in this exploratory survey. The median ordinal data from Likert scale questions (range 1–5) in the survey are presented in Fig. 1, visualising the gap between WCAG 2.0 and GAG. Lower values confirm the gap analysis. As seen in Fig. 1, most of the gap analysis was confirmed. Notable exceptions were the five questions mentioned in the previous section. The groups of people with or without disabilities had some different opinions, where PwD tended to confirm the gap more clearly (dashed line in Fig. 1).

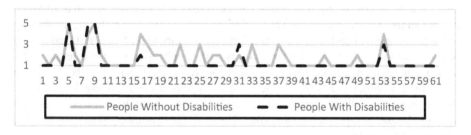

Fig. 1.   Median values of 1 or 2 (Y-axis) confirm gap in each question (X-axis).

6.3   Semi-structured Interviews

Feedback from three interview participants (IP#) can further validate the gap analysis. Quotes and comments are added under each interview question.

Interview Question 1.   Does WCAG require giving a clear indication that interactive elements are interactive? Conceptual explanation: Ensure clear distinction between elements that are interactive and elements that are not, for example ensuring that a white label on a red rectangular button is clearly distinguishable from a white title on a red rectangular background. This refers to visual affordances; being able to discern the function of an object through its appearance. IP1 said that "I don't think there are any design requirements about visual design indicating interactivity" and further, "this would be at a programmatic level, your assistive technology knows that this is interactive and can tell you." This refers to e.g. screen readers that is still not possible to use in games as the common game engines and platforms do not support these. IP2 said "I don't think there are specifics about what interactive means" in WCAG and further that a game "is very different on how you might just interact with content or search on a browser". IP3 said "I actually don't believe WCAG 2.0 covers this anyway, but 2.1 might.". Thus, this GAG is not considered by WCAG 2.0 (according to the IPs).

Interview Question 2. If a printed manual is provided on how to use a website, does WCAG require the printed manual to be duplicated online in a screen-reader accessible format? Conceptual explanation: This relates to information that is required for the use of the product but is not provided within the product itself; instead it is provided externally through an entirely different type of media. IP1 said "No, because printed material is out of the scope of WCAG, it only addresses web content." and IP3 confirmed: "No because WCAG does not cover stuff that is not web". However, IP2 said: "they need to have access to it in an alternate form. And that to me is covered by WCAG." but IP3 explained that with "WCAG for ICT, it is Section 508 that requires us to do that and not WCAG itself". Thus, this GAG is not considered by WCAG 2.0 according to IP1 and IP3.

Interview Question 3. Does WCAG require that subtitles/captions are or can be turned on before any sound is played? Conceptual explanation: Ensure that if a single option to enable/disable the display of captions for all videos throughout a product is provided, either the menu containing that option can be accessed before the first item of video content starts to play, or the option is enabled by default. As opposed to an introductory video for an application being captioned, but captions turned off by default, and having to wait until the video finishes to gain access to the application's general settings. IP1 said "I don't think it specifically requires that one way or the other." The 'before' is the keyword here, which IP2 noted: "Whether that happens at the beginning, I don't think there is any specific WCAG that requires that.". IP3 said "No it doesn't require that but you must be able to repeat it with them on". Thus, this GAG is not considered by WCAG 2.0 (according the IPs).

Interview Question 4. Does WCAG require an option for non-essential elements to be bypassed, either by making a choice upfront or through a contextual skip option? Conceptual explanation: If part of a test or process is too challenging, offer the option to skip that part of it, on the basis that if it is removed what is left still has value. IP1 said that "I would say definitely WCAG 2 does not address that at all". However, IP2 said that "to me the intent of the WCAG is to enable users to skip pass redundant information in the same way that any other user can do that.". Furthermore, IP3 seems to agree: "I don't think it is covered by WCAG" and also adds that: "to enable people with different skill level to still manage to do the game that is absolutely awesome, and it's not just disabilities, it's like different skill levels so a kid might still be able to play it". Thus, this GAG is not considered by WCAG 2.0 (according to IP1 and IP3).

7   Discussion

Below the research questions are answered by discussing the results and analysis.

7.1   Similarities and Differences Between WCAG 2.0 and GAG

GAG was built upon BBC guidelines, which was built upon WCAG 2.0. While at some abstract level, there are some similarities, there are many differences. Some of the main (D)ifferences are: (D1) WCAG focus on web only, GAG focus on games as a whole product (including printed manuals); (D2) WCAG relies on User Agents, AT and programmatic determined; from the survey comments: "WCAG throws a lot of these things to a user's assistive technology, and doesn't expect the owner/developer of the content to provide accessibility functions". GAG is more explicit and specific. (D3) WCAG levels A/AA/AAA vs GAG Basic/Intermediate/Advanced; e.g. GAG level basic which is applicable to most games (but not all due to game rules); (D4) WCAG aims for universal access, games cannot be universally accessible within limits of game rules; and (D5) GAG is best practices oriented, WCAG is conformance oriented.

7.2   Value of Gap Analysis to W3C Silver Taskforce

Clearly related to this, two comments were made by IP1 before the interview questions were asked: (1) "I believe a project like this will be an excellent first step to gather requirements."; and (2) "One of the goals of Silver and the reason we have dropped web content from the name of Silver is that we want a broader scope". The main differences above and the gap analysis with validations through interviews and survey may justify when to use GAGs for (web based) games instead of WCAG, or perhaps in combination. Using the problem statements by Silver TF[9], maintenance problem relates to D1 and D2; conformance problem relates to D3, D4, and D5.

The scale of the gap (61 guidelines) presents several options for future Silver TF investigation. If this number of guidelines could reasonably be added to the work being considered by Silver TF. As a significant number them only apply to games, whether their inclusion may hinder developers not working on games, or if they would need to be split into a separate sub-section of guidelines. Whether separate or not, if spending time duplicating guidelines that already exist elsewhere is something that adds value. And as new mechanics and input methods arise more frequently in games than other media, a question around level of maintenance.

7.3   Optimising Accessibility for Web Based Games

WCAG evaluates the web page and perhaps also Canvas and WebGL content to some extent, but when that content is a game, i.e. an application with game rules, it seems better to use GAG or other sets of guidelines for accessible games. For instance, the CEAPAT guidelines [10] are written in Spanish with obvious benefits if English is a

---

[9] https://www.w3.org/WAI/GL/task-forces/silver/wiki/Problem_Statements.

barrier. Also, if the game targets seniors [5], or is an audio game [6] or focusing on mobility and orientation [7] as well as hearing [8], the related research papers are also highly relevant to consider.

7.4   WCAG 2.1, Virtual Reality and Beyond

This study has focused on the GAGs missing in WCAG 2.0. Comments from the survey on the still unreleased WCAG 2.1 and GAG are highly relevant: (1) "'an option to adjust the sensitivity of controls' is similar to WCAG 2.1's 2.5.1 Pointer Cancellation."; (2) "WCAG considers ensuring mobile content adjusts to fit users rotating their device between portrait and landscape' is textbook WCAG 2.1's 2.6.2 Orientation."; (3) "WCAG considers avoid pressing inputs in quick succession in a limited period of time' is helped by WCAG 2.1's 2.5.1 Pointer Gestures". Going further, extended reality (XR) is a concept including e.g. augmented and virtual reality, growing both in games and other application fields. IP1 commented on this: "The accessible platform architecture working group is looking at areas of work that need focus on, accessibility focus, and we have already identified web virtual reality as a major topic in gaming as I believe a subcategory of that." As Silver TF aims to go beyond the web to apps, and GAG contains a small number of guidelines that are relevant to XR, those guidelines may be able to contribute to a starting point for XR accessibility.

7.5   Limitations

34 survey responses are not enough to speak generally nor claim any statistical significance. More replies may have been possible with a longer time for the survey, but designing the survey took more time than expected. When interpreting results, years of work with WCAG did not matter much, self-evaluation of knowledge was more important. As the survey did not require login there was no control of duplicate answers, but the survey was followed up with expert interviews where the survey results seem reasonable in comparison. The survey questions were not mandatory to answer, but only two respondents missed one question each so this should not affect the results significantly.

8   Conclusions and Future Research

Within the limitations conclusions are that there is a clear gap but WCAG 2.1 bridges a few parts. More differences were related to the Silver TF lenses. Furthermore, the study seems to offer valuable information both for the Silver update and possibly for extended reality applications. GAG as well as other guidelines for games may be used in conjunction with WCAG for web-based games. The next step could be to evaluate more thoroughly which guidelines do not apply outside of games, or it could be to conduct several case studies or workshops, where the design of Canvas and WebGL based games are discussed in-depth involving PwD with experience of WCAG who preferably also have gaming experience. Nine persons identified as disabled in the survey. Although we did not collect contact information, reaching out via the same channels could be a way to get in touch with them.

References

1. Suits, B.: The Grasshopper: Games, Life and Utopia. Broadview Press, Peterborough (2005)
2. Hughes, K.: Adapting Audio/Video Games for Handicapped Learners: Part 1. Teaching Exceptional Children, pp. 80–83, November 1981
3. Brooks, A.: Accessibility: definition, labeling, and CVAA impact. In: Brooks, A.L., Brahnam, S., Kapralos, B., Jain, L.C. (eds.) Recent Advances in Technologies for Inclusive Well-Being: From Worn to Off-body Sensing, Virtual Worlds, and Games for Serious Applications, pp. 283–383. Springer, Cham (2017). https://doi.org/10.1007/978-3-319-49879-9
4. BBC: Accessible Games Standard v1.0 (2014). http://www.bbc.co.uk/guidelines/futuremedia/accessibility/games.shtml. Accessed 04 Jan 2016
5. Ferrer, M.C., et al.: Recommended guidelines for developing video games and interfaces for seniors. Instituto de Biomecánica de Valencia (2013)
6. Garcia, F.E., de Almeida Neris, V.P.: Design guidelines for audio games. In: Kurosu, M. (ed.) HCI 2013. LNCS, vol. 8005, pp. 229–238. Springer, Heidelberg (2013). https://doi.org/10.1007/978-3-642-39262-7_26
7. Sánchez, J., Elías, M.: Guidelines for designing mobility and orientation software for blind children. In: Baranauskas, C., Palanque, P., Abascal, J., Barbosa, S.D.J. (eds.) INTERACT 2007. LNCS, vol. 4662, pp. 375–388. Springer, Heidelberg (2007). https://doi.org/10.1007/978-3-540-74796-3_35
8. Waki, A.L.K., Fujiyoshi, G.S., Almeida, L.D.A.: Games accessibility for deaf people: evaluating integrated guidelines. In: Antona, M., Stephanidis, C. (eds.) UAHCI 2015. LNCS, vol. 9177, pp. 493–504. Springer, Cham (2015). https://doi.org/10.1007/978-3-319-20684-4_48
9. AbleGamers: Includification (2012)
10. CEAPAT, Buenas prácticas de accesibilidad en videojuegos, 1st edn. Catálogo General de Publicaciones Oficiales (2012)
11. IGDA GA-SIG: IGDA GA-SIG Guidelines. https://igda-gasig.org/about-game-accessibility/guidelines/. Accessed 30 Jan 2018
12. Cavender, A., Trewin, S., Hanson, V.: General writing guidelines for technology and people with disabilities. http://www.sigaccess.org/welcome-to-sigaccess/resources/accessible-writing-guide/. Accessed: 25 Mar 2018

Gamification of Cognitive Rehabilitation

Krzysztof Dobosz[1(✉)], Magdalena Dobosz[2], and Marcin Wojaczek[1]

[1] Institute of Informatics, Silesian University of Technology, Gliwice, Poland
krzysztof.dobosz@polsl.pl, marcwoj424@student.polsl.pl
[2] Upper-Silesian Rehabilitation Center 'Repty', Tarnowskie Góry, Poland
m.dobosz@repty.pl

Abstract. Mobile applications have been introduced in the field of e-health for several years. The aim of this studies was the gamification of exercises used in the process of cognitive rehabilitation. Selected game elements have been incorporated to the mobile application. Then, three methods of evaluation was proposed: a questionnaire, the MMSE test, and a new universal factor independent on the exercise type. The factor allows the therapist to monitor and compare the progression in the rehabilitation. Pilot studies are finished, but the effect of gamification must be verified for a larger number of patients in longer time, because at present it cannot be unambiguously determined a positive influence of the gamification.

Keywords: Gamification · Cognitive impairment · Rehabilitation
Mobile application

1 Introduction

Upper-Silesian Rehabilitation Center "*Repty*" located in Tarnowskie Góry (Poland) provides rehabilitation of different kinds of neurological patients. Some of them are after a brain stroke, others are victims of unfortunate accidents, and others suffer from dementia. All of them perform a lot of exercises to stimulate different cognitive processes and to improve the quality of their brain functioning. First, we introduced exercises on tablets to activate patients and encourage further training [1]. As a part of that work, we developed the sets of small mobile applications for memory exercises. Although patients were characterized by varying degrees of cognitive impairment and manual disability, the findings were generally positive.

Next the set of mobile applications was improved and integrated in the one mobile application under the name *RehaMob* [2]. The sense of using mobile devices in the process of rehabilitation of cognitive disabilities in the Rehabilitation Center has been confirmed: for most of patients the tasks in the form of mobile application were more attractive than the traditional, paper exercises.

The aim of our current research is to incorporate game elements to the *RehaMob*. We want to investigate the influence of gamification on the process of cognitive functions rehabilitation.

K. Miesenberger and G. Kouroupetroglou (Eds.): ICCHP 2018, LNCS 10896, pp. 280–283, 2018.
https://doi.org/10.1007/978-3-319-94277-3_44

2   State of Art

The concept of gamification [3] has become popular over the last years. Gamification allows to digitally engage and motivate people to achieve their goals, change behaviors, develop skills or drive innovation [4]. Therefore, a gamification also is widely use in the e-health, what is confirmed by many papers indicated by a systematic review [5]. The most frequently studied health issue for gamified applications is chronic disease treatment and rehabilitation. A special field in this area is gamification of cognitive training, which also had a review of literature [6]. Some studies evidence that playing video games can be cognitively beneficial and stimulating for a brain. Findings in the investigation of the cognitive effects of video gaming have typically been positive. It has been confirmed that video game players outperform non-gamers on tests of working memory [7], visual attention [8, 9], and processing speed [10, 11].

3   Introducing Game Elements

Using the knowledge gathered in the book on programming game mechanics [12], existing mobile application was improved by following game elements:

- *Passing levels* - the concept of levels is undeniably a very important aspect attached to the games environment. There are three difficulty levels implemented in the *RehaMob*. Every task of each exercise implemented in the program is assigned to one of them. If the patient wants to practice on the higher levels of difficulty, first he must finish and pass all of previous levels in order to unlock the further ones. Each passed level is represented by a specific star sign (Fig. 1.a).

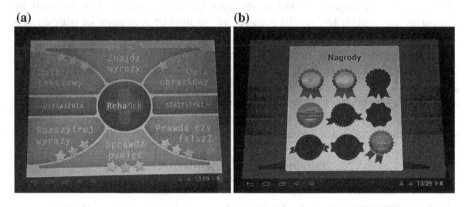

(a)   **(b)**

Fig. 1. (**a**) Passing levels, (**b**) Trophies to achieve.

- *Awards and achievements* - it provides a huge motivation and makes people happy and engaged when they win some trophy or receive some kind of badge for accomplishing a certain task. In the application almost every action performed by the user is awarded with some trophy or badge in a graphical form (Fig. 1.b).

- *Time measuring* - timer is an indispensable element of many games. This can give a lot of fun to players by introducing a kind of competition, when users are trying to get their best result in a specific time. Each of implemented exercises is equipped with a special timer which counts the whole time of performing set of questions which relates to the particular difficulty level.
- *Hints and tips* - this feature is some kind of tutorial which guides the player through the gamified environment of the application, while it is his first time of usage of this program. With the help of such hints and tips messages, which appear on the screen when the patient run the application for the first time, it is much more easier to go deeper into the game world and to familiarize with all of the rules and regulations that govern this virtual environment.
- *Collecting and storing statistics* - this aspect is crucial regarding to the research as itself, because some constructive conclusions might be formed mainly based on the results gathered from the statistics data of each user. In the application, statistics system has its own menu which is launched as the separate window.

4 Evaluation

The main objective of this work was the gamification of the rehabilitation application. Future plans include a study on the effectiveness and influence of game elements on the process of cognitive rehabilitation. In order to achieve this target it is necessary to perform an evaluation of the rehabilitation provided with the gamified tool.

The most popular way of testing the applied method is the questionnaire in which patients and therapists are asked about working with the *RehaMob*. The answers are given in a five-level Likert scale. Another most conventional used methods is the Mini-Mental State Examination (MMSE). Progress in the rehabilitation is assessed by comparing the MMSE test results gathered at the time of admission of patients to a rehabilitation center with the results achieved before they go home.

Gamified rehabilitation tool allows therapists to calculate a relative factor in the ongoing therapy. Data obtained from game elements consists of the number of games played, the number of completed tasks for each difficulty level, the best time scores for each difficulty level, etc. It is possible to calculate a universal rehabilitation factor RF, resulting from mentioned values that may be also a true assistance in the ongoing monitoring the progress of rehabilitation. RF can be calculated by the formula (1).

$$RF = \sum_{l=1}^{3} \frac{p_l}{t_l} w_l \tag{1}$$

where: p_l – number of points, t_l – the best time, w_l – weight (each one for l level).

The weight is a constant value denotes a multiplication factor which is arbitrarily determined and constant for each difficulty level. In the *RehaMob* its values are respectively: 1 for the easy, 1.25 for the normal and 1.5 for the hard difficulty level.

5   Final Remarks

First, the novelty introduced in the study is a set of game elements implemented in the rehabilitation mobile application. The second one is a proposal of universal factor independent on the exercise type. The *RF* factor allows the therapist to observe the progression in the ongoing process of rehabilitation.

The *RehaMob* is currently using on a neurological ward in the rehabilitation center. Pilot studies are finished, but the effect of gamification must be verified for a larger number of patients in a longer time, because at present it cannot be unambiguously determined a positive influence of the gamification.

Acknowledgements. Publication financed by the Institute of Informatics at Silesian University of Technology, statutory research no. BK/213/Rau2/2018.

References

1. Dobosz, K., Dobosz, M., Fiolka, T., Wojaczek, M., Depta, T.: Tablets in the rehabilitation of memory impairment. In: Miesenberger, K., Fels, D., Archambault, D., Peňáz, P., Zagler, W. (eds.) ICCHP 2014. LNCS, vol. 8547, pp. 399–402. Springer, Cham (2014). https://doi.org/10.1007/978-3-319-08596-8_61
2. Dobosz, K., Wojaczek, M., Dobosz, M., Drzastwa, A.: Rehabilitation of cognitive impairment with the RehaMob. J. Med. Inform. Technol. **24**, 239–245 (2015)
3. Deterding, S., Dixon, D., Khaled, R., Nacke, L.: From game design elements to gamefulness: defining "gamification". In: Proceedings of the 15th International Academic MindTrek Conference: Envisioning Future Media Environments, pp. 9–15. ACM (2011)
4. Burke, B.: Gamify: How Gamification Motivates People to Do Extraordinary Things. Bibliomotion, Inc., Brookline (2014)
5. Sardi, L., Idri, A., Fernández-Alemán, J.L.: A systematic review of gamification in e-Health. J. Biomed. Inform. **71**, 31–48 (2017)
6. Lumsden, J., Edwards, E.A., Lawrence, N.S., Coyle, D., Munafo, M.R.: Gamification of cognitive assessment and cognitive training: a systematic review of applications and efficacy. JMIR Serious Games **4**(2), e11 (2016)
7. Colzato, L.S., Wildenberg, M., Zmigrod, S., Hommel, B.: Action video gaming and cognitive control: playing first person shooter games is associated with improvement in working memory but not action inhibition. Psychol. Res. **77**(2), 234–239 (2013)
8. Durlach, P., Kring, J., Bowens, L.: Effects of action video game experience on change detection. Mil. Psychol. **21**(1), 24–39 (2009)
9. Green, C., Bavelier, D.: Enumeration versus multiple object tracking: the case of action video game players. Cognition **101**(1), 217–245 (2006)
10. Dobrowolski, P., Hanusz, K., Sobczyk, B., Skorko, M., Wiatrow, A.: Cognitive enhancement in video game players: the role of video game genre. Comput. Hum. Behav. **44**, 59–63 (2015)
11. Dye, M.W.G., Green, C.S., Bavelier, D.: Increasing speed of processing with action video games. Curr. Dir. Psychol. Sci. **18**(6), 321–326 (2009)
12. Zichermann, G., Cunningham, C.: Gamification by Design: Implementing Game Mechanics in Web and Mobile Apps. O'Reilly Media, Sebastopol (2011)

Designing Trainer's Manual for the ISG for Competence Project

Szilvia Paxian[1], Veronika Szücs[1], Shervin Shirmohammadi[2], Boris Abersek[3], Petya Grudeva[4], Karel Van Isacker[5], Tibor Guzsvinecz[1], and Cecilia Sik-Lanyi[1(✉)]

[1] University of Pannonia, Veszprem, Hungary
{paxian,szucs,guzsvinecz.tibor}@virt.uni-pannon.hu,
lanyi@almos.uni-pannon.hu
[2] Istanbul Sehir University, Istanbul, Turkey
shervinshirmohammadi@sehir.edu.tr
[3] University of Maribor, Maribor, Slovenia
boris.abersek@um.si
[4] ZGURA-M Ltd., Plovdiv, Bulgaria
zguraproject@gmail.com
[5] PhoenixKM, Kortemark, Belgium
info@PhoenixKM.eu

Abstract. The 3-year project "Intelligent Serious Games for Social and Cognitive Competence" targets children and youth with disabilities, teaching them on creativity and social competencies, using serious desktop and mobile games. The intellectual output (IO) 4 "Trainers manual" is based on the results and conclusions from desktop and survey findings from IO1 Scoping Report, the curriculum and learning scenarios of IO2 Suite of serious game on accessible learning objects (learning content creation) and IO3 Interactive games for mobile learning which can be reviewed/downloaded from the official project website www.isg4competence.com.

Keywords: Serious games · Disability · Assistive technologies
Trainer's manual

1 Introduction

The intellectual output IO4 "Trainers manual" document of the ISG4Competence project [1] is based on the following documents:

The IO1 Scoping Report was the first outcome of the project, and aimed at identifying context of use data (analysis of target audience characteristics and learning and training needs, tasks, and environments of use) for materials adaptation and development of a suite of serious games for students with learning difficulties.

This was realised through country reports and a consolidated survey among stakeholders and target groups in Turkey, Slovenia, Hungary, Bulgaria and Belgium, resulting in a qualitative and quantitative analysis of findings (national and comparative). Almost

K. Miesenberger and G. Kouroupetroglou (Eds.): ICCHP 2018, LNCS 10896, pp. 284–288, 2018.
https://doi.org/10.1007/978-3-319-94277-3_45

500 individuals contributed to the survey, from a wide range of target groups that were envisaged at the start already by the partnership.

The IO2 is based on the results and conclusions from desktop and survey findings from IO1 Scoping Report. It aims to produce a suite of serious games on accessible learning objects in basic skills, key skills, personal development, work preparation and work sustainability.

The aim of this document was to present the curriculum and learning scenarios framework which will be implemented through the development, iterative testing and piloting of the suite of the serious games (desktop and mobile).

2   Main Purpose of the Manual

This manual (a) describes the hardware/software requirements; (b) guides the trainers/ teachers/pedagogical staff on the implementation of the pedagogical methodology; (c) provides guidance on the used instructional approach for practical implementation at classroom settings; (d) guides trainers, teachers and pedagogical staff on how novel ICT solutions such as serious educational games; (e) provides ethics and consent forms; (f) provides pre- and post- assessment forms (Likert scale).

The potential benefits, in terms of the social context, that result from these games include: giving students (with disabilities and their peers without disabilities) ownership of their learning; opportunities for identity school activities/work through taking on alternate point of view as a role play model; freedom to fail and try again without negative consequences; chances to increase fun and joy in the classroom; opportunities for differentiated instructions; making learning visible; providing a manageable set of tasks and subtasks; inspiring students to discover intrinsic motivators for learning; motivating and engaging more into the learning process of students with learning difficulties.

As part of a strategic initiative: for example, an organisational change. Focus is on running the game at the organisational level i.e. emphasising and training goals, room for actions and success criteria in relation to a concrete change initiative. The purpose of the game is to support a change of perspective, culture, competences and focus in for example a group of learners – for example in peer learning context where a peer without disability is supporting student with learning difficulties.

Below is the list of characteristic features in the ISG4Competence [1] games (games feature all or some of these characteristics) that are of special interest from a learning perspective:

Interactivity– Interaction between the player and the interface and between the players (peer learning).

Customization – allows different ways of learning – learning as participant, learning as observer, learning from others experience.

Strong identities – the identity is connected with a specific virtual character – the identity is clearly associated with the sorts of functions, skills, and goals one has to carry out in the virtual world.

Well-ordered problems – problems in a good game is well-ordered – this is a part of good level design (see IO2 where we described learning goals, learning outcomes etc.).

Games are pleasantly frustrating – ISG4Competence games adjust challenges and give feedback in such a way that the different sort of players feels the game is challenging – they get feedback about the sort of the progress they are making.

Deep and fair – in the context of ISG4Competence games the play elements seem simple and easy to learn – and become more and more complex through levels of difficulty – and fair when it is challenging, but set up in a way that leads to success.

During the implementation process it will be beneficial and effective for the process of inclusion of serious educational games into the educational activities if following aspects are considered: Training the pedagogical staff who will be involved in the serious games implementation. Considering a technical person from the school team who will support the use of desktop computers, smartphones and tabs during the implementation phase. Consider (if possible) a second teacher or a member from the pedagogical staff who can make (written) observations during the session. Set up a group of 4–6 students (mixed with and without disabilities) that could implement a collaborative session. Consider average of time for a session with serous games between 8–12 min. Exceeding that time is not useful for educational purposes. Consider environment (classroom) with average lighting in order to have a better visibility of the screens of computers, tabs and smartphones. Avoid noisy environment which will distract the students.

3   Describing the Target Users and Beneficiaries of the Serious Games Designed

Target users of this manual are Professionals (mainly pedagogical staff) involved in education; Educational/Training centres – in the context of mainstream inclusive education; Academicians - (Special) pedagogy; Psychology; ICT/gaming/Assistive technology etc.; Training staff from non-governmental organisations/Unions/Associations of people with disabilities.

Additional beneficiaries of the content of the manual are Families of children/youth with disabilities; Intermediaries; Policy makers.

The manual can be used by any of the above mentioned target users who would like to introduce the serious educational games into following educational settings: Schools – mainstream, vocational education & training (VET), Special care centres, Education and training providers (including those in non-formal area), Public sector organizations dealing with inclusive education and Public sector – health and social care providers that offer e.g. basic soft skills trainings.

The target groups who may take benefit from ISG4Competence [1] serious game are Students with mild learning disabilities (slow rate of maturation, reduced learning capacity and inadequate social adjustment); Students with sensory impairments; Students with low level social skills; Students with specific learning difficulties (dyslexia, dyspraxia, autism spectrum disorder, Attention-deficit/hyperactivity disorder (ADHD)).

4   An Outline of the Aims of Serious Games

Game based learning is a method that will enhance the classroom learning environment by increasing motivation, increasing opportunities to develop a decision making process that forces analysing and implementing solutions, and will allow these skills to transfer to other aspects of life.

Game based teaching and learning can be quite effective if understood what it is and how it can be implemented to enhance instruction and learning. During the last decade there are many examples (see IO1 Scoping report) which prove their effectiveness towards inclusive education of students with learning difficulties.

Serious educational games have four key ingredients:

Goal: a game has to have a desired outcome.

Rules: in order to achieve the goal there has to be some parameters put into place that eliminate or make it difficult to achieve the goal.

Feedback system: this is a process whereby the player knows where they are in the system to achieve the goal.

Voluntary participation: this means that everyone involved in the game understands the rules, has a clear sense of the goal, and how to receive feedback.

When we discuss games for learning it is essential that teachers/trainers/educators see a benefit to the use of the game. Once they recognise this, and realise that a particular game can motivate students to learn, is fairly simple to implement, and can support learning targets, standards, and distinct goals can be met, then a game has great potential to actually be used in the classroom. One fundamental difference between gaming for fun vs. gaming for educational purposes is that educators start with learning goals, and gaming media choices will be made based on the games potential to meet those goals.

In the context of the ISG4Competence project [1], following social and cognitive competences are trained through the usage of serious educational games: Self-esteem and self-confidence, Motivation, Managing anger and stress, Team working, Communication, Improving own learning and Problem solving.

During their peer cooperation the students with disabilities and their peers without disability are in the explorative dialogue, whereby they can propose hypotheses explore and discuss, and the progression of their work is based on a common acceptance of the different opinions and proposals which are facilitated by the teacher/trainer.

The ISG4Competences games generate dynamic learning opportunities, engaging students in productive classroom discussions by forcing the students to be engaged, to argue and reflect upon the learning goals.

The ISG4competence serious games are applicable to support the education and training in the following educational settings: Classrooms in mainstreaming schools: used as additional approach to fulfil the learning outcomes of a particular learning subject; Extracurricular activities in the schools: used as possible alternative approach for the acquisition of basic and key competencies which cannot be effectively covered during regular activities at schools; Private lessons: used as an alternative educational approach for students who cannot attend mainstream courses; Private sessions with resource tutors, psychologist or speech therapist: use as a training method for the acquisition/improvement of basic and key competencies; Activities of youth volunteering informal groups: used as a media where peer learning support could be facilitated; Some of the games could equally be used in kindergarten settings, which do not require the knowledge of reading.

5   Main System Requirements of the Games

Before starting the implementation phase the technical manuals attached to each of the ISG serious educational games should be considered.

Consider equipment which is compatible with the technical requirements for each game.

Ensure that the batteries of smartphones and tabs are fully charged before the sessions.

Be careful with the unattended provision of equipment to the students (especially minors because they could easily destroy it).

Make a try-out with each game by yourself to ensure that the game is properly installed and that there are no bugs which may demotivate the students' participation.

All of the games (AndMath; Cars Racing; Labyrinth; "Manage Yourself"; Card Pairing Memory game; Weekend Wonderland; Into the Forest; Minecraft; Sequence; Memory) designed under the umbrella of ISG for Competence project were developed for Android, IOS, OSX, Windows or any web browser platforms, and except Minecraft all of the games are license fee free.

6   Summary

The piloting phase of the ISG for Competence project is still under progress and will have a final outline and review later this year. These outcomes will be available and downloadable from the project website. The serious games designed by the project partners will be available at Google Play and the project website. All the games will be free of charge and can be used by anyone.

Acknowledgement. The authors acknowledge the financial support of Széchenyi 2020 under the EFOP-3.6.1-16-2016-00015.

Reference

1. ISG4Competence: Intelligent Serious Games for Social and Cognitive Competence (ERASMUS+ 2015-1-TR01-KA201-022247). http://www.isg4competence.eu/

Accessibility and Usability of Self-Service Terminals, Technologies and Systems

Accessibility and Usability of Self-service Terminals, Technologies and Systems

Introduction to the Special Thematic Session

Helen Petrie[(✉)] and Jenny Darzentas

Human Computer Interaction Research Group, Department of Computer Science,
University of York, York, UK
{helen.petrie,jenny.darzentas}@york.ac.uk

Abstract. This short paper introduces the seven papers a special thematic session dedicated to discussing accessibility and usability issues of self-service terminals technologies and systems. The authors are from a mix of academic and industry backgrounds, thus bringing together a range of stakeholder perspectives. The papers include experimental investigations; user testing and feedback from real world deployments; novel interface and interaction concepts; and critical appraisals of standards and legislation as mechanisms for ensuring accessibility. To give some context to the focus on SSTs, particularly when some are being replaced by combinations of mobile app on smartphones, this introduction presents a brief account of current and past interest in the accessibility and usability of SSTs in Europe, as evidenced by the upcoming European Accessibility Act.

Keywords: Self-service terminals · Accessibility · Usability

1 Introduction

In Europe, with the soon-to-be voted European Accessibility Act (EEA), the accessibility and usability of self-service terminals, technologies and systems are in the spotlight. The Act is aimed at both ensuring the full participation of people with disabilities in society and at reducing the fragmentation of legislation governing access to products and services. Although it is referred to as The European Accessibility Act, it is more properly a proposal adopted by the European Commission for a directive. Thus, amongst other products and services, the present text of the proposed directive refers specifically to access to products and services by self-service terminals, located within the territory of the Union, including Automatic Teller Machines, ticketing machines, check-in machines and payment terminals. These are all required to comply with the requirements set out in the directive.

Overall, the proposal for a directive provides for a common EU definition of, and implementation framework for, accessibility requirements for certain products and services. It also aims to use the same accessibility requirements to provide a clear definition of the existing general accessibility obligation laid down in European law. It does not

© Springer International Publishing AG, part of Springer Nature 2018
K. Miesenberger and G. Kouroupetroglou (Eds.): ICCHP 2018, LNCS 10896, pp. 291–294, 2018.
https://doi.org/10.1007/978-3-319-94277-3_46

aim to impose detailed technical solutions to render a product or service accessible but simply to establish 'accessibility principles' [1].

At present, the proposal text has been amended and positively voted by the Council of the European Union (September 2017). The Council agreed in its meeting of 7 December 2017 on a position ('General Approach') on the European Accessibility Act. This signals that the negotiations among the three EU institutions: European Commission, the European Parliament and Council, to agree on a final text can start.

The European Commission (whose responsibility it is to bring matters before the Council of the EU and the Parliament) has been aware of issues of accessibility and usability with SSTs for some time, and has been extremely active, making use of a variety of initiatives. It has organised research and industry workshops to bring those working on the latest developments in SSTs' accessibility together and to publicise findings [2], as well as commissioned fact-finding on national rules and regulations concerning the accessibility of SSTs [3]. It has organised public consultations [4] and Flash Eurobarometers [5]; made requests (Mandates) to European Standards Organisations (Mandates 376, 420 and 473 [6]) and has funded research, e.g. [7] and e-accessibility networking e.g. [8] projects to further understand the problems as they related to SSTs, and how they might be resolved. The Commission routinely works with advocacy groups, such as the European Disability Forum [9]; AgePlatform Europe [10]; ANEC (representing consumers in standardisation) [11]; and very notably, with the PayAble platform [12] that campaigned and were successful in having (card) payment terminals included in the wording of the amended text of directive proposal.

With this as a background, it is gratifying that the call for a special session on the accessibility and usability of self-service terminals (SSTs) was well responded to and a selection of seven papers made. Of these, three are from academic based work, two from the SST manufacturing, one from an SST deployer, and one from a consultancy that specialises in accessibility issues, thus representing a good mix of both academic and industry viewpoints.

2   Special Thematic Session on SSTs

The papers selected include experimental investigations, including testing and involving users (Cederbom, Darzentas & Petrie, Jokisuu; Zaim,); real world deployments (de Groot; Sandnes); novel interface and interaction concepts (Jokisuu; Zaim); a critical look at standards as a mechanism for ensuring accessibility (Cederbom; Darzentas & Petrie; Jokisuu, Day & Rohan); new ways of interacting using apps and mobile devices and their accessibility (Zaim), and a reflection on the de-commissioning of SSTs due to mobile apps (Sandnes). Although in Europe, the use of ATMs are declining due to an increase in cashless payments, in other parts of the world, they are increasing [13]. Similarly, while many people use electronic tickets and smart phone apps in travel, some people do not have mobile devices, or cannot afford network charges, therefore many transactions are still carried out via SSTs with paper tickets, and plastic travel cards are purchased and managed (e.g. 'topped up') at self-service machines. One of the mainstay principles of the proposed EEA is that services and products should be accessible and usable by all, regardless of the type of access technology people use: e.g. apps, mobile devices, SSTs or a person-to-person service.

Some of SSTs discussed specifically refer to those in the banking sector (de Groot; Jokisuu, Darzentas & Petrie) and those used in travel (Sandnes, Darzentas & Petrie). However, the authors acknowledge, most of the issues that arise, apply, - or could apply-, to other sectors. Indeed, since the banking sector is subject to very strict security rules. These can conflict with common accessibility solutions, (such as providing voice output for the those who cannot see a screen), this work is broadly applicable to other areas and could potentially be of great value to them, for example in Healthcare where security and fraud are also high risk. Finally, it is common when talking about SSTs to divide accessibility issues into those to do with the placement of the SST (Cedebom, de Groot), those which are to do with hardware (Jokisuu; Jokisuu, Day & Rohan; de Groot) and those to do with software (Zaim; de Groot), although some overlap is always present.

3   Conclusions

In conclusion, we thank the authors for their participation in this session, that has produced an interesting cross-section of views, offering fresh perspectives to both authors as well as to readers. We feel this set of papers are both informative and thought-provoking, providing interesting results and useful good practices.

In the meantime, the self-service 'ethos' [14, 15] continues to pervade new sectors each with their own particular requirements, e.g. hospitality settings like hotels and restaurants, and healthcare settings like hospitals and doctor's surgeries. At the same time new technologies, or new combinations of technologies, are being employed to deliver services, for example, the use of biometrics [16]; moving from SSTs in kiosk enclosures to tablet computers; and from stationary to mobile SSTs, such as the roaming robot SSTs available in airports [17]; and finally possibly from SSTs as simple transaction machines to SSTs offering automated social presence (ASPs) [18]. Throughout these developments, it is vital to maintain a focus on the accessibility and usability needs of those emerging forms of SSTS. We look forward to engaging with researchers and industry in the future on this fascinating topic in forthcoming special thematic sessions at ICCHP.

Acknowledgements. The research carried out in this paper by Jenny Darzentas has been partly funded by the European Union under the Marie Skłodowska-Curie Action Experienced Researcher Fellowship Programme, as part of the Education and Engagement for inclusive Design and Development of Digital Systems and Services Project (E2D3S2, Grant No. 706396). The content reflects the authors' views and is not the views of the European Commission.

References

1. European Parliamentary Research Services: Briefing- EU legislation in progress–The European Accessibility Act, November 2017. http://www.europarl.europa.eu/RegData/etudes/BRIE/2017/603973/EPRS_BRI%282017%29603973_EN.pdf. Accessed 25 Mar 2018
2. European Commission Workshop on Accessibility of Products and Services (2017). http://ec.europa.eu/social/keyDocuments.jsp?pager.offset=0&&langId=en&mode=advancedSubmit&advSearchKey=EAAworkshop. Accessed 25 Mar 2018
3. Priestly, M.: National accessibility requirements and standards for products and services in the European single market: overview and examples. Academic Network of European Disability experts (ANED) – VT/2007/005 (2013)
4. Deloitte and External Experts, Public Consultation Analysis: Study on the socio-economic impact of new measures to improve accessibility of goods and services for people with disabilities (2013). Final Report. http://ec.europa.eu/social/main.jsp?catId=1202. Accessed 25 Mar 2018
5. Flash Eurobarometer 345 on Accessibility (2012). http://ec.europa.eu/commfrontoffice/publicopinion/flash/fl_345_en.pdf. Accessed 2 Mar 2018
6. M376, see 'eAccessibility'; M/420, see Built Environment; for M473, 'Design for All', https://www.cencenelec.eu/standards/Sectors/Accessibility/BuiltEnvironment/Pages/default.aspx. Accessed 25 Mar 2018
7. Accessible Personalised Services in Public Digital Terminals for All. http://www.apsis4all.eu/. Accessed 25 Mar 2018
8. Miesenberger, K., Velleman, E., Crombie, D., Petrie, H., Darzentas, Jenny S., Velasco, Carlos A.: The eAccess+ network: enhancing the take-up of eAccessibility in Europe. In: Miesenberger, K., Karshmer, A., Penaz, P., Zagler, W. (eds.) ICCHP 2012. LNCS, vol. 7382, pp. 325–328. Springer, Heidelberg (2012). https://doi.org/10.1007/978-3-642-31522-0_49
9. European Disability Forum. http://www.edf-feph.org/. Accessed 25 Mar 2018
10. Age Platform Europe. http://www.age-platform.eu/. Accessed 25 Mar 2018
11. ANEC. www.anec.gr. Accessed 25 Mar 2018
12. Pay-Able. http://pay-able.eu/. Accessed 25 Mar 2018
13. ACCENTURE ATMIA ATM Benchmarking Study and Industry Report (2016). https://www.accenture.com/_acnmedia/PDF-10/Accenture-Banking-ATM-Benchmarking-2016.pdf. Accessed 13 Mar 2018
14. Gershuny, J.: After Industrial Society? The Emerging Self-Service Economy. MacMillan Press, London (1978)
15. Eriksson, K., Vogt, H.: On self-service democracy: Configurations of individualizing governance and self-directed citizenship. Eur. J. Soc. Theory 16(2), 153–173 (2013)
16. Napua, J.: Growth of biometric technology in self-service situations. Fujitsu Sci. Tech. J. 47, 68–74 (2011)
17. Sillers, P.: Robots and AI: the technology coming to airports (2017). http://www.independent.co.uk/travel/news-and-advice/future-travel-airport-technology-hi-tech-chatbots-robots-augmented-reality-ai-a7961171.html. Accessed 25 Mar 2018
18. van Doorn, J., Mende, M., Noble, S.M., Hulland, J., Ostrom, A.L., Grewal, D., Petersen, J.A.: Domo arigato Mr. Roboto J. Serv. Res. 20(1), 43–58 (2016)

Standards, Guidelines and Legislation Related to Self-service Technologies: Developments Since 2013

Jenny Darzentas[✉] and Helen Petrie

Human Computer Interaction Research Group, Department of Computer Science,
University of York, York, UK
{jenny.darzentas,helen.petrie}@york.ac.uk

Abstract. The intention of the standards, guidelines and legislation discussed here, along with other initiatives mentioned, is to ensure accessibility for all is built into self-service technologies from the outset. This paper presents developments in relevant standards, guidelines and legislation since 2013. In reporting on this work, the intention to give an idea of its scope, but also to place these standards, guidelines and legislation within a critical framing that reviews both the material and its impact on efforts to make SSTs accessible to all users.

Keywords: Accessible self-service technologies · Standards
Guidelines and legislation

1 Introduction

The uses and usage of self-service technologies (SSTs) continue to proliferate and move into new areas. At the same time, the SST industry and deployments of SSTs are continually evolving, developing innovative ways to carry out everyday activities. SSTs are a recognised thriving economic sector. A recent report stated that the interactive kiosk market was valued at USD 20.37 billion in 2016 and was expected to be worth USD 30.53 billion by 2023. The same report states that the growth of this market is driven by the increasing interest of customers in self-service interactive kiosks and the enhanced experiences they provide [1].

The intention of the standards, guidelines and legislation discussed here, along with the other initiatives included, is to ensure accessibility for all is built into SSTs from the beginning. This paper presents developments in relevant standards, guidelines and legislation that have occurred since 2013. According to ANEC (the European umbrella organisation representing consumer interests in standardisation), standards can, among other things, "help to structure the digital age and the information society, and help people of all ages and abilities have equal access to products and services" [2].

This update takes 2013 as a starting point as this was the end of the EU supported eAccess + Project [3], that focused on SSTs as one of its three areas of special interest. It is especially important to review what has happened since then, as in the intervening time, work has progressed on the European Accessibility Act [4], and one of the targets

© Springer International Publishing AG, part of Springer Nature 2018
K. Miesenberger and G. Kouroupetroglou (Eds.): ICCHP 2018, LNCS 10896, pp. 295–302, 2018.
https://doi.org/10.1007/978-3-319-94277-3_47

of that Act is the accessibility of various types of SSTs. As part of the background to this development, paper reports firstly on standards-related work carried out in 2014/5 [5], that showed that for many people in Europe, SSTs were still very much a priority for the agenda on accessibility.

The standards and associated work reported here cover a range of initiatives, both worldwide, and country specific, and developments that are both horizontal (applying to a range of SSTs) and sector specific, looking at vertical sectors (e.g. financial, travel, etc.). These include both formal standards, produced by organisations such as ISO and the European Standards bodies (CEN, CENELEC and ETSI) [6] as well as implementation guides such as that of Canada's Transportation Agency, adopted from national standards. In addition, also relevant are industrial standards, for instance recommendations from the banking industries dedicated to ATMs [7].

Finally, it is interesting to note the role of legislation, as it has developed in the U.S., where litigation, eventually, appears to give impetus to accessible solutions. The forthcoming European Accessibility Act, underpinned by standards, is expected to play a similar role.

2 SSTs and Older and Disabled People

In 2015, experts working on Mandate 473 [5], were tasked to discover what are the main barriers to accessibility in Europe, and to prioritise those barriers in terms of those that would be the most important for standardisers to work on. A consultation with those directly concerned was carried out via an online survey that was addressed to disabled and older people as well as organisations that represent these populations in Europe [5].

The consultation did not include barriers that result from architectural or structural elements in the built environment, as this issue is addressed elsewhere. However, still included are any kind of products or services that may be situated in the built environment and cause difficulty there, such as touch screen controls in a lift or ticketing machines, and announcements in public transportation services.

The survey was available in 5 languages (Danish, English, French, German and Greek). In the 4-week period in September–October 2014 during which the survey was online, 899 responses were received. The age range of respondents was from 0–10 yrs to 91+, with a gender split of 52% female and 48% male respondents who self-reported the nature of their disability or impairment, with many reporting more than one. After all the responses were analysed, the results showed that SSTs came out as an important obstacle to accessibility, with 69 people also providing comments about these technologies.

Some of the reported barriers for SSTs were problems with: *touch screens*: "Most machines can only be operated through touchscreens not user-friendly for people with vision impairments as they are operated via silent touch screens, and do not have voice instruction"; the *ergonomic dimensions*, for instance the operating height: "At self-service terminals in banks the displays are often not readable, because they are too high for wheelchair users"; *cognitive load*: "menu navigation often unclear or too complicated".

People complained of difficulties with a range of machines: besides ATMs, ticket machines and self-scanning in supermarkets, they included: petrol filling; parking machines; vending machines; self-service machines for sending parcels; self-service machines for picking up packages; discrete parts of financial self-services such as the password calculator and card payment terminals; and queuing systems used in banks, post-offices and chemists.

Some respondents suggested solutions: "Auditory instruction at the push of a button would certainly be a start,of course, direct contact persons would be best - also on the telephone"; "ATMs and points of sale devices should be equipped with wireless connection so that (deaf)blind people can read the screen information with their smartphone/ Braille mobile devices"; "for queuing systems (…) there is a solution, where the user gets a little coin, and when your number is on it vibrates".

Some noted the deeper implication of not being able to use an SST independently: "old people are unable even to cope with buying a ticket for the train or bus. In many places there are no manned ticket offices anymore. Therefore, old people's autonomous mobility is being restricted." "Often companies do not have service numbers anymore and can only be reached by email or electronic contact forms, 'normal' old people cannot find access such media." "Bank services ('paying terminals') are not universally designed, which means that many lose control over own economy".

Respondents also commented that there was no uniform system for machines with the same function, for instance in cash or ticketing machines. Thus, a recommendation from the consultation was to develop a new standard to cover the accessibility of self-service machines/kiosks.

3   Standards for SSTs

Of course, standards for SSTs do exist, and one of the problems is the plethora of such standards. There are standards that are general as well as those that are sectorspecific; there are *de jure* standards, developed and endorsed by official standardisation bodies, and those which are *de facto* coming mostly from praxis rather than being officially endorsed. Also, the nature of standards varies, with some giving precise specifications, such as those found in the Americans with Disability (ADA) standards [8] and the 508 [9] regulating height and reach measurements and keypad specifications. For instance, ADA specifies that the forward or side height and reach of a kiosk or ATM should be between 15 inches and 48 inches from the ground and that numeric keys must use an ascending or descending 12-key layout, a raised dot on 5, and function keys that stand out visually from the background surface [8]. Against these, there are also performance-based standards, that give functional objectives, against which to measure SSTs. An example of performance based objectives is found the de jure standard EN301-549 - Accessibility requirements suitable for public procurement of ICT products and services in Europe [10] discussed next.

3.1　Formal Standards

Previous work from formal standards directly related to SSTs are now very old. Some of this work has been updated. In 2007 the Canadian Standards Agency issued CAN/CSA-B651.2-07 (R2017) - Accessible Design for Self-Service Interactive Devices, a standard that was reaffirmed in 2017 [11]. When originally published in 2007, this standard did not include Automated Banking Machines, which had a standard of their own CAN/CSA-B651.1 [12] based on work from 2001 with a second edition in 2009, and reaffirmation in 2015.

Moving to more generally based standards, the previously mentioned EN301 549 (latest update published in 2015) [10] is also the result of a mandate. M376 was a request from the European Commission to the European Standardisation Organisations to produce a standard for the public procurement of ICT products. Those products included "kiosks and transaction machines" and "ticketing machines". This standard uses the principle of performance based objectives. That is, they do not give specific requirements. Rather clause 4 of the standard: 'Functional performance (informative)' contains a list of user needs when accessing ICT products and services and explains how the ICT can cover that need. For instance: '4.2.1 -Usage without vision' states "Where ICT provides visual modes of operation, some users need ICT to provide at least one mode of operation that does not require vision. NOTE: Audio and tactile user interfaces may contribute towards meeting this clause."

Thus, an issue in relation to SSTs is that there is no specific standard setting out performance requirements for their design. This concerns manufacturers as it is not clear what is required for the finished product across the many sectors. However, while the scope of EN301-549 is very broad, there is substantial content that could form the basis for specifications for self-service machines. Moreover, although the result of a European initiative, EN 301 549 is recognised internationally: the U.S. Access Board that oversees accessibility matters, harmonized its 'refresh' of 2017 with EN301549 [13], and in 2016 the Australian government adopted it [14]. Extra effort has been made to make people aware of the standard, using non-traditional formats: Microsoft sponsored the work of Funka to present and explain the standard in a set of videos with multi-language subtitles [15]. In addition, the European mandated work (M376) was also complemented by a toolkit [16] that guides procurers and tenderers to fulfil requirements, that can lead to more concrete specifications.

3.2　Industry Specific Standards

Adding to the confusion over SSTs and accessibility, industry produces its own sector specific standards and within these, recommendations on accessibility issues. Two of those at the forefront are banking services and airline travel.

In Europe and North America there has been a decline in recent years in the use of ATMs due to the increase in cashless transactions. However, in other parts of the world, ATMs are increasing and are the main channel for financial services for the underbanked [17]. In 2014, the Automated Teller Machine Industry Association (ATMIA) published international industry recommendations for the ATM user interface focusing on accessibility, speed, operability, and security, and incorporating recommendations for new technologies, such as tactile and multi-touch capabilities, biometrics and HTML 5, thereby allowing accessibility technologies usually applicable to mobile devices and tablets to be extended to ATM interfaces. This is important as many assistive technologies are available via mobile devices. In July 2017, ATMIA published recommendations on 'Maximising ATM accessibility' [7]. These publications are only available to those who are members of the ATMIA organization, but their existence testifies to the awareness and concern of the industry.

In airline travel, from December 2016, the IATA rules (following US Department of Transport [18] and the Canadian Transport Agency rules [19]) state that kiosks will need to have: keyboard with embossed and colored keys, headphone jack & volume control, text-to-speech technology, braille labels and a height of screen at a maximum 48 inches. Along with this ruling, the Canadian Transport Agency issued in 2014 an 'Implementation Guide Regarding Automated Self-Service Kiosks' [20] based upon CAN/CSA B651.2-07. The Guide contains specific measurements and requirements. The story of the change to the rules originates with a litigation case from 2011 [21].

4 Legislation and Litigation

To highlight the close connection between standards and legislation, reference is made to several cases from the United States. The Americans with Disability Act, (ADA) was revised in 2010 with new specifications for SSTs. The following cases were brought against SST deployers over machines that are not accessible.

In 2017, the American Council of the Blind sued eatsa, a fast-food chain that uses automated self-service kiosks and ordering apps, there are no waiters or cashiers. Instead, patrons order their meals through a phone app or at one of the in-store ordering kiosks. These kiosks consist of tablet computer devices mounted and framed on a stand. When the food is ready, the customer's name appears on a screen along with a number. The number directs the customer to an automated dispenser where they can retrieve their food. The entire process is silent. While tablets can provide technology that make text accessible to blind and low vision users, these kiosks do not, because the audio jacks and home buttons required for accessible options are covered by the frame and no tactile features exist on the kiosks. eatsa's phone app is also incompatible with screen reader technology, and the food pickup process has no audible or tactile cues. Additionally, although the eatsa's kiosks contain an option to request employee assistance this feature, is also inaccessible to blind customers. Following legal action, eatsa, has agreed to make its hardware and software accessible in consultation with user organisations [22].

In 2017, Walmart agreed to settle a disability-rights suit that was filed in 2012 by installing equipment in its stores that will enable people in wheelchairs to read the screens at the checkout display, and on credit card terminals and thus make such purchases on their own [23].

These cases demonstrate that while manufacturers have been making their machines compatible with ADA specifications, these have mostly been aimed at users of wheelchairs. Worryingly, deployers, using current trends of lightweight kiosks (tablet computers on stands), and making their own software applications, were not aware of the needs of their low vision and non-sighted customers. Similarly, other newer self-service technologies, such as credit card (POS) terminals are not accessible to those with vision impairments.

A case brought in 2015, makes this more apparent. The case is about vending machines. The latest generation of vending machines, the Glass Front Vendor (GFV), is inaccessible to the visually impaired. The GFV does not display the availability of the products that it sells in any non-visual manner, nor does it offer any non-visual interface for the purchase of the products that it sells. GFVs are available at many places of public accommodation, for instance bus terminals and hospitals, where only self-service options are available. A supreme court ruling has judged that the Coca- cola that operates or leases the vending machines is not at fault [24]. Despite the defeat, the question of the accessibility of these SSTs has been raised. The ruling may point to deployers having to bear the responsibility of deploying accessible vending machines. This would then turn them to requesting GFVs with accessibility from the manufacturers.

This would not be the first time an entire sector or industry has had to change its way of doing things. The US Department of Transportation revised its rules in 2011 following litigation against airport check-in machines [21] Although the airline company won the litigation, there was enough groundswell for the rule change. This mandates that all airport kiosks (both airline proprietary and common-use self-service (CUSS) kiosks) installed after December 12, 2016 must be accessible until 25% of kiosks in each location at an airport are accessible. Airports and airlines will be held jointly and severally liable for shared-use automated airport kiosks that do not meet the accessibility requirements or are not maintained in working order.

5 Discussion and Conclusions

What does the future hold for accessible SSTs? On the one hand the proliferation of SSTs means that they are found in all sorts of domains, recently in hospitality settings, and in healthcare. At the same time, the self-service trend is dominant, with people becoming more familiar with it, and requesting convenience of anytime access, often with multiple language facilities and other benefits over human-delivered services. Furthermore, increasingly the younger old (60–69) are proficient technology users.

However, acceptance does not mean that the technologies are accessible. Rather, as the eatsa case shows, with new types of self-service hardware and software considerations, it important that awareness of accessibility issues are built in. Whether it be low-cost tablet computers on stands using purpose built apps, or sophisticated mobile robots delivering the self-services, it is vital that consideration is given to accessibility concerns. As is often the case, these new technologies can provide better and more varied range of access than previous hardware and software solutions. For instance, a mobile robot can come to people, instead of them being required to seek out a terminal and stand -perhaps for longer than is comfortable for them -in front of it.

In reporting on this work, the intention to give an idea of its scope, but also to place these standards, guidelines and legislation within a critical framing that reviews both the material and their impact on efforts to make SSTs accessible to all users. The success of these materials depends upon how well they are taken up and applied. A slavish approach to implementing standards results in features that tick boxes but are practically useless. A case in point is keypads as alternatives to touch screens that are placed low down on the interface, and often on the vertical fascia, so that they are difficult to find and use by those populations who need them, people who are visually impaired.

In addition, it also depends on how these standards and guidelines are developed, and how proactive they are in reflecting emerging paradigms in technology development and the ways people interact with technology. For this reason, the move to performance based standards represents a more flexible approach, which specifies the outcome required, without prescribing the method, and leaves designers able to interpret.

What is most needed is greater awareness, and earlier user testing. It is still lacking. As was noted by the plaintiffs in the eatsa case: "Technology has had a major positive impact on improving the inclusion of blind people. eatsa's concept is all about the power of technology, but the company did not think to take the added steps to make it accessible for its blind customers" [22].

Acknowledgements. The research carried out in this paper by Jenny Darzentas has been partly funded by the European Union under the Marie Skłodowska-Curie Action Experienced Researcher Fellowship Programme, as part of the Education and Engagement for inclusive Design and Development of Digital Systems and Services Project (E2D3S2, Grant No. 706396). The content reflects the authors' views and is not the views of the European Commission.

References

1. Markets and Markets. https://www.marketsandmarkets.com/PressReleases/interactive-kiosks.asp. Accessed 13 Mar 2018
2. ANEC. https://www.anec.eu/about-anec/who-we-are. Accessed 13 Mar 2018
3. Miesenberger, K., Velleman, E., Crombie, D., Petrie, H., Darzentas, J.S., Velasco, Carlos A.: The eAccess + Network: enhancing the take-up of eaccessibility in Europe. In: Miesenberger, K., Karshmer, A., Penaz, P., Zagler, W. (eds.) ICCHP 2012. LNCS, vol. 7382, pp. 325–328. Springer, Heidelberg (2012). https://doi.org/10.1007/978-3-642-31522-0_49
4. European Accessibility Act. http://ec.europa.eu/social/main.jsp?catId=1202. Accessed 13 Mar 2018
5. M473 Deliverable 2.1 parts 1 & 2. https://www.cencenelec.eu/standards/Sectors/Accessibility/DesignForAll/Pages/default.aspx. Accessed 13 Mar 2018
6. Priestly, M.: National accessibility requirements and standards for products and services in the European single market: overview and examples. Academic Network of European Disability experts (ANED) – VT/2007/005 (2013)
7. ATMIA. https://www.atmia.com/news/atmia-publishes-new-atm-accessibility-guide/5005/. Accessed 13 Mar 2018
8. ADA Standards for Accessible Design https://www.ada.gov/regs2010/2010ADAStandards/2010ADAstandards.htm#c7. Accessed 13 Mar 2018
9. https://www.section508.gov/. Accessed 13 Mar 2018
10. EN301549 (V1.1.2 (2015-04)) Accessibility requirements suitable for public procurement of ICT products and services in Europe. http://www.etsi.org/deliver/etsi_en/301500_301599/301549/01.01.02_60/en_301549v010102p.pdf. Accessed 13 Mar 2018

11. CAN/CSA-B651.2-07 (R2017) - Accessible Design for Self-Service Interactive Devices. http://shop.csa.ca/en/canada/accessibility/cancsa-b6512-07-r2012/invt/27026262007. Accessed 13 Mar 2018
12. CAN/CSA-B651.1-09 (R2015) - Accessible design for automated banking machines. http://shop.csa.ca/en/canada/accessibility/b6511-09-r2015/invt/27013202009. Accessed 13 Mar 2018
13. United States Access Board (2017). https://www.access-board.gov/guidelines-and-standards/communications-and-it/about-the-ict-refresh/overview-of-the-final-rule. Accessed 13 Mar 2018
14. Goggin, G., Hollier, S., Hawkins, W.: Internet accessibility and disability policy: lessons for digital inclusion and equality from Australia. Internet Policy Rev. **6**(1) (2017)
15. Funka: Video captions are translated into ten languages. https://www.funka.com/en/our-assignments/standardisation/arkiv. Accessed 13 Mar 2018
16. Mandate 376 Accessible ICT Procurement Toolkit (2014). http://mandate376.standards.eu/. Accessed 13 Mar 2018
17. ACCENTURE ATMIA ATM Benchmarking Study and Industry Report (2016). https://www.accenture.com/_acnmedia/PDF-10/Accenture-Banking-ATM-Benchmarking-2016.pdf. Accessed 13 Mar 2018
18. United States Department of Transportation Automated Kiosks Accessibility final rule www.regulations.gov, docket DOT-OST-2011-0177. Accessed 13 Mar 2018
19. Canadian Transportation Agency Automated Kiosks Accessibility final rule. https://www.otc-cta.gc.ca/eng/removing-communication-barriers. Accessed 13 Mar 2018
20. Canadian Transportation Agency Implementation Guide (2014). https://otc-cta.gc.ca/eng/publication/implementation-guide-regarding-automated-self-service-kiosks. Accessed 13 Mar 2018
21. Feingold, L.: Accessibility lawsuit filed against Jetblue Airways. http://www.lflegal.com/2010/10/jet-blue/. Accessed 13 Mar 2018
22. Disability Rights Advocates. http://dralegal.org/press/eatsa-agrees-make-cutting-edge-technology-accessible-blind-customers/. Accessed 13 Mar 2018
23. Kiosk Industry Whitepaper Ada Kiosk, POS Terminal & Walmart (2017). https://kioskindustry.org/whitepaper-ada-pos-terminal-walmart/. Accessed 13 Mar 2018
24. Stohr, G.: Supreme Court rejects blind man's bid for vending machine access. Bloomberg Business Week, 2 Oct 2017. https://www.bloomberg.com/news/articles/2017-10-02/supreme-court-rejects-blind-man-s-bid-for-vending-machine-access. Accessed 13 Mar 2018

Accessibility Features on BNP Paribas Fortis ATMs

Pascal De Groote[✉]

BNP Paribas Fortis – Client Advocacy, Warandeberg 3, 1000 Brussels, Belgium
Bank4all@bnpparibasfortis.com

Abstract. This paper gives an overview of the accessibility features on the BNP Paribas Fortis ATM's (Automatic Teller Machines). This document doesn't have the intention to be scientific, but can be considered as an example how the industry is taken in account the accessibility for customers with special needs. The accessibility efforts done on our ATM's is part of the program "An Accessible Bank For All". The goal of this program is to provide to our customers with a disability the opportunity to carry out their banking transactions in the most autonomous and user-friendly way possible. Within this program we've consulted organisations, representing persons with impairments, to better understand the needs of our customers with special needs. This helped us to work out a global approach to render the use of our ATM's as accessible as possible. We can divide the efforts on 3 levels: physical accessibility of the venue, accessibility of the hardware and accessibility features of the software.

Keywords: Cash withdrawal · ATM · Cash machine · Bank

1 Introduction

1.1 Our Program: "An Accessible Bank for All"

The goal of our program is to provide to our customers with a disability the opportunity to carry out their banking transactions in the most autonomous and user-friendly way possible. If cost and technical feasibility do play a certain role, we still want to offer to our customers the highest level of independence which is possible.

The program has started up in 2014 although the bank already had some accessibility features in place before that. Our efforts to improve the accessibility of our ATM's are part of this program.

More info in following video made in 2014:
https://www.youtube.com/watch?v=rayvrbbnPeI

1.2 Our Approach

To better define the needs of our customers with disabilities, we organised in 2014 a conference with organisations, representing people with disabilities (26 participants). In addition, colleagues with disabilities were consulted to gather suggestions upon the

K. Miesenberger and G. Kouroupetroglou (Eds.): ICCHP 2018, LNCS 10896, pp. 303–306, 2018.
https://doi.org/10.1007/978-3-319-94277-3_48

topic. In 2016 a feedback conference was organized to inform the organisations about our progress and to capture their comments.

The captured information was used to work out solutions and define priorities. Since the launch of the program, we continuously evaluate the solutions installed as well as the suggestions we are receiving from our customers and from our colleagues.

In addition, a helpdesk has been opened for customers and colleagues. This helpdesk will give us additional insights for finding adequate solutions and will also provide support for those using our accessibility features. Since the beginning of the helpdesk (May 2017), we did receive 67 accessibility requests/remarks.

1.3   Our ATMs

BNP Paribas Fortis has about 2.000 ATM's in Belgium. The majority of them is located in branches, but we also have ATM's on venues with high traffic, such as railway stations and shopping centres.

1.4   Footholds to Accessibility of an ATM

In order to tackle the accessibility of an ATM, we can distinguish 3 footholds:

- Physical Accessibility of the venue
- Accessibility of the hardware
- Accessibility features in the software

2   Physical Accessibility

2.1   Accessible Branches for People with Limited Mobility

221 of our branches (29%) have received a certification for their accessibility for people with limited mobility. This certification is granted by an external accessibility organisation (www.plain-pied.com). In these branches, we guarantee that the self-banking space, where our internal ATM's are located, are accessible for people with limited mobility. To receive the certification, One of the requirements is that the self-banking space has at least 1 ATM with a free space of 1,50 m, so that wheel chair users can easily use our ATM in a lateral way.

As the majority of our branches has not been evaluated yet on their accessibility, we may assume that there are more ATM's that are accessible for people with mobility issues.

3   Hardware

3.1   The Machine

Currently, our ATM's (Diebold-Nixdorf Opteva-series) are ADA (American Disability Act) compliant. The card reader is at maximum 1,22 m height. For our new machines, our Procurement department will take the accessibility into account when deciding on which vendor BNP Paribas Fortis will choose. Our goal is to have the card reader at a maximum height of 1,10 m (ISO) on our future machines. This height may not concern the physical card reader, but the NFC card reader for contactless bank cards.

3.2   Miscellaneous Accessibility Efforts

Discretion Screen. Between our ATM's in the self-banking area of the branch, discretion screens have been installed. We noticed the screens were too low and bothered wheel chair users. Therefore, we now install screens with an increased vertical space (min. 85 cm).

Discretion Numeric Keypad Cover. Some ATM's are equipped with discretion cover around the numeric keypad. In the old version of this cover, it generated a shadow on the top row of the keys. Hence, customers, mostly older customers, complained about the visibility of the keypad. Thanks to their remarks, a new cover has been developed that does not generate a shadow.

Convenience Shelf. Most customers rather have a shelf on which they can put their handbag while using the ATM. However, this tablet increases the distance to the ATM for wheel chair users and the visual impaired. To avoid the inconvenience for these customers, a new shelf has been developed that meets the needs of both our customers without impairments and those using a wheel chair or suffering from a visual impairment.

Rest Benches. Older customers suggested, it would help them if there were rest benches in the self-banking space, especially when they have to queue to use an ATM. A vandalism proof bench has been tested, and a rollout has been started in our branches that offer enough space in the self-banking area.

4   Accessibility Features in the Software

Some accessibility features have been or will be included in the software running on our ATM's. They are mainly useful for people with visual impairments.

4.1   Voice-Assisted Withdrawals

The voice assisted withdrawal is available for all users of our ATM's since 2010. This feature is activated when plugging in a standard 3,5 inch earphone into the jacket of the ATM after which the screen is switched off and the dialog is started up through the ear phones. These are the different steps:

- The user is getting instructions on how to use this feature (can be skipped for frequent users).
  - Possibility to adjust the volume.
  - The user is asked to enter his PIN.

- – Input of the amount.
- – Confirmation of the amount.
- – Notes are delivered.
- – Possibility to get a receipt.
- – End of session.
- The interaction with the machine goes through the numeric keypad, with tactile indications on the buttons: 5dot on 5, circle on "OK", cross on "Cancel" and vertical bar on "Modify"

BNP Paribas Fortis was the first bank in Belgium to offer this feature, in the meantime a second bank, Belfius, has an equivalent service.

4.2   Screen Colour Preferences

At this moment a new feature is developed on our ATM's enabling customers to choose the screen colours. Once selected, the chosen preference will be automatically activated for each session on each ATM of BNP Paribas Fortis. Next to the default colour scheme, following choices are available:

- White font on a black background
- Yellow font on a black background
- Black font on a white background

4.3   Software Buttons

In the new software, the soft buttons on the screen will be placed as low as possible on the screen. This must help wheel chair users to access these buttons.

4.4   General Readability

When designing screens for the ATM, contrast is taken into account, just as the right colour choice to avoid colour blind users experiencing problems using our ATM's.

Accessibility of Self-Service Terminals in Norway

Andreas Cederbom[1], Susanna Laurin[2], and Emil Gejrot[2(✉)]

[1] Funka Nu AB, St. Olavs Plass 2, 0165 Oslo, Norway
andreas.cederbom@funka.com
[2] Funka Nu AB, Tegnérgatan 23, 111 40 Stockholm, Sweden
{susanna.laurin,emil.gejrot}@funka.com

Abstract. This short paper outlines a project on SST accessibility conducted by Funka on behalf of the Norwegian Agency for Public Management and eGovernment (Difi). The aim of the project was to establish a set of usable guidelines for the accessible placement of SSTs in Norway. To do this, Funka reviewed and compared the relevant existing standards. From the resulting corpus, Funka culled requirements relevant to issues of placement and harmonised them. The eventual result was a step-by-step guide for the accessible placement of self-service terminals. Funka would like to continue the work on role-based filtering tools. Funka has already launched such a tool for its Swedish market, drawing on several open-source standards. Something similar could be done for SST accessibility on the basis of, for instance, the EN 301 549 European standard.

Keywords: Self-service terminals · Accessibility · Standardisation

1 Introduction

Self-service terminals are becoming increasingly ubiquitous. From ticket machines at the train station, to automated tills at the supermarket: more and more, public and private actors steer you towards fully automated machines, rather than their human counterparts. But are these technologies accessible? Much has been done to establish overarching standards for the accessibility of physical environments, as well as for the accessibility of web environments. This makes it easier to achieve accessible design in both situations. However, SSTs exist at the intersection of the two environments. For the individual user or service provider, then, it can be difficult to know which parts of which standards they should apply in order to make an SST fully accessible, regardless of the end user's physical or cognitive abilities. This difficulty is compounded by the fact that there are many different kinds of users and service providers for whom SST accessibility requirements will be relevant: SST producers, store managers, city planners, software developers, to name just a few. Standards users in these different roles will also have markedly different needs. Where some need guidance on product design matters, others will be more interested in the placement of the SST, or the conditions of its surrounding environment.

To begin addressing this issue, the Norwegian Agency for Public Management and eGovernment (Difi) asked Funka to establish a set of usable guidelines for the accessible

K. Miesenberger and G. Kouroupetroglou (Eds.): ICCHP 2018, LNCS 10896, pp. 307–310, 2018.
https://doi.org/10.1007/978-3-319-94277-3_49

placement of self-service terminals, aimed at the retail sector. This short paper describes some further reasons behind the study, as well as how it was carried out and what the subsequent results were. It will describe how Funka identified and reviewed the existing standards relevant to SST accessibility in the Norwegian context, which in turn allowed the research team to cull a set of clear requirements and establish a step-by-step guide. Finally, some avenues for future work in the realm of SST accessibility will be discussed.

2 Background

In line with the growing ubiquity of self-service terminals, some research on their accessibility has already been carried out. Mostly, this research has revolved around the operation of SST interfaces, and scholars have paid particular attention to the experiences of the visually impaired. Two oft-cited examples can serve to illustrate this: Already in 1998, Hone et al. discussed the use of speech technology to allow blind patrons to use automatic teller machines [1]. They concluded that in this case, speech technology should be discouraged for privacy reasons. Later, their conclusion was reflected in a study by Sandnes et al. on the operation of SSTs through the use of gestures. Carried out with visually impaired test subjects in Norway, this study showed encouraging results [2].

In fact, Norway is an interesting case when it comes to universal design and accessibility. In most ways, Norwegian legislation in this area requires more things of more actors than what is the case elsewhere in the Nordic region, or indeed in the EU. Most importantly, Norwegian accessibility legislation encompasses private actors as well as their public-sector counterparts. Furthermore, the law also applies to self-service terminals – albeit in a somewhat confusing fashion.

The research revealed a vast tangle of recommendations that were likely to be considered inscrutable by anyone who was not an expert in universal design or accessibility. No fewer than ten different standards with bearing on SST accessibility in Norway are identified in the regulation on the universal design of ICT solutions. Aside from overlapping each other, these standards comprised a mixture of functional performance requirements (i.e., descriptions of end users' needs) and jargon-laden technical specifications. Moreover, the standards did not appear to have been developed with any particular professional role in mind. The cumulative effect made the corpus of applicable standards – all told some 800 pages – hard to read, and even harder to understand [3].

The non-specialist user faces further barriers to applying these standards. For one thing, in Norway as elsewhere, there are fees for accessing and using standards. An individual user may well conclude that these costs are prohibitive, especially if there is no way of telling if a standard will be relevant to their particular situation, and to what degree. For another thing, even if a user purchases a standard and intends to apply it, they may find that the requirements made are outmoded, or unscientific, or both. This is a well-known problem with standards for physical accessibility. Many of them were created several decades ago, often based on little more than the experiences of one particular individual, or even just best-guess estimated measurements. In some cases, these drawbacks render standards unusable – no doubt irritating if you have already spent good money to gain access.

3 Developing a Harmonised Guide

To Funka, it became clear that the applicable standards for SST accessibility needed to be harmonised. The research team compared the standards and highlighted where they were in agreement, where they diverged and, significantly, where gaps in coverage remained. These findings were then put forward in a series of user interviews, where the respondents were given the opportunity to assess the practicability of the recommendations made. This eventually resulted in a step-by-step guide for the accessible placement of self-service terminals [4].

The guide was designed for maximum ease of use, complete with graphics and an introductory video. It is divided into four parts, not counting the introduction explaining the reasoning behind the guide and how it ought to be used. The four parts track the stages of SST interaction an end user will go through, from locating the terminal, to approaching it, and to using it. Each part contains minimum requirements, as well as best-practice recommendations.

Part 1 describes the steps that should be taken to allow a user to find the self-service terminal. These steps include signage, display lighting, tactile markings in the ground leading up to the SST, as well as visible placement. Part 2 describes how to create accessible approaches to the terminal by, for instance, ensuring that the surrounding surface is sufficiently wide and even to allow for unhindered navigation. Part 3 deals with the immediate surroundings of the terminal, pointing out the need for sufficient space around the terminal to allow for easy access and some measure of privacy for the user. Part 4, finally, lays out requirements for actual usage of the SST, taking into account aspects such as surrounding noise and lighting conditions. It also recommends that the SST is made at least partly adjustable, allowing it to be operated by users of varying height or mobility.

4 Discussion

The end product turned out to be something that could be of use not just to the selected professional role of newsagent proprietor, but also to other public and private actors charged with the placement of self-service terminals. Nevertheless, many other target audiences remained outside the scope of the online guide. For instance, the guide says nothing about requirements for industry, or for the developers of SST software. Similarly, the guide does not give equal attention to all aspects of SST accessibility, which encompasses not just placement, but also software, dimensions, light conditions, acoustics and so on.

In other words: further research is needed. Funka would like to continue this exercise on a larger scale, perhaps resulting in an interactive tool that allows the user to filter requirements from more standards, according to more potential roles. In fact, Funka has already done something in this vein for the Swedish market. We recently launched a subscription service for a tool that allows users – primarily public-sector procurers – to assemble relevant technical requirements for web development. The tool draws on EN 301 549, the European standard for accessibility in IT procurement, the Web Content Accessibility Guidelines (WCAG) 2.0, official Swedish web development guidelines and, finally, Funka's own requirements, developed in close cooperation with various disabled persons' organisations. The user can filter the requirements according to which role is relevant – such as developer, editor, UX designer or system administrator [5].

There is a barrier to doing something similar for SSTs, however. In order to create the step-by-step guide described above, Funka needed to obtain permission from the rights holders to create simplified versions of the relevant standards. This was by no means a straightforward task, and it seems unlikely that they would agree to a more far-ranging usage of the standards, in the manner of our existing requirements tool. When it comes to SST accessibility, then, a more workable solution could be to use the harmonised EN 301 549 standard – which is available to use free of charge – as the starting point for further elaboration. This elaboration could then serve as the basis for a tool that would allow the user to filter the requirements according to the needs of their role. This would also provide an opportunity to update those requirements that do not reflect actual needs in the present. Such an endeavour would entail extensive user testing, as well as the active involvement of industry representatives.

5 Conclusion

On behalf of the Agency for Public Management and eGovernment (Difi) in Norway, Funka created an easy-to-use guide for the accessible placement of self-service terminals. This turned out to be a fruitful avenue of study, not least since this facet of SST accessibility had not received as much attention as that of the operability of interfaces. However, the guide is far from all-encompassing. Further steps ought to be taken to expand the scope and applicability of the guide, possibly also outside Norway.

References

1. Hone, K.S., Graham, R., Maguire, M.C., Baber, C., Johnson, G.I.: Speech technology for automatic teller machines: an investigation of user attitude and performance. Ergonomics **41**(7), 962–981 (2010)
2. Sandnes, F.E., Tan, T.B., Johansen, A., Sulic, E., Vesterhus, E., Iversen, E.R.: Making touch-based kiosks accessible to blind users through simple gestures. Univ. Access Inf. Soc. **11**(4), 421–431 (2012)
3. Norwegian regulation FOR-2013-06-21-732. Section 4
4. Difi. Veileder for utplassering av selvbetjeningsautomater. https://uu.difi.no/krav-og-regelverk/veileder-utplassering-av-automater
5. Funka. Nytt verktyg för krav på tillgänglighet. https://www.funka.com/vi-erbjuder/stod-krav-och-test/kravunderlag-och-regelverk-/nytt-verktyg-for-krav-pa-tillganglighet/

Improving the Robustness to Input Errors on Touch-Based Self-service Kiosks and Transportation Apps

Frode Eika Sandnes[1,2(✉)]

[1] Department of Computer Science,
Oslo Metropolitan University, Oslo, Norway
frodes@oslomet.no
[2] Faculty of Technology, Kristiania University College, Oslo, Norway

Abstract. Text input is cumbersome on public self-service kiosks and apps. Applications often provide prefix-based text suggestions to speed up input, but the input must be correct. However, application specific lists are usually limited in size. For example, the Norwegian rail network comprise 324 stations. This can be exploited in the input process. Several approaches are explored herein for more flexible text input that are robust to errors.

Keywords: Self-service kiosks · Travel apps · Text entry · Error correction

1 Introduction

Public self-service kiosks have become an important part of the transport infrastructure in large cities allowing unmanned service of stations. Apps have also emerged as an alternative [1] and the two often coexist side by side. One common step is the input of destination names using text entry.

Moderate use of text input is a useful principle applicable to both touch-based self-service kiosks and smartphone apps. In some situations, one may avoid the problem altogether by other means such as QR-codes [2]. When selecting from a small list of items, such ten station names, the interface can rely on recognition and selection (see Fig. 1(a)). However, with larger item lists that cannot be fitted on a simple screenful, such as a few hundred station names, it may be impractical to perform interaction through recognition. In these instances, the relevant item can be recalled through text input (see Fig. 1(c) and (d)). However, text input on public self-service kiosks can be challenging for some users if they have limited experience using the system and feel pressure from being observed by onlookers. Also, often public kiosks have low-quality displays, dated technology or damaged displays making it hard to hit the exact targets. Visitors such as tourists may not have the local knowledge needed to select destinations with unintuitive names such as "Gardemoen" to get "Oslo Airport".

The input of text via smartphone apps is also challenging for many users due to the small screen real-estate with small virtual keys, making it challenging to hit the targets (see Fig. 1(b)).

K. Miesenberger and G. Kouroupetroglou (Eds.): ICCHP 2018, LNCS 10896, pp. 311–319, 2018.
https://doi.org/10.1007/978-3-319-94277-3_50

(a)   Taiwan High Speed Rail).

(b)   NSB travel app.

(c)   NSB ticket kiosk (alphabetical, 2006).

(d)   NSB ticket kiosk (QWERTY, 2016).

Fig. 1. Selecting travel destination.

Public kiosks and smartphone can display a similar amount of information on a single screen. Although the kiosk displays are larger than smartphone displays they are viewed from longer distances. Also, one must prevent information overload.

Text input can be challenging for individuals with disabilities. With reduced vision one may not be able to perceive the information. With motor disabilities such as tremor one may hit incorrect targets. Fitts' law explains the relationship between the time to hit a target, the distance to a target and the size of the target [3]. Users with cognitive disabilities, such as dyslexia, may have problems both decoding and encoding text [4, 5], and thus benefit from query-building aids [6].

Although the item lists are too large to be displayed on one screen, the lists can still be relatively small. When a list contains few textual elements (a few hundred) one may exploit the fact that the limitations allow fewer valid choices and hence provide stronger error correcting power than is possible with full dictionaries.

This study explored several strategies for exploiting small language models with the overall goal of achieving universal accessibility [7]. Four methods are investigated, namely how to compensate for (a) motor input error due to accidentally hitting neighboring targets, (b) the effort needed to input long words, (c) cognitive disabilities causing incorrect letter orderings and (d) a mixture of motor input error and cognitive errors. The methods are enhancements of the prefix method and users without reduced motor or cognitive function should not notice the added functionality. The issue of low vision is not addressed although transportation is a major challenge for individuals with reduced vision [8]. Kiosk interfaces targeted at users with low vision can for instance employ gestures with audio feedback to facilitate input [9, 10]. Moreover, gestures are usually relative movements and hence the problem of hitting absolute targets is avoided altogether. Alternatively, tactile feedback can be used [11].

2 Background

There has been much research into various aspects of self-service kiosks such as readiness for the technology [12], accessibility issues [13], ergonomic issues [14], service design [15], prototyping [16], evaluation techniques [17], etc. Self-service kiosks spans a range of areas such as food and catering [18], ATMs [19], healthcare [20], navigation in hospitals [21], vending machines [22], interactive public displays [23] and for public transport and ticket purchase [24]. A self-service kiosk is usually placed in a public space [25] and is meant to be usable by all and there has thus been some focus on the universal accessibility of such kiosks [26].

In previous work we have focused on making kiosks accessible to blind users, especially given the task of selecting stations [10] and adapting dynamically to the needs of the user [27]. We have also explored the effect of keyboard layout for the same task, whereby presenting the users with a familiar layout is less likely to impose unnecessary stress [28]. There is a vast literature on text entry in general [29–31].

There is a long history of research into spell checking and correcting from the more classic methods using dictionaries [32] to newer methods using Hidden Markov Models [33] and online texts [34]. Attempts have also been made to study the mistakes made by dyslexic users [35] and users with reduced motor function [36]. Geometric models have been used to relax the need to hit targets exactly [37].

3 Method

The language model comprises a list of 324 train stations acquired from timetables. The station names were converted to lowercase to simplify processing.

3.1 Motor Errors: Fuzzy Keys

To compensate for motor input errors, it is assumed that the user is using a virtual QWERTY keyboard. Moreover, it is assumed that simple motor errors are caused by missing the target, that is, the user hits one of the neighboring keys. For simplicity, it is assumed that horizontal errors are more frequent than vertical errors, especially as virtual smartphone keyboards in portrait mode have tall and narrow keys (see Fig. 1(c)).

For each keypress the two horizontally neighboring keys are considered as alternative intended keystrokes. For example, if the user enters the character C, the character X on the left and character V on the right are included into the set of potential input characters. Next, all combinations of the three possibilities for each keypress are combined and each combination is checked against the list of words. All the words with matching prefixes are added to the word suggestion list. Clearly, with one-character input there are 3 possibilities, with two input characters there are 9 possibilities, with 3, 4, 5, 6, 7 and 8 characters there are 27, 81, 243, 729, 2187 and 6561 possibilities, respectively. Imagine the user intends to write "Oslo", but starts with the right hand in a wrong position and writes "Iski". The four characters give 81 possibilities including "Uiau", "Uiai", "Uiao", "Uisu" and also the correct word "Oslo". The correct string is selected when correctly identified in the list of words.

3.2   Reducing Input Effort: Abbreviations

Prefix-based input works well with the English language where most words are not combined with other words. In other languages, such as Norwegian, compound words are built by combining words, and more words thereby share the same prefix. The user must enter long prefixes before a reliable suggestion can be made. To solve this problem abbreviation input was proposed [38]. With abbreviation-based input the user only inputs selected characters at various positions in the word. This was implemented by using the least common subsequence (LCS) algorithm.

Imagine we want to input "Lundamo". There are four words that share the same 3 letter prefix, namely Lundamo, Lunde, Lunden and Lunner. Three of these also share the same 4 letter prefix "Lund". With abbreviation-based input the user may enter the four consonants "lndm" to retrieve "LuNDaMo".

3.3   Cognitive Errors: Bag-of-Letters

Cognitive errors can cause characters to appear in the wrong sequence. To recover from such input errors the following strategy was performed. An entered prefix is matched against all the words in the list of words. A count of matching characters is maintained. If the number of matching characters equal the length of the prefix the associated word is included in the list of suggestions. Imagine the user intends to input "Oslo", but accidentally inputs "Olso". Since all the characters in Olso also are in Oslo the word is correctly identified.

3.4   Motor and Cognitive Errors: Fuzzy-Bag

An attempt was made to combine fuzzy-key and bag-of-letters. This was achieved by generating the set of potential input characters sequences using fuzzy key. Next, each of the contenders were matched against the entries in wordlist using bag-of-letters. Imagine we wish to input "Oslo", but we accidentally place the right hand incorrectly, and also accidentally swaps the two middle characters, and thus input "Iksi".

3.5   Measurements

The four methods described herein were evaluated according to the number of available suggestions at each step of the input process. The average and the maximum number of suggestions were recorded by systematically inputting the list to the system one character at a time in offline mode while recording the suggestions at each step.

4 Results

Table 1 presents the results. The data shows that the prefix method leads to the fewest suggestions. When only one key is pressed there are on average 23.4 suggestions (maximum 50). With two characters the maximum is reduced to 14 suggestions with a mean of 4.7. With three characters there is a maximum of 4 suggestions and a mean of 1.7 suggestions. In other words, the prefix method allows most stations to be entered with three keystrokes or less, although with no tolerance for errors.

Abbreviations result in more than twice as many suggestions with one key compared to the prefix method, and with three characters the mean number of suggestions is reduced to a manageable 6.1 (maximum 32). With four keystrokes this is reduced to a maximum of 10 suggestions with a mean of 2.1 suggestions. The freedom to construct a word from abbreviations comes at the expense of more suggestions.

Compensating for motor errors by incorporating neighboring keys gives a maximum of 322 suggestions (mean 81) with just one keypress. One needs to enter six characters to safely arrive at a maximum of 7 suggestions (mean of 1.2). This approach requires a larger keystroke sample to determine the word. Thus, the number of keystrokes is traded for decreased precision requirement.

With cognitive error compensation the number of alternatives with one input character gives a maximum of 202 suggestions (mean 97). This method converges slower and 7 keystrokes are needed to achieve a maximum of 9 suggestions (mean 1.8).

The combined method is different from the other methods in that it requires all the characters in the word to be entered. There are no entries for one keystroke since there are no one-letter station names, but there are a couple of two-letter stations. The mean number of suggestions is largest for words with 9 characters, although this mean is less than 10. The maximum number of suggestions of 63 is associated with 8 keystroke sequences.

An approach based on Levenshtein distances were included for completeness, where the string was compared to the prefixes of all words with the same length and all words with a Levenshtein distance less than 4 were included in the suggestion list. The levenshtein distance incorporates insertions, deletions and insertions and can thus compensate for both motor and cognitive errors. The Levenshtein approach works well with short distances but gives many suggestions for 4 and 5 keystrokes (maximum of 33 and 50 suggestions, respectively). However, users probably expect to have a reliable suggestion by the third keystroke and this approach appears to be quite a good balance as well as its simple implementation.

The robustness to both motor error and cognitive errors comes at the expense of longer suggestion lists. However, for someone who is very uncertain about how to input a word may find this method useful.

Table 1. Mean and maximum number of suggestions (M = mean, mx = maximum).

N	Prefix		Abbreviation		Fuzzy key		Bag-of-letters		Fuzzy bag		Levenshtein	
	M	mx	M	mx	M	mx	M	mx	M	mx	M	mx
1	23	50	98	202	81	322	98	202	0	0	0	0
2	5	14	24	86	24	322	36	123	0	2	5	14
3	2	4	6	32	7	71	16	65	0	4	9	24
4	1	4	2	10	3	71	8	42	1	9	14	33
5	1	3	1	4	1	23	4	26	2	20	23	50
6	1	2	1	2	1	7	3	16	5	28	7	18
7	1	1	1	1	1	2	2	9	7	42	3	7
8					1	2	1	7	7	63	2	4
9					1	1	1	3	10	43	1	3
10							1	3	7	19	1	2
11							1	2	8	19	1	1
12							1	1	5	7		
13									6	7		
14									7	7		
15									7	7		

5   Conclusions

Several strategies for making the input of destinations on self-service kiosks and mobile apps have been discussed, namely fuzzy key, abbreviations, bag-of-letters, fuzzy bag and Levenshtein distances. The flexibility and robustness to input errors comes at the expense of more input in terms of keystrokes. Overall, suggestions based on Levenshtein differences appears to provide a good balance of simplicity, few keystrokes and robustness to errors.

References

1. Dickinson, J.E., Ghali, K., Cherrett, T., Speed, C., Davies, N., Norgate, S.: Tourism and the smartphone app: capabilities, emerging practice and scope in the travel domain. Curr. Issues Tour. **17**, 84–101 (2014)
2. Huang, Y.P., Chang, Y.T., Sandnes, F.E.: Ubiquitous information transfer across different platforms by QR codes. J. Mob. Multimed. **6**, 3–13 (2010)
3. MacKenzie, I.S., Buxton, W.: Extending Fitts' law to two-dimensional tasks. In: Proceedings of the SIGCHI conference on Human Factors in Computing Systems, pp. 219–226. ACM (1992)
4. Eika, E.: Universally designed text on the web: towards readability criteria based on antipatterns. Stud. Health Technol. Inform. **229**, 461–470 (2016)
5. Eika, E., Sandnes, F.E.: Authoring WCAG2.0-compliant texts for the web through text readability visualization. In: Antona, M., Stephanidis, C. (eds.) UAHCI 2016. LNCS, vol. 9737, pp. 49–58. Springer, Cham (2016). https://doi.org/10.1007/978-3-319-40250-5_5
6. Berget, G., Sandnes, F.E.: Do autocomplete functions reduce the impact of dyslexia on information searching behaviour? A case of Google. J. Am. Soc. Inf. Sci. Technol. **67**, 2320–2328 (2016)
7. Whitney, G., Keith, S., Bühler, C., Hewer, S., Lhotska, L., Miesenberger, K., Sandnes, F.E., Stephanidis, C., Velasco, C.A.: Twenty five years of training and education in ICT design for all and assistive technology. Technol. Disabil. **3**, 163–170 (2011)
8. Sandnes, F.E.: What do low-vision users really want from smart glasses? Faces, text and perhaps no glasses at all. In: Miesenberger, K., Bühler, C., Penaz, P. (eds.) ICCHP 2016. LNCS, vol. 9758, pp. 187–194. Springer, Cham (2016). https://doi.org/10.1007/978-3-319-41264-1_25
9. Gomez, J.V., Sandnes, F.E.: RoboGuideDog: guiding blind users through physical environments with laser range scanners. Procedia Comput. Sci. **14**, 218–225 (2012)
10. Sandnes, F.E., Tan, T.B., Johansen, A., Sulic, E., Vesterhus, E., Iversen, E.R.: Making touch-based kiosks accessible to blind users through simple gestures. Univers. Access Inf. Soc. **11**, 421–431 (2012)
11. Lin, M.W., Cheng, Y.M., Yu, W., Sandnes, F.E.: Investigation into the feasibility of using tactons to provide navigation cues in pedestrian situations. In: Proceedings of the 20th Australasian Conference on Computer-Human Interaction: Designing for Habitus and Habitat, pp. 299–302. ACM (2008)
12. Liljander, V., Gillberg, F., Gummerus, J., Van Riel, A.: Technology readiness and the evaluation and adoption of self-service technologies. J. Retail. Consum. Serv. **13**, 177–191 (2006)

13. Petrie, H., Darzentas, J.S., Power, C.: Self-service terminals for older and disabled users: attitudes of key stakeholders. In: Miesenberger, K., Fels, D., Archambault, D., Peňáz, P., Zagler, W. (eds.) ICCHP 2014. LNCS, vol. 8547, pp. 340–347. Springer, Cham (2014). https://doi.org/10.1007/978-3-319-08596-8_53

14. Day, P., Rohan, C., Coventry, L., Johnson, G., Riley, C.: Reach modelling for drive-up self-service. In: Contemporary Ergonomics and Human Factors 2010: Proceedings of the International Conference on Contemporary Ergonomics and Human Factors 2010. Contemporary Ergonomics, pp. 47–55, Taylor & Francis, London (2010)

15. Darzentas, J., Darzentas, J.S.: Systems thinking in design: service design and self-services. Form Akademisk-forskningstidsskrift for design og designdidaktikk 7 (2014)

16. Schreder, G., Smuc, M., Siebenhandl, K., Mayr, E.: Age and computer self-efficacy in the use of digital technologies: an investigation of prototypes for public self-service terminals. In: Stephanidis, C., Antona, M. (eds.) UAHCI 2013. LNCS, vol. 8010, pp. 221–230. Springer, Heidelberg (2013). https://doi.org/10.1007/978-3-642-39191-0_25

17. Sandnes, F.E., Jian, H.L., Huang, Y.P., Huang, Y.M.: User interface design for public kiosks: an evaluation of the Taiwan high speed rail ticket vending machine. J. Inf. Sci. Eng. **26**, 307–321 (2010)

18. Shiba, Y., Sasakura, M.: Visual interface and interaction design for self-service orders at a restaurant. In: 2016 20th International Conference Information Visualisation, pp. 230–235. IEEE (2016)

19. van Schaik, P., Petrie, H., Japp, J.: The ATM speaks: the design and evaluation of an automatic teller machine with voice output. Adv. Assistive Technol. **3**, 223–227 (1997)

20. Lyu, Y., Vincent, C.J., Chen, Y., Shi, Y., Tang, Y., Wang, W., Liu, W., Zhang, S., Fang, K., Ding, J.: Designing and optimizing a healthcare kiosk for the community. Appl. Ergon. **47**, 157–169 (2015)

21. Wright, P., Soroka, A., Belt, S., Pham, D.T., Dimov, S., De Roure, D., Petrie, H.: Using audio to support animated route information in a hospital touch-screen kiosk. Comput. Hum. Behav. **26**, 753–759 (2010)

22. Siebenhandl, K., Schreder, G., Smuc, M., Mayr, E., Nagl, M.: A user-centered design approach to self-service ticket vending machines. IEEE Trans. Prof. Commun. **56**, 138–159 (2013)

23. Azad, A., Ruiz, J., Vogel, D., Hancock, M., Lank, E.: Territoriality and behaviour on and around large vertical publicly-shared displays. In: Proceedings of the Designing Interactive Systems Conference, pp. 468–477. ACM (2012)

24. Min, X.G., Li, G.Z., Wan, T.: Improve on the ticket vending machine for the railway. In: Advanced Materials Research, vol. 422, pp. 35–38, Trans Tech Publications (2012)

25. Tikka, H., Viña, S., Jacucci, G., Korpilahti, T.: Provoking the city—touch installations for urban space. Digit. Creativity **22**, 200–214 (2011)

26. Schreder, G., Siebenhandl, K., Mayr, E., Smuc, M.: The ticket machine challenge: social inclusion by barrier-free ticket vending machines. In: Generational Use of New Media, pp. 129–148 (2012)

27. Hagen, S., Sandnes, F.E.: Toward accessible self-service kiosks through intelligent user interfaces. Pers. Ubiquit. Comput. **14**, 715–721 (2010)

28. Sandnes, F.E.: Effects of common keyboard layouts on physical effort: Implications for kiosks and Internet banking. In: The proceedings of Unitech2010: International Conference on Universal Technologies, pp. 91–100 (2010)

29. Sandnes, F.E., Huang, Y.P.: Chording with spatial mnemonics: automatic error correction for eyes-free text entry. J. Inf. Sci. Eng. **22**, 1015–1031 (2006)

30. Sandnes, F.E.: Evaluating mobile text entry strategies with finite state automata. In: Proceedings of the 7th International Conference on Human Computer Interaction With Mobile Devices & Services, pp. 115–121. ACM (2005)

31. Sandnes, F.E., Jian, H.-L.: Pair-wise variability index: evaluating the cognitive difficulty of using mobile text entry systems. In: Brewster, S., Dunlop, M. (eds.) Mobile HCI 2004. LNCS, vol. 3160, pp. 347–350. Springer, Heidelberg (2004). https://doi.org/10.1007/978-3-540-28637-0_35

32. Peterson, J.L.: Computer programs for detecting and correcting spelling errors. Commun. ACM **23**, 676–687 (1980)

33. Li, Y., Duan, H., Zhai, C.: A generalized hidden markov model with discriminative training for query spelling correction. In: Proceedings of the 35th International ACM SIGIR Conference on Research and Development in Information Retrieval, pp. 611–620. ACM (2012)

34. Duan, H., Hsu, B.J.P.: Online spelling correction for query completion. In: Proceedings of the 20th International Conference on World Wide Web, pp. 117–126. ACM (2011)

35. Bruck, M.: The word recognition and spelling of dyslexic children. Read. Res. Q. **23**, 51–69 (1988)

36. Kane, S.K., Wobbrock, J.O., Harniss, M., Johnson, K.L.: TrueKeys: identifying and correcting typing errors for people with motor impairments. In: Proceedings of the 13th International Conference on Intelligent User Interfaces, pp. 349–352. ACM (2008)

37. Kristensson, P.O., Zhai, S.: Relaxing stylus typing precision by geometric pattern matching. In: Proceedings of the 10th International Conference on Intelligent User Interfaces, pp. 151–158. ACM (2005)

38. Sandnes, F.E.: Reflective text entry: a simple low effort predictive input method based on flexible abbreviations. Procedia Comput. Sci. **67**, 105–112 (2015)

Practical Challenges of Implementing Accessibility Laws and Standards in the Self-service Environment

Elina Jokisuu[(✉)] [iD], Phil Day [iD], and Charlie Rohan

User Centred Design, NCR Corporation, Dundee DD2 4SW, UK
elina.jokisuu@ncr.com

Abstract. Self-service technologies (SSTs) must be accessible to anyone, anywhere, anytime. This leads to an interesting challenge in terms of ensuring their accessibility to people with disabilities. There are various laws, standards and guidelines aiming to describe the minimum requirements that make SSTs accessible for everyone, for example by requiring specific height and depth to interface elements and controls, requiring private audio guidance, and requiring that interface elements are tactile enough to be discoverable and identifiable by touch. In this paper, we reflect on the experiences of implementing these various accessibility requirements from an industrial perspective, and demonstrate difficulties and successes through three different case studies. The first describes the development of the tactile symbols on ATM (Automated Teller Machine) keypad, which became a de facto standard and eventually a codified legal requirement. The second case study describes a research project to make ATM touchscreens accessible for people with visual impairments, and the impact accessibility laws and standards had on the project. The third case study takes a look at the height and depth requirements for ATMs worldwide to demonstrate the challenges of their implementation and the urgent need for harmonization. Finally, broader conclusions will be drawn between the gap that can exist between standards writers and the industries that must use them, with suggestions being made as to how this process can be improved.

Keywords: Self-service · ATM · Accessibility standards

1 Introduction

Self-service technologies (SSTs) pose an interesting challenge in terms of their accessibility to people with disabilities. By nature, SSTs are based on the principle of "walk up and use": anyone, anywhere, anytime must be able to use them without any previous experience, training or knowledge. There are various laws, standards and guidelines aiming to specify the minimum requirements for SSTs, thus ensuring they are made accessible to people with disabilities such as people with visual impairment or people who use wheelchairs. Some of these key requirements include the height and depth to interface elements and controls, providing private audio guidance, and making sure interface elements are tactile enough to be discoverable and identifiable by touch.

© Springer International Publishing AG, part of Springer Nature 2018
K. Miesenberger and G. Kouroupetroglou (Eds.): ICCHP 2018, LNCS 10896, pp. 320–326, 2018.
https://doi.org/10.1007/978-3-319-94277-3_51

One type of SSTs, namely Automated Teller Machines (ATMs), have had requirements for their accessibility for over 30 years, with some countries including them in building codes or rules for the built environment, and others having specific rules for ATMs. The benefits of these accessibility requirements are numerous. From a manufacturer's point of view, they distil the needs of certain user groups into well-researched accessibility criteria. The ensure equal access, they ensure consistency in user experience and thus allow for transferring a learnt experience, such as the keypad layout, from one machine to another, and they ensure that access to cash remains available to all, a particularly important consideration as financial services are changing with some regions reducing the number of bank branches.

However, the practical implementation of these accessibility requirements can also create challenges as their interpretations vary wildly between different countries, even though they all aim towards the same goal: making a SSTs accessible to people with disabilities. The requirements vary in both their legal status and their scope, so much so that it is very difficult to design one product or solution that meets all the requirements in these different standards.

In this paper, we reflect on the experiences of implementing these various accessibility requirements from an industrial perspective, and demonstrate difficulties and successes by use of three different case studies.

2 Case Study 1: Tactile Features on ATM Function Keys Become a De Facto Standard

The first case study describes an NCR collaboration with ONCE (the Spanish national organisation for blind and partially sighted people) to develop an easier way to identify each function key on the ATM keypad. Usually there are at least three function keys: Cancel, Clear and Enter, although some countries also have other keys (such as Help). The original customer request was to add Braille to the key surfaces in order to make them usable for people with visual impairment. However, the NCR designer pointed out that not all blind and partially sighted people can read Braille, and what is more, the use of Braille was declining, meaning that fewer and fewer users would benefit from the Braille characters. Furthermore, haptic sensation, required for reading Braille, is significantly degraded in cold conditions, a problem when many ATMs are placed outside. We therefore collaborated with ONCE in defining new, abstract tactile symbols that were easily distinguishable and could readily be learnt. We then campaigned across other regions for them also to adopt these symbols; namely a raised X for Cancel, a raised circle for Enter, and a raised line or arrow for Clear/Correct. Through this campaigning with standards bodies internationally and socialising the work with our customers, these tactile features have now become a de facto standard not only for ATMs, but also for payment machines at a retail point-of-sale. They have also been codified in several laws and standards, e.g. the UK ATM guideline [1], the US Americans with Disabilities Act (ADA) [2], and the European Bankers keyboard standard [3]. We made a deliberate decision to not attempt to restrict or protect this initiative to gain commercial advantage, but instead freely shared this innovation in order to drive market adoption and ensure a consistency of experience.

This case study illustrates the importance of collaboration between all the stake-holders: end users, manufacturers, disability advocacy groups and standards bodies. There was a practical user need driving the need for a solution, which through user acceptance became standard practice worldwide.

3 Case Study 2: Making Touchscreen PIN Entry an Accessible and Acceptable Solution

ATMs are generally used to handle financial transactions, which means the requirements for privacy and security are important and need to be considered alongside the accessibility requirements. Unfortunately, this can lead to a tension between the two. One example of this type of tension is with card slots. A recent trend is to reduce the height of the card slot opening to reduce the chance of fraudulent devices being inserted, thus improving security. However, this change means that the card slot no longer has a funnelled lead-in, which can make it more difficult for those with reduced manual dexterity or sight loss to find the slot and insert the card.

Another example of this tension is the stringent security requirements regarding entering the PIN on an ATM [4]. Blind and partially sighted people rely on the ATM vocalising the on-screen content and options, but the security requirements mean that the ATM software is not allowed to vocalise (or even know) what the user's PIN code is. When entering the PIN, traditionally blind and partially sighted users can use the tactile feedback provided by the physical keypad to input the correct numbers: the 5 key has a raised pip, the other number keys follow a prescribed layout, and the function keys have specific tactile features as well. However, when the PIN entry is performed on a touchscreen, instead of a physical keypad, these tactile features are no longer available. All that can be felt is the smooth surface of the touchscreen, and all that can be heard is an all-purpose beep to communicate that a number has been entered.

To overcome this issue, we created multiple concepts that allowed numbers to be entered on a touchscreen, while providing some level of confidence that a correct number had been entered. These concepts were evaluated with blind and partially sighted people, together with experts from the RNIB (Royal National Institute of Blind People in the UK) [5, 6]. Over the course of several years, these concepts were either dropped or refined until we had a solution that tested well and was eventually approved, gaining a Gold status in the RNIB Approved scheme.

A key point here is that many of the accessibility laws and standards explicitly state that a physical numeric keypad must be present on the ATM. For example, the US ADA has a section concerned with ATMs and fare machines; section 707. Within this section there are specific requirements on input devices:

```
707.6.1 Input Controls. At least one tactilely discernible
input control shall be provided for each function. Where pro-
vided, key surfaces not on active areas of display screens,
shall be raised above surrounding surfaces. Where membrane keys
are the only method of input, each shall be tactilely discern-
able from surrounding surfaces and adjacent keys.
```

707.6.2 Numeric Keys. Numeric keys shall be arranged in a 12-key ascending or descending telephone keypad layout. The number five key shall be tactilely distinct from the other keys.

[Excerpt from 2010 ADA Standard, 2]

These requirements were written in a proscriptive manner and assumed that the only way of making input accessible was through a physical keypad. It could therefore be argued that the standards inadvertently restricted innovation. It was particularly concerning for us as many of the blind and partially sighted individuals and groups that we worked with in the US and UK were enthusiastically embracing touchscreen technology on smartphones and tablets (helped by the mainstreaming of accessibility features in the operating system such as iOS and Android) [7].

The ADA, as do many other standards and regulations, does have a general clause to try to ensure other solutions are suitable. This so-called equivalent facilitation means that the existence of the requirement does not prevent the use of other designs or technologies as long as they provide equivalent or greater accessibility. From a practical standpoint, the manufacturer carries the responsibility of demonstrating equivalent facilitation but the problem is that the regulation provides no mechanism for demonstrating this equivalence.

During the process of refining the solution, we had many detailed discussions with legal experts, interested parties from prospective customers, and even with the US Access Board (an independent federal agency that promotes equality for people with disabilities through leadership in accessible design and the development of accessibility guidelines and standards for the built environment, transportation, communication, medical diagnostic equipment, and information technology). Unfortunately, although the attendees of the Access Board meeting agreed that there was a need for a mechanism of demonstrating equivalent facilitation, they were unable to provide this service or advise how it could be achieved. We therefore had to fall back on a court judgement – in the end this was achieved by working with the National Federation of the Blind (NFB), a customer (Cardtronics) and a court appointed arbiter (a Special Master) to have the solution assessed and judged to provide an equivalent level of accessibility [8].

This difficulty, enforced by an assumption on the part of the standards writers, contrasts with a standard such as EN 301 549 [9], which was written in a manner to describe the functional performance of Information and Communication Technology (ICT), rather than specify implementations or methods of providing this functional performance. In this standard, there are similar requirements around the need to support non-visual access (which are not quoted verbatim for reasons of copyright). However, the requirement is written in a manner that does not exclude newer technologies or methods from being used. For example, in Sect. 5.2.2 of the EN 301 549, which is concerned with the discernibility of operable parts, the requirement is written in terms of providing a means to discern each operable part. There is then a note that suggests one possible means of meeting this is to make each operable part tactilely discernible. This still enables other methods of providing accessibility features; such as have been offered by Apple, Android and others on smartphones and tablets in recent years. Without this careful level of consideration by the standards writers, it is easy to slip into being too proscriptive, and therefore constrain or stifle future innovation in accessibility features.

Another helpful approach that was taken in this standard was to differentiate between open and closed systems. A closed system can be thought of as a system that is self-contained and does not allow users to add peripherals or software to access that functionality. In terms of accessibility features, a closed system does not allow the user to use their screen reader of choice, or to plug in an alternative input or output device (such as footswitches or a Braille display). Almost all SSTs are closed, and certainly all ATMs are closed by design, as there are stringent security rules around financial transactions that would be breached by allowing this level of logical access.

Again, without this distinction between open and closed systems being made, some accessibility requirements may conflict with mandatory security requirements and therefore be unachievable. However, it is our view that a standard can provide helpful guidance without restricting innovative accessibility methods on the one hand, or enforcing unworkable accessibility requirements on the other.

4   Case Study 3: Lack of Requirements Harmonisation Causes Issues in Terms of Reach to ATM Interface

Most of the accessibility laws, standards and guidelines specify the minimum and maximum height and depth of the user interface elements/controls for self-service machines. These vary significantly across countries, despite all being driven by the same basic requirement; that of enabling everyone to be able to reach to the user interface regardless of stature (and including people who are seated as well as ambulant populations). This is illustrated with an example of the height an ATM interface should be placed at in different countries (Fig. 1).

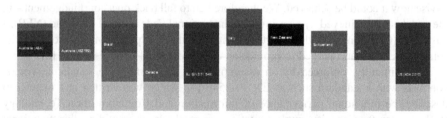

Fig. 1. Example height requirements for ATMs (the coloured block illustrates the height of the ATM interface as defined in the regulations) – wide variation around the world (Color figure online)

The lack of consistency is apparent on visual inspection of an illustration like this. Let us consider the reach heights of just a few of the countries that are illustrated here.

- Australia: 750–1200 mm (exact height varies by feature)
- France: 400–1300 mm (again varies by feature, most in 700–900, or 900–1300)
- Switzerland: 800–1100 mm

- UK: exact height varies by depth, but approximately 700–1250 mm for minimal depth
- USA: 380–1220 mm

It quickly becomes evident that there is a very small amount of common overlap between these requirements, and that this space is extremely small (200 mm of height). In fact, a 19" display with a 5:4 aspect ratio (such as is used in some current ATMs) is approximately 369 mm tall including the bezel. This display will not fit into such a height restriction, even before any other modules are added. In practice, of course, ATMs and other SSTs offer a large amount of functionality, and therefore contain multiple features and modules (e.g. input/output slots, handsets, large displays, and biometric authentication features). It is therefore a challenge for the industry to build products that meet all the requirements – even if they want to, the requirements conflict between countries.

It is evident, therefore, that there is an urgent need for harmonization between standards, to ensure consistency and thus increase the chance of these standards being adopted by the market. There has been some work in this area (e.g. harmonization between EN 301 549, US ADA and US Section 508, along with harmonization between some software standards and WCAG 2.0/2.1) and these efforts are welcome. However, there is still a great deal of inconsistency, so more work is needed in this important area.

5 Discussion and Conclusions

In summary, the growing trend towards self-service technology is likely to mean that accessibility regulations will be extended to more and more areas, for example supermarket self-checkouts. This is a welcome effort; however, it should be noted that it is vitally important that there is a concurrent effort to harmonise between the standards.

There is also another challenge; namely that of the gap that can exist between standards writers and the industries that must use them. We therefore highlight areas of the standards writing process that have worked well from our perspective:

- Harmonisation. Make every effort to harmonise with existing standards, even if that means extending the current standard. One possible example of this might be to adopt requirements for software from the W3C's Web Content Accessibility Guidelines, while extending them to differentiate between open and closed systems. This can be onerous in the short term (as was the case with the efforts of harmonisation between EN 301 549 and both section 508 update and the ADA update) but makes for a much more workable standard; thus significantly improving the likelihood of adoption by industry.
- Involve all parties, including manufacturers, and allowing enough time for them to feed back. This may necessitate multiple iterations of comment and review periods.

- Do not use proscriptive requirements which specify a particular technology or form of implementation. Instead, we would recommend a move towards more functional requirements such as the functional requirements in EN 301 549. Examples of possible implementations can then be given for the purpose of illustration, but it should be made clear that this is not a complete list; other implementations are allowed.

The authors would like to thank all those who give their time and expertise in contributing to the development of accessibility standards, and hope that this paper spurs discussion among the community.

References

1. Centre for Accessible Environments: Access to ATMs: UK design guidelines. Centre for Accessible Environments, London (2002)
2. ADA Standards for Accessible Design. https://www.ada.gov/regs2010/2010ADAStandards/2010ADAstandards.htm. Accessed 01 Mar 2018
3. European Committee for Banking Standards (ECBS): Keyboard layout for ATM and POS PIN entry devices. DEBS 100 v.3, September 2004
4. PCI Security Standards Council: Payment Card Industry PIN Transaction Security Point of Interaction Security Requirements v4.0. PCI Security Standards Council LLC (2013)
5. Jokisuu, E., McKenna, M., Smith, A.W.D., Day, P.: Improving touchscreen accessibility in self-service technology. In: Antona, M., Stephanidis, C. (eds.) UAHCI 2015. LNCS, vol. 9176, pp. 103–113. Springer, Cham (2015). https://doi.org/10.1007/978-3-319-20681-3_10
6. Jokisuu, E., McKenna, M., Smith, A.W.D., Day, P.: Touchscreen accessibility in self-service terminals. J. Technol. Pers. Disabil. 4, 114–132 (2016)
7. Chandler, E., Day, P.: Human factors and ergonomics practice in inclusive design: making accessibility mainstream In: Shorrock, S., Williams, C. (eds.) Human Factors and Ergonomics in Practice: Improving System Performance and Human Well-Being in the Real World, pp. 287–298. CRC Press (2016). ISBN: 9781472439253
8. United States District Court District of Massachusetts: Commonwealth of Massachusetts v. Cardtronics, Inc, Civil No. 03-11206-NMG, Special Master Cohen Certification Report – NCR Kalpana ATM VG Script 1.0-K, Case 1:03-cv-11206-NMG Document 417, Filed 10/25/16 (2016)
9. EN 301 549: Accessibility requirements suitable for public procurement of ICT products and services in Europe, CEN/CENELEC/ETSI (2014). http://mandate376.standards.eu/standard. Accessed 01 Mar 2018

Accessible Touch: Evaluating Touchscreen PIN Entry Concepts with Visually Impaired People Using Tactile or Haptic Cues

Phil Day ⓘ, Elina Jokisuu(✉) ⓘ, and Andrew W. D. Smith

User Centred Design, NCR Corporation, Dundee, DD2 4SW, UK
elina.jokisuu@ncr.com

Abstract. Findings are presented from a user test of several different concepts to enable personal identification number (PIN) entry on a touchscreen by people who are blind or partially sighted. A repeated measures experimental design was used for the user test, with all participants using all concepts in a randomised order. Results are presented, and wider implications of this study and the subsequent approvals are discussed.

Keywords: Self-service technology · Touchscreen accessibility
Visual impairment

1 Introduction

Accessible PIN entry on self-service terminals such as automated teller machines (ATMs) has traditionally involved the use of a physical keypad, private audio and some means of mapping all on-screen options to a number [1]. However, with the growing ubiquity of touchscreen-equipped personal devices such as smartphones and tablets, and the provision of accessibility features in mainstream products that both Apple (iOS) and Google (Android) have offered, there has been a growing adoption by some blind and partially sighted people of accessibility features that utilise touchscreen and audio. There is also an increase in touchscreen usage in self-service [2]. A research project was thus begun to investigate how a touchscreen-only ATM could be made usable for people with visual impairment, without the need for prior training or experience.

Some existing accessibility solutions are particularly well suited to a small (smartphone-sized) touchscreen; namely techniques that require moving a finger around to find each option. This quickly becomes a tedious exercise on a larger (15+″) touchscreen of an ATM. In addition, ATMs have stringent security standards. One such standard [3] means that the system cannot vocalise either during selection or when entering a PIN, and in fact the software is not allowed to know the PIN (as it is encrypted and transmitted as a block). This means that alternative solutions are required that provide accessibility while meeting the security rules.

This work continued from previous investigations in this area which included an expert review of different input modalities [4], and then a subsequent user test with 49 participants completing PIN entry, menu selection and alphanumeric entry [5, 6]. These

© Springer International Publishing AG, part of Springer Nature 2018
K. Miesenberger and G. Kouroupetroglou (Eds.): ICCHP 2018, LNCS 10896, pp. 327–334, 2018.
https://doi.org/10.1007/978-3-319-94277-3_52

previous investigations clearly demonstrated that some concepts showed promise, particularly the concept that had tactile features affixed immediately adjacent to the touchscreen. It was well received as it offered a fixed tactile reference point when using edge-to-edge glass. However, error rates for PIN entry were unacceptably high, meaning that new concepts had to be designed and then evaluated.

This paper presents the findings of evaluating these new concepts, focusing solely on PIN entry as a task as this was the most challenging scenario (due to the limited amount of feedback that can be given due to security rules). All these concepts involved some form of tactile or haptic feedback to offset the lack of auditory feedback.

2   Method

The test had 39 participants; 21 of whom categorised themselves as blind without any useful residual vision, 15 as blind with some useful residual vision, and 3 as partially sighted. 23 were male and 16 were female; age varied from 18 up to 75+, with half of the participants in the 45–64 age range.

A repeated measures experimental design was used, with all participants using all concepts in a randomised order. Participants were asked to enter a specific 4-digit PIN (2608, selected to force navigation to particularly difficult numbers). Each participant was asked to complete the PIN entry task with each concept, with ratings and open ended questions being asked on completion of each task. Finally, after using all concepts, the participant was asked some comparative questions and invited to rank them in order of preference. All questions were asked by the evaluator, and then recorded on an electronic survey (SurveyGizmo) via a tablet.

Concepts that were evaluated included:

• A tactile 'strip' with grooved features on it: the participant's finger slides from the groove onto the touchscreen (Fig. 1).

Fig. 1. Tactile strip with grooves

• A tactile 'strip' with grooves leading to holes: the participant's finger slides along the groove and touches the screen through the hole at the end of the groove (Fig. 2). The two tactile strips were used with a touchscreen running custom-developed demo software that enabled participants to enter a 4-digit PIN, while hearing the same level of audio feedback that would be possible on an ATM. Participants were also asked to use their preferred tactile strip version with added haptic vibration (which vibrated briefly when they had selected an option).

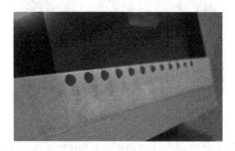

Fig. 2. Tactile strip with holes

- (Non-functional) glass with etched tactile features (Fig. 3). The etched glass concepts were non-functional (a sheet of glass on a wooden pedestal). Two versions were used: one with 0.3 mm deep and another with 0.5 mm deep etchings. Participants were asked to rate the ease of distinguishing the features and to compare them to the tactile strips. The same raised circle and X symbols were used on the etched glass as on the tactile strips, and at the same size.

Fig. 3. Tactile features etched on glass

- Haptic feedback added to touchscreen entry (Fig. 4). A box containing a touchscreen which gave a gentle pulse when the participant's finger was on a number key, with a stronger pulse when on the number 5 key. A firm press activated a key when on it. Cancel, Clear and Enter keys were all vocalised (as they are not protected by the same security rules). This was an early prototype produced by a 3rd party; details are omitted for reasons of commercial sensitivity.

Fig. 4. Touchscreen with haptic feedback

- A conventional ATM keypad for comparison: this was installed on a real ATM, had a raised pip on the 5 key, a raised X on Cancel, raised vertical bar on Clear, and a raised circle on Enter. The software on the ATM was non-functional; brief instructions were given before using the ATM, but the ATM gave no beeps or other audio feedback.

3 Results

As might be expected, the traditional ATM keypad was rated highest by overall rank (32 participants ranking it as favourite); by success rate (39 participants successfully entering the PIN); and by confidence (an average rating of 4.8 out of 5).

The haptic touchscreen was ranked least favourite by 34 participants. The biggest problem was losing orientation (for example between rows of numbers). It also had the lowest success rate: only 19 participants managed to successfully enter their PIN, with 18 stating that it would not be an acceptable solution for ATMs. The ease of use was rated as difficult (average rating of 2.15 out of 5), which was significantly lower than the other concepts (Friedman's ANOVA for the ATM PIN pad, $\chi^2 F(3) = -2.0$, p = .000; for the 'Grooves' tactile strip, $\chi^2 F(3) = 1.5$, p = .000; and for the 'Holes' tactile strip, $\chi^2 F(3) = 1.4$, p = .000).

Participants also rated the haptic touchscreen significantly worse in terms of confidence ("How confident would you be to use this PIN entry method; (a) without any practice, and (b) with practice"). Firstly, confidence without practice was rated significantly worse when comparing the haptics concept with all other concepts (compared with the ATM PIN pad, $\chi^2 F(3) = -1.912$, p = .000; compared with the 'Grooves' tactile strip, $\chi^2 F(3) = 1.250$, p = .000; and for the 'Holes' tactile strip, $\chi^2 F(3) = 1.438$, p = .000). There was also a significant difference in ratings of confidence with practice between the haptics concept and all others (compared with the ATM PIN pad, $\chi^2 F(3) = -1.600$, p = .000; compared with the 'Grooves' tactile strip, $\chi^2 F(3) = 1.338$, p = .000; and for the 'Holes' tactile strip, $\chi^2 F(3) = 1.412$, p = .000). However, based on participants' comments, the haptics concept seemed to offer some benefits for partially sighted people.

The tactile strip with grooves had a good success rate: 31 participants managed to enter the PIN successfully. Based on the ratings for ease of use, there was no significant difference between this and the ATM keypad (mean 4.7 for keypad, 4.23 for tactile strip,

$\chi^2 F(3) = -0.5$, p = .5). Similarly, most participants felt confident that they could use this PIN entry method independently (average rating 4.22/5).

The tactile strip with holes had a lower success rate for the first-time usage (only 17 managed to enter the correct PIN the first time) but 31 participants managed after a second attempt, with a similarly positive rating for ease of use (4.2 as compared with 4.23 for the strip with grooves). Again, there was no significant difference when compared with the ATM keypad, $\chi^2 F(3) = -0.6$, p = .226, or the strip with grooves, $\chi 2 F(3) = .1$, p = 1.000.

Ratings for confidence appeared to be slightly higher for the strip with holes (4.78 with practice, 4.28 without practice) than for the strip with grooves (4.68 with practice, 4.22 without practice). However, this difference between the strip concepts was not significant (without practice: $\chi^2 F(3) = -0.188$, p = 1.000; with practice: $\chi^2 F(3) = -0.075$, p = 1.000). Similarly, there were no significant differences for ratings of confidence without practice between the ATM keypad and the two strips ('Grooves' tactile strip, $\chi^2 F(3) = -0.662$, p = .130, 'Holes' tactile strip, $\chi^2 F(3) = -0.475$, p = .599) or for ratings of confidence with practice between the ATM keypad and the two strips ('Grooves' tactile strip, $\chi^2 F(3) = -0.262$, p = 1.000, 'Holes' tactile strip, $\chi^2 F(3) = -0.188$, p = 1.000). To sum up, the participants' level of confidence was equally high for the ATM PIN pad and both tactile strips but significantly lower for the haptics concept (Figs. 5, 6, 7 and 8).

When considering the addition of vibration to the tactile strip, 11 participants preferred it with vibration, 22 without. Vibration was thought to provide useful extra feedback in noisy or cold environments, or for people with hearing impairment or reduced tactile sensation, but most participants thought that it was an optional extra; a nice-to-have.

When considering the etched glass concepts, the 0.5 mm etched features were rated as easier (4.28) than the 0.3 mm variant (4.03). However, there was a clear preference for the tactile strip: 23 participants preferred the tactile strip over the etched glass, 10 preferred the etched glass, and the remainder had no preference. Participants tended to have more difficulty in distinguishing symbols on the etched glass when compared with raised features on the tactile strip concepts.

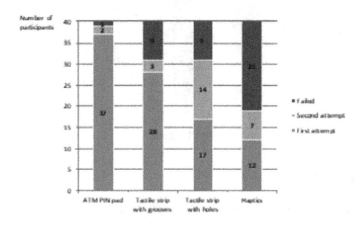

Fig. 5. Success rate (number of participants who entered PIN correctly)

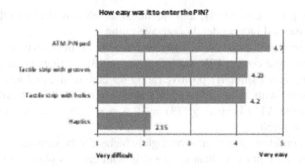

Fig. 6. Ease of use ratings

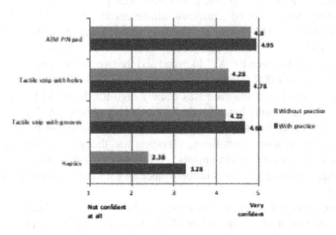

Fig. 7. Confidence ratings

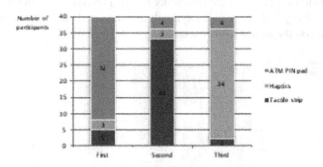

Fig. 8. Rank

4   Discussion

The touchscreen with haptics and no other tactile features was ruled out due to poor success rates, ratings and overall rank. The use of etching glass to create features that are sub-surface appeared to make it more difficult to distinguish symbols when compared with features that were raised (on the tactile strips). Etched features were included in the test as there are potential manufacturing benefits, but based on this evaluation, the approach of raised tactile features is preferred. Vibration added to a tactile strip could be useful if more than one type of vibration can be produced, for example one type of a pulse for exploring and another for entering a number, but participants in this test found it not to be essential.

There were some difficulties with the two tactile strips, mainly around remembering the order of the options (which were laid out as Cancel, 0–9, then Enter). Some participants mistook the raised circle (Enter) as zero. Similarly, some participants also mistook the first groove/hole as 1 when it is in fact Cancel. In other cases, some initially tried to press the raised features (X or o) instead of touching above them on the touchscreen. Finally, there were some participants who used the holes to count numbers rather than the tactile grooves beneath them, and therefore entered digits inadvertently.

The two tactile strips were very similar in terms of performance, and were clearly promising concepts based on the ratings. However, based on the improved first time performance, and the reduction in inadvertent digit entry, the approach using grooves only was taken forward. This had the added benefit that it enabled the whole touchscreen to be used (as the variant with holes necessarily obstructed view at the bottom of the display).

The issues discussed above were alleviated by several key improvements. The first refinement was to the form of the grooves: smooth grooves with sharper ridges in-between to encourage a finger to follow the groove, rather than following the ridge between the grooves. Another was to add subtle lines in the middle of the groove, making a tactile feature of the centre of each 'number'. In subsequent expert reviews and observations with visually impaired people, this helped in identifying the centre of each option. In addition, the raised tactile features were made more distinctive (the raised X and O) by increasing the size, weight and space around them.

Another key change was to the software behaviour. It now allows and supports exploration while instructions are playing; the version tested interrupted the speech as soon as a touch was registered, which meant that people who naturally started exploring once the layout was explained could not hear the entire set of instructions. Finally, improvements were made to the wording of instructions.

Following on from this user test, there were subsequent improvements and refinements with input from experts from the Royal National Institute of Blind People (RNIB) in the UK and the National Federation of the Blind (NFB) in the US. The solution was brought to market, and was also judged to be accessible. Firstly, it has been granted RNIB Approved gold status [7], and was also judged to meet the requirements of the US ADA by an expert from NFB as part of wider discussions between Cardtronics & NFB [8].

This study therefore demonstrates the challenges of innovating in the accessibility space; particularly when accessibility standards, guidelines and regulations are written in such a manner that assumes the use of a specific technology or solution, e.g. a physical keypad. It also serves as a case study to show the importance of having usability specialists embedded in the organisation to work on solutions that may take several years to

334   P. Day et al.

bring to fruition, along with the benefits of partnering with organisations such as RNIB in evaluating and refining a solution.

Getting approval of a solution is particularly important when it is innovative and therefore doesn't necessarily match the type of solution that might have been assumed in some accessibility standards. It should also be noted that it is very helpful if accessibility standards are written in such a way as to not be proscriptive about the type of implementation, and instead focus solely on the type of capability to be offered. This means that new technologies and methods can subsequently be used in offering more accessible products and solutions. This recommendation is not just for self-service; it can equally be applied to web, mobile and internet-based solutions, consumer electronics and the built environment.

References

1. Day, P.N., Chandler, E., Carlisle, M., Rohan, C.: Making self-service accessible: talking ATMs. In: Anderson, M. (ed.) Contemporary Ergonomics and Human Factors 2013: Proceedings of the International Conference on Ergonomics & Human Factors 2013, pp. 339–342. CRC Press, Taylor & Francis Group (2013)
2. Digital Trends, European McDonald's to replace human cashiers with touch screen computers. http://www.digitaltrends.com/computing/european-mcdonalds-to-replace-human-cashiers-with-touch-screen-computers. Accessed 1 Oct 2015
3. PCI Security Standards Council: Payment Card Industry PIN Transaction Security Point of Interaction Security Requirements v4.0. PCI Security Standards Council LLC (2013)
4. Jokisuu, E., McKenna, M., Smith, A.W.D., Day, P.: Evaluating touchscreen PIN entry with visually impaired users. In: Waterson, P., Sims, R., Hubbard, E.-M. (eds.) Contemporary Ergonomics & Human Factors 2016, pp. 290–295. Chartered Institute of Ergonomics and Human Factors, Loughborough (2016)
5. Jokisuu, E., McKenna, M., Smith, Andrew W.D., Day, P.: Improving touchscreen accessibility in self-service technology. In: Antona, M., Stephanidis, C. (eds.) UAHCI 2015. LNCS, vol. 9176, pp. 103–113. Springer, Cham (2015). https://doi.org/10.1007/978-3-319-20681-3_10
6. Jokisuu, E., McKenna, M., Smith, A.W.D., Day, P.: Touchscreen accessibility in self-service terminals. J. Tech. Persons Disabil. **4**, 114–132 (2016)
7. NCR news release, Royal National Institute of Blind People Awards NCR Technology for Commitment to Financial Inclusion. https://www.ncr.com/news/newsroom/news-releases/financial/royal-national-institute-of-blind-people-awards-ncr-technology-for-commitment-to-financial-inclusion. Accessed 31 Jan 2018
8. United States District Court District of Massachusetts: Commonwealth of Massachusetts v. Cardtronics, Inc, Civil No. 03-11206-NMG, Special Master Cohen Certification Report – NCR Kalpana ATM VG Script 1.0-K, Case 1:03-cv-11206-NMG Document 417, Filed 10/25/16 (2016)

TokenAccess: Improving Accessibility of Automatic Teller Machines (ATMs) by Transferring the Interface and Interaction to Personal Accessible Devices

Emre Zaim[(✉)] and Klaus Miesenberger

Institut Integriert Studieren, JKU Linz, Altenberger Straße 69, 4040 Linz, Austria
zaimemre@gmail.com, klaus.miesenberger@jku.at

Abstract. ATM interaction tends to be restrictive and prescriptive in the way one can interact with. The hardware (screen, keyboard, slot) and most often also the software interfaces are fixed and miss many layers of adaptability for diverse groups of users including those with disabilities. All studies on accessibility and usability underline the difficulty due to often contradictory requirements (what helps one user makes it more complex for another user) making it very hard, cost intensive and almost impossible to reach a satisfactory user experience. Therefore, considerations are vital to investigate the feasibility of transferring the interaction with ATMs as much as possible to a standard HCI and web based system and to runs as much as possible of the interaction on a personal device, which might connect ATs in a well-controlled and accessible environment. The TokenAccess approach is a feasibility study of these considerations. It provides a prototype of a technical infrastructure demonstrating the feasibility of such approach by integrating steps of interaction into already existing services such as e-banking, online check-in or eTicketing. The development of the prototype was done using a user centered design approach involving disabled colleagues and students at the Institute Integriert Studieren at the University of Linz as co-researchers and evaluators. Heuristic Evaluation, Cognitive Walkthrough and observation have been used in each step from requirements engineering towards evaluation.

Keywords: Accessibility · ATM · Mobile devices

1 Introduction

Automatic Teller Machines (ATMs) are becoming important and often the only point of access to many services in today's "self-service society". They can be found in many areas of everyday life like train stations, universities, bus stops, libraries, movie theaters, airports and banks. If not accessible, ATMs tend to build barriers, contribute to exclusion and to generate additional social/care costs [1].

ATM interaction tends to be restrictive and prescriptive in the way one can interact with them. The hardware (screen, keyboard, slots) and most often also the software interfaces are fixed and miss many layers of adaptability for diverse groups of users

K. Miesenberger and G. Kouroupetroglou (Eds.): ICCHP 2018, LNCS 10896, pp. 335–342, 2018.
https://doi.org/10.1007/978-3-319-94277-3_53

including those with disabilities [2]. Considerable research and development efforts have been made to improve accessibility and usability of ATMs over the last years providing a remarkable body of knowledge, demonstrators and best practice examples [3–7]. But still, a fully satisfying level of accessibility is not reached excluding many users, in particular those with disabilities and ageing population.

2　Problem Description

ATMs are a special type of computer system and as such, the problem of ATM accessibility is not just about the physical accessibility of the ATM but at the same time about the HCI accessibility of the ATM interface. Problems are related, but not restricted to issues as [8]:

- There might be enlargement and contrast settings, but commands change from ATM to ATM and the environments might be shady, sunny, dirty making interaction difficult or impossible.
- There might be a screen reader or self-voicing features with a plug for earphones, but unknown keyboards and interaction concepts might be hard to manage and the environment is often too noisy to manage uncommon audio-based interaction.
- Although hard to implement, there might be ergonomic buttons, slots and other hardware features at different heights and with tactile markers, but still one size does not fit all and users face considerable barriers.
- There might be easy to read, symbol/picture/video/animation support, but still, as interfaces differ considerably, good understandability is not in reach for all users.
- Several of the above issues might be addressed with profiling and personalization, but still many aspects, in particular related to contradicting hardware requirements, remain.

All studies on accessibility and usability underline the difficulty due to often contradictory requirements (what helps one user makes it more complex for another user) making it very hard, cost intensive and almost impossible to reach a satisfactory user experience. In human-computer interaction, what is "good for someone" is not always "good for someone else" [9]. Elderly people for example often have low vision and also deterioration in cognitive capacity like memory, attention span and reaction time [10]. A UI with large fonts and high contrast would be more accessible for elderly people given their low vision. Also, texts composed in simple language, pictures next to the text, didactic illustrations and slow animations might make a better UI for elderly people [11]. However, such an interface might be perceived as unpleasant and slow by users without disabilities. Blind users would need speech output, e.g. a screen reader and deaf users would need visual notifications such as closed captions and visual alerts as alternatives to sound alerts. A user without disabilities would not want to deal with all the voice descriptions and closed captions and flashing screens [9].

Even if users are willing to use ATMs, they would need more time, prior training and preparation. And even then, ATM users with disabilities feel stressed when managing the interaction in public spaces with queues of people behind them as they can't reach the expected level of efficiency and effectiveness.

3   Transferring the Interaction to the Web and Personal Accessible Devices

People with disabilities use Assistive Technologies (AT) providing access to the standard Human-Computer Interface (HCI). Access to the HCI proved to be very successful and allows personalization to the individual needs of users including those using AT. Users with disabilities invest not only in the AT tools but also in training and professionalizing usage as it is a key point for independent access to more and more systems and services information society.

Therefore, as a general principle, we can trust that integrating interfaces and interactions as much as possible into the personal HCI/AT environment will contribute to accessibility and usability. Software [12] and today, as most applications support web interaction, Web Accessibility standards [13] provide an agreed and well-known base to implement and use accessibility. Accessibility legislation and policies reference these standards. Accessibility features are available on all platforms and development frameworks. Standard applications support accessible content provision. Of course, implementation is still not perfect, but the HCI/AT based interaction provides a solid, accepted, well supported and flexible way for providing accessible user experiences. Web based solutions also allow much more flexibility in terms of timing, location and additional support. The interaction can be embedded targeted support and care environments [14].

Therefore, considerations are vital to investigate the feasibility of transferring the interaction with ATMs as much as possible to a standard HCI and Web based system and to run as much as possible the interaction on a personal device, which might connect ATs in a well-controlled and accessible environment [15]. This should allow preparing and (semi-)automating many parts of the interaction at the ATM and thereby reducing barriers and fears as well as improving control, trust and comfort.

4   The TokenAccess Concept

The TokenAccess approach is a feasibility study of these conceptual considerations. It provides a prototype of a technical infrastructure demonstrating the feasibility of such an approach by integrating steps of interaction into already existing services as e-banking, online check-in or eTicketing.

Figure 1 outlines the two-step concept of TokenAccess to decouple interaction from the ATM and the underlying technical architecture:

1. The first part of the interaction takes place in the personal accessible environment of the user. In this part, the user prepares the interaction with the ATM in his personal accessible environment using the TokenAccess web application or the TokenAccess mobile application.
2. The TokenAccess server is the central component responsible for the management and verification of tokens. The result of the interaction that the user has prepared in his personal accessible environment is encoded and stored as a "digital token" on the TokenAccess server and also sent to the user's mobile device.

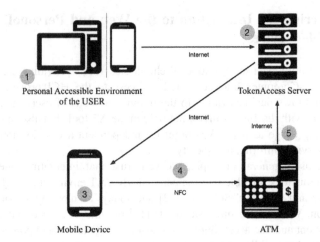

Fig. 1. Secure ATM interaction with TokenAccess bridging the process from personal environment to ATM. Image Source: [17]

3. The TokenAccess mobile application is responsible for the management and secure storage of the users' tokens on the mobile device.
4. The second part of the interaction takes place at the ATM, but reduces interaction steps to a minimum by executing the prepared interaction in a "two-tap workflow":
   a. First the user touches or comes close to the NFC reader of the ATM with his mobile device for "Identification" and "Authentication".
   b. With a second touch, the user executes the "Confirmation" step and the token stored on the mobile device is transferred to the ATM. The ATM then executes the prepared interaction stored in the token, completing the interaction.
5. Security sensitive operations like withdrawing money will implement additional communication with the TokenAccess server to validate the stored transaction.

This process of decoupling the interaction from the AT allows a first analysis of the traditional and TokenAccess based interaction with ATMs outlining where barriers in interaction can be better, more flexible and efficiently [8].

The development of the prototype was done using a user centered design approach involving disabled colleagues and students at the Institute Integriert Studieren at the University of Linz as co-researchers and evaluators. Heuristic Evaluation, Cognitive Walkthrough and observation have been used in each step from requirements engineering towards evaluation (Table 1).

The development of the prototype was done using a user centered design approach involving disabled colleagues and students at the Institute Integriert Studieren at the University of Linz as co-researchers and evaluators. Heuristic Evaluation, Cognitive Walkthrough and observation have been used in each step from requirements engineering towards evaluation.

The demonstrator (Fig. 2) provides a web interface (which could be part of online services of companies also running ATMs, e.g. eBanking). The system allows to register a personal mobile device. The transaction is prepared on the accessible web

Table 1. Comparison between traditional ATM interaction and TokenAccess interaction

	Traditional ATM interaction	TokenAccess
Identification	The bank account number is stored on the magnetic strip on the bank card and transferred to the ATM when the card is inserted into the ATM	The bank account number is stored on the mobile device and is transferred to the ATM with the first tap via NFC
Authentication	The user enters his PIN using the keypad of the ATM	Digital certificates and challenge-response based authentication. Additional authentication via PIN entry/fingerprint on the mobile device also possible
Input	The input is done using the ATM interface, e.g. the menus shown on the screen, the hardware buttons to the left and right of the screen, the keypad etc.	The same input is realized using web forms in the TokenAccess web application that is accessible by the user in his personal accessible environment
Confirmation	Using the ATM interface, similar to the input step	By touching the NFC reader of the ATM a second time, the user confirms executing the prepared interaction (the token) on the mobile device
Transaction	The ATM executes the operation (e.g. dispense money)	The ATM executes the operation (e.g. dispense cash)

Fig. 2. TokenAccess: Preparing interaction with e.g. a cash dispenser. (1) Login and create the token, (2) token pushed to the mobile device, (3) tap on or bring the mobile device near to/on a defined spot, authenticate (e.g. fingerprint or pin), redo the contact and the token is transferred to the ATM. The ATM processes the token and cash is dispensed. Image Source: [18]

page (e.g. part of eBanking) using the known and trained personal environment what avoids outlined stress factors. Using ATM based services might also become part of service provision for people with disabilities and care for improved but still secured independence. In this personal environment, a token on the server is generated, which is made available on the registered mobile device. When tabbing the ATM with the mobile device, putting the mobile device on a certain spot or simply coming near the TokenAccess application gets started, triggered by some sort of wireless connection e.g. NFC. The predefined transaction is started, which might include another step of manageable interaction (e.g. the standard pin, gesture or fingerprint) for security.

The mobile device provides feedback for confirmation of the action in different formats, e.g. visual, vibrating and a short audio (TTS) information to confirm the interaction. When finished, the token gets invalid, so no further transaction can be done with it. Also expiring dates can be defined and the amount can be restricted. All this allows a personalization of the interaction making best use of available accessible environments. Different steps in the process, due to personal needs, might be subject to adaptation, what should be supported by the framework and is subject to negotiation and contracting with the ATM or service provider.

5   Usability Study

The TokenAccess prototype has been tested using the Heuristic Evaluation Approach [16] with 10 expert users including 5 with disabilities (vision, motor and cognitive disabilities). In total, we conducted 8 test runs and the prototype was improved after each test run following the feedback from users.

Table 2 shows an overview of the results from the last round of the usability study:

Table 2. Results of the usability study

		B1	B2	C	W	M
1	Create a "withdraw money" token for single usage on the TokenAccess web interface	✓	✓	✓	✓	✓
2	Use this token to withdraw money on the TokenAccess ATM simulation	✓	✓	✓	✓	-[a]
3	Create a "withdraw money" token for multiple usages	✓	✓	✓	✓	✓
4	Use this token multiple times on the TokenAccess simulation	✓	✓	✓[b]	✓	-[a]
5	Create multiple tokens (both ATM and ticketing machine) for the same device	✓	✓	✓	✓	✓
6	Navigate the client application when there are multiple tokens on the mobile device	✓	✓	✓	✓	-[a]
7	Use these tokens on different simulations (ATM and ticketing machine) to withdraw money and buy a tram ticket	✓	✓	✗[c]	✓	-[a]

[a] The user with motor disability was not able to make use of one's hands and could not complete the tests involving the mobile device.
[b] The user with cognitive disability was able to complete the task with the help of further instructions.
[c] The user with cognitive disability was not able to complete the second part of the task due to a bug in the prototype.

The abbreviations in the table head row describe the tested user group(s):

- B1. Blind user one
- B2. Blind user two

- C. User with cognitive disability
- W. User without disabilities
- M. User with motor disability

6 Conclusion and Future Work

The TokenAccess framework allows simulating the interaction with different ATMs for various services based on ATMs. This allows discussing, rethinking and planning ATM services in an as accessible and also usable manner as possible. It uses (a) a web page for preparing the interaction, (b) one mobile device (Android) as the end user device and (c) one device (Android) simulating the ATM. Of course, for different user groups, individual users and diverse ATM applications in varying environments specific barriers might be detected. The TokenAccess framework invites to adapt the process of ATM interaction to the individual requirements, which includes technical issues but also others like personal support by care givers or other staff making ATMs part of improved independent living. It also includes taking security and privacy mechanisms into account. As TokenAccess uses as much as possible standard HCI interaction and includes personal AT solutions in known and supported environment, it helps reducing barriers to a minimum and the need to adapt the ATM itself to a minimum (e.g. physical design of the ATM and its environment, authentication). By integrating the process into existing web based systems such as eBanking or eTicketing one can make use of established, trained and already accessible procedures and modules.

The usability study allowed us to technically prove the viability of the approach and bringing it into discussion at ATM companies and banking software companies. At the moment, we expect cooperating with a banking software company for larger field testing and experimenting including organizations of different groups of people with disabilities.

References

1. Sidel, R.: ATMs fall short on disability rule. Wall Str. J. http://www.wsj.com/articles/SB10001424052970204276304577265710282201338. Accessed 18 Mar 2018
2. Blinden- und Sehbehindertenverband Österreich: Barrierefreie Geldausgabe. http://www.blindenverband.at/home/672. Accessed 18 Mar 2018
3. Tracy, E.: Safer banking tips for disabled people. BBC News Ouch Blog. http://www.bbc.com/news/blogs-ouch-31108792. Accessed 20 Mar 2018
4. Edison, T.: How blind people use the ATM. https://www.youtube.com/watch?v=Jzah0A6IC5o. Accessed 20 Mar 2018
5. Noonan, T.: Barriers to using automated teller machines. https://www.humanrights.gov.au/barriers-using-automatic-teller-machines#_Toc474344391. Accessed 20 Mar 2018
6. Pous, M.: Enhancing accessibility: mobile to ATM case study. In: 2nd IEEE International Workshop on Consumer eHealth Platforms, Services and Applications (2016)

7. Chan, C.C., Wong, A.W., Lee, T.M., Chi, I.: Modified automatic teller machine prototype for older adults: a case study of participative approach to inclusive design. Appl. Ergon. **40**, 151–160 (2009)
8. Zaim, E.: Transferring ATM interface and interaction to mobile devices for enhancing accessibility and usability. Master Thesis (2017)
9. Bergman, E., Johnson, E.: Towards accessible human-computer interaction. In: Advances in Human Computer Interaction (1995)
10. Hiroko, A., Hiroyuki, M.: Usability research for the elderly people. Oki Tech. Rev. **71**, 54–57 (2004)
11. Tarakanov-plax, A.: Design concept for ATM machine, accessible for the elderly users in Israel. In: Proceedings of the International Conference on Inclusive Design (2005)
12. ISO: ISO 9241.171:2008 Ergonomics of human-system interaction. https://www.iso.org/standard/39080.html. Accessed 25 Mar 2018
13. W3C/WAI: Web Content Accessibility Guidelines (WCAG) 2.0. https://www.w3.org/TR/WCAG20/. Accessed 25 Mar 2018
14. Madrid, R.I., Schrader, K., Ortega-Moral, M.: Improving the accessibility of public digital terminals through personalisation: comparison of direct and indirect interaction modes. In: Stephanidis, C., Antona, M. (eds.) UAHCI 2014. LNCS, vol. 8513, pp. 258–269. Springer, Cham (2014). https://doi.org/10.1007/978-3-319-07437-5_25
15. Biswas, P., Halder, A., Maheswary, K., Arjun, S.: Inclusive Personalization of User Interfaces, Smart Innovation, Systems and Technologies, vol. 65. Springer, Singapore (2017)
16. Nielsen, J., Molich, R., Heuristic evaluation of user interfaces. In: Proceedings of the SIGCHI Conference on Human Factors in Computing Systems, pp. 249–256 (1990)
17. Icons: Computer by Martin Vanco, Smartphone by João Luiz, Server by iconsmind.com. http://iconsmind.com. ATM by Luca Trinchero, all from the "Noun Project", February 2018. https://thenounproject.com/
18. Icons: Computer by Icon Solid, Smartphone by João Luiz, ATM by BomSymbols, all from the "Noun Project", February 2018. https://thenounproject.com/

Universal Learning Design

Increasing Inclusive Capacity of Vocational Education and Training (VET) Organizations with Digital Media and ICT

Harald Weber[(✉)]

Institut für Technologie und Arbeit (ITA), Trippstadter Str. 110, 67663 Kaiserslautern, Germany
harald.weber@ita-kl.de

Abstract. This paper reports on work in progress that relates to the use of digital media and ICT in educational settings, particularly in vocational education and training. While the application of digital media and information and communication technology has often been the subject of projects with a focus on classrooms and beyond, this work discusses an idea for a systematic analysis of the potentials digital media and ICT carry to increase an educational organization's inclusive capacity as a whole, not just at classroom level.

Keywords: VET · Inclusive capacity · Digital media/ICT

1 Introduction

In 2000, the Council of Ministers in Europe has made vocational education and training (VET) a priority, stating that every citizen must be equipped with the skills needed to live and work in the new information society and that special attention must be given to people with disabilities (Lisbon European Council). Inclusive education, the main instrument to provide learners with a wide spectrum of abilities and needs with equitable means to participate in education, develops and propagates at different speeds in Europe [1]. A recurring observation throughout the countries is that the educational level is often diametrical to the level of its inclusiveness – the higher the ISCED level of education [2], the lower the level of inclusion. In particular, VET in most countries lags behind the developments in ISCED levels 0 to 3. Against the background of the UN Convention on the Rights of Persons with Disabilities (UNCRPD), VET organizations are under pressure to become more inclusive. Inclusion, however, as a goal cannot be achieved comprehensively by focusing on inclusive teaching and learning at classroom level only. Rather, the whole organization needs to be taken into account to increase and maintain its inclusive capacity.

At the same time, a structural transformation of EU labour markets is visible that increasingly demands workers with advanced digital skills [3]. Traditional occupations are coming under scrutiny, while the emergence of potentially new occupations is becoming apparent [4]. An analysis reveals a strong positive correlation between jobs that are anticipated to grow in employment in the next decade, and the importance of advanced digital skills within such jobs [5]. The European Commission investigated job

K. Miesenberger and G. Kouroupetroglou (Eds.): ICCHP 2018, LNCS 10896, pp. 345–352, 2018.
https://doi.org/10.1007/978-3-319-94277-3_54

profiles of different occupations which have been traditionally penetrated less by ICT, among which VET teacher was one out of 12 occupations in focus. It is concluded that the adoption of ICT tools varies considerably among VET teachers, and that younger teachers might find it easier to adopt ICT tools than older teachers [6]. Hence, VET has to adapt to the changing labour market demands and equip their teachers with the skills necessary to educate and train the future workforce.

Those two general lines of development, inclusion and digitalization, are independent drivers of the strategic advancement of VET organizations, but there are intersecting areas with mutual impact. Particularly, digital media have an inherent potential to contribute to inclusion, and they carry pedagogical added-value such as, e.g., enabling discovery and mastery of new content knowledge, collaborative, connected learning, low-cost creation and iteration of new knowledge, use of new knowledge with authentic audiences for 'real' purposes, and enhancement of teachers' ability to put students in control of the learning process, accelerating learner autonomy [7]. Much research has been done on the use of digital media in classrooms, and also to make use of it to render teaching and learning in the classroom more inclusive. However, a focus on the classroom alone might be too narrow. A wider view on the whole organization seems more likely to be able to exploit the full potential of digital media and ICT for building up and maintaining a VET organization's inclusive capacity.

2   Research Idea

The application of digital media in education is discussed widely, yet with a clear focus on pedagogical value and often on the comparison between traditional and new media use with regard to impact on learning (e.g. [8, 9]). At the same time, developments in the area of web technologies, the internet of things, industry 4.0 etc. are discussed mainly to increase efficiency of individuals and organizations, e.g. to produce faster, cheaper or more individualized. Yet, there seem to be no thorough analyses or systematic approaches on how to gear organizational digitalization strategies and activities at both classroom- and organization-level towards the same aim, in this case towards the increase of a VET organization's inclusive capacity. Hence, it is suggested to (i) analyze VET organizations as a complex system to understand the relationships among all system elements and to recognize the role of each element to raise the system's inclusive capacity (systems approach), and then (ii) to scrutinize each of those elements that are identified as strong levers in organizational change to which extent they could benefit from the use of digital media and/or ICT.

3   State of the Art

The use of ICT and/or digital media in education to facilitate or improve inclusion has a long history. Particularly, the conference series of ICCHP (International Conference on Computers Helping People with Special Needs) started in 1989 supporting the advancement of ICT and Assistive Technologies for people with disabilities and the aging population. ICCHP has produced a wealth of scientific findings in the intersection of ICT and education, but also in many other application and life domains. The European Agency for Development in Special Needs Education run a project on Information and Communication Technology for Inclusion (ICT4I) during 2012 and 2013 which aimed to explore how ICT can be used to support learning and teaching in inclusive settings. A review of research literature was developed in the context of this project [10] that reflects the state of the art in the intersection of ICT and inclusion. ICT is also seen by UNESCO as a useful tool to improve the lives of persons with disabilities, by allowing them to participate meaningfully in activities available to the general public [11]. In the Qingdao Declaration [12], signed by Ministers of Education in May 2015, it is stated that' To achieve the goal of inclusive and equitable quality education and lifelong learning by 2030, ICT – including mobile learning – must be harnessed to strengthen education systems, knowledge dissemination, information access, quality and effective learning, and more efficient service provision..' (p. 1).

With regard to the methodology to make use of a systems approach to analyze VET organizations, there are few examples that this type of approach has been applied before to the education domain. A systems approach recognizes the interdependent and inter-active nature of elements inside and outside an organization, and takes account of that a system (here: VET organization) is more than the sum of its constituent elements (e.g. teachers, learners, infrastructure, qualification processes).

For example, Kickert [13] described a Ministry's move from classical government towards more autonomy and self-responsibility in the area of higher education, to express the complex network of inter-related, more or less autonomous actors in higher education. OECD [14] developed a systems approach to educational research and inno-vation to help governments and other stakeholders to comprehensively evaluate how the system works and how they can enhance their innovation capacity. Silvern [15] had applied a systems approach to describe feedback signal paths from outside a secondary school or school district to an occupational teacher, while Delahaye [16] applied a systems theory approach to VET, yet with a focus on the management of knowledge assets. Finally, Likar [17] indicated the importance of a systems approach in VET to address the challenge posed to learners' innovation.

4 Methodology

The methodology is split into two steps.

In a *first step* (finalized), an analysis of educational organizations was performed as an international project run by the European Agency for Development in Special Needs Education [1] in 26 countries. Small teams visited individual examples of successful organizations in VET in each of the participating countries and explored the factors that might have a positive or negative impact on VET processes and the outcomes for indi-vidual learners with special educational needs (SEN)/disabilities. The organizational outcome considered as the overall success of a VET organization was agreed as: Successful VET and transition to the open labour market for learners with SEN/disa-bilities. The analysis resulted in a system model that:

1. describes cause-effect relationship among its elements (success factors),

2. allows to identify strong and weak levers for organizational change, and
3. is applicable in a wide range of economic, policy, cultural or other contexts.

In a *second step* (work in progress), the previously identified strong levers/drivers for organizational change towards increased inclusive capacity will be analyzed. For each factor, the potential for an amplification through targeted use of digital media/ICT will be discussed. Focus will be put on those aspects where digital media/ICT are known to have benefits/strengths compared to traditional media or techniques.

The results of both steps will provide guidance on areas where a prudent use of digital media would not just increase an organization's efficiency but also contribute to an overarching leitmotif for the whole organization, in this case: inclusion.

5 R&D Work and Results

The analysis of VET organizations was based on a qualitative analysis of 28 study visits from 26 countries to extract the similarities and differences with regard to why each particular VET example was successful. This analysis lead to 1,148 individual factors, each associated with a particular example [18]. These factors were sorted under three main headings: structure/input, process and output/outcome factors. Process theory was identified as an appropriate yet flexible framework that would provide deeper insights into *why* these examples are considered successful. Outputs/outcomes in this model result from, or are produced by, a certain set of inputs/structures and a certain set of processes.

Due to the high number of factors, further segmentation was needed. The analysis grouped identical or very similar factors together and formulated a heading for each group that aimed to describe the factors it contained ('coding' phase). Through this approach, 68 success factors were joined. Some of these factors were observed in many of the visited examples, i.e. these highly frequent factors are common to many of the examples despite different economic, policy, cultural or other contexts. Consequently, these were of particular interest for further analysis, which aims to develop recommendations that would be applicable and useful in many different contexts.

Complex systems consist of elements that are also inter-linked, i.e. elements impact on each other. Hence, the set of success factors was further analyzed with regard to potential cause–effect relationships by a team of senior experts in the field of VET:

1. whether there exists a direct cause-effect relationship between them,
2. which direction this relationship has (i.e. which factor impacts on which), and
3. which impact level can be associated to this relationship.

The result of this analysis is a network of connected factors that establish a VET system model, which still reflects the key characteristics of the examples visited.

A closer look at the VET system model shows that success factors are linked to other factors with varying intensity. Some factors impact upon many factors, while others hardly impact upon any other factor. A more systematic analysis of this observation was beneficial in order to select factors for interventions that would have the potential to impact on larger parts of the VET system, i.e. they would be strong levers and therefore efficient to be used to change a system. Figure 1 shows a diagram where each dot represents one of the system elements/factors and where its location indicates the potency of a factor in organizational change.

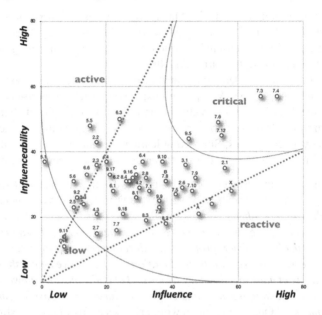

Fig. 1. Two dimensional graph of the active and passive sum for each factor (dots) in the VET system, discriminating stronger from weaker levers (structure adapted from [19, 20])

For example, factors that are influenced by a few others, but influence many other factors (see section *'active'* in Fig. 1), have the potential to impact on wider parts of the system. They are therefore considered a good and efficient starting point for interventions to initiate changes in the VET system. Factors that influence hardly any other factors (see section *'slow'*) will barely impact upon the system, and therefore should not be a priority for intervention. The factors to be found in the section *'critical'* are accelerators and catalysts, they are useful for a quick kick-off, but care is recommended as they might over-shoot or break down easily. The *'reactive'* section contains factors where changes addressed to them are likely to be only of a cosmetic nature. Finally, success factors in the middle of the figure can hardly be used for steering the whole system, but they might contribute to system self-regulation [17].

This resulting system model has been expressed as a diagram that contains all highly frequent success factors, with arrows originating from those factors that influence other factors. Due to its complexity, only excerpts will be used.

The resulting model shows the relevance to take different stakeholders into consideration to assure inclusive VET. Obviously, learners and teaching/training staff are relevant stakeholder groups, but equally VET managers and current and future employers/labour market representatives. The latter two are hardly addressed in research to explore the potentials of ICT/digital media to improve inclusion. The ongoing research work will systematically shed light on the different system elements and view them from the different stakeholders' perspectives. The system analysis resulted in the following key issues to be addressed as to increase a VET organization's inclusive capacity, itemized according to the four stakeholder groups [1]:

- Managers: Institutional leadership; Managing multi-disciplinary teams.
- Teachers/trainer: Learner-centred approaches; Using individual plans for education, learning, training and transition; Dropout reduction strategy; Matching labour market skills requirements and the learners' skills.
- Learners: Focusing on learners' capabilities; Matching work opportunities & learners' individual wishes & expectations; Having established co-operation structures with local companies for practical training and/or employment after graduation.
- Future employers/labour market representatives: Safeguarding connections with local employers/companies; Supporting learners & employers during the transition phase; Providing follow-up activities to maintain learners' employment.

VET managers, for instance, are required to develop inclusive leadership. The system analysis concluded with regard to this area that: *'Effective school leadership requires leaders to look ahead and be flexible, as well as to change the structure and duration of the VET programme to match the learners' needs, if required. Effective leaders will also offer further professional development opportunities to all staff, including teachers, to ensure quality in education. [...] Effective leadership safeguards the positive effects of multi-disciplinary teams and of coordinated teamwork. It ensures that support is provided to learners and employers during the transition phase into the open labour market.'* Ongoing research work analyses each of these constituents of the identified key issues with regard to the potentials of improving it through the use of digital media/ICT. On the example of school leadership, it will be elaborated, how digital media/ICT could support managers, e.g., to:

- be able to forecast future labour market skills relevant to learners (e.g. through automated or augmented data synthesis from official labour market statistics),
- identify and manage learners' individual needs (e.g. e-assessment for leaning),
- provide continuing/further professional development opportunities (e.g. e-learning, peer-to-peer networks),
- manage multi-disciplinary teams (e.g.. through task management applications),
- co-ordinate teamwork (e.g. through online collaboration platforms),
- extend the presence of support staff for learners placed outside the VET organization (e.g. by mentoring & guidance applications, audio/video communication).

On a methodological level, it is planned to systematically collect examples of ICT/ digital media use in these different organizational areas from a variety of countries in Europe. Through discussions, good practice will be identified and documented. In a follow-up phase, success criteria as well as inhibiting factors and structural constraints with regard to the use of ICT/digital media in the respective topic area will be discussed. Based on these intermediate results, a final phase will elaborate new ideas, tools or innovative strategies to make best use of ICT/digital media for raising inclusion capacity of educational organizations offering VET, respecting the success criteria but also the inhibiting factors and constraints. After a consultation phase of approximately 6 to 8 weeks for each topic to involve a wider audience, feedback will be summarized and fed back for final consideration. The results will then flow into a guidance document for VET organization management and educational professionals, to make best use of digital media to enhance their organization's inclusive capacity.

6 Scientific and Practical Impact

From a scientific point of view, the system model can be a rich source for further research, e.g. for transfer in other types of educational organizations. It could also serve as an inspection point to examine which wanted as well as unwanted or unexpected side effects the induction of ICT might trigger in an organization. It could help to reflect on the impact of ICT/digital media beyond the direct target group, encompassing indirect target groups, other persons affected and the whole organization. With regard to practical impact, the results will equip education managers from VET and related areas with guidance to further develop their organizations' inclusive capacity for the ultimate benefit of learners with and without disabilities.

7 Conclusion and Planned Activities

The open method of data gathering and analysis allowed the development of hypotheses on successful VET. To the best of the author's knowledge, it is the first time that a systems approach (based on the outcomes of data gathering) has been applied to gain a deeper understanding of inclusive VET. Results have been fed back to representatives of all ministries of education in the participating countries who did not report on any implausible conclusion drawn. However, no rigorous validation has taken place yet. Next steps will involve the collection of successful examples of ICT/digital media use at different points in the VET system model. A strategic network to undergo this investigation on international level has been applied for in the ERASMUS + Program. Based on these outcomes, it will be possible to explore the amplification potential of ICT/digital media more in-depth, and to derive to recommendations for targeted interventions in the context of organizational change towards inclusion.

References

1. European Agency for Development in Special Needs Education (ed.): European Patterns of Successful Practice in Vocational Education and Training – Participation of Learners with SEN/Disabilities in VET. Odense (2013)
2. UNESCO: International Standard Classification of Education, ISCED 1997. http://www.unesco.org/education/information/nfsunesco/doc/isced_1997.htm. Accessed 23 Mar 2018
3. Cedefop: The great divide: Digitalisation and digital skill gaps in the EU workforce', #ESJsurvey Insights, No. 9. Thessaloniki (2016)

4. Padur, T., Zinke, G.: Digitalisation of the world of work – perspectives and challenges facing vocational education and training 4.0. Translation from the German original (published in BWP 6/2015). https://www.bibb.de/en/36985.php. Accessed 23 Mar 2018

5. Cedefop: Rise of the machines: technological skills obsolescence in the EU, #ESJsurvey Insights, No. 8. Thessaloniki (2016)

6. European Commission: ICT for work: digital skills in the workplace. The impact of ICT on job quality: evidence from 12 job profiles. Luxembourg (2016)

7. Fullan, M., Langworthy, M.: A Rich Seam: How New Pedagogies Find Deep Learning. Pearson, London (2014)

8. Organisation for Economic Co-operation and Development (ed.): Inspired by Technology, Driven by Pedagogy: A Systemic Approach to Technology-Based School Innovations. Centre for Educational Research and Innovation. 2010, OECD Publishing, Paris (2010)

9. UNESCO IITE: Personalized Learning: A New ICT-Enabled Education Approach. IITE Policy Brief, March 2012. UNESCO IITE, Moscow (2012)

10. European Agency for Development in Special Needs Education (ed.): Information and Communication Technology for Inclusion - Research Literature Review, Odense (2013)

11. UNESCO: Accessible ICT. http://www.unesco.org/new/en/nairobi/communication-and-information/accessible-ict/. Accessed 23 Mar 2018

12. UNESCO: Qingdao Declaration. International Conference on ICT and post-2015 Education. Seize Digital Opportunities, Lead Education Transformation, 23–25 May 2015, Qingdao, the People's Republic of China. http://www.unesco.org/new/fileadmin/MULTIMEDIA/HQ/ED/pdf/Qingdao_Declaration.pdf. Accessed 23 Mar 2018

13. Kickert, W.: Steering at a distance: a new paradigm of public governance in dutch higher education, governance. Int. J. Policy Adm. **8**(1), 135–157 (1995)

14. Organisation for Economic Co-operation and Development: A systemic approach to educational research and innovation. http://www.oecd.org/innovation/policyplatform/48136016.pdf. Accessed 26 Jan 2018

15. Silvern, L.C.: Systems Analysis and Synthesis Applied to Occupational Instruction in Secondary Schools. https://files.eric.ed.gov/fulltext/ED015676.pdf. Accessed 26 Jan 2018

16. Delahaye, B.L.: The management of knowledge: a systems theory approach for vocational education and training. In: Searle, J., Roebuck, D. (eds.) Proceedings of the 10th Annual International Conference on Post-compulsory Education and Training. Australian Academic Press, Brisbane, pp. 236–243 (2002)

17. Likar, B.: Innovation in vocational education – ways of reaching the tip of the iceberg. Int. J. Innovat. Learn. **4**(4), 323–341 (2007)

18. European Agency for Special Needs and Inclusive Education (ed.): European Patterns of Successful Practice in Vocational Education and Training. Methodology Paper. EASNIE, Odense (2014)

19. Honegger, J.: Vernetztes Denken und Handeln in der Praxis. Versus, Zürich (2011)

20. Vester, F.: Die Kunst Vernetzt zu Denken. Deutsche Verlags-Anstalt, Stuttgart (1999)

Application of Smart Technologies in Music Education for Children with Disabilities

Nataliya G. Tagiltseva[1(✉)], Svetlana A. Konovalova[1(✉)], Nataliya I. Kashina[1(✉)], Lada V. Matveeva[1(✉)], Anastasia I. Suetina[1(✉)], and Inna A. Akhyamova[2(✉)]

[1] Ural State Pedagogical University, Yekaterinburg, Russia
`musis52nt@mail.ru, konovsvetlana@mail.ru, koranata@mail.ru, lada-matveeva@yandex.ru, suetina@uspu.me`
[2] Yekaterinburg Academy of Contemporary Art, Yekaterinburg, Russia
`innaah@yandex.ru`

Abstract. The article reveals the experience of introducing new tools related to the Smart-education technology segment into the educational process of the disciplines "Listening to Music" and "Musical Literature", which are included in the curricula of Russian supplementary education institutions - children's music schools and art schools: computer (multimedia) presentation, video-clavier, electronic textbooks with audio and video sections, materials of sites related to musical art. This toolkit helps promotes stimulation and activation of cognitive and creative activity, self-realization of students with special educational needs, development of their independence, ability to full artistic perception, which allows achieving the main goal of the lessons in the disciplines "Listening to Music" and "Musical Literature" - the formation of interest in musical art and creativity. It will allow teachers working in the system of additional education to effectively organize the monitoring of students' knowledge, to build individual educational trajectories, to implement personally oriented and activity-oriented methodological approaches in teaching students with special educational needs.

Keywords: Smart-education technologies · Inclusion
Children with special educational needs · Children's music school
Children's art school · Additional education of children system
"Listening to Music" · "Music Literature"

1 Introduction

In normative documents in Russia the field of education and social development focuses attention on the need to ensure the development of the individual in the innovative conditions of education and upbringing; creation of programs implementing information technologies in education [1]. Such documents include the Federal State Educational Standard for children with disabilities. The Federal State Educational Standard for children with disabilities is designed to teach such children in school. But, in Russia today such children are trained in the system of additional music education - in children's

K. Miesenberger and G. Kouroupetroglou (Eds.): ICCHP 2018, LNCS 10896, pp. 353–356, 2018.
https://doi.org/10.1007/978-3-319-94277-3_55

music schools, children's art schools. They learn to play musical instruments, listen to music and compose music.

The modern curricula of children's music schools and children's art schools include the disciplines "Listening to Music" and "Musical Literature". For children with disabilities, the study of these disciplines is primarily aimed at the formation of interest in musical art. The speech in this article will focus on teaching children who have serious disorders in the locomotor and speech spheres (cerebral palsy, speech disorders).

2 Theoretical Grounds for the Introduction of Smart-Education Technologies in Children's Music School and Art School

In modern scientific literature is used the concept of "smart education", which is defined as an educational system that provides on the basis of the Internet interaction with the environment and the process of education and upbringing for citizens to acquire the necessary knowledge, skills, abilities and competences [2].

The concept of smart education (Smart-education) is associated with a number of concepts. The term "smart technology", which appeared in the scientific literature about 40 years ago in connection with the development of aerospace technologies, was later borrowed and disseminated by other branches of science [3]. The term "smart" implies to the property of a system or process that manifests itself in interaction with the environment and gives the system and/or process the ability to respond immediately to changes in the external environment. The analysis of numerous works on the introduction of Smart-education technologies into artistic and musical didactics allows us to draw a conclusion about its great pedagogical potential.

3 Experiment to Introduce Smart-Education Technologies in Children's Music School and Art School

The main means of training in disciplines «Listening to Music» and «Music Literature» is sounding music, which can be performed by the teacher himself and broadcast to the child through Skype, or music presented in audio and video recordings, when a musical piece is performed by great musicians, conductors and vocalists.

Experimental training using Smart-education in these disciplines was conducted in children with health problems (problems with the musculoskeletal system and in the speech sphere) at the Children's Art School No. 4 in Yekaterinburg, Russia. At the lessons of "Musical Literature" and "Listening to Music", as well as at home lessons conducted using Skype, included a computer (multimedia) presentation, a video-clavier, an electronic textbook with audio and video sections.

3.1   Characteristics of Smart Education Technologies

1. A computer (multimedia) presentation is a small video film containing graphic, text and audiovisual information, united in a single structure. It is based on the existence

of a storyline, a script and the structure of navigation. This is a kind of "multimedia advertising", that is, an artistic product that contains expressiveness, plot and drama of development. The plot of such a presentation, which includes fragments of classical music, can be a child's favorite tale, the life story of a great composer or the events of a child's life [4].

2. In the educational process was also used such a modern mean as a video-clavier. Against the background of a video recording of an opera or other stage musical genre, a clavier recording of the work is entered into the video sequence, including the fixation of a musical notation. Such simultaneous listening and "tracing" the child text of the note "intact" is possible, thanks to information technology, when the sound is supplemented with a musical notation that appears on the computer screen simultaneously with the music of a particular work [2].

3. Another means of learning in the context of the problem studied in this article is the use of electronic textbooks on music with sections of audio-video. In these electronic textbooks teachers of the Children's Art School No. 4 in Yekaterinburg included special assignments for children with a delay in speech development. For example, on the theme "Musical genres" they were asked to designate a musical genre with a certain color (level 1), for a march, dance or song, select a picture in the textbook (level 2), show march, dance (fingers, hands, body). Senior students who do not have problems with intelligence, but who have with the musculoskeletal system answered the questions that were in the textbook. These are questions about composers, about the characteristic features of time/epoch, which are reflected in the work of composers, about the plot of a musical work, etc.

In children who have already shown a constant interest in musical art, teachers have developed a desire for independent search for musical information. To this end, the teacher can familiarize students with Internet sites containing information in the field of culture and art, as well as record music in mp3; Here are some of them. These are: Belcanto website (electronic resource - http://www.belcanto.ru/), site "Classic online" (electronic resource - http://classic-online.ru), site "Intermezzo" (Electronic resource - http://www.aveclassics.net/board) [3].

3.2 Unsolved Problems

In applying intellectual technologies in music education for children with disabilities, there are unsolved problems. For example, the greatest interest of children in the visual, then in the musical series. Enthusiasm for pictures, video clips, but not musical works. Desire to listen to modern pop music, etc. These problems can be solved by teachers who, in computer presentations, in tasks of electronic textbooks, should harmoniously combine the visual and auditory series. A music teacher and a child can listen to classical music together in modern arrangements, and also compose the contents of tasks, including interesting facts about the creation of classical works available on different sites [5].

4   Key Findings

Thus, the results of the introduction of Smart-education technologies into the educational process in the music and theoretical disciplines "Listening to Music" and "Music Literature" showed that these technologies have a positive impact on the emotional sphere of students with special educational needs, which is associated with the joy of creativity [6]. Correction component, at the same time, becomes for such children imperceptible. Children with serious impairments in the musculoskeletal area began to show greater interest in classical music than it was before. Many of them, became interested in various sites, they had the desire to engage in computer presentations. Children with a delay in speech development, thanks to the emotional impact of music, began to pronounce the name of their favorite musical compositions, something that had not previously been observed. These children expressed their positive attitude towards music by words and gestures. A singing of musical themes on a certain syllable to accompaniment (the task available in the electronic textbooks) allowed to form a clearer pronunciation of their words.

References

1. Mokrousov, S.I., Kashina, N.I.: Internet resource of diagnostics and accompaniment of artistically gifted students. Pedagogical Education in Russia, no. 11, pp. 72–76 (2017)
2. Kashina, N.I., Pavlov, D.N.: The problem of development of creative self-realization of college students of culture and arts in the process of musical composition activity. Innovative Projects and Programs in Education, no. 3, pp. 11–15 (2016)
3. Tagiltseva, N.G., Prisyazhnaya, E.A.: Information technologies in the professional activity of the teacher of additional education. Municipal Formation: Innovation and Experiment, no. 6, pp. 12–16 (2016)
4. Tagiltseva, N.G.: A polyartistic approach to the organization of the process of teaching music teachers in a pedagogical college. Pedagogical Education in Russia, no. 5, pp. 147–152 (2016)
5. Tagiltseva, N.G., Konovalova, S.A., Kashina, N.I., Valeeva, E.M., Ovsyannikova, O.A., Mokrousov, S.I.: Information technologies in musical and art education of children. In: Uskov, V.L., Howlett, R.J., Jain, L.C. (eds.) SEEL 2017. SIST, vol. 75, pp. 112–119. Springer, Cham (2018). https://doi.org/10.1007/978-3-319-59451-4_12
6. Konovalova, S.A.: Pedagogical model of the development of children's creative activity in music classes in conditions of additional education. Pedagogy of Art, no. 4, pp. 106–112 (2011)

Br'Eye: An Android Mobile Application to Teach Arabic and French Braille Alphabets to Blind Children in Tunisia

Amina Bouraoui[1,2(✉)] and Mejdi Soufi[3]

[1] Riadi, University of Manouba, Manouba, Tunisia
hannibal.a@topnet.tn
[2] Institut Supérieur des Technologies Médicales-ISTMT,
University of Tunis El Manar, Tunis, Tunisia
[3] Tunis, Tunisia
soufi.majdi@gmail.com

Abstract. This paper presents an Android mobile application consisting in an educational content for visually handicapped children in Tunisia. The application involves simple and various interfaces that aim to teach Braille alphabet in both Arabic and French. It uses multimodal interaction methods as well as a novel approach to help young users locate areas of interest on the screen.

1 Introduction and Motivation

According to the National Statistics Institute the prevalence of disability in Tunisia in 2014 is estimated at 2.5% [1], among which 20.2% are visually handicapped. The number of children with disabilities attending primary schools in 2017 was estimated at 3578 [2]. Visually handicapped students in particular face many problems, such as:

- The majority of blind children are enrolled in specialized schools. There are exactly five specialized schools throughout the country. Visually impaired children can attend mainstream schools in specialized or inclusive classes. There is no available data on handicapped children who do not attend school. Moreover, children with disabilities do not benefit of equal opportunities in access to education [3].
- The schools, whether private, public, specialized or inclusive, lack resources, such as trained staff for the education of children with disabilities. They also lack equipment, like Braille printers or modern Braille devices, because of their prohibitive prices.
- Depending on the available equipment, blind children do not always have the opportunity to learn Braille in good conditions, which can make their schooling ineffective and insufficient. In major cases, schools use stylus and slate to teach Braille. The child has to make a great effort to learn Braille and reverse[1] writing requires a significant and additional intellectual work. The fact that students have to learn two languages at the same time does not make things any easier.

---

[1] Arabic is read/written from right to left, however, following the international convention, Arabic Braille is read from left to right.

© Springer International Publishing AG, part of Springer Nature 2018
K. Miesenberger and G. Kouroupetroglou (Eds.): ICCHP 2018, LNCS 10896, pp. 357–364, 2018.
https://doi.org/10.1007/978-3-319-94277-3_56

- When children reach university, they are integrated with sighted students. If they choose to pursue different studies than the ones "dedicated" to them (switchboard operator, physiotherapist...), they must manage not to fall behind. Presently, the rare blind students in universities often rely on their sighted classmates to read an exam, and in most cases they answer orally.

On another level, handheld devices such as smartphones or tablets are widespread and popular especially among children, and their prices are affordable comparing to desktop, handheld computers and assistive technologies. As a matter of fact there are over 14 million mobile phones for a total population of 11 million [4].

This paper describes an application that takes advantage of the popularity of mobile devices, as well as their affordability and accessibility, to teach the basics of Braille to young children. Our application is meant to provide the student with an additional tool to practice wherever and whenever wanted.

2 State of the Art

Many research works investigated the use of a touchscreen for visually handicapped users, and studied the suitable interaction methods. Besides, there are numerous mobile applications that exploit the touchscreen of a handheld device to represent Braille code. These applications vary in objectives, interaction platforms and methods, complexity, availability, languages...etc. The majority are aimed to provide a tool for Braille text entry [5–9].

During the literature review, we focused on mobile applications that teach Braille to blind users, including children and preferably proposing Arabic Braille among other languages. We did not find works that combine these three criteria. Only one or two criteria were covered, for example: V-Braille [10] targets blind-deaf adults that are fluent in Braille, and focuses only on reading. LearnBraille [11] teaches Braille but targets sighted and adult Braille learners, while mBraille [12] targets visually impaired students, but teaches Bangla and English Braille.

The same applies to Android apps found on the Google play store. Their goal is to teach Braille to sighted users, or else they provide a Braille keyboard to blind users who already know Braille. No research work or app has been found that teaches Arabic Braille and that targets blind children at the same time.

3 Proposed Approach and Application Design

Our app (baptized Br'Eye) has been developed using Android Studio. We did not rely on the built-in accessibility features, we rather prefer to design and develop an accessible application from scratch.

There are two major disadvantages related to the use of the touchscreen for the blind: firstly, the complexity of the multi-touch gesture and secondly, the difficulty to locate specific positions on the screen. In the following paragraphs, we propose an approach that addresses these issues.

3.1   The Adaptive Finger Touch

Researchers think that a single finger touch is better suited for blind people interacting with a touchscreen [5] despite the slowness of the method. Our hypothesis is that single finger gesture and ludic software are best advised for children. Therefore, we have designed an app that accepts a single finger gesture to process a single Braille dot.

However, we also assume that children learn fast and evolve quickly, for these reasons, Br'Eye is designed to adapt and sustain more sophisticated interaction methods. The user can activate two or more dots using multi-touch gesture.

3.2   The Tactile Markers

Regarding the second concern, and since touch is important for blind children [13], it is necessary to find alternatives to help the child identifying the Braille cell layout. Hence, we have designed markers that can be placed on the screen (see Fig. 1(a)). To facilitate the use of Br'Eye, the markers can, also, be placed by an accompanying adult, family member or a teacher.

Given the wide variety of screen sizes, we designed repositionable markers cut out in an adhesive material, thereby, they can be placed, removed and replaced if needed. Any inexpensive material can be used, such as sticky thick paper, replaceable glue chips, foam …etc.

Markers are suitable for many uses and applications: for example they can be used to simulate a real Braille cell by adding relief (e.g. a glue chip on which a flat/raised Lego piece is placed). It is also possible to design a modular grid marker (3 × 2) placed on the entire Braille cell. Such a grid can serve as a guide for children.

Along with the markers we have used vibratory feedback and sounds to guide the user and alleviate the touchscreen's absence of tactile feedback.

3.3   Interface Design and Interaction Methods

The learning related interfaces have the same aspect (see Fig. 1(a)):

- the upper part of the screen is occupied by a 6-dot braille cell (3 dots × 2 columns). This area is called the Braille zone, where strictly defined areas are dedicated to the 6 braille dots represented by circular images;
- the lower part is reserved for control or data presentation widgets that are limited to two per screen. This area is called control zone.

The application offers the following input interaction methods to the user:

- a tap (simple click) gives feedback, for example in the Braille zone it will indicate the dot's state (raised or not) with an adequate message or sound; in the control zone, it will vocalize the widget label/role;
- a press (long click) permits to do an action, e.g. in the Braille zone and according to the current activity it will activate/deactivate the dot;
- a double click allows to execute a command related to the activity, this will only work in the control zone;

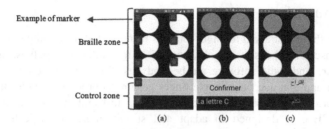

Fig. 1. Layout and markers (a), French exploring (b), Arabic testing (c)

- a swipe allows to change the present task, e.g. in learning mode it scrolls the letters;
- speech recognition allows the child to pronounce the featured letters in testing mode.

Br'Eye uses multimodal interaction for output, e.g. sound is coupled with vibration in addition to visual feedback.

We decided to make the dots visible, thus the children can involve their entourage in the learning process. Besides, the colors present a correct contrast according to the W3C recommendations [14].

3.4   Software Design and Content

The current prototype contains four main activities: learning, exploring, testing knowledge, and entertaining with a memory-like game that revises some of the studied characters. When the application is launched, the user (or the accompanying sighted adult) is invited to place the markers on the screen. A configuration activity allows the user to choose the preferred language, and a help activity explains the braille cell composition, such as the dots' names.

The Learning Activity. In this activity, the first alphabet letter is represented in the Braille zone and a corresponding sound is played. When tapping on the screen, the user senses different (strong/weak) vibrations that indicate if the dot is raised or not, while a sound is emitted (e.g. when the dot is activated, the corresponding dot number is pronounced; when the dot is deactivated, a sound mimicking emptying is played). Touching the screen does not change the pattern, it only gives feedback. The user can scroll the letters forward or backward by swiping to the left (next letter), to the right (previous letter), up (first letter), and down (last letter).

The Exploring Activity. The exploring activity allows the user to practice writing. It shows a blank braille cell, the user interacts with each dot and gets immediate, auditory and vibratory feedback. A tap leads to the same behavior as in the learning activity. A press activates or deactivates the dot (depending on its original state). The sounds and vibrations are different whether the dot is raised or not. When raising a dot the app simulates a filling sound, while the vibration is strong. When pressing a raised dot, the app simulates an emptying sound with a short vibration. The user confirms the pattern by selecting a widget or double tapping in the control zone, the activity pronounces the braille character that has been entered (Fig. 1(b)), or, if it is a wrong pattern, it pronounces an error message.

Testing User's Knowledge. To test the user's knowledge, two activities are proposed: one for reading and the second for writing:

- The "Reading" activity: a random character is suggested, rendered by a Morse-like sound representing the letter (long beep for a raised dot and short beep for an empty dot), and a vibratory feedback when the user taps the screen. The user can guess the character after activating the speech recognition by pressing the adequate button or by double tapping the screen. The activity congratulates the user if he/she finds the good letter, or gives an error message. Figure 1(c) is an example of testing the user's ability to read the Arabic character 'د'.
- The "Writing" activity presents a blank Braille cell, and pronounces a random letter. The user has to write using the same method as in the exploring activity.

The user can change the proposed letter anytime by either choosing the adequate control button or by swiping in the control zone.

Memory-Like Game. The fourth activity allows the user to play while training with a memory-like game. The screen is composed of a grid of virtual objects which are represented by sounds, vibrations, or text-to-speech. First, the user is prompted to choose the size of the grid (the number of virtual objects). At this time, the following sizes are proposed: 2×2, 3×2, 4×2, and 4×3. The objects are grouped by families of two. For example the word "cat" ("chat" in French, or "قط" in Arabic) is coupled with the sound of a cat meowing. A tap on an object gives information about it (for example the message "This is a cat"), while a press allows the user to select the object. Pairs are identified when selected one after the other. Hence, they disappear from the grid. Once all the pairs are identified, the user can start over with a different game. The families of objects proposed in one screen usually feature a single letter that has been chosen by the user.

4 Evaluation

Br'Eye has been tested in a Tunisian specialized school[2] with 8 pupils aged between 6 and 8 years old. A preliminary session has been organized to explain the general purpose of the app, and the interaction methods. Some of the children never touched or used a mobile device before, for this reason markers have been placed on each device.

The evaluation scenario is as follows: first, the pupils use learning and exploring activities to learn how to read and write letters; secondly, they use the testing activity to test their knowledge in both reading and writing. If they fail identifying a letter, then they should move to the next letter and not to make another attempt. They can also stop practicing anytime. No time constraints or language were imposed. We arranged two

---

[2] Ecole primaire Ennour, Ben Arous, Tunis.

sessions to avoid boredom and fatigue: a session for learning interaction and exploring, and another session for testing.

We monitored the sessions using traditional means, and measured times spent on different features of the software. At the end of the experiment, and with the help of teachers, we orally conducted short interviews with pupils. We adopted general guidelines explored in [15], therefore specific care has been given to the questions design: we used brief questions (inspired by QUIS [16]) that require simple answers on a scale range 1–5 (varying from a very bad appreciation to a very good one). There are five general criteria: the overall reaction to the app, the content, the learning process, the feedback and the markers. Each criterion is composed of a maximum of three related questions, for example the content criterion is composed by questions about the app's features, the quality of help and the guidance value.

4.1 Quantitative Results

The pupils have been identified by the code P_n ($1 \leq n \leq 8$). Table 1 summarizes data related to the pupils (gender and age), the different amounts of time (hours: minutes) spent on learning and testing for both reading (R) and writing (W), the chosen language and the accuracy rate percentage obtained by the child when testing. The accuracy rate is the number of correctly identified characters in relation to the total number of practiced characters.

Table 1. Quantitative results of Br'Eye evaluation

Pupil	Sex	Age	Learning		Testing		Language	Accuracy rate (%)	
			R	W	R	W		R	W
P1	M	7	0:55	0:42	0:45	0:40	Arabic	64	56
P2	M	6	1:10	1:05	0:25	0:20	French	40	35
P3	F	8	0:55	0:40	0:25	0:35	Arabic	71	75
P4	F	7	0:45	0:55	0:50	0:43	Both	55	54
P5	M	8	0:35	0:38	0:36	0:35	French	84	83
P6	M	7	0:42	0:45	0:36	0:39	Arabic	82	84
P7	F	6	0:59	1:09	0:44	0:30	Arabic	86	90
P8	M	8	0:35	0:41	0:28	0:32	French	53	60

4.2 Qualitative Results

The results of the interviews are shown in Fig. 2. We mention however, the following points that we noticed or that were reported by teachers:

- all the children showed great interest in the app, and an overall positive reaction. They were very excited, 5 out of 8 expressed the desire in pursuing the experiment;
- all of them appreciated the game integrated in the app and asked for more entertaining features;

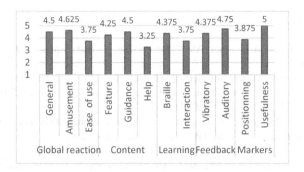

Fig. 2. Qualitative results: average scores by criterion

- 7 out of 8 wished they could learn Braille with this app or a similar one as an alternative to using the stylus that lacks precision, and demands exhausting efforts;
- 6 out of 8 highly appreciated the tactile markers while 2 suggested the use of a total grid overlay;
- by scoring 4.25 out of 5 points, the app proved to be efficient, easy to use and entertaining.

5   Conclusion and Further Works

Br'Eye uses means within reach of almost everyone and do not necessitate specialized equipment. Learning is made easier than with the conventional means currently used (wooden pieces and nails, stylus and slate), which require much more effort from children.

After the evaluation process we took note of some improvements to make and features to add. The logical continuation of this work would be to carry on the Braille teaching with more advanced features such as ligatures and diacritic marks in Arabic, and diacritic signs and letters in French, numbers and punctuation, writing and reading sentences …etc.

In the future we want to propose similar educational software tools and games. Our priority goes to education and learning through simple applications, later we want to work on improving communication between different categories of users. The handicapped user should be involved before, during and after the design and development of such applications.

We conclude by saying that the app is not available yet on Google Play, but it is freely distributed in Tunisian schools voluntarily or on demand. It could be deployed in many Arabic or French speaking countries. It can also be adapted to other languages.

References

1. Institut National de Statistiques: Atelier National sur les Statistiques du Handicap, Technical report (2016)
2. Tunisian ministry of education: School statistics 2016–2017, Technical report (2017)
3. Tunisie: Rapport National sur les enfants non scolarisés 2014: Unicef Bureau régional, Moyen-Orient et Afrique du Nord, Tunis (2015)
4. Instance nationale des télécommunications: Tableau de bord téléphone mobile. http://www.intt.tn/upload/files/TB2_Tel-Mobile%20-%20Septembre%202017.pdf. Last Accessed 02 Nov 2017
5. Alnfiai, M., Sampalli, S.: BrailleEnter: a touch screen braille text entry method for the blind. In: Shakshuki, E. (ed.) 8th International Conference on Ambient Systems, Networks and Technologies, Procedia Computer Science, vol. 109, pp. 257–264, Madeira (2017)
6. Oliveira, J., Guerreiro, T., Nicolau, H., Jorge, J., Gonçalves, D.: BrailleType: un-leashing Braille over touch screen mobile phones. In: Campos, P., Graham, N., Jorge, J., Nunes, N., Palanque, P., Winckler, M. (eds.) INTERACT 2011. LNCS, vol. 6946, pp. 100–107. Springer, Heidelberg (2011)
7. Dobosz, K., Szuścik, M.: OneHandBraille: an alternative virtual keyboard for blind people. In: Gruca, A., Czachórski, T., Harezlak, K., Kozielski, S., Piotrowska, A. (eds.) ICMMI 2017. AISC, vol. 659, pp. 62–71. Springer, Cham (2018). https://doi.org/10.1007/978-3-319-67792-7_7
8. Southern, C., et al.: An evaluation of BrailleTouch. In: Proceedings of the 14th International Conference on Human-Computer Interaction with Mobile Devices and Services, pp. 317–326. ACM, New York (2012)
9. Hewahi, N., et al.: Arabic Braille touch keyboard for Android users. Int. J. Technol. Diffus. 5 (2), 54–71 (2014)
10. Jayant, H., Acuario, C., Johnson, W., Hollier, J., Ladner, R.: V-Braille: Haptic Braille perception using a touch-screen and vibration on mobile phones. In: Proceedings of the 12th International ACM SIGACCESS Conference on Computers and Accessibility, pp. 295–296. ACM, Orlando (2010)
11. Hatzigiannakoglou, P.D., Kampouraki, M.T.: Learn Braille: a serious game mobile app for sighted Braille learners. J. Eng. Sci. Technol. Rev. 9(1), 174–176 (2016)
12. Nahar, L., et al.: Design of a Braille learning application for visually impaired students in Bangladesh. Assist. Technol. 27(3), 172–182 (2015)
13. Withagen, A., Vervloed, M.P.J., Janssen, N.M., Knoors, H., Verhoeven, L.: Tactile functioning in children who are blind: a clinical perspective. J. Vis. Impairment Blindness 104(1), 43–54 (2010)
14. Caldwell, B., Cooper, M., Reid, L.G., Vanderheiden, G.: Web content accessibility guidelines 2.0, Technical report, W3C (2008)
15. Markopoulos, P., Read, J.C., MacFarlane, S., Höysniemi, J.: Evaluating Childrens Interactive Products Principles and Practices for Interaction Designers. Morgan Kaufman Publishers Inc, San Francisco (2008)
16. QUIS 7.0. http://lap.umd.edu/quis/. Last Accessed 15 Nov 2017

Information Technologies in Teaching Pop Vocals of Teenagers with Disabilities in Motion

Nataliya G. Tagiltseva[1(✉)], Svetlana A. Konovalova[1(✉)], Liana V. Dobrovolskaya[2(✉)], Anna M. Zhukova[3], and Oksana A. Ovsyannikova[4(✉)]

[1] Ural State Pedagogical University, Yekaterinburg, Russia
{musis52nt,konovsvetlana}@mail.ru
[2] M. Kozybayev North Kazakhstan State University, Petropavlovsk, Kazakhstan
doliana@inbox.ru
[3] Tyumen State Institute of Culture, Tyumen, Russia
anya_2112@mail.ru
[4] Tyumen State University, Tyumen, Russia
sergeiovsiannikov@yandex.ru

Abstract. The article considers information technologies that can be used by children of adolescence with limited motor abilities. Such children can not often visit music schools, vocal studios and circles, but they, like many teenagers who do not have health restrictions, want to engage in contemporary forms of musical art and, in particular, pop vocals. One of the tools that allows an adolescent with limited motor abilities (cerebral palsy, upper and lower extremity dysplasia, etc.) to engage in this form of music making, to engage in creative communication with other children who are addicted to pop-performance are information technologies. Currently, Internet resources provide ample opportunities for learning pop vocals. But, the use of the abundance of Internet programs, various kinds of Internet teaching resources, however, is not yet a guarantee of its success. Therefore, adolescents who want to master pop vocals need the help of an adult teacher who, through the use of these technologies, will determine the logical sequence and appropriateness of including such resources and technologies in the learning process. The article presents the sequence of introducing teenagers with disabilities into health in the form of interrelated stages in the process of education. Receiving the teacher's advice on Skype, the child can successfully master them. Each stage is aimed at: on the development of a sense of rhythm and purity of intoning (the program "Real piano" and "Absolute Rumor."); on the upbringing of the ability to evaluate one's performance; on the formation of the ability to listen to vocal harmony (the program "Akapella maker"); on the formation of skills of ensemble performance (the program "Smule sing."). The content of the stages of teaching pop vocals of a child with disabilities in health: from elementary vocal skills to the skills of joint vocal playing with other children and is the purpose of this article.

Keywords: Children with limited motor abilities · Stages of training · Pop vocals Computer programs

© Springer International Publishing AG, part of Springer Nature 2018
K. Miesenberger and G. Kouroupetroglou (Eds.): ICCHP 2018, LNCS 10896, pp. 365–368, 2018.
https://doi.org/10.1007/978-3-319-94277-3_57

1 Introduction

Nowadays, information technologies are increasingly being included in the educational field. They are also used today in educational institutions that deal with the musical education of children. The review of pedagogical literature suggests that these technologies are also used in teaching children with disabilities and, in particular, with limited motor abilities. These technologies are especially relevant for teenagers. It is known that in adolescence the leading activity of children is communication. Teenagers communicate with each other in certain interest groups. They willingly include in their groups those children who are engaged in the same types of creativity, sports, social, research activities. However, children with limited motor capacity, being at home all the time, often can not realize themselves in these activities, as a result of which they are not accepted into adolescent communities. Therefore, one of the motives to engage in actively loved activities in children with children with disabilities in health is to gain "trust" in healthy children and to join them in a communication group.

A child with disabilities in health who wants to engage in such a favorite business every day can receive certain recommendations from a teacher who will present these recommendations via Skype. However, for the teacher himself, one must have an idea of the certain sequence of stages of such self-training of a disabled child to achieve the success of training, preserve his health and maintain interest in such activities. This training includes the training of the parent. Also, such technologies contribute to the successful teaching of music to children with cerebral palsy through the inclusion of a visual series (notes, pictures associated with the content of a musical work), or through clearly marked instructions for playing an electronic musical instrument that the child receives from the teacher via the Internet [1, 2].

For adolescents with special health abilities, those programs that contribute to the formation of their skills in pop singing are extremely relevant. This dominant of pop vocals over other vocal forms of performing is dominant in the world musical culture, which undoubtedly affects the interests of adolescent children, including those who have limited opportunities in health [3].

2 Theoretical Bases of Training Pop Vocals for Teenagers with Limited Mobility

Much less often than the work on the use of ICT in instrumental performance in the literature, there are developments of a theoretical and methodical plan for using the same technologies in vocal training. Especially this disadvantage is manifested in teaching classical vocal, in which the traditions of Italian, German, French, Russian academic singing schools are strong [4]. Vocal creativity is also taught to children with disabilities in health. It is an interesting experience to teach the vocal of a child with autism, which is disclosed in an article by Vaiouli et al. [5]. Presented ideas of the authors reveal the possibilities of teaching the child vocals with the help of visual computer tools that contribute to the formation of certain vocal skills, including those in children with disabilities.

3 The Introduction of ICT in the Process of Teaching Pop Vocals to Teenagers with Disabilities

The purpose of this article is to present a specific algorithm for the introduction and use of computer programs. At the same time, the article will show not so much the features of such programs, their characteristics and specific usage, but rather the sequence of the stages of introducing such programs for a novice pop vocalist.

In pedagogy there are various definitions of the stage-by-stage learning of one or another activity. We will reveal this technology, which was actively introduced into the learning process of novice pop vocalists- adolescents with limited ability to move. These children were trained in the system of additional musical education in the Children's Art School No. 4 in Yekaterinburg, Russia.

First stage of the work was the introduction of the program "Realpiano" and "Absolute Rumor ". It is known that auditory control is important for any musician-performer. The same control is also necessary for the pop vocalist. The most frequently repeated mistakes in the performance of pop music is not the accuracy of the intonation, when the performer then understates, then overstates the tone or even "leaves" the tone, for example, in the case of a song without accompaniment - a`capella. In connection with the need to eliminate this disadvantage, pop vocalists-disabled teenager need a thorough auditory training, which allows to accurately and purely intone any vocal work. To this end, the program is first introduced into the training (which can be for every disabled teenager in the smartphone) "Realpiano". This program allows to lose the melody of the vocal work, to repeat it in a voice, accompanying himself to "Realpiano", singing those fragments that cause the student intonational difficulties.

The next program, which was actively used to develop intonational accuracy of vocal performance, was the program "Absolute Rumor". The advantage of this program is the development of auditory skills, and not only. It contributes to the development and rhythmic feeling, so necessary to the pop vocalist due to the need to perform jazz works, complex in rhythmic, tempo and metrorhythmic terms. In this program there are tasks for the development of a sense of rhythm, namely, the learner is offered to play the rhythm offered for listening, record this rhythm with music durations, reproduce the complex rhythmic pattern with claps. At the end of the execution of the tasks, the results of the execution of the tasks of each block appear on the display. The next stage of introduction of ICT in the process of preparing of novice pop vocalists is the inclusion of such a program as "Akapella maker". The value of this program is that a children can perform the same melody of a vocal work several times, and "imposing" different performances will give him the opportunity to hear inaccuracies in sounding, in rhythmic design of the vocal work, and reveal melodic and metrorhythmic discrepancies.

At this stage it will be possible to include another, undoubtedly, useful program called Smulesing, which is not even called a program but a social network. For more colorful sounding in the recorded track, the student can include interesting sound effects: claps, flicks, fingers, rumba, maracas, etc. Another advantage of this program is the choice of the form of performance of the chosen composition: solo, duet, trio, ensemble, quartet and even chorus. In the vocal music-making the teenager can involve several performers, and the association through the program of their sounding makes it possible to create an ensemble or chorus whose participants may be in another city, state or even on another continent.

4 Key Findings

With the introduction of three stages of technology, the following results were obtained. Children - teenagers with disabilities learned to intone well, developed their possibilities in terms of ICT development, and, most importantly, found new friends in the overall creative work, which undoubtedly brings such training to pop vocal as an effective means of socializing these children. This is confirmed by performances at contests for teenagers with disabilities in the movement on vocal competitions and festivals. The pop vocals of these children included elements of the presented technology. The effectiveness of the technology is proved by concert performances of one of the winners of the television project "Voice. Children", the third season - Danila Pluzhnikova.

References

1. Tagiltseva, N.G., Konovalova, S.A., Kashina, N.I., Valeeva, E.M., Ovsyannikova, O.A., Mokrousov, S.I.: Information technologies in musical and art education of children. In: Uskov, V.L., Howlett, R.J., Jain, L.C. (eds.) SEEL 2017. SIST, vol. 75, pp. 112–119. Springer, Cham (2018). https://doi.org/10.1007/978-3-319-59451-4_12
2. Prisyazhnaya, E.A., Tagiltseva, N.G.: Information technologies in professional work of the teacher of an additional education. In: MUNICIPAL Education: Innovation and Experiment, no. 6, pp. 12–16 (2016). (in Russian)
3. Delgado, M., Humm-Delgado, D.: The performing arts and empowerment of youth with disabilities/Pedagogia Social. Revista interuniversitaria. Youth empowerment and Social Pedagogy. Universidad de Salamanca, pp. 105–120 (2017)
4. Konovalova, S.A., Korosteleva, N.I.: Actualization of the vital experience in the vocal class. Fundam. Res. **7**, 11–14 (2007). (in Russian)
5. Vaiouli, P., Grimmet, K.R., Ruich, L.: Bill is now singing: joint engagement and the emergence of social communication of three young children with autism. Autism **19**(1), 73–83 (2015)

Levumi: A Web-Based Curriculum-Based Measurement to Monitor Learning Progress in Inclusive Classrooms

Jana Jungjohann[1], Jeffrey M. DeVries[1(✉)], Markus Gebhardt[1], and Andreas Mühling[2]

[1] Technische Universität Dortmund,
Emil-Figge-Str. 50, 44227 Dortmund, Germany
jeffrey.devries@tu-dortmund.de
[2] Christian-Albrechts-Universität zu Kiel,
Christian-Albrechts-Platz 4, 24118 Kiel, Germany

Abstract. Our paper introduces and assesses the Levumi platform's web-based assessment of reading fluency. One challenges of inclusive education is meeting the needs of the learners with special education needs (SEN). Children with SEN and other risk factors face an increased risk of failing in schools and manifesting academic and social problems over the time. Web-based curriculum-based measurement (CBM) can provide an effective tool to track progress of learners and limit such risks. In particular, it can ease the challenges of test administration in inclusive classrooms through automation and providing multiple difficulty levels without the need of different paper-forms. Furthermore, Levumi can help educators track children and thus provide support for learners. Levumi takes advantage of the strengths of web-based CBM to assess reading fluency in primary school students. We confirmed the reading fluency test's test-retest reliability (n = 334), its ability to measure learning over time in individual learners with SEN (n = 8, across 14 MPs), and its applicability to learners with SEN (n = 300, including n = 46 with SEN). We evaluate Levumi's overall usefulness in assessing different types of learners, and discuss its contributions to CBM research.

Keywords: Curriculum-based measurement · Web-based assessment
Computer-based assessment · Reading fluency

1 Introduction

Since Germany signed the UN-Convention on the Rights of Persons with Disabilities in 2009, the German School system has been changing to meet new standards for inclusive classrooms. Before 2009, children with special educational needs (SEN) primarily visited special schools and were not included in the regular school system. However, an important goal of today's German school system is to reach academic inclusion, meaning that children with and without SEN learn together in the same classroom.

© The Author(s) 2018
K. Miesenberger and G. Kouroupetroglou (Eds.): ICCHP 2018, LNCS 10896, pp. 369–378, 2018.
https://doi.org/10.1007/978-3-319-94277-3_58

In inclusive classrooms, academic performance of children with and without SEN is very heterogeneous [1]. Children with SEN and other risk factors (e.g., minority or migration background) face an especially high risk of failing in schools and manifesting academic and social problems over the time (e.g., [2]). Issues relating to reading instructions are important to teachers because most students with SEN have difficulties learning to read. Indeed over the last several decades, numerous studies have reported that the vast majority of students with SEN have difficulties in learning to read [3, 4], that they achieve significant lower reading skills than their peers [5], and that this has consequences both within and outside the classroom [6]. These results were also applicable to students learning to read German [1, 7]. Reading problems might negatively affect skills related to early reading acquisition (e.g., reading fluency [8]) or in later skills (e.g., reading comprehension [9]). Reading fluency influences general reading development [10]. Because reading fluency already correlates to reading comprehension in primary school [11], it is a fundamental reading skill and an important goal in the early reading development for every student [12, 13]. Influencing factors, such as general cognitive ability, phonological awareness, speech perception and production, letter-name knowledge, rapid automatized naming, or consistency of the orthography, predict the early reading ability and individualize the learning processes [14, 15]. Additionally, specific reading fluency instruction can be differentially effective for students with and without SEN [16].

Furthermore, the heterogeneous conditions and needs in inclusive classrooms challenges teachers in new ways, such as designing effective instruction for the special needs students. In this regard, it is important that the teachers focus on individual learning growth instead of the social comparison between students [17]. Only in this way, can teachers provide targeted effective reading instruction [18]. This requires a new approach: first, teachers need to determine the individual needs of their students. Second, they choose a lesson and give it to the target student. Third, they monitor the individual learning growth and reflect upon the choice of the instruction. If learning growth is sufficient, the teacher can continue with the same instruction or focus on a new goal. If not, the teacher can adapt the method or can try another approach for that student.

Curriculum-based measurement (CBM) is a method for monitoring the learning growth of children and for supporting the teachers in effective decision-making [19]. CBM was designed in the United States to solve academic difficulties in special education [20]. CBM tests can be used very frequently during the lessons, take only few minutes, and show the slope of individual learning growth for a longer period graphically. The tasks are representative of end-year performance goals and integrate various subskills for competence in a domain (e.g., in reading or mathematics) [21]. Like any other test, CBM instruments need to possess quality criteria such as objectivity, reliability, validity, and be sensible of learning growth [22]. For classroom use, it should be simple and easy for educators to use the test and interpret the results. Additionally, it is important that multiple measurement points (MP) are comparable over time and the test is demonstrated to be invariant across these MPs [23].

The reliability and validity of CBM instruments has been shown in the classical test theory framework [24], and they are particularly useful for children with SEN [25]. More recently, computer based instruments have boosted the potential of CBM instruments [26]. Computer versions can reduce the time requirements, ease the creation of parallel test versions, and provide automatic feedback to students and teachers.

Curriculum-based measurement has also been studied in the context of German schools [27]. The first German CBM tests were pen-and-paper tests tracking reading or mathematic skills [e.g., [28]). However, in large classes pen-and-paper tests can result in a lot of additional work for teachers. Moreover, with these instruments, teachers must choose CBM tests from lower classes for children with SEN and lower ability levels (e.g., [29]), which complicates the use of the CBM instruments in inclusive classrooms [30]. Newer instruments have focused on online assessments to remedy some of these problems (e.g., [31, 32]), but such online tools often cost money for teachers or administrators [33]. Nonetheless, more research is necessary regarding the use of CBM techniques in real inclusive German classrooms [34].

The web-based platform Levumi (www.levumi.de) was founded by a multidisciplinary research team with the goal of creating a free online CBM tool to assess reading and mathematics competencies in primary education, with a focus on children with SEN, learning problems, behavior problems, or other risk factors. The three main goals of this research project are (1) to offer teachers a practical CBM tool for inclusive classrooms, (2) to improve research on CBM and the acceptance of CBM tools by teachers, and (3) to use the collected data for evaluating supporting materials for research and development in teaching and learning [33].

Levumi is currently available for teachers and researchers. Users can register on the website for free. Supporting material is also provided free of charge (e.g., [35]). Levumi tests can be used in all 16 German federal states and focus on learning goals throughout the country. Levumi runs from within any major browser. This makes it easy for teachers to use the system without having to install additional software, which usually requires administrative privileges that teachers do not have in typical school IT infrastructures. The only requirement is a permanent internet connection. In some tests, the teachers control the tests, and in other tests, the teachers activate a test for a class and the students can then take the test on their own by logging in with a personal ID code. Each such test begins with an instruction page, often with an interactive sample item, which requires multiple inputs to prevent a student from accidently starting the test.

The design of the platform is visually simple, and the tests look similar to one another in order for learners with SEN to easily work within the platform. For each item, the actual answer and whether or not it is correct is recorded. The sum of correct responses is used as the final score of the test. Immediately after each test, our mascot, a dragon named Levumi, shows each child if he or she has improved. Teachers can see graphically how each student performs in comparison both to past performance and to other students. Furthermore, the teachers get more detailed performance information, including items a student had problems with. The multiple difficulty levels allow learners with SEN to use the same tools and tests as their peers, which makes supporting all learners in an inclusive classroom much easier for teachers. Additionally, the teachers can track student information such as age, sex, migration background, and SEN.

Levumi contains tests of important indicators of overall competence in different learning domains. These learning domains are currently reading, writing, and mathematics. For each domain, several competencies can be measured with separate test types and multiple difficulty levels. The reading test structures are outlined in Fig. 1.

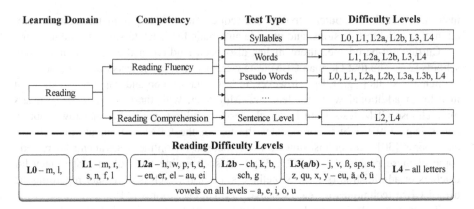

Fig. 1. Test structure of the learning domain reading in the Levumi platform

The reading domain contains two competencies: reading fluency and reading comprehension. For each competency, teachers can pick several test types and difficulty levels, which is important or practical use in class, it is very important that the teachers can easily choose a particular test and difficulty level. For each learning domain, the same difficulty structure exists across all competencies (see Fig. 1, lower part).

Each test has a unique item pool that includes approximately 40 to 200 items. All items are constructed upon theoretical models of reading acquisition. The web platform randomly orders the items for each measurement. This creates a huge number of parallel test forms for each single measurement. In some tests, additional rules are applied to produce the random item ordering. Typically, these tests involve items from multiple categories, such as item types from different dimensions. Additionally, in some tests, such as the reading fluency test, words or syllables with the same initial letter are prevented from following one another, preventing common mistakes. In these cases, items of the different categories or types were randomly in selected via round robin.

The Levumi reading fluency test measures fluency in reading aloud, a robust indicator of overall reading competence [36]. In these tests, the children read aloud items from a computer screen for one minute. Teachers rate the correct and non-correct answers by keyboard and can consider any factors specific to each learner such as a speech impairment. Reading of syllables, words, and pseudo words are assessed through separate tests. All reading fluency tests are based on the 'Kieler Leseaufbau' [37], which applies specifically to the German language. For each test, we incorporate multiple difficulties levels (L0 to L4) [38], based on a range of letters (see Fig. 1). Vowels are used in every difficulty level. The lower levels use stretchable consonants (e.g., /m/, /r/, /s/, /l/) in simple word structures. In the higher levels, the plosive, less common consonants, and consonant combinations are used with more complex word structures (e.g., /b/, /sch/, /qu/). In L4 all consonants and vowels are included. A student can be tested in a difficulty level after instruction on all contained letters. Because the teachers can choose a suitable Levumi test based upon the competency level of a student and not upon their age or grade, ease-of-use for teachers in inclusive classrooms is maintained.

As a part of the completion of test development of the reading fluency assessment for Levumi, we present four research questions. First, to verify the psychometric properties of the test in respect to the item response theory, we ask: (1) how does a Rasch model fit the Levumi syllable reading test? Next, we wish to examine the applicability of the sum scores to important theoretical questions and the general reliability of the syllable reading test and its ability to measure changes over time. Thus, our second and third research questions are: (2) do the sum scores of Levumi reading fluency test possess good test-retest reliability over 2 MPs, and: (3) can the Levumi test measure learning progress of learners with SEN over multiple MPs. Lastly, we wish to examine the applicability of the assessment to learners with special education needs, so we ask: (4) how do Levumi reading fluency test takers with SEN compare to other test takers in terms of sum scores on the syllable reading test?

2 Methods

Participants include test takers of the syllable reading fluency test on the Levumi platform in five samples. The first three samples were measured twice within a period of 7 to 10 weeks, with each representing data from a single difficulty level, L2b (n = 105), L3 (n = 97), and L4 (n = 132). The fourth sample was a small group of learners with SEN from a single class (n = 8). The fourth sample included 4 MPs of difficulty level L2b, followed by 5 MPs of L3, and lastly 5 MPs of L4 over one school year. Lastly, the fifth sample was taken from inclusive and special schools (N = 300) and included learners with SEN (n = 46; 38 with learning SEN, 7 with German SEN, and 1 other).

We calculated a full Rasch analysis for the second sample. We examined item fit scores (infit and outfit) for all test items. We further report Warm's weighted likelihood estimates (WLEs) for the first three samples.

Next, we analyzed the sum scores of each sample. First, we conducted a reliability assessment over 2 MPs in the first three samples. Second, we conducted a repeated measures ANOVA on the sum scores of the 8 participants in the fourth sample to assess the test's ability to measure learning progress. Lastly, we compared the results of SEN learners to other learners in the fifth sample.

3 Results

A graphical model check confirmed that all items performed equally across both MPs for difficulty level L3, indicating good test-retest reliability. Next, we calculated a Rasch model across both measurement points for difficulty level L3. The model possessed good data fits, with the mean square (MSQ) of the outfit ranging from .726 to 1.682 and the MSQ of the infit ranging from .911 to 1.079. Good values for the MSQ of the outfit and infit measures are between 0.5 and 1.5, while only values above 2.0 are considered harmful to measurement [39]. With only 2 of 112 items with an outfit over 1.5, we concluded the Rasch model fits our data very well. Furthermore, all three difficulty levels had good reliability within the Rasch model, $WLE_{L2b} = .919$,

WLE_{L3} = .883, and WLE_{L4} = .895. Therefore, we conclude that the Rasch models fit the data well, and the test is suitably unidimensional to use sum scores.

Sum scores at difficulty level L4 indicated a very high level of test-retest reliability for difficulties L2b and L4, r_{L2b} = .84 and r_{L4} = .85. The reliability of difficulty L3 was lower, but still high, r_{L3} = .76. This is consistent with the other reliability analyses.

Figure 2 includes all sum scores of the tracking sample of 8 learners with SEN across one school year. Each individual line represents the performance of a single learner. The left section contains MPs of difficulty L2b, the middle has L3, and the right has L4. Separate ANOVAs for each test type confirmed significant changes over time. For the L2b test, performance significantly changed from MP1 (M = 21.8, SD = 5.4) to MP4 (M = 30.8, SD = 7.9), F(3,21) = 13.49, p < .001. For the N3 test no differences over time were found, F(4,28) = 1.644, p > .10. Lastly for the L4 test, a change from MP1 (M = 24.0, SD = 7.8) to MP5 (M = 29.8, SD = 8.6) was detected, F (4,28) = 4.32, p < .01. We concluded that individual changes over different MPs are detectable.

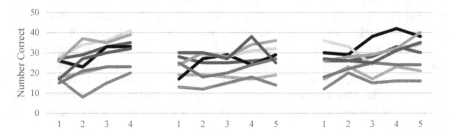

Fig. 2. Individual Tracking across Difficulty Levels L2b, L3, and L4

Lastly, the average items correctly solved for those students with SEN (M = 28.5, SD = 9.7) was no different than for those without SEN (M = 30.4, SD = 14.0), Welch's t(83.4) = 1.08, p > .25.

4 Discussion and Future Work

We assessed the quality of the syllable reading fluency test across different difficulty levels. Rasch analyses verified the test's psychometric qualities. Test-retest reliability was confirmed in a graphical model check and an analyses of sum scores. Learners with SEN performed no differently than those without SEN. Also, scores of the difficulty L2 and L4 improved significantly over the course of learning. Scores for L3 did not change, but this may represent a local plateau in the learning process.

These assessments allow for three important implications. First, good test-retest reliability indicates that any changes in student responses over the course of the school indicate changes in learner ability level not test artifacts. Second, the test is effective at measuring the learning process across multiple MPs. Lastly, equivalent test performance for learners with SEN demonstrates that the test provides a fair assessment for those learners. However, some limitations remain. We did not assess all learners, all test types, and difficulty levels. Further work should assess other test quality criteria. Levumi provides multiple tests to monitor learning growth in different learning domains. Development is nearly complete on other tests. An item-response theory based evaluation of test quality criteria is needed for other test types and difficulty levels. Simultaneously, new test types for use on the Levumi platform are being designed. These measure competencies in reading, writing, and mathematics, as well as behavior ratings. They include reading comprehension tests on the level of individual words and complete sentences comprehension, and mathematical assessments on early number sense and number sequencing tasks. Work is ongoing to create more difficult tests for use in secondary schools. Lastly, CBM behavior ratings are planned for primary and secondary schools. Similar test evaluations will be performed on the new tests.

We are also improving platform use on tablets. We have had the chance to collect pilot data for some tests with tablets. Some of these work well on tablets, but others need specific adaptions. Many participants were familiar with touch screens but require some time to familiarize themselves with Levumi. Further work should investigate if there are any mode effects between these two systems. Providing an app that displays the tests for students is also a possible improvement.

Our research established essential reliability and usefulness of a new web-based CBM technique. This platform will allow for rapid assessments and easy tracking of children with and without special education needs in all classroom types. Reliability of the tests for reading fluency was confirmed, and development continues on new tests of different competencies. Lastly, we found no difference in performance between students with and without SEN, and no differences were required in the test preparation and handling for learners with SEN.

References

1. Gebhardt, M., Sälzer, C., Mang, J., Müller, K., Prenzel, M.: Performance of students with special educational needs in Germany. Findings from PISA 2012. J. Cognit. Educ. Psychol. 14(3), 343–356 (2015). https://doi.org/10.1891/1945-8959.14.3.343
2. Jones, D.E., Greenberg, M., Crowley, M.: Early social-emotional functioning and public health: The relationship between kindergarten social competence and future wellness. J. Inf. 105(11), 2283–2290 (2015). https://doi.org/10.2105/AJPH.2015.302630
3. Kavale, K.A., Reece, J.H.: The character of learning disabilities. Learn. Disabil. Q. 15, 74–94 (1992)
4. Bental, B., Tirosh, E.: The relationship between attention, executive functions and reading domain abilities in attention deficit hyperactivity disorder and reading disorder: a comparative study. J. Child Psychol. Psychiatry 48(5), 455–463 (2007). https://doi.org/10.1111/j.1469-7610.2006.01710.x
5. National Center for Education Statistics: The nation's report card: Reading 2011 (NCES 2012-457). Institute of Education Sciences, U.S. Department of Education, Washington, D. C. (2011)
6. Taylor, C.R.: Engaging the struggling reader: Focusing on reading and success across the content areas. Nat. Teacher Educ. J. 5(2), 51–58 (2012)

7. Landerl, K., Wimmer, H.: Development of word reading fluency and spelling in a consistent orthography. An 8-year follow- up. J. Educ. Psychol. **100**(1), 150–161 (2008). https://doi. org/10.1037/0022-0663.100.1.150

8. Klicpera, C., Ehgartner, M., Gasteiger-Klicpera, B., Schabmann, A.: Voraussetzungen für das Leselernen bei lernbehinderten Kindern in der Sonderschule und bei guten und schwachen Lesern in der Grundschule: Eine Längsschnittuntersuchung zur Entwicklung des phonematischen Bewußtseins in der ersten Schulstufe. Heilpädagogische Forschung **3**, 104–108 (1993)

9. Nation, K.: Children's reading comprehension difficulties. In: Snowling, M.J., Hulme, Ch. (eds.) The Science of Reading: A Handbook, pp. 248–265. Blackwell Publishing Ltd. (2005)

10. National Institute of Child Health and Human Development: Report of the national reading panel - Teaching children to read: An evidence-based assessment of the scientific research literature on reading and its implications for reading instruction. U.S. Government Printing Office, Washington, D.C. (2000)

11. Roberts, G., Good, R., Corcoran, S.: Story retell: A fluency-based indicator of reading comprehension. Sch. Psychol. Q. **20**(3), 304–317 (2005). https://doi.org/10.1521/scpq.2005. 20.3.304

12. Hudson, R.F., Pullen, P.C., Lane, H.B., Torgesen, J.K.: The complex nature of reading fluency: a multidimensional view. Reading & Writ. Q. **25**(1), 4–32 (2008). https://doi.org/ 10.1080/10573560802491208

13. Perfetti, C.A.: Reading Ability. Oxford University Press, New York (1985)

14. Bowey, J.A.: Predicting individual differences in learning to read. In: Snowling, M.J., Hulme, Ch. (eds.) The Science of Reading: A Handbook, pp. 155–172. Blackwell Publishing Ltd. (2005)

15. Wimmer, H., Mayringer, H., Landerl, K.: The double-deficit hypothesis and difficulties in learning to read a regular orthography. J. Educ. Psychol. **92**(4), 668–680 (2000). https://doi. org/10.1037//0022-O663.92.4.668

16. Kuhn, M.R., Stahl, S.A.: Fluency: a review of developmental and remedial practices. J. Educ. Psychol. **95**(1), 3–21 (2003). https://doi.org/10.1037/0022-0663.95.1.3

17. Gebhardt, M.: Gemeinsamer Unterricht von Schülerinnen und Schülern mit und ohne sonderpädagogischen Förderbedarf. Ein empirischer Überblick. In: Kiel, E. (ed.): Inklusion im Sekundarbereich, pp. 39–52. Kohlhammer, Stuttgart (2015)

18. Jungjohann, J., Gebhardt, M.: Lernverlaufsdiagnostik im inklusiven Anfangsunterricht Lesen – Verschränkung von Lernverlaufsdiagnostik, Förderplanung und Wochenplanarbeit. In: Hellmich, F., Görel, G., Löper, M.F. (eds.) Inklusive Schul- und Unterrichtsentwicklung. Kohlhammer, Stuttgart (2018, in Press)

19. Deno, S.L.: Curriculum-based measurement: the emerging alternative. Except. Child. **52**, 219–232 (1985). https://doi.org/10.1177/001440298505200303

20. Deno, S.L.: Developments in curriculum-based measurement. J. Spec. Educ. **37**(3), 184–192 (2003). https://doi.org/10.1177/00224669030370030801

21. Fuchs, L.S.: The past, present, and future of curriculum-based measurement research. Sch. Psychol. Rev. **33**(2), 188–192 (2004)

22. Good, R., Jefferson, G.: Contemporary perspectives on curriculum-based measurement validity. In: Shinn, M.R. (ed.) Advanced Applications of Curriculum-Based Measurement (The Guilford School Practitioner Series), pp. 61–88. Guilford Press, New York (1998)

23. Gebhardt, M., Heine, J.-H., Zeuch, N., Förster, N.: Lernverlaufsdiagnostik im Mathematikunterricht der zweiten Klasse. Raschanalysen zur Adaptation eines Testverfahrens für den Einsatz in inklusiven Klassen. In: Empirische Sonderpädagogik, **7**(3), 206–222 (2015). http://www.psychologie-aktuell.com/fileadmin/download/esp/3-2015_20150904/esp_3-2015_206-222.pdf

24. Wayman, M.M., Wallace, T., Wiley, H.I., Tichá, R., Espin, C.A.: Literature synthesis on curriculum-based measurement in reading. J. Spec. Educ. **41**(2), 85–120 (2007). https://doi.org/10.1177/00224669070410020401

25. Stecker, P.M., Fuchs, L.S., Fuchs, D.: Using curriculum-based measurement to improve student achievement: review of research. Psychol. Sch. **42**(8), 795–819 (2005). https://doi.org/10.1002/pits.20113

26. Russell, M.K.: Technology-aided formative assessment of learning: new developments and applications. In: Andrade, H.L., Cizek, G.J. (eds.) Handbook of Formative Assessment, pp. 125–138. Routledge, New York, London (2010)

27. Klauer, K.J.: Lernverlaufsdiagnostik - Konzepte, Schwierigkeiten und Möglichkeiten. Empirische Sonderpädagogik **3**(3), 207–224 (2011)

28. Diehl, K., Hartke, B.: Zur Reliabilität und Validität des formativen Bewertungssystems IEL-1. Inventar zur Erfassung der Lesekompetenz von Erstklässlern. Empirische Sonderpädagogik **3**(2), 121–146 (2011). http://nbn-resolving.de/urn:nbn:de:0111-opus-93201

29. Förster, N., Souvignier, E.: Curriculum-based measurement: Developing a computer-based assessment instrument for monitoring student reading progress on multiple indicators. Learn. Disabil. Contemp. J. **9**(2), 21–44 (2011)

30. Gebhardt, M., Diehl, K., Mühling, A.: Online-Lernverlaufsmessung für alle Schülerinnen und Schüler in inklusiven Klassen. Zeitschrift für Heilpädagogik **66**, 444–453 (2016)

31. Kuhn, J.-T., Holling, H.: Number sense or working memory? The effect of two computer-based trainings on mathematical skills in elementary school. Adv. Cognit. Psychol. **10**(2), 59–67 (2014). https://doi.org/10.5709/acp-0157-2

32. Salaschek, M., Souvignier, E.: Web-based progress monitoring in first grade mathematics. Front. Learn. Res. **2**, 53–69 (2013). https://doi.org/10.14786/flr.v1i2.5

33. Mühling, A., Gebhardt, M., Diehl, K.: Formative Diagnostik durch die Onlineplattform Levumi. Informatik Spektrum **40**(6), 556–561 (2017). https://doi.org/10.1007/s00287-017-1069-7

34. Jungjohann, J., Gegenfurtner, A., Gebhardt, M.: Systematisches Review von Lernverlaufsmessung im Bereich der frühen Leseflüssigkeit. Empirische Sonderpädagogik **10**(1), 100–118 (2018)

35. Jungjohann, J., Gebhardt, M., Diehl, K., Mühling, A.: Förderansätze im Lesen mit LEVUMI (2017). https://doi.org/10.17877/de290r-18042

36. Deno, S.L., Mirkin, P.K., Chiang, B.: Identifying a valid measure of reading. Except. Child. **49**(1), 36–45 (1982)

37. Dummer-Smoch, L., Hackethal, R.: Kieler Leseaufbau. Handbuch, 9th edn. Veris, Kiel (2016)

38. Gebhardt, M., Diehl, K., Mühling, A.: Lern-Verlaufs-Monitoring LEVUMI Lehrerhandbuch. Version 1.1. (2016). https://doi.org/10.17877/de290r-17792

39. Wright, B.D., Linacre, J.M.: Reasonable mean-square fit values. Rasch Meas. Trans. **8**(3), 370 (1994) https://www.rasch.org/rmt/rmt83b.htm

Mobile Online Courses for the Illiterate: The eVideo Approach

Yasmin Patzer[1]([⊠]), Johanna Lambertz[2], Björn Schulz[2], and Niels Pinkwart[1]

[1] Humboldt-University Berlin, Unter den Linden 6, 10099 Berlin, Germany
`patzer@informatik.hu-berlin.de`
`https://cses.informatik.hu-berlin.de/en/`
[2] Arbeit und Leben Berlin-Brandenburg (DGB/VHS),
Kapweg 4, 13405 Berlin, Germany
`http://www.berlin.arbeitundleben.de`

Abstract. More than half of Germany's functional illiterates are gainfully employed adults. This paper presents the eVideo approach that aims at people with poor basic education. The course "eVideo mobile - digital media in hospitality industry" is a game-based work-related eLearning course. It is based on an inclusive eLearning platform. Basic educational skills are addressed in workplace-related interactive videos and exercises on different competency levels. In a small pilot study users were observed while using the course and afterwards questioned in interviews.

Keywords: Mobile learning · Inclusive eLearning
Functional illitracy · Poor basic education

There are about 7.5 million functional illiterates in Germany [1]. More than half of them are gainfully employed adults. Therefore offers for this target group should deal with content, which is workspace related. There are already different existing national and international projects like [2–4] that are addressing this topic. The eVideo approach [5] is aiming at this as well, with game-based work-related eLearning courses that are targeting basic educational skills, including literacy and numeracy as well as media literacy. There is already some research on eLearning and inclusion [6] as well as on game-based training in basic education [7]. In the eVideo course the user interacts with colleagues in short video sequences, completes typical work tasks and thereby solves an underlying work-related adventure. The core idea of this format is a combination of realistic workplace-related videos and exercises on different competency levels. The course of events is guided and linear and also designed for "technical novices". Nevertheless some users might need additional support.

The novelty presented in this paper is a redesign of the eVideo technology so that the educational approach is retained while the system runs on a smartphone, thereby enabling time and space independent access. This redesign has been implemented in the context of the course "eVideo mobile - digital media in hospitality industry". The course is developed to be responsive and can be used

© The Author(s) 2018
K. Miesenberger and G. Kouroupetroglou (Eds.): ICCHP 2018, LNCS 10896, pp. 379–383, 2018.
https://doi.org/10.1007/978-3-319-94277-3_59

on both tablets and desktop computers, but follows a mobile first approach. Previous eVideo courses were developed for desktop computer usage only.

The development of the mobile eVideo system followed a design science research paradigm. Contrary to former eVideo courses, the new version is technically based on the LAYA platform - an inclusive eLearning platform [8]. Structure and design of the course should allow recognition for users, who already know other eVideos. For a target group with mostly low media literacy level, this eases orientation and navigation between the courses. The challenging aspect of this combination was to bring together an existing inclusive eLearning platform, with the eVideo course concept and script (that were not designed with inclusion in mind) and then make all that usable on smartphones and accessible for users with low media literacy levels. UI design and content had to be adapted to the small screen size, without a loss of the course characteristics. A challenging point was the adaptation of the exercises with their three difficulty levels. The highest level was the most challenging, as it is not only more difficult to solve, but also contains more text than level one and two. In iterative cycles, content and layout of each exercise were designed and tested. This also required the replacement of exercise types that were unsuitable for the target users on a small screen. For instance, one exercise that was planned as drag and drop of text elements from an email was changed into a marking exercise. Otherwise the exercise would have been overloaded and confusing. Exercise types that are used in this course are single- and multiple choice, clozes, drag and drop and marking exercises.

Universal Design for Learning (UDL) has been taken into account for the development of this course. There are different levels of support for users, which address different levels of poor literacy skills on the one hand and different types of learners on the other. For instance, all videos have subtitles and all texts in the course have an additional audio alternative (see Fig. 1: loud speaker icons on the left). There is also a dictionary available that includes all potentially difficult vocabulary and technical terms used in the exercises. Besides, motivating feedback and a help function are part of each exercise and the icons used throughout the course are consistent.

The Screenshot in Fig. 1 shows exercise 3. Below the progress bar is the "Anleitung" button, which opens the instruction text for the exercise. The instruction for each exercise is read out automatically the moment it is opened. Below the instruction button, there are three more buttons: the left button (icon: magnifier) opens information that is needed to solve the exercise, the middle one (icon: question mark) is a help button and the right one (icon: book) leads to the dictionary. For this exercise, the button with the magnifier icon has the text "Phishingmerkmale" (engl. phishing characteristics) and opens a list of typical characteristics of phishing mails. After having read and/or heard those the user is asked to mark three typical characteristics of phishing mails for the easiest level. For the other two complexity levels, the e-mail is more difficult and five (level 2) or seven (level 3) characteristics have to be marked. After solving the exercise, the users get immediate feedback on their performance. If they made

Fig. 1. Screenshot exercise 3

mistakes, they get exercise specific hints. After three failed trials, the correct solution is shown and the user can continue with the course.

Motivation plays an important role for this user group as many people with poor basic education have made negative experiences connected to learning. This is addressed by a novel gamification and adaptation concept, which adapts known principles like collecting badges and trophies or recommending changes in difficulty for an inclusive user group.

A small pilot study has been conducted with nine users, who were observed while using the system for at least 50 min. Afterwards, the users were interviewed about their experience. A problem-centered guided interview was chosen, as it allows a strong focus on users' perceptions and opinions. Users were asked about computer and smartphone usage, eLearning and gamification experiences. Five users had poor basic education, the other four had no impairments. This set of participants was chosen, to make sure that the needs and requirements of the main target group of the eVideo courses were met on the one hand. And on the other hand, experts for technical development and design were asked to give their opinion on the redesigned course. All participants liked the idea, content and structure of the course and pointed out that they could easily identify with the person addressed in the interactive videos. Especially the participants with poor basic education liked the combination of text and audio in the videos as well as in the exercises. Yet, some of the users without impairments thought it rather distracting, that the audio automatically started, as they were opening and reading an instruction text. Furthermore the feedback after each exercise was perceived as motivating and encouraging no matter if the exercise was solved correctly in the first trial or not.

The users' feedback in the pilot study lead to adaptations in the course. For instance the functionality of the audio buttons was changed, to allow pausing the audios. Furthermore some instructions were changed according to the feedback.

The course can be a starting point to address poor basic education problems of employees in the hospitality industry. It should be embedded in a blended-learning context to have the best possible effect. The novel mobile version allows users to work on the course on their own and independent of location (i.e., possibly also at work). In a next step studies with more heterogeneous users are necessary to ensure, that the course is as inclusive as it aims to be. Afterwards larger empirical studies with the course and a publicly accessible version are planned in order to investigate the system effects under real conditions.

References

1. Grotlüschen, A., Riekmann, W., Buddeberg, K.: Hauptergebnisse der leo. - Level-One Studie. In: Grotlüschen, A., Riekmann, W. (eds.) Funktionaler Analphabetismus in Deutschland - Ergebnisse der ersten leo. - Level-One Studie, pp. 15–53. Waxmann, Münster, New York, München, Berlin (2012)
2. lit.voc - Literacy and vocation (n.d.): European Workplace Literacy Profile (European Core Curriculum). http://www.grundbildung-und-beruf.info/et_dynamic/page_files/637_datei.pdf?1383242976. Accessed 24 Mar 2018
3. NDS: Tasmanian Disability Sector Language, Literacy and Numeracy Skills - Action Plan 2016–2017 (2016). https://www.nds.org.au/the-workplace-literacy-project. Accessed 24 Mar 2018
4. Klinkhammer, D., Schubarth, B., Schwarz, S., Spranger, T.M., Ungerer, J.: Wie wirkt Grundbildung im Betrieb? - Erste Ergebnisse einer Studie zur Kompetenzentwicklung. In: Sozialverband VdK Deutschland e.V. (ed.) Sozialrecht+Praxis, Vol. 9/17 (2017)
5. Schulz, B., Lambertz, J.: eVideo - ein digitales Lernangebot zur arbeitsplatzbezogenen Verbesserung von Grundkompetenzen. Wege der Erreichung einer lernungewohnten Zielgruppe. In: Magazin Erwachsenenbildung.at, vol. 30. Wien (2017)
6. Patzer, Y., Sell, J., Pinkwart, N.: Anforderungen und ein Rahmenkonzept für inklusive E-Learning Software. In: Lucke, U., Schwill, A., Zender, R. (eds.) GI Lecture Notes in Informatics - Tagungsband der 14. e-Learning Fachtagung Informatik (DeLFI), pp. 257–268. Bonn, Köllen Druck+Verlag GmbH (2016)
7. Malo, S., Neudorf, M., Wist, T.: Game-based Training in der Alphabetisierung. Entwicklung eines Lernspiels für die Grundbildung. MedienPädagogik: Zeitschrift für Theorie und Praxis der Medienbildung, vol. 15, pp. 1–15 (2009)
8. Patzer, Y., Pinkwart, N.: Inclusive E-Learning - towards an integrated system design. In: Cudd, P., De Witte, L. (eds.) Studies in Health Technology and Informatics, vol. 24. IOS Press (2017)

"Let's Play Catch Together": Full-Body Interaction to Encourage Collaboration Among Hearing-Impaired Children

Naoki Komiya[1(✉)], Mikihiro Tokuoka[1], Ryohei Egusa[2,3], Shigenori Inagaki[3], Hiroshi Mizoguchi[1], Miki Namatame[4], and Fusako Kusunoki[5]

[1] Tokyo University of Science, Yamazaki, Noda, Chiba, Japan
marimo3omiram@gmail.com, 7517641@ed.tus.ac.jp,
hm@rs.noda.tus.ac.jp
[2] Japan Society for the Promotion of Science, Chiyoda-ku, Tokyo, Japan
126d103d@stu.kobe-u.ac.jp
[3] Kobe University, Tsurukabuto, Nada, Kobe, Hyogo, Japan
inagakis@kobe-u.ac.jp
[4] Tsukuba University of Technology, Amakubo, Tsukuba, Ibaraki, Japan
miki@a.tsukuba-tech.ac.jp
[5] Tama Art University, Yarimizu, Hachioji, Tokyo, Japan
kusunoki@tamabi.ac.jp

Abstract. For hearing-impaired children, interaction with others is often suppressed due to their struggle to communicate vocally, which is the primary tool of communication for most children. This limits hearing-impaired children's opportunities to develop social skills. We have developed a prototype system that supports hearing-impaired children's acquisition of social skills. This system encourages collaborative play, using visual information and full-body interaction, with the aim of supporting the hearing-impaired child's acquisition of social skills. We evaluated this system for empathy, negative feelings, and behavioral involvement. The result of this evaluation suggests that this system provides opportunities for collaboration, supporting the hearing-impaired child's acquisition of social skills.

Keywords: Collaboration · Hearing-impaired children · Full-body interaction
Social skills · Kinect sensor

1 Introduction

For all children, acquiring social skills—skills that facilitate relationships with others—is important [1]. Social skills are cultivated through interaction with others [2]. Hearing-impaired children often suppress interaction with others because it is difficult for them to communicate vocally, which is the primary means of communication for most children. Thus, they have limited opportunities to acquire and develop social skills.

Studies have been conducted using a tablet and computer as tools to support hearing-impaired children's communications [3, 4]. For example, there are tablet

© Springer International Publishing AG, part of Springer Nature 2018
K. Miesenberger and G. Kouroupetroglou (Eds.): ICCHP 2018, LNCS 10896, pp. 384–387, 2018.
https://doi.org/10.1007/978-3-319-94277-3_60

applications which support linguistic communication [3], and computer-animated characters may be employed to visually support sign language education [4]. However, these are only educational tools, and one problem with their use is that it is not possible to provide opportunities for the users to actually communicate with others. This problem must be solved in order for hearing-impaired children to acquire social skills.

It is very important to cultivate nonverbal communication skills, such as visual information processing and the use of body language. Research has shown that as with all children, hearing-impaired children should be encouraged to acquire social skills through play [5]. Therefore, we have developed a prototype system that encourages collaborative play, using visual information and full-body interaction, with the aim of supporting the hearing-impaired child's acquisition of social skills. We expect that collaboration will encourage the acquisition of social skills in hearing-impaired children.

In this paper, we describe our prototype system and the evaluative experiment conducted using both the system and a follow-up questionnaire.

2 System

Our system is play-based. Using visual and physical interactions, the system supports hearing-impaired children as they acquire social skills.

Figure 1 shows the current system, which consists of a Kinect sensor, a control PC, and a projector. In this system, the motion of several people is simultaneously detected by the sensor, and objects are manipulated based on these motions. The program starts when three learners stand in front of the sensor. The system then displays the learners on the screen; at the same time, sparks fall randomly from the top of the screen. When the learners use their bodies and bring their hands close together, the sparks are extinguished. Figure 2 shows the flow of this system. As the fallen sparks disappear by means of collaboration, the visual cues help the learners realize that collaboration is key.

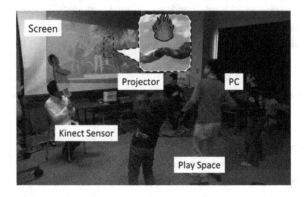

Fig. 1. System setup

(1) A spark falls   (2) Two learners bring   (3) The spark is extinguished
their hands together on the spark"

Fig. 2. System flow

3   Evaluation Experiment

Participants included 21 hearing-impaired children in years one through six of elementary school. The students participated in this system in groups of three, and then completed a 12-item paper questionnaire. The questionnaire sought responses regarding empathy (six questions), negative feelings (two questions), and behavioral involvement (four questions). For each item, the participants replied using a five-stage Likert scale.

Table 1 shows the responses from the participants about the questions. Participants' replies were classified into positive responses of "strongly agree," or "agree," and neutral or negative responses of "no strong opinion," "disagree," or "strongly disagree." We conducted an analysis of the differences between the number of positive, neutral, and negative replies for each item using a 1×2 Fisher's exact test.

Table 1. Questionnaire for examining this system

Items	SA	A	N	D	SD
1. My feelings became one with my friends who played with me*□*	15	6	0	0	0
2. I played according to the motion of my friends*□*	8	11	1	1	0
3. When I was playing, I felt that my friends adapted to my motion*□*	10	6	4	1	0
4. I felt that I was extinguishing the spark in collaboration with my friends*□*	18	2	0	0	1
5. I thought that my friends were watching my motion firmly*□	7	7	4	0	3
6. I firmly watched the motion of my friends*□*	10	6	3	1	1
7. I thought it would be nice if my friends failed[n.s.]	3	2	1	6	9
8. It was fun to play with three people*□*	20	1	0	0	0
9. I felt my friends were happy when I was happy*□*	13	5	1	2	0
10. I became happy that my friends seemed happy*□*	15	4	2	0	0
11. I felt that my friends who are playing together are good*□*	14	5	2	0	0
12. I thought enviously of my friends[n.s.]	4	7	6	1	3

$N = 21$, p *□*□ $< .01$, p *□ $< .05$, [n.s.]: not significant.
SA: Strongly agree A: Agree.
N: No strong option D: Disagree SD: Strongly disagree.

As a result of the questionnaire, it was found that active behavioral involvement and empathy among participants occurred. Figure 1 shows the experiment taking place.

The results suggest that this system could provide opportunities for collaboration to be used to support the acquisition of social skills for hearing-impaired children.

4   Conclusion and Future Work

In this paper, we analyzed our prototype system to support the hearing-impaired child's acquisition of social skills. We also evaluated the system using a questionnaire. The evaluation suggested that this system does provide opportunities to collaborate, supporting the hearing-impaired child's acquisition of social skills. In the future, we intend to further encourage collaboration by adding to the game objects that should not be extinguished or can only be extinguished through collaboration among three people.

Acknowledgements. This work was supported in part by Grants-in-Aid for Scientific Research (B).

References

1. Batten, G., Oakes, P.M., Alexander, T.: Factors associated with social interactions between deaf children and their hearing peers: a systematic literature review. J. Deaf Stud. Deaf Educ. **19**(3), 285–302 (2013)
2. Hoffman, M.F., Quittner, A.L., Cejas, I.: Comparisons of social competence in young children with and without hearing loss: A dynamic systems framework. J. Deaf Stud. Deaf Educ. **20** (2), 115–124 (2014)
3. Meinzen-Derr, J., Wiley, S., McAuley, R., Smith, L., Grether, S.: Technology-assisted language intervention for children who are deaf or hard-of-hearing; a pilot study of augmentative and alternative communication for enhancing language development. Disabil. Rehabil. Assistive Technol. **12**(8), 808–815 (2017)
4. Toro, J.A., McDonald, J.C., Wolfe, R.: Fostering better deaf/hearing communication through a novel mobile app for fingerspelling. In: Miesenberger, K., Fels, D., Archambault, D., Peňáz, P., Zagler, W. (eds.) ICCHP 2014, Part II. LNCS, vol. 8548, pp. 559–564. Springer, Cham (2014). https://doi.org/10.1007/978-3-319-08599-9_82
5. Smith, P.K., Hart, C.H.: Blackwell Handbook of Childhood Social Development. Blackwell Publishing, Malden (2002)

Motor and Mobility Disabilities: AT, HCI, Care

An Accessible Video Surveillance System for ALS People

Rim Somai$^{1(\boxtimes)}$, Meriem Riahi^2, and Faouzi Moussa^1

^{1} Faculty of Sciences of Tunis, Tunis El Manar University, Tunis, Tunisia
rimsomai@gmail.com, faouzimousssa@gmail.com
^{2} National Engineering School of Tunis, Tunis University, Tunis, Tunisia
meriem.riehi2013@gmail.com

Abstract. The commercialization of EEG devices (electroencephalography) increases the possibility of their use in different fields other than medicine. These brain computer interfaces (BCI) can be a solution for people who suffer from sever motor disabilities like amyotrophic lateral sclerosis (ALS). It offer them the ability to control a computer without any movement. In fact, the EEG signals are transformed into machine commands. Thus, it exist deferent BCI based systems. Our main objective here, is to offer a video surveillance system commanded by voluntary blinks. This voluntary blinks are detected from the EEG signals using our blink detection approach. It's based on unsupervised clustering of the blink regression parameters using the Gaussian mixture model (GMM). Based on the user tests of our system, it was well appreciated.

Keywords: BCI · EEG signals · GMM · Blinks
Polynomial regression · Video surveillance · UCD · ALS people

1 Introduction

People with special needs suffer from many difficulties related to their professional life integration which explains their high unemployment rates. These difficulties are explained by the lack of accessible solutions that take into account each kind of disability in the design process of any professional system. The ALS is known as a severe motor disability. Despite the human aspect related to this handicap, there is a lack of accessible solutions giving the possibility to ALS persons to integrate professional life. However, the Brain Computer Interfaces (BCI) could be considered as a solution for ALS people. The BCI is based on the brain signals essentially EEG signals to communicate and to control computer systems. In their survey paper, Takabi & al. surveyed some BCI available applications running in different systems and platforms which called them BCI App stores. This applications fall under numerous category like education, entertainment, gaming, meditation, relaxation training, wellness, marketing, BCI research tools, and developer's etc. [1]. Despite the big number of BCI based application and systems, there is a lack of dedicated professional BCI systems. A BCI system

© Springer International Publishing AG, part of Springer Nature 2018
K. Miesenberger and G. Kouroupetroglou (Eds.): ICCHP 2018, LNCS 10896, pp. 391–394, 2018.
https://doi.org/10.1007/978-3-319-94277-3_61

is composed of signal acquisition, signal pre-processing (the filtering), signal processing including feature extraction and translation algorithm and the graphic human interfaces [2]. The EEG signal acquisition constitutes the first step of a BCI based system. However, during the last ten years, the EEG acquisition process depended on expensive materials and on experimented users during the installation phase. Nowadays, thanks to the emergence of the new non invasive EEG headbands, BCI fields is more accessible. In effective different BCI based systems variants, the training phase (learn to control of specific EEG features) is an essential factor of system control success. In addition, the work of Amiri & al. establish a general comparison of different BCI approaches such as the P300, the slow cortical potentials (SCP), the event related desynchronization/synchronization (ERD/ERS) and the steady state visual evoke potentials (SSVEP) based BCI system, they show that the training phase can takes minutes, hours or even days [3]. The blink based BCI system is known as a simple and a powerful method that enables to command machines without requiring a long training period. In other words, ALS users can command and control a BCI system only by the power of voluntary blinks. Ma & al. proposed a BCI system that controls a multi-functional humanoid robot and four mobile robots. This hybrid BCI system used both of the Electro-oculography (EOG) i.e. eye movements and the EEG signals [4]. We propose a BCI system based on only blinks which can be used by ALS people. It's a video surveillance system. The second and third steps of a BCI system includes signal processing and translation steps known also by the BCI machine learning. The blink detection methods was subject of many research, Ochoa surveyed four most known methods to detect blinks in the EEG signals: The Blind Source Separation (BSS) method, the classical rejection or removal method, the bandpass FIR filters and the neural networks [5]. On our side, our approach was based on unsupervised clustering of the blink regression parameters using the Gaussian mixture model (GMM). It was the subject of another work. The main idea was to apply GMM clustering on blink curve parameters which are approximated by polynomial regression. After the automatic segmentation process, a prediction phase aims to classify the curve approximated parameters related to each of the unknown EEG segments. Concerning the GUIs design, the Ubiquitous computer science has given a new way of interaction. It has the ability to adapt its operation to the needs of users to increase their usability and efficiency. For the BCI system case, Klau & al shows that the famous User Centered Design (UCD) framework can be applied to the BCI systems [6]. Thus, a GUI based BCI can be evaluated by the metrics of usability: effectiveness, efficiency and satisfaction.

2   The Proposed System

We propose here a blink based video surveillance system, the architecture is shown in the Fig. 1. Like any classic BCI system, our system is composed firstly by a data acquisition phase which was done using the $Muse^1$, a low cost solution (249.00\$ USD) which integrate four channels: A1, A2, Fp1 and Fp2 (7 sensors).

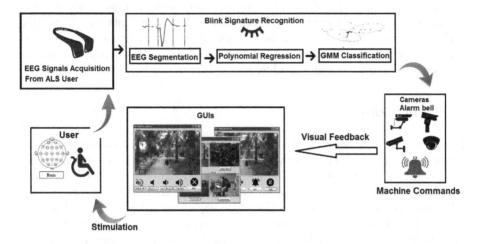

Fig. 1. The Muse based system control

Our contribution was in the modeling of specific GUIs. We present a case of a personalized stimulus for an event related potential (ERP) EEG based BCI, it's a blink based system of video surveillance. We propose a blink based paradigm that simulate the tabulation or moving cursor and the click or selection. One blink permit to navigate between interface elements, and two blinks allows to choose or to select the current element. We have developed a GUIs prototype based on the ERP paradigm. The first interface include four videos, each video is subtitled by a text button with gray background and black text (contrast about 90%). One blink permit to navigate between interface elements (the text of the current item is bold) and two blinks allows to choose or to select the current element. When one "option video" button is selected the user can pass to the related interface. The option interface is composed by the video, a return button and three category camera option: Sound, Zoom and Alarm. Five users accepted to test our detection system. Our detection method can detect any blink based on its curve, so the user doesn't need a training period. Interviewees were asked about the usefulness of the video surveillance system commanded by blinks, the usability of the blink to navigate between items and to select action, the GUIs pertinence and ergonomic: if they appreciate the disposition and chosen colors of the items of the window, the use of the icons with each text button. For the performance evaluation, the first metric of the UCD framework is the effectiveness, it means the possibility of successful control BCI system, it is expressed in percentage of correct responses [6]. In our case, the successful of the blink detection task can measure the effectiveness. Our system of blink detection was

---

^{1} http://www.choosemuse.com/.

tested and provided about 0.9310 as a recognition accuracy score. So, A system controlled by blink based paradigm is feasible. For the satisfaction metric, users were asked about the usefulness of the video surveillance system commanded by blinks, the usability of the blink to navigate between items and to select action, the GUIs pertinence and ergonomic: if they appreciate the disposition and chosen colors of the items of the window, the use of the icons with each text button. Roughly speaking, the users appreciated our video surveillance system and found it useful in their daily life.

3 Conclusion

In this paper, we propose a blink based system to control a video surveillance application. The machine learning phase consist on the automatic blink signature recolonization of any user from its first use. Then the blink are transformed to commands including the navigation and selection GUIs items. Our designed GUIs was specified to satisfy well the ALS people and followed the guidelines of the UCD framework. We obtained encouraging results following different metrics and the principal aim to integrate ALS people in the professional life was done through our system.

References

1. Takabi, H., Bhalotiya, A., Alohaly, M.: Brain computer interface (BCI) applications: privacy threats and countermeasures. In: 2016 IEEE 2nd International Conference on Collaboration and Internet Computing (CIC), 102–111. IEEE (2016)
2. Wolpaw, J.R., Birbaumer, N., McFarland, D.J., Pfurtscheller, G., Vaughan, T.M.: Brain-computer interfaces for communication and control. Clin. Neurophysiol. 113(6), 767–791 (2002)
3. Amiri, S., Fazel-Rezai, R., Asadpour, V.: A review of hybrid brain-computer interface systems. Adv. Hum.-Comput. Interact. 2013, 1 (2013)
4. Ma, J., Zhang, Y., Cichocki, A., Matsuno, F.: A novel EOG/EEG hybrid human-machine interface adopting eye movements and ERPs: application to robot control. IEEE Trans. Biomed. Eng. 62(3), 876–889 (2015)
5. Ochoa, J.B.: EEG signal classification for brain computer interface applications. Ecole Polytechnique Federale de Lausanne 7, 1–72 (2002)
6. Kübler, A., Holz, E.M., Riccio, A., Zickler, C., Kaufmann, T., Kleih, S.C., Staiger-Sälzer, P., Desideri, L., Hoogerwerf, E.J., Mattia, D.: The user-centered design as novel perspective for evaluating the usability of BCI-controlled applications. PLoS One 9(12), e112392 (2014)

Design of a Low-Cost Exoskeleton for Hand Tele-Rehabilitation After Stroke

Riccardo Candeo[1], Mauro Rossini[2], Beatrice Aruanno[1],
and Mario Covarrubias[1(✉)]

[1] Politecnico di Milano, Dipartimento di Meccanica, Milano, Italy
mario.covarrubias@polimi.it
[2] Valduce Hospital, Villa Beretta, Rehabilitation Centre, Costa Masnaga, Italy

Abstract. The impairment of finger movements after a stroke results in a significant deficit in hands everyday performances. To face this kind of problems different rehabilitation techniques have been developed, nevertheless, they require the presence of a therapist to be executed. To overcome this issue have been designed several apparatuses that allow the patient to perform the training by itself. Thus, an easy to use and effective device is needed to provide the right training and complete the rehabilitation techniques in the best way. In this paper, a review of state of the art in this field is provided, along with an introduction to the problems caused by a stroke and the consequences for the mobility of the hand. Then follows a complete review of the low cost home based exoskeleton project design. The objective is to design a device that can be used at home, with a lightweight and affordable structure and a fast mounting system. For implementing all these features, many aspects have been analysed, starting from the rehabilitation requirements and the ergonomic issues. This device should be able to reproduce the training movements on an injured hand without the need for assistance by an external tutor.

Keywords: Hand rehabilitation · Post stroke · Tele-Rehabilitation

1 Introduction

Recent researches showed that the method of using mechatronic devices and virtual reality in rehabilitation training is feasible and effective. Patients that undergo a robot-treatment of the upper limbs experience a significantly decreased motor impairment in the muscle groups exercised explicitly by the robotic actuation [3]. In this rehabilitation, the movement induced by the actuated support consists in the primary actions of the affected area; regarding the hands, these actuations are simple open-close movement actuated on the fingers to make the patient re-learn those activities that he lost because of the disease. These moves aim to re-route the signal directed to the hand to another area of the human brain, that is why this is a proper re-learning of the movement because it

© Springer International Publishing AG, part of Springer Nature 2018
K. Miesenberger and G. Kouroupetroglou (Eds.): ICCHP 2018, LNCS 10896, pp. 395–398, 2018.
https://doi.org/10.1007/978-3-319-94277-3_62

is like the first time the patient is experiencing it. Rehabilitation techniques may be divided into two different macro-regions: the passive rehabilitation and the active rehabilitation. In the passive rehabilitation, the movement of the affected regions is provided by an external source; this could be provided by a medic, or by a device or by the patient itself (In this case the rehabilitation is provided by muscles that usually do not incur in the actual movement). This kind of recovery is fundamental in the after-stroke phase as muscles are stiff and not controllable. On the other hand, in the active rehabilitation, the region affected is moved by the muscles that are usually involved in the normal movement.

2   Architecture

The software chosen to control the Arduino Board is the Arduino IDE [1], which implements functions using the C++ programming language. It allows a natural programming flexibility and fast debugging procedure. The necessity to develop an easy to use device, however, require a more user-oriented interface. That is why, although the control software used is Arduino, another software has been used to interface with the patient. This software is the game engine Unity?. It is a cross-platform game engine which is primarily used for the development of video games for computer, consoles, and mobile. The Unity version that will run the software is the 5.0.1 due to the necessity for the web interface. The web interface is TelbiosConnect? [2], and the user will interface with it through a personal area defined by its username and password.

Figure 1 shows the system components.

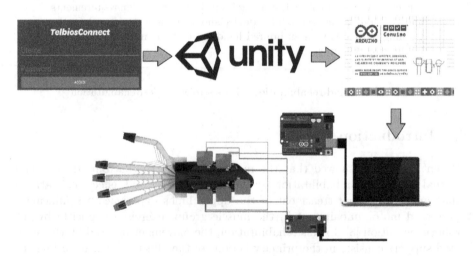

Fig. 1. Logic path of information within the whole system.

3   Results

The assessment of the primary functionalities consists of a test performed on healthy people to guarantee that the purposes that do not depend on rehabilitation have been reached. The procedure followed during the tests is the following:

1. Description of the device that is going to be tested, what is its purpose and how it is expected to perform.
2. Description of the exercises that are going to be executed.
3. Wearing the device, the instructions about how to set it into position are given step-by-step.
4. Start of the mechanical actuation, the three exercises are performed.
5. Removal of the device.
6. First comments about the device.
7. Administration of the questionnaire.

Figure 2 shows the results for Ease of use issues.

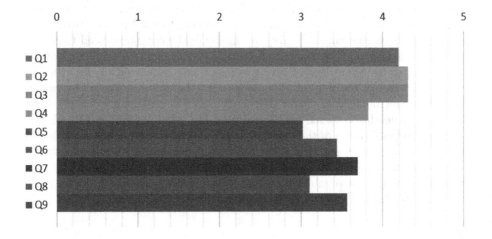

Fig. 2. Ease of use issues for the system

As can be seen from the histogram, the overall satisfaction about the ease of use of the device is pretty good. The lowest grades are the ones regarding the goodness of the movement that needs some improvements to gain a better fluidity. The last request, the ones bout the ability for the user to set the device in motion without any help, are also underperforming. However, the result from this point of view is reasonable under the aspect of simplicity of use.

Figure 3 shows the results for Tele-Rehabilitation issues.

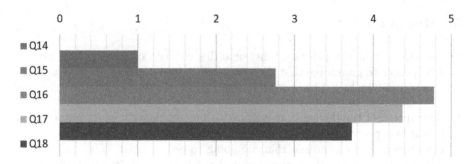

Fig. 3. Tele-Rehabilitation

4 Conclusion

The paper has been presented a system which is able to help people affected by hand impairment because of a stroke. An effective system could help millions of patients to improve their life condition and to overcome the difficulties that they, unfortunately, find in their path. The development started with research in the field which allowed to acquire the knowledge needed about strokes and their effect on the human body. Experts in the field were interviewed to gather direct information that has been useful during the design process. The solution found is an exoskeleton divided into two parts, one connected to the arm and one to the hand of the patient. The support of the arm has five servo motors that allow controlling each finger independently. The real innovation has been the use of a flexible material for 3D printing the hand support which allowed both the personalization of the device (thank to 3D printing) and a reduction in volume, complexity, weight (thank the flexible filament). The result of the design process was assessed by means of tests on healthy subjects and interview with experts in the field of rehabilitation and biomedical engineering. The outcome provides some hints for future developments.

References

1. Arduino-IDE: Arduino 1.8.1, March 2018. https://www.arduino.cc/en/Main/Software
2. Telbios-Connect: Telbios-connect, March 2018. http://www.telbios.com/telbiosconnect/
3. Volpe, B., Krebs, H.I., Hogan, N., Edelstein OTR, L., Diels, C., Aisen, M.: A novel approach to stroke rehabilitation robot-aided sensorimotor stimulation. Neurology **54**, 1938–1944 (2000)

Use of DUCK Keyboard for a Daily Use

Mathieu Raynal[✉] and Philippe Roussille

University of Toulouse – IRIT, Toulouse, France
{mathieu.raynal,philippe.roussille}@irit.fr

Abstract. This article presents the new version of the DUCK keyboard. To evaluate this new prototype, we chose an evaluation with novice users, in two steps: A first step with a copy of sentences. Then we let them get familiarized with our system for 15 days. Finally, we re-evaluate their performance after this phase of familiarization. Results shows that, after a learning phase, the participants significantly improve their input performance with the DUCK keyboard. Text input speed and accuracy have been improved.

Keywords: Soft keyboard · Touch screen · Smartphone
Visually impaired users

1 Introduction

Since the arrival of smartphones, several text entry systems have been proposed to allow blind people to enter text on these devices. Two major categories of systems are opposed: on the one hand, systems based on the Braille alphabet; on the other hand, standard soft keyboards adapted to non-visual interaction. The first Braille input systems were very time-consuming because they required a typing sequence to enter each point corresponding to the Braille character to be typed [1]. With touch screens and the use of multitouch interaction, the input of a character could be improved [2, 3]. However, these systems are still accessible to a small number of blind people, because only 10% of them know the Braille alphabet.

The most common input system used by blind people is the standard soft keyboard augmented by a screen reader (well-known systems are Talkback and Voiceover). However, these systems have a major drawback: the user must accurately enter each character. To solve this problem, we have proposed the DUCK keyboard [4]. This keyboard allows to enter different characters of the word imprecisely, then to select the word in a list of deduced words. Our first evaluation showed two main problems [5]: on the one hand, the input of short words; and on the other hand, navigation and selection in the word list. To overcome these two problems, we have proposed different solutions [6, 7].

This paper presents the new keyboard that integrates the selected solutions. Here, we have chosen for this new experiment to evaluate the performance of our system with novice users. Then we let them get familiarized with our system for 15 days. Finally, we re-evaluate their performance after this phase of familiarization. After presenting the

© Springer International Publishing AG, part of Springer Nature 2018
K. Miesenberger and G. Kouroupetroglou (Eds.): ICCHP 2018, LNCS 10896, pp. 399–406, 2018.
https://doi.org/10.1007/978-3-319-94277-3_63

improvements made to our system compared to the first study, we will present the results obtained with this new system during the two sessions.

2 Improvements to the DUCK Keyboard

Generally, the input of a word with the DUCK keyboard remains the same as initially [4]: the user enters the first character of his word precisely. Then, he continues with approximate strokes and validates the desired word using the list of deducted words.

2.1 Short Word Mode

For words of four letters or less, the user can enter the word with the short word mode: the user enters the first character of the word in the same way as for other words. Then he presses the smartphone screen with two fingers to access the list of short words associated with that first character. The list of short words can contain a maximum of 8 words. To establish the list associated with each character, we chose the 8 words most frequently used in the language. These lists are therefore static. Finally, the proposed interactions for using these lists of short words are the same as for the deduced word lists.

2.2 Interaction with Lists

For all the lists used in the DUCK keyboard (word deduction lists or static short word lists), we have taken the choice presented in [6]: the list presents the words in a linear layout. Selecting a word is done by sliding the finger over it. Lifting the finger off the screen validates the selection. Finally the voice synthesis pronounces the word that is flown over by the user's finger, and announces the selected word at the time of the final validation.

3 Protocol

We recruited 4 visually impaired users (2 women and 2 men, aged 45 years on average), for this study. These four participants work or are students in a Specialized Education Center for the Visually Impaired. Participants are regular users of smartphones and daily use an onscreen keyboard along with VoiceOver. None of the participants had participated in the first experiment, nor in the study of lists or short words.

For this experiment, participants used a Samsung Galaxy SIII, with the same features and software tools used in the first experiment. Two keyboards were presented to the participants: on the one hand, the DUCK keyboard with improvements presented previously; and on the other hand, the VODKA keyboard as it was already used during the first experiment. VODKA is a VoiceOver like keyboard that proposes the same interactions. The characters layout is the same on both keyboards.

For each exercise, participants would type a set of sentences as quickly as possible. Before starting the first session, each participant could test the system. During this period the participant learns to use the keyboard, to type one or more words, then one or more sentences, according to his wish. When the participant felt comfortable with the system, he had to enter 20 sentences. The exercise stopped after 20 min even though he had not finished typing the 20 sentences. For each sentence to be entered, the sentence was read to the participant by speech synthesis. Then, the participant had to type this sentence as quickly as possible. The user could listen again to the sentence to copy, if he wished.

After each word entered, the system checked whether the word entered corresponded to the requested word. If the word was wrong, the user had to re-enter the word until it was correct. In order to simplify the task for the participants, we did not ask them to enter exactly each word: a "homophonic" tolerance of each word was enough (for example, "sear" would be accepted even if "seer" was requested).

In order to evaluate the evolution of the participants' performances during the first uses of the DUCK keyboard, we conducted two evaluation sessions. The two sessions were separated by two weeks. A session consisted of two exercises: one with each system to be tested. Two participants started with the DUCK keyboard before performing the second with the VODKA keyboard. The other two participants did the exercises in reverse order. After the first session, the DUCK keyboard was left for the participants for two weeks. We asked them to daily use the keyboard, to make a written production corresponding to a few lines of text, like an email.

During each exercise, we recorded all the actions performed by the user (presses, releases, and movements of the finger on the screen), the instructions given by the system to the user (instructions of the exercise, sentences to be copied) as well as the lists of words presented to the user during the entry (those produced by the deduction system as well as those used for short words).

4   Results

We detail here the results obtained during the two sessions of our study. We performed Wilcoxon tests as well as Friedmann analyzes to support our results if they do not follow a normal distribution. The significance level (α) of the statistical tests was always set to 0.05.

4.1   Evolution of Text Input Speed During the Two Sessions

First, we looked at the results of the two sessions of the study. At first, we chose to consider only the first session, without training, then the second session, after the user training phase for two weeks.

The graph shown in Fig. 1 gives the text input speeds per session and keyboard. The average text input speed of each keyboard are for the first session of 0.71 characters per second (cps) for DUCK against 0.56 cps for VODKA. The Wilcoxon test showed that these speeds were significantly different ($W = 1113$, $p = 0.0478$). At the second session, the participants achieved a text input speed of 1.1 cps with the DUCK keyboard, whereas they only entered an average of 0.61 cps with the VODKA keyboard. The Wilcoxon test showed that these speeds were significantly different ($W = 859$, $p = 0.0364$).

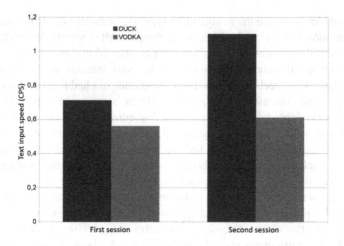

Fig. 1. Text entry speed of both keyboards during the first and second sessions

On the other hand, we can see an evolution of the input speed with the DUCK system between the two sessions. There was a significant difference between the two sessions (W = 649, p = 0.024).

4.2   Text Entry Speed According to Word Length

Figures 2 and 3 show the mean text input speed according to the length of the word to be typed, respectively in the first and second sessions.

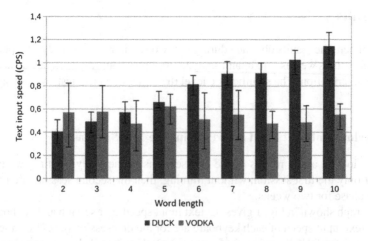

Fig. 2. Text input speed according to the word length during the first session

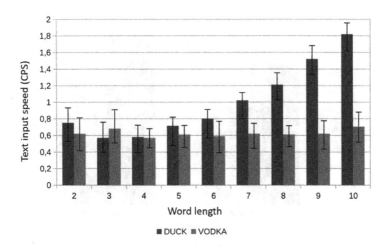

Fig. 3. Text input speed according to the word length during the second session

In Fig. 2, we can see that DUCK is more efficient than VODKA for words of four or more characters. Moreover, the text input speed is higher for the long words than in the first experiment [5]. By analyzing the input time with DUCK, we can see that the time required to validate a word in the deduction list is only 2.85 s on average, whereas it was 3.6 s in the first study. This confirms that the changes made to the interaction with the list are beneficial to the validation time, and thus allow the user to enter the words faster.

After the learning phase, during the second session, participants improved their text input speed with the DUCK system, especially for short words (see Fig. 3). There are no significant differences in entering short words between the two keyboards. This can be explained by the good use, by the participants, of the list of short words. Moreover, the decomposition of the input time, with the DUCK keyboard, between the selection phase and the validation phase shows that the users validate the word in 2.07 s during the validation phase. Thus, with the learning phase, participants reduced the time needed to validate a word in the deduction list.

4.3 Success Rate

To compare the accuracy of each keyboard, it was necessary to introduce the notion of "correct word". A word is defined as a correct word if, and only if, the word phonetically corresponds to the word requested in the sentence but exists as a real word.

To be able to compare the two keyboards, we calculated a success rate by the formula:

$$Success\ Rate = \frac{\text{Number of correct words}}{\text{Number of words entered}}$$

For both keyboards, we obtain the results presented in Fig. 4: for the first session, DUCK has a success rate of 75% against 52% for VODKA. In the second session, the success rate is 91% for DUCK against 77% for VODKA.

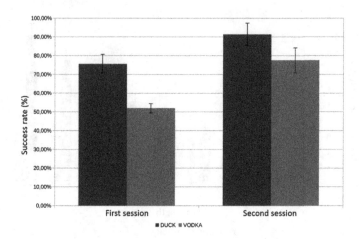

Fig. 4. Success rate of both keyboards during the first and second sessions

A Wilcoxon test indicates that there is a significant difference between precision with the DUCK keyboard and with the VODKA keyboard in the first session (W = 1070, p = 0.036), as well as for the second session (W = 2069, p = 0.032). In addition, we can also observe that for both systems, the success rate increases between the two sessions. This observation is confirmed by Wilcoxon tests which confirm a significant difference between the two sessions and for both keyboards (W = 1208, p = 0.0487 for DUCK and W = 276, p = 0.0124 for VODKA).

Given these observations, we can conclude that DUCK is more efficient than VODKA in word correction: the number of correctly entered words is greater with DUCK than with VODKA.

4.4 Use of Short Words

Finally, we were interested in using the short word mode throughout the experiment. Our first hypothesis was to consider that the activation of the short word mode allowed the user to accelerate his input.

In order to evaluate the impact of using the short word mode, we counted the number of uses of the short word mode. We split into two use cases: (a) the "useful" use, when the user must really type a short word; (b) the "useless" use, when the user activates this mode by mistake. In this case, we do not distinguish between cases when the user has consciously activated the short word mode by mistake (The user thinks to find the word in the list, but this one is not there) and when it was an involuntary movement on the screen.

To evaluate the use of the short word mode, we calculated the rate of useful use (RUF) of the short word mode by the formula:

$$RUF = \frac{number\ of\ useful\ uses\ of\ short\ word\ mode}{number\ of\ short\ words}$$

"Number of useful uses of short word mode" is the number of times the user uses this mode correctly, and "Number of short words" is the number of times the user should have used this mode.

Similarly, we also calculated the rate of useless use (RUL) of the short word mode by:

$$RUL = \frac{number\ of\ useless\ uses\ of\ short\ word\ mode}{number\ of\ words}$$

"Number of useless uses of short word mode" is the number of times the user uses this mode by mistake, and "Number of long words" is the number of words that are not in the short word lists.

We present the results we obtained in Fig. 5. The RUF is 43% for the first session, and 68% for the second session. A Wilcoxon test confirms the significant difference between the two sessions of the useful use of the short word mode ($W = 511, p = 0.036$). This is explained by a better knowledge by the users of the contents of the lists of short words during the second session.

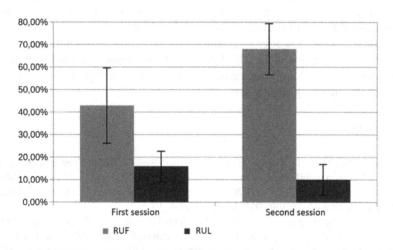

Fig. 5. Use of short word mode during the first and second sessions

Regarding the RUL, participants activated by mistake the short word mode for 16% of the words in the first session and 10% in the second session. However, this decrease is not significant ($W = 421, p = 0.280$). The participants explained at the end of the second session that the useless use of the short word mode were largely due to a problem of interaction, most often due to an uncontrolled finger movement.

5   Discussion

The aim of this experiment was to evaluate the DUCK keyboard integrating the improvements made to the use of short words and the validation of words in the deduction lists. We chose to carry out this experimentation in two sessions separated by a learning phase.

This allowed us to see the results of novice users, and then once they took control of the system for two weeks.

Overall, we can see that improvements to DUCK have been beneficial. Indeed, the system is more efficient than VODKA from the first use. The participants thus obtained a significantly higher input speed with DUCK than with VODKA in the first session. Similarly, they made fewer text entry errors with DUCK.

Through this evaluation, we were able to observe the improvement of the performances concerning the validation of the word in the deduction list. Indeed, during the first evaluation, this time was 3.5 s to validate a word [5]. In the first session of this experiment, the mean validation time was only 2.85 s to validate a word in the deduction list. This time was further reduced during the second session to 2.07 s. This reduction in validation time has made it possible to increase the user input speed with DUCK. Participants thus have higher input speeds with DUCK for words of 4 or more characters in the first session, compared to 6 characters or more in the first experiment.

In addition, the participants also assimilated the short word mode. If they only used it in 40% of the cases during the first session, they used it in two-thirds of the cases during the second session. This good use of the short word mode allows users to enter faster with DUCK, for all words regardless of their length.

Finally, we can see that after a learning phase, the participants significantly improve their input performance with the DUCK keyboard. Text input speed and accuracy have been improved. With a longer use, participants thus find advantages in using this system rather than the ones they already use.

References

1. Oliveira, J., Guerreiro, T., Nicolau, H., Jorge, J., Gonçalves, D.: BrailleType: unleashing braille over touch screen mobile phones. In: Campos, P., Graham, N., Jorge, J., Nunes, N., Palanque, P., Winckler, M. (eds.) INTERACT 2011. LNCS, vol. 6946, pp. 100–107. Springer, Heidelberg (2011). https://doi.org/10.1007/978-3-642-23774-4_10
2. Mascetti, S., Bernareggi, C., Belotti, M.: TypeInBraille: quick eyes-free typing on smartphones. In: Miesenberger, K., Karshmer, A., Penaz, P., Zagler, W. (eds.) ICCHP 2012. LNCS, vol. 7383, pp. 615–622. Springer, Heidelberg (2012). https://doi.org/10.1007/978-3-642-31534-3_90
3. Nicolau, H., Montague, K., Guerreiro, T., Guerreiro, J., Hanson, V.L.: B#: chord-based correction for multitouch braille input. In: CHI 2014, pp. 1705–1708. ACM (2014)
4. Roussille, P., Raynal, M., Kammoun, S., Dubois, E., Jouffrais, C.: DUCK: a deDUCtive keyboard. In: 3rd International Workshop on Mobile Accessibility, pp. 1–5 (2013)
5. Raynal, M., Roussille, P.: DUCK: A DeDUCtive soft keyboard for visually impaired users. Stud. Health Technol. Inf. **242**, 902–909 (2017)
6. Roussille, P., Raynal, M.: LOVIE: a word list optimized for visually impaired UsErs on smartphones. In: Antona, M., Stephanidis, C. (eds.) UAHCI 2016. LNCS, vol. 9738, pp. 185–197. Springer, Cham (2016). https://doi.org/10.1007/978-3-319-40244-4_18
7. Roussille, P., Raynal, M.: SWIFT: a short word solution for fast typing. In: Miesenberger, K., Bühler, C., Penaz, P. (eds.) ICCHP 2016. LNCS, vol. 9759, pp. 464–471. Springer, Cham (2016). https://doi.org/10.1007/978-3-319-41267-2_65

Gaze Control Toolbar: A Low-Cost Software Solution for Gaze Based Computer Interaction

David Rozado[(✉)]

Otago Polytechnic, Forth Street, Dunedin, New Zealand
david.rozado@op.ac.nz

Abstract. Gaze reactive accessibility software for computer control permits individuals with moderate or severe dysfunction of motor function to operate a computer exclusively via gaze. Unfortunately, the small size of the severely motor impaired community and the large fixed costs of developing accessibility software results in commercial gaze control software solutions being markedly expensive, with price ranges between 1,000–10,000 USD. The high price tag renders gaze control accessibility software unaffordable for a large proportion of the motor impaired population. Historically, open source gaze control software has been lacking. The few existing applications do not match the effectiveness, feature richness and software robustness of commercial solutions. In this work, an open source accessibility application for gaze control is presented that permits complete and customizable desktop computer control using only gaze interaction. The software depends merely on a low cost eye tracker geared by its manufacturer towards the gamers market (cost less than $200 per unit). Thereby, motor impaired users with limited financial means can benefit from gaze control as a means to interact with computers. The open source nature of the software also makes it possible for software developers and accessibility researchers to extend the application by adding innovative interaction methods and features stemming from accessibility research. The motivation for the creation and distribution of this software is grounded on the belief that accessibility research bears a responsibility in furthering a culture of dissemination of open source and/or low-cost assistive technologies that make the digital world accessible to all.

Keywords: Accessibility · Gaze interaction · Motor impairment
Open source assistive technologies

1 Introduction

Interaction with computers using standard input hardware such as the mouse and the keyboard is challenging or unfeasible for people with upper limb motor impairment [1]. Accessibility software, such as gaze reactive applications for computer control, strive to provide motor impaired subjects with a mechanism for interacting with electronic devices, thereby, providing greater independence and quality of life in digitally intensive societies. Unfortunately, the performance of gaze control software in terms of the information transfer rate between the human and the computer is often sub-optimal since it

© Springer International Publishing AG, part of Springer Nature 2018
K. Miesenberger and G. Kouroupetroglou (Eds.): ICCHP 2018, LNCS 10896, pp. 407–414, 2018.
https://doi.org/10.1007/978-3-319-94277-3_64

lags behind the accuracy and latency metrics achieved by standard keyboard and mouse interaction [2], albeit the gap might be narrowing [3].

An important barrier for existing gaze control software applications being widely adopted by their target audience is the cost of such technologies [4], which renders them unaffordable for a significant fraction of the motor impaired population. The lack of access to assistive technologies by those in need worldwide has been estimated as 9 out of 10, mainly due to the high price tag associated with such products [5]. This has circumscribed the usage of assistive technologies in general and gaze control accessibility software in particular to users of high socioeconomic status or to parts of the developed world where social institutions that cater to the needs of the disabled population bear the cost of accessibility products acquisition. This situation leaves a large chunk of potential beneficiaries of gaze control, those users with low socioeconomic status, underserved by existing commercial solutions [6].

The reason for the high cost of gaze control software is the small size of the target market with its subsequent modest potential for profit [7]. This creates an unfortunate economic conundrum in which the high fixed costs required for creating a gaze control software product can only be distributed among a small number of customers, which irresolubly results in high unit costs. To compound the effect of the high-priced tag associated with assistive technology products, potential users of accessibility software often have low levels of disposable income [7] due to their inability to participate in the workforce. This has led some authors to promote do-it-yourself assistive technologies solutions [8] which while perhaps appropriate in some cases are clearly sub-optimal in most scenarios since the majority of potential beneficiaries of assistive technologies lack the skills, means and know-how to create effective assistive technologies solutions for themselves.

The United Nations Convention on the Rights of Persons with Disabilities (UNCRPD) has repeatedly called for the need to expand access to assistive technologies [9] which unfortunately still remains a distant goal. Some authors have suggested that educational institutions and in particular Information Technology/Computer Science schools bear a responsibility in furthering a culture of research into low-cost assistive technologies and accessibility software [6] in order to democratize its usage. The author agrees with this view and he extends the responsibility of contributing to disseminate assistive technologies to the accessibility software research community itself. Hence, the motivation for this work.

Existing commercial accessibility software that provides control of a desktop computer via gaze interaction include, among others, *myGaze Power* and *Tobii Windows Control*. The author has found the *Tobii Windows Control* software package to be a very efficient accessibility tool for comprehensive control of a desktop computer via gaze. The reason *Tobii Windows Control* outperforms alternative commercial accessibility software is due to its offering of advanced gaze interaction techniques, such as dynamic zooming for fine grained target acquisition, robust and feature rich wrapper software, interface customizability and state-of-the-art gaze estimation accuracy (0.5° of visual angle at 60 cm from the screen for most users). Unfortunately, the *Tobii Windows Control* software commands a high price tag of around $1000 and it requires an eye tracker hardware device that costs an additional $2000, bringing the total price of this accessibility solution to over $3000, not counting additional expenses such as mechanical switches, mounting frames or advanced communication software (such as *Tobii Communicator*).

To Tobii's credit, the company has tried to create an entry-level eye control software, *Gaze Point*, that is free to download and that in their own words "opens the world of gaze interaction to everyone". The software however only permits the control of the mouse cursor by direct mapping of gaze estimation coordinates and the generation of single mouse clicks by dwelling the gaze over a target beyond a time threshold. The software does not support complex interaction tasks such as drag-and-drop, gaze based scrolling or the ability to type text through an on-screen gaze reactive keyboard with word prediction capabilities. The only available gaze interaction technique: gaze dwell time selection is clearly suboptimal in comparison with the dynamic zooming feature of *Tobii Windows Control*. For full computer access, Tobii still recommends, and most accessibility practitioners would agree, their commercial comprehensive software: *Tobii Windows Control*. In addition, even Tobii's free software, *Gaze Point*, still requires the purchase of an expensive gaze tracker which undermines the company good intentions of opening gaze interaction to everyone.

In this manuscript, an open source accessibility software solution is introduced that affords complete computer control using only gaze and which offers state-of-the-art interaction techniques rather than mere mapping of a gaze estimation vector to cursor coordinates. While the author acknowledges that commercial gaze accessibility software solutions are often quite effective in allowing efficient computer control, their biggest drawback is their cost, which renders them unaffordable for users with low levels of disposable income. Our target audience, users with severe motor impairment and low socio-economic status have been traditionally underserved by existing commercial products due to unavoidable market realities. Thereby, the aim of this work is to spread the usage of gaze control to anyone regardless of financial circumstances.

2   Hardware Requirements

The *Gaze Control Toolbar* software requires just a low-cost eye tracker such as the *Tobii Eye Tracker 4C*, the *Tobii Eye X* or the *GazePoint Eye Tracker*. Both Tobii devices cost less than $200 each. The *GazePoint* price tag is $600. The technical specifications of each device are similar, with gaze sampling frequencies in the range of 40 Hz to 90 Hz. For all supported gaze tracking hardware devices, the recommended maximum screen size for accurate gaze estimation is 27 in. with 16:9 aspect ratio. The operating distance range of the devices is 50 to 95 cm and the gaze estimation accuracy is in the range 0.5 to 1° of visual angle at 60 cm from the screen. These technical specifications are similar to more expensive eye tracking hardware devices used for commercial accessibility solutions.

3 Gaze Control Toolbar

The *Gaze Control Toolbar* (see Fig. 1) allows motor impaired users to fully control a Windows desktop computer using only their gaze and a low-cost eye tracker marketed to gamers. The software modular design permits the seamless addition of different interaction methods by potential future contributors to the code base. Our preferred and default gaze interaction method uses a 3 step target interaction procedure by which the user first selects a desired interaction action to be carried out (left mouse click, right mouse click, scrolling, etc.) by gazing at a gaze reactive taskbar on the border of the computer screen (see Fig. 1).

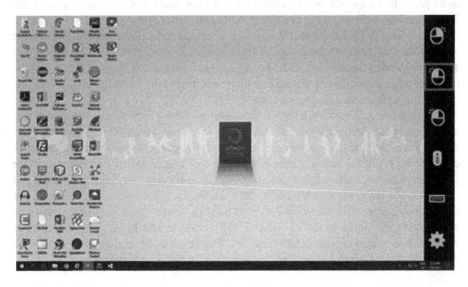

Fig. 1. The open source *Gaze Control Toolbar* user interface consist of a gaze reactive taskbar superimposed on the right side of the standard Windows user interface. The customizable taskbar contains icons representing potential interaction actions such as mouse right/left button click, scrolling or an open source on-screen keyboard (OptiKey) for typing. In the example on the left, the user has gaze selected a mouse left click action as a first interaction step. The program has highlighted in red the action in the taskbar for visual feedback purposes. (Color figure online)

In the second interaction step (see Fig. 2), the user gazes at the target on the screen on which it wants to trigger the previously gaze selected action. Given the limitations of the gaze estimation algorithms to resolve gaze position at less than 0.5° of visual angle, a zooming lens functionality around the target is invoked by the software (see Fig. 1) after a predefined time threshold is exceeded. The zoomed in window allows, as a third interaction step, the fine-grained selection of the target by means of the user fixating on the zoomed in target.

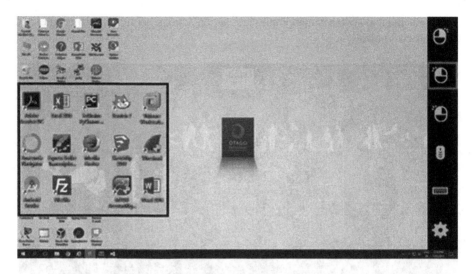

Fig. 2. In this example, the user has engaged in the second interaction step which involves gazing at the target location on the screen (in this illustration, the Firefox browser icon). The software fires up a zoomed-in window after detecting a fixation around the target location. This allows the user to fine grain select the target using a second fixation on the zoomed-in target as third interaction step.

The three-step target acquisition procedure avoids one of the historically most pervasive problems of gaze interaction: The Midas touch problem. Using the three-step target acquisition method described, a user can freely inspect a user interface without fear of generating unwanted interaction actions. Only when the user is ready to interact with a target, will the user look at the gaze reactive taskbar on the border of the screen to activate a particular interaction action, which will then be completed through the second and third steps of the target interaction procedure.

The *Gaze Control Toolbar* software also affords functionality enhancement for users with residual motor function via accessibility switches that can be mapped to specific interaction actions to speed up interaction by circumventing the need to gaze select an action on the taskbar. That is, short-circuiting the need for the first step of the interaction procedure. This permits a simpler acquisition of a target by gazing at it and activating the corresponding switch mapped to a particular action (left mouse click, right mouse click, scrolling, etc.) desired by the user. The interaction is completed by carrying out steps 2 and 3 of the previously described interaction procedure (i.e. fixating on the target and in the subsequent zoomed in window).

The *Gaze Control Toolbar* software, a comprehensive user guide, a video demo and technical documentation for developers can be found at: https://github.com/accessibilitysoftwarehub/OpenSourceWindowsGazeControl.

The *Gaze Control Toolbar* is fully customizable by users via gaze or a regular pointer device (mouse, trackpad, digital pen, etc.), providing users and caregivers with many degrees of freedom to customize the software to their particular needs and abilities (see Fig. 3). The software permits adjustment of fixation thresholds, sticky keys, zooming levels, mechanical switches mapping to interaction actions, toolbar rearrangement and crosshair customization.

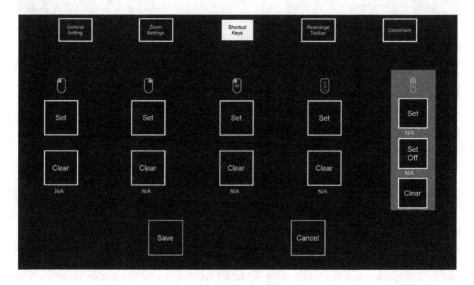

Fig. 3. The gaze control toolbar provides a gaze reactive settings interface to achieve a high degree of customizability to the specific circumstances of any given user.

4   Discussion

Accessibility technologies have often been formulated in terms that fail to successfully address socioeconomic context. Therefore, accessibility software and hardware solutions have often benefited only a small fraction of the global target population. We believe this work, addresses such affordability gap for gaze control accessibility software.

The Gaze Control Toolbar accessibility software is free so any user can take advantage of it regardless of financial circumstances. The only expense users might need to incur is the purchase of a low-cost, off-the-shelf eye tracker marketed for gamers and not for accessibility purposes. The open source nature of the project gives the user community freedom to modify the source code for customizing the software to their needs. Accessibility researchers can also easily plug-in modules containing innovative gaze interaction methods to test hypotheses about their effectiveness in comparison to alternative interaction modalities.

The Gaze Control Toolbar also suffers from the archetypical disadvantages of open source projects. The most salient one being the lack of warranted customer support, which is particularly important for accessibility software applications given their often technically complex nature. Additionally, the open source nature of the Gaze Control Toolbar also means that the source code is exposed to agents with potential malicious intentions who can look for exploits and vulnerabilities.

A natural follow-up research of this work would consist on carrying out an extensive user evaluation of the Gaze Control Toolbar with the target users: individuals with severe motor impaired. In addition, a comparative study of system performance between the Gaze Control Toolbar and existing commercial gaze control software would throw light on the competitiveness of the Gaze Control Toolbar against existing high-end commercial benchmarks.

Despite the limitations delineated above, the author strongly believes that the Gaze Control Toolbar is addressing an underserved niche market. The inescapable fact that gaze control accessibility software solutions are often unaffordable for a sizable percentage of the population highlights the importance of closing that gap. In the author's view, the accessibility research community bears a social responsibility to make accessibility technology stemming from research efforts accessible to their research subjects. Open source software led by accessibility research scholars appears to the author as precisely the type of social force that can address the underserved community of users with motor disability who cannot afford existing commercial accessibility software.

Acknowledgments. The Gaze Control Toolbar software has been created and is actively maintained by successive student cohorts of the Bachelor of Information Technology at Otago Polytechnic during the course of their degree final year capstone project. The merits of the tool is all theirs, while the shortcomings are the author's fault for having failed to provide better guidance to his students.

References

1. Istance, H.O., Spinner, C., Howarth, P.A.: Providing motor impaired users with access to standard Graphical User Interface (GUI) software via eye-based interaction. In: Proceedings of the 1st European Conference on Disability, Virtual Reality and Associated Technologies (ECDVRAT 1996), pp. 109–116 (1996)
2. Yuan, P., Gao, X., Allison, B., Wang, Y., Bin, G., Gao, S.: A study of the existing problems of estimating the information transfer rate in online brain–computer interfaces. J. Neural Eng. **10**, 026014 (2013)
3. Rozado, D.: Mouse and keyboard cursor warping to accelerate and reduce the effort of routine HCI input tasks. IEEE. Trans. Hum. Mach. Syst. **43**, 487–493 (2013)
4. Uslan, M.M.: Barriers to acquiring assistive technology: cost and lack of information. J. Vis. Impair. Blind. **86**, 402–407 (1992)
5. WHO: Assistive Technology. http://www.who.int/mediacentre/factsheets/assistive-tech nology/en/
6. Pal, J., Vallauri, U., Tsaran, V.: Low-cost assistive technology in the developing world: a research agenda for information schools. In: Proceedings of the 2011 iConference, pp. 459–465. ACM, New York (2011)
7. Bauer, S.M.: Demand pull technology transfer applied to the field of assistive technology. J. Technol. Transf. **28**, 285–303 (2003)

414   D. Rozado

8. Hurst, A., Tobias, J.: Empowering individuals with do-it-yourself assistive technology. In: The Proceedings of the 13th International ACM SIGACCESS Conference on Computers and Accessibility, pp. 11–18. ACM, New York (2011)
9. Convention on the Rights of Persons with Disabilities – Articles: United Nations Enable. https://www.un.org/development/desa/disabilities/convention-on-the-rights-of-persons-with-disabilities/convention-on-the-rights-of-persons-with-disabilities-2.html

Co-exploring Interaction Opportunities for Enabling Technologies for People with Rheumatic Disorder

Suhas Govind Joshi[(⊠)] and Jørgen Valen

Department of Informatics, University of Oslo, Oslo, Norway
{joshi,jorgeval}@ifi.uio.no

Abstract. This paper presents a case of co-design for people with rheumatic disorder to support the argument of opening up the design space to include interaction opportunities found in the physical world. The position argued for is that opening up the design space beyond common screen-based interfaces may contribute to the design of enabling technologies for people with rheumatic disorders by acknowledging their varying capabilities during both design and use. The presented results consist of one thematic analysis of home interviews and group discussions as well as one statistical analysis of the results from a formative evaluation of six conceptual prototypes developed along with the participants. The paper uses the combination of the thematic analysis, the six conceptual prototypes, and formative evaluation of performance scores and preference ratings to demonstrate how our co-design process involving users with rheumatic disorder in all phases allowed participants to discover both limitations and opportunities as they explored and co-designed alternative concepts.

Keywords: Enabling technology · Rheumatic disorder · Tangible interaction

1 Introduction

The wide range of conditions falling under the umbrella term rheumatic disorder, as well as the fluctuating nature and individually perceived manifestation of the associated physical impairments, complicates the design of enabling technologies intended to support a highly heterogeneous composition of users. Selecting specific interfaces usually involves certain assumptions about the users' capabilities for interaction. By using, for instance, a touch-based interface, we have already assumed by design that the users possess the necessary physical preconditions to perform the interaction mechanisms and finger-based gestures such as swiping and pinching.

In this paper, we argue that involving the users in all phases of the design process, and simultaneously developing a better understanding of their capabilities for interaction when selecting interface, can increase the chances for both successful and prolonged interaction for users with rheumatic disorders. We support our position by presenting a thematic analysis highlighting some of the challenges associated with rheumatic disorders and rely on data from an evaluation of six co-designed conceptual prototypes involving 15 people from the target demographic as well as 11 expert users. We explore whether opening up the design space to include interaction opportunities

© The Author(s) 2018
K. Miesenberger and G. Kouroupetroglou (Eds.): ICCHP 2018, LNCS 10896, pp. 415–423, 2018.
https://doi.org/10.1007/978-3-319-94277-3_65

found in the physical world (as opposed to just screen-based designs) may contribute to the design of enabling technologies for people with rheumatic disorders by acknowledging their varying capabilities.

The research presented in this paper expands on the previous work carried out by the authors on designing enabling technologies (e.g., [1, 2]). While many of the participants were older adults, this paper revolves around a particular set of physical impairments and does not limit the target demographic and participants to only older adults.

2 Related Work

The hundreds of conditions associated with the umbrella term rheumatic disorder can manifest themselves very differently, and the fluctuating nature of the various conditions yield highly individual and temporal experiences [3]. These fluid and often-unpredictable characteristics complicate the design of enabling technologies that are based solely on specific conditions or umbrella terms such as rheumatic disorder because the success of enabling technologies ultimately lies in the intertwining between the personal perspective of the user and the contextual circumstances [4]. The various manifestations of rheumatic disorders that may influence our physical opportunities and limitations have been outlined in the past, for instance in [5] where the characteristics of rheumatoid arthritis are described or in [6] where the effects of various conditions, e.g., Parkinson's disease are explained. Examples of how these physical symptoms of rheumatic challenges affect the opportunities to interact with technology as well as challenge the assumptions designers can make about the users' physical capabilities have been specifically discussed in the context of aging (e.g., [1, 7–11]). However, the manifestation of physical impairments such as those associated with rheumatic disorders may be equally troublesome for people who are not considered as older adults as studies are pointing towards a range of disabilities found in cases where young or middle-aged people live with physical impairments [9]. It has also been argued that enabling technologies should acknowledge that the experience of technology is a concern that involves the intertwinement of a multitude of co-existing factors, among which we find physical impairment. The authors of [8] argued that you cannot detach the intended users or users groups when raising questions about what technologies are. It is further argued that the multitude of interacting factors complicate the predictability of use and the related outcomes [4]. Thus, we draw on many different bodies of work on the relationship between physical impairment and the users' readiness towards technology, but common for all is an underlying understanding of the users' capabilities as something defined by more than just a medical diagnosis.

3 Research Methodology and Methods

The overarching methodology follows the Participatory Design (PD) approach we have previously applied in an extensive research project spanning over four years [1, 2]. The strategy emphasizes a respectful and inclusive design process and is heavily influenced by the phenomenological ideas of Maurice Merleau-Ponty [12] and his notion of the lived body. This strategy offers a framework for understanding able-bodied human-technology relationships through a phenomenological lens that focuses on how the technology meets the capable body and attempts to understand the interaction through the user's bodily experience of a phenomenon. The exact nature of how physical impairments affect the ability to engage with technology is highly subjective and something we consider as continuously evolving through life. Our approach emphasizes that participants should be able to engage in co-design activities on their own terms.

Our research was structured into two main components: data gathering and evaluation. The data gathering consisted of demonstrative interviews from the target demographic and two group discussion sessions with a local branch of the Norwegian rheumatism association with 49 users. The collected data material included audio recordings of group discussions, field notes from observations, photographs, and transcripts from interviews. This data was used in a thematic analysis where we attempted to structure essential challenges. Based on the data gathering sessions, six conceptual prototypes were co-designed with the users to serve as thinking tools. These prototypes (depicted in Fig. 1) were designed to learn more about the capabilities of the users and help us reflect about the assumptions about the users and should therefore not be considered as end-results. The prototypes were used to carry out a task-based formative evaluation of performance and preference when interacting with alternative tangible text input interfaces. The evaluation sessions were carried out at the homes or care facilities of the participants. 15 people struggling with various forms of rheumatic challenges constituted the user group (average age of 71.4 years), while 11 health practitioners or HCI experts formed the expert group. The procedure for both the thematic analysis and the evaluation are further described in the next section.

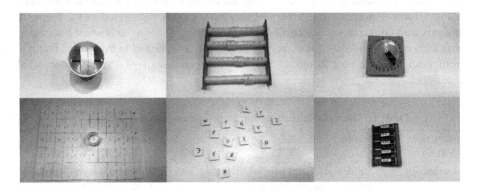

Fig. 1. The six co-designed conceptual prototypes used during the evaluation

4 Results and Analysis

The result section is divided into two main components. We present the results from a thematic inductive analysis, and we outline the primary results from a statistical analysis of the performance scores and preference ratings from a task-based evaluation of the six conceptual prototypes.

4.1   Thematic Analysis

The data used in the analysis was gathered through group discussion sessions and home interviews. We followed the approach for inductive thematic analysis outlined in [13]. The home interviews revealed interesting perspectives, for instance, one participant showing us around her home explaining adjustments made to technology at multiple points of interest in her apartment (as seen in, e.g., [14]). She had introduced several modifications to support her own capabilities for interaction, for instance using a pencil with a rubber band as an extended pen for her computer keyboard (leftmost image in Fig. 2).

Fig. 2. Examples of how homemade adjustments can support interaction with everyday objects

The thematic analysis revealed two main clusters, namely *everyday activities* and *interaction challenges*. The former cluster included all contextual and health-related concerns, particularly those found in the home setting, e.g., button on clothes and use of utensils. The latter cluster consisted of all issues related to interaction with technology. Table 1 presents a summary of this latter cluster discovered in the thematic analysis with emphasis on key challenges and involved enabling aids when interacting with technology. While we focus on only one of the two clusters in this paper, findings from both clusters contributed to the informed co-design of the six conceptual prototypes.

Table 1. Overview of challenges related to interaction with technology

Interaction challenge	Particular difficulties	Enabling accessories/aids
Reachability	Stiffness and joint pain when writing with regular computer keyboards	Homemade stylus, speech to text software
Long-term strain injuries	Fatigue from using a regular computer mouse	Ergonomic computer mouse, rolling or trackball mouse
Exhaustion	Resting arms when using mouse and keyboard	Ergonomic keyboard, speech-to-text software
Readability issues	Eye strain and fatigue when reading small text	Text-to-speech software, magnifying software
Eye-straining	Bright light from screens	Screens with adjustable light

4.2 Evaluation of Conceptual Prototypes and Statistical Analysis

The participants were given a similar text input task as commonly used on modern screen-based systems across the six devices in randomized order. To further avoid any learning effects, the task and the concepts were introduced and explained ahead of the evaluation to normalize the level of familiarity and expectancy among all participants. For each task, completion time was recorded, and all participants were also asked to rate preference, simplicity, and easiness of use during the post-evaluation interview. The rating used a relative scale, i.e., grading from least to most preferred (coded as 1–6). As such, the data consisted of both quantitative and qualitative results. Figure 3 shows two of the users as well as one group of experts participating in the evaluation.

Fig. 3. Two participants from the user group and one group of experts during the evaluation

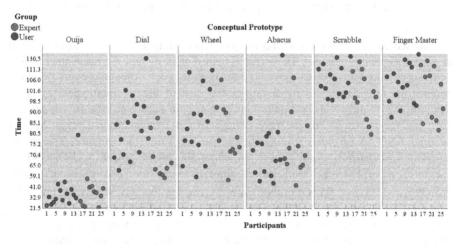

Fig. 4. Performance time for all participants sorted by conceptual prototype

The scatterplot in Fig. 4 shows the performance time for each participant across all six conceptual prototypes. An exploratory data analysis using factorial ANOVA *(group x prototype)* studied the variance in performance time across these prototypes for each group. The results indicated a statistically significant main effect for the groups, $F(1, 143) = 6.70$, $p < .005$. There was also a statistically significant main effect for the prototypes, $F(1, 143) = 60.471$, $p < .001$. The main effects for the different prototypes

$(\eta_\rho^2 = .679)$ was then subject to a post hoc analysis where we applied Bonferroni correction. The core results were that the Ouija prototype differed significantly from all other prototypes ($p < .001$ for all comparisons) and that the Scrabble and Finger Master prototypes also differed from the rest, but in the opposite direction. When comparing the variance for each prototype separately and simultaneously isolating the user group, only the Ouija prototype demonstrated a statistically significant difference from the rest at the $<.05$ level.

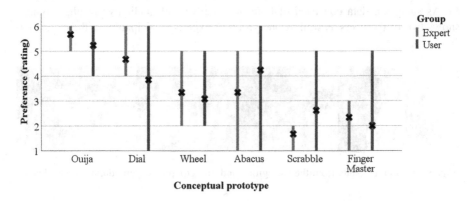

Fig. 5. Preference rating for each of the six prototypes coded by group

The second set of results presents the preference rating given on average to each of the six conceptual prototypes. These results helped us study how the mean and range of preference rating varied between users and experts for each of the prototypes. Figure 5 outlines the range bars and mean ratings for each of the six prototypes. The bars represent the minimum and maximum rating given for each prototype by experts and users, and the crosses signify the mean rating across all participants in a group. Another factorial ANOVA *(group x prototype)* was used to study the variance. The results revealed a statistically significant main effect for prototypes, $F(5, 390) = 94.19$, $p < .001$, $\eta_\rho^2 = .414$, as well as a similar result for *prototypes x group*, $F(5, 390) = 2.25$, $p < .05$. From the figure, we can see that the range was similar for only the Wheel prototype, and that a larger scale was used in the user group in all the five cases where there was a range difference between the users and experts. The extreme example would be the Scrabble prototype where the experts limited their preferences to two values only while the user group's ratings ranged across five values. Finally, we can also see that the expert group only rated the Abacus prototype ($M_{experts} = 3.38$, $SD_{experts} = 1.58$; $M_{users} = 4.24$, $SD_{users} = 1.43$) and the Scrabble prototype ($M_{experts} = 1.69$, $SD_{experts} = 1.07$; $M_{users} = 2.66$, $SD_{users} = 1.27$) lower on average than the user group.

5   Discussion

As seen in Fig. 5, the user group relied on a broader range when rating the prototype with only one exception. Our key findings emerged as we paired the statistical analysis with the qualitative data from the post-evaluation interview as well as the thematic analysis summarized in Table 1. We relied on the combination of both quantitative and qualitative results as the combination of these two diverse sets of data provided different focus of measurement and psychometric characteristic when studying a human-technology relationship in the context of enabling technologies [1, 4]. Involving contextual factors during the preference rating was particularly common within the user group (as also discussed in [4]). Accessing past subjective experiences [3] through interaction with only conceptual prototypes allowed the user group to shed light on factors not considered by the experts, e.g., long-term factors such as straining on muscles, which was reflected in their fluctuating performance rating (Fig. 4). For many of the participants, working on a computer was a necessity, but simultaneously an activity that turned exhausting and straining over time. One participant said she depended on her computer for most of her work, but she could never take on regular full-time employment relying on frequent computer use due to devastating fatigue and pain over time. One theme brought up during the home interviews and group discussions was that several challenges were related to fatigue and pain caused by poor working position, forceful keying, duration of use, and workstation setup – some of which are also mentioned in [15]. Two of our conceptual prototypes (Dial and Abacus) were subject to critique from certain participants due to the afforded working positions and quickly resulting in pain. When describing her experience with the Dial, one participant said: *"...the working position becomes completely skewed, so I get terrible pain in my shoulder region"*. However, this experience simultaneously made the participants aware of how other alternatives among the six conceptual prototypes offered new opportunities. For instance, the Finger Master prototype – despite being one of the most time-consuming and least preferred options overall – allowed participants to discover new configurations of the human-technology relation. One participant using the Finger Master noted that having the keyboard in her lap minimized straining in the shoulders and offered a more relaxed working position. Another participant praised its resemblance as it reminded her of older cell phone keypads and the mechanisms associated with text messaging.

On the other hand, there were also cases of consensus. One such case was the Ouija prototype that scored best on both performance time (Fig. 4) and preference rating (Fig. 5). Having all letters (i.e., input options) visible at all times similar to a regular keyboard was essential to most of the participants in both groups. Another reason for its high performance and preference was that it allowed the whole hand rather than just individual fingers to be used. Thus, we argue that the broader range among the users in Fig. 5 demonstrate how different people with rheumatic disorder can find both limitation and opportunities when the interaction is more configurable also regarding how it acknowledges and responds to bodily capabilities of the users.

6   Conclusion

Our overarching salutary perspective attempts to provide a positive outlook by focusing on the participants' capabilities [1], and this paper has attempted to demonstrate how users with rheumatic disorder found both limitations and opportunities when opening the space and giving them a chance to have a more proactive role in the design process. We have reported from one thematic analysis of home interviews and group discussion as well as one statistical analysis of performance and rating scores from a formative evaluation of six conceptual prototypes developed along with the participants. We have demonstrated how participants used past experiences to discover opportunities to counteract interaction challenges in current interfaces. Using even conceptual prototypes as thinking tools helped both the participants and us to easier access the subjective experiences of rheumatic disorders and supported the co-discovering of new spaces for design in the physical world tailored specifically for this user group.

References

1. Joshi, S.G.: Designing for Capabilities: A Phenomenological Approach to the Design of Enabling Technologies for Older Adults (Doctoral dissertation). Ser. Diss. Submitt. Faculty of Mathematics and Natural Sciences 1881 (2017)
2. Joshi, S.G., Bratteteig, T.: Designing for prolonged mastery. On involving old people in participatory design. Scand. J. Inf. Syst. **28**, 3–36 (2016)
3. Been-Dahmen, J.M.J., Walter, M.J., Dwarswaard, J., Hazes, J.M.W., van Staa, A., Ista, E.: What support is needed to self-manage a rheumatic disorder: a qualitative study. BMC Musculoskelet. Disord. **18**, 84 (2017)
4. Hoenig, H., Giacobbi, P., Levy, C.E.: Methodological challenges confronting researchers of wheeled mobility aids and other assistive technologies. Disabil. Rehabil. Assist. Technol. **2**, 159–168 (2007)
5. Tuntland, H., Kjeken, I., Nordheim, L.V., Falzon, L., Jamtvedt, G., Hagen, K.B.: Assistive technology for rheumatoid arthritis. Cochrane Database Syst. Rev. (2009)
6. Langdon, P., Thimbleby, H.: Inclusion and interaction: designing interaction for inclusive populations. Interact. Comput. **22**, 439–448 (2010)
7. Joshi, S.G.: Re-establishing interaction through design of alternative interfaces. Presented at the eTELEMED 2016, The Eighth International Conference on eHealth, Telemedicine, and Social Medicine (2016)
8. Blythe, M.A., Monk, A.F., Doughty, K.: Socially dependable design: the challenge of ageing populations for HCI. Interact. Comput. **17**, 672–689 (2005)
9. Putnam, M.: Linking aging theory and disability models: increasing the potential to explore aging with physical impairment. The Gerontologist **42**, 799–806 (2002)
10. Holzinger, A., Searle, G., Nischelwitzer, A.: On some aspects of improving mobile applications for the elderly. In: Stephanidis, C. (ed.) UAHCI 2007. LNCS, vol. 4554, pp. 923–932. Springer, Heidelberg (2007). https://doi.org/10.1007/978-3-540-73279-2_103
11. Hammel, J.: Assistive Technology and Environmental Intervention (AT-EI) impact on the activity and life roles of aging adults with developmental disabilities: findings and implications for practice. Phys. Occup. Ther. Geriatr. **18**, 37–58 (2000)
12. Merleau-Ponty, M.: Phenomenology of Perception. Routledge, New York (2002)

13. Braun, V., Clarke, V.: Using thematic analysis in psychology. Qual. Res. Psychol. **3**, 77–101 (2006)
14. Brereton, M.: Habituated objects: everyday tangibles that foster the independent living of an elderly woman. Interactions **20**, 20–24 (2013)
15. Baker, N.A., Rogers, J.C., Rubinstein, E.N., Allaire, S.H., Wasko, M.C.: Problems experienced by people with arthritis when using a computer. Arthritis Rheum. **61**, 614–622 (2009)

Tactile Interface to Steer Power Wheelchairs: A Preliminary Evaluation with Wheelchair Users

Youssef Guedira[1(✉)], Franck Bimbard[1], Jules Françoise[1],
René Farcy[2], and Yacine Bellik[1]

[1] LIMSI-CNRS, Univ. Paris-Sud, Université Paris-Saclay, 91405 Orsay, France
{youssef.guedira,franck.bimbard,jules.francoise,
yacine.bellik}@limsi.fr
[2] LAC-CNRS, Univ. Paris-Sud, Université Paris-Saclay, 91405 Orsay, France
rene.farcy@u-psud.fr

Abstract. Power Wheelchairs can be a necessity for many people to have a certain level of mobility. Unfortunately, some of them may not be able to use one because they cannot safely manipulate a joystick. In a previous study, we proposed a tactile interface to steer power wheelchairs and started a first round of experimentation with able-bodied users. In this paper, we present recent tests of our steering interface in both formal and informal settings with some users with mobility impairment from different profiles. In the formal tests, two wheelchair users performed three different common tasks: straight line following, 90° corner and doorway passing with both our tactile steering interface and a joystick. The steering performance of the tactile interface was close or similar to that of the joystick. We also outline lessons that we learned from these tests for future improvements.

Keywords: Tactile interface · Joystick · Power wheelchair · Evaluation

1 Introduction

Many people who need a power wheelchair cannot use one because the joystick (the most used wheelchair steering device [1]) is not well adapted to their disability. Through discussions with therapeutic assistants and residents of specialized care, a few profiles have emerged as having serious difficulties using a normal joystick:

- People with neuromuscular diseases: These users can have so little force in the hand that handling a normal joystick can be impossible for them.
- People with 'E' factor: their arms extend uncontrollably, when they experience a strong emotion. Consequently, it can hit the joystick handle and get stuck against it. In many cases, this may lead to serious accidents and injuries.
- People with tense hand posture: Spasticity, for example, can cause hand muscles to contract. Consequently, these people are not able to correctly grab a joystick handle. Therapeutic and ergonomic assistants often resort to manual modifications of the joystick handle or different types/shapes of handles.

K. Miesenberger and G. Kouroupetroglou (Eds.): ICCHP 2018, LNCS 10896, pp. 424–431, 2018.
https://doi.org/10.1007/978-3-319-94277-3_66

In [3], authors have investigated the use of alternative wheelchair steering devices aimed at users with neuromuscular diseases (mini-joystick, finger-joystick...). Yet, these steering alternatives can be too pricy making them inaccessible to many users. In addition, the reduced handling space in these devices can make them over sensitive, thus reducing the steering precision. In [2, 6], we have presented a novel steering interface on a tablet. This choice was motivated by the fact that the tactile interface would require less effort to steer compared to a joystick. Finger movement filtering can be added to the tactile interface to even smooth out the steering, by eradicating any jerkiness in steering input caused by cerebellar tremors for example. Also, graphics tablets have the potential to be a fertile ground for developing/testing various interaction techniques; we extend this idea into graphical tactile tablets [4]. They are flexible and the rise in computing power in smartphones and tablets provides a great potential for more comprehensive interfaces that can even analyze user actions and adapt to user profiles. Finally yet importantly, caregivers and users also pointed out the need of having one unique device that can serve for different tasks and control multiple artifacts in the surrounding of the user especially with the rise of home automation systems. Thus, the device that serves to steer the wheelchair can also serve as a hub for environment controls. This diminishes the number of devices the user needs to carry and lookout for as well as the differences between different user interfaces that not only should the user get used to separately but also have to be independently tweaked to suit his/her need.

2 Description of Our Steering Interface

Figure 1 gives a representation of the steering interface with the steering panel at its center. The neutral central area allows the user to rest his/her finger without moving. Depending on user preferences, it can be bigger or smaller. The tactile interface can be used with or without a passive haptic cover. It gives the user a better orientation while using the tactile interface without having to look at it. With a simple touch, the user can modify his/her speed and direction of movement: the further from the center the user points, the faster he/she goes. The stripe at the edge of the panel allows the user to change direction while keeping maximum speed. The calibration function allows the user to rescale the steering panel as well as reposition it depending on his/her specific finger motor space.

Fig. 1. Left: Passive haptic feedback cover, Right: Screenshot of the steering interface. Normally, only the active portion of the circle is colored, but we colored the whole circle to better illustrate the segmentation of speed and direction (mentioned in the next section). (Color figure online)

3   Evaluation of the Tactile Steering Interface

3.1   Previous Evaluation of the Tactile Steering and Resulting Improvements

The development of the tactile interface is done with close contact and continuous feedback from care centers and wheelchair users of various profiles: users with motor impairment, users with cerebral palsy, neuromuscular diseases… Yet it is still necessary to perform formal user testing with both subjective and objective measures. The tactile interface is mostly intended as an alternative solution for some people who cannot use a joystick or for people who can use one but would like to have a unique device to perform different tasks. Still, comparing it to the latter should give an idea about the overall performance of the tactile interface against a benchmark steering device. Later evaluations of the tactile interface will be conducted against devices like the mini-joystick in order to determine if it actually provides an overall easier steering than what is proposed in the market for people with neuromuscular diseases.

In [6], we conducted an experiment to compare the tactile interface performance with that of the joystick. The main improvements from the experiment results were the tactile steering interface now gives a large enough maximum speed stripe (double the previous one). More importantly, the oversensitivity of the interface was remediated by allowing the user to configure a number of subdivisions in both direction and speed. This should reduce the sensitivity of the interface depending on the dexterity level of the user's touch.

3.2   Recent Informal Tests of the Tactile Interface

Both wheelchair users and therapeutic assistants suggested that during the first learning stages of the steering, it could be easier for many novice users to start with fewer steering directions and work their way up to a fully continuous steering. We were able to notice that in practice during one of our visits to a care center. Under the supervision of two therapeutic assistants, and in a clear large space, we gave the tactile interface to a child with cerebral palsy (who is quite used to steering with a joystick). At first, the steering seemed too impulsive. We then limited the number of directions to only four (forward, backward, right, left). He then could steer the wheelchair more easily. Then, we progressively increased the number of directions (smooth steering with 32 directions) (Fig. 2). This gives an indication on how to proceed during the learning stages of the tactile interface steering.

Fig. 2. Screenshots, from left to right, showing different widths of forward direction subdivision when the level of subdivision is 4, 8, 16 and 32 regions for directions and 3 different speed increments.

In another visit to a care center for children with cerebral palsy, we were able to test our tactile interface with two children under close supervision of their medical and therapeutic assistants. The first one uses an electric wheelchair with an adapted joystick. His condition makes it so that his hand is too contracted and he can hardly open it. When he tried the tactile steering interface, we noticed a strong motivation effect caused by a high-tech side of the tactile interface inside the center's playground. This motivation helped him extend the index, for the first time in over six months according to his therapeutic assistant, in order to steer the wheelchair. Although we are still unable to quantify such effect or predict its durability, it shows a strength of the tactile interface that will potentially help its user in steering the wheelchair in the learning stages. The second child also, suffering from cerebral palsy, tested the tactile steering interface. He was even able, after just few minutes of familiarization, to go for a short wheelchair drive closely accompanied by his medical and therapeutic assistants and us. His assistant also showed us a communication aid app on a tablet that he uses as he has very slurred speech. She suggested that he would probably benefit from having a steering interface on his tablet.

3.3   Current Formal Evaluation of the Tactile Interface against a Joystick

The goal of this evaluation is not to prove that our tactile interface surpasses the joystick but rather get an approximate measure of how it performs when given to users with mobility impairment. Three wheelchair users tested our interface as well as the wheelchair's factory joystick to compare their performances. A stock Electric wheelchair (Sunrise Medical Salsa R2) was used and the joystick used was the one provided by the manufacturer with its factory settings. For the tactile interface, we used a Sony Xperia Z Ultra as a tablet that we connected to the wheelchair's control system by Bluetooth. We used the cover and the visual response (see Figs. 1 and 2) as the only feedback modalities. The steering circle's diameter was set to cover the whole width of the tablet and the central neutral zone's radius was set a third of the steering circle's. We also reduced the precision requirement of the steering to 5 subdivisions in speed and 256 subdivisions (a decrease of 30% compared to the previous experiment). The placement of each device was set in a position deemed comfortable by the participant. The steering interface requires only one finger touch. Therefore, to avoid accidental steering input, we asked the user to wear a glove that lets out only the finger meant for steering. For their convenience, the tests with the first and second user were done in a clear space next to their respective living areas. The test with the third participant was done in a cleared room next to our lab. To ensure the participants' safety one of the experimenters was carrying a wireless emergency stop command that halts the wheelchair if needed. For each task (Fig. 3), the participants got familiar for few minutes with both the steering device and the task track. Then, three timed trials were recorded for each task and at two different levels of speed. The first level, with maximum speed set to 0.625 m/s and the second one with maximum speed set to ~1.11 m/s. The order of the devices was alternated. The trials were taped and the data were logged for each driving wheel by a wheel encoder (precision < 1 mm and an acquisition at 100 Hz). The participants then filled a System Usability Scale (SUS) form [5] for each device. Finally, we had an informal interview about the driving experience during the tests. For the first and third participant, we will proceed task by task. Participant 2's test will be discussed further below. The first user is a regular user of electric wheelchair, with a regular joystick, with no cognitive or sensory impairment. He had already tested the second prototype of the tactile interface that allowed continuous and progressive control of the direction and speed about 1.5 years before the current study; his steering was better with a joystick. The third one is a regular user of a manual wheelchair who uses an electric wheelchair occasionally when he needs to travel long distances. For this third subject, it was the first time he tested our tactile interface.

Following a Straight Line. Participants were asked to follow a straight line of 5.7 m in a hallway (simulated by signaling cones) of width 0.9 m, corresponding to the minimum width required by building regulations concerning wheelchair accessible buildings [7]. We recorded the time it took to traverse the hallway, the average speed as well as the percentage of time the participant kept a constant speed. Figure 4 summarizes the performance figures of each participant with both devices (Fig. 5).

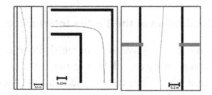

Fig. 3. Passages of the third participant using the tactile interface: in blue is the rear-end center of the wheelchair, in black the simulated wall, and in orange the simulated door edges. (Color figure online)

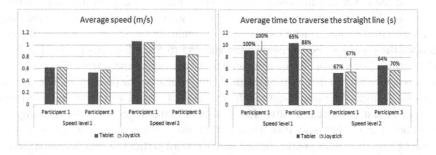

Fig. 4. Summary of the key performance figures in task 1. The percentage at the top of each column in the right graph represents the percentage of time the participant kept a constant speed over 3 trials.

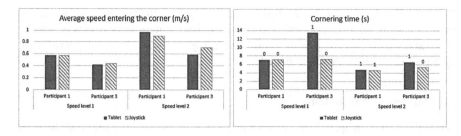

Fig. 5. Summary of key performance figures in task 2. The number at the top of each column in the right graph represents the number of collisions over 3 trials.

The first participant was able to get optimal performance in speed level 2 with both the joystick and the tactile interface. In speed level 3, the performance dropped slightly but he was slightly better performing with the tactile interface. Participant 3 however, was better performing and more stable with the joystick.

90° Corner. Participants were asked to take a 90° turn in a hallway simulated by signaling cones. The entrance to the corner was of 0.9 m width and the exit of the corner had a 1.1 m width. The minimum requirements for wheelchair accessible building [7] dictates a total of 2 m for both lengths. For each trial, we recorded the speed just before entering the corner, the time taken to complete the turn as well as the number of cones (or wall) touches. Figure 5 summarizes the performance figures of each participant with both devices.

Participant 1 had a very similar performance while using either devices especially in speed level 2. Speed level 3 was more challenging because of the tightness of the corner which explains the cone collisions. Yet, he was still able to gage the speed entering the corner and maintain a stable cornering with either devices. He also had a slightly higher speed entering the corner with the tablet, which may indicate a better sense of confidence but the cornering was a bit slower. Participant 3 had a better performance using the joystick. The speed entering the corner was higher and the cornering was faster, more stable and without touching cones.

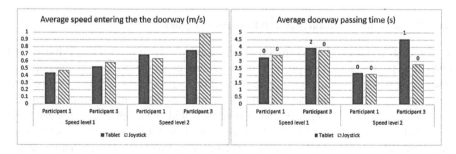

Fig. 6. Summary of key performance figures in task 3. The number at the top of each column in the right graph represents the number of collisions over 3 trials.

Doorway Passing. Participant 1 had a very similar performance using either devices. However, with the joystick, participant 3 was quicker entering the doorway, and was faster at the exit, especially with speed level 2. Figure 6 summarizes the performance figures of each participant with both devices.

3.4 Subjective Evaluation

While the first participant gave both devices 100% in the SUS, he said that, he would prefer to have the tactile interface because: (a) He felt that it required less muscular effort to steer especially in the cornering task. (b) He found it more precise. (c) He liked having the passive haptic feedback (the cover) as it provided him with a tangible delimitation of the steering area without having to look at it. The third participant gave the tablet a 90% SUS score and still preferred the joystick (SUS: 100%). In addition, he praised the fact of having the tablet as a centralized control device for the wheelchair and the environment. Both participants were able to successfully complete the tasks with both steering devices. Yet, the video recordings showed that unstable steering was mainly caused by fast and successive changing of steering input especially for participant 3. When he needed to correct the trajectory, he ended up overcorrecting. This led to a series of corrections that reduced the stability of many trials. The physics of the joystick lever make the change in steering input progressive, which smooths it out. Our Application tries to emulate this behavior but the rate of change may be too quick. We need to add a tunable input steering dampening function to slow down this rate of change.

3.5 Where There is a System's Shortcoming, There is an Improvement Opportunity

Participant 2 is a regular user of an electric wheelchair who has a lack of sensitivity at the tips of his fingers. Therefore, when he touches the tablet he does not have an immediate sensory feedback and presses harder on the screen. This caused both his finger to slip on the touch screen resulting in erratic steering and even the tablet to fall from its holder at times. This shows the importance of immediate interface feedback at the user's touch. In future improvements, we will investigate in depth how different output modalities (sound, vibration…) could improve the driving experience.

3.6 Discussion of Limitations and Lessons Learned

The biggest limitation of the current study, especially in its formal setting, is the limited number of participants. This prevents it from being generalizable over the majority of wheelchair users. A second obstacle in front of the generalizability is the level of variability amongst wheelchair users, whether it be in the motor abilities, cognitive abilities, sensory/perceptive abilities, previous experience with wheelchairs… However, the current study gives us an idea about a few points that will be helpful for both future improvements and future tests with wheelchair users. First, we can see that the tactile interface is usable by people with motor impairments to steer a power wheelchair. With proper training and fine-tuning of the steering interface, it has the potential to perform similarly to a benchmark wheelchair steering device. The duration of the training to use the tactile steering device will certainly vary from one person to another. The methodology of the training would also vary especially according to the cognitive abilities of the person, his/her previous experience steering a power wheelchair, the learning motivation... For future tests, we may have to organize a few training sessions, especially for people with cognitive impairment or cerebral palsy.

4   Conclusion

We present the evaluation of a novel tactile interface to steer power wheelchairs. The informal evaluation gave us an idea about the potential usability of our steering interface with users with various profiles. In the formal tests, we compared the performance of our steering interface to a benchmark steering device for power wheelchairs. It showed a close overall performance of the tactile interface compared to a joystick for two users who have a considerable experience with the latter. There are still some improvements that we need to make in order to accommodate the usability needs of more user profiles. Future evaluations will continue in this path to gage the level of performance of our interface. In parallel, we are working on multiple interaction techniques and pushing the boundaries of the tactile interfaces to further help people in need.

Acknowledgements. We thank the *IES Champigny-sur-Marne* and the *MAS Saint-Jean de Malte* for their continuous feedback, help and logistical support valuable to the completion of this study and the iterative development of our steering interface in general. We also thank all the subjects that participated to the experiments. Last but not least, we would like to mention that this work is supported by the "IDI 2017" project funded by the IDEX Paris-Saclay, ANR-11-IDEX-0003-02.

References

1. Lee Kirkby, R.: Wheelchair Skill Assessment and Training. CRC Press/Taylor and Francis Group, Boca Rota (2006)
2. Guedira, Y., Jordan, L., Favey, C., Farcy, R., Bellik, Y.: Tactile interface for electric wheelchair. In: Proceedings of the 18th International ACM SIGACCESS Conference on Computers and Accessibility (ASSETS 2016). ACM, New York, 313–314 (2016)
3. Pellegrini, N., Guillon, B., Prigent, H., Pellegrini, M., Orlikovski, D., Raphael, J.-C., Lofaso, F.: Optimization of power wheelchair control for patients with severe Duchenne muscular dystrophy. Neuromuscul. Disord. **14**, 297–300 (2004)
4. Buxton, W.: There's more to interaction than meets the eye: Some issues in manual input. In: Norman, D.A., Draper, S.W. (eds.) User Centered System Design: New Perspectives on Human-Computer Interaction, pp. 319–337. Lawrence Erlbaum Associates, Hillsdale (1986)
5. Brooke, J.: SUS: a 'quick and dirty' usability scale. Usability Eval. Ind. **189**, 4–7 (1996)
6. Guedira, Y. Farcy, R. Bellik, Y.: Interface Tactile pour le Pilotage de Fauteuils Roulants Electriques. Actes de la 28eme conférence francophone sur l'Interaction Homme-Machine, Fribourg, Suisse, October 2016
7. Ministère de la Transition Ecologique et Solidaire, Ministère la Cohésion des Territoires. Réglementation Accessibilité Batiment (2017). http://www.accessibilite-batiment.fr/. Accessed March 2017

Empowerment of People with Cognitive Disabilities Using Digital Technologies

Digital Inclusion Through Accessible Technologies

Introduction to the Special Thematic Session

Susanne Dirks[(✉)], Christian Bühler, and Cordula Edler

TU Dortmund University, 44227 Dortmund, Germany
Susanne.dirks@tu-dortmund.de

Abstract. Not only access to digital media but also technical skills, educational opportunities, living conditions, personal support and financial resources play an important role in digital participation. In this article, existing barriers to digital participation and current research projects, examining existing access to digital resources and developing approaches to improve in particular the participation of people with cognitive impairments through appropriate technologies, are presented and discussed. Relevant future research fields, and approaches to the participatory development of accessible technologies and the increased application of the principles of universal design, are motivated.

Keywords: e-Inclusion · Accessibility · Assistive technologies
Cognitive disabilities

1 Introduction

While the discussion about 'digital divide' or 'digital literacy' generally focuses on access to resources and competences of individuals, the term 'digital inclusion' specifically covers the issues of societal conditions for access to digital media and opportunities to acquire knowledge and skills in the use of digital media. Research and activities in digital inclusion are focused on a practical, policy-oriented approach that takes into account the needs of communities as a whole. In that sense, digital inclusion provides a framework for evaluating and examining the willingness of communities to provide access to the opportunities available to all people in the digital age. Accessibility to modern technologies is requested in the UN-CRPD and can be considered as a human right [1]. Digital media are also regarded as potentially empowering means for inclusion [2].

Digital progress has opened up new areas of exclusion and privilege, isolating some parts of the population from the digital world. Our increasingly digitalized societies require a comprehensive approach to foster digital participation of all people. According to the results of the digital inclusion survey [3], digital inclusion covers three different areas: access, adoption and application. Digital exclusion occurs when parts of the population cannot participate in the use of generally available technical possibilities due to certain personal characteristics or structural conditions. This form of exclusion results in further deteriorations in a person's life paths, such as poor health, poor lifelong income

© Springer International Publishing AG, part of Springer Nature 2018
K. Miesenberger and G. Kouroupetroglou (Eds.): ICCHP 2018, LNCS 10896, pp. 435–438, 2018.
https://doi.org/10.1007/978-3-319-94277-3_67

and an increased risk of marginalization. Still too many people are excluded from digital participation due to low income, unequal educational opportunities, cultural differences, physical or cognitive impairment or inadequate support [4].

2 Existing Barriers to Digital Participation

Although Information and Communication Technology (ICT), with its manifold communication and interaction possibilities, can contribute to overcome physical barriers, the accessibility of digital information itself is often still limited.

The main barriers that arise not only for people with disabilities but for all disadvantaged users of digital resources concern the following areas: 'access', 'skills', 'motivation', 'trust', 'confidence', 'availability', 'affordability' and 'support' [5, 6].

Depending on the nature of their disability and its severity, people with disabilities face different degrees of digital exclusion. Various studies have shown that people with impaired hearing differ only marginally in the use of digital resources from people without impairments [7, 8]. Since most of the information in the digital media is published as textual information and many video and audio resources are now subtitled, there are usually no significant digital barriers for people with impaired hearing. People with physical or visual impairments are often dependent on additional technical devices for access to digital information. Alternative input and output devices such as mouth devices, eye controls, braille displays or speech output systems facilitate independent access to digital information for these user groups. However, these technical aids can also act as barriers to digital participation as they create additional costs, maintenance efforts and further technical dependencies. In contrast, people with cognitive impairments use the Internet and other digital resources significantly less, mainly due to their limited financial resources, lack of technical skills and insufficient support options [9, 10]. Usually they have a lower-than-average income and therefore cannot afford the appropriate technical equipment. They live more frequently in homes with poor access to digital resources and often have limited reading, writing and communication skills, and, to date, there are hardly any helpful technologies available for people with cognitive impairments.

In summary, despite the technical possibilities of modern ICT, digital barriers still prevent full societal participation of people with disabilities. Especially people with cognitive impairments are still excluded from unrestricted digital participation.

3 Development of Accessible Technologies: Approaches

People with disabilities often experience barriers in the use of digital materials and technologies. Ideally, tools and contents are designed from the outset for a wide range of users with different abilities and disabilities. Unfortunately, accessibility issues are often only considered in the later phases of product development. In order to improve the accessibility of digital resources, especially for people with cognitive impairments, various aspects must be taken into account in the design and development of digital resources.

First, early and effective involvement of people with disabilities in the development processes can lead to valuable and often unexpected insights into how accessibility problems can be solved. Frédéric Vella et al. investigate how user-centered design approaches can be adapted for the development of technical solutions by and for people with disabilities. Julia Louw et al. show how the Participatory Action Research approach can be used in the development of technical solutions for the target group. New ways are being developed on how to involve people with disabilities as peer researchers in software development by Peter Heumader et al. and in usability engineering by Susanne Dirks et al.

The use of everyday technologies to support people with cognitive impairments is another important research area. Jessica Nicole Rocheleau et al. investigate the potential of existing every day technologies as assistive technologies.

As the independent use of digital resources requires a high degree of reading ability approaches to facilitate the understanding of textual content are of particular importance for digital participation of people with cognitive disabilities. Beat Vollenwyder et al. investigate the effect of Plain Language or Easy-to-Read Language on standard websites. Tereza Pařilová et al. research the development of assistance systems to support dyslectic users. Ting Wang Fu et al. work on a project that investigates strategies to support students with dyslexia.

Further research takes place in the development of assistive technologies for people with Autism Spectrum Disorder. Simone Hantke et al. and Miklos Gyori et al. investigate how the independence and quality of life of people with ASD can be improved through appropriate technical support.

The increasing life expectancy and the associated increase in the number of people with dementia results in more far-reaching demands on the cognitive accessibility of digital resources. The main research objective in this area is the development of accessible technologies that actively support people with dementia and thus enable them to maintain their independent lifestyle for a longer period of time and is represented amongst others by the works of Alexander Bejan et al.

4   Conclusion

The term digital participation refers not only to access to digital media and thus to equal access to information and communication opportunities, but also includes societal and political aspects of participation. As has been demonstrated, many current research projects address the development and evaluation of accessible technologies for the use of digital resources. As people with cognitive impairments in particular still experience severe limitations in digital participation, their interests should be brought more into focus. Henceforth, further approaches should be developed for the participatory development of accessible technologies and increased application of universal design principles in the development of accessible digital resources and tools. In addition, people with disabilities must be encouraged and supported to become more active in shaping their working and living conditions using digital resources.

References

1. Bühler, C., Scheer, B.: Barrierefreie Informationstechnik. In: Diehl, E., Degener, T. (eds.) Handbuch Behindertenrechtskonvention. Teilhabe als Menschenrecht – Inklusion als gesellschaftliche Aufgabe, vol. 1506, pp. 197–203. BpB-Schriftenreihe, Bonn (2016)
2. Bühler, C., Pelka, B.: Empowerment by digital media of people with disabilities. In: Miesenberger, K., Fels, D., Archambault, D., Peňáz, P., Zagler, W. (eds.) ICCHP 2014. LNCS, vol. 8547, pp. 17–24. Springer, Cham (2014). https://doi.org/10.1007/978-3-319-08596-8_4
3. Digital Inclusion Survey. https://digitalinclusion.umd.edu/content/what-digital-inclusion
4. Digital Inclusion for a better EU society. https://ec.europa.eu/digital-single-market/en/digital-inclusion-better-eu-society
5. Raja, D.S.: Bridging the Disability Divide through Digital Technologies. Background Paper Digital Dividends, World Development Report (2016). http://pubdocs.worldbank.org/en/123481461249337484/WDR16-BP-Bridging-the-Disability-Divide-through-Digital-Technology-RAJA.pdf
6. Edler, C.: E-Inklusion und Cognitive Accessibility, Menschen mit kognitiven Behinderungen nutzen Tablets im Alltag. In: Merz Medien und Erziehung, München, vol. 59, no. 4 (2015)
7. Dobransky, K., Hargittai, E.: Unrealized potential: exploring the digital disability divide. Poetics 58, 18–28 (2016)
8. Chadwick, D., Wesson, C., Fullwood, C.: Internet access by people with intellectual disabilities: inequalities and opportunities. Future Internet 5(3), 376–397 (2013)
9. Bühler, C., Dirks, S., Nietzio, A.: Easy access to social media: introducing the mediata-app. In: Miesenberger, K., Bühler, C., Penaz, P. (eds.) ICCHP 2016. LNCS, vol. 9759, pp. 227–233. Springer, Cham (2016). https://doi.org/10.1007/978-3-319-41267-2_31
10. Dirks, S., Bühler, C.: Participation and autonomy for users with ABI through easy social media access. Stud. Health Technol. Inform. 242, 813–819 (2017). Harnessing the Power of Technology to Improve Lives

Requirements Engineering for People with Cognitive Disabilities – Exploring New Ways for Peer-Researchers and Developers to Cooperate

Peter Heumader[1(✉)], Cordula Edler[2], Klaus Miesenberger[1,2], and Sylvia Wolkerstorfer[3]

[1] Institut Integriert Studieren, Johannes Kepler University Linz, Linz, Austria
{peter.heumader,klaus.miesenberger}@jku.at
[2] inbut, Zell u. A, Germany
cordula.edler@icloud.com
[3] Kompetenznetzwerk Informationstechnologie zur Förderung der Integration von Menschen mit Behinderungen, Linz, Austria
sylvia.wolkerstorfer@ki-i.at

Abstract. Digital technologies can improve the daily lives of people with cognitive disabilities, allowing them to participate and communicate in society. However the success of a technical product depends not only on the price or lifespan, but also on its user experience. To ensure user satisfaction when creating new technology or products, it is necessary to know their needs. This article presents methods of requirements analysis and elicitation for digital participation together with people with cognitive impairments.

Keywords: Human-machine interaction · R&D · e-Inclusion · Accessibility UCD · Cognitive disabilities

1 Introduction

The topic of human-machine-interaction for people with cognitive disabilities requires an interdisciplinary approach, taking into account methodological as well as legal, ethical and social implications that have hardly been found in research and development up to date. Up to now, computer software has only been developed sporadically with accessibility for people with cognitive disabilities in mind.

Before developing a user interface, as in any product development, understanding the requirements of the target group is an important aspect in order to obtain results that are accepted, desired and usable by the customer.

Current studies show that in general there is a persistent discrepancy between requirements engineering research and requirements engineering in practice, which leads software developers to ignore the needs of users [1]. The situation is even more serious for people with cognitive disabilities, as many methods of requirements engineering cannot be applied 1 to 1, or have never been tested before.

K. Miesenberger and G. Kouroupetroglou (Eds.): ICCHP 2018, LNCS 10896, pp. 439–445, 2018.
https://doi.org/10.1007/978-3-319-94277-3_68

Therefore, developers usually assume that the target group has suspected requirements and create the product without their direct involvement. Although there are concepts for requirements analysis for the development process of common software products, rarely one of them directly asks users with cognitive disabilities during the design phase. At the earliest when the product is almost ready, they are included in the test phase and integrated as test users. The result for the target group is often dissatisfaction and frustration due to poor user experience and product usability. This paper presents a new approach to involve people with cognitive disabilities in software development from the initial design phase to develop products that meet their needs.

2 State of the Art

Requirements engineering in today's software engineering process usually starts with a problem description and the environmental conditions of the system to be developed and ends in concrete requirements that can be implemented by software developers [1, 2]. Current state of the art techniques can be categorized in [6]:

- requirements elicitation and discovery,
- requirements modelling,
- analysis and specification.

Each category hosts different techniques and methods that can be used to determine the requirements of potential users. This paper will focus on requirements elicitation and discovery which is about describing the functionality, reliability, efficiency and usability of the system to be developed so that it suites the end users' needs [1]. Common techniques for requirement's engineering were categorized by Nuseibeh and Easterbrook [7] in the following groups:

- **Traditional techniques:** These techniques include questionnaires, surveys and analysis of existing documentation to collect the requirements of end-users [8].
- **Prototyping:** Requirements are collected by prototyping either with pen and paper or with a real software product. This allows developers, designers and end-users to work closely together and specify the requirements.
- **Group elicitation techniques:** Group techniques aim to foster stakeholder agreement and buy-in, while exploiting team dynamics to elicit a richer understanding of the needs [7]. Common examples for this techniques include brainstorming, focus groups, rapid application development and workshops.
- **Contextual techniques:** Here the requirements are gathered by observation of costumers and end-users directly at the customer's workplace. Examples for contextual techniques are participant observation where the observer gets the requirements from observing team discussions, interviews, documents and non-verbal interaction.
- **Cognitive techniques:** Cognitive techniques allow analyzing and gathering information up to the human thinking level [9]. They include protocol analysis, where an experts performs a task while thinking aloud and an observer documents the cognitive processes used to perform the task. Another method is card sorting, where stakeholders are asked to sort cards into groups.

- **Model-driven techniques:** These techniques analyze the information that is gathered by the system and use this model to drive the elicitation process.

Most of these techniques were never used in cooperation with people with cognitive disabilities, therefore many of today's systems are not developed and designed for people with cognitive disabilities. A common prejudice in the scientific community is that people with intellectual disabilities are not very reliable interview partners, as they would not be able to give valid answers in the context of surveys [15]. We would like to overcome this and show that with appropriate preparations and adapted research tools and methods the target group may gain a position to work on its own behalf. On the other hand, the involvement of the target groups as peer researchers always requires a high willingness and intuition of the researchers and developers.

3 Design and Method

For requirements elicitation of software an integrative design oriented research approach supporting and including peer researchers has to be created. This approach will be done by combining two existing design methods: Inclusive Participatory Action Research – IPAR [5] and User Centred Design – UCD [16].

- The IPAR method by Janice Ollerton is a variation of the Participatory Action Research (PAR). IPAR includes people with cognitive disabilities in all steps. IPAR provides a framework for integrative participatory action research (fusion of integrative research approaches and participatory action research). It is a practical, alternative methodology for integrative research design with accessible data collection and analysis tools. IPAR questions the traditional research relationships in which research is conducted instead of with people with intellectual disabilities.
- UCD [16] is a design methodology that puts users at the heart of the design process. In particular when it comes to systems and appliances for a mass-consumer market the involvement of user groups at all stages of research processes has proven to be essential for better usability and improved product/output quality. Studies underline that reasonable investment in UCD leads to substantial return in terms of higher efficiency, less maintenance, less complaints and higher usage/client rates.

The integration of IPAR and UCD should provide the basis for the participation of co-researchers with cognitive disabilities. In order to develop proper methods and tools as methodology, individual steps within the requirements engineering process, such as requirements elicitation methods, are selected, developed and evaluated together with people with different competencies. This is done by:

- Evaluating current methods and tools for requirements engineering: Literature research and well-known findings of existing tools will be examined and formally tested if they suit the needs of the target group.
- Developing new methods that suites the needs of the target group: This will be done by Design-Based Research. DBR uses a mix of methods to analyse and improve the methods of UCD [3].

Resulting methods and processes will be applied to a real software project where people with cognitive disabilities (peer researchers) will be involved.

4 Approach

4.1 Recruiting and Instruction

In order to select, adapt and to develop methods for requirements elicitation people with cognitive disabilities are invited to participate in a real software project as peer researchers. This was initiated with a first workshop that provided them with an overview on the goals of the project and about the working conditions. This workshop is of utter importance and should create a common understanding on the functionality and purpose of the software that is going to be developed within the software project.

4.2 Requirement Analysis and Methods

In the next step selected methods and tools for requirements elicitation will be tested and evaluated with the co-researchers. The specification can be clarified by the user perspective with use cases. These include the functional requirements described by the participants, for example what is missing, what is disturbing and what is good. In a first step, the following methods, which seem to be useful for requirement analysis, were selected:

- **Focus group:** A focus group shares their thoughts, feelings and attitudes towards an already existing software product or prototype [10]. This is especially useful as input for new software systems as feedback from users identify useful features and problems in existing systems. The focus group is a moderated group discussion. First, the topic/task of the session is determined. Usually 6–10 peer researchers or potential target group members participate in a session. They share their attitudes and thoughts, for example about an existing software product or prototype. These results help to review existing concepts and to gain new ideas and input for new software systems. A moderator chairs the session by providing help, asks questions, sums up and makes sure that the focus is not lost during the discussions. This method can be used in any phase of the UCD.
- **User stories:** This method provides an alternative to the focus group. The requirements of the user are collected at the beginning of a development by user stories of himself and formally documented to identify the extent of a system [11]. In doing so, the user goals and intentions are e.g. noted on an index card. In the simplest case, these can be just one or two sentences. Then a priority is given by the peer researcher (from 1 to 5 where 1 is the highest priority, or high, medium, low).
- **Use cases:** Here, peer researchers can have a voice from the user's perspective. They can report on their real-life experiences and share their thoughts on what applications of a system or product they needed [12]. This specifies the require-ments for a system and defines the features that the system should have for the end users. The functional variety of a product or software is broken down into under-standable and related units. Use cases are also an instrument to find out who should use the product and what the product should do for the user.
- **Storyboard:** Storyboards use illustrations/images that are shown one after the other, for example to visualize an interactive media sequence in advance [13]. It

illustrates interactions between a person and the product or software. Peer researchers are then able to use these images to contribute their own ideas and views on the required features of the software or product.

- **The Easy Cognitive Walkthrough:** This method is a modified version of the cognitive walkthrough method - a procedure in which peer researchers, as experts, with or without the support of a test moderator, perform tasks with the product that were previously described as a typical task, taking into account the expected knowledge and skills of the target group [14]. Each step is analysed by the co-researchers from the perspective of another user and thus problems and required features should be identified.

4.3 Communication Is Necessary

Inclusive requirements engineering in a software project, requires intensive communication between all participating stakeholders. This exchange can be done during daily meetings of relatively short duration, reflection rounds or workshops for the collection of requirements.

Fig. 1. Performing the focus group method with co-researchers on a prototype interface

When stakeholders, with or without cognitive disabilities are willing to exchange information and communicate within the project, requirements and needs of stakeholders are easier detected resulting in a better product.

5 Current Results

Currently the first methods are tested and evaluated with the co-researchers in a software project, dealing with the creation of a browser-extension helping people with cognitive disabilities to improve their ability to browse and understand web-content.

A preliminary evaluation of testing the different methods with end-users shows that a requirement analysis with the target group is feasible and that the people with cognitive disabilities are reliable interview partners which are quite capable of expressing their needs in this way. It is being observed that all peer researchers take their task very seriously and on the other hand they show interest and a certain degree of personal responsibility.

As can be seen in Fig. 1 the cooperation between peer researchers and developers in a focus group are quite positive. Peer researchers actively participated in the process and expressed their requirements and needs. On the other hand software developers and designer got a deeper insight in the requirements of their end users which led to new interaction and information presentation concepts. In this project the peer researchers are located in the same building as software developers and designers, which allows short communication way and fosters exchange of thoughts which is very positive.

Regarding the software development process itself an agile software development process seemed appropriate for the target group. This implies that the peer researchers and developers constantly work together on their own behalf during the project.

Acknowledgments. This project has received funding from the European Research Council (ERC) under the European Union's Horizon 2020 research and innovation programme (grant agreement No. 780529).

References

1. Gerogiannis, V.C.: Software requirements engineering: state of the art and research trends. Int. J. Manag. Appl. Sci. (IJMAS) 3(9), 66–71 (2017)
2. Pohl, K.: Requirements Engineering: Fundamentals, Principles, and Techniques. Springer, Heidelberg (2010)
3. Wang, F., Hannafin, M.J.: Using design-based research in design and research of technology-enhanced learning environments. In: Conference Paper: Annual Meeting of the American Educational Research Association, San Diego, C.A. (2004)
4. Kremsner, G.: Macht und Gewalt in den Biographien von Menschen mit Lern-schwierigkeiten – eine (forschungsethische) Herausforderung? In: Schuppener, S., Bern-hardt, N., Hauser, M., Poppe, F. (Hrsg.): Inklusion und Chancengleichheit. Diversity im Spiegel von Bildung und Didaktik, pp. 61–68, Heilbrunn (2014)
5. Ollerton, J.: IPAR, an inclusive disability research methodology with accessible analytical tools. Int. Pract. Dev. J. 2(2), Article ID 3 (2012). http://www.fons.org/library/journal/volume2-issue2/article3
6. Paetsch, F., Eberlein, A., Maurer, F.: Requirements engineering and agile software development, WET ICE 2003. In: Proceedings. Twelfth IEEE International Workshops on Enabling Technologies: Infrastructure for Collaborative Enterprises, pp. 308–313 (2003). https://doi.org/10.1109/enabl.2003.1231428
7. Nuseibeh, B., Easterbrook, S.: Requirements engineering: a roadmap. In: Future of Soft-ware Engineering, ICSE 2000, pp. 35–46. Limerick, Ireland (2000)
8. Tuunanen, T.: A new perspective on requirements elicitation methods. JITTA J. Inf. Technol. Theory Appl. 5(3), 45–62 (2003)
9. Yousuf, M., Asger, M.: Comparison of various requirements elicitation techniques. Int. J. Comput. Appl. 116(4) (2015)

10. Kontio, J., Lehtola, L., Bragge, J.: Using the focus group method in software engineering: obtaining practitioner and user experiences. In: Proceedings of the International Symposium on Empirical Software Engineering (ISESE), pp. 271–280. IEEE Computer Society, Redondo Beach, CA, August 2004

11. Moreno, A.M., Yagüe, A.: Agile user stories enriched with usability. In: Wohlin, C. (ed.) XP 2012. LNBIP, vol. 111, pp. 168–176. Springer, Heidelberg (2012). https://doi.org/10.1007/978-3-642-30350-0_12

12. Lee, J., Xue, N.L.: Analyzing user requirements by use cases: a goal-driven approach. IEEE Softw. **16**(4), 92–101 (1999)

13. Branham, S.M., Wahid, S., McCrickard, D.S.: Channeling creativity: using storyboards and claims to encourage collaborative design (2007). http://people.cs.vt.edu/mccricks/papers/bwm-cc07.pdf

14. Rieman, J., Franzke, M., Redmiles, D.: Usability evaluation with the cognitive walkthrough. In: CHI 1995 Proceedings. ACM (1995)

15. Buchner, T., König, O.: Von der Ausgrenzung zur Inklusion: Entwicklung, Stand und Perspektiven gemeinsamen Forschens. In: DIFGB (2011) Forschungsfalle Methode? Partizipative Forschung im Diskurs, Band 1, pp. 2–16, Leipzig (2011)

16. Lowdermilk, T.: User-Centered Design: A Developer's Guide to Building User-Friendly Applications. O'Reilly Media Incorporated, Sebastopol (2013)

Usability Engineering for Cognitively Accessible Software

Susanne Dirks[✉] and Christian Bühler

TU Dortmund University, Emil-Figge-Str. 50, 44227 Dortmund, Germany
susanne.dirks@tu-dortmund.de

Abstract. Since the use of software products has become an integral part of life, it has emerged that, in addition to functional requirements, the consideration of qualitative requirements plays an essential role in the usability and acceptance of software systems. In order to enable people with cognitive impairments, who are particularly affected by exclusion and disadvantage, to participate in technical development, cognitively accessible software must be developed. In the scope of various studies, usability patterns have been developed which can be used to facilitate the implementation of general usability requirements in software development. In the study presented here, the usability of four software systems, which have been developed specifically for users with cognitive impairments, was examined. In order to solve the existing problems and improve the usability of the examined systems, usability patterns and respective usage scenarios were developed and will be evaluated as part of the redesign of the systems. As the main result of the study a catalogue of usability patterns will be compiled, which contains all relevant usability patterns for the development of cognitively accessible software systems.

Keywords: Software development · Accessibility · Usability patterns
Cognitive impairment

1 Introduction

To support the adoption of digital technologies by people with cognitive impairments, software products must be usable and, in this sense, cognitively accessible. The interface design of commercial applications is often too complex and confusing and fundamental usability requirements are not fulfilled. There is general agreement that usability is a complex and multifaceted but nonetheless essential construct in software engineering. One of the common general definitions of usability is that of the International Organization for Standardization (ISO 9241). Usability of a product is "the extent to which a system, product or service can be used by specified users to achieve specified goals with effectiveness, efficiency and satisfaction in a specified context of use" [1].

In software engineering, the following definition of Nielsen [2] has become widely accepted: "Usability is the measure of quality of the user experience when interacting with something – whether a web site, a traditional software application, or any other device the user can operate in some way or another" [2]. According to Nielsen usability

© Springer International Publishing AG, part of Springer Nature 2018
K. Miesenberger and G. Kouroupetroglou (Eds.): ICCHP 2018, LNCS 10896, pp. 446–453, 2018.
https://doi.org/10.1007/978-3-319-94277-3_69

can be defined by five independent quality components: learnability, efficiency, reliability, errors and satisfaction. The goal of usability engineering is the development of processes to define usability, to measure usability outcomes and to improve the overall usability of a product.

Although more and more software developers recognize usability engineering as an important part of the design and development process and modern approaches to agile software development support the integration of usability engineering early in the development process, the majority of software products still suffer from significant restrictions with regard to usability and accessibility.

As users with cognitive impairments represent a group that is particularly affected by the lack of opportunities for digital participation, usability engineering plays a central role in the development of cognitive accessible software. Nevertheless, users with cognitive impairments are seldom regarded as a relevant end user group and therefore not involved in usability engineering processes. For the group of users with cognitive impairments, the relationship between users and technological products is of particular importance. The potential users of software products should be consistently involved in the development processes in the sense of participative development. The requirements of the users as well as their limitations and wishes must be determined in a participative manner before the beginning and have to be checked repeatedly in the course of the technical development. Particularly for people with cognitive impairments or seniors, special challenges are often imposed on the design of assistive devices. In many cases, the final design of products or apps designed for users with cognitive limitations is perceived as unaesthetic and stigmatizing [3]. However, if the potential users of the system are involved in the development right from the start, both the functional and design-related aspects can be continually reviewed and adapted.

Building on the work of Folmer et al. [4] and Vieritz et al. [5], the described project investigates which of the generally accepted usability patterns are relevant for the development of cognitively accessible software products and how they could be compiled into a pattern library.

2 Background

There is a large set of software design principles, some of which are considered particularly relevant for usability engineering. The most common usability attributes used in software development are based on the quality aspects of usability formulated by Nielsen [2]: learnability - how quickly and easily a user can deal with an unknown system, combined with the ease of remembering the way a system operates; efficiency of use - the number of tasks per time unit that the user can perform with the system; reliability in use - the error rate resulting from the use of the system and the time required for recovery and satisfaction - the subjective contentment of users with the system.

The usability attributes proposed by Nielsen can be assigned to specific usability patterns. Since the influential work of the 'Gang of Four' [6], design patterns have played an important role in software development. Originally developed by Alexander [7] for the fields of architecture and urban planning, the idea of creating reusable concepts for problem solving was subsequently applied to many other fields and processes. In software development, design patterns are regarded as tried-and-tested solutions to recurring design problems. They describe essential design decisions and their use should make a design flexible, reusable, extensible, easier to use and change resistant. In recent years, the use of so-called 'usability patterns' has also become established in the field of usability engineering. According to Juristo et al. [8] usability pattern is "a functional solution pattern for a typical interaction problem in a specific usage context". Here, interaction problems are understood as problems, requirements or wishes that users have when interacting individually with a system, for example, during the execution and control of actions, during input or during the interpretation of outputs. Functional solution patterns are abstract functional features or functions of a system that solve such interaction problems.

According to the usability framework proposed by Folmer and Bosch [9] the mapping between usability attributes, like 'user satisfaction' and related usability patterns, like 'multi channelling' or 'undo' is mediated by usability properties, like 'user control' or 'adaptability'. A comprehensive literature survey done by Folmer and Bosch revealed that there seems to be a common understanding that a usability attribute is a precise and measurable component of the abstract concept 'usability' [10]. A usability property, in turn, can be understood as a rather concrete form of usability requirement in relation to a certain solution area. Therefore, usability properties can be used as requirements during the design phase. The aim of usability patterns is the consideration of usability requirements in the process of requirement development and early development. In most cases, the assignment between usability attribute and usability pattern is not one-to-one, a pattern can be assigned to several usability attributes or design principles or several patterns can support the same attribute. Figure 1 shows an example of the mapping of usability patterns and usability properties as proposed by Folmer et al. [4] for the usability principle 'satisfaction'.

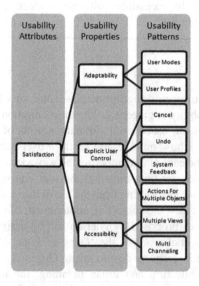

Fig. 1. Mapping of usability patterns

It can be concluded that the use of proven, ergonomically sensible solution patterns in usability engineering seems to be groundbreaking. In the complex application world of software engineering, patterns can offer easy-to-understand, clear and concrete solution proposals. Furthermore, they can make ergonomic knowledge and experience tangible and reusable.

3 Study

During the last few years, various projects for the development of cognitively accessible software have been carried out at the Chair of Rehabilitation Technology at the TU Dortmund University, e.g. Knoffit [11], Mediata [12], Via4All [13] or eJo [14].

Although detailed field studies, user surveys and user tests have been carried out in all projects, the final versions of the products still had noticeable usability problems. Some of the problems reported by the user group with cognitive impairments can only be solved by substantial changes in the software architecture. As Folmer et al. [4] stated, especially changes related to user-system interactions are associated with significant changes in the system architecture. In order to reduce the effort resulting from changes after completion of the software, it needs to be investigated which usability properties are particularly relevant for users with cognitive impairments and which of them require substantial changes in software architecture when detected late in the development process.

3.1 Usability Analysis

In the first part of the project, all usability requirements and corresponding results of the preliminary and final evaluations of the relevant projects were analyzed in order to identify remaining usability problems. Thorough analysis of the results showed that the learnability of a software system plays a particular role in usability for users with cognitive limitations. Learnability is a usability attribute, which according to Folmer et al. [4] can be related to many different usability patterns. Furthermore, it could be shown that the usability attributes reliability and accessibility are relevant for users with cognitive impairments as well. Even though accessibility in the context of software development is regarded rather as a usability property than a usability attribute and thus not on a par with qualities like learnability or satisfaction, it was evident that accessibility for users with cognitive impairments is an essential prerequisite for usability. For people with cognitive impairments it is essential that the systems are compatible with assistive technologies, so that for example a screen reader can be used for reading out important content to the user. The Mediata system, which provides spoken language or a text-free image selection as alternative input options for web search, was rated significantly better in terms of accessibility and learnability than the Knoffit system, which did not provide these input modalities.

The usability analysis of the more complex software systems like Via4all or EJO, showed that for users with cognitive impairments it was important that the system could be adapted to their personal preferences and that clear and easy-to-understand messages were displayed in case of errors. Since none of the systems had implemented any of the corresponding patterns, such as the 'wizard' or 'context sensitive help' pattern, it was not possible to determine how relevant these patterns are for the respective user group.

In the field of software development, usability requirements are usually regarded as non-functional requirements. Therefore, they are often only partially considered during the software planning phase. However, based on extensive empirical studies, in recent years some research groups have moved on to regard usability requirements as equally important as functional requirements. For example, Juristo et al. [8] have suggested that usability requirements that have an influence on software architecture should be referred to as 'functional usability requirements'. The usability problems for users with cognitive impairments essentially concern the usability attributes, which have been described as software architecture relevant in the aforementioned research projects. Therefore, it seems plausible that the usability of software systems for people with cognitive impairments can be improved using suitable usability patterns.

Table 1 gives an overview of the most prominent usability problems and the respective usability patterns that can be applied to solve these problems.

Table 1. Identified usability problems and related usability patterns

Usability problem	Description	Usability pattern
Missing feedback	User gets stuck in the process and needs feedback on the actual status of the system	System feedback pattern, context sensitive help
Software not compatible with assistive technology	User needs to use alternative output channels (e.g. text-to-speech) or to enlarge text	Adaptable view, settings
Missing help for error correction	User needs help to correct wrong input	Undo, field validation
No adjustable preferences	User wants to save her preferred system configuration	User profile, user modes
Missing shortcuts	User want to create shortcuts to operate the system more efficiently	Shortcuts, user modes

3.2   Usability Pattern Catalogue

The aim of the second part of the project is the compilation of a catalogue of usability patterns for the development of cognitively accessible software. At present, this part of the project is not yet completed.

Since usability patterns are intended to facilitate the implementation of usability requirements, they must have an internal structure that allows developers to easily understand and apply them in different usage situations. The usual way of documenting design patterns using more than 13 different criteria [6] has proven to be too extensive as well as not specific enough for practical application. In the corresponding literature, many different documentation schemata can be found, so part of the work in this project phase will consist of creating a suitable documentation schema for usability patterns for the development of cognitively accessible software. A suitable documentation scheme for usability patterns for the development of cognitively accessible software should cover at least the following criteria: name, assignment to corresponding usability attribute, problem description, solution, example, consequences and risks.

The key outcome of the described project will be library of usability patterns and usage scenarios that are essential for the development of cognitively accessible software. Table 2 shows a preliminary description of the System Feedback usability pattern.

Table 2. Description of system feedback usability pattern

Name	System feedback pattern
Corresponding usability attribute	Learnability
Problem	User gets stuck in the process because continuation actions are unclear
Solution	User needs to receive a feedback on how to continue Provide feedback using the **system feedback pattern** Use a trigger or positive feedback loops to induce change of behavior
Example	Login – user does not touch the login button, but waits for system response
Consequences and risks	Efficiency might be affected as user has to wait for system feedback, but other users are not affected as feedback is only given when required action is not carried out

To assess the impact of the pattern-based approach, usage scenarios for all identified usability problems will be created and solutions based on the assigned usability patterns will be given. All identified usability problems will be modelled as usage scenarios and then used for redesign and re-evaluation of the examined software systems.

It can be assumed that the usability of the tested systems can be considerably improved by applying the developed usability patterns in the redesign process. Figure 2 shows a comparison of the original login interface of the Mediata App [12] and its enhancement in the re-design with the addition of a contextual system feedback.

Fig. 2. Login screen Mediata App - before and after redesign

The usability requirements of two of the four software systems that are currently still under development will be reformulated and the systems will be redesigned based on the compiled pattern catalog.

4 Discussion

The aim of the study presented here was to investigate usability patterns that play a special role in the development of cognitively accessible software. Based on several research projects on the development of software for people with cognitive impairments, typical usability problems for users with cognitive impairments have been identified. The majority of the usability problems found in the described study were related to the usability attributes 'learnability', 'adaptability' and 'reliability'. Moreover, the user group of people with cognitive impairments perceived usability problems caused by limited accessibility of the software as particularly restrictive. Since the accessibility of software systems has not been sufficiently considered in existing studies, there are currently virtually no usability patterns for the problems caused by accessibility violations. In further studies, special attention must therefore be given to these aspects.

As the project continues proposals for improving the cognitive accessibility of software products using usability design patterns will be developed and evaluated. After evaluation of the created patterns a library of usability design patterns suitable for the development of cognitively accessible software will be compiled. This usability pattern library can then be used to address and solve typical usability problems in software development as early as in the design phase. This will hopefully broaden the understanding and simplify the implementation of cognitively accessible software and improve the usability of software products for people with cognitive impairments.

Through increased efforts in developing design patterns for the implementation of accessibility needs, software may be developed that specifically addresses the needs of people with disabilities and contributes to ensuring that all users can use all software products without any barriers.

References

1. ISO Online Browsing Platform. https://www.iso.org/obp/ui/#iso:std:63500:en. Accessed 20 Jan 2018
2. Nielsen, J.: Usability Engineering. Academic Press Inc., Boston (1993)
3. Ziefle, M., Schaar, A.K.: Technology acceptance by patients: empowerment and stigma. In: van Hoof, J., et al. (eds.) Handbook of Smart Homes, Health Care and Well-Being, pp. 167–177. Springer, Switzerland (2017). https://doi.org/10.1007/978-3-319-01583-5_34
4. Folmer, E., van Gurp, J., Bosch, J.: Software architecture analysis of usability. In: Bastide, R., Palanque, P., Roth, J. (eds.) DSV-IS 2004. LNCS, vol. 3425, pp. 38–58. Springer, Heidelberg (2005). https://doi.org/10.1007/11431879_3
5. Vieritz, H., Schilberg, D., Jeschke, S.: Merging web accessibility and usability by patterns. In: Miesenberger, K., Klaus, J., Zagler, W., Karshmer, A. (eds.) ICCHP 2010. LNCS, vol. 6179, pp. 336–342. Springer, Heidelberg (2010). https://doi.org/10.1007/978-3-642-14097-6_54

6. Gamma, E., Helm, R., Johnson, R., Vlissides, J.: Design Patterns: Elements of Reusable Object-Oriented Software. Addison-Wesley, Reading (1995)
7. Alexander, C., Ishikawa, S., Silverstein, M., Jacobson, M., Fiksdahl-King, I., Shlomo, A.: A Pattern Language: Towns, Buildings, Construction. Oxford University Press, New York (1977)
8. Juristo, N., Moreno, A.M., Sanchez-Segura, M.-I.: Guidelines for eliciting usability functionalities. IEEE Trans. Softw. Eng. **33**(11), 744–758 (2007)
9. Folmer, E., Bosch, J.: Usability patterns in software architecture. In: Jacko, J.A., Stephanidis, C. (eds.) Human-Computer Interaction: Theory and Practice Proceedings HCI, vol. 1, pp. 93–97. LEA, London (2003)
10. UI Design Patterns. http://ui-patterns.com/patterns. Accessed 20 Jan 2018
11. Schaten, M., Lexis, M., Roentgen, U., Bühler, C., de Witte, L.: User centered design in practice – developing software with/for people with cognitive and intellectual disabilities. In: Encarnação, P., Azevedo, L., Gelderblom, G.J. (eds.) Assistive Technology: From Research to Practice: AAATE 2013. IOS Press (2013)
12. Dirks, S., Bühler, C.: Participation and autonomy for users with ABI through easy social media access. In: Cudd, P., de Witte, L.P. (eds.) Harnessing the Power of Technology to Improve Lives, Proceedings of the 14th European Conference on the Advancements of Assistive Technology, Studies in Health Technology and Informatics, vol. 242. IOS Press (2017)
13. Via4All Project Website. http://www.via4all.de/start. Accessed 20 Jan 2018
14. Brausch, C., Bühler, C., Feldmann, A., Padberg, M.: Supported employment – electronic job-coach (EJO). In: Miesenberger, K., Bühler, C., Penaz, P. (eds.) ICCHP 2016. LNCS, vol. 9758, pp. 142–149. Springer, Cham (2016). https://doi.org/10.1007/978-3-319-41264-1_20
15. Röder, H.: Usability Patterns – Eine Technik zur Spezifikation technischer Usability-Merkmale. http://www.iste.uni-stuttgart.de/fileadmin/user_upload/iste/se/people/roeder/Holger_Roeder-Dissertation-Usability_Patterns.pdf. Accessed 20 Jan 2018

Strengthening Participatory Action Research Approach to Develop a Personalized Mobile Application for Young Adults with Intellectual Disabilities

Julia S. Louw[✉] [iD]

National University of Ireland, Galway (NUIG), Galway, H91 TK33, Ireland
julia.louw@nuigalway.ie

Abstract. Participation in social inclusion activities has been reported to be an important determinant of health for people with disabilities and has a number of benefits particularly for young adults with intellectual disabilities (ID). However, young adults with ID often have difficulty making friends and are excluded from taking part in social activities in society, therefore they struggle to sustain friendships over time. This paper reports on a study that investigates how a mobile application can help young adults with ID make friends, build social relationships and participate successfully within their communities. Using a participatory research design, we developed a prototype of a mobile app to introduce social inclusion activities for young adults with ID. Parents, service providers, staff and young adults with ID provided input on features of the prototype. To evaluate the impact of the mobile app, pre- and post-intervention measures will be collected. This experiential opportunity will encourage young adults with ID with self-determination when they interact with others but more importantly, give a sense of independence when they engage in real-world social environments.

Keywords: Participatory research · Young adults · Intellectual disabilities
Social inclusion

1 Introduction

It is estimated that one billion people are in need of assistive products, with the majority being older individuals and people with disabilities, [16, 20]. According to the World Health Organization (WHO) assistive products including Assistive Technology (AT) enable people to live healthy, productive, independent and dignified lives; to participate in education, the labour market and in social and civic life [20, p. 1]. Without access to assistive products and technology these individuals may suffer exclusion, may be at risk of isolation and poverty, and they may become a burden to their family and on society [20]. Particularly young adults with moderate to severe intellectual disabilities (ID) are most often ignored and marginalized. Thus, the UN Convention on the Rights of Persons with Disabilities (CRPD) underscore the importance of all people with disability to have the right to all areas of participation and inclusion [17].

© Springer International Publishing AG, part of Springer Nature 2018
K. Miesenberger and G. Kouroupetroglou (Eds.): ICCHP 2018, LNCS 10896, pp. 454–461, 2018.
https://doi.org/10.1007/978-3-319-94277-3_70

Over the years an emerging importance of the role and use of digital tools to improve and increase participation and social inclusion for people with disabilities has evolved [8]. Dekelver et al. [5] noted, that too few scholars and publications refer to the use of ICTs and digital tools by young adults with intellectual disabilities, thus highlighting the limited opportunities and often exclusion from electronic information and services for these individuals. Parsons [12] however highlights that the commitment of key stakeholders to the benefits of assistive technology is critical, to facilitate the successful adoption of assistive devices by young adults with intellectual disability.

Still, too little informed discussion, public debate or critical analysis and in-depth research exists that involve key holders in a step-by-step participatory approach to examine the potential and implication of assistive devices such as mobile technology for young adults with intellectual disabilities [7]. This study implements the pilot of a mobile application for young adults with intellectual disabilities to assess its use through the perceptions of key stakeholders that include service providers, staff, parents, guardians and people with intellectual disabilities.

2   Aim of the Study

The aim of the research study is to examine to what extent social inclusion initiatives for young adults with ID between the ages of 18 to 30 years can be sustained over time. The research questions investigate:

- To what extent can a social inclusion mobile app and introduction to social media enhance social inclusion for young adults with ID?
- Further, can the mobile app and social media help sustain social inclusion activities over time?

3   Study Design and Measures

3.1   Research Approach

The study adopts a research design based on the principles of Participatory Action Research (PAR), which is suitable for working with key stakeholders that include a multidisciplinary team of researchers, service providers, staff, parents, guardians and young adults with ID [1, 6]. PAR involves practitioners in the research process from the initial design and implementation of the project through data gathering and analysis to final conclusions and actions arising out of the research [19]. Therefore, from the proposal writing and ethics application stage of the study, researchers and service providers participated in the conceptualization of the study as well as preparing the ethics application. This involved consultations with service providers, to provide input on the practical implications of implementing an intervention that involve a mobile application for young adults with ID who participate in Day services offered by the service provider. Also, service providers assisted in addressing specific concerns related to confidentiality and privacy issues related to the inclusion of a social media component for the study. Subsequently, with the guidance and input from service providers, ethics approval of the study was successfully obtained. This participatory approach has been applied during the development of the mobile app that is described in more detail in the Preliminary Findings section.

To match the mobile application to the young people's needs and to understand how the functionality can best be met, a full day training is planned that will include gathering information of the current level of social participation, familiarization of the mobile app and role play social situations with the support of the mobile app [4]. During the planned training, each participant will receive a tablet pre-loaded with the social activity themes, a protective case for the device as well as a charger.

3.2 Measures

Pre- and post-intervention measures will be collected. The San Martin Quality of life (QoL) scale will be used to assess and collect information before and after the intervention [18]. This scale is suitable for those with the lowest levels of functioning who are frequently unable to communicate their feelings, thoughts, and preferences. In addition, during the intervention direct observations from support workers will be documented and noted, with descriptions and interpretations of the participants' levels and signs of increased interactions.

With consent and permission of participants, digital images will be used to elaborate on the experiences of social participation in their communities. This documentation forms a basis for the PhotoVoice technique, a qualitative strategy that allows individuals to create their own narratives and to communicate this to staff, family and friends [13, 14]. PhotoVoice methodology is strongly rooted in the notion of 'participation'. Thus, at the heart of the participatory approach is the aim of increasing the involvement of marginalized groups in decision-making that affects their own lives [2]. Lastly, on a social media platform, participants will be asked to share selected photographs should they prefer and consent to do so, and use this platform to help improve their networking and self-determination [3]. According to Darcy et al. [4] in their study on using a mobile technology platform, positive feedback was received with a parent reporting that her daughter loved taking pictures and enjoyed photographing people like her family, especially her young nephew, her dog and cat and then share this with them on her mobile phone.

4   Preliminary Findings

Thus far, the prototype of the mobile app has been completed and consultations have been conducted with key stakeholders. The development of the mobile app was done by a team that include the researcher who is a qualified Research Psychologist, an academic staff member from the National University of Ireland, Galway (NUIG) with a background in Engineering and a clinician who us a qualified Behavior Analyst based in the School of Psychology at NUIG. Valuable input and feedback was received and suggestions made on how functional the app is to support young adults with ID. Below, a detailed description of the features of the prototype as well as a summary of the feedback and suggestions that was noted in the form of field notes after each consultative meeting:

4.1   Features of the Prototype

The overall objective of the mobile app is to support young adults with ID to engage socially with peers with more ease. Therefore, the prototype includes the following functionality:

- it has been written in the computer language called 'Ionic' suitable for Android devices but also transferable to an iOS platform;
- it has eight pre-loaded social inclusion themes representative of various social topics, as well as an additional ninth theme that has no assigned topic. This ninth theme means that a participant can create their own social theme that may not be included in the first eight themes;
- examples of the themes include topics such as 'going shopping; learn a sport, etc'. each theme signifies any social activity related to that specific theme for example, the theme named 'learn a sport' may signify an activity such as 'learn to swim' or 'learn the rules of tennis';
- each theme allows for staff or parent interaction in the form of support when finalising individualised prompts or guided instructions;
- questions are included on evaluating the overall functioning of the app, as well as the social validity of each activity when completed. The response to these questions take the form of colourful 'emojis' and is done in the form of a likert scale 'yes, maybe, no';
- capability is included that capture the date and time when an activity is marked complete;
- lastly, a startTimer and stopTimer capability for each activity is included.

4.2   Feedback from Consultations

The following feedback was received from meetings and discussion and suggestions made by key stakeholders during consultations and meetings that included young adults and their support workers:

- reduce the number of screenshots to a minimum of 3 to 5;
- add a functionality that translate 'Text-To-Speech' for each of the prompts;
- add an option to upload their own picture of their participation in the social activity;
- add an option to edit, change or delete prompts and pictures;

The mobile app has subsequently been revised to include all the suggestions made by the key stakeholders. In addition, the app includes a screenshot with an overview of the general guidelines of how the app works.

5 Discussion

The preliminary findings here provide valuable information related to using a participatory research approach [1, 19], when implementing an intervention study that focus on developing a mobile app to support young adults with ID with social inclusion activities in their communities. Key stakeholders included researchers, service providers, staff, parents and young adults with ID who provided input on the practical and functional use of the prototype of a mobile app.

Regarding the feedback and suggestions made, specifically in relation to the features of the prototype: firstly, key stakeholders expressed concern that with too many screen-shots to navigate through the app, young adults with ID may become overwhelmed and confused, therefore they suggested to reduce the number of screen shots to no more than five. This suggestion derived during the consultation when staff gave the tablets to two young adults with ID to explain how the app works. The young adult was not able to continue further after the 5th screenshot and became very agitated. After several attempts to get this young adult to try using the app again, he simply lost interest. From the initial seven screen shots, the revised prototype has been adjusted to only three screens shots to navigate through each activity. Second, to accommodate young adults with ID on the spectrum from mild to profound ID, stakeholders advised to include text-to-speech capabilities particularly for individuals with difficulty in speech and reading abilities. In this way, once the prompt has been completed, young adults are able to listen to the prompts as often as they like and at their own convenience without the oversight of the parent or staff member. Thirdly, the prototype initially had copyright approved Google images to illustrate the nine themes, but the key stakeholders indicated that this is problematic. Many young adults with ID only associate with images and pictures that they are personally familiar with. Therefore, the prototype has been adjusted in such a way that it also allows the capability for young adults to take a photograph of their choice each time when a new prompt for an activity is written. Finally, the suggestions to add the editing capability was critical, as some adults with ID can at times become distressed with viewing images of themselves, therefore it was important to be able to delete this depending on how comfortable they felt with having their picture as part of the prompt.

Regarding the other features of the app, for example making provision for parent and staff interaction, was to include support in the form of typing in prompts that will be played back to young adults via the text-to-speech capability, and that will guide them through an activity. It was suggested for these messages to be a short phrase or single words, as young adults with ID find it difficult to remember instructions or guidelines that are given in long extended text or explanations. Also, the two young adults present in the consultations were asked to select the same theme but their parents had to give input of what prompts would be more suitable for each of them. Each young adult's prompts were different based on their own ability and preference, even though they selected to partake in the same social activity. This is a unique feature of the app that specifically addressed the personal individual needs of young adults with ID.

Interestingly, staff highlighted the difference in benefits of the prototype for young adults with mild to moderate ID versus severe to profound ID. In the former, they noted that the basic features of the prototype will be able to address issues that go beyond facilitating social interactions for this group since they are more often already socially immersed in their communities. On the other hand, by using the prototype among young adults with severe to profound ID, they will be able to benefit more with practicing and understanding social skills such as understanding verbal and non-verbal cues, etc. However, this assumption by staff that young adults with mild ID is already being integrated socially into their communities is questionable. Research shows that people with ID in general have become more visible in society due to the move from institutionalized settings to community settings [20] and this may be what staff has been noticing. With this in mind, service providers need to focus on individual life skills to improve social inclusion on the whole when working with people with ID. Overmars [11] highlights that, to create a suitable environment for social inclusion it is important that people with an ID have or develop skills to nurture the interaction with people in their communities, and this inevitably implies that community members also try to adapt to the skills of people with ID. But often this does not happen; instead the expectation is that people with ID fit and adjust into society and as a result, no reciprocal relationships are formed.

It was important to include a startTimer and stopTimer capability. This feature allows for the recording of time spent on each individual activity. Also, the time spent on each step or prompt is recorded and the number of times each step or prompt have been repeated. This information can be used to inform staff and parents of what prompts may be too difficult to understand or formulated and thus may need to be revised. In the case of specifically young adults with severe to profound ID, the time spent on a prompt is also an expression of their likes or dislikes since their verbal abilities is limited. For them, far more support is needed from a staff member or caregiver when entering a prompt, but with the text-to-speech and the visual images by way of taking pictures of the activity they participate in, a response will be triggered, which serves as an indication of their expression of how they feel. Another benefit of the timer on the activities and prompts is that staff and parents will be able to have a better record of the young adult with ID's emotional well-being because often when they leave the Day service to go home to their parents, a quick verbal update is given of the day's events. But with the mobile app that has this feature, an in-depth understanding is communicated through the app instead of the verbal exchange where key information may leave out important information to report. Also, with staff changes this information will come in handy in addition to the written and verbal reporting during the intake of a new service user or transferring from one to another staff member.

Encouraging to note is the adoption of, and the level of acceptance and willingness of young adults with ID to engage with digital technology as noted with the young adults present in the consultations and by key stakeholders. These young adults were very comfortable with handling the device, which they did with ease. In fact, the parents who participated in the consultations confirmed that their children own their personal device, that is mostly tablets and for some of them, this has become an invaluable item that they came to depend on to keep busy by listening to music, watching their favorite program, or search the internet. However, what is generally neglected in the development of digital tools is related to that of 'accessibility' and 'usability' [6]. Too often socially and normative constructed notions are directly transferred to the development of technology creating a bigger gap in addressing the needs of individuals in the general population and people with disabilities [9, 10]. Söderström and Ytterhus [15] noted that technologies for people without disabilities are often associated with independence, competence, belonging and freedom. Equally, assistive or disability-focused technologies are more likely to be associated with dependency, restraint, difference and dependency.

6   Outcomes and Impact

This intervention has the potential to enable young adults with ID to partake in social activities with greater ease. It aims to create more opportunities to observe, practice and refine social skills as well as model appropriate social behaviour. It will improve the networking and development of healthy social relationships and help to build healthy interpersonal relationships. Young adults with ID will gain self-confidence and a sense of independence when engaging in real-world social environments. Further, it will promote better health and quality of life for the young person with ID and their family. Thus, the efficacy of a research project that uses ICT via a mobile application, the introduction to a social media component and including a photovoice technique as a unique and innovative method to reveal real life experiences and enhance social relationships, will empower marginalized individuals such as young adults with intellectual disabilities immensely.

Acknowledgement. This research was supported by funding from the charity RESPECT and the People Programme (Marie Curie Actions) of the European Union's Seventh Framework Programme (FP7/2007-2013) under REA grant agreement no. PCOFUND-GA-2013-608728

References

1. Bergold, J., Thomas, S.: Participatory research methods: a methodological approach in motion. Forum: Qual. Soc. Res. **13**(1), 191–222 (2012)
2. Blackman, A., Fairey, T.: The PhotoVoice Manual: A Guide to Designing and Running Participatory Photographic Projects, London, United Kingdom (2007)
3. Cumming, T.M.I., Strnadova, J., Knox, M., Parmenter, T.: Mobile technology in inclusive research: tools of empowerment. Disabil. Soc. **29**(7), 999–1012 (2014)
4. Darcy, S., Maxwell, H., Green, J.: Disability citizenship and independence through mobile technology? A study exploring adoption and use of a mobile technology platform. Disabil. Soc. **31**(4), 497–519 (2016)
5. Dekelver, J., Kultsova, M., Shabalina, O., Borblik, J., Pidoprigora, A., Romanenko, R., et al.: Design of mobile applications for people with intellectual disabilities. In: Kravets, A., Shcherbakov, M., Kultsova, M., Shabalina, O. (eds.) Creativity in Intelligent Technologies and Data Science. CCIS, vol. 535, pp. 823–836. Springer, Cham (2015). https://doi.org/10.1007/978-3-319-23766-4_65
6. Denzin, N., Lincoln, Y.: Introduction: The Discipline and Practice of Qualitative research. The Landscape of Qualitative Research. Theories and Issues, pp. 1–45 (2003)
7. Ellis, K., Goggin, G.: Disability, locative media, and complex ubiquity. In: Ekman, U., Bolter, J.D., Diaz, L., Sondergaard, M., Engberg, M. (eds.) Ubiquitous Computing, Complexity and Culture, pp. 272–287. Routledge, New York (2015)

8. Goggin, G.: Disability and mobile internet. First Monday, **20**(9) (2015). http://firstmonday.org/ojs/index.php/fm/article/view/6171/4906. https://doi.org/10.5210/fm.v20i9.6171

9. Jaeger, P.: Disability, human rights, and social justice: the ongoing struggle for online accessibility and equality. First Monday, **20**(9) (2015). http://firstmonday.org/ojs/index.php/fm/article/view/6164/4898. https://doi.org/10.5210/fm.v20i9.6164

10. Louw, J.S.: E-inclusion: social inclusion of young adults with intellectual disabilities-a participatory design. Stud. Health Technol. Inform. **242**, 269–272 (2017)

11. Overmars-Marx, T., Thomése, F., Verdonschot, M., Meininger, H.: Advancing social inclusion in the neighbourhood for people with an intellectual disability: an exploration of the literature. Disabil. Soc. **29**(2), 255–274 (2014)

12. Parsons, S., Daniels, H., Porter, J., Robertson, C.: Resources, staff beliefs and organisational culture: factors in the use of information and communication technology for adults with intellectual disabilities. J. Appl. Res. Intellect. Disabil. **21**(1), 19–33 (2008)

13. Powers, M., Freedman, D., Pitner, R.: A Photovoice Facilitator's Manual, South Carolina, United States (2012)

14. Schalock, R.L., Verdugo, M.A.: Handbook on Quality of Life for Human Service Practitioners. American Association on Mental Retardation, Washington, DC (2002)

15. Söderström, S., Ytterhus, B.: The use and non-use of assistive technologies from the world of information and communication technology by visually impaired young people: a walk on the tightrope of peer inclusion. Disabil. Soc. **25**(3), 303–315 (2010)

16. UNICEF: Children and Young People with Disabilities Fact Sheet (2013)

17. United Nations Convention on the Rights of Persons with Disabilities (UNCRPD) (2006). http://www.un.org/disabilities/convention/conventionfull.shtml. Accessed 12 Jan 2018

18. Verdugo, M.A., Gomez, L.E., Arias, B., Navas, P., Schalock, R.: Measuring quality of life in people with intellectual and multiple disabilities: validation of the San Martin scale. Res. Dev. Disabil. **35**(2014), 75–86 (2013)

19. Whyte, W.: Participatory Action Research. Sage Publications Inc., Thousand Oaks (1991)

20. World Health Organization (WHO): The GATE Initiative: Equipping, Enabling and Empowering. Improving Access to Assistive Technology for Everyone, Everywhere (2016)

Adaptation of User-Centered Design Approaches to Abilities of People with Disabilities

Marine Guffroy[1(✉)], Yohan Guerrier[2(✉)], Christophe Kolski[2(✉)], Nadine Vigouroux[3(✉)], Frédéric Vella[3(✉)], and Philippe Teutsch[1(✉)]

[1] Le Mans Université, CREN, EA 2661, Le Mans, France
{marine.guffroy,philippe.tetutsch}@univ-lemans.fr
[2] Univ. Valenciennes, LAMIH, CNRS UMR 8201, 59313 Valenciennes, France
{Yohan.Guerrier,Christophe.Kolski}@univ-valenciennes.fr
[3] IRIT, UMR CNRS 5505, Univ. Paul Sabatier, Toulouse, France
{vigourou,Frederic.Vella}@irit.fr

Abstract. The goal of this paper is to report how the adaptation of user centered (UCD) design approaches meet the specificities of impaired persons and their ecosystem for the design of interactive systems. Adapted UCD methods are illustrated through three case studies involving different impairments. The discussion reports the success of the different design processes.

Keywords: User-centered design · Disabled person · Assistive system

1 Introduction

The literature is rich concerning user-centered design (UCD) approaches [1, 2]. They promote the involvement of users in each stage of the methodological approach. In case of assistive systems design, the use of generic UCD approaches is not applicable for being used for people with certain kinds of impairments. Several studies have shown the high abandonment rate of assistive technologies [3]. The reasons are various: insufficient representation from potential users, environmental barriers dependent of the disability, difficulties to express the needs, including the needs of ecosystem (informal and familial caregivers, teachers and so on) [4].

2 State of the Art

UCD involves focusing on the user's needs, carrying out a task analysis and designing iteratively. However, UCD methods are not completely appropriate to involve the disabled people in the participatory design. Indeed [5] have evaluated a set of methods and techniques according to two criteria: the disability and the age. For instance, how to adapt a questionnaire to make it accessible to a person with cognitive disorders? What solutions can be put in place to allow disabled people to participate in the design stages despite their difficulties [6]? This paper will consider different types of disabled persons. These are sometimes at the crossroads of both criteria. For example, children with ASD

© Springer International Publishing AG, part of Springer Nature 2018
K. Miesenberger and G. Kouroupetroglou (Eds.): ICCHP 2018, LNCS 10896, pp. 462–465, 2018.
https://doi.org/10.1007/978-3-319-94277-3_71

are both children and users with communication difficulties; person who suffers stroke can be older, have communication disorders and visual impairment. This paper will report how some methods of the UCD have been adapted to overcome limitations of participation in the design through three illustrations for people with cognitive/communication problems.

3   Case Studies Involving Different Types of Disabilities

Three case studies present illustrations of adaptations of UCD approaches dedicated for disabled users. For each, we explain the profile of the target users, the needs of adaptation of the UCD approach, the UCD approach used, the main results obtained.

3.1   Adaptation of Evaluation Stage for Chidren with Autism Disorders

The aim of çATED project [7] is to provide a digital organizer on tablet to children with autism spectrum disorders (ASD), see Fig. 1(a), and to help the public gradually appropriate the tool in a user instrumentation process. Despite the communication difficulties of the target audience, the project has shown that the public, as well as its human ecosystem, could participate during the prototype evaluation phase.

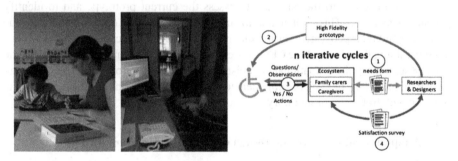

Fig. 1. (a) Work and observation session on the application between a child with ASD and the engineer, (b) user-centered design and test of the ComMob system dedicated to users with cerebral palsy in real environment with members of the ecosystem, (c) adapted UCD

Children with ASD have difficulty communicating and working with others. Design and evaluation methods based on communication, such as brainstorming or focus groups, are not recommended [8]. In addition, the work sessions to design or evaluate the tools dedicated to these children can be long and tiring for them. As proof, school activities usually do not exceed twenty minutes. However, in order to evolve in their living environment, children with ASD are accompanied by their ecosystem (family, medical and educational teams).

The goal is to enable children with ASD to contribute to the evaluation of the tool dedicated to them. Study proposes to extend the classic user-centered evaluation model to a shared evaluation model between the central user and his or her human ecosystem. The extended ecosystem evaluation method was implemented during 18 months in a specialized classroom for 6 children with ASD. The ecosystem included the teacher, two school assistants and an embedded engineer. Finally, the children are involved in the return of use on the user interface. The data collected via each of the actors complement each other.

3.2 Adaptation of UCD for the Design of CECI System

The CECI (Environment Control and Integrated Communication) system [9] is an assistive technology which allows people with motor impairment and/or language disorders to communicate with their ecosystem (occupational therapists and family caregivers) and to control their digital environment.

Persons who suffer cerebral palsy, traumatic brain injury, and stroke are the target users. They communicate with their ecosystem using facial expression, sign language (eyes, head, thumb, etc.) and/or disorders language. Sometimes visual or cognitive impairment can be also identified.

Without adaptation of the UCD, their participation in the design process can be limited or impossible. The proposition is that the ecosystem may be involved in the UCD (Fig. 1c) process to report the needs, to understand the behaviour in the customizing or in the trials made by the disabled end user. Firstly, the patient needs form is written by the ecosystem. For that, the caregivers ask questions to patient. These needs are then translated into functionalities, features, pictograms or audio messages. Then, the Hi-Fi prototypes are given to the end user to assess the current prototype and to identify potential new needs. This implementation of UCD consisted in a co-design between the end users and their ecosystem during the trial of the assistive technology in all phases. As illustration, the design of the CECI system for a person suffering locked-in syndrome took 18 sessions with occupational therapists for each iterative prototype. This co-design took 9 months. This method is implemented for two patients with Locked-In Syndrome and one with traumatic brain injury.

3.3 Adaptation of UCD for the Design of ComMob for Users with CP

A communication support, named ComMob (communication and Mobility) was carried out according to an adapted UCD approach, Fig. 1(b). It allows the user to prepare and formulate a set of sentences using pictograms.

Our focus is on users with athetoid Cerebral Palsy (CP). This type of disability is characterized by involuntary which greatly reduce the precision in the gestures. In addition, these people have speech problems. When the speech problems of the target users are important, the approach used should facilitate the search for solutions to improve the communication with the actors of their ecosystem, as well as with systems. The process must be adapted in this sense, giving a large part to the technical and user-centered tests throughout the project.

An adapted UCD approach, in which the designer has the target profile, has been performed; he was representative of the end users. His role was central in each stage, particularly during the needs analysis, the modeling and the prototyping, and throughout the project during technical and user-centered tests. Tests on the field were made in a public place and involved requests for help from him, using the ComMob system, from

281 people [10]. From the test results, it has been possible to progressively improve ComMob. The project lasted about two years. The direct involvement of the designer having the targeted profile in all stages has allowed successive evolutions taking into account in a detailed way the needs.

4   Discussion and Research Perspective

The three examples of interactive system show that adaptations of UCD are efficient. Indeed these systems have been designed and are used in real context. These three cases demonstrate that the design process needs to involve the end disabled users but also their ecosystem. The participation of the caregivers, the specialized teachers but also the family is essential to avoid abandonment. The methods "Questionnaires", "User trials", "Prototyping and participatory design" have been co-realized by the end user and the ecosystem for the case studies 1 and 2. In the case study 3, the designer is an end user. This suggests extending the work of [3] by proposing UCD approaches dedicated to one or several types of disabilities.

References

1. Norman, D.A.: The Design of Everyday Things. Basic Books, New York (2013)
2. https://www.iso.org/obp/ui/#iso:std:iso:9241:-210:ed-1:v1:en
3. Phillips, B., Zhao, H.: Predictors of assistive technology abandonment. Assistive Technol. 5(1), 36–45 (1993)
4. Guffroy, M., Vigouroux, N., Kolski, C., Vella, F., Teutsch, P.: From human-centered design to disabled user & ecosystem centered design in case of assistive interactive systems. Int. J. Sociotechnol. Knowl. Dev. (in press)
5. Antona, M., Ntoa, S., Adami, I., Stephanidis, C.: User requirements elicitation for universal access. In: Stephanidis, C. (ed.) The Universal Access Handbook, pp. 1–14. CRC Press (2009)
6. Benton, L., Johnson, H., Ashwin, E., Brosnan, M.J., Grawemeyer, B.: Developing IDEAS: supporting children with autism within a participatory design team. In: Konstan, J.A., Chi, E.H., and Höök, K. (eds.) CHI Conference on Human Factors in Computing Systems, CHI 2012, Austin, TX, USA, pp. 2599–2608. ACM (2012)
7. Guffroy, M.: Adaptation des méthodes d'évaluation classiques à un jeune public avec Troubles du Spectre Autistique. In: Proceedings IHM 2017, pp. 53–60. ACM, Poitiers (2017)
8. Frauenberger, C., Good, J., Alcorn, A., Pain, H.: Supporting the design contributions of children with autism spectrum conditions. In: Schelhowe, H. (ed.) The 11th International Conference on Interaction Design and Children, IDC 2012, UNK, Bremen, Germany, pp. 134–143. ACM (2012)
9. Vella, F., Sauzin, D., Truillet, F.P., Vigouroux, N.: Design and evaluation of multi-function scanning system: a case study. In: Miesenberger, K., Fels, D., Archambault, D., Peňáz, P., Zagler, W. (eds.) ICCHP 2014. LNCS, vol. 8548, pp. 188–194. Springer, Cham (2014). https://doi.org/10.1007/978-3-319-08599-9_29
10. Guerrier, Y., Naveteur, J., Kolski, C., Poirier, F.: Communication system for persons with cerebral palsy. In: Miesenberger, K., Fels, D., Archambault, D., Peňáz, P., Zagler, W. (eds.) ICCHP 2014. LNCS, vol. 8547, pp. 419–426. Springer, Cham (2014). https://doi.org/10.1007/978-3-319-08596-8_64

Automated vs Human Recognition of Emotional Facial Expressions of High-Functioning Children with Autism in a Diagnostic-Technological Context: Explorations via a Bottom-Up Approach

Miklos Gyori[1,2(✉)] ⓘ, Zsófia Borsos[1,2] ⓘ, Krisztina Stefanik[1,2] ⓘ,
Zoltán Jakab[1] ⓘ, Fanni Varga[1] ⓘ, and Judit Csákvári[1] ⓘ

[1] ELTE University, Ecseri Road 3, Budapest 1097, Hungary
gyorimiklos@elte.hu
[2] MTA-ELTE 'Autism in Education' Research Group,
Ecseri Road 3, Budapest 1097, Hungary
maszk@barczi.elte.hu

Abstract. Early detection of autism spectrum conditions (ASC) is an important goal. Automated facial expression recognition is a promising approach and has implications for assistive and educational technologies, too. This study was an initial exploration of (1) the inter-rater reliability of human recognition of facial emotions of high functioning (HF) children with ASC; (2) the relationship between human and automated recognition of facial emotions; and (3) a 'bottom-up' approach on identifying ASC/typical development (TD) differences, from a screening serious game context. Thirteen HF, kindergarten-age children with ASC and 13 children with TD, matched along age and IQ, participated. Emotion recognition was administered on video-recordings from sessions of their playing with the serious game. Results showed lack of inter-rater reliability in human coding, confirming some advantages of machine coding. The simple bottom-up cross-sectional exploratory analysis did not reveal any ASC/TD difference. This is in contrast with our and others' previous results, indicating such differences when aggregating emotion data from wider time-windows in machine-coded data-sets. This suggests that this second approach may be a more promising one to identify autism-specific emotion expression patterns.

Keywords: Autism spectrum conditions · Emotional facial expressions
Screening · Serious game

1 Background

1.1 Autism Spectrum Conditions, Technology-Aided Early Recognition

Autism spectrum conditions (ASC) are atypical pathways of neurocognitive development, manifested in atypical patterns of social and communication skills, and the overall organization of own behaviors and interests [1, 2]. Resulting adaptation difficulties

© Springer International Publishing AG, part of Springer Nature 2018
K. Miesenberger and G. Kouroupetroglou (Eds.): ICCHP 2018, LNCS 10896, pp. 466–473, 2018.
https://doi.org/10.1007/978-3-319-94277-3_72

persist in evolving forms throughout the life from early childhood, and imply specific support and educational needs. Early detection of the presence of ASC is an important goal: it has been demonstrated that early-starting assistive and educational intervention has significant and lasting benefits [3]. 'High functioning' (HF) children with ASC (those cases where ASC is accompanied by typical level of intellectual and language abilities) represent a specific challenge for early recognition: they tend to receive diagnosis later than the more affected cases, typically only at school age [4, 5].

Recently, a wide range of technological solutions, including a variety of computer-based approaches have been experimented with to enhance early detection (screening and/or diagnosis) [6], but no breakthrough has taken place so far in this field. The present study and the project serving as its broader context were motivated by utilizing automated emotional facial expression recognition technology in early recognition of cases of ASC, with a special emphasis on HF ones. While effective early recognition has indirect positive impact on the affected individuals by allowing earlier intervention and support, automated emotional facial expression recognition technology seems to have assistive and educational potential, too.

1.2 Emotional Facial Expressions in Autism

Atypical patterns of emotional facial expressions are important parts of autism-related behaviors [1, 2], and they clearly contribute to the social and communication difficulties experienced by individuals on the autism spectrum. Yet, systematic and detailed evidence on emotional facial expressions in ASC is rare and not yet conclusive: greater variety of affect expressions, more negative and incongruous emotions, more neutral, flat or idiosyncratic expressions, atypical inter- and intrapersonal integration of emotions were all demonstrated in various studies [7]. Interpretation of these results is made complicated by the fact that they are from studies which are heterogeneous in terms of sample size, subject characteristics and research paradigms.

1.3 Automated Facial Expression Recognition for Diagnostic, Assistive and Educational Solutions

Surprisingly, a very few published studies have explored emotional facial expression characteristics in ASC by using automated facial expression recognition technologies. Recent evidence has come from young adults with ASC, from interactive social situations [8]; and from high functioning young children with ASC, from a digital serious game context [7, 9]. These studies found differences in various emotion intensity patterns between subjects with ASC vs TD, showing that automated facial emotion recognition has a potential role in screening/diagnostic technologies in autism.

As we discussed in more details elsewhere [7], this technology hold promises for assistive and educational solutions for people with ASC, too. Many people with autism experience difficulties in communicating their own emotions, and assistive technologies may exploit facial expression recognition to help social partners read out their emotional states better; while educational technologies may use automated facial expression recognition technologies in order to help the person with ASC become (more) aware of their own affective states and express them more effectively [10].

1.4 The SHAKES Project: Objectives and Main Results to Date

The project serving as the context of this study is aimed at implementing and validating a social serious game based software system for screening for HF cases of ASC at kindergarten age. An estimation of the risk of the presence of ASC in the player is to be done on the basis of mouse states, gaze focus and emotional facial expressions data. A full game prototype was implemented with data recording but, as yet, without risk estimation. A user experience study, a raw data quality study, and a first ASC/typical development (TD) comparison study have been completed on this prototype [7, 9, 11], demonstrating a promising potential of the system for the aimed screening purpose.

2 Objectives of the Present Study

The study reported here was aimed at providing preliminary insights about two issues which are of key importance for the project: the relationship between human and machine coding, and the feasibility of a simple, fundamentally bottom-up approach for finding differences between the intensities of emotional facial expressions shown by the two groups. The first issue relates to one of the preassumptions the project has been built on: namely, that machine coding of facial emotions outperforms human coding along such crucial dimensions as reliability, speed, cost-effectiveness. The second issue has relevance to the potential approaches to data processing and analysis: from among the 3 such 'core' approaches we identified (see them later, at Conclusions), the bottom-up strategy, explored here, appears conceptually the simplest.

Therefore, the present study was aimed at the following three exploratory research questions:

1. What is the inter-rater reliability of human recognition of emotional facial expressions of HF children with ASC, from the digital game context;
2. What is the relationship (again, inter-rater reliability) between the human and the automated recognition of facial emotions; and
3. Whether a simple 'bottom-up' exploration of the machine-coded emotion expression data reveals any ASC/TD differences.

3 Methods

Subjects: 13 high-functioning, kindergarten-age children with ASC and 13 TD children, matched along age and IQ, participated in the study. Their characteristics are shown in Table 1. The sample was the same as in [7]. For each child, a questionnaire screening for ASC, the Social Communication Questionnaire (SCQ) [12] was completed by one of the parents. Mann-Whitney test showed significant difference between the two groups in the total SCQ score ($z = -4,414$; $p < 0,001$). Allocation into ASC vs TD groups was based on former diagnosis, but was also controlled by administering the ADOS (Autism Diagnostic Observation Schedule, [13]) and the ADI-R (Autism Diagnostic Interview – Revised, [14]) with each child.

Table 1. Sample characteristics (adapted from [7])

Variables	ASC group (9 male/4 female)			TD group (6 male/7 female)		
	Mean (SD)	Min	Max	Mean (SD)	Min	Max
Age (months)	58.38 (8.45)	43	70	57.15 (6.74)	43	68
Leiter-R Brief IQ	118 (14.61)	98	139	118.53 (15.61)	98	145
SCQ score	20.46 (6.25)	8	29	0.62 (0.51)	0	1

Game Script and Presentation: The main theme of the game has been adapted from a developmental psychological study by Sodian and Frith [15], which examined the ability to use deception and sabotage as social strategies in children with and without autism. The scheme of the game script and the specific themes and functions of the scenes are shown in Table 2. The mean total game time was 24.81 min in the ASC group, 24.28 min in the TD group [7].

Table 2. Game script outline (adapted from [9])

	Theme	Function
1	Perceptual preferences	To evoke emotional and gaze responses
2	Introduction and instructions, 1	To familiarize with characters, task, controls
3	Sabotage in co-operative context	To evoke emotional, behavioral, gaze responses
4	Sabotage in competitive context	
5	Sabotage in co-operative context	
6	Sabotage in competitive context	
7	Introduction and instructions, 2	To familiarize with characters, task, controls
8	Deception in co-operative context	To evoke emotional, behavioral, gaze responses
9	Deception in competitive context	
10	Deception in co-operative context	
11	Deception in competitive context	
12	Closing	To close the session

Technological Setting: The game prototype was running on a standard desktop-mounted, binocular eye-tracking PC (Eyefollower 2 by LC Technologies). A web-camera, positioned below the monitor, made video recordings of the players' face.

Human recognition of emotional facial expressions: a group of independent raters (7 students in the special needs education BA programme at ELTE University, Budapest) coded video recordings of faces of children, recorded while playing with the screening serious game, covering the entire game session. The coding scheme was an adapted version of the FACES [16]. Coders had to locate the transitions 'points' of dominant emotions first. Then they had to locate the plateaus of the intensity of the dominant emotion between such transition points. Finally, for each such emotional plateau, they had to estimate the intensities of the same 7 basic emotions which were coded by the automated system, too: neutral, happy, sad, angry, surprised, scared, disgusted.

Two independent raters coded the recording of each of the 3 children with ASC and the 3 TD children; coders were blind to the condition of the child. Although the FACES coding scheme is less time-consuming than other human emotion coding schemes, such as Ekman's Facial Action Coding System [17], coding one recording required 3–15 h.

Automated recognition of emotional facial expressions was done on the video recordings from the total sample of 26 children, again covering the entire game session in each case. The Noldus FaceReader v5.1 system was used for this purpose, which attempts to estimate the intensities of 7 basic emotions (see above) in each frame of the video-recording.

4   Results

4.1   Inter-rater Reliability of Human Recognition of Facial Emotions

Spearman's rank correlation coefficients were calculated for each coded video recording for the following emotion variables: overall valence, overall intensity, intensities of neutral, happy, sad, angry, surprised, scared, disgusted, and the dominant emotion. From among the total of 60 coefficients calculated (10 emotion variables $\times$ 6 subjects), only 4 indicated significant positive relationship (happy: subject ASC2 $r = 0.322$ $p = 0.016$; ASC3 $r = 0,526$ $p < 0,001$; NT3 $r = 0,341$; $p = 0,010$; and surprised: subject ASC1 $r = 0,290$; $p = 0,045$). This indicates that human coding was highly unreliable in the coded cases, in both groups.

4.2   Relationship Between Human and Machine Recognition of Facial Emotions

Since human coding was found to be highly unreliable, it was meaningless to calculate its relationship to machine coding; therefore, these analyses were rejected.

4.3   Exploration of ASD/TD Differences, by Machine Coding

To explore potential 'cross-sectional' ASC/NT differences in intensities of displayed emotions throughout the game session, mean intensities of emotions and confidence intervals (95%) were calculated and plotted by data points, in each of the two groups. This was done for the following emotions, coded by the FaceReader: neutral, happy, sad, angry, surprised, scared, disgusted. This procedure, without revealing any statistically relevant difference between the two groups, indicated that the emotion intensity group means exhibited a very fast fluctuation.

To have a better view on the nature of our data, therefore, we plotted individual curves and their means in the same diagrams. This method revealed that individual emotion intensity time series themselves showed a high degree of variation at data points and along time. Therefore, to eliminate such high-frequency changes, emotion intensity means and confidence interval margins were smoothed by averaging in shifting time-windows. This manipulation left only slowly changing components in the emotion intensity data-set, thereby making intensity data from the two groups and the seven emotions more easily comparable.

Several time-windows and shifting steps have been explored for this purpose. The resulting emotion curves did not indicate any statistically relevant difference in the intensities of the specific emotions between the two groups, at any particular time-point within the game time. Also, in line with our previous findings [9], they indicated somewhat sub-optimal and progressively decreasing quality of raw emotion data. Data plotted in Fig. 1, for illustration, was obtained using a 30-second-long averaging time-window that was moved by steps of 0.3 s over the 'scared' emotion data series.

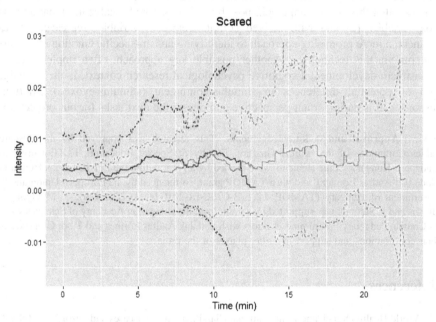

Fig. 1. Means and confidence intervals of the intensities of the 'scared' emotion for the two groups, coded by machine coding (solid red line: ASC group mean, solid green line: TD group; dotted lines: confidence intervals). (Color figure online)

5   Conclusions and Perspectives

Our results clearly confirmed some advantages of machine emotion expression coding above human coding of facial emotions. Human coding is not only highly resource-demanding and time-consuming, but also proved to be highly unreliable (in terms of inter-rater reliability) in this study. It is important to note that another human emotional facial expression coding system, Ekman's Facial Action Coding System [17], has proven to be highly reliable, but it is extremely resource-intensive. This again points to the clear advantages of machine emotion expression recognition systems in terms of reliability, speed, and efficiency.

The simple bottom-up cross-sectional exploratory analysis approach, aimed at revealing any particular time-point (or narrow time-window) within the game session with statistically relevant ASC/TD difference in emotion intensity, did not reveal any such difference in any of the analyzed emotions. This, on the one hand, suggests that such a simple strategy to identify diagnostically relevant emotion expression differences between the facial expressions of children with autism and typically developing children requires further methodological refinements – or may not be a promising approach.

On the other hand, this negative finding is in contrast with our [7] and others' [8] results, indicating such differences when aggregating emotion data from much wider time-windows within machine-coded emotion data-set. Together, this pattern of results suggests that this second approach, possibly combined with analyzing dynamic emotion variables [7] and with derived complex emotion variables represents, at the moment, a more promising approach to identifying autism-specific emotion expression patterns via this technology. Another possible key approach, often implemented in mainstream developmental cognitive psychological research context, is the investigation of potential differences in stimulus-contingent (stimulus-evoked) emotional responses. It is an important perspective and one of the next tasks for our project, too.

Ethical Approval and Acknowledgements. This research was approved by the Research Ethics Committee of the 'Barczi Gusztav' Faculty of Special Education, ELTE University, Budapest, Hungary. Some elements were funded by a grant within the EIT ICT Labs Hungarian Node (PI: András Lőrincz), and via a TÁMOP grant, co-financed by the European Union and the government of Hungary (TÁMOP 4.2.1./B-09/KMR-2010-0003). The work of M Gyori, Zs Borsos and K Stefanik was supported by a grant from the Hungarian Academy of Sciences within its Content Pedagogy Programme. Authors wish to thank András Lőrincz and Tibor Gregorics for their contributions and support in earlier phases of the project.

References

1. World Health Organization: International Classification of Diseases and Disorders, 10th edn. Author, Geneva (1993)
2. APA [American Psychiatric Association]: Diagnostic and Statistical Manual of Mental Disorders, 5th edn, (DSM-5). American Psychiatric Association, Washington DC (2013)
3. Chawarska, K., Macari, S., Volkmar, F., Kim, S.H., Shic, F.: Autism in infancy and early childhood. In: Volkmar, F., Rogers, S., Paul, R., Pelphrey, K. (eds.) Handbook of Autism and Pervasive Developmental Disorders. Willey, Hoboken (2014)
4. Brett, D., Warnell, F., McConachie, H., Parr, J.R.: Factors affecting age at ASD diagnosis in UK: no evidence that diagnosis age has decreased between 2004 and 2014. J. Autism Dev. Disord. **46**, 1974–1984 (2016)
5. Daniels, A.M., Mandell, D.S.: Explaining differences in age at autism spectrum disorder diagnosis: a critical review. Autism **18**, 583–597 (2014)
6. Bölte, S., Bartl-Pokorny, K.D., Jonsson, U., Berggren, S., Zhang, D., Kostrzewa, E., et al.: How can clinicians detect and treat autism early? Methodological trends of technology use in research. Acta Paediatr. **105**(2), 137–144 (2016)

7. Borsos, Z., Gyori, M.: Can automated facial expression analysis show differences between autism and typical functioning? In: Cudd, P., de Witte, L. (eds.) Harnessing the Power of Technology to Improve Lives. Studies in Health Technology and Informatics, pp. 797–804. IOS Press, Amsterdam (2017)

8. Owada, K., Kojima, M., Yassin, W., Kuroda, M., Kawakobo, Y., Kuwabara, H., Kano, Y., Yamasue, H.: Computer-analyzed facial expression as a surrogate marker for autism spectrum social core symptoms. PLoS ONE **13**(1), e0190442 (2018)

9. Gyori, M., Borsos, Z., Stefanik, K., Csákvári, J.: Data quality as a bottleneck in developing a social-serious-game-based multi-modal system for early screening for 'High Functioning' cases of autism spectrum condition. In: Miesenberger, K., Bühler, C., Penaz, P. (eds.) ICCHP 2016. LNCS, vol. 9759, pp. 358–366. Springer, Cham (2016). https://doi.org/10. 1007/978-3-319-41267-2_51

10. Grossard, C., Grynspan, O., Serret, S., Jouen, A.-L., Bailly, K., Cohen, D.: Serious games to teach social interactions and emotions to individuals with autism spectrum disorders (ASD). Comput. Educ. **113**, 195–211 (2017)

11. Gyori, M., Borsos, Z., Stefanik, K.: Evidence-based development and first usability testing of a social serious game based multi-modal system for early screening for atypical socio-cognitive development. In: Sik-Lányi, C., Hoogerwerf, E.J., Miesenberger, K. (eds.) Assistive Technology: Building Bridges. Studies in Health Technology and Informatics, pp. 48–54. IOS Press, Amsterdam (2015)

12. Rutter, M., Bailey, A., Lord, C.: The Social Communication Questionnaire: Manual. Western Psychological Services, Los Angeles (2003)

13. Lord, C., Rutter, M., DiLavore, P.C., Risi, S.: Autism Diagnostic Observation Schedule. Western Psychological Services, Los Angeles (1999)

14. Le Couteur, A., Lord, C., Rutter, M.: The Autism Diagnostic Interview-Revised. Western Psychological Services, Los Angeles (2003)

15. Sodian, B., Frith, U.: Deception and sabotage in autistic, retarded and normal children. J. Child Psychol. Psychiatry **33**, 591–605 (1992)

16. Kring, A.M., Sloan, D.M.: The facial expression coding system (FACES): development, validation, and utility. Psychol. Assess. **19**(2), 210–224 (2007)

17. Cohn, J.F., Ekman, P.: Measuring facial action. In: Harrigan, J.A., Rosenthal, R., Scherer, K. R. (eds.) The New Handbook of Methods in Nonverbal Behavior Research, pp. 9–64. Oxford University Press (2005)

Assessing Support Needs for Developing an App-Based Assistive System for Enhancing Independence in the Autism Spectrum: Results from a Mixed-Mode Study

Miklos Gyori[1,2](✉) ⓘ, Judit Csákvári[1] ⓘ, Márta Molnár[1,2] ⓘ,
Ágnes Havasi[1,2] ⓘ, Fanni Varga[1] ⓘ, Krisztina Stefanik[1,2] ⓘ,
and Anita Virányi[1] ⓘ

[1] ELTE University, Ecseri road 3, Budapest 1097, Hungary
gyorimiklos@elte.hu
[2] MTA-ELTE 'Autism in Education' Research Group,
Ecseri road 3, Budapest 1097, Hungary
maszk@barczi.elte.hu

Abstract. The DATA project is intended to develop a compound digital assistive system, including a mobile app set, for increasing independence in people with autism. The objective of this study was to explore this target group's support needs, as a basis for the system designing process. A mixed-mode study was implemented, with an on-line survey (N = 147), and with 3 focus groups. The support need profiles were different across levels of functioning, with only minor differences between profiles provided by parents vs professionals. One's awareness of support methods emerged as an important factor.

Keywords: Autism · Independence · Mobile app · Support needs assessment

1 Background

Autism spectrum conditions (ASC) are defined by atypical limitations in social communication, in overall adaptive and flexible organization of behaviors and interests, and by atypical sensory sensitivities [1]. These characteristics and the arising difficulties in social adaptation, social participation and daily living skills arise in early childhood, in individual patterns, and keep evolving throughout life. Support needs are highly variable on the spectrum.

Up-to-date evidence-based interventions in ASC are comprehensive psycho-educational approaches, applied in individualized ways to enhance autonomy, competence and development [2]. Autism-specific assistive technologies focus dominantly on certain cognitive and/or communication areas, and their assistive functions are often combined with educational ones.

Evidence shows that various digital tools have assistive and educational potentials for people with ASC [3]. While the offer of 'autism-apps' is broad [4], as they may

K. Miesenberger and G. Kouroupetroglou (Eds.): ICCHP 2018, LNCS 10896, pp. 474–477, 2018.
https://doi.org/10.1007/978-3-319-94277-3_73

allow the transportation of key elements of support into focus situations across different contexts [5], systematic assessment of the target user group's support needs has been published only rarely.

2 Objectives

The objective of the DATA (Digital Autonomy supporT in the Autism spectrum) project is to develop a digital assistive system for increasing autonomy and independence in the daily life of people on the autism spectrum. The concept of the system builds on the HANDS system [5]: its main components are a set of assistive mobile applications, used by the user with ASC, and a browser-based content management and monitoring service, used by a supporting user ('assisted user/assisting user dyads'). As a key challenge, we attempt to provide a solution for (assisted) users from the broadest possible range of the autism spectrum. Development will take place through 2 prototypes and the final, to-be-publicized product. A strictly evidence-informed design-development-evaluation process is implemented.

The objective of this study was to gain evidence on the target group's support need profiles, as an input for system designing and for designing user training and support methods. The product design process is, now, driven by the conclusions from a literature review and from this study.

3 Methods

A mixed mode study was implemented: a quantitative on-line survey and a qualitative study based on focus groups. Recruitment of respondents and participants was done via autism-related websites and mailing-lists.

In the quantitative study, respondents were 83 parents (mean age: 44.4 years) of a child or an adult with ASC (mostly between 4–18 years), 61 educational professionals (mean age: 40.89 years) working with people with ASC, and 3 persons who were both parents and professionals; a total of 147. Only 3 people with ASC provided data, these were omitted from statistical analysis. Table 1 shows the overall structure of the questionnaire. Data were analyzed statistically, following data quality control.

Table 1. The overall structure and the main foci of the on-line questionnaire.

(Main) items	Focus	Respondent group(s)
1–4	Basic demographics	All
5–9	Everyday use of digital tools	All
10–12	Basic profiling of child/client with ASC	Parents, professionals
13–18	Respondent/child/client with ASC use of digital tools	All
19–24	Support needs and assistive tools	All
25–26	User training and user support preferences	All

In the qualitative study, 5 parents of children with ASC took part in the 'Parents' group; 5 educational professionals in the 'Professional' group, and 4 high-functioning young adults with ASC in the 'Participatory' group. Groups were mediated by the first author.

Data from the focus groups were processed by qualitative content analysis. Transcriptions of the recordings were annotated independently by 3 experts. Foci of annotation were (i) support need domains; (ii) preferred means of support; (iii) preferred contexts of support. Then a consensus text was formed by merging those parts of the 3 annotations where at least 2 experts found a part of text relevant, along the same focus. This consensus text was further analyzed and consensually interpreted by the 3 experts.

4 Results

In the quantitative analysis, the main focus was on the support need profiles provided by parents vs professionals, for low-, mid-, and high-functioning individuals with ASC. Chi-square tests show that profiles are significantly different across levels of functioning, as expected, and there are only few significant differences between profiles provided by parents vs professionals; see Fig. 1.

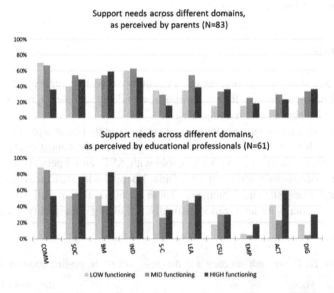

Fig. 1. Support needs of people with ASC, as perceived by parents and educational professionals. (Abbreviations: COMM: communication, SOC: Social skills, BM: behavioral management, IND: Independence, S-C: Self-care, LEA: Learning, CSU: Community service use, EMP: Employment related skills, ACT: Daily and leisure activities, DIG: Digital skills.)

In qualitative findings, too, parents' and professionals' perspectives were close to each other. As an interesting difference, while parents and professionals focused more on the means and the contexts of needed support, the Participatory group focused more on domains of support needs, such as managing intimate relationships. Importantly, we found that the awareness and knowledge on evidence-based, effective intervention techniques in supporting people with ASC strongly determined the perception of support needs, means, and contexts, in all stakeholder groups.

5 Conclusions and Perspectives

Support need profiles were clearly different in the low-, mid- and high functioning (supported) user groups. A consistent pattern of preferred foci of support emerged. Focus groups suggested that a better understanding of support methods may help identify individual support needs. As of limitations, we failed to access a significant number of respondents with ASC in the quantitative study, and had only high functioning young adults with ASC in the Participatory focus group. However, we collected information about low- and mid-functioning individuals from parents and professionals, indirectly.

The above-summarized results allowed us to draw 4 main conclusions for the design process: (1) a weighted list of support needs; (2) the implementation of 3 distinct default user personas for low-, mid-, and high-functioning users; (3) putting special emphasis on principles and key methods of evidence-based intervention in the developed user training and support toolkit; and (4) that the mixed-mode study design proved highly productive. The key test of the results of this study, however, will be, clearly, the system development and evaluation processes.

Acknowledgements. This research complies with the guidelines of the Research Ethics Committee of the 'Barczi Gusztav' Faculty of Special Education, ELTE University. The project is funded via an EFOP grant, co-financed by the EU and the government of Hungary (EFOP-1.1.5-17-2017-00007). The work was supported by a grant from the Hungarian Academy of Sciences within its Content Pedagogy Programme.

References

1. APA [American Psychiatric Association]: Diagnostic and Statistical Manual of Mental Disorders, 5th edn, (DSM-5). American Psychiatric Association, Washington DC (2013)
2. Howlin, P.: The effectiveness of interventions for children with autism. J. Neural Trans. Suppl. **69**, 101–119 (2005)
3. Grynszpan, O., Weiss, P.L., Perez-Diaz, F., Gal, E.: Innovative technology-based interventions for autism spectrum disorders: a meta-analysis. Autism **18**(4), 346–361 (2014)
4. Kim, J.W., Nguyen, T.Q., Gipson, S.Y.M.T., et al.: Smartphone apps for autism spectrum disorder—Understanding the evidence. J. Technol. Behav. Sci. **3**(1), 1–4 (2018)
5. Gyori, M., Stefanik, K., Kanizsai-Nagy, I.: Evidence-based development and evaluation of mobile cognitive support apps for people on the autism spectrum: methodological conclusions from two R+D projects. In: Sik-Lányi, C., Hoogerwerf, E.-J., Miesenberger, K. (eds.) Assistive Technology: Building Bridges: 13th European AAATE Conference. Studies in Health Technology and Informatics, vol. 217. pp. 55–62. IOS Press, Amsterdam (2015)

DysHelper – The Dyslexia Assistive Approach User Study

Tereza Pařilová(✉) ⬤

Masaryk University, 602 00 Brno, Czech Republic
parilova@mail.muni.cz

Abstract. The aim of this article is to focus on user experience with Dys-Helper, the dyslexia assistive web extension designed for Czech and other phonetic languages. We conducted this research with university and high school students over 18 years old. Firstly, we describe the design of the extension (invented in 2016 at Masaryk University) and then focus on describing the various stages of the practical user experience, which consisted of individual user testing, the reading two types of texts, followed by discussion with users. The results indicate that the extension is generally welcomed. Although Dys-Helper has its limits, user experience research shows that it has a significant potential to affect reading problems positively and can be easily used, also in consideration of needs that may change over time.

Keywords: Dyslexia · Assistive technology · User study

1 Introduction

Dyslexia is defined as a specific learning disorder and manifests more or less in all known languages. Several hypotheses of its background were studied but this question has still not been fully answered Most discussed its genetic background, especially with the DYX1C1 gene on chromosome 15, but others have been discussed as well [1, 2]. Prenatal states and development also seems to be crucial. There is not much to be done to prevent a child from the risk of becoming a dyslexic person. There are many approaches that can indicate whether a child is at considerable risk or can uncover dyslexia symptoms in its early stage, but we do not have any assistive technology that would help those already suffering from reading problems whilst allowing them to keep reading (as restricting written information has a negative effect on cognitive processes and states). The only "solutions" we have are mainly based on teachers' support, reading huge amount of adequate literature, using colored filters, etc. But in the digital age, dyslexia may have a negative influence on education and social integration. It can impede the academic and social success of many users [3].

Reasons for studying individual dyslexic symptoms (problems), designing an assistive technology and testing it with dyslexic users were the following:

- In decades of 20th century dyslexia had been incompatible with the social environment in former Socialist states.

© Springer International Publishing AG, part of Springer Nature 2018
K. Miesenberger and G. Kouroupetroglou (Eds.): ICCHP 2018, LNCS 10896, pp. 478–485, 2018.
https://doi.org/10.1007/978-3-319-94277-3_74

- There is a huge gap between empirical studies of dyslexia within most frequent foreign languages (e.g. English, Spanish) and non-world languages, like Czech, Polish, Swedish, etc.
- For many languages there is no basis to build on, for instance deep studies of language complexity versus individuality of dyslexia.

Therefore, in this article we briefly present the DysHelper assistive tool to give an idea of how it works and then we focus on a small user study which shows how important individualism of dyslexia is and how inventing dyslexia assistive technology focusing on individualism may be important to make dyslexic life easier.

2 Dyslexia

Dyslexia affects up to 20% of the worldwide population, depending on the type of alphabet and language complexity [4]. The symptoms can manifest in overlapping letters, switching letter order, or letter rotation due to visual and/or visuo-phonological dysfunction (therefore slow reading) and makes text comprehension harder. The problems of dyslexia lie also in the individual brain information flow. Dyslexia results from miscommunication between the left and right hemisphere in the corpus callosum, the only place that connects the hemispheres and where the visual path crosses [5]. For this reason, dyslexia can be highly individual because the flow of information through the corpus callosum is weak, could be unsystematic and asynchronous [6]. Huge differences can be found within children compared to adults, as the role of brain plasticity and a person's vocabulary is important as well. We still have no possibilities to heal dyslexia, but we can endeavor to help to "rehabilitate" reading and make it easier through well designed assistive technology that could customize text visually.

2.1 Available Solutions Aiming at Dyslexia

Nowadays, there are several tools or approaches that can be used by dyslexic users when they cannot read a text without assistance. Most of all, it is any tool having a text-to-speech system built in [7]. However, if all users use this solution, they will totally overcome written information and it may have a negative impact, especially on children. Another way of accessing online text is via the use of the DysWebxia service [8]. The web service removes all pseud-necessary elements (commercials, huge coloring, formatting). The problem here arises with text formatting because the whole webpage (html attributes) changes and its visual form moves. Open Dyslexic is a font introduced by Abelardo Gonzalez1 in 2011 [9]. The design is based on existing dyslexic friendly fonts such as Comic Sans. Each letter has thicker and thinner parts; however, similarity remains as the thicker/thinner lines are steady and therefore ignore different visual effect of letter patterns. Lukeš [10] presents a friendly reader interface through an application which combines a reading aloud mode, a text highlighting mode, a color and font mode, etc. These solutions have been implemented before as independent tools. However, the main problem with letter similarity is still not being solved. Changing font type can help marginally to change the visual attributes of text, but visually similar letters will still remain similar (for instance oddball, `oddball`, oddball). Plus, if for example a child of primary school age uses a reading app and eliminates reading, it can lead to lowering cognitive skills. It should be used only as a secondary help in critical situations. A very similar tool was discussed in a paper of Athènes et al. [11], but the idea of fragmenting words is sketched here – unfortunately with a steady (syllabic) concatenation system (no individualism taken into account). None of the solutions, except DysHelper, solve the main problem of letter similarity and closeness of such letters causing dyslexia symptoms.

2.2 DysHelper

The discussed assistive extension for Chrome web browser was introduced in [4]. DysHelper does not have to be installed; it only needs to be downloaded. It comprises a set of tests that should evaluate which letters and letter patterns cause large reading problems to each dyslexic user. The tests can be re-taken any time. The level of errors from which the text should be customized is defined (e.g. 50% of errors in pattern o-d-b) and according to the test results the customization is done. The customization is based on inserting a fragmenting sign shaped as a short dash (-). A piece of customized text may look like the one in Fig. 1.

Inkluze, te-dy sp-olečné vzdělávání dětí s různými handicapy, byla zave-d-ena v září roku 2016. Ře-ditelé škol se p-otýkali s ne-d-ostatkem p-eněz na p-o-dpůrná o-patření, která mají dětem p-omo-ci začlenit se d-o kolektivu. Pře-d schválením vyhlášky o inkluzi v ro-c-e 2015 se 68 pro-c-ent ře-ditelů škol d-omnívalo, že na sp-olečné vzdělávání chybějí p-eníze.

Fig. 1. Design of text customized based on a dyslexic's need. Fragmentation signs (-) can be seen between letters p, o, d, e, c, etc.

Technically, regular expressions are used to find letter patterns that are meant to be fragmented. We can shortly write it as follows: Let M be a pair of letters, a letter pattern respectively. Then M_1, M_2...M_n is a set of letter patterns pre-defined to be searched for. The definition of patterns M_1, M_2...M_n comes from the test results. Each user obtains a unique ID which represents the user's results (generally what needs to be fragmented and what not). When the user downloads DysHelper (or any time it is enabled), he/she is asked for the unique ID. Then the user is paired with information what and how to fragment and text modification can start.

3 Methodology

Our methodology is based on crucial research questions: Does visual fragmentation of problematic letter patterns help dyslexic people to read more quickly? Does visual fragmentation of problematic letter patterns help dyslexic people to eliminate letter errors? Does both faster reading and fewer errors make the text more comprehensible?

3.1   Design

We designed the research in three main stages:

- individual testing,
- text reading,
- discussion.

Stage "text reading" contained three sub-parts: reading the original unmodified text; reading modified text no. 1; reading modified text no. 2. Two modified texts were chosen to eliminate distortion that could be caused by brain plasticity (the hypothesis here was that the first text could be confusing due to new text image and with paradoxically longer reading time, while the second text could be easier and therefore faster to read after the first text). We tried to keep the off time between modification no. 1 and no. 2 as short as possible so that the brain of the participant remembers special fragmentation signs and applies brain plasticity ability.

We asked the users to read all texts out loud (to coordinate objectivity and validity of reading time and errors) while measuring time of reading for each text and checking errors, and correct comprehension during the discussion stage.

We chose a newspaper text, selecting no technical or expert expressions to make sure that it is not a factor of results distortion. The unmodified text was the same for all users to ensure reliability of the results.

The second part of our study covered reading modified text no. 1 and no. 2. The text for each user was modified according to the previously mentioned rules and individual test results, setting the fragmentation sign per threshold 60%. So, the results for each user looked different. For fragmentation, we again used a newspaper text but different segments. Using the same fragment as for the original reading could very possibly affect the results of reading time and comprehension. To make all texts objective, we used a script searching for as many similar texts as possible – we had texts that corresponded in a number of problematic letter patterns and in an average length of words. As for the average length of words, according to the analytical results of the Natural Language Processing Laboratory of Masaryk University [12], the average length of word in Czech text is 5.54 letters and according to the Czech dictionary it is 8.11 letters. We chose to have a length of 7 graphemes, which seems to be optimal in consideration of the average length and good for smooth fragmentating.

Each piece of text differed slightly in the number of letters because for text comprehension we had to keep sentences as a unit and make them understandable. Speed of reading was then normalized towards number of letters so that final reading times objectively show real reading time counted per same number of letters.

After each text was read, we asked participants about the content of the text, and a couple of questions specific to the given article in order to check comprehension of the text.

At the end, we had a brief discussion with each participant where we asked their feeling about fragmented text, their observations or any tips they could have to help us improve the idea of DysHelper.

This research with participants was done in a quiet room, on the same day time (afternoons) and under the same conditions. This was done in order to keep conditions for each participant as similar as possible to make the research valid.

3.2   Users

Through the Teiresiás Centre, the Support Centre for Students with Special Needs, we addressed users that had been diagnosed with dyslexia. Also, we used the Information system of Masaryk University to inform other students with dyslexia who may not necessarily be registered within the Teiresiás Centre and who could also share the information about our research with their dyslexic friends and classmates. Six participants were students of different faculties of Masaryk University (2 females and 4 males, mean age 22.67, SD = 1.6). Four of our participants were high school students in the last grade of Gymnasium who participated because they heard about our research from our colleague and were interested in helping (1 female and 3 males, mean age 19.25, SD = 0.43). Together we had 3 females and 7 males, mean age 21.3, SD = 2.1. Obligatory requirements were:

- Age over 18 due to ethical reasons.
- Proof of dyslexia as a clinical disorder. The proof was possible to accept either from pedagogical and psychological counselling offices or the Teiresiás Centre, where potential dys are being tested for Masaryk University (prospective and current) students. Pseudo-anonymity was guaranteed to users that would be willing to participate in our study. Informed consent was signed by both sides, the leader of the research and each participant.

4   Results

As mentioned, we recorded the time of reading of each text and number of errors made while reading (including snagging). Throughout we were checking text comprehension. Table 1 summarizes reading time of each participant for each text. To keep our participant anonymous, we numbered them 1 to 10.

Participants no. 6, 7, 9 and 10 had first modified text faster than the original text. On the other hand, participants no. 1, 2, 3, 4, 5 and 8 had the first modified text slightly slower then the original text. As we expect, it might be due to specific visual image to which participants were not used to. Regardless, for 4 out of 10 participants the modified text no. 1 was faster, especially in case of participants no. 9 and 10 it was significant.

When comparing times of modification no. 1 and modification no. 2, in all cases the second modification was read faster then the first one. This phenomenon might be, as already mentioned, due to inurement to visual difference, (participants reported that they do not even mention special signs in text any more).

Looking at reading times of the original text and modification no. 2, except participant no. 2 and 3, times were faster in modification 2 compared to the original text.

Table 1. An overview of reading times (in secs.) for each text – original without modification, modified text no. 1 and no. 2 (both using fragmentation signs)

Participant	Original text	Modification no. 1	Modification no. 2
1	3.59	4.17	3.51
2	1.53	2.20	2.00
3	2.30	2.52	2.51
4	2.18	2.31	2.04
5	2.26	2.34	2.23
6	4.37	4.16	3.59
7	2.28	2.16	2.12
8	3.15	3.20	3.09
9	2.57	2.32	2.28
10	3.17	2.37	2.34

The original text read by participants no. 2 and no. 3 still remains faster out of all three texts. It could be due to several reasons:

- Dyslexia really is very individual and some dyslexic people might need different approach than DysHelper offers.
- Reading texts may need to be longer to get more significant results in these cases (to find some evidence, if even existing within such dyslexic people).
- Such dyslexic people may not need any "help" as their dyslexia is not serious.

However, let us look at the number of errors in each text. Not only reading time is crucial to conclude whether assistive technology has any positive impact on reading. In Table 2, we can see the number of errors for each text, the original one and the modified ones for each participant.

Table 2. Overview of number of errors for each text made by each user while reading.

Participant no.	Original text	Modification no. 1	Modification no. 2
1	9	8	2
2	8	8	6
3	6	8	6
4	11	7	2
5	9	5	1
6	3	2	2
7	15	8	2
8	11	6	0
9	3	3	0
10	5	4	1

Looking at errors for each participant and text, we see that, again, participants no. 2 and no. 3 do not have significant increase or decrease of errors, while the rest of participants show a significant decrease of errors from the original text to modification no. 1 and also from modification no. 1 to modification no. 2. Especially the difference between modification no. 1 and no. 2 can be seen as crucial.

To see understanding context and content of texts, we asked what the text was about (topic; we asked to paraphrase its content) plus we asked questions focusing on more detailed information from each text. Paraphrasing content was not a problem for anyone taking part in our research. However, when asking specific questions, participants no. 4, 7 and 8 had trouble answering questions concerning the original text. When looking at number of errors in reading the original text within these participants, it is obvious that they were having trouble because the number of errors in the original text reading is very high (11, 15 respectively). For these participants, answering questions regarding modificated texts, no other misunderstandings were found.

Discussing with participants, we found out that they really appreciate texts with fragmentation signs. It does not disturb them; on the contrary, it helped some of them to read words as a unit (they normally read just the first part of words and then make mistakes and misunderstand context because they are confusing ends of nouns, verbs, adverbs, etc.).

5   Conclusions

Concerning DysHelper testing, we performed a pilot study to verify our hypothesis that designed accommodation and customization of text is relevant to individual dyslexic users' needs. Brain plasticity of users facilitates this. We are aware of the small number of participants; however, results should be taken as a building block for further testing and optimizing the DysHelper function to make text more accessible to people with dyslexia. Also, our proposal can be a steppingstone to finding variations of the accommodation process for specific languages (anti-phonetic, orthographic, etc.).

To brain plasticity, this means that the stimulus must be repeated (therefore it is not possible to follow brain plasticity within the first modified text and it is not possible to say that the first text should be read already faster. This explains why the first modified text is a little slower than the original one within two participants; however, the second modified text is getting faster in reading time within all participants). To conclude, except two participant all reading times were getting faster and the number of errors was decreasing. Except these two mentioned participants, they understood context well in the original text, and all of the participants (including the two) properly understood the content of the modified texts.

This research helped us to prove our hypotheses on dyslexics reading and further research is now being done to accommodate DysHelper to other languages and to design an assistive technology that would help to modify also offline texts, study materials, printed beletry, etc.

Acknowledgments. We would like to thank to our participants who helped us to prove our hypothesis and maintain our idea for further research in area of assistive technologies. This result was achieved in the context of specific research on Masaryk University: Large Computational Systems - Models, Analysis, and Verification VII.

References

1. Schulte-Körne, G., Grimm, T., Nöthen, M.M., Müller-Myhsok, B., Cichon, S., Vogt, I.R., Propping, P., Remschmidt, H.: Evidence for linkage of spelling disability to chromosome 15. Am. J. Hum. Genet. **63**, 279–282 (1998). https://doi.org/10.1086/301919
2. Zhang, Y., Li, J., Tardif, T., Burmeister, M., Villafuerte, S.M., McBride-Chang, C., Li, H., Shi, B., Liang, W., Zhang, Z., Shu, H.: Association of the DYX1C1 dyslexia susceptibility gene with orthography in the Chinese population. PLoS ONE **7**, e42969 (2012). https://doi.org/10.1371/journal.pone.0042969
3. Tanaka, H., Black, J.M., Hulme, C., Stanley, L.M., Kesler, S.R., Whitfield-Gabrieli, S., Reiss, A.L., Gabrieli, J.D.E., Hoeft, F.: The brain basis of the phonological deficit in dyslexia is independent of IQ. Psychol. Sci. **22**, 1442–1451 (2011). https://doi.org/10.1177/0956797611419521
4. Pařilová, T., Mrváň, F., Mižík, B., Hladká, E.: Emerging technology enabling dyslexia users to read and perceive written text correctly. Res. Comput. Sci. **117**, 173–183 (2016)
5. Casanova, M., El-Baz, A., Elnakib, A., Giedd, J., Rumsey, J., Williams, E., Switala, A.: Corpus callosum shape analysis with application to dyslexia. Transl. Neurosci. **1**, 124–130 (2010). https://doi.org/10.2478/v10134-010-0017-8
6. Hynd, G.W., Hall, J., Novey, E.S., Eliopulos, D., Black, K., Gonzalez, J.J., Edmonds, J.E., Riccio, C., Cohen, M.: Dyslexia and corpus callosum morphology. Arch. Neurol. **52**, 32–38 (1995)
7. Is Text-to-Speech Technology Beneficial for Struggling Readers?. http://www.gettingsmart.com/2015/06/is-text-to-speech-technology-beneficial-for-struggling-readers/. Accessed 18 Mar 2018
8. Rello, L.: DysWebxia: a model to improve accessibility of the textual web for dyslexic users. ACM SIGACCESS Access. Comput. **102**, 41–44 (2012)
9. OpenDyslexic—Free, OpenSource Dyslexia Typeface. https://opendyslexic.org/. Accessed 18 Mar 2018
10. Lukes, D.: Dyslexia friendly reader: prototype, designs, and exploratory study. In: 2015 6th International Conference on Information, Intelligence, Systems and Applications, IISA, pp. 1–6. IEEE (2015)
11. Athènes, S., Raynal, M., Truillet, P., Vinot, J.-L.: Ysilex: a friendly reading interface for dyslexics. In: International Conference on Information & Communication Technologies from Theory to Applications, Tunisia (2009)
12. Frequency of letters, bigrams, trigrams, length of words. https://nlp.fi.muni.cz/web3/cs/FrekvencePismenBigramu. Accessed 18 Mar 2018

Introducing an Emotion-Driven Assistance System for Cognitively Impaired Individuals

Simone Hantke[1,2(✉)], Christian Cohrs[3], Maximilian Schmitt[1],
Benjamin Tannert[3], Florian Lütkebohmert[3], Mathias Detmers[3],
Heidi Schelhowe[3], and Björn Schuller[1,4]

[1] ZD.B Chair of Embedded Intelligence for Health Care and Wellbeing,
University of Augsburg, Augsburg, Germany
simone.hantke@informatik.uni-augsburg.de
[2] Machine Intelligence and Signal Processing Group, Technische Universität
München, Munich, Germany
[3] Working Group on Digital Media in Education, University of Bremen,
Bremen, Germany
[4] GLAM – Group on Language, Audio and Music, Imperial College London,
London, UK

Abstract. Mental, neurological and/or physical disabilities often affect individuals' cognitive processes, which in turn can introduce difficulties with remembering what they have learnt. Therefore, completing trivial daily tasks can be challenging and supervision or help from others is constantly needed. In this regard, these individuals with special needs can benefit from nowadays advanced assistance techniques. Within this contribution, a language-driven, workplace integrated, assistance system is being proposed, supporting disabled individuals in the handling of certain activities while taking into account their emotional-cognitive constitution and state. In this context, we present a set of baseline results for emotion recognition tasks and conduct machine learning experiments to benchmark the performance of an automatic emotion recognition system on the collected data. We show that this is a challenging task that can nevertheless be tackled with state-of-the-art methodologies.

Keywords: Speech-driven assistive technology · Disabilities · Affect
Speech and emotion recognition

1 Introduction

Technology is growing rapidly and opens a new world of opportunities in different areas of health care. In this context, a wide range of applications for many health conditions such as dementia [26], depression [2], or Parkinson's disease [28] are being developed. Nowadays mobile communications and network technologies for health care entail the usage of portable devices with the capability to create,

K. Miesenberger and G. Kouroupetroglou (Eds.): ICCHP 2018, LNCS 10896, pp. 486–494, 2018.
https://doi.org/10.1007/978-3-319-94277-3_75

analyse, store, retrieve, and transmit data in real-time between the users, for the purpose of improving individuals' safety and quality of life [9].

As well as being applied to improve life quality, these systems are capable of facilitating the communication between clinicians and patients [28]. In this regard, remote monitoring systems have amongst others been proposed for asthma patients [15], the tracking of patients with dementia [14], or to support treatment of sleep apnoea [8]. Such assistance systems can also be adapted for unobtrusively recognising stress from human voice [13], to perform suicide prevention [12], or to enable individuals with special needs to both join the workforce and aid them at their job [24].

This contribution focuses on people with cognitive impairments which need special ways to learn new things and keep them in mind. Especially at their workplace, there is necessity to recall working steps in mind to fulfil the work without becoming injured or to avoid inappropriate actions. For these individuals it is often hard to learn new tasks, as they are not able to abstract the work process. Therefore, a special explanation right at the machine or workstation is needed [23]. Another characteristic of this target group is their weak ability in staying focused [23]. Often, small things like music or statements of a colleague can distract these individuals from their work-task. Furthermore, the ability to stay focused or other abilities differ from their normal behaviour according to their emotional status and their health constitution [11].

Psychological research results on people with cognitive disabilities indicate a relation between the voice and articulation on the one hand, and the emotional status on the other hand [11,25]. In this regard – within the German national *Emotional sensitivity Assistance System for people with disabilities (EmotAsS)* project – a language-driven, workplace integrated, assistance system is being developed. The first-of-its kind system aims at supporting individuals with mental, neurological, and/or physical disabilities in the handling of certain activities while taking into account their emotional-cognitive constitution and state.

2   Exemplary Application Area

The first application of the proposed system will be located at the working shelter with disabled employees working in a cleaning department. The complexity of the given tasks within this department lies in the nature of having the knowledge – and more importantly remembering – the different usages and compositions of the cleaning devices for the different tasks to perform, e. g., cleaning the workshop areas, the bathrooms, or the offices. Therefore, the cleaning trolley needs to be prepared with its special equipment depending on these different tasks. For the employees, the proposed system can make it easier to learn and remember how to equip the trolley correctly.

We imagine the following situation: Alex is an employee of the cleaning department and was given the task to clean the wood workshop. Alex is unsure about the required supplies and embarrassed to ask the supervisor again. Fortunately, the proposed assistance system can provide the answer, so Alex asks the speech-driven system instead. The integrated emotion recognition component

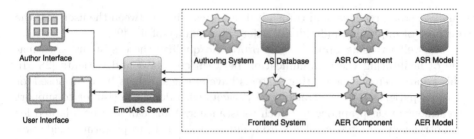

Fig. 1. Overview of the hardware and software components of the assistance system (AS), including the automatic speech recognition (ASR) and automatic emotion recognition (AER) component.

detects that Alex seems to be in a bad mood. In this regard, the system will present longer and more detailed descriptions on the task Alex likes to perform. After a few shown working steps the system detects that Alex' mood has brightened and now presents slightly shorter and less detailed descriptions how to equip the trolley. With the help of the assistance system, Alex was able to perform this task without help of the supervisor, which facilitate independent work, and thus strengthen self-confidence.

3   The System

The system is composed of several hardware elements, consisting of a central server-system and several thin-clients. The applied software elements are divided into a web-application, which provides the assistance and authoring frontends to the end users (here: disabled employees of the sheltered workplace) and authors (here: care-taking personal), and the automatic speech and emotion recognition sub-systems. The authoring and frontend system was implemented as a web application to enable the system to be accessible from several devices such as notebooks and tablets, granting the users mobility during daily use, as well as easy integration into daily work-life. Speech and emotion recognition is processed by a powerful multi-core i7-System, which runs the webserver for the authoring and frontend as well. Clients access the system via web browser. Speech data and recognition results are provided to clients and server via TCP sockets and web-sockets. To be agile as well as structured in its development, the system was implemented via the web application framework Ruby on Rails.

The authoring interface acts as the management system (cf. Fig. 1) and allows creating and accessing user profiles of both end users and authors, instructions for work steps and devices, adding or editing interventions, and accessing frontend statistics. Finally, all data is stored in a database. The assistance frontend is the 'face' of the system, offering instructions, records speech of the end users and passes it to the *automatic speech recognition* (ASR) and *automatic emotion recognition* (AER) components. ASR provides verbal content detected in speech and the assistance system compares the content with commands specified in the database. In addition, the frontend system also offers control inputs via a specialised keyboard without the need for speech input. This allows users with speech disabilities to use the assistance system to a certain degree. Simultaneously, AER is processing the speech recordings of a user, detecting *arousal* (describing how strong or weak an emotion is) and *valence* (describing how positive or negative an emotion is) within the speech sample. Depending on the emotion recognised, the frontend will display emotion-specific content to the user.

4   Emotional Speech Data Collection

To develop the assistance system, emotional speech data from disabled employees were recorded at a workplace shelter as described in detail in [7]. Seventeen participants (ten female and seven male, ages range from 19 to 58 years with a mean age of 31.6 years, and standard deviation of 11.7 years) agreed to take part in the experiment and provided data relating to their personal and health issues including their form of disability. As there are strict ethic restrictions on the data, no further details on the disability of the subjects can be given, but can be clustered into mental, neurological, and physical disabilities: thirteen participants are mentally disabled, three neurological, and one has multiple disabilities.

Taking into account the daily or even hourly mood changes of the participants, a special recording set-up was developed, as not to add undue stress. To achieve a high, but also realistic audio quality, the recordings took place in a working room with equal set-up and conditions for each recording session. The participants had to sit down in front of the recording equipments. An experimental supervisor, an internal occupational therapist, and an internal psychologist of the shelter were sitting next to the participants all the time to communicate and help them through the given tasks. The recorded data consists of spontaneous speech and was recorded by giving the participants different tasks related to different contents [7]. In this way, questions were raised about professional life and certain tasks to be accomplished. The tasks were designed in such a way that the mood of the participants can be shown and their emotions are being provoked. To ensure a professional management of possibly expressed emotions, the tasks were performed in supervision of a psychologist.

The data was annotated by 29 annotators using the crowdsourcing platform iHEARu-PLAY [6]. Labels were gathered giving the annotators the choice to select from the six basic emotions (anger, disgust, fear, happiness, sadness, and surprise), as well as 'neutral' [7]. Moreover, each utterance was annotated on a 5-point likert scale, to represent the intelligibility of the speech, so the data can be used for automatic speech recognition tasks.

5   Automatic Speech and Emotion Recognition

For both the ASR and AER subsystems, the recorded voice is first chunked on the client side, using the *WebRTC Voice Activity Detector*[1]. The resulting

---

[1] https://pypi.python.org/pypi/webrtcvad.

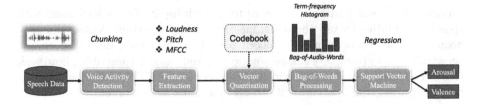

Fig. 2. Schematic overview of the automatic emotion recognition system.

chunks of a duration of approximately 2 to 5 s are then sent to the server via a TCP socket.

The ASR subsystem was integrated using the open-source toolkit KALDI [16]. MFCCs as the most commonly used speech features were extracted and normalised on chunk level. The *acoustic model* consists of a state-of-the-art *maxout* Deep Neural Network [29] and was trained on 160 h of German broadcast news [27]. As a *language model*, a *4-gram Kneser-Ney backoff language model* is used [10], trained on 307 million running words from German newspaper articles. A grapheme-to-phoneme conversion is used to generate a pronunciation model for words not present in the training data of the acoustic model. Evaluation on the *NoXi* database of video chat recordings [1] shows a *word error rate* of approximately 30%.

The AER subsystem processes the incoming speech in the way as illustrated in Fig. 2: first, 65 acoustic features are extracted from small blocks (frames) of the chunk. The features are defined in the COMPARE feature set [22] and include prosodic features, such as *loudness* and *pitch*, *spectral* descriptors, and *Mel-frequency cepstral coefficients* (MFCC), which are a feature widely-used in speech analysis [21]. Then, the acoustic features of one chunk are summarised using the *bag-of-audio-words* (BoAW) approach, which has been proven to be very suitable for the task at hand [19]. In this method, the low-level descriptors (LLDs) from each frame are quantised using a 'codebook' of audio words, previously learnt from data of the same domain using clustering. After this step of *vector quantisation*, the frequencies of each audio word within the whole utterance are counted, resulting in a so-called *term-frequency histogram* or BoAW. For the proposed AER system, we used a codebook of size 1 000 and 10 assignments per frame. This fixed-length histogram is then the input to a *support vector regression*, predicting continuous values for the emotional dimensions arousal and valence. Using the in-the-wild database SEWA of naturalistic and spontaneous humans emotions [17], *concordance correlation coefficients* of .47 and .43 are achieved for arousal and valence, respectively [20]. The implementation of the whole AER subsystem uses only the open-source tools OPENSMILE [4], OPENXBOW [20], and LIBLINEAR [5].

Evaluating the proposed system, extensive machine learning experiments were run on the collected database. As the basic emotions disgust, fear, and surprise are sparse, only the categories anger, happiness, and sadness were

Table 1. Class distribution and classification results on the EmotAsS database (*A(nger)*, *H(appiness)*, *N(eutral)*, *S(adness)*) in terms of unweighted average recall (UAR) [%]; *C*: complexity of the SVM, *CS*: codebook size.

Class distribution				ComParE + SVM			BoAW + SVM			Fusion
	Train.	Devel.	Test	Σ	C	Devel.	Test	CS	Devel.	Test	Test
A	125	50	272	447	10^{-6}	34.2	41.3	250	38.7	36.4	43.4
H	743	965	650	2358	10^{-5}	37.8	43.1	500	40.5	36.5	
N	2287	2842	2024	7153	10^{-4}	28.2	38.4	1000	39.8	38.1	
S	187	329	153	669	10^{-3}	29.9	35.4	2000	38.1	41.3	
Σ	3342	4186	3099	10627	10^{-2}	29.9	33.1	4000	37.9	39.2	

considered for the performed experiments, together with a neutral background class. For the experiments – also employed as a baseline in the Interspeech 2018 ComParE Challenge [22] – we split the data into three partitions, training, development, and test partition, with five subjects in each split. Both the ComParE acoustic feature set consisting of 6373 *supra-segmental* acoustic features and BoAW representations of the corresponding 130 LLDs were considered. A support vector machine (SVM) was used as a classifier. Both the complexity of the SVM and the codebook size for the BoAW approach were optimised; the model was re-trained on the fusion of the training and the development set to receive the final performance estimate on the test set. Results in terms of the *unweighted average recall (UAR)* are given in Table 1 for different hyperparameters. For BoAW, the complexity has been optimised on the development set for the shown configurations. Moreover, a late fusion of the predictions of both models was evaluated, considering for each data instance the prediction with the larger confidence. Fusing the outputs of the two models performing best on the test set gives a UAR of 43.4%, slightly outperforming the single models. These results show both that AER for the atypical speech data is a quite challenging task but that it is yet feasible with a potential for improvement.

6   Conclusions and Outlook

A novel speech-driven, emotionally sensitive assistance system has been introduced to support mentally, neurologically and/or physically disabled people at their workplace. Successful baseline experiments evaluating the automatic emotion recognition component have been performed in earlier work [3,7,18] and were herein expanded by performing novel BoAW experiments, leading to a UAR of 43.3% (4 emotion classes) on the collected data and promising a large margin for improvement considering recent machine learning techniques such as *generative models* and *transfer learning*. Furthermore, primary usability evaluations with the target group are currently ongoing, giving first insights into the promising success of the system. Future work will take into account recent machine learning techniques and focus on comparing the gathered speech emotion recognition results with facial emotion expression observations.

Acknowledgement. The research leading to these results has received funding from the German national BMBF IKT2020-Grant under grant agreement No. 16SV7213 (EmotAsS). We thank all iHEARu-PLAY users for donating their annotations.

References

1. Cafaro, A., Wagner, J., Baur, T., Dermouche, S., Torres, M.T., Pelachaud, C., André, E., Valstar, M.: The NoXi database: multimodal recordings of mediated novice-expert interactions. In: Proceedings of International Conference on Multimodal Interaction, Glasgow, Scotland, pp. 350–359 (2017)
2. Cummins, N., Vlasenko, B., Sagha, H., Schuller, B.: Enhancing speech-based depression detection through gender dependent vowel-level formant. In: Proceedings of Conference on Artificial Intelligence in Medicine, Stockholm, Sweden, pp. 3266–3270 (2017)
3. Deng, J., Xu, X., Zhang, Z., Frühholz, S., Grandjean, D., Schuller, B.: Fisher kernels on phase-based features for speech emotion recognition. In: Jokinen, K., Wilcock, G. (eds.) Dialogues with Social Robots. LNEE, vol. 999, pp. 195–203. Springer, Singapore (2017). https://doi.org/10.1007/978-981-10-2585-3_15
4. Eyben, F., Weninger, F., Groß, F., Schuller, B.: Recent developments in openSMILE, the Munich open-source multimedia feature extractor. In: Proceedings of International Conference on Multimedia, Barcelona, Spain, pp. 835–838 (2013)
5. Fan, R.E., Chang, K.W., Hsieh, C.J., Wang, X.R., Lin, C.J.: Liblinear: a library for large linear classification. J. Mach. Learn. Res. **9**, 1871–1874 (2008)
6. Hantke, S., Eyben, F., Appel, T., Schuller, B.: iHEARu-PLAY: introducing a game for crowdsourced data collection for affective computing. In: Proceedings of International Workshop on Automatic Sentiment Analysis in the Wild, Satellite of Conference on Affective Computing and Intelligent Interaction, Xi'an, China, pp. 891–897 (2015)
7. Hantke, S., Sagha, H., Cummins, N., Schuller, B.: Emotional speech of mentally and physically disabled individuals: introducing the EmotAsS database and first findings. In: Proceedings of INTERSPEECH, Stockholm, Sweden, pp. 3137–3141 (2017)
8. Isetta, V., Torres, M., González, K., Ruiz, C., Dalmases, M., Embid, C., Navajas, D., Farré, R., Montserrat, J.M.: A new mHealth application to support treatment of sleep apnoea patients. J. telemedicine and telecare **10**, 14–18 (2015)
9. Istepanian, R., Laxminarayan, S., Pattichis, C.S.: M-Health. Springer, Heidelberg (2006). https://doi.org/10.1007/b137697
10. Kneser, R., Ney, H.: Improved backing-off for M-gram language modeling. In: Proceedings of International Conference on Acoustics, Speech and Signal Processing, Detroit, USA, pp. 181–184 (1995)
11. Krannich, D., Zare, S.: Concept and design of a mobile learning support system for mentally disabled people at workplace. In: Proceedings of International Conference on E-Learning in the Workplace, New York, USA, pp. 1–6 (2009)

12. Larsen, M.E., Cummins, N., Boonstra, T.W., O'Dea, B., Tighe, J., Nicholas, J., Shand, F., Epps, J., Christensen, H.: The use of technology in suicide prevention. In: Proceedings of International Conference on Engineering in Medicine and Biology Society, Milan, Italy, pp. 7316–7319 (2015)
13. Lu, H., Frauendorfer, D., Rabbi, M., Mast, M.S., Chittaranjan, G.T., Campbell, A.T., Gatica-Perez, D., Choudhury, T.: Stresssense: detecting stress in unconstrained acoustic environments using smartphones. In: Proceedings of Conference on Ubiquitous Computing, Pittsburgh, USA, pp. 351–360 (2012)
14. Miskelly, F.: Electronic tracking of patients with dementia and wandering using mobile phone technology. Age Ageing **34**, 497–498 (2005)
15. Namazova-Baranova, L.S., Molodchenkov, A.I., Vishneva, E.A., Antonova, E.V., Smirnov, V.I.: Remote monitoring of children with asthma, being treated in multidisciplinary hospital. In: Proceedings of International Conference on Biomedical Engineering and Computational Technologies, Novosibirsk, Russia, pp. 7–12 (2015)
16. Povey, D., Ghoshal, A., Boulianne, G., Burget, L., Glembek, O., Goel, N., Hannemann, M., Motlicek, P., Qian, Y., Schwarz, P., Silovsky, J., Stemmer, G., Vesely, K.: The Kaldi speech recognition toolkit. In: Proceedings of International Workshop on Automatic Speech Recognition and Understanding, Hawaii, USA, 4 p (2011)
17. Ringeval, F., Schuller, B., Valstar, M., Gratch, J., Cowie, R., Scherer, S., Mozgai, S., Cummins, N., Schmitt, M., Pantic, M.: Avec 2017: real-life depression, and affect recognition workshop and challenge. In: Proceedings of the 7th Annual Workshop on Audio/Visual Emotion Challenge, Mountain View, USA, pp. 3–9 (2017)
18. Sagha, H., Deng, J., Gavryukova, M., Han, J., Schuller, B.: Cross lingual speech emotion recognition using canonical correlation analysis on principal component subspace. In: Proceedings of International Conference on Acoustics, Speech, and Signal Processing, Shanghai, P. R. China, pp. 5800–5804 (2016)
19. Schmitt, M., Ringeval, F., Schuller, B.: At the border of acoustics and linguistics: bag-of-audio-words for the recognition of emotions in speech. In: Proceedings of INTERSPEECH, San Francisco, USA, pp. 495–499 (2016)
20. Schmitt, M., Schuller, B.: openXBOW-introducing the passau open-source cross-modal bag-of-words toolkit. J. Mach. Learn. Res. **18**, 1–5 (2017)
21. Schuller, B.: Intelligent Audio Analysis. Springer, Heidelberg (2013). https://doi.org/10.1007/978-3-642-36806-6
22. Schuller, B.W., Steidl, S., Batliner, A., Marschik, P.B., Baumeister, H., Dong, F., Hantke, S., Pokorny, F., Rathner, E.M., Bartl-Pokorny, K.D., Einspieler, C., Zhang, D., Baird, A., Amiriparian, S., Qian, K., Ren, Z., Schmitt, M., Tzirakis, P., Zafeiriou, S.: The INTERSPEECH 2018 computational paralinguistics challenge: atypical & self-assessed affect, crying & heart beats. In: Proceedings of INTERSPEECH, Hyderabad, India, 5 p (2018, to appear)
23. Thiel, O.: Das Familienhandbuch des Staatsinstituts für Frühpädagogik - Lernschwierigkeiten (2010)
24. Verbrugge, L.M., Sevak, P.: Use, type, and efficacy of assistance for disability. J. Gerontol. Ser. B: Psychol. Sci. Soc. Sci. **57**, 366–379 (2002)
25. Vogt, T.: Real-time automatic emotion recognition from speech. Ph.D. thesis, University of Bielefeld (2010)
26. Vuong, N.K., Chan, S., Lau, C.T.: mHealth sensors, techniques, and applications for managing wandering behavior of people with dementia: a review. In: Adibi, S. (ed.) Mobile Health. SSB, vol. 5, pp. 11–42. Springer, Cham (2015). https://doi.org/10.1007/978-3-319-12817-7_2

27. Weninger, F., Schuller, B., Eyben, F., Wöllmer, M., Rigoll, G.: A broadcast news corpus for evaluation and tuning of German LVCSR systems. arXiv.org arXiv:1412.4616, 4 p. (2014)
28. Zapata, B.C., Fernández-Alemán, J.L., Idri, A., Toval, A.: Empirical studies on usability of mHealth apps: a systematic literature review. J. Med. Syst. **39**, 1 (2015)
29. Zhang, X., Trmal, J., Povey, D., Khudanpur, S.: Improving deep neural network acoustic models using generalized maxout networks. In: Proceedings of International Conference on Acoustics, Speech and Signal Processing, Florence, Italy, pp. 215–219 (2014)

Assistive Technology App to Help Children and Young People with Intellectual Disabilities to Improve Autonomy for Using Public Transport

Jesus Zegarra Flores[1(✉)], Emilie Cassard[2], Claude Christ[2],
Nadia Laayssel[2], Gilbert Geneviève[2], Jean-Baptiste de Vaucresson[2],
Remi Coutant[2], Jean Paul Granger[2], and Jean-Pierre Radoux[1]

[1] Medic@, Département de recherche d'Altran, Parc d'Innovation, Boulevard Sébastien Brandt,
Bât Gauss, CS 20143, 67404 Illkirch, France
{jesus.zegarraflores,jeanpierre.radoux}@altran.com
[2] ADAPEI du Territoire de Belfort, 11 route de Phaffans, 90380 Roppe, France
{e.cassard,c.christ,n.laayssel,jb.devaucresson,r.coutant,
jp.granger}@adapei90.fr, gilbert.genevieve90@orange.fr

Abstract. Children and young adults with intellectual disabilities experience problems to go from one place to another using public transport because of the complexity of its network. Different learning activities are practiced in order to make them learn a path and to take the right bus. For example, the creation of small paper books as learning tools which describe the actions to do in a chaining way using pictograms, texts, colors, landmarks, photos and times. Additionally, specialists do the path as many times as it is necessary with the children completing the learning process. However, unexpected situations while the person is doing the path by himself can induce to errors not allowing the person to arrive to the destination. In order to help people to reduce the errors and to propose a learning tool, an app called "Assist Motion" has been created. This work has been done in collaboration between ADAPEI Belfort and Altran Technology. The app was developed in Android operating system with the function to save the steps of the path with specific information and to reuse it to visualize the different steps sequentially as a learning tool. This information associated to the GPS coordinates proposes navigation, emergency and surveillance systems. Tests with specialists and disabled children have been done showing a good acceptance of our first approach.

Keywords: GPS · App · Intellectual disability · Transport

1 Introduction

Children and young people with intellectual disabilities face many problems in order to go from one place to a destination by taking public transport buses or metro stations. The complexity of the public transport network and the management of unexpected situations make this task difficult. In order to find solutions to these problems, we are working in narrow collaboration with the specialists from the transportation workshop

© Springer International Publishing AG, part of Springer Nature 2018
K. Miesenberger and G. Kouroupetroglou (Eds.): ICCHP 2018, LNCS 10896, pp. 495–498, 2018.
https://doi.org/10.1007/978-3-319-94277-3_76

from the ADAPEI Belfort (http://adapei90.fr/), which is an association dedicated to improve autonomy for people with intellectual disabilities in different activities. In this article, we will present the first implementation with encouraging results.

Most of the current work for cognitive impaired people relies on the use of the GPS systems to improve pedestrian wayfinding and navigation; for example, Liu et al. [1], have been working on creating outdoor navigation solutions for improving wayfinding experiences to reach destinations more intuitively than standard navigation systems.

Their studies show comparison between landmark based directions and turning based directions using Markov Decision Process to select the best guiding system. Moreover, using "Wizard–of-Oz", they have performed many tests in indoor environments [2]. Gomez et al. [3] propose a method in which the system adapts to the user in terms of route calculation and interface design.

The caregivers or professionals can create the path using a tool on the computer finding landmarks using Google Street View. The problem about images from Google Street View is that these are, mostly not updated. Moreover, sometimes, GPS coordinates of addresses taken from standard navigation systems do not correspond to the accurate position.

2   Use Case: Transportation Workshop in ADAPEI

The specialist teachers create the sequential information in a paper book by using different software tools. However, the creation of a path is normally time-consuming; doing the path, recovering information (like photos) and after editing in a software.

The small book serves to teach to the disabled children (between 14–20 years old) the different steps to arrive from one place to another, taking the bus, and the adaptation of this information by using pictograms and vocabularies which can be understood by every person; for example, images representing: wait for the bus number 2, getting into the bus at 3 o'clock, getting off at the next bus station, yellow background color to indicate a morning activity or dark color to indicate a night activity.

In order to learn the path, the children do the path with the specialists as many times as it is necessary. Specialists indicate points of interest (train stations, movie theaters, commercial centers, etc.) that are clear landmarks. An observed problem is that, for long distances, inside the bus, children are not attentive and they occasionally forgot to push on the "stop button" to indicate the bus driver to stop at the next bus station to get off.

3   Our Approach: "Assist Motion" App

The app can be interpreted as a system to save the path with different useful information (text, photo, GPS coordinates, etc.), to visualize the path showing this information in a sequential way (learning tool) and to use this information for proposing a navigation and emergency system.

The prototype has been developed in Android operating system. Saving the path involves to type the information of the action to do, selecting the time at which the person has to do the action and to choose the pictograms (for instance: get on, take the bus, validate the ticket taken, etc.); moreover, the photo of the landmark (for example: photo of bus station or pedestrian crossing) and the GPS coordinates (Fig. 1, menu on the left) can be added. All the journey sequence information is stored in a special folder having the .txt file and the images files of every landmark. Firstly, specialists will save the path step by step (walking and taking the bus) because they have a better understanding of the preferences (vocabulary and pictograms) of every child.

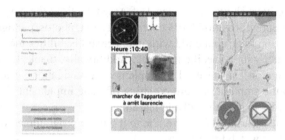

Fig. 1. On the left, menu to save and collect the information; on the center, menu showing the step information and, on the right, map showing the GPS coordinates of the path and the emergency buttons. (Color figure online)

Two other user interface interaction have also been programmed. Firstly, to visualize all the information of every step, as on the center of Fig. 1 (step 1). Secondly, the navigation interface (Fig. 1, on the right) in which there is the possibility to call an assigned person by a button and also to send a SMS having the information of latitude and longitude.

First tests with medium and deep intellectual disability children, including autism, (between 14–20 year old) have been done to validate the pertinence of the user interface to visualize the step information.

4   Results

The first tests have been done with the specialists of the transportation workshop; a first path with one change of bus and 11 steps have been registered taking into account the pedestrian crossing, bus stops and destination. The weather conditions were a rainy day in the morning and no difficulties were observed to use the app. The app also allows adding landmarks at any time between the house and the bus station.

The specialists have indicated that the app is very intuitive and easy to use. They have also expressed that the gain in time of the creation of the electronic book is substantial, 70% faster compared to the current method used (paper book).

The app has been tested in different kinds of Android Systems and versions (low and high cost Smart Phones) with no problems and the delay time to show the photos was always less than 1 s. Moreover, the vocalization (text to speech) of the information is useful for the children who are not able to read.

In order to make the child learn to get ready to "get off" and push on the "stop button", the GPS coordinates of the previous station is saved, when the person is close to the landmark in the bus, the information is delivered as a specific sound (alarm) to recall.

5 Conclusions and Future Work

In this article, we have shown the concept of Assist Motion: the possibility to save a path adding different information (GPS coordinates, text, photos, pictograms, time) and reuse the information to teach a child with intellectual disabilities the steps to go from one place to another with a specific interface. Additionally, thanks to the GPS coordinates, this information can be used to implement a navigation system alerting, for example to push the stop button before getting off. The implementation of this alarm will be done in order to aid to recall and learning.

According to the learning objective, the tool will be programmed to switch from a learning process to a watchdog process.

Future work will include sharing the path created to other users in a collaborative way. Moreover, the information of the schedule time will be added automatically in real time to help the person manage real time variations in arrival buses.

The creation of this app will allow us to study the gain in autonomy of the children and young people and also to increase the possibility to go to unfamiliar places.

Additionally, the creation and use of a bracelet can be considered. For example, in a case of unexpected situation, the bracelet connected to the Smart Phone can detect the high stress level of the child to send the position information to an assigned person who can help.

References

1. Liu, A.L., Hile, H., Borriello, G., Brown, P.A., Harniss, M., Kautz, H., Johnson, K.: Customizing directions in an automated wayfinding system for individuals with cognitive impairment. In: Proceedings of the 11th International ACM SIGACCESS Conference on Computers and Accessibility, pp. 27–34. ACM, October 2009
2. Liu, A.L., Hile, H., Kautz, H., Borriello, G., Brown, P.A., Harniss, M., Johnson, K.: Indoor wayfinding: developing a functional interface for individuals with cognitive impairments. Disabil. Rehabilit. Assist. Technol. 3(1–2), 69–81 (2008)
3. Gomez, J., Montoro, G., Torrado, J.C., Plaza, A.: An adapted wayfinding sy tem for pedestrians with cognitive disabilities. Mob. Inf. Syst. 2015 (2015)

Technology Evaluation for Improving Independence with Activities of Daily Living

Jean Des Roches[1] and John Magee[2]([✉])

[1] Seven Hills Foundation, Worcester, MA 01603, USA
jdesroches@sevenhills.org
[2] Clark University, Worcester, MA 01610, USA
jmagee@clarku.edu

Abstract. We present a pilot case study evaluating the deployment of touch screen tablets in supported living situations to help improve the independence of individuals in their daily lives. Supported individuals who required prompting and reminders for their activities of daily living were provided with tablets in their homes supported by staff members who could set up daily reminders. This paper discusses the needs of supported individuals and staff, the deployment of the technology, and observations of the intended user population. Our focus here is on the observation of adaptation and abandonment factors of the technology by supported individuals and support staff.

Keywords: Activities of daily living · Supported environments
Technology adoption and abandonment

1 Introduction

Seven Hills Community Services provides housing for people with developmental disabilities, autism, and brain injury. Currently, SHCS serves over 500 adults residentially and operates more than 100 homes throughout Massachusetts. These include homes for individuals with significant behavioral health needs as well as individuals on the autism spectrum, individuals with complex medical needs, and individuals with brain injury.

We sought to evaluate an assistive technology that would help these individuals become more independent in various areas of their lives. Our consultations with behavioral specialists and support staff highlighted some areas of concern that could be addressed with the use of technology. Technology concerns included privacy and HIPPA compliance, ease of use of the tablet interface and the staff portal, and the level of training required.

Our needs in searching for an appropriate technology included effectiveness, ease of use, affordability, and the availability of technical support.

To be effective, the solution had to come with the right set of tools to help foster the growth in independence we were seeking. Much of the support given by

© Springer International Publishing AG, part of Springer Nature 2018
K. Miesenberger and G. Kouroupetroglou (Eds.): ICCHP 2018, LNCS 10896, pp. 499–503, 2018.
https://doi.org/10.1007/978-3-319-94277-3_77

staff is in the form of simple reminders, which is something we could automate. "For example, if a person with dementia leaves their home, a reminder message could tell them to lock the front door. This technology can also remind both caregiver and patient of appointments" [1].

Ease of use for both the individual and the staff or caregiver becomes an important determinant of how effective the device will be over time. If the individual feels the device is useful and unobtrusive, they will be more likely to accept and use the device. If staff finds the device cumbersome to interact with or find the learning curve is onerous, they will use the device begrudgingly or not at all. Barriers to adopting new technologies include: "lack of institutional support, lack of financial support, and, most importantly, lack of time to learn new technologies" [2,3]. The biggest obstacle for us was the "time to learn new technologies".

2   Systems, Users, and Context

2.1   Systems

Our pilot study involves the TouchStream Solutions tablet device (Fig. 1 Left). The system provides the following key features for our supported individuals: reminders, task analysis (step-by-step instruction) to support more difficult tasks, automated recording of medical information such as glucose readings and blood pressure readings, scanning of QR codes to indicate accurate completion of specific tasks. The software also has the capability to push surveys to the devices, which we have used to get feedback about the usefulness of the device. Staff configure the system using a portal from a separate computer or tablet, allowing them to monitor compliance, view reporting, receive alerts on missed tasks, set notification thresholds on medical information, and input new tasks, reminders or calendar events remotely (Fig. 1 Right).

Fig. 1. Left: TouchStream tablet. Right: Staff interface.

The product vendor describes their system as: "a tablet-based monitoring system that helps people live independently and gives their families peace of mind. The system provides assistance managing medications, chronic health conditions, doctor appointments, and activities of daily living" [4]. The physical device is an Asus 8″ tablet that has been pre-configured so that the assistive software is always presented as the user interface.

2.2 Users

Our users include both supported individuals and support staff. The majority of individuals using the device are over the age of 50, each of whom is challenged with mild to moderate intellectual disabilities. They face various behavioral and cognitive challenges such as anxiety over scheduling and changes to their routines, memory deficits, and deficits in acquiring new skills. The users could interact effectively with the tablet after minimal instruction. The staff charged with setting up the devices have technical skills that range from beginner to intermediate levels, and there was no prior experience using a platform such as TouchStream. Their typical duties are to help all individuals navigate their activities of daily living, medical concerns, and community involvement.

2.3 Context (Environment)

Residences are carefully designed to give each individual the experience of living in their own home. A typical facility would be similar to a single-family home with common areas and private bedrooms. There are always 2–3 support staff members on site. The supported individuals face typical concerns: getting to the dentist on time, remembering to put on sun-screen, drinking enough water every day, or remembering to call family.

3 Pilot Evaluation

Our expectation was that we would utilize the tablets to promote individual independence by having the tablet present reminders and task analysis support, to reduce reliance on staff. Tablets were placed in the common area of the home, as we did not have funding for individual devices to be placed in each of the individuals' rooms. Because the devices were in public areas, and due to HIPPA regulations, we were not able to list personal information, such as specific medication reminders, on a device in public view.

Therefore, reminders included things such as "time to drink more water"; "time for your daily vitamin" or "put on your sunscreen before leaving the house". QR labels were added to some items, such as the sunscreen tube, so that the individual was forced to scan the lotion's QR label at the tablet to record the date and time the individual was contemplating using the lotion.

Our pilot evaluation was conducted in stages. The first stage lasted three months with one device each in three separate homes. We quickly observed that the outcomes we experienced depended on the needs of the individuals in the home balanced with the adoption of the device by staff. One home, using the device with just one individual, quickly lost interest in the device after the individual reportedly "showed little interest". The second home thought it was useful, reported that the individuals "mostly" paid attention to the device, and felt they could support continuing with the device. The staff in the third home reported that they "needed" to see this trial continue and remarked on how helpful and enjoyable the individuals found the device. The trial in the third home was extended to one year.

After the initial trial, we also decided to pilot the device for one year in an additional home which had been upgraded to a "smart-home" with other available technology. We observed slower adoption with the staff in the smart-home. Although staff in each home was given identical training, and even with the smart-home staff receiving extra support from tablet vendor's tech support team, staff were not timely in reporting concerns or asking questions, which resulted in the under-utilization of the devices. Subsequent discussions indicated that the initial challenges in implementation in the smart-home were a direct result of the staff's comfort level with new technology and not an issue with the individuals, the system, or tech support.

Once we resolved obstacles to effective adoption of the system, we expanded to two devices per home. We also added devices that automatically record medical readings from a glucose meter and blood-pressure cuff. There is a separate study underway to determine if these medical devices will produce fewer errors and omissions than the manual medical reporting system currently in use.

After observing positive outcomes in the first stage of the trial, we added an additional home to the one-year trial. Each participant in this home has his or her own device, in contrast to the other locations where devices were shared among participants. The current stage of the trial consists of eight devices in three homes participating for one year.

3.1   Role of the Staff

The role of the staff was designed and expected to be twofold. First, staff would identify and program in those tasks that they were accustomed to prompting the individuals to complete. Secondly, staff were expected to make sure the devices remained charged and in proper working order. It wasn't until the trials began that it became obvious that the devices were as useful for staff reminders as for individuals. Staff found it useful to be reminded about various compliance issues, for example, recording the water temperature from the faucets once a month.

3.2   Adoption and Abandonment Issues

In some cases, poor adoption by supported individuals was due to poor adoption rates by the staff. Some felt that "they were too busy to ask questions", so if they didn't know how to do something, rather than ask, they just ignored the device.

In other cases, devices were readily adopted by some individuals in a home while others, in that same home, avoided using it. Some just didn't like the talking tablet, but couldn't articulate exactly why that was, while others perhaps did not receive the reinforcement necessary from staff to make using the device part of their daily routine. One individual had a psychological issue (hearing voices) which was temporarily exacerbated when the device was implemented.

4   Conclusions and Future Direction

One must be certain that the technology is actually helping the user to be more independent and to assure that the user is comfortable with and appreciates the benefits afforded by using the technology. Additionally, staff perception of their role needs to evolve from being there to help individuals to being there to help individuals become more independent. Individuals have unique abilities and situations; larger trials will be needed to generalize the technologys effectiveness for the various populations we support.

We envision that this type of device can have a positive role in helping individuals to become more independent. One way we could have ensured higher acceptance would have been to work more closely with our behavioral specialists in order to design skill acquisition plans around the use of the device. We believe our pilot study demonstrates that these solutions could be scaled to a larger number of our supported individuals without unreasonable burdens of staff time and training. We hope to build a pool of participants that will facilitate longitudinal studies that will benefit the individuals and fill in significant gaps in accessibility research [5, 6].

Acknowledgments. We thank our participants, support staff, behavioral specialists, assistive technology specialist, and the technical support staff at Touch Stream Solutions.

References

1. Sauer, A., Sauer, A.: Technology innovations for those living with dementia. Alzheimer's net (2014). http://www.alzheimers.net/9-22-14-technology-for-dementia/. Accessed 1 Feb 2018
2. Butler, D.L., Sellbom, M.: Barriers to adopting technology for teaching and learning. In: Educause Quarterly, pp. 22–28. Educause, November 2002
3. Yusif, S., Soar, J., Hafeez-Baig, A.: Older people, assistive technologies, and the barriers to adoption: a systematic review. Int. J. Med. Inf. **94**, 112–116 (2016)
4. TouchStream Solutions. http://TouchstreamSolutions.com. Accessed 29 Jun 2017
5. Dee, M., Hanson, V.L.: A pool of representative users for accessibility research: seeing through the eyes of the users. ACM Trans. Access. Comput. (TACCESS) **8**(1), 4:1–4:31 (2016)
6. McIntyre, L., Hanson, V.L.: BESiDE - the built environment for social inclusion through the digital economy. In: Proceedings of the SIGCHI Conference on Human Factors in Computing Systems Extended Abstracts (CHI 2013), pp. 289–294. ACM (2013)

Recognizing Everyday Information Technologies as Assistive Technologies for Persons with Cognitive Disabilities

Jessica Nicole Rocheleau[1(✉)], Virginie Cobigo[2],
and Hajer Chalghoumi[2]

[1] School of Computer Science, Carleton University, Ottawa, Canada
jessicarocheleau@cmail.carleton.ca
[2] School of Psychology, University of Ottawa, Ottawa, Canada

Abstract. In this short paper, we shed light on the potential for everyday Information Technologies (IT) to serve as Assistive Technologies for Cognition (ATC) for persons with cognitive disabilities. We present the results of a review and thematic analysis of definitions of ATC included in peer-reviewed journal articles and conference proceedings published within the last decade. We then provide a critical analysis of researchers' descriptions of ATC, emphasizing the need for definitions of these technologies that are inclusive of everyday IT. The discussion provided in this paper may serve to broaden current conceptualizations of ATC and IT, thus promoting greater access and accessibility of technologies for persons with cognitive disabilities.

Keywords: Intellectual and developmental disability · Dementia
Cognitive assistive technology · Information and communication technology

1 Introduction

Cognitive disabilities refer to significant limitations in a person's intellectual functioning. They may result from intellectual and developmental disabilities (e.g. Down syndrome, autism spectrum disorders), stroke, traumatic brain injuries or dementia [1]. Persons with cognitive disabilities encounter challenges in their everyday life due to limitations in their memory, reasoning, information processing or communication abilities [1]. Information Technologies (IT)—such as computers, smartphones, and tablets—are able to support the cognitive functioning, independence and well-being of persons with cognitive disabilities, and may therefore be considered as Assistive Technologies for Cognition (ATC) for these users [2]. Unfortunately, technology developers and policy-makers often do not recognize IT as ATC when used by persons with cognitive disabilities, thus reducing the funding, usability and use of IT for this population of users with special needs [2]. To minimize barriers to technology use for persons with cognitive disabilities, there is a need to identify the similarities and differences between IT and ATC in their ability to support these users. In this paper, we examine current definitions of ATC, and discuss the extent to which they also describe the functions of IT. The discussion provided in this paper may serve to broaden

© Springer International Publishing AG, part of Springer Nature 2018
K. Miesenberger and G. Kouroupetroglou (Eds.): ICCHP 2018, LNCS 10896, pp. 504–508, 2018.
https://doi.org/10.1007/978-3-319-94277-3_78

technology developers' and policymakers' conceptualizations of ATC and IT, thus promoting greater access and accessibility of technologies for persons with cognitive disabilities.

2   Method

We conducted a literature review to explore the definitions of ATC within peer-reviewed journal articles and conference proceedings. Our review was guided by the following research question: What are the main functions of ATC? We used the following steps to conduct our review: (1) identifying data sources, (2) identifying keywords, (3) identifying screening criteria, (4) conducting the search, and, (5) extracting the data [3].

Given the exploratory nature of our study, we limited our data sources to Google Scholar. Google Scholar was selected as the main data source because it indexes scholarly articles from a wide range of fields that research on ATC tends to occur (e.g., rehabilitation, psychology, human-computer interaction). The search was conducted between March 2 and 7, 2018 using the following terms: *assistive technology for cognition*, *cognitive assistive technology*, *cognitive orthotic*, and *cognitive prosthetic*. To ensure the inclusion of the most relevant and recent definitions of ATC, we narrowed our search to papers published within the last decade (i.e., January 2008 to March 2018). To reduce the proportion of grey literature in our search, we focused on the first 200 results for each term [4]. We reviewed the full text of all English, peer-reviewed journal articles and conference proceedings identified from the search, and extracted excerpts in which the authors clearly endeavoured to define ATC. Since we were specifically interested in technologies supporting cognitive functioning, we excluded general definitions of assistive technology.

We qualitatively analysed the definitions of ATC using an inductive, thematic approach. The first author independently reviewed the definitions of ATC, and developed a list of descriptive codes. Afterwards, these codes were grouped into themes representing the main functions of ATC. Finally, the first and third author collaboratively reviewed and refined the themes.

3   Findings

3.1   Study Selection and Characteristics

Our search yielded 58 unique definitions of ATC, the largest proportion of which were from works in the field of neuro-rehabilitation (27.6%). A total of 481 unique publications were excluded because (1) they were not peer-reviewed journal articles or conference proceedings (n = 145), (2) we could not identify a segment of the text that defined ATC (n = 287), (3) they were not available in English (n = 28), or (4) they could not be accessed through two institutional libraries (n = 21).

3.2   Main Functions of ATC

Our thematic analysis revealed four main functions of ATC; Table 1 presents the themes and example definitions of ATC that represent each of the main functions of these technologies[1].

Table 1. Example definitions of ATC representing each function.

Function	Definitions
Increase or maintain users' cognitive functioning	"… Assistive technologies for cognition can generally be categorised into those that augment or compensate for information processing deficits (i.e., perceptual and communication aids) and those that augment or compensate memory and executive function impairments (i.e., memory aids and prompting systems)" [5]
Match users' environment with their functional abilities	"External aids, often termed assistive technology for cognition (ATC) are tools or devices that either reduce the cognitive demands of a task or transform the task or environment to match the users' abilities" [6]
Facilitate caregiving	"A *cognitive orthotic* is a tool assigned to the patient and potentially configured by the caregiver that serves as link between the two, relaying the caregiver's assistance to the patient and providing feedback to the caregiver about the activities completed (or neglected) by the patient" [7]
Enhance users' independence and well-being	"Assistive Technology for Cognition (ATC)… has the advantage of being highly customizable, so that one can directly assist each patient in performing his [activities of daily living] … these kinds of tools have positive social impacts, as they represent modernity, and are commonly perceived as making life more simple and enjoyable" [8]

4   Discussion

We conducted a review of 58 peer-reviewed publications on ATC to determine the main functions of these technologies. Our findings reveal that ATC serve multiple functions: (1) increasing or maintaining users' cognitive functioning, (2) reducing the cognitive demands of everyday tasks, (3) informing caregivers on the person's daily well-being and functioning, and (4) supporting independent living.

Our literature review revealed notable discrepancies within researchers' definitions of ATC. Firstly, many researchers solely emphasize the potential for ATC to help persons with cognitive disabilities to accomplish memory-related tasks. Cognitive disability not only refers to memory impairments, but also deficits in communication, problem solving, or planning. Future definitions of ATC should be inclusive of all

---

[1] Please contact the authors for a full list of references included in this review.

aspects of cognitive functioning. Furthermore, there are notable inter-disciplinary disparities in researchers' approach to defining ATC. While most researchers in the fields of rehabilitation and medicine emphasize the users' cognitive deficits in their description of the function of ATC, other researchers regard ATC as environmental tools that minimize the complexity of tasks. We recommend that future definitions of ATC apply the social model of disability, therefore highlighting the potential for accessible technologies to reduce environmental obstacles to performing daily activities.

The ATC functions described in the reviewed definitions can all be met by everyday IT [2]; therefore, we argue that IT can function as assistive technologies when used by persons with cognitive disabilities. For example, a smartphone may act as a digital assistant for persons with cognitive disabilities, enabling them to set reminders for everyday activities and to contact their caregivers when they need assistance. However, IT are not commonly regarded as ATC because they are not built specifically for persons with cognitive disabilities. As a result, persons with cognitive disabilities are often deemed ineligible in programs funding assistive technologies. However, they have expressed preferences towards mainstream technologies to support their daily activities because they are perceived as less stigmatising than specialized ATC [2]. In addition, mainstream technologies that are developed for a sizeable market tend to be less expensive than assistive technologies designed specifically for persons with disabilities.

We only used one search tool (Google Scholar) when conducting our review. Future work should extend our search to other search engines. Nevertheless, the current research sheds light on key concepts within a broad range of definitions of ATC. The knowledge gained from our review may help technology developers and policy-makers to understand and identify the typical functions of these technologies.

References

1. Bohman, P.R., Anderson, S.: A conceptual framework for accessibility tools to benefit users with cognitive disabilities. In: Proceedings of the 2005 International Cross Disciplinary Workshop on Web Accessibility, W4A, pp. 85–89. ACM (2005)
2. Institute of Medicine Committee on Disability in America. https://www.ncbi.nlm.nih.gov/books/NBK11418/. Accessed 24 Mar 2018
3. Arksey, II., O'Malley, L.: Scoping studies: towards a methodological framework. Int. J. Soc. Res. Methodol. 8(1), 19–32 (2005)
4. Haddaway, N.R., Collins, A.M., Coughlin, D., Kirk, S.: The role of Google Scholar in evidence reviews and its applicability to grey literature searching. PLoS ONE 10(9), e0138237 (2015)
5. O'Neill, B., Moran, K., Gillespie, A.: Scaffolding rehabilitation behaviour using a voice-mediated assistive technology for cognition. Neuropsychol. Rehabil. 20(4), 509–527 (2010)
6. Wang, J., Ding, D., Teodorski, E.E., Mahajan, H.P., Cooper, R.A.: Use of assistive technology for cognition among people with traumatic brain injury: a survey study. Mil. Med. 181(6), 560–566 (2016)

7. La Placa, M., Pigot, H., Kabanza, F.: Assistive planning for people with cognitive impairments. In: Proceedings of Workshop on Intelligent Systems for Assisted Cognition Hosted by International Joint Conference on Artificial Intelligence, IJCAI (2009)
8. Sablier, J., Stip, E., Jacquet, P., Giroux, S., Pigot, H., Mobus Group, Franck, N.: Ecological assessments of activities of daily living and personal experiences with Mobus, an assistive technology for cognition: a pilot study in schizophrenia. Assist. Technol. 24(2), 67–77 (2012)

MemoRec – Towards a Life-Theme-Based Reminiscence Content Recommendation System for People with Dementia

Alexander Bejan[(✉)], Christian Plotzky, and Christophe Kunze

Furtwangen University, Robert-Gerwig-Platz 1, 78120 Furtwangen, Germany
{beja, plan, kuc}@hs-furtwangen.de

Abstract. In line with statistical predictions, the age-correlated condition of dementia may become a major societal challenge in the 21st century.

As technology-supported reminiscence therapy is a potentially effective way to maintain the well-being of people with dementia, we propose a reminiscence recommender system that aims to lower the caregiver burden and allow for the efficient conduction of individually tailored reminiscence sessions.

This paper describes the underlying technologies of the MemoRec system as well as the promising results of the preliminary study.

Keywords: Recommender systems · Reminiscence therapy · Dementia

1 Introduction

With the worlds' population growing ever older, the age-correlated condition of dementia will presumably be one of the key health-related challenges of the 21st century. As statistical institutions predict a significant rise of the elderly population, many citizens are also likely to develop dementia symptoms [1].

In this light, interventions for persons with dementia (PwD) focusing on well-being – such as activating pleasant memories in so-called reminiscence therapy (RT) sessions (with analogue or digital content) – are regarded as efficient [2, 3] and good practice in line with human-centered care for PwD [4].

The MemoRec assistive reminiscence system aims to enhance – the highly sought-after [5] – technology-supported RT approach by providing caregivers with an automatic tool that helps them to conduct spontaneous RT sessions tailored to the personal life themes of the participating PwD. In essence, MemoRec uses a specific recommender algorithm to match the PwD's individual biographies – which were digitized and transferred into a graph database in a previous step – with potentially relevant audio-visual content (audio, video, text) from a dedicated content pool. It then presents the ranked results to the caregiver in an easy to use front-end. Based on that, the caregiver should easily be able to trigger reminiscence by showing appropriate content to the PwD, regardless of knowing the personal biography of the PwD or not.

© Springer International Publishing AG, part of Springer Nature 2018
K. Miesenberger and G. Kouroupetroglou (Eds.): ICCHP 2018, LNCS 10896, pp. 509–513, 2018.
https://doi.org/10.1007/978-3-319-94277-3_79

2 State of the Art

Originating back in the late 1950s, the theory of psychosocial development postulates a struggle between "ego integrity" versus "despair" in elderly people. In order to turn this "crisis" to a favorable outcome, a person has to feel a sense of accomplishment pertaining to his or her past life [6]. Evidently, affirmative "life-reviewing" memories are an integral part of this well-being-fostering process [7]. For PwD, the creation of new memories is impaired, but the recall of autobiographical memories – especially from a specific time frame – still works to a certain extent [8]. Besides the correct time period, RT contents have to adhere to the personal life themes of the PwD (e.g. profession, birth and living places, interests, hobbies, etc.) and their individual significance in order to trigger reminiscence [9].

On the technological side, recommender systems [10] are frequently used in search engines (e.g. Google), social IT (e.g. social networks, dating portals, movie databases), commercial IT (e.g. web shops) or content-providing systems (e.g. streaming portals), in which users seek a filtered, efficient and effective prediction regarding items in a vast information pool and for a certain context. Depending on the prediction type as well as other parameters (e.g. the dataset size), several techniques can be implemented independently or in combination to create an appropriate "user-item-recommendation" function. Commonly used state-of-the-art algorithms are the dynamic learning approaches of "collaborative" filtering and "content-based" filtering or the more static domain-specific "knowledge-based" filtering [11].

Current multimedia RT approaches, e.g. the CIRCA project [12], put a heavy focus on different devices and different forms of interaction, but show a lack of automatic – potentially workload-reducing – recommendation of the reminiscence content itself. Albeit digital RT content seems to be well-suited for recommender systems, caregivers have to choose or even compose the contents for the session manually in most cases. As proof of concept, one of the few recommender systems for RT content, "REMPAD", uses content-based recommendation with overall positive results [13]. Nonetheless, it does not use different media formats – a gap that MemoRec aims to fill.

3 System Description

As part of the multimedia RT project InterMem [14, 15], the life theme based recommender system MemoRec was conceived as a component of an interactive RT system. Following the identification of a life theme ontology (e.g. "profession", "home", "language", "interests") extracted from 40+ PwD biographies, a first iteration of the test system was developed in a user-centered design approach.

At its core, MemoRec not only provides a recommendation back-end, but also a "control" front-end for the caregiver and a RT "presentation" front-end for the PwD. Both front-ends are implemented using the Ionic web-app framework. The back-end includes the Neo4j graph database – holding the PwD life themes as well as the content information –, a life theme parser, the recommender algorithms themselves and an event-coordination database. The front-end for the caregiver lets him or her choose the highest ranked content items from an ordered list (and also rate their effectiveness afterwards), whereas the RT front-end presents the chosen images to the PwD on a suitable display. The system's modules are loosely coupled over standardized interfaces (e.g. RESTful, JSON, CSV interfaces) in order to allow for an easy integration of new modules (see Fig. 1).

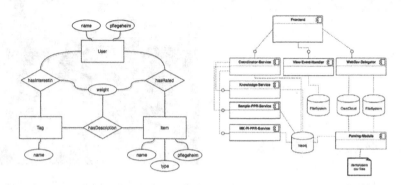

Fig. 1. Left side: MemoRec ER diagram; Right side: MemoRec system diagram

The main algorithm is a modified personalized page rank (PPR) algorithm [16] working on the life theme holding user-item-graph database. The structure of the graph consists of three parts: user-nodes (PwD), item-nodes (content) and life-theme-nodes – the latter nodes being connected with both user-nodes as well as item-nodes. Life-theme-nodes thus represent the individually weighted interests ranging from "−1" (lack of interest) to "3" (vested interest) of the particular PwD. As the caregiver requests recommendations for a certain PwD, a chosen amount of "random walkers" begin to traverse the graph starting from the particular user-node. Depending on the PwD's preferences, the walkers are more likely to visit higher-weighted life-theme-nodes and thus more frequently end up at more likely suited item-nodes. The PPR algorithm counts the frequency of the visits to the item-nodes and calculates a ranked list to be shown in the front-end. If positive feedback is given by the caregiver, the particular item-node is being directly connected to the user-node, further raising the probability of frequent visits to this important content-item.

4 Methods and Results of the Initial Feasibility Study

As large display surfaces seem to be effective for activating PwD [17], MemoRec was initially tested using a custom-built 4 × 55-in. "monitor wall" in one of the InterMem dementia care partner institutions. In addition, a Microsoft Surface Pro 12-in. tablet PC served as control front-end for the caregiver. The one-shot case study sample consisted of n = 4 of the institutions' PwD. The system was "fed" the life themes of each test person and then used by the caregiver as an assistive reminiscence content tool in the ensuing RT sessions (up to 30 min for each PwD).

Every session was directly observed (from a vantage ground outside of the field of vision of the caregiver-PwD-tandem; see Fig. 2) while textual notes were taken for later qualitative data analyses. In addition, MemoRec itself logged the time, content item, rating, as well as the PwD ID. As a final step, interviews assessing the usability and the (subjective) quality of recommendations were conducted with the caregiver.

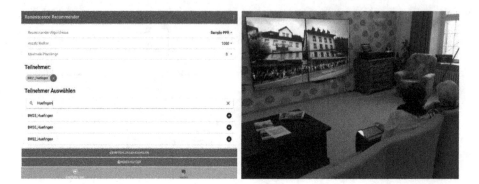

Fig. 2. Left side: MemoRec participant selection screen; Right side: initial live evaluation

On one hand, the recommended audio-visual content items seemed to elicit positive feelings and trigger reminiscence in most cases. On the other hand, some recommendations were misleading, particularly regarding the life-theme "home": although one particular PwD's home was Bavaria, MemoRec gave a picture from the Black Forest a top three ranking, as the life-theme-node "home" didn't hold the correct property. Ultimately, the interview yielded a predominantly positive perception from the point of view of the caregiver: MemoRec was described as intuitive as well as easy to use while having a high potential when improved properly.

5 Discussion

In summary, the preliminary study showed that it is feasible to use MemoRec as an assistive RT tool to automatically find well-suited reminiscence content for a given PwD, but for valid test results, further iterations, more objective measures (incl. a baseline condition) and a higher number of test persons are needed (especially regarding the "learning from feedback" feature of the recommender that cannot be tested otherwise).

Further complications (and with that potential points of improvement) are the recommender-specific "cold start problem", as the number of items in the content pool were not sufficiently high (i < 100) and the "knowledge engineering problem", as the life theme ontology did not seem to be optimal, as seen in the misleading "home"-related recommendation.

Apart from algorithm-related improvements, an automatic multimedia web content crawler to widen the content pool as well as an automatic tagging system are to be implemented as future modules. Such additions may help the caregivers to further concentrate on the important inter-personal aspects of RT and be less burdened by the time-consuming collection, maintenance and manual selection of reminiscence content.

Acknowledgments. We especially thank all of our test persons, colleagues and partners, as well as the Federal Ministry of Education and Research (project InterMem, 16SV7322).

References

1. Alzheimer's Disease International: World Alzheimer Report (2016). https://www.alz.co.uk/research/WorldAlzheimerReport2016.pdf. Accessed 21 Mar 2018
2. Pinquart, M., Forstmeier, S.: Effects of reminiscence interventions on psychosocial outcomes: a meta-analysis. Aging Ment. Health **16**, 541–558 (2012)
3. Lazar, A., Thompson, H., Demiris, G.: A systematic review of the use of technology for reminiscence therapy. Health Educ. Behav. **41**, 51S–61S (2014)
4. Kitwood, T.M.: Dementia Reconsidered: The Person Comes First. Open University Press, Maidenhead (2012)
5. Sixsmith, A., Gibson, G., Orpwood, R., Torrington, J.: Developing a technology 'wish-list' to enhance the quality of life of people with dementia. Gerontechnology **6**, 2–19 (2007)
6. Erikson, E.H.: Identity and the life cycle: selected papers. Psychol. Issues **1**, 1–171 (1959)
7. Butler, R.N.: The life review: an interpretation of reminiscence in the aged. Psychiatry **26**, 65–76 (1963)
8. Fromholt, P., Larsen, S.F.: Autobiographical memory and life-history narratives in aging and dementia (Alzheimer type). In: Conway, M.A., Rubin, D.C., Spinnler, H., Wagenaar, W.A. (eds.) Theoretical Perspectives on Autobiographical Memory. ASID, vol. 65, pp. 413–426. Springer, Dordrecht (1992). https://doi.org/10.1007/978-94-015-7967-4_24
9. Subramaniam, P., Woods, B.: The impact of individual reminiscence therapy for people with dementia: systematic review. Expert Rev. Neurother. **12**, 545–555 (2012)
10. Aggarwal, C.C.: Recommender Systems: The Textbook. Springer, New York (2016). https://doi.org/10.1007/978-3-319-29659-3
11. Adomavicius, G., Tuzhilin, A.: Toward the next generation of recommender systems: a survey of the state-of-the-art and possible extensions. IEEE Trans. Knowl. Data Eng. **17**, 734–749 (2005)
12. Astell, A.J., Alm, N., Gowans, G., Ellis, M.P., Dye, R., Campbell, J., Vaughan, P.: Working with people with dementia to develop technology: the CIRCA and Living in the Moment projects. PSIGE Newsl. **105**, 64–69 (2009)
13. Yang, Y., Caprani, N., Bermingham, A., O'Rourke, J., Collins, R., Gurrin, C., Smeaton, A. F.: Design and field evaluation of REMPAD: a recommender system supporting group reminiscence therapy. In: O'Grady, M.J., Vahdat-Nejad, H., Wolf, K.-H., Dragone, M., Ye, J., Röcker, C., O'Hare, G. (eds.) AmI 2013. CCIS, vol. 413, pp. 13–22. Springer, Cham (2013). https://doi.org/10.1007/978-3-319-04406-4_3
14. Klein, P., Uhlig, M.: Interactive memories. In: Proceedings of the 9th ACM International Conference on PErvasive Technologies Related to Assistive Environments, PETRA 2016 (2016)
15. Interactive Memories. http://www.intermem.org. Accessed 21 Mar 2018
16. Lofgren, P.A.: Efficient algorithms for Personalized PageRank (2015)
17. Bejan, A., Gündogdu, R., Butz, K., Müller, N., Kunze, C., König, P.: Using multimedia information and communication technology (ICT) to provide added value to reminiscence therapy for people with dementia. Zeitschrift für Gerontologie und Geriatrie **51**, 9–15 (2017)

How to Use Plain and Easy-to-Read Language for a Positive User Experience on Websites

Beat Vollenwyder[1]([envelope]), Andrea Schneider[2], Eva Krueger[2],
Florian Brühlmann[1], Klaus Opwis[1], and Elisa D. Mekler[1]

[1] Center for Cognitive Psychology and Methodology, Department of Psychology,
University of Basel, Basel, Switzerland
{beat.vollenwyder,florian.bruehlmann,klaus.opwis,elisa.mekler}@unibas.ch
[2] Swiss Federal Railways, Bern, Switzerland
{andrea.schneider,eva.krueger}@sbb.ch

Abstract. Plain Language and Easy-to-Read Language are two approaches to reduce language complexity, which are also applied in the context of Web Accessibility. While Easy-to-Read Language was specifically designed to meet the needs of people with cognitive and learning disabilities, benefits for users with a variety of abilities have been reported. However, studies have also found unintended side-effects on non-disabled users, such as reduced text liking and intention to revisit a website compared to variants in conventional language. The present study addresses this issue by testing two approaches combining conventional with Easy-to-Read Language against a Plain Language variant, as well as a control group in conventional language. In an online study, 308 non-disabled participants read three texts presented in one of the four language variants. Measurements of performance indicators as well as subjective responses show that Easy-to-Read language may be implemented without unintended side-effects.

Keywords: Plain Language · Easy-to-Read Language
User Experience

1 Introduction

Language complexity is an often-underestimated factor in Web Accessibility. Early research and development within Web Accessibility mainly focused on perceptibility and operability. In recent years, aspects that support understandability, such as content design, structure and wording, have gained increasing importance [1,2]. While understandability is often discussed in the context of cognitive and learning disabilities, benefits for users with a variety of abilities have been reported [3–6].

The Web Content Accessibility Guidelines 2.0 address language complexity in a rather broad sense: Unusual words (criterion 3.1.3) as well as abbreviations (criterion 3.1.4) should be explained, while the overall reading ability

K. Miesenberger and G. Kouroupetroglou (Eds.): ICCHP 2018, LNCS 10896, pp. 514–522, 2018.
https://doi.org/10.1007/978-3-319-94277-3_80

required to understand the text should not exceed lower secondary education (criterion 3.1.5). More specific recommendations to reduce language complexity are proposed with the concepts of *Plain Language* and *Easy-to-Read Language*. Both approaches differ regarding their formalisation and their intended audience. *Plain Language* has its roots in efforts to improve government information and focuses on clear and precise writing [7]. It is centred on the user's goals and tries to make the content easily scannable and understandable by avoiding long, convoluted sentences and jargon. There is no clearly defined target group, as writings in Plain Language aim at being understandable for as broad an audience as possible. *Easy-to-Read Language*, in contrast, was specifically designed to meet the needs of people with cognitive and learning disabilities [8]. However, Easy-to-Read Language also benefits a potentially larger audience, such as people with low language skills or auditory disabilities [1]. Texts in Easy-to-Read Language attempt to be as simple as possible. Guidelines include the use of very clear sentence structures, making only one statement per sentence and avoiding difficult words. Additional recommendations for optimal readability exist. Easy-to-Read Language is characterised by the rule to present one sentence per line, turning the text presentation into a list-form [9].

Research generally reports that Easy-to-Read Language benefits users with cognitive and learning disabilities [8]. However, studies have found unintended side-effects on non-disabled users [5,10]. While non-disabled users also seem to benefit from better text understanding, they prefer conventional language with regards to text liking. Further, their intention to revisit a website was reduced when Easy-to-Read Language was applied [10]. Importantly, these findings contrast recent studies that showed no drawbacks of implementing other Web Accessibility criteria [11]. Because non-disabled users arguably represent the main user base of most websites, practitioners are very sensitive to potential trade-offs and will not implement controversial recommendations [12]. Hence, further research is necessary to find solutions suitable for all user groups [1,5].

The present work addresses potential unintended side-effects by proposing a dynamic and a static approach for combining conventional with Easy-to-Read Language (see Sect. 2.2). The contribution is three-fold: (1) Different approaches for countering potential negative side-effects of reducing language complexity are tested in an experimental design. (2) Thanks to a collaboration with the Swiss Federal Railways, a real-world example of practical relevance is studied. (3) The theoretical and practical discourse about the application of Plain and Easy-to-Read Language on websites is advanced.

2   Method

2.1   Participants and Design

A total of 336 participants completed an online study. A priori power analysis suggested a minimum sample size of 280 participants. Recruitment was conducted by the recruiting-service TestingTime, targeting a balanced sample in terms of age and gender. Participants received a payment of 10 Swiss Francs (about 8.50 Euros) for completing the study. Twenty-eight participants were subsequently excluded from the sample: Seven participants indicated that they did not answer the questionnaire seriously, 14 participants completed the questionnaire in less than 10 min and one participant's response time exceeded one hour. Finally, 6 participants were excluded because they did not fully answer the cloze test to estimate their level of literacy.

In total, 308 non-disabled participants (age $M = 41.8$, $SD = 16.0$, range 18–79; 165 women, 140 men, 3 non-binary or not specified) were included in the analysis. On average, the study took 21 min ($SD = 8.5$ min) to complete. The study consisted of a one-factorial between-subjects design with four conditions. Experimental groups did not significantly differ with regards to age, gender distribution or literacy.

2.2   Materials

The selection of texts for the study was based on the experiences of call agents working in the contact centre of the Swiss Federal Railways, covering common questions by customers. For these topics, texts with a length of approximately 300–400 words (i.e., a reading time of about 2 min) were screened. Three text samples A (excerpt of terms of conditions), B (excerpt of privacy policy) and C (advertisement letter) were selected and subsequently translated by a professional translator into a Plain Language and an Easy-to-Read variant. The Easy-to-Read variant was translated according to the ruleset of the "Forschungsstelle Leichte Sprache" of the University of Hildesheim [9]. The translation was tested by four reviewers with cognitive disabilities. Based on the reviewers' qualitative feedback, the Easy-to-Read text was deemed adequate and accessible. Additionally, the texts were analysed with the German version of the Flesch-Reading-Ease formula [13], which provides a readability score ranging from 0 (very easy) to 100 (very difficult). This analysis showed a decrease of text difficulty for the translations compared to the original text in conventional language. Descriptives for all texts and variants are presented in Table 1.

Next, four variants of a website were prepared to present the texts: (1) A control group, where the original text was presented in *conventional* language. (2) A condition in *Plain Language* text. (3) A combination of the original text with a *dynamic presentation of the Easy-to-Read text* (ETR Dynamic). Specifically,

Table 1. Descriptives for all texts and language variants including word count and the Flesch-Reading-Ease score ranging from 0 (very difficult) to 100 (very easy).

	Conventional language		Plain Language		Easy-to-Read Language	
	Words	Flesch score	Words	Flesch score	Words	Flesch score
Text A	352	45	932	72	739	81
Text B	302	41	450	61	543	73
Text C	175	70	252	80		

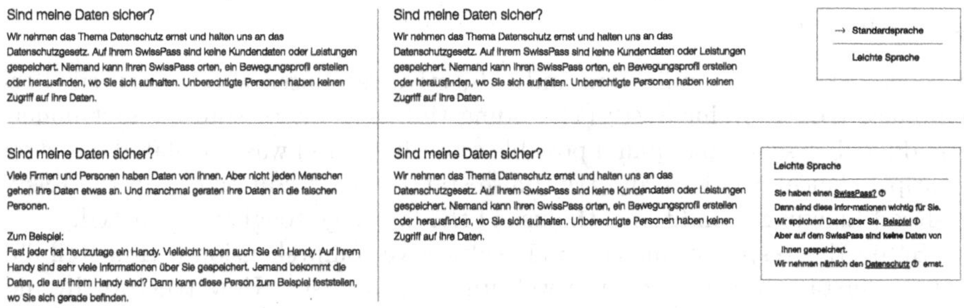

Sind meine Daten sicher?

Wir nehmen das Thema Datenschutz ernst und halten uns an das Datenschutzgesetz. Auf Ihrem SwissPass sind keine Kundendaten oder Leistungen gespeichert. Niemand kann Ihren SwissPass orten, ein Bewegungsprofil erstellen oder herausfinden, wo Sie sich aufhalten. Unberechtigte Personen haben keinen Zugriff auf Ihre Daten.

Sind meine Daten sicher?

Wir nehmen das Thema Datenschutz ernst und halten uns an das Datenschutzgesetz. Auf Ihrem SwissPass sind keine Kundendaten oder Leistungen gespeichert. Niemand kann Ihren SwissPass orten, ein Bewegungsprofil erstellen oder herausfinden, wo Sie sich aufhalten. Unberechtigte Personen haben keinen Zugriff auf Ihre Daten.

→ Standardsprache
Leichte Sprache

Sind meine Daten sicher?

Viele Firmen und Personen haben Daten von Ihnen. Aber nicht jeden Menschen gehen Ihre Daten etwas an. Und manchmal geraten Ihre Daten an die falschen Personen.

Zum Beispiel:
Fast jeder hat heutzutage ein Handy. Vielleicht haben auch Sie ein Handy. Auf Ihrem Handy sind sehr viele Informationen über Sie gespeichert. Jemand bekommt die Daten, die auf Ihrem Handy sind? Dann kann diese Person zum Beispiel feststellen, wo Sie sich gerade befinden.

Sind meine Daten sicher?

Wir nehmen das Thema Datenschutz ernst und halten uns an das Datenschutzgesetz. Auf Ihrem SwissPass sind keine Kundendaten oder Leistungen gespeichert. Niemand kann Ihren SwissPass orten, ein Bewegungsprofil erstellen oder herausfinden, wo Sie sich aufhalten. Unberechtigte Personen haben keinen Zugriff auf Ihre Daten.

Leichte Sprache

Sie haben einen SwissPass? ①
Dann sind diese Informationen wichtig für Sie.
Wir speichern Daten über Sie. Beispiel ①
Aber auf dem SwissPass sind keine Daten von Ihnen gespeichert.
Wir nehmen nämlich den Datenschutz ① ernst.

Fig. 1. Screenshot of all four conditions. Top Left: Conventional language. Bottom Left: Plain Language. Top right: ETR Dynamic. Bottom right: ETR Static.

participants had the option to actively adapt the text complexity for each paragraph. To do so, a language toggle was presented next to each paragraph, with the original text selected as default option. To provide participants the flexibility to read only certain parts of the text in Easy-to-Read Language, changes on a per paragraph basis were favoured over adapting the entire text. (4) A combination of the original text with a *static presentation of the Easy-to-Read text* (ETR Static), displayed in an additional box next to the original text. Screenshots of all four conditions are presented in Fig. 1.

For texts A and B, the visual design from the original website of the Swiss Federal Railways was recreated. All four conditions were identical in terms of website elements, such as pictures and the navigation bar. Text C was presented as an e-mail newsletter. It was assumed that e-mails have limitations with regards to the presentation of additional interactive elements. Therefore, only a variant in conventional and in Plain Language was created.

Finally, multiple choice and true/false statements were developed for measuring text understanding of texts A and B [10]. The study was then pre-tested with 10 participants (age $M = 37.14$, $SD = 15.40$, range 22–68; 3 women, 7 men), who were asked to provide detailed feedback regarding the presentation of the texts and the text understanding measurement.

2.3   Procedure

Participants were first asked to provide demographic information and complete a cloze test to estimate their literacy level [14]. All participants read all three texts. Each text was randomly presented in one of the four language conditions. Texts were presented in counterbalanced order. Participants could return to the questionnaire whenever they were ready to rate the text they had just read (see Sect. 2.4). Finally, participants had to indicate whether their responses were serious and had the opportunity to comment on the study.

2.4   Measures

Various performance indicators and subjective responses were measured. Performance indicators included: (1) reading time and (2) a score for text understanding. The score (maximum possible score 40 points) was calculated based on multiple choice questions and true/false statements. Additionally, in the Easy-to-Read Language conditions, the use of the language toggle was tracked.

Subjective responses included: (1) subjective comprehension ("How well did you understand the text on the website?"), (2) trust ("How trustworthy did you find the information on the website?") and (3) two items for text liking ("I like the style in which text on the website has been written", "The writing style of the text on the website is appealing.") that were adopted from [10]. All questions were answered on a 7-point Likert scale. (4) Perceived aesthetics was measured with the short version of the Visual Aesthetics of Websites Inventory (VisAWI, [15]). (5) The pragmatic (PQ) and hedonic quality (HQ) of the website was assessed with the short version of the AttrakDiff [16]. In the Easy-to-Read Language conditions, participants additionally rated the helpfulness of the Easy-to-Read text ("How helpful were the additional texts for your understanding?").

3   Results

3.1   Performance Indicators

Planned contrasts revealed that reading time differed significantly between conditions for text A. As shown in Table 2, participants spent significantly less time reading the conventional language condition compared to the experimental conditions ($F(1, 262) = 5.71$, $p < .05, \eta^2 = 0.017$). Texts B and C did not differ significantly in terms of reading duration. Text understanding did not differ between conditions and texts.

3.2   Subjective Responses

With regards to subjective comprehension, a Kruskal-Wallis test indicated significant differences between conditions for texts A ($\chi^2(3) = 19.27$, $p < 0.001, \eta^2 = 0.058$), B ($\chi^2(3) = 14.55$, $p < .01, \eta^2 = 0.043$) and C ($\chi^2(1) = 6.66$, $p < .01, \eta^2 = 0.020$). Conover-Imans's pairwise comparisons with a Holm correction for multiple comparisons revealed lower subjective comprehension for conventional language versus Plain Language for texts A ($p < .001, d = 0.79$), B ($p < .01, d = 0.52$), and C ($\chi^2 = 6.66$, $p < .01, \eta^2 = 0.020$). Further, Plain Language scored better on subjective comprehension compared to ETR Dynamic for texts A ($p < .01, d = 0.61$) and B ($p < .01, d = 0.64$).

In terms of pragmatic quality, planned contrasts showed significant differences between conditions for text A and text C. Conventional language scored lower compared to all experimental conditions for text A ($F(1, 262) = 5.83$,

$p < .05, \eta^2 = 0.011$) and text C ($t(270) = 2.02$, $p < .05, d = 0.25$). Further, higher PQ ratings were found for text A ($F(1, 262) = 4.68$, $p < .05, \eta^2 = 0.006$) for Plain Language compared to the Easy-to-Read conditions. Ratings for trust, text liking, perceived aesthetics and hedonic quality did not differ significantly between conditions and texts.

Table 2. Means and standard deviations for all dependent variables as a function of language conditions.

		Conventional	Plain	ETR Dynamic	ETR Static
Text A	Reading Time[a]	135.99 (85.77)	182.31 (122.88)	185.45 (179.28)	183.97 (164.42)
	Text Understanding	28.79 (5.40)	29.83 (5.13)	29.05 (5.57)	30.08 (6.82)
	Sub. Comprehension[b]	5.37 (1.37)	6.24 (0.76)	5.61 (1.27)	5.81 (1.11)
	Trust	5.75 (1.22)	5.92 (1.17)	5.94 (1.01)	5.89 (1.27)
	Text Liking	4.53 (1.40)	4.65 (1.75)	4.34 (1.58)	4.55 (1.55)
	VisAWI	4.94 (1.04)	4.98 (1.08)	4.66 (1.25)	4.95 (1.14)
	PQ[c]	4.80 (1.33)	5.48 (1.06)	4.91 (1.41)	5.25 (1.19)
	HQ	4.40 (1.15)	4.44 (1.17)	4.38 (1.26)	4.61 (1.11)
Text B	Reading Time	96.22 (46.91)	110.48 (65.63)	104.29 (51.57)	112.23 (56.34)
	Text Understanding	26.05 (4.38)	26.88 (4.26)	26.00 (4.75)	26.32 (4.20)
	Sub. Comprehension[b]	5.92 (1.28)	6.46 (0.78)	5.79 (1.27)	6.19 (0.79)
	Trust	5.76 (1.13)	5.75 (1.32)	5.70 (1.44)	5.96 (1.18)
	Text Liking	5.01 (1.26)	5.09 (1.38)	5.15 (1.21)	4.98 (1.56)
	VisAWI	4.94 (0.91)	4.94 (1.09)	5.15 (1.05)	5.03 (1.21)
	PQ	5.36 (1.06)	5.57 (1.09)	5.34 (1.14)	5.43 (1.04)
	HQ	4.69 (0.97)	4.74 (1.12)	4.85 (1.11)	4.78 (1.23)
Text C	Reading Time	63.62 (70.73)	63.85 (31.80)		
	Sub. Comprehension[b]	6.38 (0.82)	6.60 (0.75)		
	Trust	6.18 (0.89)	6.01 (1.19)		
	Text Liking	5.39 (1.24)	5.03 (1.65)		
	VisAWI	5.09 (1.10)	4.94 (1.21)		
	PQ[c]	5.59 (1.05)	5.83 (0.86)		
	HQ	4.99 (1.03)	4.88 (1.29)		

Note. [a] Reading Time for conventional language significantly shorter than in all other conditions.
[b] Subjective comprehension for Plain Language significantly higher than in all other conditions.
[c] Pragmatic quality for Plain Language significantly higher than in all other conditions.

3.3   Helpfulness of Dynamic and Static Easy-to-Read Texts

Most participants noticed the presence of the additional Easy-to-Read texts for text A (dynamic = 54.6%, static = 85.9%) and text B (dynamic = 61.9%, static = 81.2%), which was more pronounced in the static condition. Both Easy-to-Read variants were deemed moderately helpful for text A (dynamic $M = 4.66$, $SD = 1.70$; static $M = 5.00$, $SD = 1.82$) and text B (dynamic $M = 4.97$, $SD = 1.55$; static $M = 4.89$, $SD = 1.65$). In the dynamic condition, all participants had used the language toggle at least once for text A (toggle uses $M = 3.12$, $SD = 2.51$, range 1–14) and text B (toggle uses $M = 3.17$, $SD = 1.95$, range 1–7).

4   Discussion

Results show that the proposed approaches combining Easy-to-Read Language with conventional language did not result in the unintended side-effects on text liking reported in previous studies [5, 10]. As most participants noticed the additional texts, these approaches seem to be discrete enough to prevent a negative impact on User Experience. However, whereas no negative effects on text liking or perceived aesthetics were found, no significant benefits for text understanding in the Easy-to-Read conditions were observed either. The moderate helpfulness ratings of the additional texts suggest that the information provided might not have been appropriate in the present situation or that the writing style did not appeal to users. Both factors may have reduced the active use of the additional Easy-to-Read texts. Further, as suggested by the longer reading time, too much text was perhaps presented at once, thus reducing the utility of the provided information. Nevertheless, it is important to note that the review group did rate the Easy-to-Read text as accessible. Hence, it is arguably more important to further improve the presentation of additional Easy-to-Read text for the needs of users with cognitive and learning disabilities. As long as there are no drawbacks for other users, a maximum of inclusion can be attained this way. Hence, it is essential to involve potential end users in the development process [2]. As all participants in the study used the language toggle at least once, this concept seems to work for non-disabled participants. It remains to be seen whether this also holds true for users with cognitive and learning disabilities, or if the static presentation or other solutions are preferable options.

For the Plain Language variant, multiple advantages compared to the conventional language text were found, which also applied for non-disabled users. The positive effects on subjective comprehension and pragmatic quality suggest that the Plain Language text was deemed more understandable and more suitable for users' needs. While this effect was merely subjective and did not translate into higher text understanding scores for the present sample, this might contribute to a better overall User Experience due to a positive perception of self-efficacy [17]. Perhaps, a combination of Plain Language and Easy-to-Read texts could make full use of the potential of the approaches discussed in the present paper.

5   Conclusion

The present study demonstrated that Easy-to-Read Language may be implemented without unintended side-effects. While positive effects for people with cognitive and learning disabilities could be retained, no negative effects on other users emerged. Further work should investigate an optimal implementation of the proposed approaches and strive to extend the positive effects for as broad an audience as possible.

Acknowledgements. This study was registered with the Institutional Review Board of the University of Basel under the number D-012-17. Research was supported by the Swiss Federal Railways.

References

1. Miesenberger, K., Petz, A.: "Easy-to-read on the web": state of the art and needed research. In: Miesenberger, K., Fels, D., Archambault, D., Peňáz, P., Zagler, W. (eds.) ICCHP 2014. LNCS, vol. 8547, pp. 161–168. Springer, Cham (2014). https://doi.org/10.1007/978-3-319-08596-8_25
2. Cognitive and Learning Disabilities Accessibility Task Force: Cognitive Accessibility User Research (2017). https://w3c.github.io/coga/user-research/
3. Ruth-Janneck, D.: Experienced barriers in web applications and their comparison to the WCAG guidelines. In: Holzinger, A., Simonic, K.-M. (eds.) USAB 2011. LNCS, vol. 7058, pp. 283–300. Springer, Heidelberg (2011). https://doi.org/10.1007/978-3-642-25364-5_21
4. McCarthy, J.E., Swierenga, S.J.: What we know about dyslexia and Web accessibility: a research review. Univ. Access Inf. Soc. **9**(2), 147–152 (2009)
5. Karreman, J., van der Geest, T., Buursink, E.: Accessible website content guidelines for users with intellectual disabilities. J. Appl. Res. Intellect. Disabil. **20**(6), 510–518 (2007)
6. Boldyreff, C., Burd, E., Donkin, J., Marshall, S.: The case for the use of plain English to increase web accessibility. In: Proceedings 3rd International Workshop on Web Site Evolution, WSE 2001, pp. 42–48. IEEE (2001)
7. Skaggs, D.: My website reads at an eighth grade level: why plain language benefits your users (and you). J. Libr. Inf. Serv. Distance Learn. **11**(1–2), 96–105 (2016)
8. Fajardo, I., Ávila, V., Ferrer, A., Tavares, G., Gómez, M., Hernández, A.: Easy-to-read texts for students with intellectual disability: linguistic factors affecting comprehension. J. Appl. Res. Intellect. Disabil. **27**(3), 212–225 (2013)
9. Bredel, U., Maaß, C.: Leichte Sprache. Theoretische Grundlagen. Orientierung für die Praxis. Dudenverlag, Berlin (2016)
10. Schmutz, S., Sonderegger, A., Sauer, J.: Easy-to-read language in disability-friendly web sites: effects on nondisabled users. Appl. Ergon. (in press)
11. Schmutz, S., Sonderegger, A., Sauer, J.: Implementing recommendations from web accessibility guidelines: would they also provide benefits to nondisabled users. Hum. Factors: J. Hum. Factors Ergon. Soc. **58**(4), 611–629 (2016)
12. Ellcessor, E.: <ALT="Textbooks">: web accessibility myths as negotiated industrial lore. Crit. Stud. Media Commun. **31**(5), 448–463 (2014)
13. Flesch, R.: A new readability yardstick. J. Appl. Psychol. **32**(3), 221–233 (1948)
14. Grotjahn, R.: The C-Test: Current Trends. Peter Lang, Bern (2014)
15. Moshagen, M., Thielsch, M.: A short version of the visual aesthetics of websites inventory. Behav. Inf. Technol. **32**(12), 1305–1311 (2013)

16. Hassenzahl, M., Monk, A.: The inference of perceived usability from beauty. Hum.-Comput. Interac. **25**, 235–260 (2010)
17. Tuch, A.N., Trusell, R., Hornbæk, K.: Analyzing users' narratives to understand experience with interactive products. In: The SIGCHI Conference, pp. 2079–2088. ACM Press, New York (2013)

Modeling and Quantitative Measurement Method of the Tripartite Interpersonal Distance Dynamics for Children with ASD

Airi Tsuji[1(✉)], Takuya Enomoto[2,3], Soichiro Matsuda[1], Junichi Yamamoto[3], and Kenji Suzuki[1]

[1] University of Tsukuba, 1-1 Tennodai, Tsukuba, Ibaraki 305-8573, Japan
{tsuji,matsuda}@ai.iit.tskuba.ac.jp, kenji@ieee.org
[2] Meisei University, 2-1-1 Hodokubo, Hino-shi, Tokyo 191-0042, Japan
[3] Keio University, 2-15-45 Mita, Minato-ku, Tokyo 108-8345, Japan
takuya.enomoto@keio.jp, yamamotj@flet.keio.ac.jp

Abstract. In this paper, We focused on the measurement method of the tripartite interpersonal distance in the social development supporting for children with autism spectrum disorder (ASD), and tried quantitatively measurements of interpersonal distance dynamics between three-person using motion capture. We report on the modeling and measurement about the tripartite interpersonal distance dynamics.

Keywords: ASD · Interpersonal distance · Motion capture

1 Introduction

Children with Autism Spectrum Disorders (Children with ASD) are defined as those who have difficulty with social communication and interactions according to DSM-5 issued by the American Psychiatric Association [1]. The social communication skills of children with ASD are known to be improved through appropriate comprehensive developmental support [7]. Interpersonal distance or physical proximity are types of nonverbal communication that has been measured in the psychological field [2,5,6]. However, those methods was limited to measurement of interpersonal distance between a two person. The actual situation surrounds them, which they not only need to communicate with teacher or therapist but also friends. The tripartite interpersonal distance dynamics requires quantitative measurement method. Kendon's F-formation [4] clarified the knowledge about the position and direction about a group composed by multiple people. The ATR group also clarifies the walking speed is influenced by the number of members and density of space [9]. We aim to support the developmental support program for children with ASD, develop the quantitative measurement method of the tripartite interpersonal distance dynamics from previous research. In this paper,

© Springer International Publishing AG, part of Springer Nature 2018
K. Miesenberger and G. Kouroupetroglou (Eds.): ICCHP 2018, LNCS 10896, pp. 523–526, 2018.
https://doi.org/10.1007/978-3-319-94277-3_81

we constructed a model of tripartite interpersonal distance and sat up the measurement system on the support room to measure the dynamics of tripartite interpersonal distance during the therapy.

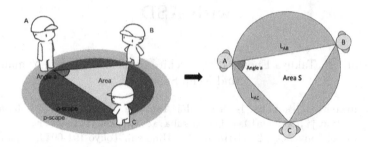

Fig. 1. Tripartite interpersonal distance model

2   Method

In order to quantify the intent and dynamics of individual members on the group constructed by three people, we modeled them. The triangle is inscribed in the o-space shown in Fig. 1. Vertices are the positions of the members A, B, and C. The inscribed triangular area in Eq. (1).

$$\Delta S_A = \frac{1}{2} L_{AB} L_{AC} sin\theta_a \tag{1}$$

L_{AB} represents the distance from A to B in the Fig. 1, and L_{AC} similarly represents the distance from A to C. $Sin\theta_a$ is from the Angle a in the Fig. 1.

In accurately measuring the positions of the three person, the trunk is small in preschool children with ASD targeted by this study. Furthermore, they often takes unexpected behaviors. Measurement using only the camera is capable, but not stable. In this study, we will use the motion capture system to acquire the head position and shoulder position. However, in children with ASD, wearing the markers suits are difficult for hypersensitivity. We decided to use the marker cap using the previous research [8] for position measurement of the head in this research. We also attached choulder marker for measurement of head direction.

3   Experiment

Preliminaly experiment was conducted to investigate whether changes in interpersonal distance between the three people could be measured. Two children with ASD and one therapist participated in the experiment. Measurements were taken for 10 min before and after of the 1 h therapy. During the measurement, the therapist was instructed not to be actively involved to children. Children with ASD were suggested to take free action using toys. Therapy room was fenced to prevent children from running. Hypotheses of this experiment is the interpersocal distance approaches by therapy. That is, the inscribed triangular area (Area) is reduced. It is also conceivable that the interior angle of two ASD children will expand. The details of the children with ASD participants are shown in Table 1. Both of them are male.

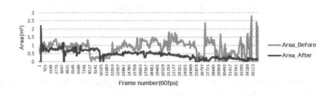

Fig. 2. Experimental result of area

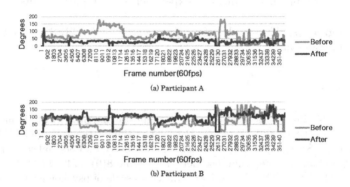

(a) Participant A

(b) Participant B

Fig. 3. Experimental result of angle

4 Result

Figure 2 shows the area of the triangle formed by experiment participants A, B, C before and after the therapy. Gray line indicates before, Black line means after. Figure 3 shows the individual angles of both children participants.

5 Discussion

Since the decrease in Area (Fig. 2) was seen by therapy, there is a possibility that area dynamics means that the dynamics of interpersonal distance between the

Table 1. Participant characteristics

Participant	CA	DA	Diagnosis	K-Degree [3]
A	10 y, 4 mo.	11 y, 2 mo.	ASD	39
B	10 y, 2 mo.	10 y, 4 mo.	ASD	21

three persons. However, in order to take account of the phenomenon of motion due to fatigue, it is also necessary to consider individual movements. About Angle, the therapist did not change much. Because there is a reversal among children participants, there is a possibility that the relationship has changed (Fig. 3(a), (b)). Further analysis is necessary. In addition, since it is conceivable that information on the face and body orientation is required in verifying the angle, the data of the markers attached to the shoulder are also under analyzing.

6   Conclusion

In this paper, we constructed a model of the tripartite interpersonal distance dynamics for children with ASD. The results that the inscribed triangular area (Area) of the after of therapy is reduced compared with the before of 1 h therapy. In the future, we planned additional experiments more participants.

Acknowledgments. This work was supported by JST CREST Grant Number JPMJCR14E2, Japan.

References

1. American Psychiatric Association, et al.: Diagnostic and Statistical Manual of Mental Disorders (DSM-5®). American Psychiatric Publications, Virginia (2013)
2. Gessaroli, E., Santelli, E., di Pellegrino, G., Frassinetti, F.: Personal space regulation in childhood autism spectrum disorders. PLoS One **8**(9), e74959 (2013)
3. Ikuzawa, M., Matsushita, Y., Nakase, A.: Kyoto scale of psychological development 2001. Kyoto International Social Welfare Exchange Centre, Kyoto (2002)
4. Kendon, A.: Spatial organization in social encounters: the f-formation system. In: Conducting Interaction: Patterns of Behavior in Focused Encounters (1990)
5. Pedersen, J., Livoir-Petersen, M., Schelde, J.: An ethological approach to autism: an analysis of visual behaviour and interpersonal contact in a child versus adult interaction. Acta Psychiatr. Scand. **80**(4), 346–355 (1989)
6. Rogers, A.L., Fine, H.J.: Personal distance in play therapy with an autistic and a symbiotic psychotic child. Psychother. Theory Res. Pract. **14**(1), 41 (1977)
7. Rogers, S.J., Estes, A., Lord, C., Vismara, L., Winter, J., Fitzpatrick, A., Guo, M., Dawson, G.: Effects of a brief early start denver model (ESDM)-based parent intervention on toddlers at risk for autism spectrum disorders: a randomized controlled trial. J. Am. Acad. Child Adoles. Psychiat. **51**(10), 1052–1065 (2012)
8. Tsuji, A., Matsuda, S., Suzuki, K.: Interpersonal distance and face-to-face behavior during therapeutic activities for children with ASD. In: Miesenberger, K., Bühler, C., Penaz, P. (eds.) ICCHP 2016. LNCS, vol. 9759, pp. 367–374. Springer, Cham (2016). https://doi.org/10.1007/978-3-319-41267-2_52
9. Zanlungo, F., Brščić, D., Kanda, T.: Spatial-size scaling of pedestrian groups under growing density conditions. Phys. Rev. E **91**(6), 062810 (2015)

Utilizing Multiple Representation System to Improve Reading Comprehension for Students with Learning Disabilities

Ting-Fang Wu[1](✉), Ming-Chung Chen[2], and Hui-Shan Lo[3]

[1] Graduate Institute of Rehabilitation Counseling,
National Taiwan Normal University,
162, Sec. 1 Hoping East Rd., Taipei, Taiwan
tfwu@ntnu.edu.tw
[2] Department of Special Education, National Chiayi University,
300, Syuefu Rd., Chiayi, Taiwan
mtchen@mail.ncyu.edu.tw
[3] Department of Special Education, National Taiwan Normal University,
162, Sec. 1 Hoping East Rd., Taipei, Taiwan
80209003E@ntnu.edu.tw

Abstract. Reading skill is an important ability for students, and students acquire knowledge through reading. However, it is difficult for students with learning disabilities (LD) to read effectively without any support. The purpose of this study was to develop a Multiple-representation system, which provided different kinds of cognitive supports for reading and to examine the effects of cognitive supports by comparing the reading performance of students with LD in the situations of with and without cognitive supports. The "Multiple-representation system" includes six cognitive support strategies. The result demonstrated that the participants performed better when reading with cognitive supports. The "Multiple-representation system" provides learners with LD an individualized cognitive supports adapted to their needs in digital learning environment.

Keywords: Learning disabilities · Cognitive support strategies

1 Introduction

Reading is an important ability for students, and students acquire knowledge through reading. However, it is difficult for students with learning disabilities (LD) to read effectively without any support. These difficulties prevent students with LD from acquiring knowledge through general curriculum [1]. LD is a group of disorders that affect comprehension, speech production, attention, reading, writing, reasoning, and/or calculate. Children with LD represent 3%–5% of school-aged students, and there are over 80% of students with LD demonstrate reading difficulties [2].

Students with reading difficulties need extra cognitive support strategies to help them read. The cognitive support strategies include 'bottom-up' and 'top-down' approach [3]. The bottom-up approach provides supports to the specific word in order to

K. Miesenberger and G. Kouroupetroglou (Eds.): ICCHP 2018, LNCS 10896, pp. 527–530, 2018.
https://doi.org/10.1007/978-3-319-94277-3_82

compensate readers' limitations in decoding and accessing lexical meaning. The top-down approach provides concept mapping, text summarization, and background knowledge. Previous studies have reported various effective strategies, such as word-recognition instruction methods [4], reciprocal teaching [5], and concept map drawing [6]. Therefore, the purpose of this study is to develop a 'Multiple-representation System', which provides different kinds of cognitive supports for reading. In addition, the effects of cognitive supports were examined through comparing the reading performance of LD students with and without cognitive supports.

2 Experiment

2.1 Participants

There were 22 participants with grade 5 and 6 participated in this study with their parental consents. The participants were recruited from the elementary schools in Taipei Metropolitan area. All participants attended regular class. Students with LD were diagnosed and identified by the local education authority based on the specific criteria below: (a) intellectual quotients were normal; (b) significant intra-individual differences were found between skills; (c) significant difficulties in academic performance, such as hearing comprehension, oral expression, word recognition, reading comprehension, writing, and calculation, were not improved after intervention provided in regular education. Meanwhile, no neurological deficits, intellectual delay, physical impairments, or cultural disadvantage were reported.

2.2 Instrument

A self-developed system 'Multiple-representation system' was used to provide individualized cognitive supports for special needs learners. The system of readers and editors adopt the same computer-based development tools programed with Microsoft Visual Studio and the file system is developed using Extensible Markup Language (XML). XML provides a highly variable storage format that allows system designers to easily modify article settings. This system can create a suitable reading environment. The following cognitive support strategies were available: ① Text-to-speech function ② a video explanation of the key concept ③ pictures of the key concepts ④ an annotate of a key word ⑤ marked key point ⑥ a concept map of the article.

   To exclude the effect of learning experience, the authors chose the 'Peculiar kind of animals of Taiwan' as the reading topics. The articles would introduce the appearance, habits of peculiar kind of animals in Taiwan via word, picture, or video. The number of characters in the article and the length of article were similar. Each article was accompanied by a reading comprehension test of ten or twelve single-choice questions focusing on reading comprehension. The accuracy rate ranged from 0 to 100%. The higher rate means the better reading performance.

2.3   Procedure

Each participant was asked to read six articles, three without cognitive supports and three with cognitive supports. There was no time limit for reading the articles in both reading conditions. After every reading session, each participant is required to complete a reading comprehension test. SPSS 20.0 for Windows was used to analyze the data. Paired-sample *t* test was conducted to analyze the accuracy rate on reading comprehension test.

3   Results

The accuracy rates of the reading comprehension tests are demonstrated in Table 1. The result showed the mean accuracy rate of reading comprehension test without cognitive support and with cognitive support were 47.5% and 59.4%. The result demonstrated that the participants performed significantly better when reading with cognitive supports ($p < 0.001$).

Table 1. Accuracy rate of the reading comprehension tests

ID	Strategies	Without cognitive support (%)				With cognitive support (%)			
		1	2	3	M	1	2	3	M
S1	Mark main points	0	10	17	9	17	25	25	22
S2	Video explanation	80	80	42	67.3	42	58	92	64
S3	Mark main points	30	40	0	23.3	50	25	50	41.7
S4	Text-to-speech	40	40	25	35	33	42	25	33.3
S5	annotate of keyword	50	60	42	50.7	33	17	50	55.3
S6	Video explanation	50	50	58	52.7	75	42	33	50
S7	Video explanation	40	30	75	48.3	100	83	75	86
S8	Video explanation	90	80	67	79	50	75	58	61
S9	Text-to-speech	50	40	17	35.7	67	58	17	47.3
S10	Video explanation	60	30	58	49.3	83	50	75	69.3
S11	Concept map	60	30	67	52.3	58	83	50	63.7
S12	Text-to-speech	80	70	92	80.7	67	100	83	83.3
S13	Video explanation	30	30	8	22.7	58	42	58	58
S14	Video explanation	70	40	92	67.3	83	92	75	83
S15	Video explanation	70	40	67	59	83	33	58	78
S16	Video explanation	60	0	75	58.3	83	83	83	80
S17	Video explanation	10	40	17	22.3	33	33	50	44.3
S18	Video explanation	40	20	42	34	33	50	50	49.7
S19	Video explanation	40	30	50	40	50	75	58	61
S20	Video explanation	70	40	25	45	83	92	58	77.7
S21	Video explanation	40	50	67	52.3	75	83	83	80.3
S22	Text-to-speech	50	50	83	61	75	83	83	80
Mean					47.5				59.4

4 Discussion and Conclusions

According to the result, the students with LD can read effectively through appropriate cognitive support strategies. Among those cognitive support strategies, 63.6% (14/22) students chose the strategies of video explanation. Among those students, one of them chose video explanation indicated that using video explanation not only improved reading comprehension, but also increase attention span on reading. The other 4 students who chose the text-to-speech indicated that providing auditory feedback can help them keep on the track of reading. Only one student chose the concept mapping strategies and indicated that concept mapping make it easier to understand the structure of the article, and it's helpful for predicting the answers of the reading tests.

Based on the above results, we found that each student with LD prefer their own strategies on supporting reading. This paper shows that the 'Multiple-representation System' provides the students with LD an individualized cognitive supports adapted to their needs in digital the learning environment. The system provides a flexible system to suit the individual need of LD. In future study, we might explore the possibility in integrating strategies of remedy and compensation into a system to improve reading skills of students with LD.

References

1. Lerner, J.: Learning and Related Disorders: Characteristics and Teaching Strategies, 10th ed. Houghton Mifflin Company, Boston (2006)
2. Hallahan, D.P., Lloyd, J.W., Kauffman, J.M., Weiss, M.P., Martinez, E.A.: Learning Disabilities: Foundations, Characteristics, and Effective Teaching. Allan & Bacon, Boston (2004)
3. Rose, D.H., Meyer, A.: Teaching Every Student in the Digital Age: Universal Design for Learning. Association for Supervision and Curriculum Developmental, Alexandria (2002)
4. Hung, L.Y., Huang, K.Y.: Two different approaches to radical-based remedial Chinese reading for low-achieving beginning readers in primary school. Bull. Spec. Educ. **31**, 43–71 (2006)
5. Ledere, J.M.: Reciprocal teaching of social studies in inclusive elementary classroom. J. Learn. Disabil. **33**(1), 91–106 (2000)
6. Chang, K.E., Sung, Y.T., Chen, I.D.: The effect of concept mapping to enhance text comprehension and summarization. J. Exp. Educ. **71**(1), 5–23 (2002)

Augmented and Alternative Communication (AAC), Supported Speech

DIGA OLÁ: An Augmentative and Alternative Communication (AAC) Mobile Application for People with Language and Speech Impairments

Tânia Rocha$^{(\boxtimes)}$, Paulo Silva, Maria Barreira, and João Barroso

INESC TEC and University of Trás-os-Montes and Alto Douro, Vila Real,
Portugal
{troch,jbarroso}@utad.pt, paulomms_96@hotmail.com,
alexandra-goncalvesb@hotmail.com

Abstract. In this paper an augmentative and alternative communication mobile application for people with language and speech impairments, called *Diga Olá*, is presented. With this mobile application, we aimed to assist people with speech and language impairment in their communication process, by presenting an alternative mobile solution in Portuguese language. The main results achieved on a preliminary user assessment were: first-rate performance, higher satisfaction and total autonomy in their interaction with the solution presented.

Keywords: Augmentative and alternative communication (AAC)
Mobile application · Android · Accessibility assessment · User tests
Speech impairment

1 Introduction

Communication is the process of sending and receiving information among people, facilitating the spread of knowledge and information. Moreover, is the foundation of all human relationship, as it helps people to express their ideas and feelings, and, at the same time, helps to understand emotion and thoughts of others. Communication is not only fundamental in personal, but in business and educational relationships [1].

However, there are people who have difficulties in the communication process because of a speech or language impairment, often incurred at birth, childhood, later due to an illness or accident, or even due to aging. A person with speech and language disorders is characterized as an individual with difficulty in interaction and communication with other individuals, in the ability to understand and be understood, and even to express their feelings. It mainly affects the ability to pronounce words clearly and understand words spoken or written. Many people with speech disorders have no problem understanding or reasoning. However, it may also involve voice disturbances, including tone, volume, or quality [2]. These groups of individuals need accessible tools to aid their communication needs.

With this in mind, many technologies are developed with the objective of facilitating tasks and problem solving [3], covering several areas, including communication

K. Miesenberger and G. Kouroupetroglou (Eds.): ICCHP 2018, LNCS 10896, pp. 533–538, 2018.
https://doi.org/10.1007/978-3-319-94277-3_83

and health. Specifically, in the context of speech therapy intervention, therapists use technologies are able to motivate their patients for training, but also optimizing their own method of work. In this sense, the concept of assistive technologies (AT) gains importance, which translates into a set of resources that make the autonomy of people with disabilities possible and the accomplishment of daily tasks, with an active participation in society [4, 5].

In this paper, it is described the development and evaluation of an AAC mobile application for people with language and speech impairments to use to facilitate their communication process.

2 Related Studies

The specific area that aimed at expanding communication skills using AT is entitled Augmentative and Alternative Communication (AAC). AAC includes all forms of communication (other than oral speech) that are used to express thoughts, needs, wants, and ideas and is used by those with a wide range of speech and language impairments, including congenital impairments such as cerebral palsy, intellectual impairment and autism, and acquired conditions such as amyotrophic lateral sclerosis and Parkinson's disease. AAC can be a permanent addition to a person's communication or a temporary aid [6, 7].

In this context, there are many examples of digital AAC solutions, such as: Talk Board, Phaphoons, Avaz Australia, Verbally, Bia Project and Vox4All. Specifically, the TalkBoard application, created by Mark Ashley, aimed to assist communication as a visual alert board. The application can easily be customized with the user's images and symbols and it can be used by teachers, speech therapists and parents of people with autism, language and communication impairments, physical disability, such as cerebral paralysis. TalkBoard is very similar to a traditional vocalizer, while being easy to use and providing a wide range of customization options for each type of user. This application is only available for the iPad and iPhone devices, which narrows down the group of possible users [8].

Plaphoons application is a communication tool created by Fressa Project. The application allows to create communication screens and structure forms of symbols, letters and words to create messages. These messages can be viewed directly on the computer screen, to be printed or heard by a synthesized or digitized voice. It can work directly as computer-mind communication screen, and activated using the mouse. There is also the option of using it with voice communicator, through voice synthesis features and/or recorded voices [9].

The Avaz Australia application was designed by the company Avaz to facilitate communication in children with special needs, such as Down syndrome, Angelmans syndrome, cerebral palsy and other speech disabilities. Avaz lets users communicate through imagens, each image has a certain sound and a corresponding word. Thus, a user can create messages and listen to them through a set of images. Users can customize each image and the appropriate sound [10].

The Verbally application was developed by the company with the same name. It is an easy to use application for the iPad. This application allows users to communicate with little physical effort. To do this simply select the word you want, or write it manually, and the word that was wrote is played to the user [11].

The BIA Project is an AAC Portuguese application, targeted to children with cerebral palsy. To be used, users must installed an independent paid software, Adobe Air and register on the official website. The application is available for Android, IOS, Windows and Linux. The application is available in 5 languages: Portuguese, Chinese, German, English, French and Spanish. It has about 36 categories which are associated with colors and pictograms. The interaction with this application is made through the selection of pictograms but the user cannot select a different pictogram without the vocalization of the previous one selected. The application allows the creation of new categories, add new images as well as small sound files [12].

Vox4all is an AAC application for mobile devices, such as smartphones and tablets. This application has several features, user can always customize them, highlighting the simple and intuitive help. It is available in 4 languages: Portuguese, Brazilian Portuguese, English and Spanish [13].

Overall, all these digital solutions features are similar: by allowing users to communicate by pointing and/or clicking in the pictogram related to the word he/she want to use, one at a time, or by writing the word; and, permit customization of images (or pictograms, depending of the method used) and sounds. All applications require installation. Regarding, language used, Phaphoons and Vox4all uses a Portuguese/ Brazilian vocalization (but is not accurate for Portuguese users). Bia Project could overcome the barrier language as it uses Portuguese language vocalization, however to be used, users must install internal paid software, adding other issues regarding the acquisition of the solution.

3 Presenting *DIGA OLÁ* Application

In this context, an augmentative and alternative communication (AAC) solution for people with language and speech impairments, called Diga lá, is presented. Diga Olá is a mobile free application that offers an interactive interface, by presenting several user options that helps in the communication needs of the daily routine and can be used rather than the broadly used printed communication boards (black and white or color pictograms charts) (Fig. 1).

Fig. 1. Diga Olá's main screen.

Diga Olá application differs from similar applications because lets users communicate not only by selecting pictogram (one at a time), but also use complete sentences, that can be created by selecting and joining different pictogram and/or categories (Fig. 2) or by writing text, save them in a database and use later on with only one click. The major asset is the most used phrases are saved and the user do not need to enter the same sentence again. Every sentence enter by the user is confirmed and saved. Another feature presented, is the possibility of adding written text and the app translate to audio through a vocalizer (uses synthesized or digitized voice). Specifically, it uses Portuguese language vocalization and not Portuguese/Brazilian pronunciation as others applications. All these features can be customized by the user.

Fig. 2. Diga Olá's main AAC categories screen

In consequence, the application presented intends to improve the AAC solutions, by providing an simple and accessible interface, with four primary features: Information, users can find a description of the application and directly access our social network page, having access to the chat, where we can respond any questions related with the interaction; Write Option, allows users to type text and consequently hear it; Let's Talk Option, has buttons of the various communication categories corresponding to the daily routines; and, finally, Settings Options, users must register in the first interaction to be able to customize all interfaces. It is an application for Android, needs installation, does not need Internet connection and if the user does not want to customize the app it does not need to register.

4 Diga Olá's Prototype Validation

After we finish the implementation, we wanted to observe and assess how users interacted with the application, in order to analyze the level of performance and autonomy that these users can achieve with the proposed application. In order to do so, we performed a preliminary user test evaluation as specified below.

4.1 Participants

The assessment was carried out by nine participants with different ages: six children (three girl and three boy), age range 6 to 15; and three adults (one men and two women), age range 24 to 26 years. All participants had speech and language impairments associated to intellectual disability (for example, Down syndrome). According to DSM–V, the intellectual disability presented can be classified according to severity levels, between mild to moderate. These participants were selected by a speech therapist, a special education teacher and a psychologist, according to the average rate of literacy and primary education: three participants were in the 9th grade; two, in the 7th grade; and, four, in the 4th grade. Furthermore, within the group: seven participants can read and write and two expressed difficulties in this respect. All participants were volunteers and had permission of their parents or tutors to participate in the usability assessment.

Furthermore, three speech therapists were also invited to participate and give their input to improve the application.

4.2   Experimental Design

All participants (with speech impairments and speech therapists) used the application in two assessment moments: one with specific tasks to assess usability, and other to run freely with the application (to assess user experience).

4.3   Procedure and Apparatus

Participants were seated comfortably with a smartphone, with the application installed, in a controlled environment. After explained the aim of the assessment tasks, they started to interact with the application. The evaluator/observer did not help in the interaction. A smartphone Samsung Galaxy S6 Edge was used, Internet connection is not needed.

4.4   Results and Discussion

To measure usability of the application, it was performed a user tests assessment, in which it was registered effectiveness, efficiency and satisfaction variables. The results of this evaluation (user tests) were analyzed by age range. Overall, showed that DIGA LÁ application allowed an autonomous and easy communication. All participants completed the tasks successfully and without effort. They commented that the interaction was simple, easy and satisfactory. No one gave up and liked to use the application without specific tasks (second moment of assessment). They asked if they could use the application after finishing the tests, with each other's. The speech therapists also gave positive feedback regarding interaction. Also, they considered as a major asset the application ability of save and reuse sentences, allowing users to quickly communicate, without having to enter and assemble the phrase gradually, which they considered as a demanding process. They mentioned: "In a normal app the user has to choose, for example, the word/ pictogram "I", then "Want", "To Eat" and finally "Bread", and in every occasion they need this sentence has to choose/write all over again, pictogram by pictogram. It is very interesting that your app allows to have I WANT TO EAT, in the library of sentence available and the user only have to choose the food, without having to register or customize". Furthermore, they ask if it was possible to make the application available for them to use with other participants in other institution.

5 Conclusions and Future Work

The main results achieved on a preliminary user assessment showed that users had first-rate performance (concluded all tasks defined with success, no one dropout, did not showed any difficulties in interaction), higher satisfaction and total autonomy in their interaction with the solution presented.

As future work, we intend to expand the number of people to reproduce the results in order to allow a more autonomous communication for this specific target group. And, replicate the user tests to other groups with speech and language impairments, such as: diverse forms of aphasia or dysarthria, people who suffer strokes and/or the elderly. Also, to study other kind of interaction, such as: eye tracking activation, for example to allow the use by people with motor impairments and include alternative languages other than Portuguese.

Acknowledgments. This work was supported by Project "NIE – Natural Interfaces for the Elderly/ NORTE-01-0145-FEDER-024048" financed by the Foundation for the Science and Technology (FCT) and through the European Regional Development Fund (ERDF).

References

1. Hauser, M.D.: The Evolution of Communication. Bradford BOOK/The MIT Press, Cambridge/London (2000). 4th print. https://books.google.pt/books?id=QbunyscCJBoC&printsec=frontcover&dq=The+evolution+of+communication&hl=pt-PT&sa=X&ved=0ahU KEwjSzsPTh4XaAhWDuhQKHcvkC68Q6AEIJzAA#v=onepage&q=The%20evolution%20of%20communication&f=false
2. Bergin, S.: Communication disorders: breaking through the barriers. Ensign, pp. 46–50, February 1991
3. Importance of Technology, How did technology changed our life – and what is the future? http://eimportanceoftechnology.com/
4. British Educational Communications and Technology Agency - BECTA.: The impact of ICT in Schools: Landscape Review, Coventry (2007). http://dera.ioe.ac.uk/1627/
5. Ribeiro, J., Almeida, A.M., Moreira, A.: A utilização das TIC na Educação de Alunos com Necessidades Educativas Especiais: resultados da aplicação piloto do inquérito nacional a Coordenadores TIC/PTE. Indag. Didact. 2(1), 94–124 (2010)
6. America Speech-Language-Hearing Association. http://www.asha.org/public/speech/disorders/AAC/
7. Communication Matters/ISAAC (UK). Foccus on…What is AAC? Introduction to Augmentative and Alternative Communication 3rd edition (2015). https://www.communicationmatters.org.uk/sites/default/files/downloads/focuson/What%20is%20AAC.pdf
8. Talk board. http://cintiappires.blogspot.com.br/2012/09/comunicacao-alternativa-utilizando.html
9. PlaPhoons, Tecno Accessible. www.tecnoaccesible.net/content/plaphoons
10. Avaz Australia, Avaz. http://www.avazapp.com/
11. Verbally. https://itunes.apple.com/pt/app/verbally/id418671377?mt=8
12. Bia Project. http://cm-castrodaire.pt/bia/index.php/software
13. Vox4all. http://arca.imagina.pt/folhetos/vox4all-br.pdf

Progress to a VOCA with Prosodic Synthesised Speech

Jan-Oliver Wülfing$^{(\boxtimes)}$ and Elisabeth André

Human Centered Multimedia, University of Augsburg,
Universitätsstrasse 6a, 86159 Augsburg, Germany
{wuelfing,andre}@hcm-lab.de
http://www.hcm-lab.de

Abstract. Providing people, who cannot or almost not articulate themselves vocally, with a Voice Output Communication Aid (VOCA) with prosodic features would allow them to express their daily needs and intentions emotionally. We outline first steps towards such a prosodic VOCA, the EmotionTalker.

Keywords: AAC · Synthetic speech · Prosody · Emotion

1 Introduction

If individuals with Complex Communication Needs (CCN) are not able to express themselves vocally, they mostly rely on methods of Augmentative and Alternative Communication (AAC). Methods to communicate that are given to them at hand typically include high-tech devices, such as Voice Output Communication Aids (VOCA). Customary VOCAs sound natural and comprehensible, but what they do not provide to individuals with CCN is the option to change the emotional content of speech dynamically (Higginbotham 2010), (Hoffmann and Wülfing 2010).

Our overall objective is to provide individuals with CCN with a means to convey their ideas and needs in an expressive manner during their daily routine (e.g. at work, at school, or in leisure). Such a prosodic VOCA is supposed to elicit a higher degree of attention from the interlocutors. Based on these considerations, we implemented a VOCA with prosodic features, the EmotionTalker.

2 Motivation

Attitudes towards individuals with CCN using a conventional VOCA are discussed by Mullennix and Stern (2010). Their work suggests that non-disabled people have negative attitudes towards individuals with CCN (e.g. less liked and less accepted). Since they have to invest more effort when listening, they tend to be more reserved towards individuals with CCN. This puts the individual with CCN in a more excluded situation than her or his non-disabled peer.

© Springer International Publishing AG, part of Springer Nature 2018
K. Miesenberger and G. Kouroupetroglou (Eds.): ICCHP 2018, LNCS 10896, pp. 539–546, 2018.
https://doi.org/10.1007/978-3-319-94277-3_84

Breen (2014) addresses the importance of an expressive voice in Text-to-Speech (TTS) systems. He has shown that, at least, for conversational agents, the interlocutor would prefer a more dynamic style of the TTS when listening. Also Portnuff (2006) - a VOCA user - puts forward that a prosodic VOCA, which is, in its basics, an expressive TTS, would have benefits for both the individual with CCN and their interlocutors.

Although the topic of emotional utterances is hardly addressed in research on AAC (Pullin and Hennig 2015), there are a couple of innovative applications to be mentioned:

ExpressivePower[TM1] co-developed by AssistiveWare B.V. and Acapela Group Babel Technologies SA enables individuals with CCN to create buttons with special emotive expressions and sounds, such as whining or questioning tones. This application has been developed with a particular focus on children using Prolongo2Go, a symbol-based communication application.

The VOCA, Tango[2], developed by BlinkTwice Inc. - it is no longer being manufactured - offered the option to convey tones as well, i.e. it allowed individuals with CCN, for example, to select a whispering or shouting voice. Shouting is a very rare VOCA feature despite the fact that vocally speaking individuals often have to speak in a louder manner (for example, in a cafeteria or pub). Tango gave individuals with CCN also the possibility at hand to save the pronunciation for each word in a dictionary.

3   User Sensitive Inclusive Design

Our research target is the design of a prosodic Voice Output Communication Aid for individuals who use high-tech devices in order to communicate as they want to modulate their utterances. Since our target group is very diverse in respect to the characteristics of their impairments, a traditional user-centered design approach does not apply. Inspired by an approach developed Newell (Newell et al. 2011) called the User Sensitive Inclusive Design, we tried to develop a more empathic view - being more sensitive - while working with the target group, rather than treat them as "subjects" in experiments. Due to the limited mobility of individuals with CCN, arranging meetings with them was a complex task often requiring a significant amount of travel by the experimenter. Furthermore, during the interviews, we had to take into account the great variety of impairments and communication aids. A particular challenge was to find a way to present information about the envisioned prosodic Voice Output Communication Aid most effectively to the participants.

As a first step towards an prosodic VOCA, we investigated how individuals with CNN communicated emotions in their daily life and whether a system that produces prosodic speech could be of benefit to them. To shed light on this question, we recruited five participants (see Table 1) that also helped us testing a first version of the prosodic VOCA.

---

[1] www.assistiveware.com/innovation/expressivepower (accessed 11/09/17).

[2] www.spectronics.com.au/product/tango-2 (accessed 11/09/17).

Table 1. Overview of the participants

	Sex	Age	Disability	Communication method
P1	f	8	CP	Tobii C15
P2	f	10	CP	Accent1000
P3	m	15	CP	Tobii I12
P4	f	45	CP	EcoTalker
P5	f	56	ASD	Facilitated communication

While the speaking ability of the five participants is limited to single sounds, they do not have disorders in language understanding. Four of our participants (P1–P4) are suffering from cerebral palsy (CP) and use VOCAs to communicate, especially when talking to foreigners. Three participants (P1–P3) use symbol- and letter-based software on their devices, except P4 who has a reading and writing disorder and relies on symbol-based software only. In addition, she employs a grid to operate her VOCA, a keyboard finger guide for better fine-motor coordination. P1 and P3 control their VOCA via eye tracking technology. The fifth participant (P5) has an autistic spectrum disorder (ASD), and instead of using a VOCA, she uses methods of Facilitated Communication (Table 1). This is a type of communication where a disabled person is supported by a facilitator who leads her or his hand across a communication board, for example. The muscles of people with CCN are often weak and therefore they are only capable of initiating the input and require help to complete it.

Due to the limited mobility of our users, the conduction of a focus group study where several people gather ideas at the same place was no option. Instead, we offered our participants a meeting in an environment that was most conveniant to them. The interview with P2 and P4 was conducted at home. During the conversation with P2, her sister and her mother were present as well. P1 and her mother were met in a special education center. The interview with P3 and his speech and language therapist was conducted in conjunction with a logopedics session. P5 was interviewed at the university. She was accompanied by her personal assistant.

The participants were asked whether there are situations in which they would like to be able to communicate emotions. They mentioned situations, such as watching a movie (to express fear) or having a meal or a drink. Furthermore, they would find it useful to express emotions, such as sadness or anger, when somebody does not understand them. Also they would like to be able to communicate emotions when talking about school (dislike and like of peers). Based on the input provided by the participants, we generated a list of prestored utterances for the VOCA to be developed that could be easily accessed by the participants.

During our communication with the participants, we found out that the participants relied on conventional VOCAs to communicate the content of speech and employed additional modalities, such facial expressions, gestures, and sound, to convey the emotions associated with the content of speech. Despite other means of communicating emotions, our participants found it desirable to be able to express emotions via speech as well and welcomed our idea to develop a VOCA with prosodic speech.

4   The R&D Work

Our VOCA named EmotionTalker was designed as a standalone application for PC and tablet. Its front-end (see Fig. 1) consists of an ordinary keyboard in QWERTZ- or ABC-layout. In order to annotate utterances with the emotion to be conveyed, we placed three emoticons in the upper right corner. These emoticons enable individuals with CCN to annotate the typed utterance as happy, sad, or angry before synthesising. The grey button is clicked to open up this selection and double clicked to switch back to the neutral style. The users can see their utterances in the description field left to the emoticons.

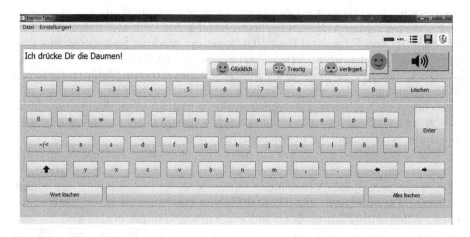

Fig. 1. The front-end of the EmotionTalker showing 'I cross the fingers for you'

The VOCA also allows individuals with CCN to switch between different menus and layouts. The upper five buttons in the right corner offer users to switch from QWERTZ- to ABC-layout. The 'category'-menu gives users fast access to prestored phrases in categories, such as school, work, or leisure. To adapt the VOCA to their needs, users have the possibility to save phrases themselves. In addition, we decided to implement a dice since individuals with CCN mostly have movement disorders and cannot roll a dice (for example, when playing ludo).

To synthesise prosodic speech, we used Cereproc's Ltd. CereVoice synthesiser (Aylett and Pidcock 2007). Text can be annotated with SSML[3]. A sample

---

[3] www.w3.org/TR/speech-synthesis11 (accessed 11/28/2017).

sentence, such as 'I cross the fingers for you', looks in a happy tone in SSML as follows:

```
<?xml version='1.0'?>
<parent>
<prosody pitch="high" rate="fast" volume="+60">
"I cross the fingers for you"
</prosody>
</parent>
```

The attributes 'pitch', 'rate' etc. of the tag 'prosody' enable us to modulate different characteristics of the tone. We produced several variants of utterances by modifying these attributes and asked our participants to assess how well a variant portrayed a happy, sad and angry tone. The best variants were implemented.

5   Our Study

A first version of EmotionTaker has been tested with the participants mentioned above. Depending on their skills, participants had the chance to control EmotionTalker themselves or with the help of the experimenter.

Fig. 2. A participant playing ludo when she uses the EmotionTalker

The graphical user interface of EmotionTalker was easy to use. Text input via the touch keyboard was intuitive and did not require further explanation. P5 appreciated the distance between the single keys. Due to the limited motor skills of individuals with CCN, keys in the neighborhood of the target are often hit by mistake. One recommendation by her was to display a list of word proposals after pressing a key to speed up communication. The option to store own predefined sentences was well received by our participants. P3 suggested to maintain a list of sentences along with the emotional state to be expressed.

The participants had not problems to map the symbols onto the intended emotional state. They were not in favour of using a higher number of symbols since the selection in daily life should not take too much time.

We also conducted perception tests with the speech output produced by EmotionTalker. In order to make sure that vocal emotions were conveyed in a natural manner, we abstained from the communication of extreme emotions. It turned out, however, that participants were not always able to recognise the subtle emotional states EmotionTalker was supposed to convey. A particular challenge was to manipulate the EmotionTalker voice in such a way that it conveyed the intended emotion with great expressivity without resulting into a voice that appeared to belong to a different person.

Overall, our participants agreed that a prosodic VOCA like EmotionTalker would be of great benefit to them. For example, P2 said: *"I enjoy to tell my mom that I love her - in a happy sound."* And P3 told us: *"I love it to talk with friends about football in an excited and louder manner,"* - he was referring to the angry voice that was presented to him.

With P2, we also tested EmotionTalker during two daily life situations: having a meal and playing ludo (Fig. 2). Even though she had found EmotionTalker easy to use, she rarely used it in these two situations. For example, P2, who was able to eat by herself, did not use EmotionTalker during a meal with her family because using the VOCA while eating was hard. During the game of ludo, she liked to use the dice integrated into EmotionTalker. However, emotions were communicated mostly through facial expressions, gestures and sound since typing took too long. These observations show that the design of a VOCA that may be used during daily activities still remains a challenge.

6   Exploring the Impact

Our study indicates that a prosodic featured VOCA bears great potential to improve the communicative competence of individuals with CCN. Such a VOCA would help satisfy, at least, some pragmatic conversational goals of such users (Todman and Alm 2003). For example, Todman and Alm emphasise the need to incorporate pragmatic features in VOCAs to enable smoother interactions of individuals with CNN. A VOCA like EmotionTalker would provide individuals with CCN with capabilities to deal with unexpected situations, such as confusion or irritation, in a more efficient manner by choosing appropriate emotional backchannels.

Another factor, which is mentioned by Wickenden (2011), is that individuals with CCN often get no attention when they want to say something. EmotionTalker would also mitigate this handicap since an emotional voice helps capture a listener's attention.

7   Conclusion

In this paper, we presented first results for EmotionTalker, a VOCA that provides people with CCN with an additional channel to communicate their emotions. Due to their limited mobility, the recruitment of participants for our study was a challenge. We therefore met our participants at locations that were most conveniant to them including their private homes. This way we also got a realistic impression of the participants' physical condition and the environment in which EmotionTalker could be employed. Overall, the participants were very positive towards EmotionTalker. They thought that the ability to communicate emotions outweighs the additional effort required to select the appropriate icons. Nevertheless, more work is required to enable an easy selection of the emotional states to be conveyed in naturalistic environments.

In the future, we will investigate how to speed up the input of emotional states in order to enable users to produce prosodic speech in daily environments. One idea would be exploit other modalities, such as facial expressions, to determine the user's emotional state based on our previous work on automated emotion recognition (Wagner et al. 2015) and enhance the user's emotional expression by prosodic speech. Furthermore, it would be desirable to offer speech output to the participants that conveys not only emotions in a convincing manner, but also matches their personality.

Acknowledgement. We would like to thank Franziska Kerstiens for her help with the preparation and the conduction of the studies. The work presented here is partially supported by PROMI - Promotion inklusive and the employment centre.

References

Aylett, M.P., Pidcock, C.J.: The CereVoice characterful speech synthesiser SDK. In: Pelachaud, C., Martin, J.-C., André, E., Chollet, G., Karpouzis, K., Pelé, D. (eds.) IVA 2007. LNCS (LNAI), vol. 4722, pp. 413–414. Springer, Heidelberg (2007). https://doi.org/10.1007/978-3-540-74997-4_65

Breen, A.: Creating expressive TTS voices for conversation agent applications. In: Ronzhin, A., Potapova, R., Delic, V. (eds.) SPECOM 2014. LNCS (LNAI), vol. 8773, pp. 1–14. Springer, Cham (2014). https://doi.org/10.1007/978-3-319-11581-8_1

Higginbotham, J.: Humanizing vox artificialis: the role of speech synthesis in augmentative and alternative communication. In: Mullennix, J.W., Stern, S.E. (eds.) Computer Synthesized SpeechTechnologies - Tools for Aiding Impairment, pp. 50–70. IGI Global, Hershey (2010)

Hoffmann, L., Wülfing, J.-O.: Usability of electronic communication aids in the light of daily use. In: Proceedings of the 14th Biennial Conference of the International Society for Augmentative and Alternative Communication, Spain, Barcelona, p. 259 (2010)

Mullennix, J.W., Stern, S.E.: Attitudes toward Computer synthesized speech. In: Mullennix, J.W., Stern, S.E. (eds.) Computer Synthesized Speech Technologies - Tools for Aiding Impairment, pp. 205–218. IGI Global, Hershey (2010)

Newell, A.F., Gregor, P., Morgan, M., et al.: User-sensitive inclusive design. Univ. Access Inf. Soc. **10**, 235–243 (2011). https://doi.org/10.1007/s10209-010-0203-y

Portnuff, C.: AAC: a user's perspective, Webcast available as part of the AAC-RERC Webcast Series (2006). http://aac-rerc.psu.edu/index.php/webcasts/show/id/3. Accessed 10 Jan 2018

Pullin, G., Hennig, S.: 17 ways to say yes: toward nuanced tone of voice in AAC and speech technology. Augment. Altern. Commun. **31**(2), 170–180 (2015)

Todman, J., Alm, N.: Modelling conversational pragmatics in communications aids. J. Pragmat. **35**, 523–538 (2003)

Wagner, J., Lingenfelser, F., André, E.: Building a robust system for multimodal emotion recognition. In Konar, A., Aruna Chakraborty, A.: Emotion Recognition: A Pattern Analysis Approach, pp. 379–410. Wiley (2015)

Wickenden, M.: Whose voice is that?: Issues of identity, voice and representation arising in an ethnographic study of the lives of disabled teenagers who use Augmentative and Alternative Communication (AAC). Disabil. Stud. Q. **31**, 4 (2011)

The Role of Accessibility for Acceptance and Usage of an Internet-Based Speech Intervention

Vanessa N. Heitplatz[(⊠)] and Ute Ritterfeld

Department of Language and Communication, TU Dortmund University,
Dortmund, Germany
{vanessa.heitplatz,ute.ritterfeld}@tu-dortmund.de

Abstract. Within a collaborative effort of technicians, speech therapists and psychologists "ISi-Speech" has been developed as an Internet-based speech-training tool. This tool aims at improving the speech of people with degenerative neurological impairments such as acquired dysarthria in, for example, Parkinson's Disease. ISi-Speech is characterized by a theory based design of training elements which take specific challenges in speech therapy as well as motivational elements into account. To ensure acceptance and long-time usage of a training system members of the target group have been involved in the design and formative evaluation process at various times in the project. Specifically, we focus on accessibility as one elementary factor of technology acceptance. Based upon the concept of the Universal-Design and Web-Accessibility-Guidelines 2.0 we implemented accessibility requirements that will be introduced and discussed in this paper.

Keywords: Accessibility · Acceptance of technology · Parkinson's disease

1 Introduction

Current statistics reveal that life expectancy has been on the rise and prevalence for degenerative diseases increases with age [1, 2]. Some of those neurological disorders are associated with speech impairments such as in Parkinson's Disease. The resulting speech disorder is often characterized by reduced intelligibility of spoken language, hereby effecting everyday communication and eventually even contributing to social isolation [3]. In many cases patients are not aware to which extent the intelligibility of their speech is affected and tend to misinterpret problems in interpersonal communication. Awareness of speech and intentional training of intelligibility are important measures to sustain communication skills of patients as long as possible.

ISi-Speech (Individualized Speech Technology in Rehabilitation for People with Speech Disorders) is an Internet-based training system to support the rehabilitation of people with acquired dysarthria. Currently it is constructed as a personalized Website with integrated motivational parameters which are adaptable to the abilities and opportunities of the user.

The stand-alone system is - independent from a clinical context - usable on various output devices such as tablets, smartphones or computers. This technological variability

K. Miesenberger and G. Kouroupetroglou (Eds.): ICCHP 2018, LNCS 10896, pp. 547–553, 2018.
https://doi.org/10.1007/978-3-319-94277-3_85

allows for tailoring the system towards personal preferences. In addition, it allows to include more or less media savvy persons and even those individuals who just started to use one of these devices. Older people who are often not familiar with new technologies nevertheless tend to exert prejudices towards using such devices. Acceptance of technologies is an often neglected aspect in successfully implementing new technologies. It is therefore of outmost importance to understand the users' needs and to remove barriers in order to support their participation [4, 5]. For this paper we focus on accessibility as one factor of technology acceptance and demonstrate how the layout of the ISi-Speech system was designed by applying the requirements of the Web-Accessibility-Guidelines and ideas of the Universal-Design.

2   The ISi-Speech Training System

As ISi-Speech intends to enable individuals with speech impairments to train their language independent from face-to-face instruction, its success heavily depends on the frequency and intensity of usage. Here ISi-Speech makes a unique contribution in targeting the motivation system that triggers usage. We deeply believe that a potentially effective training system that is not used deliberately must fail. Since the required logopedic exercises are often perceived as boring or exhausting many patients indeed display a lack of sustained motivation to perform them as often as required [5, 6]. In these cases, usage depends on external gratification provided by a therapist and hereby contradicts the original intention of self-controlled and independent usage of technology.

With ISi-Speech we intend to harvest the intrinsic motivational dynamics embedded in games [7]. Specifically, we implement gamification elements such as precise, immediate, and informative feedback, adaptability and transparency of goals, and monitoring features as important elements to trigger intrinsic motivation. With this approach we are in line with the self-determination-theory (SDT), developed by Deci and Ryan [8] and proven successful in many domains over the last decades. The theory postulates three conditions for personal growth as main aspects for intrinsic motivation: autonomy, competence and relatedness [3]. ISi-Speech includes different kinds of logopedic exercises to improve articulation, voice therapy or exercises to practice voice volume. The therapists are able to control the exercises by making certain settings to pretend specific training sessions. Therapists as well as patients have the possibility to monitor the results by obtaining statistics on their usage. After every training session results are summarized as right and wrong answers as well as time needed to conclude the task. The progress is hereby visible for both, the patient and his/her therapist.

To assure acceptance and usability of ISi-Speech an elaborate formative evaluation process with members of the target group is implemented [9]. It allows for step-by-step evaluation within the design process, providing immediate feed-back for modification Potential end-users with Parkinson's Disease were invited to participate in three one-day workshops over a period of two years. Two workshops have been already completed, the third will take place soon. In the two workshops 17 end-users recruited through Parkinson self-aid groups tested ISi-Speech. Individuals age ranged between 54 and 84 years, all had been previously diagnosed with Parkinson's Disease but were still mobile enough to attend the workshop. 15 persons have already signed up for the upcoming third workshop. To evaluate the application, a mixed-method design of scientific observation during testing-time, a standardized post hoc survey in combination with semi-structured interviews after testing the application are applied to get insights into the user's experiences regarding the training system. In addition, media competence, technology commitment [10], and perceived para-social interaction with the system [11] was controlled.

Results indicate a vast diversity of media knowledge in the testers who participated in the previous workshops: Half of them already use mobile media like smartphones and tablets but others don't use any technology yet and were rather reluctant to use ISi-Speech on tablets and computers. One tester even canceled the testing when he learned that the testing will require usage of a tablet or a computer. The results of the workshops clearly show that the patients have negative attitudes towards computers and tablets, which may affect motivation and performance of testing ISi-Speech. In addition, observations reveal operating problems by using for example mouse and headphones by using desktop computers. Half of the tester prefer to use tablets over computers for more intuitive control and perceived easier handling. Beside this hardware problem we identified orientation difficulties while navigating through the system and information overload in the main menu. In addition, it was pointed out that essential information was missing because "help"- or "next"-buttons were hard to find and written text, especially the headlines, was too small to read. If users did find information regarding the "help-button" they were sometimes confused because of too long texts and too complex graphics or images. Altogether many users needed help while they were testing the training-system. As a result, we collected and organized all the reported and observed impasses and glitches to compile a list for technological modification of the layout and interface of the website with the aim to increase accessibility within the last project phase. We hereby shifted our attention to the implementation of Universal Design ideas to fulfill the needs of potential end-users for a clear and usable website-design (Table 1).

Table 1. Implementation of WCAG 2.0 requirements in ISi-Speech

WCAG 2.0 principle	Implementation to ISi-Speech
Perceivable	- Text alternatives in cases of graphics for training success, icons or other non-text - Use of color only if it indicates an action as can be seen in Fig. 2 - Visual presentation satisfies requirements of minimum contrast rates

To further follow the principles of the Web Accessibility Guidelines [16] we substantially modified the original layout-design and the navigation of ISi-Speech (see Fig. 1). Elements like navigation, contrasts, headlines, overview, and script were redesigned according to the principles of WCAG 2.0 (see Fig. 2). Contrast could be improved. We also decided to use color only in visual means of conveying information or to indicate an action as requested in the guidelines. Every button which requires action (for example to choose or start an exercise) is now better visible for users due to its dark blue color. To conform principle three (understandable) we used easy language as far as possible, which includes the participation of symbols like a pen at the headline "meine Aufgaben" [my exercises] or the wrench as symbol for "meine Einstellungen" [my adjustments]. Further design will also apply easy language to instruct, describe exercises, and provide suitable information for better guidance through the website.

Fig. 1. Main menu before revision (Source: ISi-Speech homepage)

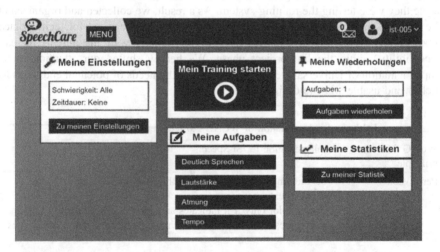

Fig. 2. Main menu after revision of WCAG 2.0 principles (Source: ISi-Speech homepage)

Considering the target group for usage of ISi-Speech, cognitive impairments are often accompanying symptoms of Parkinson's Disease. So-called mild cognitive impairments are often measureable throughout the illness and at a later stage dementing processes are not unlikely [18, 19]. Against this background it is of utmost important to design an easy and understandable access to ISi-Speech to create motivation for usage of the system and increase long-time acceptance of this technology. With respect to the health technology acceptance model [15] results of our ISi-Speech user-workshops reveal that testers often were located between acceptance stage two (being aware of technology, having feelings about technology) and stage three (intention to try out). To fully satisfy all Guideline principles many more adjustments such as reducing complex information and giving more help-options in easy language if necessary, will have to be applied before another evaluation workshop will take place.

3 Outlook

The Convention on the Rights of People with Disabilities requests accessibility of new technology in an early development process for all persons as precondition for the participation of people with disabilities [13]. The principles of the Universal Design serve as concept which grants all people the advantages by higher comfort, understandable language or straight and transparent layout-design for better using conditions [12, 14, 17]. Therefore, Universal Design was not particularly designed for special needs, but as universal guidance for the inclusion of as many people as possible. In developing a rehabilitation tool, we firmly believe in the improvement gained by the application of Universal Design. According to our experiences WCAG 2.0 principles are well understood by design developers and guide optimization to put requirements of accessibility and Universal Design into action. Even if the currently addressed target group for ISi-Speech are individuals with Parkinson's Disease, the system might be adapted for other patient groups such as peoples with neurodegenerative diseases or cognitive impairments to improve their speech.

Furthermore, theory such as the Technology Acceptance Model claim rationality in the user current research as well as our intermediate evaluation of ISi-Speech repeatedly demonstrate a gap between the design process in creating new technologies and the wide range of users' fears and needs towards their usage that substantially inhibit their efficiency [e.g., 20–22]. Results of our user-workshops demonstrated initial problems in operating and using hardware. Although we are not able to solve all hardware skill problems we take responsibility to ensure the best possible, easy access and usage of our website to prevent frustration and abortion. Our intention is the rigorous involvement of potential end-users at various stages of the design process to guide a better understanding of the users' needs and enable them through Universal Design principles to independent and self-determined usage.

References

1. Statistisches Bundesamt (Destasis). Behinderte Menschen (2018). https://www.destatis.de/DE/ZahlenFakten/GesellschaftStaat/Gesundheit/Behinderte/Tabellen/GeschlechtBehinderung.html;jsessionid=8865A3EDBE9A44AA65FC6717F4484B35. InternetLive2
2. Hoffmann, E., Menning, S., Schelhase, T.: Demografische Perspektiven zum Altern und zum Alter. In: Böhm, K., Tesch-Römer, C., Ziese, T. (Hrsg.) Gesundheit und Krankheit im Alter, pp. 21–30 (2009). http://www.gbe-bund.de/pdf/Ge-sundh_Krankh_Alter.pdf

3. Mühlhaus, J., Frieg, H., Bilda, K., Ritterfeld, U.: Game-based speech rehabilitation for people with Parkinson's Disease. In: Antona, M., Stephanidis, C. (eds.) UAHCI 2017. LNCS, vol. 10279, pp. 76–85. Springer, Cham (2017). https://doi.org/10.1007/978-3-319-58700-4_7

4. Mader, S., Levieux, G., Natkin, S.: A game design method for therapeutic games. Paper Presented at the 2016 8th International Conference on Games and Virtual Worlds for Serious Applications, (VS-Games) (2016)

5. Hainey, T., Conolly, T., Stansfield, M., Boyle, E.: The differences in motivations of online game players and offline game players: a combined analysis of three studies at higher education level. Comput. Educ. **57**, 2197–2211 (2011)

6. Gage, H., Grainger, L., Ting, S., Williams, P., Chorley, C., Carey, G., Borg, N., Bryan, K., Castelton, C., Trend, P., Kaye, J., Jorda, J. Wade, D.: Specialist rehabilitation for people with Parkinson's Disease in the community: a randomized controlled trial. Health Serv. Deliv. Res. **51**(2) (2014). https://www.journalsli-brary.nihr.ac.uk/hsdr/hsdr02510/#/full-report

7. Ritterfeld, U.: Von video games zu health gaming. In: Dadaczynski, K., Schiemann, S. (Hrsg.) Gesundheit spielend fördern. Potenziale und Herausforderungen von digitalen Spieleanwendungen für die Gesundheitsförderung und Prävention, pp. 173–190. Beltz, Weinheim (2016)

8. Deci, E.L., Ryan, R.M.: Self-determination theory: a macrotheory of human motivation, development, and health. Can. Psychol. Assoc. **49**(3), 182–185 (2008)

9. Ritterfeld, U., Muehlhaus, J., Frieg, H., Bilda, K.: Developing a technology-based speech intervention for acquired dysarthria. In: Miesenberger, K., Bühler, C., Penaz, P. (eds.) ICCHP 2016. LNCS, vol. 9758, pp. 93–100. Springer, Cham (2016). https://doi.org/10.1007/978-3-319-41264-1_12

10. Neyer, F.J., Felber, J., Gebhardt, C.: Entwicklung und Validierung einer Kurzskala zur Erfassung von Technikbereitschaft. Diagnostica **58**(2), 87–99 (2012)

11. Schramm, H., Wirth, W.: Testing a universal tool for measuring parasocial interactions across different situation and media. Findings from three studies. J. Media Psychol. **22**(1), 26–36 (2010)

12. Bühler, C.: Technology for inclusion and participation – technology based accessibility (TBA). In: Antona, M., Stephanidis, C. (eds.) UAHCI 2016. LNCS, vol. 9737, pp. 144–149. Springer, Cham (2016). https://doi.org/10.1007/978-3-319-40250-5_14

13. United Nations: Convention on the Rights of Persons with Disabilities (2017). https://www.un.org/development/desa/disabilities/convention-on-the-rights-ofpersons-with-disabilities.html

14. Global Universal Design Commission: Creating Voluntary Universal Design Standards (2017). http://www.globaluniversaldesign.org/sites/default/fi-les/docs/about/creating-volunta ry-ud-standards.pdf

15. Hastall, M.R., Dockweiler, C., Mühlhaus, J.: Achieving end user acceptance: building blocks for an evidence-based user-centered framework for health technology development and assessment. In: Antona, M., Stephanidis, C. (eds.) UAHCI 2017. LNCS, vol. 10279, pp. 13–25. Springer, Cham (2017). https://doi.org/10.1007/978-3-319-58700-4_2

16. World Wide Web Consortium: Web Content Accessibility Guidelines (2008). https://www.w3.org/Translations/WCAG20-de/WCAG20-de-20091029/

17. Bühler, C.: "Accessibility" über Desktopanwendungen hinaus – Barrierefreiheit. Informatik-Spektrum **40**(6), 501–510 (2017)

18. Witt, K., Kalbe, E., Erasmi, R., Eberbach, G.: Nichtmedikamentöse Therapieverfahren beim Morbus Parkinson. Nervenarzt **88**(1), 383–390 (2017)

19. Aybek, S., Gronchi-Perrin, A., Berney, A., Catalano Chiuve, S., Villemure, J., Burkhard, P., Vingerhoets, F.: Long-term cognitive profile and incidence of dementia after STN-DBS in Parkinson's disease. Mov. Disord. **22**(7), 974–981 (2007)

20. Davis, F.: A Technology Acceptance Model for Empirically Testing New End-User Information Systems. Massachusetts Institute of Technology (1980). https://dspace.mit.edu/handle/1721.1/15192

21. Hastall, M.R., Eiermann, N., Ritterfeld, U.: Formal and informal carers' views on ICT in dementia care: insights from two qualitative studies. Gerontology **13**(1), 53–58 (2014)

22. Conti, D., Nuovo, S.D., Buono, S., Di Nuovo, A.: Robots in education and care of children with developmental disabilities: a study on acceptance by experienced and future professionals. Int. J. Soc. Robot. **9**(1), 51–62 (2017)

Towards a Deep Learning Based ASR System for Users with Dysarthria

Davide Mulfari$^{(\boxtimes)}$, Gabriele Meoni, Marco Marini, and Luca Fanucci

University of Pisa, Pisa, Italy
davide.mulfari@ing.unipi.it

Abstract. In this paper, we investigate the benefits of deep learning approaches for the development of personalized assistive technology solutions for users with dysarthria, a speech disorder that leads to low intelligibility of users' speaking. It prevents these people from using automatic speech recognition (ASR) solutions on computers and mobile devices. In order to address these issue, our effort is to leverage convolutional neural networks toward a speaker dependent ASR software solution intended for users with dysarthria, which can be trained according to particular user's needs and preferences.

Keywords: Deep learning · Assistive technology
Speech recognition · Dysarthria

1 Introduction and Motivation

The term *dysarthria* refers to a set of neuromotor disorders affecting the control of the motor speech articulators, whose malfunction is caused by the lack of control over the speech-related muscles, the lack of coordination among them, or their paralysis. In particular, spastic dysarthria is characterized by strained phonation, imprecise placement of the articulators, incomplete consonant closure, and reduced voice onset time distinctions between voiced and unvoiced stops [2]. These factors lead to low intelligibility of users speaking and prevent people with speech disabilities from using Automatic Speech Recognition (ASR) solutions on computers and mobile devices.

Such pieces of software are intended for speakers without speech disabilities and currently they are not optimal for recognizing dysarthric speech because the pronunciation of dysarthric speakers deviates from that of non-disabled speakers in many respects. Indeed the usage of ASR platforms trained on normal unimpaired speech is not useful: when a standard ASR system is used for dysarthric speech [1], the Word Error Rates (WER) are between 26.2% and 81.8% higher than the normal speech WER. Several related works also investigated the effort of creating specialized ASR solutions for users with dysarthria instead of using speech recognition tools designed for non-disabled speakers. According to [5], it is easier for people with dysarthria to utter isolated words rather than a

K. Miesenberger and G. Kouroupetroglou (Eds.): ICCHP 2018, LNCS 10896, pp. 554–557, 2018.
https://doi.org/10.1007/978-3-319-94277-3_86

continuous sequence of words. This is more effective when the size of the ASR vocabulary is small and includes only simple words with one or two syllables in order to boost recognition rates with reduction or minimisation of dysarthric ASR errors. Therefore, isolated-word and small vocabulary ASR models are in greater demand speech recognition in the presence of disabilities [5].

In order to address the aforementioned issues, we propose a speaker dependent ASR solution tailored to the specifics of dysarthric users which leverages the knowledge from strategies in the field of artificial intelligence and deep learning. This approach seems to be promising even if an effective implementation for people with speech impairments has to be demonstrated yet [4]. Therefore in this paper, our major contribution is to investigate the potential benefits of deep learning techniques to create a basic speech recognition model that recognizes just a few number of keywords. Its practical application is a simple speech recognition software acting as an interface to access computers, e.g., controlling a mouse pointing, performing basic actions in a desktop environment. We believe that such a vocal aid may serve as an alternate computer access method for users with dysarthria, in particular for those who are unable to use keyboards or traditional input devices.

To achieve this, we arranged an initial speech commands dataset consisting of several hundreds of audio files of a person with spastic dysarthria saying a precise set of Italian words. TensorFlow, an open source deep learning framework, has been used in order to organize our training dataset and to create our speech model working on specialized kinds of convolutional neural networks (CNN) [3]. As motivated in the rest of the paper, this training configuration gives us 86% accuracy values considering a custom testing dataset, which is unrelated with the training audio data. In our opinion, this may be an initial, promising approach that we plan to extend and to better investigate in future work, with the collaboration of many Italian students with dysarthria attending our university.

2   Proposed Approach

Nowadays, deep learning represents one of the key trends for Information and Communication Technologies and allows conceiving computational models that are composed of multiple processing layers to learn representations of data with multiple levels of abstraction. These methods are based on deep neural networks (DNNs) (i.e., neural networks composed of more than one hidden layer) and have dramatically improved the state-of-the-art in pattern recognition problems, including image classification, speech recognition, visual object recognition, assets detection and many other domains.

In this section, we employ a particular type of DNNs, that are convolutional neural networks, in an ASR application scenario with the aim of recognizing just a few number of utterances within a personalized vocabulary. A CNN is composed of one or more convolutional layers pooling or sub-sampling layers, and fully connected layers (with this final type being equivalent to those used in DNNs). The aim of these layers is to extract simple representations at high resolution from the input data, and then converting these into more complex representations, but at much coarser resolutions within subsequent layers. For these reasons, CNNs are mainly designed for image classification problem, which is the task of assigning an input image to one label from a fixed set of categories.

In our research activity, we have worked on TensorFlow, an open source deep learning framework developed at Google, to employ CNN to classify audio data (utterances) within precise classes. The process leverages knowledge from the field of image classification, by converting audio i.e., a one-dimensional continuous signal across time, into a 2D spatial problem. TensorFlow's utilities solve that issue by defining a window of time our speech commands should fit into, and converting the audio signal in that window into an image. This is done by grouping the incoming audio samples into short segments, just a few milliseconds long, and calculating the strength of the frequencies across a set of bands. Each set of frequency strengths from a segment is treated as a vector of numbers, and those vectors are arranged in time order to form a two-dimensional array. This array of values can then be treated like a single-channel image, called spectrogram [3]. To prove this approach on a disabled speech, a training dataset has been collected from one male adult with spastic dysarthria. Our choice is also motivated by the lack of an Italian database containing voiceprints for users with speech disabilities. The recording were collected using a desktop microphone connected to a personal computer (PC) over a standard USB connection. On the PC side, we have implemented a Java desktop application to facilitate the task of creating our vocal dataset: at fixed time interval, the software shows a string (i.e., a word) on the device's screen and it prompts end user to utter it. Audio signals were sampled at 16 kHz sampling frequency and were encoded in many 16 bit little-endian PCM WAVE files. Each recording consists of an isolated production of each of 12 words required for our test vocabulary. Summarizing, our training dataset consists in 3000 audio contribution equally split into 12 classes. The training process of the speech model is of critical importance and has been executed on a single desktop NVIDIA CUDA Linux environment with the following hardware configuration: CPU: I7-7700K processor, RAM: 32 GB DDR4, GPU: NVIDIA GeForce GTX 1070 8 GB (6.1 compute capability level), Storage: 4 TB SATA III Hard disk drive. During the training procedure, TensorFlow framework automatically added a special class, called *unknown*, to our training database: this class containing common types of background noise and it has been designed to separate speech data from non-vocal commands during the recognition stage.

2.1   Results

We conducted early experiments to investigate the accuracy level of the speech model previously considered. We worked on a speaker dependent ASR solution: in our analysis, we have only considered utterances from the person with spastic dysarthria mentioned above. Our testing dataset consist in 130 audio files and it was split into 13 classes, including the unknown category. Figure 1 summarizes our results in a bar graph. On x-axis, we report each class (utterance) from our ASR vocabulary (Italian words), while the accuracy percentage is shown on

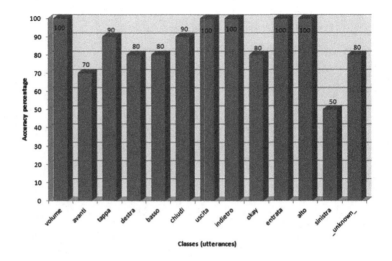

Fig. 1. Bar chart summarizing results.

y-axis. Globally, we have appreciated a 86% accuracy level: we believe that it is a good result toward the creation of a vocal interface allowing the end user to control a computer-based system with his voice.

3 Conclusion

A speaker - dependent ASR system for users with dysarthria has been presented in this paper. Its key feature is to bring together deep learning technologies and convolutional neural networks. Early results shows promising results thanks to a dedicated training procedure based on TensorFlow framework. In future works, we plan to better investigate the proposed approach with the collaboration of many Italian disabled students attending our university.

References

1. Joy, N.M., Umesh, S.: Improving acoustic models in TORGO Dysarthric speech database. IEEE Trans. Neural Syst. Rehabil. Eng. **26**, 637–645 (2018)
2. Polur, P.D., Miller, G.E.: Effect of high-frequency spectral components in computer recognition of dysarthric speech based on a mel-cepstral stochastic model. J. Rehabil. Res. Dev. **42**(3), 363 (2005)
3. Sainath, T.N., Parada, C.: Convolutional neural networks for small-footprint keyword spotting. In: Sixteenth Annual Conference of the International Speech Communication Association (2015)
4. Tejaswi, S., Umesh, S.: DNN acoustic models for Dysarthric speech. In: 2017 Twenty-Third National Conference on Communications (NCC), pp. 1–4. IEEE (2017)
5. Young, V., Mihailidis, A.: Difficulties in automatic speech recognition of dysarthric speakers and implications for speech-based applications used by the elderly: a literature review. Assist. Technol. **22**(2), 99–112 (2010)

Fig. ...

... Only ... we have ... predicted a ... summary levels we believe limit is ...

5 Conclusion

References

1. ...
2. ...
3. ...
4. ...

Art Karshmer Lectures in Access to Mathematics, Science and Engineering

Art Karshmer Lectures in Access to Mathematics, Science and Engineering
Introduction to the Special Thematic Session

Dominique Archambault[1]($\boxtimes$), Katsuhito Yamaguchi[2],
Georgios Kouroupetroglou[3]®, and Klaus Miesenberger[4]®

[1] Université Paris 8-Vincennes-Saint-Denis, THIM (E.A. 4004 CHArt),
Saint-Denis, France
dominique.archambault@univ-paris8.fr
[2] Nihon University, Tokyo, Japan
eugene@gaea.jcn.nihon-u.ac.jp
[3] National and Kapodistrian University of Athens, Athens, Greece
koupe@di.uoa.gr
[4] Johannes Kepler University, Linz, Austria
klaus.miesenberger@jku.at

Abstract. Access to mathematical expressions have always been a particular problem for blind and partially sighted people, and more widely persons with a print disability, including those with dyscalculi, dyslexia, dyspraxia and other perception or processing disorders. This has a distinct negative effect in terms of careers possibilities for print disabled people, since it excludes them not only from mathematical studies, but from all fields that require mathematical knowledge, including all scientific areas as well as areas using statistics. Since a couple of decades many researches have been carried out to provide assistive tools that help visually impaired people to overcome this challenge. This session, created 16 years ago by Art Karshmer, includes in ICCHP 2018 eight full and four short interesting and novel relative papers.

Keywords: Accessibility to mathematics · Science
Engineering and technology

In memoriam of Pr Arthur I. Karshmer (1945–2015),
the founder and long serving chair of this STS

Professor Arthur I. Karshmer, our dear colleague, mentor and Computer Science guru, started a thematic session about access to Mathematics and Science at ICCHP in 2002 in Linz [3], aiming at *"new approaches to offer blind students a better access to math, to provide tools for doing math as well as to support teachers in teaching math."* Since then, a session about access to Mathematics has always been present at ICCHP conference, that he chaired until 2014. A total of 89 papers have been published in these sessions.

© Springer International Publishing AG, part of Springer Nature 2018
K. Miesenberger and G. Kouroupetroglou (Eds.): ICCHP 2018, LNCS 10896, pp. 561–564, 2018.
https://doi.org/10.1007/978-3-319-94277-3_87

1   ICCHP 2002, Linz

An analysis of the papers presented in the first STS organised by Art in 2002 shows essentially papers about 2 main topics: one was the reading of math expressions and the other about experiences of access to Maths studies by blind students. It was very interesting to analyse how these students could succeed in studies including mathematical contents.

Indeed at this time only very few students managed to access mathematical studies. In 2002, a group of researchers working in this field had a meeting, invited by Art Karshmer, and we agreed the hypothesis that there was no reason that mathematical semantics would not be understood because of blindness [2]. We identified as the biggest barrier the way to access to mathematical content, the non visual notation in itself. Indeed there are some very talented blind mathematicians, but a blind student with an average level usually cannot cope. Based on this hypothesis many works have been carried out about how to improve the understanding of mathematical expressions in non visual modalities.

2   ICCHP 2018, Linz

Sixteen years later, the questions covered have been shifted to another level. We don't have much statistics to show that the number of students with visual impairment have really been increasing in the last years. More research need to be conducted ! Even if some progresses have been done we have to question a bit further. Indeed it is not enough to understand a mathematical expression, but to work in a scientific field, it is also necessary to manipulate this expression, to calculate. It's not the only question of how to understand a formula but what can I do with it, how do I solve a problem [1]. During the last decade, several teams have been carrying out some research in this direction. Then, even with better tools, the question of appropriation of these tools by pupils and teachers is challenging, especially in inclusive education. We have to investigate this topic, too. How to create conditions for technology to improve the real practice?

2.1   Editing Mathematical Expressions

In 2018's session, several papers concern tools allowing to edit maths expressions. Two are focusing on the manipulation of expression to solve problems.

- Neil Soiffer – *"The Benetech Math Editor: An Inclusive Multistep Math Editor for Solving Problems"* – proposes an editor with innovative functions helping students in the problem solving.
- Paúl Mejía, Luiz César Martini, Julio Larco and Felipe Grijalva – *"CASVI: A Computer Algebra System aimed at Visually Impaired People"* – a calculus software which could be seen as an audio front end for Maxima.

The question of inclusion is present in those two papers, but it appears more directly in the following one. Indeed, at school, inclusion supposes that students with visual impairment are able to deliver works that their sighted teachers and peers can read. It is the same with inclusion in a work environment. This paper proposes a tools, based on LaTeX allowing people with visual impairment to render their expression in a graphical way so it can be transmitted to sighted people (teachers, colleagues, etc).

- Giuseppe Melfi, Thorsten Schwarz and Rainer Stiefelhagen – *"An Inclusive and Accessible LaTeX Editor"* – first report a comparison of existing LaTeX editors in terms of accessibility and finally propose to develop their own, especially designed for being used with specific Assistive Technology.

Also about LaTeX, the following paper deals with the accessibility of PDF documents generated from LaTeX sources. Producing PDF/UA documents from LaTeX has been a problem since a long time, and the authors aim at developing a LaTeX package for that. They start, in this paper, with the question of embedded mathematical expressions.

- Tiziana Armano, Anna Capietto, Sandro Coriasco, Nadir Murru, Alice Ruighi, Eugenia Taranto – *"An automatized method based on LaTeX for the realization of accessible PDF documents containing formulae"* – propose a LaTeX package allowing to embed formulas in a document so they can be read properly by a screen reader.

The next paper deals also with inclusion. Working on the topic of access to chemistry diagrams, they note that it is very difficult to make accessible the chemistry handbook in use in The Netherlands.

- Dorine in't Veld and Volker Sorge – *"The Dutch Best Practice for Teaching Chemistry Diagrams to the Visually Impaired"* – propose a national repository where one can find a catalogue of accessible molecule diagrams, that can be used for teaching chemistry to visually impaired students.

Finally, two other papers propose tools for maths editors.

- Richard Stanton, Enrico Pontelli and Phoebe Toups Dugas – *"Exploring a Novel Inexpensive Tangible Interface for Non-Visual Math and Science"* – describe a way of localising blocks that can be used for supporting novel approaches to teach a number of science and math concepts to visually impaired students.
- Katsuhito Yamaguchi and Masakazu Suzuki – *"Localization Scheme of Assistive Tools for Print-Disabled People to Access STEM Contents"* – propose a model for localising the maths editor ChattyInfy to Vietnamese.

2.2   Visualisation of Digital Data

Another aspect of access to maths that is more and more investigated by researchers is the visualisation of digital data. Indeed visualisation of data is very important and seeing the shape of a figure brings much more information to most people than a table a figures. We can see at first sight if a progression is slow or fast, in what direction it goes, while it's very hard to get this from the list of numbers themselves. The question raised by these papers is: how can we provide such functionality to people with visual disabilities?

- Tetsuya Watanabe and Hikaru Mizukami – *"Effectiveness of Tactile Scatter Plots - Comparison of non-visual data representations"* – compared 3 methods of data visualisation, 2 based on tactile representation and one being data table used with a screen reader.
- Tomás Murillo-Morales and Klaus Miesenberger – *"Techniques for Improved Speech-based Access to Diagrammatic Representations"* – create aural representations of diagrams, proposed to the user in a dialogue-based interaction.
- Jonathan R. Godfrey, Paul Murrell and Volker Sorge – *"An Accessible Interaction Model for Data Visualisation in Statistics"* – provide SVG representations, with annotations, which can be explored by users.

2.3 Teaching Programming

Recently, interesting researches about access to computer programming started to appear. In this session, we have one paper about teaching to programming blind beginners. They have proposed to use blocks representing main algorithms instructions, that users can assembly to create programs [4]. In this paper they extend this work with the concept of subroutine.

- Mariko Tsuda, Tatsuo Motoyoshi, Kei Sawai, Takumi Tamamoto, Hiroyuki Masuta, Ken'ichi Koyanagi, and Toru Oshima – *"Improvement of a Tangible Programming Tool for the Study of Subroutine Concept"*.

Second paper is at the opposite of teaching programming... This time it's not for beginners but for students interested by software engineering and architecture: how to access UML representations?

- Claudia Loitsch, Karin Müller, Gerhard Jaworek, Stephan Seifermann, Jörg Henß, Sebastian Krach and Rainer Stiefelhagen – *"UML4ALL Syntax - A Textual Notation for UML Diagrams"* – present a way of presenting UML diagrams so they can be accessible to screen readers.

References

1. Karshmer, A.I., Bledsoe, C.: Access to mathematics by blind students. In: Miesenberger, K., Klaus, J., Zagler, W. (eds.) ICCHP 2002. LNCS, vol. 2398, pp. 471–476. Springer, Heidelberg (2002). https://doi.org/10.1007/3-540-45491-8_90
2. Archambault, D., Stöger, B., Fitzpatrick, D., Miesenberger, K.: Access to scientific content by visually impaired people. In: Upgrade, vol. VIII, no. 2, pp. 29–42, April 2007. http://www.upgrade-cepis.org/issues/2007/2/upgrade-vol-VIII-2.html
3. Archambault, D.: Non visual access to mathematical contents: state of the art and prospective. In: Proceedings of the WEIMS Conference 2009 The Workshop on E-Inclusion in Mathematics and Science, pp. 43–52 (2009)
4. Motoyoshi, T., Tetsumura, N., Masuta, H., Koyanagi, K., Oshima, T., Kawakami, H.: Tangible programming gimmick using RFID systems considering the use of visually impairments. In: Miesenberger, K., Bühler, C., Penaz, P. (eds.) ICCHP 2016. LNCS, vol. 9758, pp. 51–58. Springer, Cham (2016). https://doi.org/10.1007/978-3-319-41264-1_7

The Benetech Math Editor: An Inclusive Multistep Math Editor for Solving Problems

Neil Soiffer[✉] [iD]

Talking Cat Software, Portland, OR 97229, USA
soiffer@alum.mit.edu

Abstract. WYSIWYG editors for entering math in documents have existed for over 20 years. A few of these are accessible, but almost all are geared towards entering a single expression, not to the process of solving a math problem. The Benetech math editor introduces two simple and unique ideas that are very useful in the middle and high school settings for solving math problems. The first idea allows a student to cross out or cancel subexpressions; the second allows them to annotate their work so the teacher or other reviewer knows the student's reasoning.

Keywords: Mathematics · Accessibility · Visually impaired · Braille · Education

1 Introduction

WYSIWYG math editors date back to the beginnings of window-based operating systems with releases of MathType (also built into Microsoft Word) and Expressionist in 1987. Since then, most math editors have had a similar design that allows access via palettes to the large number of characters, symbols, and notations used in mathematics. Graphing and smart drag and drop that understands some semantics have been added to a few editors (e.g., Theorist, DUDAMATH, Graspable Math) since then. These editors allow a user to perform actions like dragging a term across an equal sign; doing that will change the sign of the term. A few commands such as expand and simplify that are part of much more sophisticated symbolic manipulation systems may also be part of the editors that understand semantics. However, the basic structure of most editors remains the same as it was 20 years ago.

DUDAMATH, Graspable Math and Theorist (now LiveMath) differ from most editors in that they have a history mechanism so that the derivation of the answer is shown (Fig. 1). Each step (drag and drop, simplify, etc.) creates a new line. DUDA-MATH and Graspable Math just show the results; LiveMath also records the command used to the right of the modified expression (Fig. 1c).

Math accessibility has improved significantly over the last decade; JAWS, NVDA +MathPlayer, and Safari+VoiceOver will read and navigate math encoded in MathML in a browser. NVDA+MathPlayer will also work with Word and PowerPoint when

© Springer International Publishing AG, part of Springer Nature 2018
K. Miesenberger and G. Kouroupetroglou (Eds.): ICCHP 2018, LNCS 10896, pp. 565–572, 2018.
https://doi.org/10.1007/978-3-319-94277-3_88

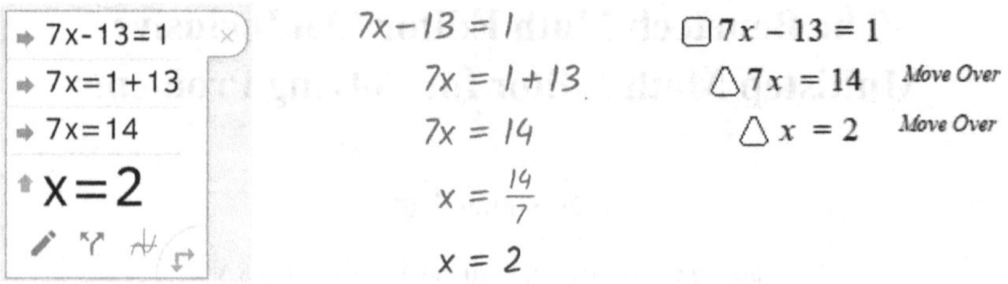

⇒ 7x-13=1 ×	$7x - 13 = 1$	☐ $7x - 13 = 1$
⇒ 7x=1+13	$7x = 1 + 13$	△ $7x = 14$ *Move Over*
⇒ 7x=14	$7x = 14$	△ $x = 2$ *Move Over*
⇑ X=2	$x = \frac{14}{7}$	
✐ ˥ ⊬ ↱	$x = 2$	
a: DUDAMATH	b: Graspable Math	c: LiveMath

Fig. 1. DUDAMATH, Graspable Math and LiveMath examples

MathType is also installed. All of them also can generate braille math codes on refresh-able braille displays.

WYSIWYG Math editors however remain largely inaccessible. Three exceptions to this are ChattyInfty [14], WIRIS's editor [13], and Pearson's Accessible Math Editor [3]. ChattyInfty supports creating an entire document, not just math. It is TeX-based and makes use of TeX commands to enter math characters and notations. ChattyInfty is self-voicing. WIRIS's editor is web-based. It is a traditional WYSIWYG editor in that it has a large number of palettes for math notation and special characters. It is mostly acces-sible, but has some accessibility issues such as some characters not being spoken when navigating the expression. Neither ChattyInfty nor the WIRIS editor support braille math codes. Pearson's editor is also a traditional palette-based editor that works in a browser. Pearson's editor is unique in that it supports both braille input and output. Both the visual display and braille display are always in sync and dots 7 and 8 are used to indicate the current insertion point or selection as is done for text. The Pearson editor was developed to be an accessible editor for state and national tests. Internally, it uses content MathML which allows it to more easily verify an answer even when the answer is entered differ-ently than the stored answer (e.g., terms are in a different order).

Work has also been done to make specific subject areas accessible to vision impaired students. Both [1, 5] describe systems that present digits in a grid to make elementary math operations such as addition and multiplication easier to navigate and solve. Some simple algebra problems are also handled by those systems by breaking the equation into parts and allowing a predefined set of operations (e.g., "add and simplify") to be applied to them. In [2], Almasri et al., use that same idea for solving beginning linear algebra problems such as adding matrices. These systems appear to be specific to their subject matter and are not general math editors. All are speech-based and do not make use of a braille display.

For those with physical disabilities, speech input is a possible alternative. MathTalk [9] was an early attempt at speech input using Dragon Dictate (now using Dragon Natu-rally Speaking). Both Pearson's editor and TextHELP's EquatIO [6] support speech input but do so in very different manners. EquatIO makes use of Google's speech recog-nition and tries to correct for the engine not being tuned towards math. Pearson's editor makes use of Dragon Naturally Speaking and so requires letters to be spoken as "alpha", "bravo", etc. None of these systems has reported error rates or user studies; speech input for math remains a research topic.

Although some math editors have a template for crossing out a selection, a literature search did not turn up any instances of math editors where cross outs were meant to be used for anything other than decorations, nor were instances found where users could add annotations to their work other than the automatic annotations added by Theorist/LiveMath. These two new and simple but powerful ideas form the basis of the Benetech multistep math editor discussed in the next section.

2   Benetech Math Editor

The Benetech math editor is an open source project funded by Benetech with the ultimate goal of being a inclusive math editor for use by students to solve math problems. Its genesis is the recognition that:

1. Although most text-based assignments use a document editor of some sort (e.g., Google Docs, MS Word, or Apple Pages), most math assignments are handwritten. However, solving/simplifying most math problems involves a large amount of copying expressions, a task at which computers are very good.
2. Students with disabilities often have trouble handwriting math expressions. They also often face challenges organizing their work (Fig. 2) which makes it difficult for teachers to assess their level of knowledge.

Fig. 2. Sample messy homework teachers see

The Benetech math editor divides the work area into two sections: A math editor and a history section that records each step. The math editor is a traditional math editor that is accessible to students who use screen readers. Students manipulate the expression by crossing out, copying, pasting, and entering math. After they have finished a step (e.g., adding something to both sides of an equation), they explain what they have done by either typing or using speech which is converted to text. They then move on to the next step. This will put the current expression and explanation into the history section, cleanup/remove any cross outs, and put the cleaned-up equation into the current editor. This mimics what a student would do on paper. In contrast to [1, 2], students are free to do as little or as much manipulation as they feel comfortable doing in each step; the explanation is generated by the student and should reflect their work. The history section provides a record of the what the student has done, complete with an explanation of what/why they have done it so that a teacher can review the student's work. Previous steps can be moved back to the math editor if changes need to be made. An example of a solved problem is shown in Fig. 3. Both the editor and the history section are accessible to students using screen readers.

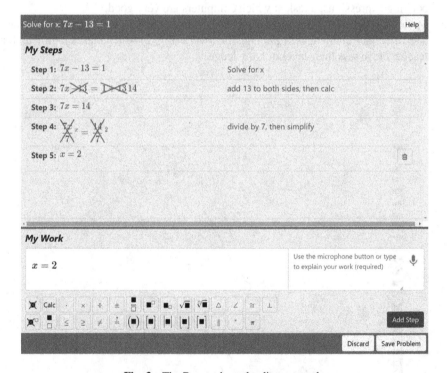

Fig. 3. The Benetech math editor example

When adding or subtracting from both sides of an equation, some students are taught to use the already familiar 2D paradigm for adding numbers. Figure 4 shows an example of its use (palette button below 'Calc' button in Fig. 3).

Fig. 4. Before and after of using alternative to crossing out

Like cross outs, these are cleaned up when adding a step.

Students who are learning pre-algebra and algebra are the initial target group for the Benetech math editor. The palette items were chosen based on an analysis of what characters/symbols are used in pre-algebra and algebra textbooks [11]. Minimizing the number of entries to only the most used (99.95% of all non-keyboard characters in textbooks) greatly simplifies access to those who must access information linearly. An option to select from a full set of symbols along with a way of including new symbols in the limited palette will be added in addition to palettes customized to other subject areas. In the meantime, the editor allows users to use AsciiMath and TeX commands such as "<=" and '\alpha' (with auto-complete) to enter any character.

As can be seen in Fig. 3, the palette includes a "calc" button. This numerically evaluates a selected expression, crosses that selection out, and places the result to the right of the crossed-out selection. In the United States, calculators are common in math classrooms and their use has been allowed in high stakes tests for many years, so a simple calculator was incorporated into the editor.

3 User Testing/Feedback

Informal initial user testing with both students and teachers to validate the concepts and receive feedback on the editor's design was performed. None of the students had identified disabilities, but some had handwriting issues and some were "organizationally-challenged". This is a common problem with middle school aged children (Fig. 2) and is a characteristic often associated with people who have ADHD and/or dysgraphia. Some of the teachers who evaluated the editor were teachers of students with visual impairments (low vision and blindness) and/or learning disabilities.

The feedback from the initial testing was generally very positive. In one round of testing with five students and one teacher, four out of five students who previously said paper was their first choice for doing math said they preferred the math editor over using pencil and paper. Here are some comments from students and teachers:

- "I like that it's digital because it helps people with messy handwriting – now my teacher doesn't have to guess what I wrote."
- "I like that the 'cross out' gets cleared up for me."
- "Being able to delete is so much better than erasing!"
- "I also like that it makes things more organized because my teacher sometimes has trouble following my work, especially when there's not enough space to show my work in the provided space."
- "Using Google Docs in a similar fashion is a lot more tedious" - teacher
- "The describing – necessitating the explanation of work is so critical" – teacher

- "I will always prefer paper, probably because that's how I've been doing math for decades, but I would use this tool interchangeable with pencil/paper" – teacher
- "I think that it would be wonderful as a 'Show Work' feature whereby students and teacher could communicate the different approaches to problems' solutions" – teacher.

We received some suggestions and comments on what should be added to the editor:

- Several students wanted to be able to pick part of the expression and work on it as a subproblem. Isolating a part of the problem is likely to be particularly useful for students with learning disabilities as it reduces distractions and minimizes working memory load [8].
- Teachers liked that the editor didn't do manipulations for the students – they wanted to see any errors students made so they could correct conceptual mistakes.
- Most teachers were OK with the "calc" button.
- Related to the calculator idea, teachers want control over what automatic features are available for each problem. For example, in more advanced math subjects, most teachers would be OK for most problems with commands like "move over" and "expand" or semantic drag-and-drop as is done in LiveMath, etc. Teachers want the ability to control the feature set at the granularity of a single problem.

4 Implementation

The Benetech editor is web-based and makes use of mathlive as the underlying editor and math display engine. Accessibility was added to the display engine by including a visually hidden area that contains MathML. This allows JAWS, NVDA+MathPlayer, Safari+VoiceOver, TextHELP and any other MathML-aware AT to read, navigate, and produce braille output on a refreshable display for the static math in the history section. Feedback from expert users who were blind helped refine the navigation model so users can quickly navigate the interface to review, enter, and activate buttons using headings, tabs, and regions. All palette entries along with the "Add Step" button have keyboard equivalents.

The interactive math editor was modified to make use of aria-live regions so that commands such as arrow keys announce important changes. For example, moving into a fraction announces not just the character that follows the new insertion point, but also that it is at the start of the numerator. Deletions are also announced as are changes in the display (e.g., "=" followed by ">" turns into "≥").

There are three problems with the current support for aria-live regions in at least JAWS, NVDA, and Safari: MathML is not interpreted as MathML; the aria-live change does not appear on a braille display; and it is not possible to embed SSML or some other speech markup language to improve the speech for math. There has been some discussion about screen readers adding alerts to the braille display, but they would need to interpret MathML so that the alert uses a braille math code instead of brailling the words. Many of the same problems occur if aria-label is used to indicate the math to speak. It appears that the only current path to generating braille for editable math is to follow the path the Pearson editor [3] took and directly write braille math to the refreshable display; the Benetech editor does not do this yet.

Supporting synchronized highlighting also faces problems due to an unfinished Web Speech API browser recommendation from 2012 [12]. All major browsers except IE11 support basic parts of the speech output recommendation, but speech cues and marks are not supported by most browsers. Marks are used to generate callbacks to signal that something should be highlighted. However, browsers do support callbacks at word boundaries and that can be used for synchronized speech highlighting. This is more complicated than using marks because many words used in math (e.g., "begin fraction") do not correspond to anything displayed on the screen.

5 Future Work

The Benetech math editor is in its infancy. User testing will guide future development of the UI and feature set. The ability to pick some part of a problem and work on it in isolation has already been identified as a need. Because an overall goal is to make the editor universally accessible, we plan on adding the following in the future:

- Synchronized highlighting of the speech to aid students who are dyslexic; coloring of parts of the static display of math will also be added for those who indicate they are severely dyslexic.
- Speech input of math to enable use by those who are physically disabled.
- Braille output from the editor; braille output for the math in the history section is supported now via the use of MathML;
- Braille input of math.

An aspect that hasn't been addressed yet is columnar layout. This is used in elementary arithmetic along with more advanced topics such as systems of equations, synthetic division, and matrices. MathPlayer's navigation [10] supports place markers and columnar navigation, and similar support is planned for the interactive editor. The "enhanced" navigation mode in MathPlayer understands the structure of the math, so moving by terms is supported, but support to deal with missing terms so that like terms are aligned in systems of equations needs to be supported.

Support for touch screens is a natural extension to the editor as cross outs are a natural gesture on a touch screen. Similarly, drag-and-drop (if allowed for the problem), particularly on a touch screen, is a natural feature to add.

The editor can be used on its own, but to be most useful, it should be part of a full math curriculum suite of tools that deals with other aspects of math such as plotting, recording scores, etc. To this end, we have had some positive talks with other groups about integration into their suite of educational tools.

Acknowledgements. The Benetech math editor is funded in part by Benetech, its donor base, and the U.S. Department of Education, Office of Special Education Programs (Cooperative Agreement #H327B100001) grant to Benetech's DIAGRAM Center. Opinions expressed herein are those of the author and do not necessarily represent the position of the U.S. Department of Education or Benetech.

Sue-Ann Ma and Jason Schwab (Benetech) both contributed to the design, development, and student testing of the Benetech math editor. Arno Gourdal developed the underlying open source mathlive editor. He has been particularly helpful in fixing bugs and adding new features to mathlive to support the Benetech math editor.

References

1. Alajarmeh, N., Pontelli, E., Burgert, T.: A multi-layer universally designed workspace for tracking students skills and mastery transition in mathematics manipulation in inclusive education.In: 2014 IEEE Frontiers in Education Conference (FIE) Proceedings (2014)
2. Almasri, B., Elkabani, I., Zantout, R.: An interactive workspace for helping the visually impaired learn linear algebra. In: Miesenberger, K., Fels, D., Archambault, D., Peňáz, P., Zagler, W. (eds.) ICCHP 2014. LNCS, vol. 8547, pp. 572–579. Springer, Cham (2014). https://doi.org/10.1007/978-3-319-08596-8_89
3. Dooley, S.S., Park, S.H.: Generating Nemeth Braille output sequences from content MathML markup. J. Technol. Pers. Disabil. 156–160 (2016)
4. DUDAMATH. www.dudamath.com. Accessed 22 Jan 2018
5. Elkabani, I. A multilingual interactive workspace for helping the visually impaired learn and practice algebra. In: Proceedings of the Conference Universal Learning Design, Linz, pp. 21–30 (2016)
6. EquatIO. http://www.texthelp.com/en-us/products/equatio. Accessed 22 Jan 2018
7. Graspable Math. http://www.graspablemath.com. Accessed 22 Jan 2018
8. Gulley, A.P., Smith, L.A., Price, J.A., Prickett, L.C., Ragland, M.F.: J. Vis. Impairment Blind. 111(5), 465–471 (2017)
9. McClellan, N.: Voice math with MathTalk using either dragon NaturallySpeaking or microsoft speech engine. In: CSUN Conference Proceedings (2005)
10. Soiffer, N.: A study of speech versus braille and large print of mathematical expressions. In: Miesenberger, K., Bühler, C., Penaz, P. (eds.) ICCHP 2016. LNCS, vol. 9758, pp. 59–66. Springer, Cham (2016). https://doi.org/10.1007/978-3-319-41264-1_8
11. Soiffer, N.: Improving usability of math editors. In: W4A 2018 International Web for All Conference, Lyon, France, April 2018, to be published
12. Web Speech API Specification. http://w3c.github.io/speech-api/webspeechapi.html. Accessed 26 Mar 2018
13. WIRIS editor description. http://www.wiris.com/editor. Accessed 25 Mar 2018
14. Yamaguchi, K., Suzuki, M.: Accessible authoring tool for DAISY ranging from mathematics to others. In: Miesenberger, K., Karshmer, A., Penaz, P., Zagler, W. (eds.) ICCHP 2012. LNCS, vol. 7382, pp. 130–137. Springer, Heidelberg (2012). https://doi.org/10.1007/978-3-642-31522-0_19

CASVI: A Computer Algebra System Aimed at Visually Impaired People

Paúl Mejía[1,2(✉)], Luiz César Martini[2], Julio Larco[1,2], and Felipe Grijalva[3]

[1] Departamento de Eléctrica y Electrónica,
Universidad de las Fuerzas Armadas ESPE, Sangolquí, Ecuador
{phmejia,jclarco}@espe.edu.ec

[2] School of Electrical and Computing Engineering, University of Campinas,
Campinas, Brazil
{paulmeji,martini,jclarco}@decom.fee.unicamp.br

[3] Departamento de Electrónica, Telecomunicaciones y Redes de Información,
Escuela Politécnica Nacional, Quito, Ecuador
felipe.grijalva@epn.edu.ec

Abstract. The biggest barrier for visually impaired people to pursue a bachelor of science degree is not the blindness itself but the access to mathematical resources. Resources such as *Computer Algebra Systems* (CAS) are not accessible, which means that even the execution of elementary math becomes a challenging task. In this paper, we present *Casvi*, a CAS for visually impaired people, which allows to perform symbolic and numeric computation using the *Maxima*'s math engine. *Casvi* offers modules for algebra, linear algebra, differential calculus, integral calculus among others. Moreover, it provides an intuitive user interface based on synthetic speech and non-speech sounds.

Keywords: Accessibility · Visually impaired · Engineering education

1 Introduction

According to the 2015 Building a Grad Nation report [1], the high school dropout rate of students with disabilities in the U.S. is nearly 40% and this trend worsens in higher education. Bachelor of Science degrees are particularly hard for them to pursue since most resources (e.g. specialized softwares) lacks of accessibility.

Among these resources, *Computer Algebra Systems* (CAS) such as *Matlab*, *Wolfram Mathematica* and *Maxima* have become indispensable tools in engineering. In general, CAS software allows symbolic computation over mathematical expressions. However, they are not accessible to the visually impaired people, which in turn means that executing the most basic mathematical operation in such softwares becomes a challenging task, even with the help of screen readers. This barrier makes imperative to build a bridge between the existent CAS tools and the unsighted people to allow writing, editing, evaluating and solving mathematical expressions. Moreover, since visually impaired students are increasingly attending regular schools, it is very important that these tools are also accessible

© Springer International Publishing AG, part of Springer Nature 2018
K. Miesenberger and G. Kouroupetroglou (Eds.): ICCHP 2018, LNCS 10896, pp. 573–578, 2018.
https://doi.org/10.1007/978-3-319-94277-3_89

to teachers who are not particularly familiar with Braille [2]. In light of this, we propose a blind-friendly CAS based on *Maxima's* math engine[1]. We named the system *Casvi*. *Casvi* performs a large set of mathematical operations and offers an intuitive user interface through synthetic speech and non-speech sounds, and allows blind students to save the mathematical expressions on disk for later use.

2   Prior Works

The process of presenting accessible mathematical content to blind people is based on tactile methods (e.g. direct conversion to Braille), audible methods (e.g. using TTS; Text-To-Speech), or the combination of both [3–6]. Other methods allow to perform an automatic translation from linearized mathematical formulas to Braille code, and use Latex, MathML, or HTML to render the math equation, thus enabling the interaction between a blind student and a sighted tutor [7,8]. Some methods introduce their own mathematical Braille which includes new symbols making it possible to represent mathematics in a linear form [9]. There are also methods in which a sighted person processes and converts the mathematical content into a format understandable to blind people [10].

There are tools that provide extensive mathematic functionality (e.g. *Maxima*), and according to Archambault [2], making these tools accessible to blind people is the next step towards a complete math accessibility. Although this is a challenging task, there are works [11,12] that tackle this problem at least for basic math operations. However, none of them can solve mathematical expressions involving more complex operations such as derivatives.

One way to deal with this problem is to create a front-end application with accessibility features that first solves the mathematical operations using an existing math engine (e.g. *Maxima*), and then communicates the results to blind users in an understandable way. This is precisely the aim of the *Casvi* project. It was created as an alternative to blind people who wish to evaluate a mathematical formula or solve it symbolically.

3   CASVI: Computer Algebra System

Figure 1 (left) summarizes how *Casvi* performs symbolic and numeric computation using the *Maxima's* math engine. *Casvi* allows to perform roots of equations and polynomials calculations, matrix and linear algebra operations, calculus, Laplace transform, arithmetic manipulations, logarithms and trigonometric operations, Taylor series, among others. It also incorporates a text editor for data entry, a user interface based on synthetic speech messages as well as non-speech sounds, and the capability to store and retrieve previously saved scripts.

3.1   Data Entry

Casvi offers two ways of entering data: through menus or through the text editor. The former allows to enter expressions using interactive voice menus (invoked

---

[1] http://maxima.sourceforge.net/.

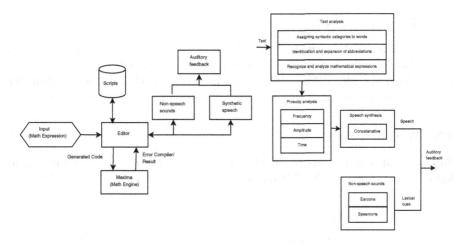

Fig. 1. Basic block diagram of *Casvi* (left). *Casvi* auditory feedback process (right).

by `Alt+key` or `Ctrl+key` combinations). For instance, the user can access the calculus interactive voice menu by pressing `Alt+C`. On the other hand, the text editor allows to enter characters, mathematical expressions and commands supported by the system. It is worth mentioning that every time a key is pressed, the user receives a TTS feedback telling her which key has been pressed.

3.2 Maxima Math Engine

For performing a mathematical calculation, *Casvi* first generates the corresponding *Maxima* code. Then, the *Maxima*'s math engine interprets the generated code. In the absence of any error (e.g. syntax errors), the results are calculated and returned to the *Casvi* editor.

3.3 Presenting and Verbalizing Mathematics

Figure 1 (right) shows the process of conversion of the information provided by *Maxima* into an auditory feedback composed by a synthetic speech part and/or non-speech sounds. The synthetic speech generation has 3 stages: text analysis, prosody analysis, and speech synthesis. In the first stage, besides assigning syntactic categories to words, we identify and expand abbreviations, and recognize and analyze mathematical expressions. Then, the prosody analysis stage aims to avoid ambiguity by assigning phonological features having a variable relationship to the words [13] such as frequency, amplitude, and time. Finally, we use a concatenative speech synthesis to generate the final speech signal. Besides speech, we use non-speech sounds (i.e. lexical cues) which has proven to be effective for conveying information regarding the structure of mathematical expressions [14]. Specifically, we use *earcons* and *spearcons*.

3.4   Store Information

Both mathematical expressions initially entered by the user and the returned results obtained by the math engine can be modified, deleted, or stored in a plain text script file. Before saving a script, *Casvi* checks the file's content for syntax errors and then eliminates them (not without first warning the user).

3.5   Workflow Example

Suppose that a user wants to calculate the integral $\int cos(x)dx$. The user should follow the workflow in Fig. 2 (left) by executing the following steps:

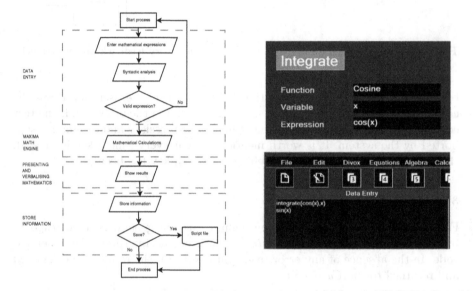

Fig. 2. *Casvi* workflow (left). *Casvi* user interface of a mathematical expression (top right). *Casvi* editor showing the integral operation and its result (bottom right).

1. Press `Alt+C` to activate the Calculus interactive voice menu. The user will listen the message *"Calculus"*.
2. Using the arrow keys, navigate through the voice menu until hearing *"Integrate"*. Then, press `Enter` to open the user interface to define the integral.
3. Enter the required parameters (see Fig. 2 top right). Use the `TAB` key to navigate through the parameters and to hear its auditory description.
4. Press `ENTER` to proceed with the calculation of $\int cos(x)dx$.

Once the integration is done, the user will receive the following audio message:

- "The results is" *(synthetic speech)* **(pause)**
- "sin of" *(synthetic speech)* **(pause)**

- "open parentheses" *(spearcon)* (pause)
- "x" *(synthetic speech)* (pause)
- "close parentheses" *(spearcon)*.

At the same time, the integral operation as well as its result will be displayed in the text editor (see Fig. 2 bottom right).

4 Conclusion

The purpose of *Casvi* is to encourage the visually impaired students to pursue engineering degrees by offering a blind-friendly computational tool for solving mathematical problems. Currently, we are performing usability tests to improve the user experience.

References

1. Civic Enterprises, the Everyone Graduates Center: Building a grad nation. Technical report (2015)
2. Archambault, D.: Non visual access to mathematical contents: state of the art and prospective. In: Proceedings of the WEIMS Conference, pp. 43–52 (2009)
3. Ferreira, H., Freitas, D.: Enhancing the accessibility of mathematics for blind people: the AudioMath project. In: Miesenberger, K., Klaus, J., Zagler, W.L., Burger, D. (eds.) ICCHP 2004. LNCS, vol. 3118, pp. 678–685. Springer, Heidelberg (2004). https://doi.org/10.1007/978-3-540-27817-7_101
4. Karshmer, A., Gupta, G., Pontelli, E.: Mathematics and accessibility: a survey. In: International Conference on Computers Helping People with Special Needs, pp. 664–669 (2007)
5. Raman, T., Gries, D.: Audio formatting - making spoken text and math comprehensible. Int. J. Speech Technol. **1**(1), 21–31 (1995)
6. Suzuki, M., Tamari, F., Fukuda, R., Uchida, S., Kanahori, T.: INFTY: an integrated OCR system for mathematical documents. In: Proceedings of the 2003 ACM Symposium on Document Engineering, pp. 95–104. ACM (2003)
7. Barbieri, T., Mosca, L., Sbattella, L.: Learning math for visually impaired users. In: Miesenberger, K., Klaus, J., Zagler, W., Karshmer, A. (eds.) ICCHP 2008. LNCS, vol. 5105, pp. 907–914. Springer, Heidelberg (2008). https://doi.org/10.1007/978-3-540-70540-6_136
8. Gopal, D., Wang, Q., Gupta, G., Chitnis, S., Guo, H., Karshmer, A.: Winsight: towards completely automatic backtranslation of Nemeth code. In: Stephanidis, C. (ed.) UAHCI 2007. LNCS, vol. 4556, pp. 309–318. Springer, Heidelberg (2007). https://doi.org/10.1007/978-3-540-73283-9_35
9. Schweikhardt, W., Bernareggi, C., Jessel, N., Encelle, B., Gut, M.: LAMBDA: a european system to access mathematics with braille and audio synthesis. In: Miesenberger, K., Klaus, J., Zagler, W.L., Karshmer, A.I. (eds.) ICCHP 2006. LNCS, vol. 4061, pp. 1223–1230. Springer, Heidelberg (2006). https://doi.org/10.1007/11788713_176
10. Suzuki, M., Kanahori, T., Ohtake, N., Yamaguchi, K.: An integrated OCR software for mathematical documents and its output with accessibility. In: Miesenberger, K., Klaus, J., Zagler, W.L., Burger, D. (eds.) ICCHP 2004. LNCS, vol. 3118, pp. 648–655. Springer, Heidelberg (2004). https://doi.org/10.1007/978-3-540-27817-7_97

11. Sanmiguel, J.M.P., Martini, L.C.: Mathematics software programming resources aimed at visually impaired users - Matvox. In: Advances in Information Technology and Applied Computing, ICISCA, Indonesia, pp. 310–314 (2012)
12. Campoverde, P.H.M., Martini, L.C.: Application of mathematical finance program designed for visually impaired users. In: Advances in Information Technology and Applied Computing, ICISCA, Indonesia, pp. 315–320 (2012)
13. Fitzpatrick, D.: Mathematics: how and what to speak. In: Miesenberger, K., Klaus, J., Zagler, W.L., Karshmer, A.I. (eds.) ICCHP 2006. LNCS, vol. 4061, pp. 1199–1206. Springer, Heidelberg (2006). https://doi.org/10.1007/11788713_173
14. Bates, E., Fitzpatrick, D.: Spoken mathematics using prosody, earcons and spearcons. In: Miesenberger, K., Klaus, J., Zagler, W., Karshmer, A. (eds.) ICCHP 2010. LNCS, vol. 6180, pp. 407–414. Springer, Heidelberg (2010). https://doi.org/10.1007/978-3-642-14100-3_61

An Inclusive and Accessible LaTeX Editor

Giuseppe Melfi[(⊠)], Thorsten Schwarz, and Rainer Stiefelhagen

Karlsruhe Institute of Technology, Karlsruhe, Germany
{giuseppe.melfi,thorsten.schwarz,rainer.stiefelhagen}@kit.edu

Abstract. In this paper, we discuss the reasons which led us to propose LaTeX as mathematical notation to visually impaired students and why there is need for an accessible LaTeX editor. We performed an accessibility test for a selection of three LaTeX editors, to investigate their capabilities to satisfy the needs of these users. The evaluation of the results showed that it was necessary to develop an own editor. The first prototype was preliminarily tested, proving that, paying attention to the GUI library and the development environment, it is possible to develop a GUI with a high level of compatibility with assistive technologies like screen readers and magnifiers. The editor achieved a satisfying ranking in the user-tests which encourages further development of the software.

Keywords: Accessibility to mathematics · LaTeX · Accessible editor

1 Introduction

Education in mathematics is important at all school levels. At university, knowledge of math is the basis for many subjects in particular in the fields of mathematics, sciences, or engineering. It is well known, that mathematical notation for the visually impaired students is a challenge which has not been completely solved by the current assistive technology (AT) yet.

There are two main aspects regarding mathematical notations that have to be considered to produce educational materials and ATs fully accessible and easy to use in the mathematical environment. The first one is the large set of different symbols used in math, that for example makes it impossible to design a character mapping one-to-one in Braille. The second aspect is the large use of subscripts, superscripts, and multi-line notation, while the screen readers are based on the linearising of the information.

2 State of the Art in R&D

In response to the problem experienced by people with visual impairment accessing mathematical materials, different solutions with different approaches have been developed in the last two decades, an extended review can be found in the work of Archambault et al. [2]. Currently, there is not a global standard for mathematics notation for Braille. Each country has an own notation and there

© Springer International Publishing AG, part of Springer Nature 2018
K. Miesenberger and G. Kouroupetroglou (Eds.): ICCHP 2018, LNCS 10896, pp. 579–582, 2018.
https://doi.org/10.1007/978-3-319-94277-3_90

are notations based both on six-dot and eight-dot Braille. In some cases, a compact Braille math code was developed and distributed together with a complete system including plug-in, editor or reader like for the LAMBDA project [1] and the LEAN Math Notation [4]. Unfortunately, only parts of users are fluent in Braille and in any case they have to learn a large set of new symbols, which poses an additional challenge for a student who is already involved with the tasks of the university. Furthermore, a symbolic notation specifically developed for visually impaired users can hinder inclusive education. The direct collaboration with a professor or a fellow student when using a specific Braille notation system could be difficult, particularly during a laboratory or a practice.

For these considerations, the use of LaTeX as a possible solution of the mathematical notation for people with visual impairment was proposed [3,5,7]. The first advantage is that LaTeX is widespread in particular in the university context which facilitates the communication and interoperability with sighted persons. Second, the tags of the markup language are quite easy to learn. The main disadvantage of the use of LaTeX is that reading and writing is extremely cumbersome due to linearization and to the use of special characters.

3   Methodology of Our R&D

Considering the advantages of the use of LaTeX, we proposed this markup language to our students of STEM subjects as the mathematical notation for tactile learning material as well as a method for writing homework and exams. Thus, it was necessary to identify a LaTeX editor, accessible both for screen readers and magnifiers, easy to use and, if possible, cross-platform. We tested two mainstream products: Texmaker (free and cross-platform) and TeXnicCenter (only for Windows but judged as a good editor for blind students [3,6]); and a third editor, BlindMath [8], purposely developed as AT.

The details about the accessibility tests conducted for these three editors are available at this web page[1] where it is also possible to download the editor topic of this paper. Resuming, Texmaker failed all tests, so it seems not a suitable option for our purpose. The other two editors are possible options for screen reader users but not for magnifier users. BlindMath received the best score in our tests, but it is important to highlight two disadvantage of this editor. First, the LaTeX code is not easy to debug. The rendering of the LaTeX code is delegated to the browser plug-in which does not provide the compiler output, not showing where or what the error is. Second, it is not possible to save the output of the editor as PDF.

After evaluating the tests' results, we decided to develop an own editor, in order to offer the students a more optimized and comfortable working environment. We present the results of a usability test conducted for the first prototype of the editor in Sect. 5.

---

[1] SZS-LaTeX Editor http://services.szs.kit.edu/szslatex/.

4   Development of the SZS-Editor for LaTeX

The SZS-Editor is a cross-platform editor and is built to handle standard LaTeX input files. This preserves the inclusion of a student who can share his files with the colleagues and vice-versa, and the possibility to work on the same document in a collaborative way. The GUI of the editor is based on the wxWidgets[2] library. The reason for this choice is the high compatibility with the ATs typically in use at SZS[3] and by its students, with respect to other GUI libraries[4].

The main features of the editor are the following:

Hidden LaTeX Header. In a typical LaTeX document, it is possible to distinguish two different main blocks of code. In the header, the global properties of the document are described, and this part is automatically hidden to facilitate the revision and to ease the use of the editor by beginners in LaTeX. The header is still editable with a second window accessible from the menu.

Simplified Log of Compiling. The standard output of the LaTeX compiler is verbose and uncomfortable to quickly check it with a screen reader or a magnifier. The SZS-Editor summarizes the log in a few lines.

A **Go-to-line** and a **Auto-completion LaTeX-code** functionality.

Code Folding. With this feature, the user can selectively hide and display sections of the currently edited file which is particularly useful during the revision of a document. The editor can fold the code between two dollar '$' symbols (used in LaTeX to open and close the mathematics environment) or between two brackets '{...}'. For example, it is possible to fold the following long equation: $y=(\frac{\sqrt{a}}{b})^{\frac{1+\omega}{z}}$ as $EQ1$ or $y=(\frac{ARGV1}{b})^{ARGV2}$. This feature is also useful to copy/paste/cut some parts of the LaTeX code in the document and for learning and understanding a long formula, folding one by one every part of it.

Focus Manager. During the development of the GUI, particular attention was paid to switch the focus automatically through the interface to facilitate the use of the editor.

5   Usability Test

We evaluated the first version of the editor with three students for a preliminary user test. It was also a good opportunity to gather feedback from the participants for further development of the software. With a preliminary questionnaire, we collected some basic information about the knowledge and experience with LaTeX. All the participants had a basic knowledge of LaTeX, two had already used an editor before (TeXnicCenter).

---

[2] wxWidgets: Cross-Platform GUI Library, https://www.wxwidgets.org/.

[3] SZS: German acronym for Study Centre for the Visually Impaired - Karlsruhe.

[4] The first prototypes of the editor were developed also with Qt library. For a short comparison, see the web page of the SZS-Editor: http://services.szs.kit.edu/szslatex/.

With five short tasks, the users had the possibility to explore all the features of the editor described in Sect. 4. After each task, they were asked how much the feature was useful. The **Auto-completion** functionality and the **Focus manager** got an average score of 3 in a scale range from 0 (not useful) to 4 (very useful); the **Code folding** got an average score of 3.3 and the **Go-to-line** feature got 4. Finally, the global usability of the editor was evaluated with a standard System Usability Scale, receiving a score of 96.

6   Conclusion and Future Work

Developing the first version of the SZS-Editor with the wxWidgets GUI library, we obtained a user interface fully accessible with the ATs used by our students. The satisfying ranking achieved in the user-tests encourages further development of the software. In particular, our work focuses on the improvement of the PDF preview (for partially sighted users), and on a useful auto-completion function for the common LaTeX commands (for blind users). The current version is in use by one student, who used it for the development of a written exam, a seminar report and a presentation.

Acknowledgement. We thank Sebastian Peter for being our voluntary partially sighted user for alpha tests and for his useful feedback.

References

1. Alistair, E., McCartney, H., Fogarolo, F.: Lambda: a multimodal approach to making mathematics accessible to blind students. In: 8th International ACM SIGACCESS Conference on Computers and Accessibility, pp. 48–54 (2006)
2. Archambault, D., Stöger, B., Fitzpatrick, D., Miesenberger, K.: Access to scientific content by visually impaired people. Upgrade **8**(2), 14 (2007)
3. Borsero, M., Murru N., Ruighi, A.: LaTeX as solution to the problem of access to texts with formulas by visually impaired people. In: GuIT Meeting, ArsTeXnica, no. 22, pp. 12–18 (2016). http://www.integr-abile.unito.it/articoli/latex-acc.pdf
4. Gardner, J., Christensen, C.: More accessible math. In: Miesenberger, K., Karshmer, A., Penaz, P., Zagler, W. (eds.) ICCHP 2012. LNCS, vol. 7382, pp. 124–129. Springer, Heidelberg (2012). https://doi.org/10.1007/978-3-642-31522-0_18
5. Gonzúrová, W., Hrabák, P.: Blind friendly LaTeX. In: Miesenberger, K., Karshmer, A., Penaz, P., Zagler, W. (eds.) ICCHP 2012. LNCS, vol. 7382, pp. 138–141. Springer, Heidelberg (2012). https://doi.org/10.1007/978-3-642-31522-0_20
6. Maneki, A., Jeans, A.: LaTeX: what is it and why do we need it? In: Future Reflections - A Magazine for Parents and Teachers of Blind Children, vol. 31, no. 2 (2012). https://nfb.org/images/nfb/publications/fr/fr31/2/fr310212.htm
7. Bexten, E.M., Jung, M.: LATEX at the university of applied sciences Giessen-Friedberg — experiences at the institute for visually impaired students. In: Miesenberger, K., Klaus, J., Zagler, W. (eds.) ICCHP 2002. LNCS, vol. 2398, pp. 508–509. Springer, Heidelberg (2002). https://doi.org/10.1007/3-540-45491-8_95
8. Pepino, A., Freda, C., Ferraro, F., Pagliara, S., Zanfardino, F.: "BlindMath" a new scientific editor for blind students. In: Miesenberger, K., Klaus, J., Zagler, W.L., Karshmer, A.I. (eds.) ICCHP 2006. LNCS, vol. 4061, pp. 1171–1174. Springer, Heidelberg (2006). https://doi.org/10.1007/11788713_169

An Automatized Method Based on LaTeX for the Realization of Accessible PDF Documents Containing Formulae

Tiziana Armano, Anna Capietto, Sandro Coriasco[(✉)], Nadir Murru,
Alice Ruighi, and Eugenia Taranto

Department of Mathematics, University of Turin,
Via Carlo Alberto 10, 10123 Torino, Italy
{tiziana.armano,anna.capietto,sandro.coriasco,nadir.murru,alice.ruighi,
eugenia.taranto}@unito.it

Abstract. Assistive technologies for visually impaired people (screen readers and braille displays) perform satisfactorily with regard to digital documents containing alphabet characters, but they still have a long way to go as far as formulae and graphs are concerned. In general, the most spread digital documents are in PDF format. However, in the case of mathematical contents, they are not accessible at all, since formulae are usually unreadable by screen readers. Currently, a standard and fast method for inserting accessible formulae into a PDF document is still lacking despite it is a very important issue for spreading accessible digital scientific documents. In this paper, we propose a method for automatically generating a PDF document with mathematical contents accessible by assistive technologies for visually impaired people. Specifically, we have developed a LaTeX package that produces a final PDF document where the formulae are totally accessible by screen readers and braille displays.

Keywords: Accessibility of formulae · Assistive technology · LaTeX
PDF document · Visually impaired people

1 Introduction

In this paper, we propose a method for automatically generating a PDF document with formulae accessible by assistive technologies for visually impaired people. Assistive technologies (screen readers and braille displays) perform satisfactorily with regard to digital documents containing alphabet characters, but they still have a long way to go as far as formulae and graphs are concerned. A comprehensive overview about this problem can be found in [1,2].

Many studies have been conducted in order to improve the accessibility of digital documents with mathematical contents. For instance, MathPlayer ensures accessibility of formulae inserted by using MathType in Word documents [10]. Another way for creating accessible mathematical documents is given by the

© Springer International Publishing AG, part of Springer Nature 2018
K. Miesenberger and G. Kouroupetroglou (Eds.): ICCHP 2018, LNCS 10896, pp. 583–589, 2018.
https://doi.org/10.1007/978-3-319-94277-3_91

MathML language (see [4] for further information). However, accessibility of such documents is heavily affected by the versions of browsers, operating systems and screen readers, making this solution very unstable. A system used by blind people for reading and writing mathematics is the LAMBDA system (Linear Access to Mathematics for braille Device and Audio-synthesis). Mathematical language in LAMBDA is designed so that every symbol can be directly translated into words. For further details on LAMBDA we refer to [5]. Unfortunately, this system does not help to spread accessible digital documents, since it is only used by visually impaired people and it is not a standard for the realization of documents by sighted people. A very used language for producing scientific documents is the LaTeX language, which is a standard in the scientific community. Assistive technologies can directly manage LaTeX documents. In this case, visually impaired people need to learn LaTeX in order to understand the commands. However, there are software which facilitate LaTeX comprehension and usability; one of them is BlindMath [9]. Moreover, some converters from LaTeX to braille exist, see, e.g., [3,8].

In general, the most spread digital documents are in PDF format. However, in the case of mathematical contents, they are not accessible at all, since formuale are usually unreadable by screen readers because (such as images) they are bidimensional. None of the above systems allows to directly produce accessible formulae in PDF documents. This could be possible only performing specific tasks. For instance, using the Word editor, if each formula is manually tagged by the author (by using the alternative text), such a comment will be kept when the corresponding PDF file will be generated and it will be read by the screen reader. However, this procedure does not help to improve the presence of accessible PDF documents, since it is a very boring and time consuming method. It is very hard to think that an author performs these actions for the realization, e.g., of a book. Currently, a standard and fast method for inserting accessible formulae into a PDF documents is still lacking despite it is a very important issue for spreading accessible digital scientific documents. In [11] standard guidelines for accessibility of PDF documents are presented. Moreover, in [6,7], an overview about accessibility of PDF documents is provided with a focus on mathematical contents. In these works, the author also proposes possible solutions and guidelines for producing accessible formulae by embedding LaTeX and MathML codes. However, a working and definitive method is not provided.

In this paper, we show a LaTeX based method for an automatized production of accessible PDF documents with mathematical contents. Specifically, we have developed a LaTeX package that produces a final PDF document where the formulae are totally accessible by screen readers and braille displays.

2   Description of the LaTeX Package 'Axessibility'

When a PDF document is generated starting from LaTeX, formulae are not accessible by screen readers and braille displays. They can be made accessible by inserting a hidden comment, i.e., an actual text, similarly to the case of web pages or Word documents. This can be made, e.g., by using the LaTeX package pdfcomment.sty or using an editor for PDF files like Adobe Acrobat Pro. In any case, this task must be manually performed by the author and it is surely inefficient, since the author should write the formulae and, in addition, insert a description for each formula. Note also that the package pdfcomment.sty does not allow to insert special characters like 'backslash', 'brace', etc, in the comment. Moreover, with these solutions, the reading is bothered since the screen reader reads incorrectly the formula and then the correct comment of the formula. In Fig. 1, we show the LaTeX code for generating a PDF document containing a simple formula with a comment manually inserted. When the screen reader accesses the PDF document, the formula will be read 'square root 1 plus 5 2 begin fraction numerator 1 plus square root of 5 over 2 end fraction', i.e., before reading the correct comment 'begin fraction numerator 1 plus square root of 5 over 2 end fraction' the screen reader reads incorrectly the formula 'square root 1 plus 5 2'.

```
\documentclass[a4paper,11pt]{article}

\usepackage{pdfcomment}

\begin{document}

A simple formula:

\begin{equation}
\pdftooltip{\frac{1 + \sqrt{5}}{2}}
{begin fraction numerator 1 +
square root of 5 over 2 end fraction}
\end{equation}

\end{document}
```

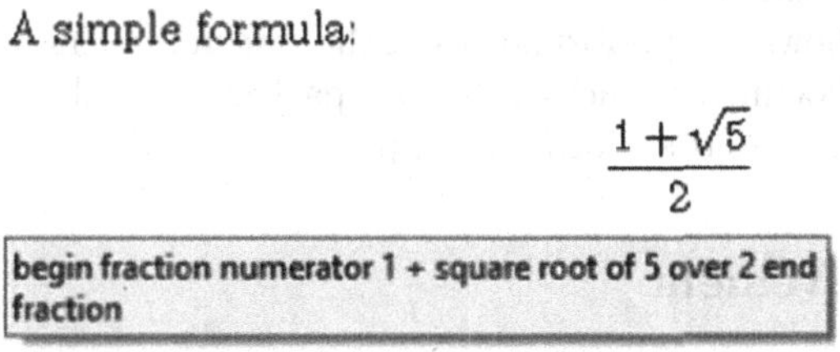

A simple formula:

$$\frac{1+\sqrt{5}}{2}$$

begin fraction numerator 1 + square root of 5 over 2 end fraction

Fig. 1. LaTeX commands for generating a simple formula in a PDF document using the package pdfcomment.sty and the corresponding PDF output

There are also some LaTeX packages that try to improve the accessibility of PDF documents produced by LaTeX. In particular the packages accsupp.sty (available at https://ctan.org/pkg/accsupp) and accessibility_meta.sty (available at https://github.com/AndyClifton/AccessibleMetaClass) has been developed in order to obtain tagged PDF documents. However, both packages do not solve the problem of the accessibility of formulae. The package accsupp.sty develops some interesting tools for commenting formulae using also special characters (possibility that is not available in the pdfcomment.sty package). This is not an automatized method, though, since the comment must be manually inserted by the author. The package accessibility_meta.sty is an improved version of the package accessibility.sty. This package allows the possibility of inserting several tags for sections, links, figures and tables. However, even if these tags are recognized by the tool for checking tags of Acrobat Reader Pro, they are not always recognized by the screen readers. Moreover, this package does not manage formulae and it is not uploaded in the official CTAN repository (some errors may appear when compiling a LaTeX file using this package).

Our package, named axessibility.sty, solves completely this problem, since it is able to automatically produce an actual text corresponding to the LaTeX commands that generate the formulae. This actual text is hidden in the PDF document but the screen reader reads it without reading any incorrect sequence before.

The package axessibility.sty uses the command '\BeginAccSupp' defined in the existing package accsupp.sty. Such a command has been modified in order to obtain an actual text readable the by screen reader.

We have treated the most used environments for inserting formulae, i.e., 'equation', 'equation*', '\[', '$$', '\(', '$'. Hence, any formula inserted using one of these environments is accessible in the corresponding PDF document.

In Fig. 2, we show the LaTeX code for generating the same PDF document shown in Fig. 1. We can observe that, in this case, the author has to write the formula without adding anything else. In Fig. 2, we also show some lines of the source code of the PDF file, where there is the actual text automatically generated by our package. The screen reader will read correctly the LaTeX command '\frac {1 + \sqrt {5}}{2}'. Moreover, we have created a JAWS dictionary that provides the reading in the natural language in the case that the user does not know the LaTeX commands.

A video that shows the performances of the screen readers NVDA and JAWS on a sample PDF document generated by our package is available at http://www. integr-abile.unito.it/demo-accformulae.php.

3   User Involvement

The package has been evaluated by four visually impaired people, named subjects A, B, C and D. They are all blind, but it is noticed that, while two of them are blind from birth and know the braille code, the others became blind during their life and they do not use the braille code. Thus, during the tests two used a refreshable braille display and two did not. Subjects A and C used the screen reader NVDA, whereas subjects B and C used JAWS. Moreover, subjects A

```
\documentclass[a4paper,11pt]{article}

\usepackage{accformulae}

\begin{document}

A simple formula:
\begin{equation}
\frac{1 + \sqrt{5}}{2}
\end{equation}

\end{document}
```

```
stream
BT
/F15 10.9091 Tf 134.765 704.247
Td [(A)-333(simple)-334(form)28(ula:)]TJ
ET
/S/Span
<</ActualText(\040\\frac\040{1\040+\040\\sqrt\040{5}}{2}\040)>>
BT
/F15 10.9091 Tf 280.489 691.232
Td [(1)-222(+)]TJ/F21 10.9091 Tf 18.788 9.024 Td [(p)]TJ
ET
q
1 0 0 1 308.368 700.475 cm
[]0 d 0 J 0.436 w 0 0 m 5.455 0 1 S
Q
BT
/F15 10.9091 Tf 308.368 691.232 Td [(5)]TJ
ET
q
1 0 0 1 280.489 686.579 cm
[]0 d 0 J 0.436 w 0 0 m 33.333 0 1 S
Q
BT
/F15 10.9091 Tf 294.428 676.369 Td [(2)]TJ
ET
```

Fig. 2. LaTeX commands for generating a simple formula in a PDF document using the package axessibility.sty and the corresponding source code of the PDF output (note that code \040 stands for the space in the PDF source)

and B have a very good knowledge of the LaTeX language, subject B is an intermediate user, while subject D is a beginner. Some information about the participants are summarized in Table 1.

All the participants tested some PDF documents produced by using our package. All of them have been able to read correctly the formulae inside the document; indeed, they observed that, when a formula is encountered, the screen reader reads the corresponding LaTeX commands. They also noticed that in the

Table 1. Participants to the evaluation

Subject	Screen reader	Braille display	LaTeX user
A	NVDA	Yes	Expert
B	JAWS	Yes	Expert
C	NVDA	No	Intermediate
D	JAWS	No	Beginner

PDF document the formula is not marked by dollars (or by the used environment) as in a LaTeX document. Participants A and B reported that in the braille display delivers what the screen reader reads. The heading levels are still lacking in the PDF documents.

The PDF documents have been accessed by Acrobat Reader DC, since it is the most used PDF viewer and it is well integrated with screen readers. If different PDF viewers are used, it is possible that the formulae are not read correctly.

Participants B and D also tested the JAWS dictionary that we have realized. They have been able to read correctly the formulae, with the difference that in this case they are read in natural language. Participant B reported that in the braille display it is still written the corresponding LaTeX commands of the formulae.

Finally, participants A and B successfully used the package for generating themselves an accessible PDF document containing formulae.

4 Conclusion

We have developed a LaTeX package that automatically generates comments to formulae when the PDF document is produced by LaTeX. The comments are hidden in the PDF document and they contain the LaTeX commands that generate the formulae. In this way, an accessible PDF document containing formulae is generated. Indeed, screen readers are able to access the comment when processing a formula and reading it. Moreover, we have created a JAWS dictionary that provides the reading in the natural language in the case that the user does not know the LaTeX commands.

As future work, we intend to release the package axessibility.sty on the official CTAN repository. In the final version of the package, we will add all the environments used for inserting formulae (for instance, in the current version of the package, the environment 'align' is not managed). Another issue, which we would like to address, concerns the heading levels. Currently a PDF file produced by LaTeX does not contain heading levels (and the existing packages, like accessibility.sty, do not fix this problem). Finally, we aim at developing a LaTeX package that produces PDF/UA documents.

Acknowledgements. The authors wish to thank the bank foundation 'Fondazione Cassa di Risparmio di Torino', LeoClub (Biella, Italy), and the several volunteers with visual impairment who provided their fundamental contribution.

References

1. Archambault, D., Stoger, B., Fitzpatrick, D., Miesenberger, K.: Access to scientific content by visually impaired people. Upgrade **8**(2), 14 (2007)
2. Armano, T., Capietto, A., Illengo, M., Murru, N., Rossini, R.: An overview on ICT for the accessibility of scientific texts by visually impaired students. In: Proceedings Conference SIREM-SIE-L 2014, pp. 119–122, Perugia, Italy (2014)
3. Batusic, M., Miesenberger, K., Stoger, B.: LaBraDoor, a contribution to making mathematics accessible for the blind. In: Proceedings of 6th International Conference on Computers Helping People with Special Needs, ICCHP 1998, Oldenbourg, Wien, Munchen (1998)
4. Bernareggi, C., Archambault, D.: Mathematics on the web: emerging opportunities for visually impaired people. In: Proceeding W4A 2007 Proceedings of the 2007 International Cross-Disciplinary Conference on Web Accessibility (W4A), Banff, Canada, pp. 108–111 (2007)
5. Bernareggi, C.: Non-sequential mathematical notations in the LAMBDA System. In: Miesenberger, K., Klaus, J., Zagler, W., Karshmer, A. (eds.) ICCHP 2010. LNCS, vol. 6180, pp. 389–395. Springer, Heidelberg (2010). https://doi.org/10.1007/978-3-642-14100-3_58
6. Moore, R.: Ongoing efforts to generate tagged PDF using pdfTEX. TUGboat **30**, 170–175 (2009)
7. Moore, R.: PDF/A-3u as an archival format for accessible mathematics. In: Watt, S.M., Davenport, J.H., Sexton, A.P., Sojka, P., Urban, J. (eds.) CICM 2014. LNCS (LNAI), vol. 8543, pp. 184–199. Springer, Cham (2014). https://doi.org/10.1007/978-3-319-08434-3_14
8. Papasalouros, A., Tsolomitis, A.: A direct TeX-to-Braille transcribing method. J. Sci. Educ. Stud. Disabil. **20**, Article ID 5 (2017)
9. Pepino, A., Freda, C., Ferraro, F., Pagliara, S., Zanfardino, F.: "BlindMath" a new scientific editor for blind students. In: Miesenberger, K., Klaus, J., Zagler, W.L., Karshmer, A.I. (eds.) ICCHP 2006. LNCS, vol. 4061, pp. 1171–1174. Springer, Heidelberg (2006). https://doi.org/10.1007/11788713_169
10. Soiffer, N.: MathPlayer: web-based math accessibility. In: Assets 2005 Proceedings of the 7th International ACM SIGACCESS Conference on Computers and Accessibility, New York, USA, pp. 204–205 (2005)
11. Uebelbacher, A., Bianchetti, R., Riesch, M.: PDF accessibility checker (PAC 2): the first tool to test PDF documents for PDF/UA compliance. In: Miesenberger, K., Fels, D., Archambault, D., Peñáz, P., Zagler, W. (eds.) ICCHP 2014. LNCS, vol. 8547, pp. 197–201. Springer, Cham (2014). https://doi.org/10.1007/978-3-319-08596-8_31

An Accessible Interaction Model for Data Visualisation in Statistics

A. Jonathan R. Godfrey[1], Paul Murrell[2], and Volker Sorge[3(✉)]

[1] Massey University, Auckland, New Zealand
A.J.Godfrey@massey.ac.nz
[2] University of Auckland, Auckland, New Zealand
paul@stat.auckland.ac.nz
[3] University of Birmingham, Birmingham, UK
V.Sorge@cs.bham.ac.uk

Abstract. Data is everywhere and its communication and understanding is an important pre-requisite for the full participation of individuals in the information age. Good data visualisation is commonly used to great effect for the sighted world, but are practically useless to a blind audience. Blind people are at risk of being left behind if efforts are not made to improve the access to information that is not traditionally conveyed in text, whether that text be accessed in braille, audio, or a computer's screen reading software. Our work aims to provide an accessible way for blind users to easily, efficiently, and most importantly accurately, explore and query the data contained in diagrams such as bar charts, box plots, time series, and many more. We employ the statistical software environment R not only as a means to generate accessible diagrams, but also as a way for blind users to directly interact with data in the same way as their sighted peers by supporting immediate data visualisation via screen reading and interactive exploration.

1 Introduction

It has been argued in [8] that blind people need to become producers of graphics, not just consumers of the information in those graphics if they are to have the same opportunities and outcomes in education and employment as their sighted peers take for granted. If blind people are to have employment prospects similar to those of their sighted peers, they must have confidence producing graphs independently, effectively, and efficiently. They must know that graphs produced for an audience look like the graphs that their audience expects to see.

This is particularly true in areas where working with graphics is an integral part of everyday tasks. Data is ubiquitous in many disciplines and its manipulation and effective communication via visualisation are vital for understanding connections and reaching informed conclusions. Consequently handling data and using statistical tools are ever more prevalent in job descriptions in sectors like finance, tech, and biotech. Unless efforts are made to improve access to statistical tools and information, blind people are at risk of being excluded from these opportunities entirely.

© Springer International Publishing AG, part of Springer Nature 2018
K. Miesenberger and G. Kouroupetroglou (Eds.): ICCHP 2018, LNCS 10896, pp. 590–597, 2018.
https://doi.org/10.1007/978-3-319-94277-3_92

Attempts to deal with this problem have mostly been aimed at providing a means for the blind person to understand the analyses completed by other people or agencies. Use of human resources to create accessible graphs (cf. [4,6]) are generally slow and expensive. Efforts to make more use of modern computer technology solutions to make scientific diagrams accessible have lead to the use of sonification and haptic feedback for mathematical graphs and charts [1,20] or using audio exploration and highlighting of graphs on touch screens [3]. While sonification can be applied to statistical graphs [16], it generally offers a "different" view of the data not necessarily compatible with that of the sighted co-worker. It has also been argued that there is a need for blind authors to be able to make and modify graphs [2]. A similar argument could be made for approaches using image analysis [12,18] that allow users to read and interact with graphs but give them no means of manipulating them.

The goal of our work is to provide support for a fully accessible workflow to enable blind users to develop statistical models independently in a process of refinement via data manipulation and visualisation. We thereby want to give the blind user exactly the same tools as their sighted peers. We achieve this by combining the R statistical software application [14] with a JavaScript library for screen reading semantically annotated SVG diagrams [17] in a web browser.

2   Statistical Graphics

Broadly speaking, statistical graphics fall into two categories; information is depicted using either areas/regions or points, but in both cases, it is the comparison between areas or points that should convey the salient features within the data being represented to the intended audience in a way that is possible but less efficient or effective in prose. We have initially concentrated on working with a number of particularly important diagrams, that can roughly be divided into two groups.

Discrete Data Graphs. Representatives of this category are for example bar charts and boxplots. Examples for both are given on the left in Fig. 1. As for the majority of examples we present, they are generated from sample data on air quality given in R and can therefore be easily reproduced. Histograms are a common form used to represent the frequency of data points in different categories. Particular types of bar charts include histograms, where data is clustered

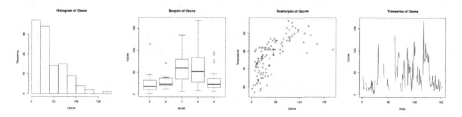

Fig. 1. Discrete and continuous graphs: histogram, boxplot, scatterplot, and time series.

into discrete intervals that are given on the x axis, while the frequency of points in each interval is given along the y axis. Thus a histogram uses area to convey information to represent frequencies as an effective visual medium. Boxplots on the other hand use both areas and points to convey different aspects of the data being represented.

Continuous Data Graphs. Although these graphs and their underlying data are not necessarily continuous in a strictly mathematical sense, they are meant to visually convey information that relies on the continuous interpretation of all data. That is, contrary to the discrete graphs, where, for instance, single bars conveyed interesting information in their own right, in continuous data graphs the visual representation of single data points is meaningless without considering their relationship to some or all other data points in the graph. Therefore, we can say that while the data can be discrete, their interpretation has to be continuous. Examples of these kind of diagrams are scatter plots or time series as given in Fig. 1. The data is discrete, in the sense that there is a finite number of data points that are clearly distinct. However, when reading the graph one is not concerned with the single points and their value, but rather with the curve represented by the overall arrangement of the points in the two-dimensional grid, as well as with respect to the uniformity distribution data points or clusters they form. Consequently, presenting data point by point to a blind reader would be absolutely useless.

3   Creating Accessible Diagrams

Our goal is to support blind users to work with statistical models, both by manipulating them and visualising data, while perceiving the same information as their sighted peers. While for the model manipulation we have chosen the R statistical software application [14], the visualisation is achieved by producing accessible SVG graphics in a browser.

R is a programming language and software environment for statistical computing that allows the efficient manipulation of statistical data and their visualisation offering a host of different diagrams and rendering options. As R is commonly used by working statisticians, both in academia and industry, integrating the ability to generate accessible graphics directly should decrease the hurdle for adoption. R has multiple graphics systems [10]; we use the grid system together with the *gridSVG* package [11] as output device, as it provides sufficiently detailed hierarchical structures in the SVG to support the type of interactive navigation that we aim to achieve.

This navigation relies on annotating the SVG with an XML structure that effectively describes the semantic components of a diagram in hierarchical graph structure. We use the *BrailleR* [7] package—an R add-on specifically targeted at blind users—to extract detailed information, such as data ranges, grammatical constructs, etc. to generate speech strings that are embedded into the XML annotation. This structure is then used by a JavaScript library called DIAGcess [17], which enables the interactive exploration of the SVG diagrams in any browser, with screen reading, synchronised highlighting and magnification.

4   Interaction Model for Data Exploration

The typical workflow for a working statistician in a statistical software environment like R is a recurring process of model refinement which consists of repeated data generation and manipulation, data inspection and visualisation, which in turn leads to an adaptation of the data and modification of the current statistical model. To adequately support this workflow for blind people we have to interlink the work in the statistical computation package with a means for interactive data inspection. Interactive work in R can be conducted in a number of environments, such as (1) directly in a terminal shell, (2) within a text editor that can support specialist modes for R programming like Emacs, (3) or in a integrated development environment like the dedicated as RStudio [19]. Aside from RStudio, these environments are accessible to blind users either via general screen readers or more dedicated libraries such as BrailleTTY [9] or Emacspeak [15].

Data visualisation in R is directly supported by offering a number of graphics devices to display output, generally in a bitmap format or in vector formats like PDF or SVG. Visualisation can be done directly from within R's working environment, which leads to a new pop up window containing a canvas with the visualisation graph. Unfortunately, this canvas is entirely inaccessible, even for vector based graphics devices. To make data visualisation accessible we generate the SVG diagrams in R together with the XML annotation necessary for *DIAGcess*. As the latter needs JavaScript to run we have decided to displaying visualisations in a browser tab instead of the R canvas. Consequently BrailleR offers a call to generate accessible diagrams, which sends the SVG and XML annotations to the browser. The newly opened browser tab is automatically focused, meaning that the R user can directly start exploring the visualisation. Once the graph has been inspected the user can close the tab shifting focus back to the R environment.

The visualised data can then be explored using a hierarchical navigation model, which breaks down the data exploration over multiple layers of abstraction, starting from a summary of the entire diagram all the way down to the exploration of small details. *DIAGcess* supports this model with a simple arrow key navigation between elements. If an element is composed of multiple children, it can be further explored by using the down arrow key. Left/right arrows then allow the user to move between the children of this layer, drilling further down if possible and so desired, or back up on the more abstract layer using the up arrow key. In each step the components of the diagram under consideration are screen read either with a short or detailed description, depending on the user's preference settings, and the elements that are currently described are also visually emphasised in the SVG using highlighting and magnification.

Our navigation model for statistics diagrams is currently geared towards the types of two dimensional data visualisations that we currently support and is broadly similar for all the diagrams. It can be divided into a common and a plot-specific part, where the latter provides different means of data exploration depending on the type of diagram. We generally work with at least three layers that comprise: (1) top level summary, (2) major component layer, and (3) single

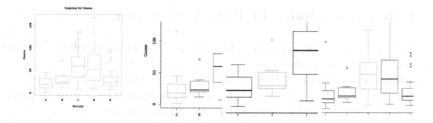

Fig. 2. Step-wise exploration of the Ozone boxplot.

component exploration. The top level summary is the root of our tree and is constituted of the entire diagram. This corresponds to the left-most diagram in Fig. 2. During exploration all diagram components are highlighted in yellow and the accompanying speech string read by the screen reader is then "5 boxplots for Ozone" or in verbose mode "5 boxplots for Ozone for Months 5 to 9".

5   Data Exploration Model

As mentioned the particular navigation model for data exploration depends on the type of data visualisation we work with. Nevertheless the basic structure of the exploration follows the pattern depicted in Fig. 2. First the entire data content is summarily presented. When diving deeper, single data elements can be explored step by step, and if available, the user can delve for additional details. Obviously both descriptions and level of details differ for different visualisation methods, but most importantly, what constitutes a data element differs for discrete or continuous graphs.

Exploration of Discrete Visualisations. Defining elements is a relatively easy task for discrete graphs. We simply take all the discrete elements (e.g., bars, boxplots) to define the navigational layer. Since their visual components are grouped in a single group element in SVG, which we can refer to them directly in our XML annotation structure. The single elements of the graph can then be explored step by step from left to right.

For example, Fig. 2 presents the exploration of three single boxplots for Ozone values over the given months. There are altogether five boxplots, which can be stepped through, with synchronised highlighting and magnification as well as aural descriptions of the form "Boxplot for month 5. Quartiles 1, 11, 18, 32, 45. 1 outlier." or in verbose mode "Boxplot for month 5 for 26 data points. Minimum 1, lower quartile 11, median 18, upper quartile 32 and upper whisker 45. 1 outlier at 115." Note, that there are a wide range of words in common use for some ideas and we aim to provide easy customisation in the future.

For each boxplot the user can dive even deeper into the structures, exploring four different components: medians, estimates of lower and upper quartiles, lower and upper whisker ends, and the presence of outliers. The exploration of the rightmost boxplot of our example would result in (1) "Median 23", (2) "Lower quartile 16 and upper quartile 36", (3) "Minimum 7 and upper whisker 47", and (4) "4 outliers at 96, 78, 73, 91".

Outliers are frequently the most interesting points of a data set as they seem to differ by a substantial amount from the rest of the data. They are often points worthy of investigation in order to understand why they differ and can lead to significant discoveries. Moreover, for very large data sets the number of outliers can be considerably large. We therefore offer one further level of exploration to allow the user to step through the points one by one.

Exploration of Continuous Visualisations. To enable a meaningful exploration in the case of continuous data graphs, some additional processing to fit our navigation model is needed. To be more specific, in order to consider exposing particular properties of graphs we often break up their data into separate components. This is often done quite artificially, but in many instances we can exploit discontinuities to discretise the curve. If these are not available, we have the option of breaking the curve recursively into equally spaced parts, introducing potentially multiple additional layers into the navigation model.

6   Testing and User Feedback

Our testing during development has been done on all major operating systems. Most of the blind people contacted for assistance with evaluation are Windows users who are blind and making use of at least one of JAWS [5] and NVDA [13] screen readers. Our development phase testing has been conducted in a variety of browsers (Chrome, Firefox, Safari, IE11, Edge, Opera, Konqueror), but our evaluators commonly used Firefox, Google Chrome, or Internet Explorer as their default browser. There are known technical limitations with some browsers which cannot render SVG content. Unfortunately, use of older operating systems and associated browsers by some evaluators is a problem to acknowledge. In order to overcome this problem, we suggested use of Firefox so that we could get feedback on the interactive exploration.

We asked a group of 10 power users to test our implementation and in particular the generated statistical diagrams. While many of these users have a good background in mathematics, most had little knowledge of R. All users have offered favourable feedback on the interactive exploration approach we have taken. Three of these users are blind and either are completing or have completed a PhD in statistics or a closely related discipline, while two more blind users are vastly experienced in programming and managing web content; this pair of respondents both knew what they were doing in terms of the interactivity, but did not fully understand the data information conveyed. One of these respondents decided that text strings were too long but failed to navigate them in details with NVDA review mode.

One of the former group of users took the simple code demonstration we offered and extended it beyond our request; he was able to experiment to the point he could replicate some bugs we had already encountered during development. These issues have been rectified and we are confident that once developments are incorporated into the public release versions of packages we depend on, this user's experiments will lead to the desired outcome. We did not direct users towards a particular mode of operating R; there are many ways of doing so and personal preferences ought to show any deficiencies in our work. Our own development phase testing ensured the accessible content could be obtained using R in a variety of modes commonly used by blind users (R in terminal mode and in the R GUI console) and in some modes not commonly used by blind users (from the shell (bash, tcsh), Emacs, and RStudio; all within Ubuntu).

Only one blind student currently engaged in an introductory course was able to give feedback. This was favourable; she was able to understand the graph's content and interactivity. Several novice users felt they would not have sufficient of the material being covered to make any useful contribution. One respondent from this group came forward and noted that she needed to know a lot more about the way the graph looked in a spatial sense before she would understand the information being conveyed by the interactive exploration. Once she was given the instructions that would have suited a student who was either in or had completed an introductory course she positively benefited from the interactivity.

Other feedback included that blind users want information on their refreshable braille displays as well as explore with a variety of feedback mechanisms including sonification of the content. These features are not yet implemented, but provision of braille via a refreshable display is a high priority.

7   Conclusions and Future Work

Our work aims to increase the effectiveness and efficiency of blind people to interact with statistical material. We have placed a great deal of emphasis on the ability to generate the accessible version of statistical graphs with as little extra work as possible being needed by the blind user. The navigation model provides users familiar with the data model a means for inspecting the visualisation without the need for additional hardware or software. Technically at present, the production of accessible statistical diagrams works well for the gridSVG package as it provides sufficiently rich SVG, however the objective is to extend it also to other renderers in R as well as to a host of other statistical graphs.

Development of the presented work benefited from feedback from a number of interested blind users during the development phase. While our initial user studies were aimed at power users and experts, we are currently planning a user study with school children that learn about graphs like histograms and boxplots. This should not only allow us to obtain more statistically relevant feedback but also give us an idea how adequate the textual descriptions of the diagrams are for early learners. Currently, they have been provided by experts for experts, which might not necessarily be the correct level for school children. Nevertheless, our evaluation to date shows that the interaction we offer does help blind people who understand the content, while there is still demand for additional information like Braille feedback and sonification. But despite these limitations we believe the work is a significant step towards providing blind people with greater access to statistical diagrams and we feel it goes some considerable way to enabling both students and professionals greater possibilities to equally participate in education and employment.

References

1. Brown, L., Brewster, S., Ramloll, S., Burton, R., Riedel, B.: Design guidelines for audio presentation of graphs and tables. In: Proceedings on Auditory Display (2003)
2. Calder, M., Cohen, R., Lanzoni, J., Xu, Y.: PLUMB: an interface for users who are blind to display, create and modify graphs. In: ASSETS 2006, pp. 263–264 (2006)
3. Cohen, R., Meacham, A., Skaff, J.: Teaching graphs to visually impaired students using an active auditory interface. ACM SIGCSE Bull. **38**(1), 279–282 (2006)
4. Ferres, L., Verkhogliad, P., Lindgaard, G., Boucher, L., Chretien, A., Lachance, M.: Improving accessibility to statistical graphs: the iGraph-Lite system. In: ASSETS 2007, pp. 67–74 (2007)
5. Freedom Scientific: JAWS Version 18. St. Petersburg, FL (2016)
6. Gardner, J., Bulatov, V.: Making scientific graphics accessible with ViewPlus IVEO. In: Proceedings of the 2008 International Conference on Technology and Persons with Disabilities (2008)
7. Godfrey, A.J.R.: BrailleR: Improved Access for Blind Users. Massey University (2016). R package version 0.24.2
8. Godfrey, A.J.R., Loots, M.T.: Advice from blind teachers on how to teach statistics to blind students. J. Stat. Educ. **23**(3), 1–28 (2015)
9. Mielke, D., Pitre, N., Doyon, S.: BRLTTY. http://mielke.cc/brltty/
10. Murrell, P.: R Graphics. The R Series. Chapman & Hall/CRC Press, Boca Raton (2011)
11. Murrell, P., Potter, S.: The gridSVG package. R J. **6**(1), 133–143 (2014)
12. Nazemi, A., Murray, I.: A method to provide accessibility for visual components to vision impaired. Int. J. HCI **4**(1), 54 (2013)
13. NVDA Team. NVDA Version 2017.1 (2017)
14. R Core Team. R: A Language and Environment for Statistical Computing. R Foundation for Statistical Computing, Vienna, Austria (2017)
15. TV Raman. Emacspeak. http://emacspeak.sourceforge.net
16. Siegert, S., Williams, R.: sonify: Data Sonification - Turning Data into Sound (2017). R package version 0.0-1
17. Sorge, V.: Polyfilling accessible chemistry diagrams. In: Miesenberger, K., Bühler, C., Penaz, P. (eds.) ICCHP 2016. LNCS, vol. 9758, pp. 43–50. Springer, Cham (2016). https://doi.org/10.1007/978-3-319-41264-1_6
18. Sorge, V., Lee, M., Wilkinson, S.: End-to-end solution for accessible chemical diagrams. In: Proceedings of the 12th W4A Conference, pp. 6:1–6:10. ACM (2015)
19. RStudio Team. Rstudio: integrated development for R. RStudio Inc., Boston (2015). http://www.rstudio.com
20. Yu, W., Kangas, K., Brewster, S: Web-based haptic applications for blind people to create virtual graphs. In: Proceedings of HAPTICS 2003, pp. 318–325. IEEE (2003)

UML4ALL Syntax – A Textual Notation for UML Diagrams

Claudia Loitsch[1(✉)], Karin Müller[1], Stephan Seifermann[2],
Jörg Henß[2], Sebastian Krach[2], Gerhard Jaworek[1],
and Rainer Stiefelhagen[1]

[1] Karlsruhe Institute of Technology, Karlsruhe, Germany
Claudia.loitsch@kit.edu
[2] FZI Research Center for Information Technology, Karlsruhe, Germany

Abstract. UML-based software modelling addresses the needs of sighted people but creates barriers for visually impaired people. Textual representations are a general premise to make modelling languages accessible for people with blindness, but their degree of accessibility differs. This paper presents the UML4ALL syntax designed to address the sequential way of working of blind people using screen reader technology. The proposed UML notation comprises four principles introduced in this paper. An evaluation with sighted and visually impaired people showed that the UML4ALL syntax has a good usability for both target groups.

Keywords: UML · Textual notation · Accessibility · Disability
UML4ALL

1 Introduction

The Unified Modeling Language (UML) is widely recognized and an integral part of computer science and software development. UML facilitates describing the structure and the behaviour of software by means of visual diagrams. Structure diagrams represent static elements of a software system and include – for instance – class, component or package diagrams. In higher education, class diagrams are used frequently [8]. Behaviour diagrams such as activity diagrams or use case diagrams illustrate the functionality of a system from different perspectives. Behaviour diagrams are more commonly applied in practise to provide a simple and graphical representation what the system is supposed to do. Figure 1 shows a class diagram with four classes (i.e. Zookeeper, Zoo, Animal, Giraffe and Zebra) where the class Animal has the attribute name of type String. Giraffe and Zebra are specialized animals. This generalisation is represented by the "is a" relation illustrated by a closed, not filled arrow. Unidirectional associations between classes are illustrated by an open arrow with a label indicating the meaning of a relation. Structure diagrams are primarily used for documenting a software architecture and the domain model.

The example shown in Fig. 1 is simple compared to the complexity of the UML specification [10]. However, it illustrates how visual UML modelling can support discussing requirements of software with business analysts or customers, sketching

© Springer International Publishing AG, part of Springer Nature 2018
K. Miesenberger and G. Kouroupetroglou (Eds.): ICCHP 2018, LNCS 10896, pp. 598–605, 2018.
https://doi.org/10.1007/978-3-319-94277-3_93

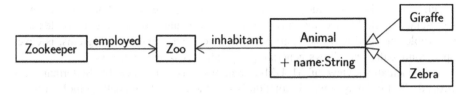

Fig. 1. Example of a UML class diagram. Rectangles represent classes and lines relations.

behaviour of systems as well as documenting aspects of the software. Such graphical software-development techniques produce barriers for visually impaired people. Blind computer scientists cannot access UML diagrams created solely in visual representations by themselves. Additional effort is necessary to translate UML diagrams into an accessible representation to enable an inclusive working environment within so-called diversity teams consisting of people with different abilities, for instance in seeing.

State of the technological development of making UML accessible for blind people comprises verbose verbal descriptions, tactile print outs, table-based formats [4, 8], hierarchical tree structure [4, 6] haptic 3D representations [2] or audio-haptic representations. Providing verbal descriptions or producing tactile print outs is time-consuming, requires expert knowledge to apply guidelines (e.g. to simplify the complexity [15]) and is mostly done as an afterthought, which makes collaborations in software development more difficult. However, providing tactile representations of UML is necessary for learning the (visual) concepts of UML [11].

Specific audio-haptic representations that allow an accessible ad hoc presentation as well as interaction were also developed. Those approaches enable blind people to access UML diagrams without additional effort to translate the visual representation into an accessible format manually. However, the workload when exploring large diagrams on tactile displays is high [7]. We assume that using textual notations of UML diagrams is a more efficient method for blind developers to create and edit UML diagrams. As we will show in Sect. 2, a multitude of textual notations are available. Some of them were developed for usability aspects, others to make UML more accessible. However, the accessibility and usability of such notations are rarely in the focus of research. More specifically, many of the available existing textual UML notations are not optimal for blind people who use screen reader technologies. Correspondingly, we present the UML4ALL syntax designed to accommodate the needs and preferences of blind people.

The remainder of this paper is structured as follows: Sect. 2 describes existing textual representations of UML. Section 3 introduces the proposed UML4ALL syntax. Section 4 presents the evaluation of the proposed textual UML representation. Finally, the paper is concluded in Sect. 5.

2 Previous Work

A multitude of textual UML notations have been designed for different purposes. One can distinguish between UML notations which focus either on quickly generating visual UML graphs or on supporting programming [13]. Textual representations targeting to make UML modelling accessible for people with blindness are under-represented [12]. Most commonly known in the context of making UML textually accessible for blind users is PlantUML[1]. It covers many types of diagrams, is developed continually and allows generating a graphic by a blind person.

A systematic review of 31 UML notations was performed by Seifermann and Groenda [13] to analyze which notation is suitable for UML modelling tools allowing creating, editing and exporting UML diagrams both graphically and textually. The results of this survey show, UML notations provide very different means to edit diagrams, have very different UML coverage and focus predominantly on generating a visual graph for documentation purposes.

How well textual UML notations (i.e. yUML, PlantUML, Umple, Earl Grey) are suited to accommodate blind people and their individual way of working was further investigated by Petrausch et al. [12]. The notations were analysed to assess their accessibility, easy comprehensibility and technical feasibility. Among others, they investigated whether associations shall be represented as textual imitations of graphical elements such as lines and arrows (e.g. - >), verbose textual descriptions (e.g. association class 1, class 2) or if specific element types (e.g. class, attributes, visibility) shall be represented in separated blocks or in compact notations.

Petrausch et al. further developed guidelines for accessible textual UML notations [12]. In summary, the guidelines cover five topics: (1) usability of the textual notation, (2) accessibility support for visually impaired, (3) language realization, (4) concrete syntax and (5) functional interaction between notation and tools. They emphasized, creating a language which is easy to learn and intuitive to use by blind persons must be consistent and consider their specific way of working. Currently, there is no UML notation available supporting the specific way of working of blind people using screen reader technology. Because of this, we created the UML4ALL syntax presented subsequently.

3   UML4ALL Syntax

The UML4ALL syntax[2] was developed within the Cooperate project[3], which aims at facilitating UML-based software development in a cooperative and collaborative manner between people with and without visual impairments [9]. This is realized by supplying a bidirectional generation of textual and graphical representations of UML diagrams by following a model-based approach [14].

For the textual representation, we developed the UML4ALL syntax by following the guidelines mentioned in the previous section. The usability aspect emphasized in [12] was integrated always having in mind that the language should be usable for people with visual impairment. In Sect. 4, we present the evaluation of the developed UML notation with respect to usability criteria.

---

[1] Web page of the PlantUML project: http://plantuml.com/.

[2] Web page of the UML4ALL-Syntax: http://www.uml4all.net/en/index.html.

[3] Web page of the Cooperate project: https://www.cooperate-project.de/index.php/en/.

The UML4ALL syntax supports the way of working of screen reader users, reading content line-by-line with a screen reader by text-to-speech or Braille. The sequential principle is a crucial design choice of the UML4ALL syntax and involves mentioning most important or general information first followed by more specific details. Providing a consistent and clear syntax structure is just as much important to facilitate blind people in understanding the semantics of UML elements as well as finding specific information such as roles or cardinalities.

Aforesaid design considerations are realized by four basic concepts described in the subsequent paragraphs: unique identification of diagram types, usage of meaningful keywords, clear and consistent structure within each diagram and a prefix-like notation of elements. The subsequent listing shows the UML4ALL syntax notation of the example class diagram "Zoo" introduced in the beginning of this paper:

```
1  @start-clsd "Zoo"
2  class Animal {
3    public name : string
4  }
5  class Giraffe
6  class Zebra
7  class Zoo
8  class Zookeeper {
9    feed (animal : Animal)
10 }
11 isa (Giraffe, Animal)
12 isa (Zebra, Animal)
13 asc employed (Zookeeper, Zoo) card [1..* : 1..1]
14 asc inhabitant (Animal, Zoo) card [0..100 : 1..1]
15 @end-clsd
```

3.1   Unique Identification of Diagram Types

Facilitating sequential reading of UML diagrams makes it necessary to provide textual information to allow blind users identifying certain concepts easily, for instance by using a unique title. As a result, all diagrams start and end with a tag including a unique identifier of the diagram type followed by a title. For instance, the identifier "clsd" represents class diagrams, "uscd" stands for use case diagram or "seqd" is used for sequence diagrams. After the start tag, a diagram title is given in quotation marks. In the example above, the start and the end tag of the class diagram "Zoo" is shown in lines 1 and 15 respectively. This helps screen reader users to quickly identify the type of UML diagram presented. This is not supported by many other textual UML notations such as PlantUML.

3.2   Usage of Meaningful Keywords

In the UML4ALL syntax, we use human-readable keywords to represent all UML elements. We omit all textual imitations of graphical structures (e.g. arrows) and use a concise vocabulary of words to improve learnability and retentiveness. As the code gets quite verbose if we use whole words such as association, we used easy to learn abbreviations for key words such as "asc" for association or "ext" for extension. If possible, we use terms known from programming languages such as "class" to indicate a UML class (line 2) or "public" to specify the visibility of an element (line 3). For other elements (e.g. associations), we define human-readable keywords such as "isa" to define a generalization relation (line 11), or asc for an association (line 13). A complete list of keywords used in each diagram can be obtained from the UML4All web page[4].

3.3   Clear and Consistent Structure Within Each Diagram

Each diagram follows a clear structure to ensure that screen reader users can quickly find required information. As shown in (line 2 to 10), a diagram represented in UML4ALL syntax first describes the objects used in a diagram including their specifications such as attributes or methods. Thereafter, relations between objects are defined (line 11 to 14). Encapsulated objects must again adhere to this structure.

3.4   Prefix-like Notation of Elements

A distinctive characteristic of the UML4ALL syntax is the prefix-like notation. Correspondingly, for UML elements (i.e. relations) the operators precede the operands. Although this notation does not follow a natural language, it supports screen reader users because the most important piece of information (i.e. type of UML element) is presented first. As shown the example above (line 14), an association is introduced with the operator/keyword "asc" followed by a name "inhabitant" describing the association further, followed by the involved classes "Animal" and "Zoo" – both representing the operands. Additional information such as roles or cardinalities are attached to the end of an element and follow again the prefix-like notation.

4   Evaluation

We evaluated the UML4ALL syntax in an online questionnaire to assess the usability. The questionnaire was organized in four parts:

1. Participants were asked general questions about the ability to see, age, profession and experiences with UML in general and with textual UML notations.
2. Participants were asked to familiarize with the UML4ALL syntax by reading a tutorial online.

---

4 Keywords of the UML4ALL-Syntax listed: http://www.uml4all.net/en/tables.html.

3. Participants were requested to answer five UML modelling questions. All UML examples used were presented in UML4ALL syntax. Each modelling question targeted a specific concept of the UML4ALL syntax.
4. In the fourth part, participants had to assess the usability of the UML4ALL syntax. We used the system usability scale (SUS) which collects a subjective assessment of usability on a ten-item Likert scale [5].

We evaluated the syntax for class and use case diagrams. However, the diagram type assessed by a participant was randomized to reduce the effort necessary to familiarize with the UML4ALL syntax and the questionnaire at all.

4.1 Participants

In total, 14 participants completed the online questionnaire. There were two conditions. Half of the participants had no visual impairment and the other half was visually impaired (six blind people and one person was severely visually impaired). Table 1 shows the distribution of participants with respect to their age and profession. The participants were not familiar with the UML4ALL syntax.

Table 1. Age groups and profession of participants.

Profession	Age groups			
	18–19	30–45	46–60	60+
Student	3			
Researcher	1	4		
Software developer		4	1	1

4.2 Results

Overall, the average SUS score for both conditions is high (M = 75, SD = 12.58). Based on Bangor et al. [1], this result indicates a good usability of the UML4ALL syntax. Moreover, the standard deviation is acceptable and the data relatively close to the mean. An independent-samples t-test was performed to compare average SUS score for sighted and visually impaired condition. There was no significant difference in the SUS scores for sighted participants (M = 72.6, SD = 12.58) and visually impaired participants (M = 74.27, SD = 14.24); t(12) = 0.22, p = 2.18. These results suggest that the UML4ALL syntax works equally good for sighted as well as visually impaired people.

4.3 Discussion

The methodology we used for the evaluation was rather difficult because users must familiarize with the UML4ALL syntax by reading a tutorial and afterwards, they were directly required to perform five modelling tasks. Nevertheless, the overall results from the evaluation are positive und show a good usability. We expect, a longer training phase with the UML4ALL syntax and a more practical task would further improve the results.

The questionnaire SUS allows only to indicate a usability tendency. Individual items cannot be interpreted by applying the SUS [5]. Moreover, we cannot derive specific usability problems accompanied with the UML4ALL syntax from the results. Evaluating specific usability problems would require a real end-user test and observations by test facilitators. This was not the objective of the presented test.

Textual UML notations are a promising way for making UML diagrams accessible. However, exploring complex diagrams linear (line-by-line) in a textual manner is a demanding task and requires high mental workload [7]. With the UML4ALL syntax we do not attempt to solve this problem. The UML4ALL syntax is designed to support the way of working of screen reader users. With the UML4ALL syntax we created the foundation for representing graphical UML diagrams in a textual manner that is usable by visually as well as sighted people. The results support this aspect because we received compatible SUS scores for both conditions.

In the Cooperate project, the UML4ALL syntax is used as an integrated textual editor of the Eclipse IDE. The editor supports common editor capabilities such as auto-completion, quick fixes, or presenting the UML diagram as a hierarchical tree in the outline view. It can be expected; so-called tooling will improve the efficiency and subjective satisfaction when working with the UML4All syntax.

5 Conclusion

Conventional software developing based on text-based source code is accessible for blind people who use screen readers and Braille displays. However, graphical technologies such as UML-based software modelling create barriers for visually impaired people and hinder them participating in cooperative work activities within diversity teams. The UML4ALL syntax presented herein supports modelling UML text-based for both sighted and visually impaired people. Together with bi-directional editing capabilities and tooling developed in the Cooperate project, UML4ALL demonstrates how work processes can be designed more inclusively to support individual abilities by avoiding the need for manually translating visual documents into accessible formats in a posterior process. Future work can apply the concept developed for UML to other graphs used in common applications, for instance PowerPoint.

References

1. Bangor, A., Kortum, P., Miller, J.: Determining what individual SUS scores mean: adding an adjective rating scale. J. Usability Stud. **4**(3), 114–123 (2009)
2. Doherty, B., Cheng, B.H.C.: UML modeling for visually-impaired persons. In: HuFaMo@MoDELS (2015)
3. Groenda, H., Seifermann, S., Müller, K., Jaworek, G.: The cooperate assistive teamwork environment for software description languages. Stud. Health Technol. Inf. **217**, 111–118 (2015)
4. Horstmann, M., Lorenz, M., Watkowski, A., Ioannidis, G., Herzog, O., King, A., Evans, D. G., Hagen, C., Schlieder, C., Burn, A.M., King, N., Petrie, H., Dijkstra, S., Crombie, D.: Automated interpretation and accessible presentation of technical diagrams for blind people. New Rev. Hypermedia Multimedia **10**(2), 141–163 (2004). https://doi.org/10.1080/13614560412331326017

5. Brooke, J.: SUS: a retrospective. J. Usability Stud. **8**(2), 29–40 (2013)
6. King, A., Blenkhorn, P., Crombie, D., Dijkstra, S., Evans, G., Wood, J.: Presenting UML software engineering diagrams to blind people. In: Miesenberger, K., Klaus, J., Zagler, Wolfgang L., Burger, D. (eds.) ICCHP 2004. LNCS, vol. 3118, pp. 522–529. Springer, Heidelberg (2004). https://doi.org/10.1007/978-3-540-27817-7_76
7. Loitsch, C., Weber, G.: Viable haptic UML for blind people. In: Miesenberger, K., Karshmer, A., Penaz, P., Zagler, W. (eds.) ICCHP 2012. LNCS, vol. 7383, pp. 509–516. Springer, Heidelberg (2012). https://doi.org/10.1007/978-3-642-31534-3_75
8. Müller, K.: How to make unified modeling language diagrams accessible for blind students. In: Miesenberger, K., Karshmer, A., Penaz, P., Zagler, W. (eds.) ICCHP 2012. LNCS, vol. 7382, pp. 186–190. Springer, Heidelberg (2012). https://doi.org/10.1007/978-3-642-31522-0_27
9. Müller, K., Petrausch, V., Jaworek, G., Henß, J., Seifermann, S., Loitsch, C., Stiefelhagen, R.: UML4ALL: gemeinsam in diversity teams software modellieren. Informatik-Spektrum **40**(6), 562–572 (2017). https://doi.org/10.1007/s00287-017-1073-y. (in German)
10. Object Management Group (OMG): Unified Modeling Language™ Version 2.5 (2015)
11. Petrausch, V., Jaworek, G., Müller, K.: Inklusives lehrmaterial für die unified modeling language (UML). In: Perspektiven im Dialog: XXXVI. Kongress für Blinden - und Sehbehindertenpädagogik. Edition Bentheim, Graz (2016). (in German)
12. Petrausch, V., Seifermann, S., Müller, K.: Guidelines for accessible textual UML modeling notations. In: Miesenberger, K., Bühler, C., Penaz, P. (eds.) ICCHP 2016. LNCS, vol. 9758, pp. 67–74. Springer, Cham (2016). https://doi.org/10.1007/978-3-319-41264-1_9
13. Seifermann, S., Groenda, H.: Survey on the applicability of textual notations for the unified modeling language. In: Hammoudi, S., Pires, L.F., Selic, B., Desfray, P. (eds.) MODELSWARD 2016. CCIS, vol. 692, pp. 3–24. Springer, Cham (2017). https://doi.org/10.1007/978-3-319-66302-9_1
14. Seifermann, S., Henß, J.: Comparison of QVT-O and henshin-TGG for synchronization of concrete syntax models. In: Eramo, R., Johnson, M. (eds.) Proceedings of the 6th International Workshop on Bidirectional Transformations (Bx 2017), CEUR Workshop Proceedings, vol. 1827, pp. 6–14. CEUR-WS.org (2017)
15. The Braille Authority of North America: Guidelines and Standards for Tactile Graphics (2011). http://www.brailleauthority.org/tg/web-manual/index.html

Localization Scheme of Assistive Tools for Print-Disabled People to Access STEM Contents

Katsuhito Yamaguchi[1(✉)] and Masakazu Suzuki[2]

[1] Junior College Funabashi Campus, Nihon University,
7-24-1 Narashinodai, Funabashi, Chiba 274-8501, Japan
eugene@gaea.jcn.nihon-u.ac.jp
[2] Institute of Mathematics for Industry, Kyushu University,
744, Motooka, Nishi-Ku, Fukuoka 819-0395, Japan
msuzuki@kyudai.jp

Abstract. To facilitate the spread of accessible e-books, especially books in STEM much more in developing countries, an efficient/ systematic scheme to localize producing/reading tools should be established. Here, multilingual support in our tool to produce accessible STEM contents and problems in localizing it are discussed. Our new localization scheme and the localization for Vietnamese as a model case are shown.

Keywords: DAISY · STEM · Localization · Print-disabilities
Developing country

1 Introduction

It is said that 90% of visually disabled people live in the developing countries. Recently, accessible e-books are becoming gradually available even in those countries. For instance, "the Accessible Books Consortium (ABC)" provides training and technical assistance in developing countries such as India, Bangladesh, Nepal and Sri Lanka since 2015 in the production and distribution of books in accessible formats [1].

As is well known, in Western countries, "DAISY (Digital Accessible Information System)" [2] (or accessible EPUB3 that is essentially DAISY4) has already held the position of the international standard for accessible e-books. Many excellent tools to produce and to read DAISY/accessible EPUB3 books are available. Certainly, DAISY is also a key technology in the activities for developing countries mentioned above. However, to facilitate the spread of accessible books much more in such countries, even now, we have several problems. For instance, a text-to-speech (TTS) engine for their local language is usually not available or of low quality. It is rather hard to produce accessible books in text DAISY or multimedia DAISY (DAISY3 or accessible EPUB3) with TTS technology.

In those countries, it is particularly difficult for print-disabled people to obtain accessible e-books in STEM (science, technology, engineering and math).

© The Author(s) 2018
K. Miesenberger and G. Kouroupetroglou (Eds.): ICCHP 2018, LNCS 10896, pp. 606–610, 2018.
https://doi.org/10.1007/978-3-319-94277-3_94

Recently, our group, NPO: "Science Accessibility Net (sAccessNet)" [3] has been working on developing tools to produce accessible STEM contents for developing countries by localizing our software. In this paper, the current situation of STEM accessibility is briefly reviewed. Next, multilingual support in our tool to produce/read multimedia-DAISY STEM books and problems in localizing such tool are discussed. Finally, our new localization scheme and a model case of the localization are shown.

2 STEM Accessibility

For the past more-than-20 years, various computerized approaches have been tried to improve STEM accessibility. In 1994, T. V. Raman reported on his "Audio System for Technical Readings" which could read out math documents in LaTeX format with DEC Talk synthesizer. It might be the very first trial in this field [5]. While LaTeX plays an important role in STEM accessibility even now, recently, MathML has become a key technology in assistive tools for print-disabled people to access STEM. For instance, DAISY has adopted MathML to represent math contents [2].

For about 20 years, sAccessNet and our research group, "Infty Project," [4] have been also developing assistive tools for print-disabled people to access STEM contents. "ChattyInfty" [3,4] is an accessible math-document editor with a TTS voice. Using it, print-disabled people not only can read but also author a STEM document easily for themselves in an intuitive manner. It can help them with both accessing and doing math. It uses Microsoft Speech API, Ver.5 (SAPI5) as a TTS engine.

The current version, "ChattyInfty3" can be used as an authoring tool for accessible STEM books since the edited result can be saved as a multimedia DAISY/accessible EPUB3 book. Combining ChattyInfty3 with our OCR software for STEM documents "InftyReader" [3,4,6], users can convert a STEM document quite efficiently into multimedia DAISY/accessible EPUB3.

3 Multilingual Support in ChattyInfty

We have been releasing the Japanese and English versions of ChattyInfty since the very beginning of it. To release both the English and the Japanese versions efficiently/systematically, in ChattyInfty, not only tables to assign aloud reading math symbols/formulas but also captions in menu items and dialogs are all stored in an independent file on a main program. Thus, in principle, we could customize ChattyInfty3 for each local language. We have actually developed its French, Italian, Czech and Turkish (trial) versions during the last four years.

In 2016, a research group in India inquired of us if a Hindustani version of ChattyInfty could be developed. We thoroughly examined the possibility. Unfortunately, however, we concluded that it should not be so easy to realize since the character set in Hindustani was quite different from European languages/Japanese. To treat Hindustani, we must reform thoroughly the editor program of ChattyInfty, itself. Thus, this plan is suspended for the present.

4   New Localization Scheme in ChattyInfty

Through the experience of trying to develop the Hindustani version, we concluded that we should give a much better localization scheme for ChattyInfty3. As the first step to realize that, we have recently implemented the following new features in ChattyInfty3.

(1) Unicode can be used on its main window so that users can input a text in their local language if characters are included in Unicode.
(2) The definition file for reading aloud math symbols and formulas, "Read-Setting.txt," is also represented in Unicode so that users can prepare its local-language version.
(3) STEM terminology in menu items can be also replaced with local names. Ordinary menu items such as "File" might be OK even if they were represented in English. In developing countries, users are usually familiar with the menu items in English; however, names of technical symbols and math formulas such as "Square Root" should be represented in their local manner.
(4) Any SAPI5 voices can be selected for speech output.

As a model case of the localization, in cooperation with "Assistive Technology Developing Organization (ATDO)" [7], we have worked on developing the Vietnamese version in 2017 [8]. Vietnamese is represented in alphabet with various (different eight types) accent marks; those characters are all included in Unicode. Using an application named "Unikey," we can input Vietnamese easily with the ordinary keyboard. Vietnamese SAPI5 TTS engines are rather of low quality but available, anyhow. Thus, considering such situations, we have judged the localization should be possible.

In May 2017, ATDO, sAccessNet and a user group in Vietnam held meetings in Hanoi to discuss how we have taken responsibility for completing the mission. The ATDO and Vietnamese members were to undertake the following jobs.

(1) They would translate the English versions of the definition file, ReadSetting.txt and its manual into Vietnamese.
(2) They would list up menu items that should be represented in Vietnamese and give us their local names.
(3) They would also prepare sample STEM documents in Vietnamese to test how the software would work.

In addition to the list mentioned previously, we revised ChattyInfty so that Unikey could be used to input. We would incorporate the Vietnamese version of ReadSetting.txt and the indicated local names of the menu items into the software.

Those jobs were completed by the mid October 2017, and we held workshops at the Hanoi School for the Blind in the end October 2017 to demonstrate how the Vietnamese version of ChattyInfty worked. The participants confirmed that they could write and read various math expressions with Vietnamese speech output. A blind high-school student who participated in the workshop said that he was so happy that he could write any math expressions freely.

However, we willingly admit that our scheme is not useful enough, yet. For the moment, we (the software developer) must execute a build process to incorporate ReadSetting.txt and the local names of the menu items in the software. Furthermore, we cannot check it for ourselves if a local TTS engine works properly. Each TTS engine has its own characteristics, and even if the same definition file for aloud reading were incorporated, actual speech output would be different from each other, depending on a used engine. Unexpected errors in reading could occur due to an inappropriate description in ReadSetting.txt. Thus, in cooperation with a local-user community, we must check speech output for various sample files and do necessary corrections. It requires us to exchange data with the local-user community over and over. It is obviously impossible for us to work on all requested localization for ourselves. Thus, we must give a much more efficient/systematic method to allow each local-user community to do most of necessary jobs just for themselves.

To achieve the objective, we are now developing a build tool for end users to allow themselves to perform the process to incorporate the ReadSetting.txt and the local names of the menu items in the software without any help of the developer. It will be included in the ChattyInfty3 package by the ICCHP2018.

5   Conclusion

When our localization scheme is completed, if the local version of ReadSetting.txt and the local names of the menu items were just prepared, users could customize ChattyInfty easily for themselves so that it could treat STEM contents in their own languages. We believe that our software could contribute to improve accessibility, especially STEM accessibility much more in developing countries.

References

1. ABC. http://www.accessiblebooksconsortium.org/portal/en/
2. The DAISY Consortium. http://www.daisy.org/
3. sAccessNet. http://www.sciaccess.net/en/
4. Infty Project. http://www.inftyproject.org/en/
5. Raman, T.V.: Audio system for technical readings. Dissertation, Cornell University (1994). Springer, Berlin (1998)
6. Suzuki, M., Yamaguchi, K.: Recognition of E-born PDF including mathematical formulas. In: Miesenberger, K., Bühler, C., Penaz, P. (eds.) ICCHP 2016. LNCS, vol. 9758, pp. 35–42. Springer, Cham (2016). https://doi.org/10.1007/978-3-319-41264-1_5

7. ATDO. http://atdo.website/english/
8. Yamaguchi, K., Kanahori, T., Suzuki, M., (Hamada) Makio, M.: Activities to provide accessible STEM E-books for the developing countries. In: The 33rd CSUN Assistive Technology Conference, EDU-058, San Diego (2018)

Improvement of a Tangible Programming Tool for the Study of the Subroutine Concept

Mariko Tsuda[✉], Tatsuo Motoyoshi, Kei Sawai, Takumi Tamamoto,
Hiroyuki Masuta, Ken'ichi Koyanagi, and Toru Oshima

Department of Intelligent Systems Design Engineering,
Toyama Prefectural University, Toyama 939-0398, Japan
t754013@st.pu-toyama.ac.jp

Abstract. We developed a tangible programming education tool "P-CUBE2" to aim at learning benefits of subroutine such as to create a function once and then reuse it. The target user of this tool are visual impairments and inexperienced persons who are not familiar with PC operation. We introduced the function mat, utterance function blocks and HIRAGANA (Japanese character) blocks so that user can learn subroutine concept. Users can create the function of utterance by combining and placing these blocks which on the function mat. The created function of utterance can be called on the main mat. By these operation, the user can control a robot which outputs sound as a controlled object. In this research, we introduce the system configuration of the P-CUBE2 and report the result of experiment for evaluation of the tool operability.

Keywords: Tangible programming tool · Subroutine concept
Visual impairments

1 Introduction

Personal computers (PC) installed programming software are often using in programming education. On the other hand, we developed P-CUBE which is a tangible [1] block type programming education tool [2] that user can learn programming without operating PCs. In addition, research and development such as E-Block [3], material programming [4] and GLICODE [5], which have an easy to use interface have been conducted even for low age groups. The user can learn three learning elements of sequential, conditional branch, and loop using these tool [6]. Since, users cannot learn a concept of "subroutine" using these tool. The subroutines are introduced in the field of actual information education. So, the purpose of this research is to add subroutine as a learning element of P-CUBE, and to confirm whether user can learn the benefits of a subroutine using P-CUBE which added function (hereinafter referred to P-CUBE2) [7]. In order to learn the concept of subroutine, we introduced a robot that outputs sound as a controlled object, and we created P-CUBE2 which can set the conversation contents using utterance function blocks.

K. Miesenberger and G. Kouroupetroglou (Eds.): ICCHP 2018, LNCS 10896, pp. 611–618, 2018.
https://doi.org/10.1007/978-3-319-94277-3_95

2   P-CUBE2

2.1   System Configuration of P-CUBE2

P-CUBE2 consists of two program mats and programming blocks which have
RFID systems. One of the program mat is the function mat which is newly
introduced in P-CUBE2, and another is the main mat. Figure 1 shows a system
configuration of P-CUBE2.

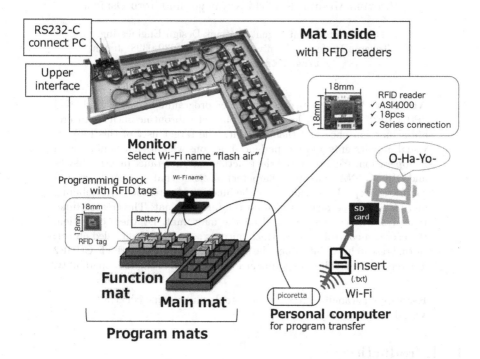

Fig. 1. System configuration of P-CUBE2.

RFID tags is attached to each side of programming block. The RFID reader
"ASI4000IIC" of 18 are installed in the main mat to read the position information
of the programming blocks on the main mat and function mat. The function mat
has 8 separated by wooden frames and the main mat has 10 cells which users can
make a main program. The function block is put on the left end of the function
mat and three hiragana blocks is put on the right side of the function block.
Users can create two functions in the function mat in this system.

2.2   Programming Block

There are four kinds of the programming block. Figure 2 shows each of programming blocks.

(i) **Hiragana Blocks.** The Hiragana block is a block that controls the utterance of the controlled object. The shape of Hiragana block is a wooden cube

chamfering the upper part of it. One hiragana block is assigned one line of characters among 50 letters of Hiragana. Each surface of the hiragana block is assigned to one hiragana pronunciation. For example, the upper surface of the block indicates "KA" sound, and each side surface indicates "KI", "KU", "KE", and "KO".

(ii) Function Blocks. F1 to F4 are set in the function blocks of side as function name. The function block has the same shape of the hiragana block.

(iii) IF Blocks. The IF block is used to branch the utterance contents when the blue switch attached to the top of the controlled object turns ON or OFF. There are two types of IF blocks, "IF START" means the start point of the conditional branch and "IF END" means the end point. The left side of the IF START block to which convex information is given using the EVA sponge indicates the state of which the switch is ON. The right side of the IF START block not using the EVA sponge indicates the state of which the switch is OFF.

(iv) LOOP Block. The LOOP block is same block when P-CUBE system.

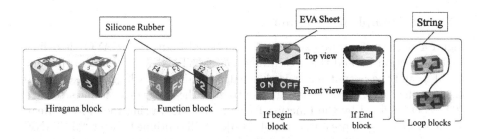

Fig. 2. Programming blocks of P-CUBE2. (Color figure online)

2.3   Controlled Object

Figure 3 shows a controlled object. The arduino Ethernet is built in the controlled object as a microcomputer. Furthermore, speech synthesis "LSI ATP3011F4-PU" which can make text data uttered was built in the arduino. The controlled

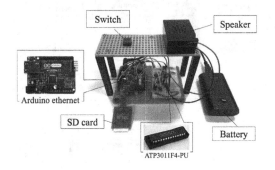

Fig. 3. Controlled object. (Color figure online)

object outputs sound data that words set in the program mat using LSI. The blue switch which is installed at an upper portion of the controlled object can be controlled by the conditional branch block.

2.4 Programming Operation

The programming procedure of P-CUBE2 is as follows.

1. Select a function block
2. Place a function block on the left end of the function mat
3. Select Hiragana blocks
4. Place hiragana blocks on the right side of the function block
5. Make a main program on the main mat using the same type of function block
6. Repeat steps 1 to 5
7. Read and transfer the position information of programming blocks to a controlled object via a PC
8. Execute a program.

2.5 An Example of Program

Figure 4 shows a program example of conditional branch. "OHAYO" is defined for the function F1 and the speech function "MATANE" is defined in the function F2, and the output result is changed depending on whether the switch to be controlled is pressed or not. The output of the program continues to utter "OHAYO" defined by the function F1 while not depressing the switch. Meanwhile, as long as user press it, controlled object will continue to utter "MATANE" defined in function F2. The function block can set a utterance content. For example, a control object can speak "OHAYO" a control object can "O", "HA" and "YO" of Hiragana Blocks on the function mat. "OHAYO" means Good morning and "MATANE" means See you in Japanese. Users can create program of the controlled object only placing programming blocks on the main mat based on program structure.

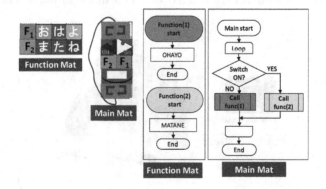

Fig. 4. Example of a conditional branch program.

3 Design of Programming Blocks Related Subroutine Concept

We created utterance function blocks and hiragana blocks as programming blocks. Figure 5 shows utterance function block and the Hiragana block.

3.1 Utterance Function Block

The current function block is represented by a combination of "F" representing Function and a number on the side of the block. The students of first year of secondary education (12–13 old years) learn a number used in mathematical problems called function in Japan [8]. Therefore, we created the function block incorporating object oriented (utterance function block) so as not to confuse program function with mathematical function.

The utterance function block is a block having the same usage method and meaning as the function block explained so far. The shape is a cube and each side has a groove of about 0.16 in. The block of material is white wood (specific gravity 0.45) and the mass is about 1 oz. In order to mean the concept of utterance we add urethane resin that imitated lips of human to the blocks' side. By imitating the feel of the real space object (lip), it is thought that it makes it easier to grasp the meaning (utterance) of the block. We applied Braille representing 1 to 4 to the chamfered portion and convex information by silicon so as to correspond to the four kinds of functions. The groove processing of each side block was applied so as not to impair the fit feeling of the block.

3.2 Hiragana Block

We adopted CUD (color universal design) in the Hiragana block and considered color usage so that information is properly transmitted to those who are different from ordinary in color appearance. The character is black, and the background color where characters overlap is white. By clarifying light and darkness and not superimposing colors, we consider that letter information will be specifically conveyed. The block of shape is hexagonal prism, the material is balsa (specific gravity 0.1), and the mass is about 1/3 oz. The information of the five letter hiragana of the vowel "a" to "o" was given to the side face of the hexagonal prism. The convex information of the arrow is given to the remaining side face to express the character flow.

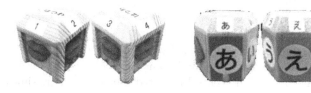

Fig. 5. Utterance function block and hiragana block.

4   Survey on Operability of Blocks

4.1   Programming Workshop Using P-CUBE

We conducted a programming workshop "Let's makes a program to run a mobile robot." for visually impaired children at the event "Jump to science summer camp 2017 [9]." The workshop participants were six high school students and seven junior high school students who have no experience in programing. Seven of them uses braille and the remaining six use extended character point. All participants are engaged only in creating program (placing programming blocks). We know that visually impaired children feel a sense of incompatibility with the block floating when they put the blocks in a wooden frame. In this paper, we define the sense of fitting blocks into wooden frames as "feeling of fit".

4.2   Experimental Overview

In order to evaluate the feeling of fit in each block of the added hiragana block and utterance function block, we carry out some program task and question-naire survey for subjects. In addition, we conduct survey on tool operation as using P-CUBE2 and scratch. The scratch is visual programming language [10]. Subjects were 8 college students who never used programming tools for the pro-gramming beginners. We conduct a questionnaire before the experiment. After that, we explain the specification of each tool and set up time to refer to the prepared manual. Next, we conduct each of the four tasks and a questionnaire to investigate the operational feeling of the tool after completing all the tasks. We compare the operational feeling of both tools by questionnaire. Figure 6 shows examples of program creation of tasks. The output result of the program was audio data.

4.3   Results

Their response to free description type questionnaire answer about operability of each tool is as the following.

P-CUBE2

- I felt that ingenuity was applied to the shape of the mat and the block so that it was easy to fit in the wooden frame.
- The hole size of the mat and the size of the block are just right.
- It was not tight.

Scratch

- I was able to programming by visually assembling blocks.
- It was easy to understand program because it is color-coded for each function.
- I felt inconvenience when even if I adjusted the cursor many times, I was not able to fit icon in the frame.

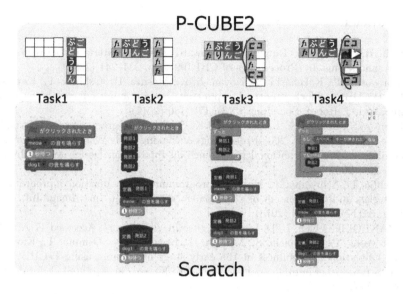

Fig. 6. Example of answer of tasks.

From these results, we consider the discomfort caused by floating the block could be improved. Also, like Scratch, it can be said that there is no inconvenience to fit in the target position such as not being able to fit the cursor. However, there was an opinion that "It is hard to find hiragana". In addition, we also set up questions to select learning elements that can be learned by both tools. Half of subjects selected not only sequential, conditional branch, loop, and subroutine but also variables. It was suggested that variables can also be learned.

5   Discussion and Conclusion

We developed P-CUBE2 which is a tangible block type programming education tool, and is intended to add subroutine as programming concept into
P-CUBE. We introduce the function mat, utterance function blocks and
HIRAGANA blocks to P-CUBE so that user can learn subroutine using
P-CUBE2. In previous studies, P-CUBE2 is suggested a tool that can learn
the concept of subroutines [7]. In this paper, we surveyed on operability of tool
which P-CUBE2 and scratch. In scratch, users were perplexed by the cursor
operation but they were not perplexed by block operation in P-CUBE2. Little
as yet researched about the mechanism of usefulnesses to use tangible programming tool. Therefore, we are working on analysis of tool operation. In the future,
we will continue verifying the learning effect of P-CUBE2.

References

1. Ishii, H., Ullmer, B.: Tangible bits: towards seamless interfaces between people, bits, and atoms. In: Proceedings of CHI 1997, pp. 234–241 (1997)
2. Motoyoshi, T., Kakehashi, S., Koyanagi, K., Masuta, H., Oshima, T., Kawakami, H.: P-CUBE - block type tool supporting programming education for visually impaired. J. Robot. Soc. Jpn. **33**(3), 172–180 (2015)
3. Horn, M.S., Solovey, E.T., Jacob, R.J.K.: Tangible programming for informal science learning. In: IDC 2008 Proceedings of Making TUIs Work for Museums. Proceedings of 7th International Conference on Interaction Design & Children, pp. 194–201 (2008)
4. Hachijo, T., Ashiyama, K.: Materials programming - visualization of programs with materials and development of development environment. Inst. Image Inf. Televis. Eng. **37**(17), 223–226 (2013)
5. EZAKI GLICO CO., LTD. http://cp.glico.jp/glicode/en/. Accessed 17 Apr 2018
6. Motoyoshi, T., Kakehashi, S., Masuta, H., Koyanagi, K., Oshima, T., Kawakami, H.: Validation of usefulness at the early stage of learning using P-CUBE which block type programming tool. J. Jpn. Soc. Fuzzy Theory Intell. Inform. **27**(6), 909–920 (2015)
7. Tsuda, M., Motoyoshi, T., Tetsumura, N., Sawai, K., Tamamoto, T., Masuto, H., Koyanagi, K., Oshima, T.: A tangible programming tool incorporating the concept of functions as a learning element of programming In: The 18th International Symposium on Advanced Intelligent Systems (2017)
8. Middle School Course of Study Guide Mathematics Edition - Ministry of Education, Culture, Sports, Science and Technology. http://homepage.kokushikan.ac.jp/rio/user/kks_rio/COS/h20mid1.pdf
9. Science accessibility net, Jump to science summer camp (2017). http://jump2science.org/files/sc2017/SC2017_Report.pdf
10. Scratch. https://scratch.mit.edu. Accessed 17 Apr 2018

Exploring a Novel Inexpensive Tangible Interface for Non-visual Math and Science

R. Stanton, E. Pontelli$^{(\boxtimes)}$, Phoebe O. Toups Dugas, and M. Manshad

Department of Computer Science, New Mexico State University, Las Cruces, USA
{rstanton,epontell}@cs.nmsu.edu, phoebe.toups.dugas@acm.org,
mmanshad@gmail.com

Abstract. Tangible interaction enables *physical* manipulation of digital data, making it ideal to support visually impaired students. Visually impaired students are frequently integrated in mainstream courses, collaborating with sighted peers and instructors. This paper describes a *tangible block localization and tracking* method, using small inexpensive sensor packages that detect color placed on an interaction surface—i.e., a standard flat-screen display. The system recursively subdivides the display surface into regions of distinct colors that the sensor package can distinguish. Once located, the sensor package can be tracked by moving the color pattern underneath to follow it, re-expanding the pattern as needed to capture the sensor package if it moves too fast. The novel tracking infrastructure supports novel approaches to teach a number of science and math concepts to visually impaired students.

Keywords: Assistive technologies · Tangible interfaces

1 Introduction

Tangible interfaces enable direct manipulation of digital data [3], without necessarily relying on a visual display, a characteristic that offers exciting interaction modalities for individuals with visual disabilities. *Non*-digital tangible manipulatives (e.g., blocks, pins, bands) are commonly used in the early education stages of visually impaired children, especially in math and science. Visually impaired individuals can explore and learn without overloading the communication channels that are more commonly employed by existing assistive technologies and/or instructors (e.g., audio). Owing to their typical design, that of an open space with tangible objects, multiple users can simultaneously manipulate an information space, enabling forms of collaborative learning.

The development of *digital tangible interfaces* has been widely explored in the research literature. Nevertheless, the unique set of circumstances that arise in the *education of visually impaired students*, especially students located at remote sites or students that lack mobility pose new challenges in the development of effective digital tangible solutions, especially in the context of *tracking technologies*, which must first localize a tangible before they can track it. The practical needs and requirements of such students are at odds with prior localization technologies.

© Springer International Publishing AG, part of Springer Nature 2018
K. Miesenberger and G. Kouroupetroglou (Eds.): ICCHP 2018, LNCS 10896, pp. 619–627, 2018.
https://doi.org/10.1007/978-3-319-94277-3_96

We develop a new localization algorithm for simple hardware that can be embedded in tangible blocks, enabling visually impaired and sighted users to work in the same information space, supporting learning, and accounting for the unique constraints of working with distributed students. The localization technique uses a simple and inexpensive color sensor, embedded in a tangible block, to identify its location when placed on top of a display surface (e.g., computer screen), which is normally laid flat on a table. The algorithm locates the sensor package on the screen by rapidly subdividing the screen space into easily detectable colors using a quadtree partitioning [5] pattern. Once located, the sensor's movement can be tracked by displaying a color pattern masked to be under the tangible (where the user cannot see it). By using only a screen and a computer, the system is portable; the screen also enables sighted users (e.g., instructors) to easily work with visually impaired students.

Our long-term project, *Tangible Interactive Multimodal Manipulatives (TIMMs)*, is a framework aimed at providing visually impaired students with a tangible "window" into the information normally provided by visual interfaces. We expect to ultimately build a tangible interface comprised of small, block-like tokens that are used in combination with a display surface designed to facilitate interaction and collaboration. The present research aims at developing a component of the project, its localization technology, which must be amenable to the unique needs and requirements outlined below. Future work will develop tangible tracking based on the localization technology, and build educational software on top of the tangible tracking system.

2   Motivation and Needs

The present research is developed specifically for visually impaired learners, potentially situated at remote locations, tackling graphical mathematical content. This imposes a number of constraints on the design of a tangible educational platform, and renders a number of prior approaches unsuitable.

2.1   Classroom Technologies

Classrooms are enabled by a number of traditional technologies that do not directly support visually impaired learners: pen/pencil, personal computers, projectors, etc. As an ongoing working example, we consider that, in mathematics, one of the most important topics involves graphing functions and building diagrams, something to which traditional technologies and visual interfaces are well-suited. An instructor can easily show sighted students a graph and how it transforms in response to changes in the original function. Visually impaired students receive very little to no benefit from this teaching tool, however, and there are very few alternatives that can convey the same information.

Manipulatives support visually impaired students' learning. During the construction of a graph, a visually impaired student typically locates two points on a corkboard, inserts a pin at each point, and then wraps a rubber band around them to construct a tactile line. These pins fall off if not placed correctly and carefully. If a pin is removed by mistake, the rubber bands can also fall off causing the loss of the representation. Because the representation is static and difficult to change, students find it difficult to explore manipulations. In typical practice, students are allowed up to *three days to construct a graph* during an exam; often students choose to skip that part of the exam.

In highly populated areas, the concentration of visually impaired students is sufficient to sustain specialized schools for visual disabilities. Instead, rural students must be accommodated in standard public schools, where visually impaired learners work with sighted learners. The small number of qualified special education teachers creates a challenge in regions where the visually impaired student population is sparse and small. Thus, there is a challenge in ensuring that each student is served by a trained special educator, forcing special educators to serve a distributed audience of students.

2.2 Needs and Requirements

Based on these considerations, we explore the unique needs and requirements that drive the design of a localization system for tangibles for visually impaired students. First, a TANGIBLE MEDIUM is required, enabling visually impaired students to manipulate information with physical objects, rather than visual interfaces. A TANGIBLE MEDIUM would augment and extend the existing classroom technologies, building on known practice. In our ongoing example of graph construction, pairs of tangibles can serve to represent any straight line without the need for non-digital manipulatives. A TANGIBLE MEDIUM reduces reliance on the audio channel, which is frequently already overloaded by other assistive technologies (e.g., screen readers) and used by instructors. Second, there is a need for SIMULTANEOUS SUPPORT of visually impaired and sighted users working in collaboration. Due to the extant state of education and its distributed nature, visually impaired students must frequently work alongside sighted students. In addition, educators are normally sighted. Thus, the TANGIBLE MEDIUM also needs to support sighted users, optimizing their senses while enabling collaboration. Since the system will be in use by multiple users, a large display and interaction surface is ideal. Finally, any developed system needs to be PORTABLE, since many educators serve a few students at multiple distributed schools. This means that any system that relies on large pieces of equipment or extensive setup is, by default, unusable in the present context. Since there is little control over the education environment, localization must be robust for a variety of lighting conditions, which eliminates many camera-based solutions.

2.3 Related Work

There is an extensive body of work concerning tangible interfaces, though the majority of them are not focused on the needs of individuals with visual impairments. Some of the set ups proposed in the literature are either build on expensive hardware or require continuous camera tracking, which conflicts with the specific needs of students who desire a continuous contact with the device (thus causing occlusion). The closest proposal presented is Leigh et al.'s Tangible, Handheld, and Augmented Window (THAW) [4], which uses a color pattern on a monitor that is interpreted by a smartphone camera. Developed in parallel with our own system, THAW can create interactions between a computer screen and the phone screen. Cuypers et al. [2] proposed a similar technique to determine the position and orientation of a smartphone on an interactive surface. We take the tracking methods utilized in this category as inspiration for our own work, which we attempt to simplify for use with simple sensors.

3   Localization System and Algorithm

Our tangible-locating system is composed of a set of sensor packages (i.e., tangibles) and an associated display surface. Communicating algorithms operate on the packages and surface to locate the packages. When integrated into a tangible block, the system supports the needs and requirements of the present context. The algorithm is executed manually and assumes that the sensor packages are actively awaiting messages before the program is run (future iterations will allow dynamically adding packages). When activated, the display surface algorithm subdivides the screen space using novemtree partitioning, in nine colors (Fig. 2). As the sensor detects and reports a color, the algorithm further subdivides the region containing color that was identified, making it possible to clear unused portions of the screen for information display.

3.1   Hardware Description

The present tangible-locating system is based on a simple sensor that reads the color of light combined with a flat monitor for display. A sensor package consists of an Arduino Fio with an RGB Sensor [1], XBee radio, and LiPo battery. The sensor packages are embedded in 3D-printed tangible blocks with the sensor facing down (Fig. 1). As a display surface, we used a 40-in. Samsung television at 1920 × 1080 resolution (~55 DPI). A computer executes the display surface algorithm.

Fig. 1. A tangible with sensor package embedded in the 3D-printed enclosure

The sensor package runs a simple program waiting for color data requests. On request, it will take RGB readings and send them back. A calibration phase (described in the next section) is necessary if the display surface or its brightness is changed.

3.2 Display Surface Algorithm

The display surface algorithm, running on the connected computer, uses readings from the sensor packages to direct partitioning of the display and localize the sensor, using the following phases: (1) Run calibration and record baseline RGB values for each color; (2) Divide the display into 3×3 grid and fill with the distinct colors; (3) When triggered, repeat until the specified number of iterations (n, described below) have been completed: **(a)** Get RGB values from all sensors; **(b)** Identify the colors under each; **(c)** Re-partition the identified rectangles at 1/9th the previous scale; (4) Return upper-left x, y pixel values of identified rectangles.

The algorithm requires a fixed number of iterations (n) be specified in advance. A higher number of iterations (n) will ideally locate the sensor within a smaller area: $screen\_width/3^n \times screen\_height/3^n$. For resolutions up to 2560×1440 on a 40-in. display (DPI = 73.43), the algorithm can reduce the search space to less than a $1\,cm \times 1\,cm$ square in 4 iterations. However performing more iterations increases the likelihood of a partition edge or intersection ending up beneath the sensor, which could be mis-identified. Because the sensor package's reporting is dependent on characteristics of the display surface's color gamut and its brightness, it is necessary to calibrate the system when these change. During calibration, the user places one or more sensor packages on the display. The display then flashes each of the nine colors in sequence, and the value of each RGB channel is then stored. The color from future readings is identified by finding the most similar of the calibration readings.

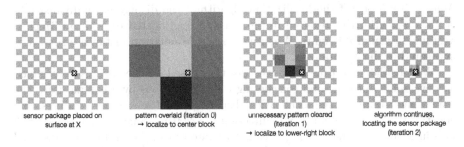

sensor package placed on surface at X

pattern overlaid (iteration 0)
→ localize to center block

unnecessary pattern cleared (iteration 1)
→ localize to lower-right block

algorithm continues, locating the sensor package (iteration 2)

Fig. 2. The sensor package is located on the surface at the black-and-white ×. In each iteration, 8/9 of the screen is made available for displaying information

4 Tracking Algorithm

Once localized, a sensor package may be actively tracked above the display surface. This tracking method utilizes the same sensor package configurations described previously. The display surface utilizes a square image of fixed size divided into a 3×3 grid of different, distinct colors. After localization, the tracking pattern is rendered underneath the tangible. From this point, the program continually requests updates from the color sensor. By matching each reading to the nearest of the collected calibration readings, it is possible to infer whether the sensor has been moved and in which direction.

A concern related to the frequency of messages is the choice of colors used in the 3×3 grid. For obvious reasons, simple color-matching schemes used with similar colors will often produce erroneous tracking results, potentially causing the tracking pattern to move away from the actual tangible. For our prototype we used a set of colors generated by the SciencesPo mèdialab tool, i want hue [6], using the full range of colors. This set was chosen from 8 potential sets of nine colors, each generated by i want hue. Then, an empty square of the same dimensions as the tracking pattern was rendered on the screen. The sensor was placed somewhere in this square, after which we had the system flash the pattern for 100 ms and collected a reading from the sensor to determine if the sensor had identified the correct color. This was repeated approximately 200 times for each color set. The set we ultimately chose identified the correct color 89.86% of the time.

5   Performance

We empirically determined the accuracy and time-to-fix for our localization system, as well as evaluated its tracking speed. For both sets of tests, we used a 40-in. LED television running as second monitor at 1920×1080 ($\sim$55 PPI) resolution. For the localization accuracy tests, we reduced the testing area to 1917×999 to avoid interference from the operating system UI or other interface widgets; the tracking speed tests were run over the full area of the screen. With 3 iterations of the localization algorithm, the display is subdivided into a 27×27 grid, this resulted in the sensor being located to a 71×37 pixel rectangle ($32\,\text{mm} \times 17\,\text{mm}$). When we discuss Manhattan distance errors, it is measured in these rectangles.

We calculate the time to fix the position based on the timings determined in developing our code and considering the expectations by a human user. The total time to update the localization display, poll all sensors for readings, and identify the corresponding color/direction is $\sim$200 ms. Since we perform $n = 3$ readings, and the first reading does not require a pause, each fix cycle required approximately 600 ms.

The present localization system clamps all results to the measured rectangle. To assess accuracy of the localization algorithm, we determine two accuracy values to report: (1) the percentage of results in the correct rectangle and (2) the distance of the measured points to the ground truth in terms of the number of rectangles away the result is. As seen in Fig. 3, most localization tests were correct or only off by one. To collect data points, the software was configured to locate tangibles in response to a mouse click. For the accuracy tests, we

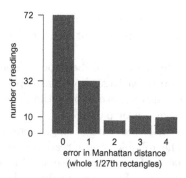

Fig. 3. Histogram of number of readings versus error

performed the following repeatedly: (**1**) At the time of the first mouse click, the x,y coordinates of the mouse cursor are recorded; (**2**) then, the sensor package is centered over the same location as the cursor, and the cursor is moved away; (**3**) on the next mouse click event, the localization system is run and the position of the identified section of screen area is recorded. One drawback of this testing methodology is the introduction of random human error. We expect this to introduce minor random error into the resulting data: a Manhattan distance of 1–2.

For the analysis, 150 readings were taken. These were analyzed by Manhattan distance between the identified rectangle and the correct one; it was noted that for Manhattan distances 4 and above (10/150 readings), the number of readings dropped to 1–2, suggesting they were outliers. This set of outliers were removed, producing 137 usable readings. Overall, the results are positive, 72 of the 137 readings were correct (52.6%), 32 (23.4%) were one rectangle off (Manhattan distance of 1), and 8 were off by two (5.8%); in combination, these account for 112 of 137 readings (81.8%) (Fig. 3). Given the size of the rectangles and the size of the tangible, these readings are all potentially valid, that is, the tangible would be located over the rectangle recognized.

We analyze the tracking method in terms of the speeds at which it can track sensor packages above our display, and in terms of the system reliability. An initial keypress prompts the system to record the starting location. Immediately following this we move the tangible in a straight line. After covering some distance over the surface of the screen, we trigger the end of the recording via another keypress and the speed is calculated. If the system is unable to keep the tracking pattern beneath the sensor, we flag this by pressing another key and immediately ending the recording. The number of times such tracking failures occur is recorded.

By collecting the information above, we are able to approximate the speed at which the sensor packages can be reliably tracked moving in a single direction and see how reliable the tracking method is. For each recording, the speed at which sensor packages were moved was adjusted based on observing whether or not the sensor was lost in the prior reading; if the sensor was not lost, we move it slightly faster during the next recording. Sensor packages were moved in different directions for each recording, but without any change in direction for that recording's duration.

We collect two sets of results as described above. The first set consists of 204 recordings using a single sensor package above the display surface. The second set is recorded based on two sensors moved above the display surface concurrently, with 228 recordings for each sensor package.

Of all the recordings collected with a single sensor, 176 were not flagged as unreliable, or 86%. The reliable sensor readings were moved an average of 18.17 cm across the display surface. From these, the highest speed was 5.63 cm/s and the average was 3.02 cm/s. From the readings flagged as unreliable, they were moved an average of 4.24 cm before the tracking pattern was lost.

The proportion of reliable readings to unreliable for the concurrent sensors was significantly different from that of the single sensor recordings—approximately 66.8%. When taking these reliable recordings, the concurrent sensors were moved an average of 12.83 cm. The highest speed of reliable recordings was 7.07 cm/s. The average speeds for the sensors was 2.81 cm/s.

From these results we can see that, in the current state of the tracking method, achieving similar reliability with different numbers of sensors requires moving the sensors at a slower speed due to the greater potential for misidentifying colors or otherwise losing the location of one of the sensor packages.

6   Discussion and Conclusions

We argue for the suitability of our system within the context of visually impaired student education based on the needs and requirements derived from observations on the state of education for such students. The combination of a collection of sensor packages with any display screen that could be laid flat comprises our tangible medium. Because such a display can be of any size and multiple tangibles can be localized above it, we likewise establish a collaborative interaction space. The system uses the display screen, briefly, during localization. The system is portable, making it ideal for itinerant educators.

The most obvious point of comparison for our novemtree partitioning method of localization is Leigh et al.'s THAW method [4]. Using the camera of an Apple iPhone, Leigh et al. were able to locate the phone's position above the screen to within an average of 6.33 mm. Using a cheaper hardware setup on a larger screen, we were able to locate a sensor package to a 33 mm × 17 mm rectangle using 3 readings per point.

We have described a tangible-tracking technology designed to support visually impaired students collaborating with sighted instructors and peers. The validated algorithm we describe will be of use to others with similar needs. The present locating technology is sufficient to accomplish math teaching for visually impaired students. Near future work develops applications to teach linear equations, as in our earlier example.

Using the novemtree algorithm and hardware within 3D-printed tangible blocks, we hope to provide a less cumbersome, more accessible input modality for visually impaired learners. The present research is one step in a larger research agenda to support visually impaired student learning. Future versions of the system may further support students by offering tangibles that can move themselves on the surface or extendable cables that can be stretched between tangible blocks.

References

1. Avago Technologies. APDS-9960 Digital Proximity, Ambient Light, RGB and Gesture Sensor. Data Sheet AV02-4191EN (2013)
2. Cuypers, T., Francken, Y., Vanaken, C., Van Reeth, F., Bekaert, P.: Smartphone localization on interactive surfaces using the built-in camera. In: Proceedings of the ProCams, vol. 2, pp. 3–4. Citeseer (2009)
3. Ishii, H., Ullmer, B.: Tangible bits: towards seamless interfaces between people, bits and atoms. In: Proceedings of the ACM SIGCHI Conference on Human Factors in Computing Systems, CHI 1997, pp. 234–241. ACM, New York (1997)
4. Leigh, S., Schoessler, P., Heibeck, F., Maes, P., Ishii, H.: THAW: tangible interaction with see-through augmentation for smartphones on computer screens. In: Proceedings of the Ninth International Conference on Tangible, Embedded, and Embodied Interaction, TEI 2015, pp. 89–96. ACM, New York (2015)
5. Samet, H.: The quadtree and related hierarchical data structures. ACM Comput. Surv. **16**(2), 187–260 (1984)
6. SciencesPo MediaLab. I Want Hue: Colors for Data Scientists (2017). http://tools.medialab.sciences-po.fr/iwanthue. Accessed 20 Jan 2017

Effectiveness of Tactile Scatter Plots: Comparison of Non-visual Data Representations

Tetsuya Watanabe[1]([⊠]) and Hikaru Mizukami[2]

[1] Faculty of Engineering, University of Niigata, Niigata 950-2181, Japan
t2.nabe@eng.niigata-u.ac.jp
[2] Graduate School of Science and Technology, University of Niigata,
Niigata 950-2181, Japan

Abstract. The goal of making a scatter plot is to visually identify the type of relationship between two quantitative variables quickly. To explore whether a scatter plot can achieve this goal when it is made in the form of a tactile graph and presented to blind people, we conducted an experiment in which x-y data sets were presented to blind participants in three data representations: tactile graph, tactile table, and electronic table, and the participants were asked to identify the type of relationship between two variables. Under all presentation conditions, the correct rates were high: it was 92.5% for the tactile graph condition and 85.0% for the tactile table and electronic table conditions. Tactile graphs were understood with the shortest time, tactile tables with the second shortest, and electronic tables needed the longest time. This differences were due to the different strategies for identifying the relationships. Both tactile graph and tactile table conditions gained higher subjective ratings than the electronic table condition.

Keywords: Blind people · Tactile graph · Tactile table · Screen reader
Scatter plot

1 Introduction

In everyday life, we often discuss the relationship between two quantitative variables such as heights and weights, temperature and ice cream sales, and working hours and accepted papers. To visually identify the type of relationship between two quantitative variables quickly, scatter plots are usually used. For blind people, visual graphs are transformed into a tactile form. Our research question is whether a scatter plot can achieve its goal when it is made as a tactile graph and presented to blind people. To explore this issue, we conducted an experiment in which twelve x-y data sets were presented to 10 blind participants in three data representations: tactile graph, tactile table, and electronic table, and the participants were asked to identify the type of relationship between two variables. We measured the reading time and correct rate, recorded the reasons for identifying reported by the participants, and discussed the effectiveness of tactile scatter plots based on these experimental results. The data for the first three participants were reported at ICCHP 2012, where the trend that the

K. Miesenberger and G. Kouroupetroglou (Eds.): ICCHP 2018, LNCS 10896, pp. 628–635, 2018.
https://doi.org/10.1007/978-3-319-94277-3_97

relationships were identified the fastest with tactile graphs among three data representations was shown [1]. In this report, we added seven more participants and observed this trend statistically.

2 Related Work

A few studies have been conducted on the readability of tactile graphs. Goncu et al. investigated the effectiveness of grid lines in tactile bar charts and found that adding grid lines and values to a bar chart was preferred [2]. Additionally, they compared four data representations, horizontal tactile bar charts, vertical bar charts, tactile tables, and vertical bar charts with audio description. The blind participants preferred tactile tables over tactile charts. Watanabe and Inaba explored which texture was suitable to fill tactile bars on capsule paper [3]. As the result, black and dark gray colors and the dot patterns whose inter-dot spacings were 1.5 mm or less were found to be suitable in terms of exploring times and subjective ratings. Yu and Brewster compared virtual haptic bar charts and conventional tactile bar charts on paper in terms of correct rate, reading time, and mental workload [4]. The result was that the number of correct answers was significantly higher with the virtual haptic system, but more reading time was spent with the system which led to significantly heavier workload.

Araki and Watanabe compared the accuracy of reading tactile pie charts and reading tactile band charts with sighted and blind students as participants [5]. They were presented with a set of tactile pie charts and band charts with individual division ratios and asked to answer the ratio. The results from sighted participants showed that the error sizes in reading pie charts were smaller than those in reading band charts and that there was little difference between the reading times of the two charts. The results from a blind participant showed similar trend to those from sighted participants except for the reading times.

Engel and Weber analyzed 69 tactile charts to develop design guidelines for tactile charts [6]. These tactile charts were collected from publications and tactile graphics guidelines. The types of these tactile graphs were bar charts, line charts, pie charts, area charts, and scatter plots. The first three chart types occupied 90% of the charts analyzed whereas scatter plots occupied merely 4%. This implies the low use rate of tactile scatter plots and, thus, researches on tactile scatter plots are scarce.

In this paper, we focus on tactile scatter plots and explore if tactile graphs are more useful than tactile tables or reading numerical data with a screen reader.

3 Experiment

3.1 Stimuli

For three data representation methods, tactile graph, tactile table, and electronic table, different data sets of four types of relationship, linear, quadratic, inverse proportion, and non-correlated, were assigned, thus in total 12 data sets were prepared. Each data set was comprised of 20 x values, and 20 y values. For all of the 12 data sets, the x values ranged from 0.5 to 10 by 0.5 step. For the nine data sets, y values were determined in the following two steps. First, the y values were calculated by inputting the x value into one of the three functions, linear, quadratic, and inverse proportion functions. Then, errors up to 10% of each y value were added in order to imitate observed (not idealistic) data and to prevent the participants from easily calculating y values from the x values and the functions. The error values were determined based on the values calculated by the random function of Microsoft Excel. The non-correlated data were also produced using the random function. The range of y values of all the data sets was from 0 to 120.

The tactile graphs and tactile tables were made with a braille embosser (ESA 721, JTR), the most popular embosser in Japan [7]. The dimension of all the tactile graphs was 147 × 200 mm (width x height). Electronic tables (text files) were voiced with a screen reader (either of PC-Talker, JAWS, or VDMW) that worked on a laptop personal computer with Windows 7 operating system. Three types of data representations are shown in Fig. 1.

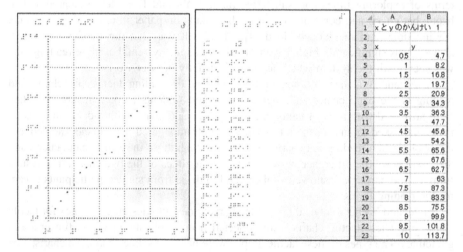

Fig. 1. A tactile graph (left), tactile table (middle), and electronic table (text file, right) used in the experiment.

3.2   Participants

Participants were 10 blind people aging from 19 to 27 with an average of 22.0 years. All of them had a grade 1 disability (mostly totally blind) and used braille every day. All of them had learned mathematics by means of braille textbooks including tactile graphs at a school for the blind.

3.3   Procedure

The experiment was carried out in a quiet room one by one. The participant sat on a chair in front of a table and touched the stimuli (tactile graphs and tactile tables) and used a personal computer on the table.

Prior to the experiments, the explanation of the four relationships' features was given to the participant. They were notified in advance that each data set had errors and differed from idealistic values.

For each presentation condition, four stimuli representing one of the four relationships were presented to the participant all together. The participant was allowed to touch the tactile graphs or tactile tables or use the computer freely until they understood all the relationships of the four stimuli. Then, they were instructed to report the answers and to explain the reason(s) for answering so. The experimenter used a stopwatch to measure the time from the start of touching the stimuli or using the computer to the start of answering as reading time.

To read an electronic table, five participants used their own laptop personal computer (OS: Windows 7) and the other five used a laptop personal computer that the experimenters prepared (Vostro 1500, Dell. OS: Windows 7. Screen Reader: PC-Talker 7).

There were six permutations to present three conditions. To each permutation, two or one participant(s) was/were assigned.

After the three representations were tested, the participant was instructed to rank the readability of each representation, from one: most readable to three: least readable, except for the first three participants.

4 Results

4.1 Reading Time

The reading times for the three representation conditions averaged over the 10 participants are shown in Fig. 2. Tactile graphs were understood with the shortest time, tactile tables with the second shortest, and electronic tables needed the longest time. As the time differences among the participants and among the representation conditions were very large, we used a nonparametric Friedman test and found a significant difference in the reading time among the representation conditions ($S = 9.8, p < 0.01$). As pairwise comparison tests, the Wilcoxon signed-rank test with the Ryan's method was repeatedly used. The tests showed significant differences between tactile graph and electronic table conditions.

4.2 Correct Rate

The correct rates for the three representation conditions averaged over the 10 participants are shown in Fig. 3. It shows a ceiling effect. For six out of 10 participants, the correct rate was 100% for all the three representation conditions. Overall correct rate was 92.5% for the tactile graph condition and 85.0% for the tactile table and electronic table conditions. A Friedman test did not reveal a significant difference in the correct rate among the representation conditions ($S = 0.6$).

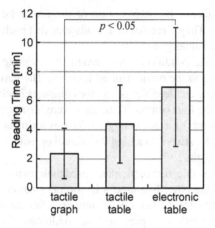

Fig. 2. Reading time.

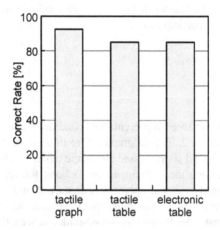

Fig. 3. Correct rate.

4.3 Reasons for Identifying

In the experiment, the participants were instructed to report the reasons for identifying the four relationships. As a result, the characteristics that distinguished each relationship from the others and the methods to find such characteristics under each representation condition were collected. Linear and quadratic functions had some characteristics in common. Tactile tables and electronic tables had some methods in common. The characteristics that distinguished each relationship are listed in Table 1.

Out of these characteristics, the plot arrangements were perceived under the tactile graph condition (in Table 1, "TG" cells are marked with *) and the ratios and differences were calculated under the tactile table and electronic table conditions (in Table 1, "Table" cells are marked with *).

Table 1. Observed features of each function. TG is the abbreviations for tactile graph and Table means both tactile and electronic tables.

Functions	Characteristics	TG	Table
Linear and quadratic functions	As x grows larger, y grows larger, i.e. the graph line runs from lower left to upper right	*	*
Linear function	Plots distribute linearly	*	
	The ratio of y to x is mostly constant		*
	Differences between neighbouring y values are mostly constant		*
Quadratic function	Plots approach the x axis (i.e. y values approach zero) as x values become close to zero	*	
	As x grows larger, the ratio of y to x grows larger		*
	Differences between neighbouring y values become larger as x grows larger		*
Inverse proportion	Plots approach the x axis (i.e. y values approach zero) as x becomes larger	*	
	As x grows larger, y grows smaller	*	*
	Y is very large when x is close to zero		*
	Differences between neighbouring y values are very large when x is close to zero		*
	Differences between neighbouring y values become smaller as x grows larger		*
Non-correlated	Plots distribute randomly	*	
	It felt as if there were multiple grahps or it were a circle	*	
	Differences between neighbouring y values are unstable		*

4.4   Subjective Rating

The subjective ratings for the three representation conditions averaged over the seven participants are shown in Fig. 4. The longer the bar is, the higher the subjective rating is. Both tactile graph and tactile table conditions gained higher ratings than electronic table condition. However, a Friedman test did not show a significant difference in the subjective rating among the representation conditions ($S = 5.4$).

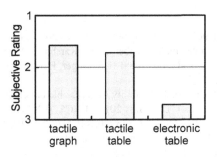

Fig. 4. Subjective rating.

5 Discussion

For the correct rate, a ceiling effect was observed and the differences among the three conditions were small (Fig. 3). Contrastingly, for the reading time, a significant difference were observed among the three conditions (Fig. 2). Thus, in this section, the differences in reading time are discussed based on the reasons for identifying four relationships.

The differences in reading time between the tactile graph condition and the two table conditions stemmed from the different strategies for identifying the four relationships. As described in the result section, under the tactile graph condition, the plot arrangements were tactually perceived very quickly. On the other hand, under the two table conditions, the ratios and differences had to be calculated mentally. This strategy needed quite a time because the calculation had to be repeated until the characteristics of the relationships were understood. Additionally, understanding the characteristics was hindered due to the errors included in the data.

Though the difference was not significant, the reading times under the tactile table condition were much shorter than those under the electronic table condition. When reading the table data, moving fingers to the next line or column took shorter times than pressing the arrow keys and listening to the speech on a computer. Moreover, with tactile tables two hands were available. This also speeded up the movement of the focusing cells.

6 Conclusion

The experimental results have shown that tactile graphs enabled blind people to identify the relationship between two variables more quickly than tactile and electronic tables. This was due to the difference in identifying strategies: To identify the relationship between x and y in tactile tables, the ratio of y to x and differences between neighbouring y values must be calculated repeatedly. On the other hand, the shapes of graphs can be understood tactually in shorter times.

Acknowledgements. This work was supported by JSPS KAKENHI Grant Number 17H02005F.

References

1. Watanabe, T., Yamaguchi, T., Nakagawa, M.: Development of software for automatic creation of embossed graphs. In: Miesenberger, K., Karshmer, A., Penaz, P., Zagler, W. (eds.) ICCHP 2012. LNCS, vol. 7382, pp. 174–181. Springer, Heidelberg (2012). https://doi.org/10.1007/978-3-642-31522-0_25
2. Goncu, C., Marriott, K., Hurst, J.: Usability of accessible bar charts. In: Goel, A.K., Jamnik, M., Narayanan, N.H. (eds.) Diagrams 2010. LNCS (LNAI), vol. 6170, pp. 167–181. Springer, Heidelberg (2010). https://doi.org/10.1007/978-3-642-14600-8_17
3. Watanabe, T., Inaba, N.: Textures suitable for tactile bar charts on capsule paper. Trans. Virtual Reality Soc. Japan **23**(1), 13–20 (2018)

4. Yu, W., Brewster, S.: Multimodal virtual reality versus printed medium in visualization for blind people. In: Proceedings of the of ASSETS 2002, pp. 57–64 (2002)
5. Araki, K., Watanabe, T.: Comparison of reading accuracy between tactile pie charts and band charts. In: The 15th ACM SIGACCESS International Conference on Computers and Accessibility, Bellevue, Washington, USA, October 2013
6. Engel, C., Weber, G.: Analysis of tactile chart design. In: Proceedings of the of PETRA 2017, pp. 197–200 (2017)
7. Oouchi, S., Sawada, M., Kaneko, T., Chida, K.: A survey on making and using tactile educational materials in schools for the blind. Bull. Nat. Inst. Spec. Educ. **31**, 113–125 (2004)

Techniques for Improved Speech-Based Access to Diagrammatic Representations

Tomas Murillo-Morales[(⊠)] and Klaus Miesenberger

Johannes Kepler University, Linz, Austria
{Tomas.Murillo_Morales,Klaus.Miesenberger}@jku.at

Abstract. Natural language interfaces (NLIs) are a novel approach to non-visual accessibility of diagrammatic representations, such as statistical charts. This paper introduces a number of methods that aim to compensate for the lack of sight when accessing semantically-enhanced diagrams through a Web-based NLI.

Keywords: Diagram semantics · Accessibility · Natural language interface

1 Introduction

Diagrams help humans with problem solving and understanding. Graphic representations of a problem exploit the natural perceptual, cognitive, and memorial capacities of the human visual system [1]; the brain finds it easier to process information if it is presented as an image rather than as words or numbers [2]. Therefore, properly graphically displaying information simplifies its understanding, assisting the sighted reader in building their mental model of the problem and easing the problem solving process. For instance, whereas looking through a large numerical table takes a considerable amount of mental effort, the same information properly displayed in a visual manner (e.g. in a scatterplot) may be grasped in a matter of seconds.

Diagrams are thus commonplace in science, journalism, finance, and many aspects of daily life. However, blind persons are generally excluded from accessing them. Visually impaired persons need to make use of assistive technologies and alternative representations of visually perceivable information, ranging from simple textual descriptions of the graphic to practically equivalent tactile transcriptions. Nevertheless, current non-visual methods of accessing diagrams are either too simplistic (linear text descriptions, audification approaches, surface haptic displays), too expensive or cumbersome to produce (tactile shape displays, tactile hard-copies, multimodal approaches, force-feedback devices), or still in their early infancy (vibrotactile displays, interactive systems, natural-language-based systems). This lack of comprehensive, inexpensive, and easy-to-use approaches has resulted on graphical information being described as the "last frontier in accessibility" [3].

Communicative images are a novel approach to accessibility of graphics that may help solve many of these drawbacks for a sizable number of graphic domains. They can be defined as two-dimensional objects (graphics) integrated with a dialogue interface which are equipped with an associated knowledge database [4]. Image semantics are

K. Miesenberger and G. Kouroupetroglou (Eds.): ICCHP 2018, LNCS 10896, pp. 636–643, 2018.
https://doi.org/10.1007/978-3-319-94277-3_98

described in a structured way by means of ontologies using semantic categories, their properties and relationships. A dialogue interface (natural language interface, NLI) then lets users efficiently retrieve the underlying knowledge by means of natural language queries. NLIs do not require any specific software or hardware, and therefore communicative images can be accessed online the same way blind people are used to navigate the Web in a usual manner. Therefore, communicative graphics have the potential of emerging as a holistic approach to the accessibility of many conventional graphics, freeing users from having to employ cumbersome, domain-dependent methods.

The serial nature of speech has an obvious disadvantage over tactile or some sonification approaches which do not impose such a cognitive load on the reader's processing capabilities. Interestingly enough, in spite of this fact blind readers much prefer speech feedback when navigating e.g. link diagrams, and other means are preferred only rarely [5]. However, being a novel approach, communicative graphics have not been thoroughly evaluated, and so far their domain of applicability has been limited to simple photographical content accessed by means of controlled natural language queries.

We have previously introduced broadening efforts to include domains other than photography in communicative images by defining a hierarchical formal semantic knowledge base in the form of ontologies underpinning visualization domains i.e. diagrams along with an accessible Web user interface to semantically-enhanced graphics based on natural language (Fig. 1) [6]. In addition, an authoring tool for seamless creation of semantic formal markup given a vector graphic has been developed, allowing authors to associate ontological instances and property occurrences to any number of a given vector graphic's constituent elements such as paths, shapes, or text elements [7].

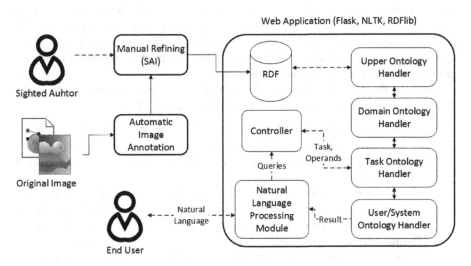

Fig. 1. Block diagram of our current prototype of a framework for speech-based access to graphics

The hierarchical knowledge base is made up of four main layers [8]: (1) an upper ontology describing syntactic aspects of visualization common across domains, (2) several domain ontologies underpinning broad visualization domains, such as statistical charts and maps, (3) task ontologies describing analytical low-level tasks that can be performed on a given domain which may then be combined to form high-level activities, and (4) user/system ontologies defining user-made and system annotations on individual graphic elements that ease non-visual access to a diagram, allowing users to customize diagram navigation to their specific needs.

A server-side controller, written in Python, is in charge of inferring the task to be performed according to which keywords are present in a user's subquery after a Natural Language Processing module has tagged each part-of-speech component of the original query. The controller then tries to select the most appropriate task among those low-level tasks that can be performed on the current domain according to the semantic information stored in the task ontology level. If relevant, the operands and operators of the end SPARQL query are also fetched by the controller from the provided list of keywords. At the moment, different input text fields, one per available low-level task, have been implemented in the Web user interface in order to simplify the natural language processing [6]. In the end prototype we are planning to combine them into a single text field with more profound back end language understanding capabilities.

In this paper, we outline some of the components of the semantic hierarchy that aim to improve the efficiency and user experience of navigating and performing analytical tasks on diagrams in a non-visual manner, and discuss their implementation into a Web-based accessible interface.

2 Cognitive Benefits of Diagrammatic Representations

The initial phase before building the supporting knowledge base and its accompanying user interface consisted on an exhaustive study on the cognitive benefits that diagrammatic representations offer sighted persons in problem solving. Only after understanding these cognitive benefits it could be attempted to implement non-visual methods that compensate for the lack thereof.

Some of the particular reasons why sighted persons prefer diagrammatic representations to linear descriptions for problem solving are [9, 10]:

1. **Resemblance preservation:** Diagrams possess the ability of directly resembling what they represent, as opposed to linear descriptions, in which the reader has to imagine the entities that are being described. This resemblance may take place in two different ways:
   a. **Literal resemblance:** many diagrams literally preserve the topology and geo-metric relationships of what is being represented, including the relative size and position between elements. This is the case in pictures and most maps.
   b. **Homomorphic resemblance:** diagrams using this type of resemblance use topology and geometric relationships metaphorically to represent abstract relationships with similar abstract properties.

2. **Indexing:** diagrams avoid large amounts of search for the elements needed to make a problem-solving inference by grouping all information that is used together, which avoids the need to use and match symbolic elements. Besides locational indexing, they also allow two-dimensional indexing, this is, the ability of locating an object by its coordinates on the two-dimensional plane. For example, two-dimensional indexing allows a sighted reader to find the values of a given point in a scatterplot by matching its location to horizontal and vertical positions on the plot's axes.

3. **Breadth-then-depth search:** when visualizing data, lots of information can be acquired in parallel from a wide area. The perceptual abilities of the human sight al-low persons to scan, recognize, and recall images rapidly. This leads to the ability of intentionally focusing the attention into a narrower, more detailed part of the whole image that the reader finds especially interesting. The capacity to gain a quick overview first, followed by the possibility of effortlessly filtering out uninteresting elements and obtaining details of the relevant ones makes visual data dis-play a much more efficient means of retrieving information than linear representations. This cognitive aspect of visualization is very well known in data visualization research, from where the so-called "visual information-seeking mantra", that aims to replicate it, stems: overview first, zoom and filter, then details on demand [11].

4. **Computational off-loading:** Diagrams automatically support a large number of perceptual inferences by means of sight, which are extremely easy for sighted humans. Perceptual inferencing depends on the visual and spatial properties of the diagram encoding the underlying information in a way that capitalizes on automatic processing to convey the intended meaning. For example, the relationship between the two variables in a line chart (i.e. the trend) can be inferred immediately by means of sight. Diagrams also allow mental animation, i.e. mentally activating components in the representation of the system in a serial manner [12].

These cognitive advantages make proper data display a critical aspect to data analysis. Properly displaying information can make a difference by enabling people to understand complex matters and find creative solutions [2]. For example, it has been proven that students learn better when textual materials are enhanced with the inclusion of didactical graphics [13]. This applies not only to information retention, but also to deep comprehension, which finally turns into better solving skills [14]. It is thus paramount for technologies that aim to enable non-visual access to graphics to provide their users with alternative methods making up, at least to a certain extent, for the loss of these critical benefits.

3   Dialogue-Based Access to Diagrams: The User/System Level

The first three levels of our hierarchy depicting the semantics of diagrams were previously discussed in previous publications by the authors: [6, 8]. Here, we focus on semantic markup added to the supporting ontologies at the domain and user/system levels in order to make up for the loss of cognitive benefits presented in the previous section.

Literal Resemblance Preservation: Most visual attributes with the ability of carrying information in diagrams, such as shape, size, and color, cannot be accurately represented by aural means. Therefore, we have resorted to describing them by means of textual descriptions. A number of visual attributes have been included as datatype properties of the upper ontology in our hierarchy, and thus any graphic object may be enhanced with semantics depicting their visual properties. A user can then inquire information about objects sharing a certain visual attribute (e.g. "blue bars" in a bar chart) or ask about the visual properties of objects (e.g. "color of current bar"). When a user performs a filtering query according to visual attributes, the system controller detects it and chooses a standard low-level filtering task with the visual attribute as the operand and "equals" as its implicit operator (unless a label with the same value as the attribute exists, in which case the labelled elements are given priority). The filtering task itself is then performed by the task ontology handler, which is further delegated to the domain and upper level ontology handlers until the relevant semantic instances are finally obtained from the knowledge base via a SPARQL query, sent back to the controller and then output to the user via a simple natural language processing module.

Moreover, any graphical object might be given a user- or author- defined label with extra information (e.g. a certain object in a map might be pre-tagged as "Germany", or users may choose to add a custom tag themselves). More on this can be read later. Special tasks may be also performed on objects carrying certain attributes. For example, of the Y coordinate value of Graphic_Object A is smaller than that of Graphic_Object B, A is said to be below B.

Homomorphic Resemblance Preservation: Metaphorical relationships between objects are included at the domain ontology level as object or datatype properties. For instance, a marriage between two persons, depicted in a family tree link diagram by a horizontal link connecting them, may be represented by the Family Tree ontology with an object property occurrence: (A, married_to, B). User tasks based on these properties can then be added at the Task ontology level. For example, the query "who is married to A?" would be interpreted as a Filtering low-level task that returns all subjects X of the triples in the domain ontology having the form (X, married_to, A).

Indexing: Graphic elements may be assigned ordinal values when they are meant to be navigated in a given order. For example, points in a line chart can be annotated from left to right (by adding occurrences of the has_order datatype property) so the user can navigate the entire line and perform tasks on each point consecutively. Navigation can be performed in a hierarchical fashion as well, since graphic objects (elementary or composite) belonging to composite objects are clearly identified in the supporting ontology in a recursive manner. Users may then issue "go to next/previous element" or "go one level up/down" queries in order to sequentially navigate through the graphic. Clusters of elements may be labelled using a common label for all elements in the cluster. These indexing features are implemented as object and datatype properties that support analytical and navigational tasks on the graphic. For instance, the following query performed on a bar chart: "average sales in January" can be performed as the system is able to first filter those bars labelled by the "January" label.

When a user moves from one graphic element to another, the "is_current_node" datatype property of the system ontology level has its subject updated to the current element by the system's controller. The user may at any time issue a "where am I?" query, and every relevant property of the current element will be output, such as labels and user annotations, in order to help blind users with orientation while navigating complex graphics.

Breadth-then-depth search: A summary of the whole graphic can be requested by the user for certain domains, upon which the most salient features of the graphic are given to the user in order to obtain an initial, high-level overview of its content. For example, a bar chart overview includes its title, what it axis represent, the contents of its legend, a list of its labels, its extreme values, and, if bars are grouped, the average value of each group. Once the user is familiar with the general aspects of the graphic, low-level tasks can be performed [6], or the user may choose to navigate the graphic in a sequential, object-by-object manner, as previously described. Summaries are automatically computed by the system's controller on a domain-dependent basis.

Computational off-loading: The author's intention when designing the graphic, such as the general trend of a line chart, is a vital piece of information that sighted users can generally infer from observing the graphic. This implicit information can be explicitly marked in the supporting ontology so blind readers acquire quick insight of the graphic's semantics, as previously described in [6].

Another powerful method for offloading the user's working memory consists on user-defined home nodes. A home node is a distinctive element of the graph, analogous to a landmark, that is used as a base for exploration and to which users may return when lost [15]. The user may select any graphic object of the diagram of special interest as the current 'home node', and the system controller will update the subject of the "is_home_node" property occurrence to the current individual. The output to any further query performed by the user will try to relate to the home node. For instance, in bar charts, if a bar is chosen as the current home node every further query that outputs a numerical value will be compared to the home node's value. In weighted graphs, the sum of weights of the shortest path from the home node to the current node may be given, and so on. This way, relationships between distant elements of interest can be quickly inferred in a non-visual manner without the user having to remember every intermediate step.

I addition, users may add a number of personal textual annotations to the current graphical instance during exploration of the diagram. These custom tags are then added by the controller to their graphical object instance via the "has_user_label" datatype property. When this element's labels are output to the user during navigation or after performing an analytical task, the user-defined labels are given as well. This helps the user with remembering previously visited elements and understanding the general structure of the graphic.

Finally, a number of navigational shortcuts are provided to the user to provide some computational unload while navigating a complex diagram. Besides the "where am I?" command, quick jumps to the first and last node, as well as the home-node, are also provided by the system. Moreover, the user may jump to the nodes with the highest and lowest values of the diagram e.g. the tallest and shortest bars in a bar chart. In the future, we would also like to let the user ask about the evolution of a section of a graph e.g. whether a line chart has an increasing/decreasing tendency within two selected points.

4 Conclusions and Further Work

This paper has introduced a number of techniques for improved natural-language-based access to diagrams, supported by a semantic knowledge base in the form of hierarchical ontologies, that aim to make up for a number of known cognitive benefits that visualizing information provides to sighted users. Thus far we have applied most of these techniques to bar charts, and have implemented a first prototype of an accessible Web interface that groups common tasks that may be performed on them. We are now working on evaluating the current prototype with sighted and blind users. Evaluation will likely reveal which of these techniques can be improved and whether users find them useful in supporting analytical tasks performed on bar charts.

Besides adding more supported domains to the current prototype (line charts, scatterplots, link diagrams, etc.) we are also working on reinforcing it with other non-visual methods to improve navigation. For instance, we would like to find out whether non-speech sounds, such as short beeps or musical notes, can be useful in recognizing different landmarks, previously visited nodes, or some other salient features of a diagram by visually impaired users.

References

1. Lewandowsky, S., Spence, I.: The perception of statistical graphs. Sociol. Methods Res. **18** (2–3), 200–242 (1989)
2. Cukier, K.: Show me. New ways of visualising data. The Economist, February 2010. http://www.economist.com/node/15557455. Accessed 5 July 2017
3. Gardner, J.: Can mainstream graphics be accessible? Inf. Technol. Disabil. E-J. **14**(1) (2014)
4. Kopecek, I., Oslejsek, R.: Communicative Images. In: Dickmann, L., Volkmann, G., Malaka, R., Boll, S., Krüger, A., Olivier, P. (eds.) SG 2011. LNCS, vol. 6815, pp. 163–173. Springer, Heidelberg (2011). https://doi.org/10.1007/978-3-642-22571-0_19
5. Ferres, L., Lindgaard, G., Sumegi, L., Tsuji, B.: Evaluating a tool for improving accessibility to charts and graphs. ACM Trans. Comput.-Hum. Interact. (TOCHI) **20**(5), 28 (2013)
6. Murillo-Morales, T., Miesenberger, K.: Non-visually performing analytical tasks on statistical charts. In: Cudd, P., de Witte, L. (eds.) Studies in Health Technology and Informatics, vol. 242, pp. 339–346. IOS Press (2017)
7. Murillo-Morales, T., Plhák, J., Miesenberger, K.: Authoring semantic annotations for non-visual access to graphics. J. Technol. Persons Disabil. **6**, 398–413 (2018)
8. Murillo-Morales, T., Miesenberger, K.: Ontology-based semantic support to improve accessibility of graphics. In: Sik-Lányi, C., Hoogerwerf, E.J., Miesenberger, K. (eds.) Studies in Health Technology and Informatics, vol. 217, pp. 255–260. IOS Press (2015)
9. Larkin, J.H., Simon, H.A.: Why a diagram is (sometimes) worth ten thousand words. Cogn. Sci. (1987). https://doi.org/10.1111/j.1551-6708.1987.tb00863.x
10. Goncu, C., Marriott, K., Aldrich, F.: Tactile Diagrams: Worth Ten Thousand Words? In: Goel, A.K., Jamnik, M., Narayanan, N.H. (eds.) Diagrams 2010. LNCS (LNAI), vol. 6170, pp. 257–263. Springer, Heidelberg (2010). https://doi.org/10.1007/978-3-642-14600-8_25
11. Shneiderman, B.: The eyes have it: a task by data type taxonomy for information visualizations. In: IEEE Symposium on Visual Languages, Boulder, 3–6 September, pp. 336–343. IEEE Computer Society Press (1996). https://doi.org/10.1109/vl.1996.545307

12. Hegarty, M.: Mental animation: inferring motion from static displays of mechanical systems. J. Exp. Psychol.: Learn. Mem. Cognit. **18**(5), 1084–1102 (1992)
13. Levin, J., Anglin, G., Carney, R.: On empirically validating functions of pictures in prose. In: Willows, D., Houghton, H.A. (eds.) The Psychology of Illustration: Basic Research, vol. 1, pp. 51–85. Springer, New York, NY, USA (1987). https://doi.org/10.1007/978-1-4612-4674-9_2
14. Hochpöchler, U., Schnotz, W., Rasch, T., Ullrich, M., Horz, H., McElvany, N., Baumert, J.: Dynamics of mental model construction from text and graphics. Eur. J. Psychol. Educ. (2013). https://doi.org/10.1007/s10212-012-0156-z
15. Brown, A.J.: Non-Visual Interaction with Graphs. Ph.D. thesis, University of Manchester (2008)

The Dutch Best Practice for Teaching Chemistry Diagrams to the Visually Impaired

Dorine in 't Veld[1] and Volker Sorge[2](✉)

[1] Tactile Reading Dedicon, The Hague, The Netherlands
dorineintveld@dedicon.nl
[2] Progressive Accessibility Solutions Ltd., Birmingham, UK
v.sorge@progressiveaccess.com

Abstract. We report on a project to develop a best practice for representing molecule diagrams for teaching Chemistry to blind and visually impaired students in Dutch secondary education. The goal was to provide both a resource for inclusive curriculum development for chemistry teachers and a source of reference for visually impaired students. Technically our solution provides a repository of commonly occurring chemical structures via a web site with interactive, fully accessible molecule diagrams together with a thematic volume of corresponding tactile images. The repository was created in close collaboration with chemistry teachers, one partially sighted, and a blind student. We report on the technical solution to generate the web accessible diagrams in Dutch, some of the necessary adaptations as well as the initial deployment of the catalogue.

1 Introduction

In The Netherlands only very few blind students choose STEM subjects. While it is currently a matter of research, whether this is due to the attitude and prejudices of teachers or students, the lack of accessible learning materials or other influencing factors, in chemistry, where the curriculum heavily depends on the graphical depiction of molecule structures, the lack of accessible resources has certainly significant influence, as there was up to now no standard for adapting structural diagrams for blind readers.

STEM education in The Netherlands uses the BINAS [2] handbook. Although Dedicon, the national resource centre for VI students, has a dedicated educational department to make study material accessible, it is currently not possible to make the Binas handbook accessible in one of their standard formats for blind readers, due to the large tables and many drawings, diagrams, and pictures.

In this project we set out to improve this situation at least for chemistry, by developing a catalogue of accessible molecule diagrams, that will serve as best practice for accessible chemistry in secondary and tertiary education. It consists of a web platform of interactive diagrams together with an accompanying thematic volume of tactile images. For the former we employ *DIAGcess*, a platform

K. Miesenberger and G. Kouroupetroglou (Eds.): ICCHP 2018, LNCS 10896, pp. 644–647, 2018.
https://doi.org/10.1007/978-3-319-94277-3_99

independent web tool to convert images of structural formulas into SVG graphics, which the blind user can navigate with their screen reader, getting speech output in each step.

The development was informed and driven by user needs: We were working closely with a blind student who just did his final secondary school exam in Chemistry. As there was no standardised way for notating structural formulas, the student and his teacher had been working with their own ad hoc notation. For the exams however, he was forced to work independently along his sighted peers. The exam was prepared by a special commission, that drew up a solution for images of structural formulas. But, since the student had not been able to practise with them beforehand, it meant that he had to sit his exam using untested and unfamiliar notation. In addition to the student's input and testing, we were working with two chemistry experts: a former teacher and coach of the student, and a chemistry teacher who is partially sighted himself.

In this paper we will give an overview of the technical background of our solution, discuss some of the issues that arose during localisation which seem to be particular to complex STEM content where rarely specialised dictionaries exist, and summarise the overall catalogue together with initial user responses.

2   Technical Background

Our approach is based on a procedure to generate interactive, web accessible chemical diagrams fully automatically [5]. It either uses image analysis to replace inaccessible bitmap graphics by accessible diagrams [6] or renders chemical identifiers or file formats as accessible scalable vector graphics (SVG) directly.

In our work we use the latter method starting with MOL files, a chemical file format that specifies molecules in terms of coordinate positions of atoms and bonds. They are typically generated with specialist chemistry drawing programs (in our case ChemSketch [1]) and can be used to import chemical drawings directly into office documents. The procedure then transforms this basic information into a web accessible diagram in a sequence of steps:

(i) Semantic enrichment computes detailed and precise information on the depicted chemical molecule and its components. In addition meaningful names for single components are computed using online web services that generate common chemical names given the specification of a compound.

(ii) Diagrams are rendered in SVG format, which scales lossless and supports interactive features in a web browser as well as offers facilities to attach rich semantic information. We thereby faithfully reproduce the layout of the input diagrams as given by the coordinate information of the MOL file.

(iii) A matching navigation structure is computed that contains a hierarchical model of the molecule, comprising a top-level overview, an intermediate level of major components and a lowest level of atoms and bonds. Expert speech rules together with the computed chemical names are employed to generate descriptions explaining components and their composition on the various levels.

The resulting SVG together with the navigation structure can then be integrated into a web site. The *DIAGcess* JavaScript library in the page allows users to explore diagrams interactively while supporting speech output, synchronised highlighting and magnification. This enables users to step-by-step navigate the molecule at different levels, while exposing the computed descriptions via a screen reader. All these operations are implemented browser, screen reader, and platform independent, exploiting HTML5 and WAI-ARIA standards.

3 Localisation and Customisation

As all the scientific descriptions for the diagrams are automatically generated, good localisation was a major component of this project. We thereby distinguish two types of speech: (i) descriptions of the molecule structures, and (ii) assigning the correct names for the molecule and its major components. The speech strings of type (i) are generated recursively using declarative speech rules and give structural descriptions comprised of the basics like bond types and atoms together with chemical orderings, substitution positions etc. Although not as trivial as translating simple message strings, localisation of the speech rules can be achieved relatively quickly with the help of a native speaker and chemical expert. Indeed for our project we had the help of a Dutch native speaker who was formerly a chemistry teacher.

To compute speech of type (ii) we employ the help of dedicated web services that can name structures, given sufficient chemical information. In particular, we employ the publicly available web APIs of ChemSpider [4] and PubChem [3] to name both an entire molecule and its components, i.e., aliphatic chains, ring systems and functional groups. Since the number of possible chemical structures is rather large (e.g., ChemSpider has a database of over 63 million structures) localisation via manually creating a lookup table is not really feasible.

While these databases often provide multiple names for compounds, such as common names, trade names for drugs or IUPAC names (which follow a standardised nomenclature that uniquely describes a molecule, however, in many cases chemists prefer common, traditional names over IUPAC) they are generally given in English only. ChemSpider has German and French names for many structures, but can only provide names in some other languages for very common compounds. And even then we only very rarely get a common name in Dutch. Consequently we developed a number of techniques to localise naming information automatically into Dutch. In particular, we heuristically try to localise English names using the following methods: (i) Wikipedia language links, (ii) Google translate while avoiding auto correction, (iii) and, as for IUPAC names these techniques generally fail, we decompose the names into alpha and non-alpha components (i.e., parentheses, dashes, numbers and Greek letters) and attempt to localise alpha components only.

Although automatic naming proved to be correct in the majority of cases, there was some need for customisation. One was due to incorrectness of the databases used. E.g., ChemSpider claims incorrectly that the Dutch name of

Butane is *butanen* instead of *butaan*, which had to be added to a correction table. In addition, the teachers that provided had a strong preference for certain names for molecules over other also commonly used ones, which prompted us to add option to specify a naming preference, e.g., preferring IUPAC names to others, or to simply provide a custom molecule name directly.

For the molecule drawings themselves, there was little need for customisation as we were effectively directly translating teachers' drawings via the provided MOL files. However, additional provision had to be made for displaying partial molecules, i.e., structural formulas with a not fully specified rest element, was implemented, as these are often used as important teaching tools to describe entire classes of chemical structures.

4 The Catalogue

The final catalogue itself is available at https://goedekennis.dedicon.nl/dossiers/structuurformules. It consists of a collection of web pages divided into seven different categories of organic molecules commonly used in teaching together with an eighth category of exercises that contain molecules with detailed descriptions only but without any chemical names. In addition there are pages with instructions on how to navigate the diagrams as well as explanations on how to read and interpret diagrams. The thematic volume with tactile images contains the diagrams given on the website.

In a sister project we also developed a standardised solution for drawing, based on skeleton formulas, i.e., structural formulas where carbon and hydrogen atoms are omitted to reduce the size of diagrams. Since this is also used by sighted students and teachers, it helps blind students to communicate their work.

As the subject is rather specialised there are currently few students to test with. However, both the website and the thematic volume will be further evaluated starting in February, when another blind student will prepare for his final exams. Our hope is that the best practice will lead to growing uptake of chemistry among visually impaired children, similar to what we have seen in Mathematics in the last 15 years, since the publication of a best practise for that subject.

References

1. ACD/Labs. Chemsketch. http://www.acdlabs.com/chemsketch/
2. Binas. 6e ed havo/vwo informatieboek, 2013. https://www.noordhoffuitgevers.nl/voortgezet-onderwijs/methoden/binas
3. Kim, S., et al.: Pubchem substance and compound databases. Nucleic Acids Res. **44**(D1), D1202–D1213 (2016)
4. Pence, H.E., William, A.: Chemspider: An online chemical information resource. J. Chem. Edu. **87**(11), 1123–1124 (2010)
5. Sorge, V., Lee, M., Wilkinson, S.: End-to-end solution for accessible chemical diagrams. In: Proceedings of the 12th Web for All Conference, p. 6. ACM (2015)
6. Sorge, V.: Polyfilling accessible chemistry diagrams. In: Miesenberger, K., Bühler, C., Penaz, P. (eds.) ICCHP 2016. LNCS, vol. 9758, pp. 43–50. Springer, Cham (2016). https://doi.org/10.1007/978-3-319-41264-1_6

Correction to: The Inaccessibility of Video Players

Gian Wild

Correction to:
Chapter "The Inaccessibility of Video Players" in:
K. Miesenberger and G. Kouroupetroglou (Eds.):
Computers Helping People with Special Needs, **LNCS 10896,**
https://doi.org/10.1007/978-3-319-94277-3_9

In the originally published version of the paper, the affiliation of the author was not mentioned. As the author is the head of the company which created and markets one of the products mentioned and rated in her paper, her potential conflict of interest was not disclosed. The corrected version of the paper states her affiliation.

The updated online version of this chapter can be found at
https://doi.org/10.1007/978-3-319-94277-3_9

K. Miesenberger and G. Kouroupetroglou (Eds.): ICCHP 2018, LNCS 10896, p. E1, 2018.
https://doi.org/10.1007/978-3-319-94277-3_100

Author Index